Course	Business Law I & II
Course Number	**Law 2510 & 2520**
	WILLIAM PATERSON UNIVERSITY
	ACCOUNTING & LAW DEPARTMENT

http://create.mheducation.com

ISBN-10: 1308251602   ISBN-13: 9781308251608

Contents

Online Supplements

Credits

Online Supplements

CHAPTER

3

The U.S. Legal System

LEARNING OBJECTIVES

After reading this chapter, you will be able to answer the following questions:

1 What are the different types of jurisdiction a court must have before it can render a binding decision in a case?

2 What is venue?

3 How is our dual court system structured?

4 What are the threshold requirements that must be met before a court will hear a case?

5 What are the steps in civil litigation?

CASE OPENER

Questionable Jurisdiction over Caterpillar

James Lewis, a resident of Kentucky, sustained an injury while operating a Caterpillar bulldozer. He filed suit against Caterpillar, a company incorporated in Delaware but with its principal place of business in Illinois. Lewis also filed suit against the supplier of the bulldozer, Whayne Supply Company, whose principal place of business was Kentucky. Lewis filed his case in a Kentucky state court, alleging defective manufacture, negligence, failure to warn, and breach of warranty. Lewis and Whayne Supply Company agreed to settle out of court. Caterpillar then filed a motion to exercise its right of removal (its right to move the case from the state to the federal court system), arguing that the federal court had jurisdiction over the case because Caterpillar and Lewis were from different states. Lewis disagreed with Caterpillar's contention, claiming that because he had not completed his settlement with Whayne, the case still included a defendant (Whayne) from Lewis's state, Kentucky. Thus, Lewis argued, federal courts did not have jurisdiction over the case.

The court agreed with Caterpillar's argument and moved the case to a federal district court. Shortly thereafter, Lewis and Whayne finalized their settlement agreement, and the district court dismissed Whayne from the lawsuit. The federal district court granted Caterpillar a favorable judgment. Lewis, however, appealed the district court's decision, renewing his argument that the district court did not have jurisdiction over the case. The court of appeals agreed with Lewis, holding that because Whayne was a defendant in the case at the time that Caterpillar moved the case from state to federal court, the diversity of citizenship necessary to give the federal court jurisdiction over the case was absent. Thus, a state court should have resolved the dispute. Consequently, the appellate court vacated the district court's decision. Caterpillar then appealed to the U.S. Supreme Court.

1. What factors determine whether the state or federal court system hears a case?
2. If you were a businessperson with Caterpillar, why might you prefer a federal court to hear the dispute with Lewis instead of a state court?

The Wrap-Up at the end of the chapter will answer these questions.

As the opening scenario illustrates, when a dispute arises, parties in this country do not simply "go to court." They often must choose between federal and state court systems. This chapter examines these systems, as well as the trial procedures that apply in civil cases.

Jurisdiction

The word jurisdiction comes from the Latin terms *juris*, meaning "law," and *diction*, meaning "to speak." A useful way to understand jurisdiction is to think of it as referring to courts' power to hear cases and render decisions that bind the parties before them. A court must have several types of jurisdiction to decide any particular case.

L01

What are the different types of jurisdiction a court must have before it can render a binding decision in a case?

ORIGINAL VERSUS APPELLATE JURISDICTION

Trial courts, or courts of original jurisdiction, have the power to hear and decide cases when they first enter the legal system. In these courts, the parties present evidence and call witnesses to testify. Most state court systems refer to trial courts as *courts of common pleas* or *county courts*. The federal system calls them *district courts*.

Courts of appellate jurisdiction, or appellate courts, have the power to review previous judicial decisions to determine whether trial courts erred in their decisions. Appellate courts do not hold trials. Rather, appellate judges review transcripts of trial court proceedings and occasionally consider additional oral and written arguments from each party.

Appellate courts handle primarily questions of law, not questions of fact. A *question of law* is an issue concerning the interpretation or application of a law. In contrast, a *question of fact* is a question about an event or characteristic in a case. For example, whether a student yelled racial slurs on a college campus is a question of fact. On the other hand, whether the First Amendment protects the student's right to utter racial slurs is a question of law.

Only judges can decide questions of law. Questions of fact are determined in the trial court. In a *bench trial* (a trial with no jury), the judge decides questions of fact; in a *jury trial*, the jury decides questions of fact. Appellate courts can, however, overrule trial courts' decisions on questions of fact, but only when the trial court's finding was clearly erroneous or when no trial evidence supports the trial court's finding.

Legal Principle: **The court in which a case is first heard is called the *court of original jurisdiction*, and the court to which a decision made by that court is appealed is called the *court of appellate jurisdiction*.**

JURISDICTION OVER PERSONS AND PROPERTY

In personam jurisdiction (literally, "jurisdiction over the person") is a court's power to render a decision affecting the rights of the specific persons before the court. Generally, a court's power to exercise *in personam* jurisdiction extends only over a specific geographic region. In the state court system, a court's *in personam* jurisdiction usually extends to the state's borders. In the federal system, on the other hand, each court's jurisdiction extends across its geographic district.

A court acquires *in personam* jurisdiction over a person (the plaintiff) when she files a lawsuit with the court. The court acquires jurisdiction over the person the plaintiff is suing (the defendant) when it gives him a copy of the complaint and a summons. The complaint specifies the factual and legal basis for the lawsuit and the relief the plaintiff seeks. The summons is a court order that notifies the defendant of the lawsuit and explains how and when to respond to the complaint.

Service of process is the procedure by which courts present these documents to defendants. Traditionally, courts use personal service: An officer of the court hands the summons and complaint to the defendant. Recently, however, courts have employed other methods of service, including *residential service,* in which a court representative leaves the summons and complaint with a responsible adult at the defendant's home, and *service by certified* or *ordinary mail.*

There has even been one case in which a court of appeals upheld service of process by e-mail to be appropriate. The facts of the case, however, created an unusual situation in which no other means of service was really possible. Rio Properties, Inc., operators of the Rio All Suites Resort Casino in Las Vegas, Nevada, decided to put some of its gaming activities on the Internet and discovered that a Costa Rican company, Rio International Interlink (RII), was operating an online, international sports book that allegedly infringed on Rio Properties' registered trademark. When the court attempted to serve RII at its U.S. address, the court found that it was only an address for an international courier that was not authorized to accept service on behalf of the company, and the court could not find any address for the company in Costa Rico. Rio Properties then filed a motion for alternative service of process with the court for permission to serve RII via its e-mail address, and the motion was granted by the district court. The court of appeals upheld the validity of the district court's order, noting that the Constitution does not require any specific means of service, only a means of service "reasonably calculated to provide notice and an opportunity to respond."[1] Because the method seemed to be the method of service most likely to reach RII, the court found that it clearly met the standard.

> To read more about how the choice of where to incorporate relates to jurisdiction, please see the **Connecting to the Core** activity on the text website at www.mhhe.com/kubasek3e.

If the defendant is a corporation, courts generally serve either the president of the corporation or an agent that the corporation has appointed to receive service. Most states require that corporations appoint an agent for service when they incorporate. Corporations are subject to *in personam* jurisdiction in three locations: the state of their incorporation, the location of their main offices, and the geographic areas in which they conduct business.

Courts have *in personam* jurisdiction only over persons within a specific geographic region. In the past, a state court could not acquire *in personam* jurisdiction over out-of-state defendants unless it served the defendants within the court's home state. Thus, defendants who injured plaintiffs could evade legal action by leaving the state and remaining outside its borders. To alleviate this problem, most

---

[1] *Rio Properties, Inc. v. Rio International Interlink,* 284 F.3d 1007 (2002).

states have enacted long-arm statutes, which enable the court to serve defendants outside the state as long as the defendant has sufficient minimum contacts within the state and it seems fair to assert long-arm jurisdiction over him or her. The U.S. Supreme Court established this "minimum-contacts" standard in the 1945 case *International Shoe Co. v. State of Washington.*[2]

Each state has its own minimum-contact requirements, but most state statutes hold that acts like committing a tort or doing business in the state are sufficient to allow the state to serve a defendant. In the opening scenario, the company sold products in Kentucky, and its products caused an injury in that state. These two facts were sufficient minimum contacts to allow the Kentucky court to serve Caterpillar, even though it was an out-of-state company.

BUT WHAT IF . . .

WHAT IF THE FACTS OF THE CASE OPENER WERE DIFFERENT?

Recall that in the Case Opener, the company sold products in Kentucky and its products caused an injury in that state. Let's say, in the Case Opener, that Caterpillar did not sell products in the state of Kentucky, but its products did cause an injury in that state. Could a Kentucky court still exercise *in personam* jurisdiction over Caterpillar and serve the company? Why or why not?

In contrast to the situation in the opening scenario, the Florida appellate court did not find minimum contacts with that state to enable a foreign corporation to sue Columbia University, located in New York City, for a tort that allegedly occurred in New York. The court found that the fact that Columbia had alumni associations in Florida, owned some interactive classrooms in that state, and offered some online classes to residents did not constitute sufficient minimum contacts for a lawsuit in which none of the tortious acts were alleged to have occurred in the state.[3]

As the E-Commerce and the Law box (next page) illustrates, the Internet has created complications for the courts in determining when an Internet presence creates in-person jurisdiction over a website operator. There is a need to protect companies from being dragged to an infinite number of courts even though their customer bases may be nationwide; at the same time, there is a need to not impinge on the sovereignty of states by curtailing the conditions under which defendants may be commanded to appear in a state's court.

If a defendant has property in a state, a plaintiff may file suit against the defendant's property instead of the owner. For example, suppose a Utah resident had not paid property taxes on a piece of land she owned in Idaho. Idaho courts have *in rem* jurisdiction (Latin for "jurisdiction over the thing") over the property. Thus, an Idaho state court has the power to seize the property and sell it to pay the property taxes in an *in rem* proceeding.

Courts can also gain quasi *in rem* jurisdiction, or *attachment jurisdiction,* over a defendant's property *unrelated* to the plaintiff's claim. For example, suppose Charlie, a Massachusetts resident, ran a red light while he was vacationing in California and collided with Jessica's car. Suppose further that Jessica suffered extensive injuries from the accident

---

[2] 326 U.S. 310.
[3] *Trustees of Columbia University v. Ocean World, SA,* 2009 WL 1212229, Ct. App. Fla.

THE SLIDING-SCALE STANDARD FOR INTERNET TRANSACTIONS

Does a business that has Internet contact with a plaintiff in a different state satisfy the minimum-contact standard? Anyone who engages in transactions over the Internet should be concerned about this question.

A federal district court established the following "sliding-scale" standard in the 1997 case *Zippo Mfg. Co. v. Zippo Dot Com, Inc.*:*

[T]he likelihood that personal jurisdiction can be constitutionally exercised is directly proportionate to the nature and quality of commercial activity that an entity conducts over the Internet. This sliding scale is consistent with well developed personal jurisdiction principles.

At one end of the spectrum are situations in which a defendant clearly does business over the Internet. If the defendant enters into contracts with residents of a foreign jurisdiction that involve the knowing and repeated transmission of computer files over the Internet, personal jurisdiction is proper.

At the opposite end are situations in which a defendant has simply posted information on an Internet website that is accessible to users in foreign jurisdictions. A passive website that does little more than make information available to those who are interested in it is not grounds for the exercise of personal jurisdiction.

The middle ground is occupied by interactive websites at which a user can exchange information with the host computer. In such cases, the exercise of jurisdiction is determined by examining the level of interactivity and commercial nature of the exchange of information that occurs on the website.

* 952 F. Supp. 1119, 1124 (W.D. Pa. 1997).

---

and successfully sued Charlie for $200,000 in a California state court. The California court can exercise quasi *in rem* jurisdiction over Charlie's California vacation home by seizing it, selling it, and transferring $200,000 to Jessica to satisfy her judgment against Charlie. If Charlie's vacation home is worth more than $200,000, however, the court must return the excess proceeds to Charlie.

SUBJECT-MATTER JURISDICTION

Subject-matter jurisdiction is a court's power to hear certain kinds of cases. Most industrialized countries have a single court system, with courts that have the power to hear both national law cases and local law cases. In contrast, the United States has both a state and a federal court system. Subject-matter jurisdiction determines which court system may hear a particular case. Cases may fall under state jurisdiction, exclusive federal jurisdiction, or concurrent jurisdiction. Exhibit 3-1 illustrates the subject-matter-jurisdiction divisions.

Exhibit 3-1

Subject-Matter-Jurisdiction Divisions

Exclusive Federal Jurisdiction
- Admiralty cases
- Bankruptcy cases
- Federal criminal prosecutions
- Cases in which one state sues another state
- Claims against the United States
- Federal patent, trademark, and copyright claims
- Other claims involving federal statutes that specify exclusive federal jurisdiction

Concurrent Federal Jurisdiction
- Federal-question cases
- Diversity-of-citizenship cases

State Jurisdiction
- All cases not falling under exclusive federal jurisdiction

Exclusive Federal Jurisdiction.   The federal court system has exclusive jurisdiction over very few cases: admiralty cases, bankruptcy cases, federal criminal prosecutions, lawsuits in which one state sues another state, claims against the United States, and cases involving federal copyrights, patents, or trademarks. Additionally, federal courts have exclusive jurisdiction over claims arising under federal statutes that specify exclusive federal jurisdiction.

State Jurisdiction.   The state court system has a broad range of jurisdiction; state courts have the power to hear all cases not within the exclusive jurisdiction of the federal court system. State courts also have exclusive jurisdiction over certain cases, such as cases concerning adoption and divorce. Most cases, therefore, fall under state court jurisdiction.

The Caterpillar case fell under state court jurisdiction because its subject matter—product liability and negligence—did not place the case under the exclusive jurisdiction of the federal court system.

Concurrent Federal Jurisdiction.   Concurrent federal jurisdiction means that both state and federal courts have jurisdiction over a case. Concurrent jurisdiction covers two types of cases: federal-question and diversity-of-citizenship cases. *Federal-question* cases require an interpretation of the United States Constitution, a federal statute, or a federal treaty. For example, suppose a plaintiff alleges that a Florida campaign financing law violates his First Amendment free speech rights. Because this case raises a federal question, it falls under concurrent jurisdiction, and both state and federal courts have the power to hear it.

A *diversity-of-citizenship* case must satisfy two conditions: (1) The plaintiff(s) does (do) not reside in the same state as the defendant(s), and (2) the controversy concerns an amount in excess of $75,000. Courts use the location of a party's residence to determine whether diversity of citizenship exists. Most federal court cases are based on diversity of citizenship.

A business may reside in two states: the state of its incorporation and the state of its principal place of business. Thus, in the opening scenario, Caterpillar was a resident of Delaware, the state where it incorporated, and of Illinois, the state of its primary place of business.

Diversity must be complete, however, for a case to fall under concurrent jurisdiction. In the Caterpillar case, Lewis argued that diversity was not complete because both he and the supply company, the second defendant he originally sued, were residents of Kentucky. The appellate court agreed with his argument and overturned the district court's decision because the district court lacked subject-matter jurisdiction.

BUT WHAT IF . . .

WHAT IF THE FACTS OF THE CASE OPENER WERE DIFFERENT?

Recall that in the Case Opener, Caterpillar was a resident of Delaware, the state where it incorporated, and of Illinois, the state of its primary place of business. Let's say that Whayne was not a defendant in the case. How would Whayne's absence affect the diversity of the case? What court, or courts, would have jurisdiction over the case?

Legal Principle: **Concurrent jurisdiction exists whenever there is a federal question or diversity of citizenship and at least $75,000 at issue.**

When a case falls under concurrent jurisdiction, the plaintiff initially chooses which court will hear the case by filing in whichever court system the plaintiff wishes the case to be heard in. If a plaintiff files the case in a state court, however, the defendant has a *right of removal.* This right entitles the defendant to transfer the case to the federal court system. Thus, either party to a case involving concurrent jurisdiction has the ability to ensure that the case will be heard in the federal court system: The plaintiff can file the case in federal court initially, or the defendant can transfer the case to federal court by exercising her right of removal if the case is initially filed in state court. In the opening scenario, Caterpillar exercised its right of removal, and the state trial court moved the case to a federal district court.

Sometimes it is not easy to determine whether a case falls under concurrent jurisdiction, as Case 3-1 illustrates.

CASE 3-1   UNITED STATES SUPREME COURT
130 S. CT. 1181 (2010)

HERTZ CORP. v. FRIEND

Two residents of California filed a lawsuit against Hertz Corporation on behalf of a group of people arguing that the company's labor practices were illegal. The corporation was labeling workers as managers and thereby exempting them from receiving overtime pay for overtime hours worked. Hertz had the case removed to a federal court, which is allowed due to the Class Action Fairness Act. The act allows such a move when there is diversity among the parties of a class action lawsuit and the monetary amount in question is over $5 million. The plaintiffs argued that while Hertz had its headquarters in New Jersey and was incorporated in Delaware, it was still a citizen of California and thus was not diverse from any of the plaintiffs. The district court in California applied the "total activity/place of operations" test, a test that considered a huge number of factors relating to a company to try to determine its principal place of business. Some of these factors include where most "business functions" take place, where most of the company executives work, where most of the sales take place, and where most of the workers are employed. Eventually, the district court determined that Hertz's principal place of business was California, because much of its business took place there, and remanded the case to the state court. The Ninth Circuit affirmed, and Hertz appealed to the United States Supreme Court.

JUSTICE BREYER: The District Court concluded that it lacked diversity jurisdiction because Hertz was a California citizen under Ninth Circuit precedent, which asks, *inter alia,* whether the amount of the corporation's business activity is "significantly larger" or "substantially predominates" in one State. Finding that California was Hertz's "principal place of business" under that test because a

plurality of the relevant business activity occurred there, the District Court remanded the case to state court. The Ninth Circuit affirmed. . . .

2. The phrase "principal place of business" in §1332(c)(1) refers to the place where a corporation's high level officers direct, control, and coordinate the corporation's activities, *i.e.,* its "nerve center," which will typically be found at its corporate headquarters.

a. A brief review of the legislative history of diversity jurisdiction demonstrates that Congress added §1332(c)(1)'s "principal place of business" language to the traditional state-of-incorporation test in order to prevent corporations from manipulating federal-court jurisdiction as well as to reduce the number of diversity cases.

b. However, the phrase "principal place of business" has proved more difficult to apply than its originators likely expected. After Congress' amendment, courts were uncertain as to where to look to determine a corporation's "principal place of business" for diversity purposes. If a corporation's headquarters and executive offices were in the same State in which it did most of its business, the test seemed straightforward. The "principal place of business" was in that State. But if those corporate headquarters, including executive offices, were in one State, while the corporation's plants or other centers of business activity were located in other States, the answer was less obvious. Under these circumstances, for corporations with "far-flung" business activities, numerous Circuits have looked to a corporation's "nerve center," from which the corporation radiates out to its constituent parts and from which its officers direct, control, and coordinate the corporation's activities. However, this test did not go far enough, for it did not answer what courts should do when a corporation's operations are not far-flung but rather limited to only a few States. When faced with this question, various courts have focused more heavily on where a corporation's actual business activities are located, adopting divergent and increasingly complex tests to interpret the statute.

c. In an effort to find a single, more uniform interpretation of the statutory phrase, this Court returns to the "nerve center" approach: "[P]rincipal place of business" is best read as referring to the place where a corporation's officers direct, control, and coordinate the corporation's activities. In practice it should normally be the place where the corporation maintains its headquarters—provided that the headquarters is the actual center of direction, control, and coordination, *i.e.,* the "nerve center," and not simply an office where the corporation holds its board meetings.

   i. Three sets of considerations, taken together, convince the Court that the "nerve center" approach, while imperfect, is superior to other possibilities. First, §1332(c)(1)'s language supports the approach. The statute's word "place" is singular, not plural. Its word "principal" requires that the main, prominent, or most important place be chosen. And the fact that the word "place" follows the words "State where" means that the "place" is a place *within* a State, not the State itself. A corporation's "nerve center," usually its main headquarters, is a single place. The public often considers it the corporation's main place of business. And it is a place within a State. By contrast, the application of a more general business activities test has led some courts, as in the present case, to look, not at a particular place within a State, but incorrectly at the State itself, measuring the total amount of business activities that the corporation conducts there and determining whether they are significantly larger than in the next-ranking State. Second, administrative simplicity is a major virtue in a jurisdictional

statute. A "nerve center" approach, which ordinarily equates that "center" with a corporation's headquarters, is simple to apply *comparatively speaking*. By contrast, a corporation's general business activities more often lack a single principal place where they take place. Third, the statute's legislative history suggests that the words "principal place of business" should be interpreted to be no more complex than an earlier, numerical test that was criticized as too complex and impractical to apply. A "nerve center" test offers such a possibility. A general business activities test does not.

   ii. While there may be no perfect test that satisfies all administrative and purposive criteria, and there will be hard cases under the "nerve center" test adopted today, this test is relatively easier to apply and does not require courts to weigh corporate functions, assets or revenues different in kind, one from the other. And though this test may produce results that seem to cut against the basic rationale of diversity jurisdiction, accepting occasionally counterintuitive results is the price the legal system must pay to avoid overly complex jurisdictional administration while producing the benefits that accompany a more uniform legal system.

   iii. If the record reveals attempts at jurisdictional manipulation—for example, that the alleged "nerve center" is nothing more than a mail drop box, a bare office with a computer, or the location of an annual executive retreat—the courts should instead take as the "nerve center" the place of actual direction, control, and coordination, in the absence of such manipulation.

d. Although petitioner's unchallenged declaration suggests that Hertz's "nerve center" and its corporate headquarters are one and the same, and that they are located in New Jersey, not in California, respondents should have a fair opportunity on remand to litigate their case in light of today's holding.

Judgment in favor of Hertz, with decision of Circuit Court of Appeals VACATED and REMANDED.

CRITICAL THINKING

The Supreme Court decided that the previous test used to determine a company's principal state of residency was too open to different interpretations by different courts. Do you think the new test solves that problem? Why or why not?

ETHICAL DECISION MAKING

How does this decision affect the future of class action lawsuits between corporations and employees? Which party benefits from the new test designed by the Supreme Court?

Wachovia Bank N.A. v. Schmidt
United States Supreme Court
126 S. Ct. 941 (2006)

When plaintiff Schmidt and other citizens of South Carolina sued Wachovia National Bank, an institution with its headquarters in North Carolina and branches in many states, including South Carolina, in a state court of South Carolina, the bank immediately attempted to exercise its right of removal to have the case moved to the federal court system. Ultimately, the United States Supreme Court had to decide which state a federally chartered bank was considered a citizen of for purposes of diversity jurisdiction. The Court noted that corporations are deemed citizens of the state in which they are incorporated and the state that is their principal place of business. Federally chartered banks, however, are slightly different from corporations in that they are not incorporated in any state. Congress, therefore, deemed that these banks would be considered citizens of states in which they are "located." The high court agreed with the bank that "located" must refer to the state in which its main office, as specified in its articles of incorporation, is located. To agree with the plaintiffs—that banks were located in every state in which they have branches—would dramatically reduce the availability of federal jurisdiction to federally chartered banks, making the federal court system dramatically less accessible to these banks than it is to state banks and state incorporated corporations, which the Court felt would not be what Congress had intended.

The Case Nugget illustrates how the courts have had to struggle with determining the citizenship of another entity that has a presence in many states: federally chartered banks.

While the question of which court system will hear a case is a matter that we think of as arising once a dispute has occurred, sometimes companies' decisions about where to locate are influenced by their knowledge about the court system in a state they are considering. And some organizations actually encourage companies to take a state's court system into account. As you already know, companies take into account the laws of the states where they are considering locating and doing business. Another factor some businesses consider is whether a state's courts seem hospitable to businesses. The American Tort Reform Association (ATRA), a national organization based in Washington, D.C., attempts to eliminate some of the "legal guesswork" for businesses by creating a list of the nation's top "Judicial Hellholes" each year. ATRA identifies its top hellholes as places where the law is applied in an "inequitable manner, generally against defendants in civil lawsuits."[4] One state in particular, West Virginia, continues to top the ATRA charts and was named the number-one Judicial Hellhole in the United States for both 2007 and 2008. ATRA mentions that one of West Virginia's major legal shortcomings is that it happens to be only one of two states in the country that does not "guarantee the right to appeal a civil verdict."[5]

Also crippling West Virginia's ability to offer a favorable business environment is its reputation as being a lawsuit- and plaintiff-friendly state. For example, a judge in West Virginia recently ordered the DuPont company to pay $196 million in punitive damages and $55 million for site cleanup and to commit $130 million to medical monitoring and testing after several West Virginia citizens filed suit against the company, claiming one of its plants contaminated their city and posed serious health risks, even though at the time of the verdict none of the residents were ill or showed health effects. High-profile and high-award cases like the DuPont case, coupled with an arguably flawed judicial system, could be enough to deter businesses from locating in West Virginia in the future. The DuPont case demonstrates that, as with any business decision, the costs and benefits of doing business in a particular state and legal climate need to be evaluated before moving forward.

Venue

L02

What is venue?

Once a case is in the proper court system, **venue** determines which trial court in the system will hear the case. Venue is a matter of geographic location determined by each state's

---

[4] www.atra.org/reports/hellholes/.
[5] Ibid.

statutes. Usually, the trial court where the defendant resides is the appropriate venue. If a case involves property, the trial court where the property is located is also an appropriate venue. Finally, if the focus of the case is a particular incident, the trial court where the dispute occurred is an appropriate venue. The plaintiff initially chooses from among the appropriate venues when she files the case.

If the location of the court where the plaintiff filed the case is an inconvenience to the defendant or if the defendant believes it will be difficult to select an unbiased jury in that venue, he may request that the judge move the case by filing a motion for a change of venue. The judge has the discretion to grant or deny the motion.

For example, one particular reason a defendant might choose to request a change of venue is negative pretrial publicity. In May 2008, Sholom Rubashkin, the manager of the nation's largest kosher slaughterhouse, was arrested in an immigration raid, and he now faces roughly 100 charges ranging from document fraud and identity theft to child-labor and minimum-wage violations. The scale of the raid, which led to the arrest of approximately 400 of Rubashkin's employees, and the severity of Rubashkin's charges attracted national media attention. Fearing that he would not be able to receive a fair trial or an unbiased jury,[6] Rubashkin filed a request to have his trial moved from Iowa to either Minneapolis or Chicago. A federal district court judge disagreed with Rubashkin, and denied his initial request for a new venue. However, the judge did acknowledge that publicity may increase even more as the trial draws near and mentioned that she may allow Rubashkin to renew his argument for a new venue at that time.

Legal Principle: **Venue is appropriate in the county where the defendant resides or where the incident took place over which the lawsuit arose.**

The Structure of the Court System

The U.S. legal system has two parallel court structures: a federal system and a state system. Once a plaintiff files a case in one of the systems, the case remains in that system throughout the appeals process. The only exception to this rule occurs when a party to a lawsuit appeals the decision of a state supreme court to the U.S. Supreme Court.

L03

How is our dual court system structured?

THE FEDERAL COURT SYSTEM

The federal court system derives its power from Article III, Section 2, of the U.S. Constitution and consists of three main levels: trial courts, intermediate appellate courts, and the court of last resort. Exhibit 3-2 on the next page illustrates this system.

Federal Trial Courts.   In the federal court system, the trial courts, or courts of original jurisdiction, are U.S. district courts. The United States has 94 districts; each district has at least one trial court of general jurisdiction. Courts of general jurisdiction have the power to hear a wide range of cases and can grant almost any type of remedy. Almost every case in the federal system begins in one of these courts.

A small number of cases, however, do not begin in trial courts of general jurisdiction. For cases concerning certain subject matter, Congress has established special trial courts of limited jurisdiction. The types of cases for which Congress has established these special trial courts include bankruptcy cases, claims against the U.S. government, international trade and customs cases, and disputes over certain tax deficiencies.

In an extremely limited number of cases, the U.S. Supreme Court functions as a trial court of limited jurisdiction. These cases include controversies between states and lawsuits against foreign ambassadors.

---

[6] www.nytimes.com/2008/10/31/us/31immig.html?hp; and seattletimes.nwsource.com/html/businesstechnology/2008881497_apkosherslaughterhousetrial.html.

Exhibit 3-2   The Federal Court System

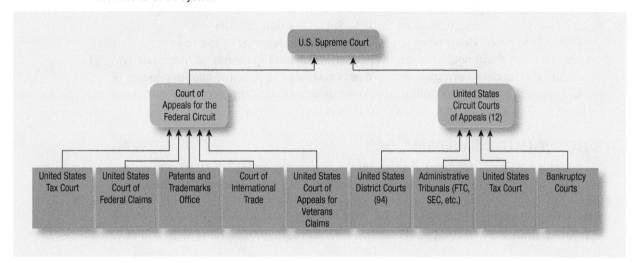

Intermediate Courts of Appeal.   The U.S. circuit courts of appeal make up the second level of courts in the federal system. The United States has 12 circuits, including a circuit for the District of Columbia. Each circuit court hears appeals from district courts in its geographic area. Additionally, a federal circuit court of appeals hears appeals from government administrative agencies. Exhibit 3-3 illustrates the geographic circuit divisions.

Exhibit 3-3   The Circuits of the Federal Court System

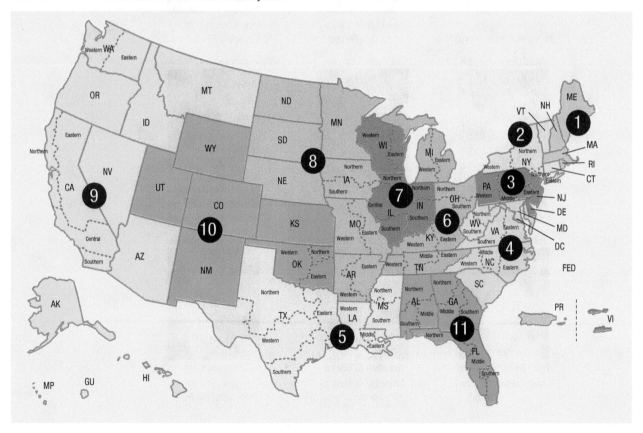

The Court of Last Resort.   The U.S. Supreme Court is the final appellate court in the federal system. Nine justices, who have lifetime appointments, make up the high court. Exhibit 3-4 shows the nine justices on the U.S. Supreme Court in 2010.

The U.S. Supreme Court hears appeals of cases from the court of last resort in a state system. The Court will not, however, hear cases considering questions of pure state law. The Court also functions as a trial court in rare occasions. The structure and functioning of the U.S. Supreme Court system differ from those of similar courts in other countries, as the Comparing the Law of Other Countries box illustrates.

STATE COURT SYSTEMS

No uniform state court structure exists because each state has devised its own court system. Most states, however, have a structure similar to the federal court system's structure.

State Trial Courts.   In state court systems, most cases begin in a trial court of general jurisdiction. As in the federal system, state trial courts of general jurisdiction have

Exhibit 3-4

U.S. Supreme Court Justices, 2010

Associate Justice

Elena Kagan
Appointed in 2010 by
President Barack Obama

Associate Justice

Antonin Scalia
Appointed in 1984 by
President Reagan

Associate Justice

Anthony M. Kennedy
Appointed in 1988 by
President G.H.W. Bush

Associate Justice

Sonia Sotomayor
Appointed in 2009 by
President Barack Obama

Chief Justice

John G. Roberts
Appointed in 2005 by
President G.W. Bush

Associate Justice

Clarence Thomas
Appointed in 1991 by
President G.H.W. Bush

Associate Justice

Ruth Bader Ginsburg
Appointed in 1993 by
President Clinton

Associate Justice

Stephen G. Breyer
Appointed in 1994 by
President Clinton

Associate Justice

Samuel Alito
Appointed in 2006 by
President G.W. Bush

In Taiwan, the country's core laws are called the "organic law of the court." These laws stipulate that the country relies on a "three-level and three-instance" court system. In other words, cases begin at one of the district court and may then move to a high court and finally to the Supreme Court. The Supreme Court is the court of last resort. Thus, at first glance, Taiwan's system appears similar to the U.S. federal system, and with respect to matters not involving interpretation of the the country's constitution, it is. But Taiwan's system also has an additional court that is absent from the U.S. system.

While Taiwan's Supreme Court is the court of last resort for civil and criminal cases, the Supreme Court is not responsible for interpreting the country's constitution. This responsibility falls to the Constitutional Court of the Judicial Yuan.

The Constitutional Court of the Judicial Yuan is a council composed of 15 grand justices. The president of Taiwan chooses the Judicial Yuan president and vice president from among the active justices, and both individuals serve terms that last four years. Seven of the fifteen members serve eight-year terms. This court also has a few additional powers, such as the ability to impeach the president and vice president of the republic.

Cases heard by the Supreme Court are presented to five judges, including a Supreme Court president who not only attends to administrative concerns but also acts as a presiding judge over the fellow members of the court.

the power to hear all cases over which the state court system has jurisdiction except those cases for which the state has established special trial courts of limited jurisdiction. Most states have a trial court of general jurisdiction in each county. The names of these courts vary by state, but most states refer to them as *courts of common pleas* or *county courts.* In some states, these courts have specialized divisions: domestic relations, probate, and so on.

Most states also have trial courts of limited jurisdiction. Usually, these courts can grant only certain remedies. For example, small claims courts, a common type of court of limited jurisdiction in most states, may not grant damage awards larger than a specified amount. Other courts of limited jurisdiction have the power to hear only certain types of cases. For example, probate courts hear only cases about asset and obligation transfers after an individual's death.

Intermediate Courts of Appeal.   Intermediate courts of appeal, analogous to federal circuit courts of appeal, exist in approximately half the states. These courts usually have broad jurisdiction, hearing appeals from courts of general and limited jurisdictions, as well as from state administrative agencies. The names of these courts also vary by state, but most states call them *courts of appeal* or *superior courts.*

Courts of Last Resort.   Appeals from the state intermediate courts of appeal lead cases to the state court of last resort. Most states call this court the *supreme court,* although some states refer to it as the *court of appeals.* Because approximately half the states lack intermediate courts of appeal, appeals from trial courts in these states go directly to the state court of last resort.

LO4

What are the threshold requirements that must be met before a court will hear a case?

Threshold Requirements

Before a case makes it to court, it must meet three *threshold requirements.* These requirements ensure that courts hear only cases that genuinely require adjudication. The three requirements are standing, case or controversy, and ripeness.

STANDING

A person who has the legal right to bring an action in court has standing (or *standing to sue*). For a person to have standing, the outcome of a case must personally affect him or her. For example, if you hire a landscaper to mow your lawn every week and she fails to show up every other week, you have standing to sue your landscaper. But if your friend hired the landscaper to mow his lawn, you lack the standing to sue on your friend's behalf because you do not have a personal stake in the outcome of the case. The American legal system requires that a plaintiff have a personal stake in the outcome of the case because, the theory goes, the plaintiff's personal stake stimulates her to present the best possible case.

Standing requirements are subject to frequent litigation when citizen groups sue to enforce environmental laws. For example, the standing of the plaintiff, Friends of the Earth (FOE), was a central issue in the 2000 U.S. Supreme Court case *FOE v. Laidlaw Environmental Services.*[7] In the case, FOE filed a lawsuit against Laidlaw, alleging that it had violated the Clean Water Act by discharging excessive amounts of pollutants into a river.

Writing for the majority, Justice Ginsburg cited three factors plaintiffs need for standing: (1) The plaintiff must have an injury in fact that is concrete and actual or imminent; (2) the injury must be fairly traceable to the challenged action of the defendant; and (3) it must be likely that the injury will be redressed by a favorable decision.[8] In applying those criteria to the Laidlaw case, the Supreme Court found that FOE members' testimony that they were afraid to fish and swim in a river they previously enjoyed satisfied the first two criteria. The Court held that although the FOE members would not directly receive money from a penalty against Laidlaw, they would benefit because the penalties would deter Laidlaw and other companies from polluting the river in the future.[9] The Court ruled in FOE's favor and assessed Laidlaw a $405,800 penalty payable to the U.S. Treasury.

CASE OR CONTROVERSY

The case or controversy (or *justiciable controversy*) requirement ensures that courts do not render advisory opinions. Three criteria are necessary for a case or controversy to exist. First, the relationship between the plaintiff and the defendant must be adverse. Second, actual or threatened actions of at least one of the parties must give rise to an actual legal dispute. Third, courts must have the ability to render a decision that will resolve the dispute. In other words, courts can give final judgments that solve existing problems; they cannot provide rulings about hypothetical situations.

RIPENESS

The case or controversy requirement is closely linked to the ripeness requirement. A case is *ripe* if a judge's decision is capable of affecting the parties immediately. Usually the issue of ripeness arises when one party claims that the case is moot—in other words, there is no point in the court's hearing the case because no judgment can affect the situation between the parties.

In the Laidlaw case cited previously, Laidlaw also argued that the case was moot because by the time the case went to trial, the company had complied with the requirements of its discharge permits. Thus, Laidlaw argued, the only remedy left to the courts—a penalty Laidlaw must pay to the government—would not affect the plaintiffs. The Supreme Court

[7] 120 S. Ct. 923 (2000).
[8] Ibid.
[9] Ibid.

disagreed, ruling that the fact that a defendant voluntarily ceases a practice once litigation has commenced does not deprive a federal court of its power to determine the legality of the practice, because such a ruling would leave the defendant free to return to his old unlawful practices. Thus, the Court found the case was not moot because imposing a penalty on the defendant would have an important deterrent effect.[10]

Legal Principle: **Before a case can be heard, it must meet the three threshold requirements of standing, case or controversy, and ripeness.**

Steps in Civil Litigation

L05

What are the steps in civil litigation?

The U.S. litigation system is an adversary system: a neutral fact finder—a judge or jury—hears evidence and arguments that opposing sides present and then decides the case on the basis of the facts and law. Strict rules govern the types of evidence fact finders may consider. Theoretically, fact finders make informed and impartial rulings because each party has an incentive to find all relevant evidence and make the strongest possible arguments on behalf of her or his position.

Critics of the adversary system, however, point out several drawbacks: the time and expense each lawsuit requires, the damage a suit may cause to the litigating parties' relationship, and the unfair advantage to those with wealth and experience using the court system.

Dare I hit "send"? Email was simpler before it became discoverable.

stus.com

THE PRETRIAL STAGE

The *rules of civil procedure* govern civil case proceedings. The Federal Rules of Civil Procedure apply in all federal courts. Each state has its own set of rules, but most states' rules are very similar to the Federal Rules of Civil Procedure. In addition, each court usually has its own set of local court rules.

Informal Negotiations.   The initial attempt to resolve a business dispute is usually informal: a discussion or negotiation among the parties to try to find a solution. If the parties are unable to resolve their dispute, one party often seeks an attorney's advice. Together, the attorney and client may be able to resolve the dispute informally with the other party.

Pleadings.   The first formal stage of a lawsuit is the *pleading stage.* The plaintiff's attorney initiates a lawsuit by filing a *complaint* in the appropriate court. The complaint states the names of the parties to the action, the basis for the court's subject-matter jurisdiction, the facts on which the plaintiff bases his claim, and the relief the plaintiff seeks. The pleadings prevent surprises at trial; they allow attorneys to prepare arguments to counter the other side's claims. Exhibit 3-5 shows a typical complaint.

Service of Process.   To obtain *in personam* jurisdiction over a defendant and to satisfy due process, a court must notify the defendant of the pending lawsuit. Service of process occurs when the defendant is given a copy of the complaint and summons by a process server or by certified or ordinary mail.

[10] Ibid.

EXHIBIT 3-5
Typical Complaint

THE COURT OF COMMON PLEAS OF CLARK COUNTY, NEVADA

Bob Lyons and Sue Lyons, Plaintiffs

v.

Christine Collins, Defendant

COMPLAINT FOR NEGLIGENCE

Case No.

Now come the plaintiffs, Bob Lyons and Sue Lyons, and, for their complaint, allege as follows:

1. Plaintiffs, Bob Lyons and Sue Lyons, both of 825 Havercamp Street, are citizens of Clark County, in the state of Nevada, and defendant, Christine Collins, 947 Rainbow Ave., is a citizen of Clark County in the state of Nevada.

2. On May 1, 2001, the Defendant built a wooden hanging bridge across a stream that runs through the plaintiffs' property at 825 Havercamp Street.

3. Defendant negligently used ropes in the construction of the bridge that were not thick enough to sustain human traffic on the bridge.

4. At approximately 4:00 p.m., on May 20, 2001, the plaintiffs were attempting to carry a box of landscaping stones across the bridge when the ropes broke, and the bridge collapsed, causing plaintiffs to fall seven feet into the stream.

5. As a result of the fall, plaintiff, Bob Lyons, suffered a broken arm, a broken leg, and a skull fracture, incurring $160,000 in medical expenses.

6. As a result of the fall, plaintiff, Sue Lyons, suffered two broken cervical vertebrae, and a skull fracture, incurring $300,000 in medical expenses.

7. As a result of the fall, the landscaping stones, which had cost $1,200, were destroyed.

8. As a result of the foregoing injuries, plaintiff, Bob Lyons, was required to miss eight weeks of work, resulting in a loss of $2,400 in wages.

9. As a result of the foregoing injuries, plaintiff, Sue Lyons, was required to miss twelve weeks of work, resulting in a loss of $3,600 in wages.

WHEREFORE, Plaintiffs demand judgment in the amount of $467,200, plus costs of this action.

Harlon Elliot

Attorney for Plaintiff

824 Sahara Ave.

Las Vegas, Nevada 89117

JURY DEMAND

Plaintiff demands a trial by jury in this matter.

The complaint explains the basis of the lawsuit to the defendant. The summons tells the defendant that if he or she does not respond to the lawsuit within a certain period of time, the plaintiff will receive a default judgment. A default judgment is a judgment in favor of the plaintiff that occurs when the defendant fails to answer the complaint and the plaintiff's complaint alleges facts that would support such a judgment.

Defendant's Response.   The defendant responds to the complaint with an answer. In this document, the defendant denies, affirms, or claims no knowledge of the accuracy of the plaintiff's allegations.

A defendant uses an *affirmative defense* when her or his answer admits that the facts contained in the complaint are accurate but also includes additional facts that justify the defendant's actions and provide a legally sound reason to deny relief to the plaintiff.

For example, if a woman sued a man for battery because he punched her in the face, he might claim that he hit her only because she aimed a gun at him and threatened to shoot. His claim that he was acting in self-defense is an affirmative defense.

If the defendant plans to raise an affirmative defense, he must raise it in his answer to give the plaintiff adequate notice. If he fails to raise an affirmative defense in the answer, the judge will likely not allow him to raise it during the trial.

Upon receiving the complaint, if the defendant believes that even though all the plaintiff's factual allegations are true, the law does not entitle the plaintiff to a favorable judgment, the defendant may file a motion to dismiss, or *demurrer.* (A motion is a request by a party for the court to do something; in this instance, the request is to dismiss the case.) In deciding whether to grant a motion to dismiss, a judge accepts the facts as stated by the plaintiff and rules on the legal issues in the case. Judges generally grant a motion to dismiss only when it appears beyond a doubt that the plaintiff cannot prove any set of facts to justify granting the judgment she seeks.

If the defendant believes he has a claim against the plaintiff, he includes this counterclaim with the answer. As Exhibit 3–6 shows, the form of a counterclaim is identical to the form of a complaint. The defendant states the facts supporting his claim and asks for relief.

EXHIBIT 3-6

Defendant's Answer and Counterclaim

THE COURT OF COMMON PLEAS OF CLARK COUNTY, NEVADA

Bob Lyons and Sue Lyons, Plaintiffs v. Christine Collins, Defendant ANSWER AND COUNTERCLAIM FOR BREACH OF CONTRACT Case No.

Now comes the defendant, Christine Collins, and answers the complaint of plaintiff herein as follows:

First Defense

1. Admits the allegations in paragraphs 1 and 2.

2. Denies the allegation in paragraph 3.

3. Is without knowledge as to the truth or falsity of the allegations contained in paragraphs 4, 5, 6, 7, 8, and 9.

Second Defense

4. If the court believes the allegations contained in paragraph 3, which the defendant expressly denies, plaintiffs should still be denied recovery because they were informed prior to the construction of the bridge that there should be no more than one person on the bridge at one time and that no individual weighing more than 200 pounds should be allowed to walk on the bridge.

Counterclaim

5. On April 15, the parties agreed that Defendant would build a wooden hanging bridge across a stream that runs through the defendants' property at 825 Havercamp Street, in exchange for which plaintiffs would pay defendant $2,000 upon completion of construction.

6. On May 1, 2001, the Defendant built the agreed upon ornament, wooden, hanging bridge across a stream that runs through the defendants' property at 825 Havercamp Street, but Plaintiffs failed to pay the agreed upon price for the bridge.

7. By their failure to pay, plaintiffs breached their contract and are liable to defendant for the contract price of $2,000.

WHEREFORE, defendant prays for a judgment dismissing the plaintiffs' complaint, and granting the defendant a judgment against plaintiff in the amount of $2,000 plus costs of this action.

Melissa Davenport

Attorney for Defendant

777 Decatur Ave.

Las Vegas, Nevada 89117

If the defendant files a counterclaim, the plaintiff generally files a reply. A reply is an answer to a counterclaim. In the reply, the plaintiff admits, denies, or claims a lack of knowledge as to the accuracy of the facts of the defendant's counterclaim. If the plaintiff plans to use an affirmative defense, she must raise it in the reply.

Pretrial Motions.   The early pleadings establish the legal and factual issues of the case. After the pleadings, the plaintiff or defendant may file a motion to conclude the case early, eliminate some claims, or gain some advantage. A party may move, or request, that the court do almost anything pertaining to the case. For example, if the plaintiff files a suit about the right to a piece of property, she may move that the court prohibit the current possessor of the land from selling it. Courts may grant or deny such motions at their discretion.

When a party files a motion with the court, the court sends a copy to the opposing attorney, who may respond to the motion, usually by requesting that the judge deny the motion. In many cases, the judge rules on the motion immediately. In other cases, the judge holds a hearing at which the attorneys for both sides argue how the judge should decide the motion.

Two primary pretrial motions are a motion for judgment on the pleadings and a motion for summary judgment. Once the parties file the pleadings, either party can file a motion for judgment on the pleadings. The motion is a request for the court to consider that all the facts in the pleadings are true and to apply the law to those facts. The court grants the motion if, after this process, it finds that the only reasonable decision is in favor of the moving party.

Either party can file a motion for summary judgment after the discovery process (described below). The motion asserts that no factual disputes exist and that if the judge applied the law to the undisputed facts, her only reasonable decision would be in favor of the moving party. The difference between this motion and a motion for judgment on the pleadings is that in a motion for summary judgment, the moving party may use affidavits (sworn statements from the parties or witnesses), relevant documents, and depositions or interrogatories (a party's sworn answers to written questions) to support his motion. The judge grants the motion if, after examining the evidence, she finds no factual disputes. If, however, she finds any factual issues about which the parties disagree, she denies the motion and sends the case to trial.

Discovery.   After filing the initial pleadings and motions, the parties gather information from each other through discovery. The discovery process enables the parties to learn about facts surrounding the case so that they are not surprised in the courtroom. Three common discovery tools are interrogatories, requests to produce documents, and depositions.

Interrogatories are written questions that one party sends to the other to answer under oath. Frequently, a *request to admit certain facts* accompanies interrogatories. Attorneys work with their clients to answer interrogatories and requested admissions of facts.

A request to produce documents (or other items) forces the opposing party to produce (turn over) certain information unless it is privileged or irrelevant to the case. Parties may request documents such as photographs, contracts, written estimates, medical records, tax forms, and other government documents. In tort cases, the defendant frequently asks the plaintiff to submit a mental- or physical-examination report.

Finally, the parties may obtain testimony from a witness before trial through a deposition. At a deposition, attorneys examine a witness under oath. A court reporter (stenographer) records every word the witnesses and attorneys speak. Both parties receive a copy of the testimony in document form. Depositions provide information and may also set up inconsistencies between a witness's testimony at the deposition and his testimony at trial. If a party discovers an inconsistency in the testimony of one of the other party's witnesses, she can bring the inconsistency to the fact finder's attention to diminish the witness's credibility. The parties may also use depositions when a witness is elderly, moving, or ill such that he may be unavailable at the time of the trial.

If a party does not comply with requests for discovery, the court may admit the facts the other party sought to discover. Attorneys who feel that certain material is outside the scope of the case often argue that the material is irrelevant to the case. If the court disagrees, however, the party must supply the requested information. Although these discovery tools are important in the United States, not all countries have a discovery process.

In discovery, as in other areas, technology is having an impact. It is estimated that 90 percent of all documents and communications are created and maintained in electronic formats. In December 2006, the Federal Rules of Civil Procedure were amended to reflect changes in technology. Parties are now required to "make provisions for disclosure or discovery of electronically stored information"[11] at the start of the litigation process, and they must develop a discovery plan during their pretrial conferences. Once it appears that litigation is imminent, litigants have an obligation not to delete or destroy electronic files that may be discoverable. However, "absent exceptional circumstances, a court may not impose sanctions . . . on a party for failing to provide electronically stored information lost as a result of the routine, good-faith operation of an electronic information system."[12]

Parties who might become embroiled in litigation, however, probably should not count on using the good-faith exception because the consequences of destroying electronic data can be significant. For example, in the sex discrimination case of *Zubulake v. UBS Warburg LLC,*[13] the judge found that the company's employees had intentionally deleted e-mail messages, lost a number of backup tapes, and failed to produce files as requested. As a sanction, she issued an *adverse-inference* instruction to the jury, basically telling them that they could assume that any documents not produced would have been harmful to the company's case. The jury ultimately awarded the woman $29.3 million in damages.

Morgan Stanley had to pay an even bigger price for its failure to meet its obligations for electronic discovery of relevant e-mail messages and documents. In *Coleman Holdings Inc. v. Morgan Stanley & Co.,*[14] the firm produced more than 1,300 pages of e-mail messages but failed to reveal in a timely fashion the existence of 1,423 backup tapes. In that case, the court also issued an adverse-inference instruction, stating that Morgan Stanley would have to bear the burden of proving that it lacked knowledge of the fraud. The jury found in favor of the plaintiff and awarded damages in the amount of $1.6 billion. Morgan Stanley also had to pay the U.S. Securities and Exchange Commission $15 million in fines for failure to comply with discovery requirements in a related commission investigation.

What organizations can learn from these cases is that as soon as they reasonably anticipate that litigation will occur, they must suspend their routine policy for retaining and destroying documents and put in place a "litigation hold" to make sure that documents that might be relevant to the lawsuit are preserved. Some plaintiffs' lawyers are now sending *litigation-hold demand* letters to potential defendants, making it almost impossible for a firm to claim that relevant documents were innocently deleted.

---

[11] Rule 16(B), Federal Rules of Civil Procedure.

[12] Rule 37(F), Federal Rules of Civil Procedure.

[13] 231 F.R.D. 159, 2005 U.S. Dist. LEXIS 1525 (S.D.N.Y., Feb. 2, 2005).

[14] 2005 WL 679071 (Fla. Cir. Ct., Mar. 1, 2005).

Pretrial Conference.   A pretrial conference precedes the trial. A pretrial conference is an informal meeting of the judge with the attorneys representing the parties. During this conference, the parties try to narrow the legal and factual issues and possibly work out a settlement. If the parties cannot reach a settlement, the attorneys and the judge discuss the administrative details of the trial: its length, witnesses, and any pretrial stipulations of fact or law to which the parties agree.

THE TRIAL

If a plaintiff seeks at least $20 in monetary damages, the Seventh Amendment to the U.S. Constitution entitles the parties to a jury trial. The plaintiff must, however, demand a jury trial in his or her complaint. Following the English tradition, most civil trials have 12 jurors; however, in many jurisdictions the number of required jurors has been reduced by the legislature. In some jurisdictions, fewer than 12 jurors may be allowed if both parties consent. If the plaintiff seeks an equitable remedy (an injunction or other court order) or if the parties have waived their right to a jury, a judge serves as the fact finder in the case.

Trials have six stages: jury selection, opening statements, examination of witnesses, closing arguments, conference on jury instructions, and posttrial motions. The following sections describe these stages.

Jury Selection.   The jury selection process begins when the clerk of the courts randomly selects a number of potential jurors from the citizens within the court's jurisdiction. Once the potential jurors have reported for jury duty, the voir dire, or jury selection, process begins. The voir dire process selects the jurors who will decide the case, as well as two or three "alternate jurors" who will watch the trial and be available to replace any juror who, for some legitimate reason, must leave jury duty before the trial ends.

During voir dire, the judge and/or attorneys question potential jurors to determine whether they are able to render an unbiased opinion in the case. If a potential juror's response to a question indicates that she or he may be biased, either attorney may challenge, or ask the court to remove, that potential juror "for cause." For example, a lawyer could challenge for cause a potential juror who was a college roommate of the defendant. In most states, each party has a certain number of peremptory challenges. These peremptory challenges allow a party to challenge a certain number of potential jurors without giving a reason.

Peremptory challenges, however, may lead to abuse. For example, in the past, attorneys have used peremptory challenges to eliminate a certain class, ethnic group, or gender from the jury. In the 1986 case *Batson v. Kentucky,*[15] the U.S. Supreme Court ruled that race-based peremptory challenges in criminal cases violate the equal protection clause of the Fourteenth Amendment to the U.S. Constitution. (Chapter 5 discusses the amendments to the Constitution in more detail.) The Supreme Court later extended the ban on race-based challenges to civil cases. In Case 3-2, the U.S. Supreme Court addressed the issue of whether the equal protection clause covers gender-based challenges.

The voir dire process has become more sophisticated over time. In cases involving significant amounts of money, rather than relying on their instinct or experience during jury selection, attorneys use professional jury selection services to identify demographic data to help select ideal jurors.

---

[15] 476 U.S. 79 (1986).

Jury selection firms also provide additional services, including mock trials and shadow juries. Jury selection firms set up mock trials by recruiting individuals who match the demographics of the real jury to listen to attorneys' arguments and witnesses' testimony. These mock trials give attorneys a sense of how their approach to the case will appear to the actual jurors. If the mock jury is not receptive to a particular argument or witness's testimony, the attorneys can modify their approach before trial.

Parties also often hire jury selection firms to provide shadow juries. Like a mock trial, a shadow jury uses individuals whose demographics match the demographics of a trial's real jurors. A shadow jury, however, sits inside the courtroom to watch the actual trial. At the end of each day of the trial, the shadow jury deliberates, giving the attorneys an idea of how the real jurors are reacting to the case. If the shadow jury finds the opposing side to be winning, the attorneys can modify their strategy.

Many attorneys believe that these services increase their clients' chances of winning cases. Critics argue, however, that jury selection services give an unfair advantage to one side when only one party can afford these services.

CASE 3-2   UNITED STATES SUPREME COURT
114 S. CT. 1419 (1994)

J.E.B. v. ALABAMA, *EX. REL. T.B.*

The State of Alabama filed a complaint for paternity and child support against J.E.B. on behalf of T.B., the unwed mother of a minor child. The court called a panel of twelve males and twenty-four females as potential jurors. Only ten males remained after three individuals were removed for cause. The state used its peremptory challenges to remove nine male jurors, and J.E.B. removed the tenth, resulting in an all female jury. The trial court rejected J.E.B.'s objection to the gender-based challenges, and the jury found J.E.B. to be the father. J.E.B. appealed, and the court of appeals affirmed the trial court's ruling that the Equal Protection Clause does not prohibit gender-based challenges. The Alabama Supreme Court declined to hear the appeal, and J.E.B. appealed to the U.S. Supreme Court.

JUSTICE BLACKMUN: Discrimination in jury selection, whether based on race or on gender, causes harm to the litigants, the community, and the individual jurors who are wrongfully excluded from participation in the judicial process. The litigants are harmed by the risk that the prejudice which motivated the discriminatory selection of the jury will infect the entire proceedings. The community is harmed by the State's participation in the perpetuation of invidious group stereotypes and the inevitable loss of confidence in our judicial system that state-sanctioned discrimination in the courtroom engenders.

As with race-based *Batson* claims, a party alleging gender discrimination must make a prima facie showing of intentional discrimination before the party exercising the challenge is required to explain the basis for the strike. When an explanation is required, it need not rise to the level of a "for cause" challenge; rather, it merely must be based on a juror characteristic other than gender and the proffered explanation may not be pretextual.

Equal opportunity to participate in the fair administration of justice is fundamental to our democratic system. It reaffirms the promise of equality under the law—that all citizens, regardless of race, ethnicity, or gender, have the chance to take part directly in our democracy. When persons are excluded from participation in our democratic processes solely because of race or gender, this promise of equality dims, and the integrity of our judicial system is jeopardized.

REVERSED and REMANDED in favor of J.E.B.

CRITICAL THINKING

The defendant was contesting the removal of males from the jury. Does this fact weaken the Court's reasoning? Explain.

ETHICAL DECISION MAKING

Which values does this decision tend to emphasize?

Opening Statements.   Once the attorneys have impaneled, or selected, a jury, the case begins with opening statements. Each party's attorney explains to the judge and jury which facts he or she intends to prove, the legal conclusions to which these facts lead, and how the fact finder should decide the case based on those facts.

The Examination of Witnesses and Presentation of Evidence.   Following opening statements, the plaintiff and defendant, in turn, present their cases-in-chief by examining witnesses and presenting evidence. The plaintiff has the burden of proving the case, meaning that if neither side presents a convincing case, the fact finder must rule in favor of the defendant. Thus, the plaintiff presents her case first.

The procedure for each witness is the same. First, the plaintiff's attorney questions the witness in *direct examination.* The plaintiff's attorney asks the witness questions to elicit facts that support the plaintiff's case-in-chief. Questions must relate to matters about which the witness has direct knowledge. Attorneys cannot elicit "hearsay" from the witnesses. *Hearsay* is testimony about what a witness heard another person say. Hearsay is impermissible because the opposing attorney cannot question the person who made the original statement to determine the statement's veracity.

The federal rules of evidence also prohibit attorneys from asking leading questions. Leading questions are questions that imply a specific answer. For example, an attorney cannot ask a witness, "Did the defendant come to your office and ask you to purchase stock from him?" Instead, attorneys must ask questions such as, "When did you first encounter the defendant?"

After direct examination, opposing counsel may *cross-examine* the witness. Opposing counsel, however, may ask only questions related to the witness's direct examination. On cross-examination, attorneys can ask leading questions. Attorneys try to show inconsistencies in the witness's testimony, cast doubt on the claims of the plaintiff's case, and elicit information to support the defendant's case.

After cross-examination, the plaintiff's attorney may conduct a *redirect examination,* a series of questions to repair damage done by the cross-examination. At the judge's discretion, opposing counsel has an opportunity to *re-cross* the witness to question his testimony on redirect examination. The parties follow this procedure for each of the plaintiff's witnesses.

Immediately following the plaintiff's presentation of her case, the defendant may move for a directed verdict. This motion is a request for the court to direct a verdict for the defendant because even if the jury accepted all the evidence and testimony presented by the plaintiff as true, the jury would still have no legal basis for a decision in favor of the plaintiff. The federal court system refers to a motion for a directed verdict as a *motion for a judgment as a matter of law.* Courts rarely grant motions for a directed verdict because plaintiffs almost always present at least *some* evidence to support each element of the cause of action.

If the court denies the defendant's motion for a directed verdict, the defendant then presents his case. The parties question the defendant's witnesses in the same manner as they questioned the plaintiff's witnesses, except that the defendant's attorney conducts direct and redirect examination and the plaintiff's attorney conducts cross-examination and re-cross-examination.

Closing Arguments.   After the defendant's case, the attorneys present closing arguments. In the *closing argument,* each attorney summarizes evidence from the trial in a manner consistent with his or her client's case. The plaintiff's attorney presents her closing

Civil procedure in Japan differs significantly from American civil procedure. The Japanese legal system has no juries and no distinct pretrial stage. Instead, a trial is a series of discrete meetings between the parties and the judge. At the first meeting, the parties identify the most critical and contested issues. They choose one and recess to gather evidence and marshal arguments on the issue.

At the next meeting, the judge rules on the chosen issue. If the judge decides against the plaintiff, the case is over. If the plaintiff wins, the process continues with the next issue. The process continues until the plaintiff loses an issue or until the judge decides all issues in the plaintiff's favor, resulting in a verdict for the plaintiff.

In addition, the discovery process in the Japanese court system is not as simple as it is in the United States. To obtain evidence, parties must convince the judge to order others to testify or produce documents. The judge can fine or jail parties who refuse to comply with such orders. Additionally, if a party does not comply with the judge's requests for discovery, the judge may admit the facts the other party sought to discover.

argument first, followed by the defendant's attorney, and the plaintiff has the option to present a rebuttal of the defendant's closing argument.

Jury Instructions. In a jury trial, the judge "charges the jury" by instructing the jurors how the law applies to the facts of the case. Both sides' attorneys submit statements to the judge explaining how they believe he should charge the jury. The judge's instructions are usually a combination of both sides' suggestions.

Different types of cases require different standards of proof. In most civil cases, the plaintiff must prove her case by a *preponderance of the evidence;* in other words, she must show that her claim is more likely to be true than the defendant's claim. In some civil cases, particularly cases involving fraud or oral contracts, the plaintiff must prove her case by *clear and convincing evidence,* a higher standard of proof. Criminal cases have an even higher burden of proof: The prosecution must prove its case *beyond a reasonable doubt.*

After the judge charges the jury, the jurors retire to the jury room to deliberate. Once they reach a decision, they return to the courtroom, where the judge reads their verdict and discharges them from their duty.

Trial procedures in the United States are quite different from trial procedures in other countries, as the Comparing the Law of Other Countries box illustrates.

Posttrial Motions. Once the trial ends, the party who received the favorable verdict files a *motion for a judgment in accordance with the verdict.* Until the judge enters the judgment, the court has not issued a legally binding decision for the case.

The party who loses at trial has a number of available options. One option is to file a *motion for a judgment notwithstanding the verdict,* or *judgment non obstante verdicto,* asking the judge to issue a judgment contrary to the jury's verdict. To grant the motion, the judge must find that, when viewing the evidence in the light most favorable to the nonmoving party, a reasonable jury could not have found in favor of that party. In other words, as a matter of law, the judge must determine that the trial did not produce sufficient evidence to support the jury's verdict. This motion is similar to a motion for a directed verdict, except the parties cannot make this motion until *after* the jury issues a verdict. The federal court system refers to this motion as a *motion for judgment as a matter of law.*

The losing party can also file a *motion for a new trial.* Judges grant motions for a new trial only if they believe the jury's decision was clearly erroneous but they are not sure that the other side should necessarily have won the case. A judge often grants a motion for a new trial when the parties discover new evidence, when the judge made an erroneous ruling, or when misconduct during the trial may have prevented the jury from reaching a fair decision.

APPELLATE PROCEDURE

Either party may appeal the judge's decision on posttrial motions or on her or his final judgment. Sometimes, both parties appeal the same decision. For example, if a jury awarded the plaintiff $10,000 in damages, the plaintiff and the defendant may both appeal the amount of the judgment. Appellate courts, however, reverse only about 1 out of every 10 trial court decisions on appeal.

To be eligible for appeal, the losing party must argue that a prejudicial error of law occurred during the trial. A prejudicial error of law is a mistake so significant that it likely affected the outcome of the case. For example, a prejudicial error could occur if the judge improperly admitted hearsay evidence that allowed the plaintiff to prove an element of her case.

To appeal a case, the attorney for the appealing party (the appellant) files a notice of appeal with the clerk of the trial court within a prescribed time. The clerk then forwards the record of appeal to the appeals court. The record of appeal typically contains a number of items: the pleadings, a trial transcript, copies of the trial exhibits, copies of the judge's rulings on the parties' motions, the attorneys' arguments, jury instructions, the jury's verdict, posttrial motions, and the judgment order.

The appellant then files a brief, or written argument, with the court. Appellants file briefs to explain why the judgment in the lower court was erroneous and why the appeals court should reverse it. The attorney for the party who won in the lower court (the appellee) files an answering brief. The appellant may then file a reply brief in response to the appellee's brief. Generally, however, appellants do not file reply briefs.

The appeals court then usually allows the attorneys to present oral arguments before the court. The court considers these arguments, reviews the record of the case, and renders a decision.

An appellate court may render four basic decisions. The court can accept the lower court's judgment by *affirming* the decision of the lower court. Alternatively, if the appellate court concludes that the lower court's decision was correct but the remedy was inappropriate, it *modifies* the remedy. If the appellate court decides that the lower court was incorrect in its decision, it *reverses* the lower court's decision. Finally, if the appeals court thinks the lower court committed an error but does not know how that error affected the outcome of the case, it *remands* the case to the lower court for a new trial.

An appellate court usually has a bench with at least three judges. Appellate courts do not have juries; rather, the judges decide the case by majority vote. One of the judges who votes with the majority records the court's decision and its reasons in the *majority opinion.* These decisions have precedential value—that is, judges use these prior appellate court decisions to make decisions in future cases. Also, these decisions establish new guidelines in the law that all citizens must follow. If a judge agrees with the majority's decision, but for different reasons, she may write a *concurring opinion,* stating the reasons she used to reach the majority's conclusion. Finally, judges disagreeing with the majority may write a *dissenting opinion,* giving their reasons for reaching a contrary conclusion. Attorneys arguing that a court should change the law frequently cite dissenting opinions from previous cases in their briefs. Likewise, appellate judges who change the law often cite dissenting opinions from past cases.

For most cases, only one appeal is available. In states with both an intermediate and a final court of appeals, a losing party may appeal from the intermediate appellate court to the state supreme court. In a limited number of cases, the losing party can appeal the decision of a state supreme court or a federal circuit court of appeals to the U.S. Supreme Court.

Appeal to the U.S. Supreme Court.   Every year thousands of individuals file appeals with the U.S. Supreme Court. The Court, however, hears, on average, only 80 to 90 cases each year. To file an appeal to the U.S. Supreme Court, a party files a petition asking the Court to issue a **writ of certiorari,** an order to the lower court to send to the Supreme Court the record of the case. The Court issues very few writs.

The justices review petitions and issue a writ only when at least four justices vote to hear the case (the *rule of four*). The court is most likely to issue a writ in four instances: (1) The case presents a substantial federal question that the Supreme Court has not yet addressed; (2) multiple circuit courts of appeal have decided the issue of the case in different ways; (3) a state court of last resort has ruled that a federal law is invalid or has upheld a state law that may violate federal law; or (4) a federal court has ruled that an act of Congress is unconstitutional. If the Supreme Court does not issue a writ of certiorari, the lower court's decision stands.

CASE OPENER WRAP-UP

Questionable Jurisdiction over Caterpillar

The timing of events was crucial to the outcome of the Caterpillar case. At the time Lewis filed the case in the state court system, one of the defendants and the plaintiff were from the same state, so the state court system had jurisdiction. Once the supply company reached an agreement with Lewis, the other defendant, Caterpillar, filed a motion to exercise its right of removal because diversity of citizenship existed in the absence of the Kentucky defendant. But the agreement was not final at the time of the motion because the agreement was subject to the insurer's approval. Thus, the appellate court ruled that because the supply company was still a party to the agreement, the federal court system could not exercise jurisdiction over the case.

The U.S. Supreme Court, however, overruled the appellate court. The Supreme Court ruled that the state court should not have granted Caterpillar's initial motion to remove the case because at the time of removal, the insurer had not accepted the settlement agreement, the supply company remained a party in the case, and, therefore, the diversity of citizenship was not complete. The Supreme Court held further, however, that the district court's error in hearing the case was not fatal because the settlement agreement was approved and the case satisfied the jurisdictional requirements by the time the federal court issued its decision. The Court ruled that to require the district court to send the case back to the state system would be an undue waste of judicial resources.

Why might Caterpillar have wanted to move the case to the federal court system? First, the case involved product liability claims. Data suggest that average damage awards in product liability cases tend to be higher in state courts than in federal courts. Second, Caterpillar may have feared local prejudice. While all judges must strive for neutrality, out-of-state defendants may fear that state judges are slightly biased in favor of in-state parties.

KEY TERMS

answer 53

appellate court 39

brief 61

case or controversy 51

complaint 40

counterclaim 54

court of appellate
  jurisdiction 39

court of original
  jurisdiction 39

default judgment 53

defendant 40

deposition 55

directed
  verdict 59

discovery 55

in personam
  jurisdiction 40

in rem jurisdiction 41

interrogatories 55

jurisdiction 39

long-arm statute 41

mock trial 58

motion 54

motion for judgment on the
  pleadings 55

motion for summary
  judgment 55

motion to dismiss 54

peremptory challenge 57

personal service 40

plaintiff 40

prejudicial error of law 61

pretrial conference 57

quasi *in rem* jurisdiction 41

reply 55

request to produce
  documents 55

ripeness 51

service of process 40

shadow jury 58

standing 51

subject-matter
  jurisdiction 42

summons 40

trial court 39

venue 46

voir dire 57

writ of certiorari 62

SUMMARY OF KEY TOPICS

In personam jurisdiction is the power of a court to render a decision affecting a person's legal rights. *Subject-matter jurisdiction* is the power of a court to render a decision in a particular type of case. The three forms of subject-matter jurisdiction are state, exclusive federal, and concurrent.

Jurisdiction

Venue is the geographic location of the trial.

Venue

The U.S. has two parallel court structures: the state and federal systems. The federal structure has *district courts* (trial courts), *circuit courts of appeal,* and the *U.S. Supreme Court.* The state court structure varies by state, but generally includes courts of common pleas (trial courts), state courts of appeal, and a state supreme court.

The Structure of the Court System

Standing: For a person to have the legal right to file a case, the outcome of the case must personally affect that person.

Threshold Requirements

Case or controversy: There must be an issue before the court that a judicial decision is capable of resolving. Parties cannot ask the judge for an "advisory opinion."

Ripeness: The case cannot be moot; it must be ready for a decision to be made.

The stages of a civil trial include the pretrial, trial, posttrial, and appellate stages.

Steps in Civil Litigation

Pretrial includes consultation with attorneys, pleadings, the discovery process, and the pretrial conference.

The *trial* begins with jury selection, followed by opening statements, the plaintiff's case, the defendant's case, closing arguments, jury instructions, jury deliberations, the jury's verdict, and the judgment.

After the trial, parties may file *posttrial motions.*

The parties may then file *appeals* to the appropriate appellate court and, in some cases, to the U.S. Supreme Court.

POINT / COUNTERPOINT

Is the Adversarial System the Most Effective Approach to Justice?	
YES	**NO**
Proponents of the adversarial system argue that justice is best served when each individual's rights and freedoms are protected. The adversarial system requires that the fact finder remain a neutral and objective party, free from bias. The parties are responsible for developing their own individual theories of the case. By allowing individuals to decide what information they wish to present as a part of their case, the system allows them to take a more active role in the legal process.	Critics of the adversarial system argue that the quest for truth should be central to the administration of justice. By pitting parties against one another in the courtroom, the adversarial system becomes more interested in solving controversies than discovering the truth. Since the parties are allowed to decide what evidence they do and do not wish to present to the fact finder, it is likely that a decision will be rendered on the basis of incomplete and biased information.
In addition to promoting individual rights, the adversarial system also helps prevent the abuse of power by the finder of fact. Proponents argue that excluding finders of fact from question asking and evidence collection prevents them from reaching a premature decision or abusing their power.	In addition to overemphasizing controversy, the adversarial system creates a wealth disparity between parties. For example, if Suzie the secretary decides to sue her employer, Giant Corporate Entity, the sheer size and financial strength of her opponent puts her at an immediate disadvantage. While Suzie may be able to afford an attorney, it is likely that her employer will be able to afford a team of attorneys, paralegals, and support staff. The adversarial system quickly goes from a "system designed to protect individual rights" to a system that primarily protects the rights of the wealthy few who can afford better attorneys and fund a lengthy litigation.
In response to critics who argue that the adversarial system is more about resolving a dispute than finding the truth, proponents argue that by pitting the two sides against one another, the truth will emerge. The parties involved in the litigation have a stronger motivation to uncover and disclose the facts relevant to the case than does any neutral party (such as the judge in the inquisitorial system). Individual rights and zealous advocacy will best lead to the administration of justice.	Rather than having the adversarial system, the country would be better served by an inquisitorial system. In the inquisitorial system, the finder of fact, not the parties, is responsible for gathering evidence and investigating. The finder of fact has the opportunity to gather as much information as necessary before rendering an opinion. In the inquisitorial system, the truth, not the controversy, guides the way.

QUESTIONS & PROBLEMS

1. Explain the two types of jurisdiction that a court must have to hear a case and render a binding decision over the parties.

2. Explain the differences between trial courts and appellate courts.

3. Identify and define the alternative tools of discovery.

4. Explain the three threshold requirements a plaintiff must meet before he or she can file a lawsuit.

5. Missouri was International Shoe Corporation's principal place of business, but the company employed between 11 and 13 salespersons in the state of Washington who exhibited samples and solicited orders for shoes from prospective buyers in Washington. The state of Washington assessed the company for contributions to a state unemployment fund. The state served the assessment on one of International Shoe Corporation's sales representatives in Washington and sent a copy by registered

mail to the company's Missouri headquarters. International Shoe's representative challenged the assessment on numerous grounds, arguing that the state had not properly served the corporation. Is the corporation's defense valid? Why or why not? [*International Shoe Co. v. Washington,* 326 U.S. 310 (1945).]

6. Nicastro, the plaintiff, was using a metal-shearing machine in New Jersey when he hurt his hand. The machine was produced by J. McIntyre Machinery, Ltd., which manufactured the machine in England, where the company is based. However, Nicastro brought the company to court in New Jersey because that is where the injury occurred. The company argued that it could not be brought to court in New Jersey because the court did not have personal jurisdiction over it due to the company's lack of minimum contacts in the state. Nicastro said that the company's distributor for the United States sold the equipment in the country, company officials attended trade shows in the country, even if they were not in New Jersey, and the record shows that one machine ended up in New Jersey. Ultimately, the company knew that its U.S. distributor could potentially sell its products in any state and that any product could somehow end up in any state. On the other hand, the company did not travel to, advertise, or contact any residents of New Jersey. Do you think the company is subject to personal jurisdiction in the state of New Jersey? How do you believe the Supreme Court ruled in this case? Why? [*J. McIntyre Machinery, Ltd. v. Nicastro,* 131 S. Ct. 2780 (2011).]

7. The plaintiff, a Texas resident, and the defendants, Colorado residents, were cat breeders who met at a cat show in Colorado. Subsequently, the plaintiff sent two cats to the defendants in Colorado for breeding and sent a third cat to them to be sold. A dispute over the return of the two breeding cats arose, and the plaintiff filed suit against the defendants in Texas. The defendants alleged that the Texas court lacked personal jurisdiction over them because they did not have minimum contacts within the state of Texas.

The Texas statute provides that the Texas court could exercise jurisdiction over an out-of-state defendant only if (1) the defendant has purposefully established minimum contacts with the forum state and (2) the exercise of jurisdiction comports with traditional notions of fair play and substantial justice. The defendants were not residents of Texas and had no business in Texas. The only contact the defendants had with Texas was a single trip they made to Texas to pick up two other cats, not related to the litigation, that they were going to take to a cat show. During that same visit, the defendants took a cat unrelated to the lawsuit to see a Texas veterinarian, and the plaintiff's husband assisted the defendants with a web page for their business. The trial court found that sufficient minimum contacts had been established. The defendants appealed. How do you believe the appellate court would rule in this case, and why? [*Hagan v. Field,* Court of Appeals of Texas, Fifth District, Dallas, 2006 Tex. App. LEXIS 393.]

8. Gucci America discovered that Wang Huoqing, a man living in China, was running multiple websites selling counterfeit Gucci products. Huoqing was selling intellectual property that was protected in Gucci's registered trademarks without permission. Gucci decided to hire a private investigator to order counterfeit Gucci merchandise from Huoqing's sites. Once the investigator received the merchandise at his address in California, Gucci filed a lawsuit against Huoqing for copyright infringement in a federal district court in California. Huoqing was notified of the lawsuit in an e-mail. However, he never appeared in court, so Gucci asked the court to make a default judgment. In turn, the court needed to decide whether it had the personal jurisdiction over the case involving Huoqing since he lived in China and his only contact with the United States was through sales over the Internet. The court decided that it would have jurisdiction over a person who had sufficient minimum contact with residents within the state. Courts have to apply a three-prong test to decide whether someone has had sufficient minimum contact with their forum: (1) Did Huoqing purposefully direct his activities and transactions with the forum or resident thereof or engage in an act whereby he was purposefully benefited by engaging in the activities in the forum, subsequently receiving the benefits and protections of its laws? (2) Did the lawsuit claim relate to Huoqing's forum-related activities? (3) If the court exercised jurisdiction, would doing so be reasonable? [*Gucci America v. Wang Huoqing,* F. Supp. 3d (2011).]

9. Jones lived in California, and for four years received weekly psychotherapy and dream counseling over the telephone from Williams, a licensed therapist living in New Mexico. Williams made several trips to California at Jones's request to provide additional treatment. For one year, Jones also received shamanic counseling over the phone from Williams's wife, Ritzman. Jones eventually ceased treatment and decided to sue Williams and Ritzman for medical malpractice. However, he filed the suit in California. Subsequently, the defendants moved to have the complaint dismissed for lack of personal jurisdiction. How do you think the court decided? [*Jones v. Williams,* 660 F.Supp.2d 1145 (2009).]

10. The plaintiffs, parents of underage children, sued the Advanced Brands and Importing Co., an importer of alcoholic beverages, seeking an injunction prohibiting advertisers from advertising its beers and damages in the form of compensation for the money spent by their children on illegal purchases of beer. The parents argued that the advertising campaign of the defendant causes underage children, like theirs, to illegally purchase the defendant's beer. The trial court dismissed the claim, in part, based on lack of standing, and the parents appealed. Do you think the appellate court found that they had standing? Why or why not? [*Alston v. Advanced Brands and Importing Co.,* 494 F.3d 562 (6th Cir. 2007).]

Looking for more review materials?

The Online Learning Center at **www.mhhe.com/kubasek3e** contains this chapter's "Assignment on the Internet" and also a list of URLs for more information, entitled "On the Internet." Find both of them in the Student Center portion of the OLC, along with quizzes and other helpful materials.

9 Negligence and Strict Liability

LEARNING OBJECTIVES

After reading this chapter, you will be able to answer the following questions:

1   What are the elements of negligence?

2   What are the doctrines that help a plaintiff establish a case of negligence?

3   What are the defenses to a claim of negligence?

4   What are the elements of strict liability?

CASE OPENER

The Case of the Collapsing Dock

Defendants Jack and Claire Lein owned and lived on Willow Creek Farm from 1980 through 2004. The farm manager, Stewart, and his girlfriend, plaintiff Tambra Curtis, also lived on the farm during this time.

While Curtis was walking across a wooden dock located on the farm, the dock collapsed, and she fell, suffering a hairline fracture to her tibia. Consequently, Curtis brought a personal injury suit against the Leins, hoping to collect damages for her personal injury. After Curtis's injury, the defendants destroyed the dock, claiming that the soon-to-be new owners of the farm planned to build a school on the property and, thus, there was no reason to replace the broken dock. Because there was no longer any evidence of the condition of the dock, the plaintiff invoked the doctrine of *res ipsa loquitur* to support her case of negligence. Curtis asserted that a wooden dock does not give way unless the creators were negligent in their creation and maintenance of the structure. The trial court granted the defendants summary judgment and ruled that the doctrine of *res ipsa loquitur* did not apply. According to the court, *res ipsa loquitur* did not apply because the dock could have collapsed for reasons other than negligence. The plaintiff appealed.

The Washington Court of Appeals affirmed the lower court's ruling, both courts concluding that *res ipsa loquitur* did not apply, but for different reasons. In contrast to the trial court, the court of appeals reasoned that the doctrine of *res ipsa loquitur* could be applied as evidence of negligence but that the plaintiff still had the burden of proving that the flaws in the dock's construction were discoverable by the defendants.

After the court of appeals affirmed the ruling of the trial court, the plaintiff sought review.[1]

1. Suppose you are the judge in this case. Do you think that Jack and Claire had a duty of care to protect Curtis? Why or why not?
2. How do you think the court ruled on review? Why?

The Wrap-Up at the end of the chapter will answer these questions.

[1] *Curtis v. Lein,* 169 Wn. 2d 884, 239 P.3d 1078, 2010 Wash. LEXIS 809 (2010).

Introduction to Negligence and Strict Liability

In the previous chapter we discussed intentional torts, wrongs in which an individual took an action that he or she should have known would harm another person. In this chapter, we consider two other types of torts: negligent and strict-liability torts. These torts are generally committed when an individual fails to maintain a duty of care to another individual.

Suppose Ross uses a piece of wood to smack Joey, the mailman, on the face. Ross has committed battery. If Ross is building a tree house in his yard, however, and accidentally drops a piece of wood on Joey, who is delivering Ross's mail, Ross's action lacks intent, so there is no battery. Yet he might be negligent.

Allegations of negligence are made in a wide variety of circumstances. For example, people have alleged negligence when incidents of teenage violence occurred. The parents of Marcos Delgado, Jr., filed a claim of negligence against a movie theater when it admitted 13-year-old Raymond Aiolentuna without an adult to the R-rated movie *Dead Presidents.* After the movie, Aiolentuna emerged from the theater, walked one block, and shot Delgado. Delgado's parents argued that the movie theater was negligent because it did not enforce the movie ratings system. The court, however, ruled in favor of the movie theater.[2] In another instance, the families of the victims of the 1999 Columbine school shootings in Colorado sued the two alleged shooters and the gun manufacturer for negligence. What exactly is required to establish a successful negligence claim?

In this chapter, we begin by examining the elements of negligence. Then we consider the methods that courts have adopted to help plaintiffs make successful negligence claims. Next, we examine the defenses that defendants to negligence claims can raise. Finally, we consider strict-liability torts.

Elements of Negligence

Negligence is behavior that creates an unreasonable risk of harm to others. In contrast to intentional torts, which result from a person's willfully taking actions that are likely to cause injury, negligent torts involve the failure to exercise reasonable care to protect another's person or property.

Sometimes, however, harm occurs because an individual suffers an **unfortunate accident,** an incident that simply could not be avoided, even with reasonable care. For example, suppose Jonathan is driving on the highway when he suffers a stroke. Because of the stroke, he crashes into two other vehicles. He is not, however, liable for damages

LO1

What are the elements of negligence?

[2] *Delgado v. American Multi-Cinema Inc.,* 99 C.D.O.S. 4772, Los Angeles Superior Court (1999).

caused by the accident. Yet if Jonathan had some type of warning that the stroke was going to occur, he might be liable for the accident.

To win a negligence case, the plaintiff must prove four elements: (1) duty, (2) breach of duty, (3) causation, and (4) damages. (See Exhibit 9-1.) A plaintiff who cannot establish all four of these elements will be denied recovery.

DUTY

The plaintiff must first establish that the defendant owes a *duty* to the plaintiff. In some particular situations, the law specifies the duty of care one individual owes to another. In most cases, however, the courts use the reasonable person standard to determine the defendant's duty of care. The reasonable person standard is a measurement of the way members of society expect an individual to act in a given situation. To determine the defendant's duty of care, the judge or jury must determine the degree of care and skill that a reasonable person would exercise under similar circumstances. The judge or jury then uses this standard to evaluate the actions of the individual in the case.

Let's return to the personal injury case in the opening scenario. What duty of care do you think a reasonable person in the position of the farm owners would owe Curtis?

When courts attempt to determine whether a reasonable person would have owed a duty to others, they consider four questions:

1. How likely was it that the harm would occur?
2. How serious was the harm?
3. How socially beneficial was the defendant's conduct that posed the risk of harm?
4. What costs would have been necessary to reduce the risk of harm?

BUT WHAT IF. . .
WHAT IF THE FACTS OF THE CASE OPENER WERE DIFFERENT?

Let's say, in the Case Opener, that the farm owners knew that the dock was extremely dangerous but figured no one would ever make it out to the dock because it was out of the way. What standard would a court apply to this case? What would be the likely outcome?

In many situations, it is far from clear what a reasonable person would do. For example, if a reasonable person saw an infant drowning in a shallow swimming pool, what would she do? In most situations like this one, the law holds that individuals have no duty to rescue strangers from perilous situations.

Exhibit 9-1
Elements of Negligence

To prove negligence, a plaintiff must demonstrate:
1. *Duty:* The standard of care a reasonable person owes another.
2. *Breach of duty:* Failure to live up to the standard of care.
3. *Causation:* (a) Actual cause (cause in fact)—the determination that the plaintiff's harm was a direct result of the defendant's breach of duty; and (b) proximate cause (legal cause)—the extent to which, as a matter of policy, the defendant will be held liable for the consequences of his actions.
4. *Damages:* A compensable loss suffered by the plaintiff.

In some cases, however, the courts hold that individuals have a duty to aid strangers in certain types of peril. For example, if Sam negligently hits Janice with his car and, as a result, Janice is lying in the street, Sam has a duty to remove her from that dangerous position. Similarly, employers have a special duty to protect their employees from dangerous situations.

The courts generally hold that landowners have a duty of care to protect individuals on their property. Similarly, businesses have a duty of care to customers who enter business property. It is important, therefore, for future business managers to be knowledgeable about this duty. Businesses should warn customers about risks they may encounter on business property. Some risks, however, are obvious, and businesses need not warn customers about them. For example, a business need not inform customers that they could get a paper cut from the pages of a book.

The courts generally hold that businesses have a duty of care to protect their customers against foreseeable risks about which the owner knew or reasonably should have known. For example, in *Haywood v. Baseline Construction Company,* a woman who tripped over lumber on the front porch of the House of Blues restaurant in Los Angeles sued for negligence. The business's attempt to warn customers by marking the lumber with yellow construction tape was insufficient to avoid the determination of negligence; the woman was awarded $91,366 in damages. Similar to *Haywood,* the Case Opener at the beginning of this chapter raises the question of the duty of care that landowners owe to individuals who are on their property with their permission.

Businesses and corporations are also obligated to provide products to consumers that are safe from foreseeable harm or injury. Failure to care for customers' safety can mean serious legal and financial repercussions for business owners and CEOs, especially if a company knowingly offers products or services that contain defects. For example, in early 2009, the Centers for Disease Control (CDC) traced hundreds of reported cases of salmonella-related sickness back to food products containing peanut substances manufactured by Peanut Corporation of America. Upon further investigation by the Food and Drug Administration (FDA), documents revealed that Peanut Corporation knew that its products tested positive for salmonella, on multiple occasions, over a time period of nearly two years. Rather than taking preventive measures to guarantee that its tainted peanut products didn't reach the public, Peanut Corporation instead decided to ship the contaminated goods.

So far, Peanut Corporation of America's bad judgment has resulted in 9 deaths and over 600 reported cases of illness. Many families of those who died or fell ill from the salmonella outbreak caused by Peanut Corporation are now filing suit and claiming negligence on the part of the company for turning a blind eye to laboratory results that confirmed salmonella's existence in its products. Other companies, such as Kellogg and King Nut, which manufactured products using peanut substances provided by Peanut Corporation, are finding themselves included in the lawsuits. Peanut Corporation has since shut down all its manufacturing plants and has filed for Chapter 7 bankruptcy. The FDA and the FBI have launched a criminal investigation and are looking into the activities of Peanut Corporation of America.[3]

Sometimes it can be difficult to tell when there is a duty of care between a business and its customers. For example, a man brought a negligence suit against AT&T, his cellular phone provider, for not providing information about the cell phone's calls when he was searching for his missing mother. Ernest Frey had bought the cell phone for his mother

[3] http://minnesota-lawyer.com/death-attorney/pritzker-law-firm-files-lawsuit-against-peanut-corporation-of-america/; "FDA Investigates PCA Plant for Salmonella Contamination," *Candy Industry* 174, no. 2 (February 2009), p. 12; and www.newsinferno.com/archives/4793.

A commonly offered explanation for the increasing occurrence of violence is the increased violence portrayed in the media. Some plaintiffs try to hold owners of certain websites liable under negligence theories for violent acts committed by teenagers. For example, in *James v. Meow Media,* a 14-year-old boy took six guns to school and shot three of his classmates to death. The parents of the deceased classmates brought suit against several Internet websites and the creators and distributors of various video games. The parents argued that these defendants had a duty of ordinary care to the slain girls.

The courts have been consistent, however, in finding that it was not foreseeable that a boy who played certain video games

and viewed certain websites would murder three of his classmates. In similar cases, courts have ruled that defendants (such as website owners, creators and distributors of video games, and directors and producers of movies) do not have a duty to protect a person from the criminal acts of a third party unless there is a special relationship that requires that the defendant act with that duty.

Although it appears that website owners, manufacturers, and producers will not be held liable, plaintiffs continue to bring suits against these groups of people. Can you think of an argument for why these groups of people might owe a duty of care to these plaintiffs?

after seeing an advertisement about the enhanced safety brought about by carrying a cell phone. When his mother went missing, he contacted the police and then AT&T to find out the location of any recent calls made from her phone. A call had been made, but AT&T refused to give Ernest Frey the location of the call without a subpoena. By the time Ernest's mother was found, after a subpoena had been issued for the cellular tower location, she was dead from a fatal injury. The U.S. district court refused to dismiss the case and found that there might be both a contractual duty of care to Ernest and his mother and a common law duty of care because the representative from AT&T was made aware of the urgency of the situation and the danger to Ernest's mother. Although previous cases involving landline telephone companies were found to lack a duty of care, the district court decided that there were enough important differences between landline and cellular telephones, as well as between the specifics of this case and the previous cases, to merit review by a trial court.[4]

Professionals have more training than ordinary people. Thus, when professionals are serving in their professional capacity, courts generally hold that they have a higher duty of care to clients than does the ordinary person. A professional cannot defend against a negligence suit by claiming ignorance of generally accepted principles in her or his field of expertise. Clients who feel that they have suffered damages as a result of a professional's breach of her duty of care can bring a negligence case against her. These actions are referred to as *malpractice cases,* and they are discussed in greater detail in Chapter 11.

BREACH OF DUTY

Once the plaintiff has established that the defendant owes her a duty of care, she must prove that the defendant's conduct violated that duty. This violation is called a *breach of duty.* For example, the driver of an automobile owes the other passengers in his car a duty of care to obey traffic signs. If he fails to stop at a stop sign, he has violated his duty to follow traffic signs and has therefore breached his duty of care. Once a duty of care has been established, it seems as if determining whether a breach of that duty occurred would be a simple task. Kathleen Turner believed that when she was hit by a foul ball at a baseball game there had been a clear breach of duty by the stadium. The Nevada Supreme Court found that Mandalay Sports Entertainment and the Las Vegas 51s had a limited duty of care to their patrons, which they fulfilled by putting up barriers in areas of high

---

[4] *Frey v. AT&T Mobility, Inc.,* 2008 U.S. Dist. LEXIS 72335 (N.D. Okla. 2008).

risks and providing written and audio announcements about the danger of foul balls. So, although there was a duty of care, that duty of care was fulfilled and the defendants were not negligent.[5] Looking back at the Case Opener, one can see the challenges of proving breach of duty when evidence of the breach is lacking. Because the defendants in the Case Opener destroyed the wooden dock that allegedly caused the plaintiff's personal injury, the plaintiff had to invoke the doctrine of *res ipsa loquitur* to try to prove breach of duty. The doctrine of *res ipsa loquitur* is discussed later in this chapter.

CAUSATION

Causation is the third element of a successful negligence claim, and it has two separate elements: actual cause and proximate cause. The plaintiff must prove both elements of causation to be able to recover damages.

The first element, actual cause (also known as *cause in fact*), is the determination that the defendant's breach of duty resulted directly in the plaintiff's injury. The courts commonly determine whether a breach of duty actually caused the plaintiff's injury by asking whether the plaintiff would have been injured if the defendant had fulfilled his or her duty. If the answer is no, then the actual cause of the plaintiff's injury was the defendant's breach. Actual cause is sometimes referred to as "but-for" causation because the plaintiff argues that the damages she suffered would not have occurred *but for* (except because of) the actions of the defendant. For example, in the personal injury case in the opening scenario, Curtis argued that *but for* the flawed construction and maintenance of the wooden dock, she would not have injured her tibia.

Proximate cause, sometimes referred to as *legal cause,* refers to the extent to which, as a matter of policy, a defendant may be held liable for the consequences of his actions. In most states, proximate cause is determined by foreseeability. Proximate cause is said to exist only when both the plaintiff and the plaintiff's damages were reasonably foreseeable at the time the defendant breached his duty to the plaintiff. Thus, if the defendant could not reasonably foresee the damages that the plaintiff suffered as a result of his action, the plaintiff's negligence claim will not be sustained because it lacks the element of proximate causation.

For example, if a defective tire on a vehicle blows out, it is foreseeable that the driver may lose control and hit a pedestrian. It is not foreseeable, however, that the pedestrian may be a scientist carrying a briefcase full of chemicals that may explode on impact, causing a third-floor window to shatter and injuring an accountant at his desk. In most states, the accountant would not succeed if he sued the tire manufacturer for negligence. The tire failure is not considered a proximate cause of the accountant's injury because the contents of the pedestrian's briefcase were highly unusual. The pedestrian, however, would be eligible to recover damages from the tire manufacturer because hitting a pedestrian is a foreseeable consequence of tire failure. Thus, the defect in the tire is a proximate cause of the pedestrian's injury.

Palsgraf v. Long Island Railroad Company is one of the most well-known cases addressing the issue of proximate cause (see Case 9-1).

BUT WHAT IF. . .

WHAT IF THE FACTS OF THE CASE OPENER WERE DIFFERENT?

Let's say, in the Case Opener, that the dock looked extremely rickety and looked as if it hadn't been touched for years. Would this alone have been enough for Curtis to foreseeably know that the dock was unsafe and would most likely collapse?

---

[5] *Turner v. Mandalay Sports Entertainment, LLC,* 180 P.3d 1172 (Nev. 2008).

CASE 9-1   PALSGRAF v. LONG ISLAND RAILROAD COMPANY
NEW YORK COURT OF APPEALS
248 N.Y. 33 (1928)

Mrs. Palsgraf was waiting for a train on a platform of a railroad. When a different train came into the station, two men ran to get on that train before it left the station. While one of the men safely reached the train, the other man, who was carrying a package, jumped on the already moving train but seemed as though he was going to fall off the train. The guard on the moving train tried to help pull the man onto the train, while another guard off of the train pushed the man from behind. Consequently, his small package wrapped in newspaper, which contained fireworks, fell upon the rails, causing the fireworks to explode. The shock of the explosion dislodged scales at the other end of the platform, and the falling scales hit Mrs. Palsgraf, causing injuries for which she brought suit against the railroad.

JUDGE CARDOZO: Nothing in the situation gave notice that the falling package had in it the potency of peril to persons thus removed. Negligence is not actionable unless it involves the invasion of a legally protected interest, the violation of a right. "Proof of negligence in the air, so to speak, will not do." If no hazard was apparent to the eye of ordinary vigilance, an act innocent and harmless, at least to outward seeming, with reference to her, did not take to itself the quality of a tort because it happened to be a wrong, though apparently not one involving the risk of bodily insecurity, with reference to someone else. "In every instance, before negligence can be predicated of a given act, back of the act must be sought and found a duty to the individual complaining, the observance of which would have averted or avoided the injury." "The ideas of negligence and duty are strictly correlative" (Bowen, L. J., in *Thomas v. Quartermaine*, 18 Q. B. D. 685, 694).

The argument for the plaintiff is built upon the shifting meanings of such words as "wrong" and "wrongful," and shares their instability. What the plaintiff must show is "a wrong" to herself, i.e., a violation of her own right, and not merely a wrong to someone else, nor conduct "wrongful" because unsocial, but not "a wrong" to any one. We are told that one who drives at reckless speed through a crowded city street is guilty of a negligent act and, therefore, of a wrongful one irrespective of the consequences. Negligent the act is, and wrongful in the sense that it is unsocial, but wrongful and unsocial in relation to other travelers, only because the eye of vigilance perceives the risk of damage. If the same act were to be committed on a speedway or a race course, it would lose its wrongful quality. . . . [W]rong is defined in terms of the natural or probable, at least when unintentional (*Parrot v. Wells-Fargo Co.* [The Nitro-Glycerine Case], 15 Wall. [U.S.] 524). . . . Here, by concession, there was nothing in the situation to suggest to the most cautious mind that the parcel wrapped in newspaper would spread wreckage through the station. If the guard had thrown it down knowingly and willfully, he would not have threatened the plaintiff's safety, so far as appearances could warn him. His conduct would not have involved, even then, an unreasonable probability of invasion of her bodily security. Liability can be no greater where the act is inadvertent.

Negligence, like risk, is thus a term of relation. Negligence in the abstract, apart from things related, is surely not a tort, if indeed it is understandable at all. . . . Negligence is not a tort unless it results in the commission of a wrong, and the commission of a wrong imports the violation of a right, in this case, we are told, the right to be protected against interference with one's bodily security. But bodily security is protected, not against all forms of interference or aggression, but only against some. One who seeks redress at law does not make out a cause of action by showing without more, that there has been damage to his person. If the harm was not willful, he must show that the act as to him had possibilities of danger so many and apparent as to entitle him to be protected against the doing of it, though the harm was unintended. Affront to personalty is still the keynote of the wrong.

The law of causation, remote or proximate, is thus foreign to the case before us. The question of liability is always anterior to the question of the measure of the consequences that go with liability. If there is no tort to be redressed, there is no occasion to consider what damage might be recovered if there were a finding of a tort.

REVERSED and COMPLAINT DISMISSED.

CRITICAL THINKING

Why does the court believe that Mrs. Palsgraf should not be awarded damages? Are you persuaded by these reasons? Why or why not?

ETHICAL DECISION MAKING

Think about the WPH process of ethical decision making. It may seem unfair that Mrs. Palsgraf was unable to collect damages for her injuries. Study the list of values or purposes for a decision. Which value do you think the court was upholding through its decision? Which value is in conflict with this favored value? With which value do you most agree?

The decision in *Palsgraf* set out the rule of foreseeability that is followed by most states today. However, a different definition of proximate cause is followed in a small minority of states. Courts in a few states do not distinguish actual cause from proximate cause. In these states, if the defendant's action constitutes an actual cause, it is also considered the proximate cause. Therefore, in these few states, both the pedestrian-scientist and the third-floor accountant would be able to recover damages from the tire manufacturer in the previous example.

Legal Principle: **Proximate cause is defined in the majority of states as foreseeability of both the plaintiff and his or her injury, whereas in the minority of states proximate cause is the same as actual cause.**

DAMAGES

Damages are the final required element of a negligence action. The plaintiff must have sustained compensable injury as a result of the defendant's actions. Because the purpose of tort law is to compensate individuals who suffer injuries as a result of another's action or inaction, a person cannot bring an action in negligence seeking only nominal damages. Rather, a person must seek compensatory damages, or damages intended to reimburse a plaintiff for her or his losses. In the opening case scenario, Curtis sought compensatory damages for her personal injury.

In typical negligence cases, courts rarely award punitive damages, or *exemplary damages,* which are imposed to punish the offender and deter others from committing similar offenses. Instead, courts usually award punitive damages in cases in which the offender has committed gross negligence, an action committed with extreme reckless disregard for the property or life of another person.

Plaintiff's Doctrines

The plaintiff has the burden of proving all four elements of a negligence case. Direct evidence of negligence by the defendant, however, is not always available. For example, there may have been no witnesses to the negligent conduct and other evidence may have been destroyed. Therefore, two doctrines have been adopted by courts to aid plaintiffs in establishing negligence claims: *res ipsa loquitur* and negligence per se.

L02

What are the doctrines that help a plaintiff establish a case of negligence?

RES IPSA LOQUITUR

Res ipsa loquitur literally means "the thing speaks for itself." The plaintiff uses this doctrine to allow the judge or jury to infer that more likely than not, the defendant's negligence was the cause of the plaintiff's harm, even though there is no direct evidence of the defendant's lack of due care. To establish *res ipsa loquitur* in most states, the plaintiff must demonstrate that:

1. The event was a kind that ordinarily does not occur in the absence of negligence.
2. Other responsible causes, including the conduct of third parties and the plaintiff, have been sufficiently eliminated.
3. The indicated negligence is within the scope of the defendant's duty to the plaintiff.

Proof of these three elements does not require a finding of negligence, however; it merely permits it. Once the plaintiff has demonstrated these three elements, the burden of proof shifts to the defendant, who must prove that he was not negligent to avoid liability.

German law is concerned with the defendant's ability to foresee, understand, and avoid danger. Both mental and physical capabilities are taken into account. For example, the duty-of-care standard stipulates that "physical and mental disabilities or defects, panic, or confusion" exempt the defendant from being found negligent. Also, although the distinction is not recognized by a statute, the courts distinguish between conscious and unconscious negligence. *Conscious negligence* requires knowledge that the offense is about to occur and that it is an actual offense. *Unconscious negligence* occurs when the defendant is either unaware that the act constitutes an offense or unaware that the act is occurring at all. In such cases, the defendant is found not guilty by reason of unconscious negligence.

One of the earliest uses of *res ipsa loquitur* was the case of *Escola v. Coca Cola.*[6] In that case, the plaintiff, a waitress, was injured when a bottle of Coca-Cola that she was removing from a case exploded in her hand. From the facts that (1) bottled soft drinks ordinarily do not spontaneously explode and (2) the bottles had been sitting in a case, undisturbed, in the restaurant for approximately 36 hours before the plaintiff simply removed the bottle from the case, the jury reasonably inferred that the defendant's negligence in the filling of the bottle resulted in its explosion. The plaintiff therefore recovered damages without direct proof of the defendant's negligence. Plaintiffs in numerous accident cases have subsequently used the doctrine where there has been no direct evidence of negligence. The defendant's best response to this doctrine is to demonstrate other possible causes of the accident. Think back to the opening case scenario: The plaintiff, Curtis, chose to invoke the doctrine of *res ipsa loquitur* because the wooden dock, which allegedly caused her personal injury, had been destroyed. Without the necessary evidence of negligence, Curtis had to rely on *res ipsa loquitur.*

Case 9-2 illustrates a plaintiff's attempt to use *res ipsa loquitur.*

[6] 24 Cal. 2d 453, 150 P.2d 436 (1944).

CASE 9-2	DISTRICT OF COLUMBIA v. WAYNE SINGLETON, ET AL.

COURT OF APPEALS OF MARYLAND
NO. 77 WITH 425 MD. 398, 41 A.3D 717 (2012)

In 2008, Wayne Singleton and his eight-year-old son, Jaron, were traveling on a bus for a school field trip to Six Flags. Wayne fell asleep on the way, and while he was asleep, the bus became "airborne" and drove off the road into a wooded area. The bus eventually collided with a tree. Singleton was asleep when the bus went off the road but woke up for the collision. Jaron was awake the whole time but did not understand the situation. Wayne sued the District of Columbia, due to the negligence of its employee. At the trial, only Wayne and his son were presented as witnesses. They did not call the bus driver or any other passenger or driver as a witness to provide evidence for why the bus went off the road. Due to this lack of evidence, Wayne invoked res ipsa loquitur to infer evidence for the negligence of the driver. The trial court disagreed and granted the District's motion for judgment.

JUSTICE HARRELL: With regard to a negligence action based on a perceptually single-vehicle accident, res ipsa loquitur ("res ipsa" or "the doctrine") will be available "if the accident or injury is one which ordinarily would not occur without negligence on the part of the operator of the vehicle" and "the facts are so clear and certain that the inference [of negligence] arises naturally from them." Res ipsa loquitur (literally, "the thing speaks for itself") allows generally a plaintiff to establish a prima facie case of negligence when direct evidence of the cause of the accident is unavailable and the circumstantial evidence permits the drawing of an inference by the fact-finder that the defendant's negligence was the cause. "The rule is not applied by the courts except where the facts and circumstances and the demand of justice make its application essential, depending upon the facts and circumstances in each particular case." Nonetheless, the plaintiff retains his or her burden to prove the defendant's negligence. A defendant confronted properly with a res ipsa inference is obliged to go forward with his case, shouldering what has been described as the "risk of non-persuasion." In effect, res ipsa loquitur allows the plaintiff to present the question of negligence to the fact-finder, notwithstanding a lack of direct evidence bearing on causation.

To invoke successfully the doctrine, the plaintiff must establish that the accident was "(1) of a kind that does not ordinarily occur absent negligence, (2) that was caused by an instrumentality exclusively in the defendant's control, and (3) that was not caused by an act or omission of the plaintiff." Additionally, although not an indispensable requirement of res ipsa, "one of the circumstances which calls for the application of the doctrine is when the facts surrounding the accident are more within the knowledge of the defendant than within the knowledge of the plaintiff."

To satisfy the exclusive-control requirement, the evidence adduced must demonstrate that no third-party or other intervening force contributed more probably than not to the accident. We iterated in Holzhauer that a res ipsa inference of the defendant's negligence is not permissible where an intervening force may have precipitated the accident. The existence of that potentiality "weakens the probability that the injury is attributable to the defendant's [negligent] act or omission." In proving the absence of other, more-probable causes of the accident, the plaintiff "is not required to exclude every possible cause for [his] injuries other than that of negligence; [he] is only required to show a greater likelihood that [his] injury was caused by the defendant's negligence than by some other cause."

In sum, res ipsa loquitur requires the conclusion that, "by relying on common sense and experience, the incident more probably resulted from the defendant's negligence rather than from some other cause."

Respondents failed to show that negligence attributable to the District more probably caused the accident than other potential causes. This deficiency stems from their inability to recount personally the events leading to the bus leaving the travel-portion of Route 50 and their apparent decision not to adduce other reasonably available evidence that could have cast light on that inquiry (e.g., testimony from the bus driver, other bus passengers, motorists who witnessed the accident, emergency responders, or possibly the police accident report, if admissible in whole or in part). Respondents' attorney stated during oral argument before this Court that he spoke with witnesses, indicating that obviously some of these witnesses were known and accessible. Nonetheless, Respondents envisage that the nature of the accident entitled them merely to prove that the bus left the road and rest, taking advantage of res ipsa loquitur to plug the hole in the doughnut. Their position, however, belies the doctrine's requirement that plaintiffs' evidence must show that the defendant's negligence, and not a third-party causation or force, more probably than not caused the accident, given the particular circumstances of the accident.

In Hanes v. State ex rel. Lamm, we said that "[w]here a motor vehicle leaves the roadway without a prior collision and thereby causes injury or damage, the courts, as a general rule, are prepared to draw an inference of negligence from the occurrence, assuming, of course, that all the other conditions of applicability are met." Requiring plaintiffs to show that a motor vehicle left the roadway, without an antecedent collision, is not an absolute threshold condition for applying res ipsa loquitur. Rather, it represents one conception of the exclusive-control element of res ipsa whereby plaintiffs must demonstrate that the defendant's negligence, and not an intervening act such as another vehicle, more likely than not caused the accident.

We are persuaded also by the Supreme Court of Connecticut's case of Chasse v. Albert, where a sleeping passenger in a vehicle that left the road sued, on a negligence theory, the administratrix of the deceased driver's estate. The only evidence regarding the accident came from another driver, who was 150 yards away and uninvolved in the accident. The Supreme Court of Connecticut affirmed the trial court's directed verdict against the passenger, noting that the paucity of evidence did not warrant an inference of negligence: "[M]any possibilities, other than negligence on the part of the operator, existed as to the cause of the accident here. The doctrine of res ipsa loquitur was not available to the plaintiff in this situation."

Here, Respondents' perhaps unnecessarily bare-bones case-in-chief failed to eliminate sufficiently other causes of the accident, and failed to evince that the bus driver's negligence was the most probable causative factor. Respondents point out that their testimony established that the driving conditions were dry and that there were tire marks on Route 50 where the bus "jumped the median." This evidence, however, is ambiguous. Tire marks do not demonstrate necessarily that the speed of the bus was excessive relative to the ambient physical conditions or even the posted limit on that section of the road (there was no evidence of the latter or the speed of the bus as it crossed the median). "Tire-skid" marks, if that is what Singleton observed, could indicate also a sudden emergency, such as a tire blowout, avoiding another vehicle or other moving obstacle, an unforeseen medical emergency, or a mechanical failure unrelated to inadequate maintenance. Although plaintiffs are not required to exclude all other potential causes of the accident, Respondents' limited evidence here established only that "the probabilities are at best evenly divided between negligence and its absence," in which case "it becomes the duty of a court to direct a jury that there is no sufficient proof." Therefore, the trial court granted properly the District's motion for judgment.

Respondents' evidence failed to evince that the District's bus driver's negligence more probably than not caused the bus to leave the road because other potential causes were not explored or excluded sufficiently. Thus, we cannot say their evidence is "so clear and certain that the inference [of negligence] arises naturally."

Our conclusion that res ipsa loquitur is inapplicable in the present case is buoyed by Respondents' apparent tactical decision to avoid reasonably available witnesses. Application of res ipsa loquitur is justified, in some circumstances, by a defendant's superior access to identification of the facts surrounding the accident. Failing to produce reasonably available and likely probative witnesses, where substantive and direct evidence is otherwise lacking, leads to the inference that the facts surrounding the happening of the accident were equally accessible to the plaintiff and the defendant.

Here, Respondents failed to produce apparently reasonably accessible witnesses that might have supplemented their limited evidence with additional direct or circumstantial evidence of negligence. Although it is understandable that Respondents may have been loathe to call the bus

driver, a listed defense witness and inferentially hostile to Respondents' case, Respondents' testimony established the existence of other potential witnesses: the other passengers on the bus, motorists "who actually saw the accident" and pulled over to help the accident victims, and emergency responders; nor did Respondents offer a copy of the police accident report. It may be inferred that Respondents had equal access as the defendant to the facts surrounding the accident. Therefore, Respondents may not rely upon res ipsa loquitur to satisfy their burden to adduce a prima facie case of negligence and thus defeat the District's motion for judgment.

. . . Respondents' inferred equal access to a fuller presentation of the facts of the accident cements our conclusion that the Circuit Court granted properly the District's motion for judgment.

REVERSED in favor the Defendant.

CRITICAL THINKING

What evidence does the judge say the defendants ought to have brought to court? Do you think this evidence would have helped them?

ETHICAL DECISION MAKING

Suppose you were a representative for the District of Columbia. The plaintiff's attorney has contacted you, claiming that the district was liable for the employee's negligence in this case. What would your response to the plaintiff's attorney be?

Business owners need to be mindful when selecting employees to work for their companies. When an employee engages in unlawful actions, it is the business owner who may actually end up in costly litigation. For example, when trash collector Christopher McCowen was found guilty for the murder and rape of well-known fashion writer Christa Worthington, the family of the deceased filed a $10 million lawsuit against his employer, Cape Cod Disposal. Worthington's family alleged that Donald Horton, the owner of Cape Cod Disposal, failed to use reasonable care when hiring McCowen and negligently sent the former criminal to collect Worthington's trash at her home. A background check after the murder revealed that McCowen had a violent past that included burglary, grand theft, felony assault, and trafficking of stolen property. Additionally, McCowen had been issued several restraining orders for threats against women. In 2007, Horton and the Worthington family settled for an undisclosed amount. Business owners may avoid negligent hiring and wrongful-death claims by using proper preemployment screening techniques. Many companies utilize background checks, call references, and verify previous employment to safeguard themselves and their employees against potential injury and liability.[7]

> To see how paying and receiving a negligence judgment relates to income taxation, please see the **Connecting to the Core** activity on the text website at www. mhhe.com/kubasek3e.

NEGLIGENCE PER SE

Negligence per se (literally, "negligence in or of itself") is another doctrine that helps plaintiffs succeed in negligence cases. Negligence per se applies to cases in which the defendant has violated a statute enacted to prevent a certain type

---

[7]www.nytimes.com/2006/11/17/us/17cape.html; www.boston.com/news/local/articles/2005/05/18/cape_writers_family_sues_over_death/; and www.entrepreneur.com/tradejournals/article/161024244.html (all accessed March 3, 2009).

of harm from befalling a specific group to which the plaintiff belongs. If the defendant's violation causes the plaintiff to suffer from the type of harm that the statute intends to prevent, the violation is deemed negligence per se. The plaintiff does not have to show that a reasonable person would exercise a certain duty of care toward the plaintiff. Instead, the plaintiff can offer evidence of the defendant's violation of the statute to establish proof of the negligence.

For example, if Ohio passes a statute prohibiting the sale of alcohol to minors, and a minor runs a red light and kills two pedestrians while driving under the influence of alcohol sold to him illegally, the liquor store's violation of the statute prohibiting the sale of alcohol to minors establishes negligence per se on the part of the store. The families of the pedestrians do not need to establish that a reasonable person would have a duty not to sell alcohol to a minor.

A defendant who complies with legislative statutes, however, can still be held liable if a reasonable person would have exercised a more stringent duty of care toward the plaintiff. The legislative statutes are minimum, not sufficient, standards for behavior.

Before examining the defenses against negligence claims, compare the definition of negligence in the United States with its definition in South Africa, as described in the Comparing the Law of Other Countries box on the next page.

SPECIAL PLAINTIFF'S DOCTRINES AND STATUTES

In addition to recognizing *res ipsa loquitur* and negligence per se, some states have established other doctrines or statutes to aid plaintiffs in negligence suits. For example, suppose an airplane taxiing at Reagan National Airport in the winter runs off the runway and into the Potomac River due to the negligence of the airline. Some bystanders observe the crash and jump into the water to rescue the crash survivors. If any of the bystanders are injured while attempting to rescue the survivors, many courts will hold the airline liable for their injuries under what is known as the *danger invites rescue* doctrine.

Many states have also enacted statutes to aid plaintiffs in successfully establishing specific kinds of negligence claims. For instance, many states have dram shop acts, which allow bartenders and bar owners to be held liable for injuries caused by individuals who become intoxicated at the bar. Other states have passed laws that hold hosts liable for injuries caused by individuals who became intoxicated at the hosts' homes.

BUT WHAT IF. . .

WHAT IF THE FACTS OF THE CASE OPENER WERE DIFFERENT?

Let's say, in the Case Opener, that Curtis was a guest on the farm and became intoxicated at a gathering held on the farm. She wandered to the dock and improperly used it, causing it to collapse. Who is liable for the collapse of the dock and Curtis's injuries?

Defenses to Negligence

The courts' doctrines of *res ipsa loquitur* and negligence per se help the plaintiff in a negligence case, but the courts permit certain defenses that relieve the defendant from liability even when the plaintiff has proved all four elements of negligence. Defendants can successfully rebut negligence claims with contributory negligence, comparative negligence, assumption of the risk, and other special negligence defenses.

L03

What are the defenses to a claim of negligence?

South Africa's legal system is a combination of selected legal traditions—from Roman to Dutch to German. The Roman *actiones legis Aquiliae* influences South Africa's statutes concerning liability. Under this Roman tradition, certain cases concerning liability mandate the presence of *culpa,* or negligence. South African law dictates that individuals can be found negligent in three different ways.

Negligence is first defined as failure to observe an accepted standard of conduct. In other words, individuals must exercise care and foresight with regard to others. A failure to do so indicates negligent behavior. Second, negligence is determined by whether the defendant could have prevented the consequent damages. The law expects individuals to take precautions to avoid harm or damage. Finally, South African law outlines the extent to which one can be found negligent in a crisis situation. In such instances, individuals have a duty to do what is "reasonably" expected. Because of the obvious ambiguity associated with this definition, South African law cites the American "doctrine of sudden emergency" as a standard for determining negligence in crisis situations. Encompassing all three of these definitions is an implicit duty of the individual to take precautions to prevent harm.

CONTRIBUTORY NEGLIGENCE

Contributory negligence, a defense once available in all states but replaced today in some states by the defense of comparative negligence (discussed in the next section), applies in cases in which the defendant and the plaintiff were both negligent. The defendant must prove that (1) the plaintiff's conduct fell below the standard of care needed to prevent unreasonable risk of harm and (2) the plaintiff's failure was a contributing cause to the plaintiff's injury. How can defendants use contributory negligence in a case? Some defense lawyers argue that if a plaintiff involved in a car accident failed to wear her seat belt, that failure constitutes contributory negligence because her action contributed to her injuries.

If the defendant successfully proves contributory negligence, no matter how slight the plaintiff's negligence, the plaintiff will be denied any recovery of damages. Because this defense seems unfair, many states have adopted the last-clear-chance doctrine. This doctrine allows the plaintiff to recover damages despite proof of contributory negligence as long as the defendant had a final clear opportunity to avoid the action that injured the plaintiff.

For example, suppose that Samantha and Nicole, in their cars, are facing each other while stopped at a red light. The light turns green, and Nicole starts to turn left at the intersection. Samantha sees Nicole start to turn, but she still continues to travel straight through the intersection and crashes into Nicole's car. Although Samantha had the right-of-way at the intersection, she could have avoided hitting Nicole's car by braking or swerving. Thus, according to the last-clear-chance doctrine, Nicole could recover damages.

Legal Principle: **If the court finds that (1) the plaintiff's conduct fell below the standard of care needed to prevent unreasonable risk of harm and (2) the plaintiff's failure was a contributing cause of the plaintiff's injury, the defendant will not be liable for the plaintiff's injuries unless the plaintiff can prove that the defendant had the last opportunity to avoid the accident.**

COMPARATIVE NEGLIGENCE

The adoption of the last-clear-chance doctrine, however, leaves many situations in which an extremely careless defendant can cause a great deal of harm to a plaintiff who is barred from recovery due to minimal contributory negligence. Thus, most states have replaced the contributory negligence defense with either pure or modified comparative negligence.

According to a pure comparative negligence defense, the court determines the percentage of fault of the defendant. The defendant is then liable for that percentage of the plaintiff's damages.

Courts calculate damages according to modified comparative negligence in the same manner, except that the defendant must be more than 50 percent at fault before the plaintiff can recover.

Twenty-eight states have adopted modified comparative negligence, thirteen have adopted pure comparative negligence, and nine have adopted contributory negligence. Every state has adopted one of these three defenses. Thus, the parties to a negligence suit cannot choose among them.

ASSUMPTION OF THE RISK

Another defense available to defendants facing negligence claims is called assumption of the risk. To use this defense successfully, a defendant must prove that the plaintiff voluntarily and unreasonably encountered the risk of the actual harm the defendant caused. In other words, the plaintiff willingly assumed as a risk the harm she suffered. There are two types of this defense. *Express assumption of the risk* occurs when the plaintiff expressly agrees (usually in a written contract) to assume the risk posed by the defendant's behavior. In contrast, *implied assumption of the risk* means that the plaintiff implicitly assumed a known risk.

The most difficult part of establishing this defense is showing that the plaintiff assumed the risk of the *actual* harm she suffered. A 1998 case against the Family Fitness Center illustrates an unsuccessful attempt to use assumption of the risk as a defense against a negligence claim.[8] In that case, the plaintiff was injured when a sauna bench on which he was lying collapsed beneath him at the defendant's facility. The trial court granted summary judgment in favor of the defendant on the basis of assumption of the risk. The plaintiff had signed a contract that included the following provision: "Buyer is aware that participation in a sport or physical exercise may result in accidents or injury, and Buyer assumes the risk connected with the participation in a sport or exercise and represents that Member is in good health and suffers from no physical impairment which would limit their use of FFC's facilities." The appellate court overturned the trial court's decision because the type of injury the plaintiff suffered was not the type of risk he had assumed. The court held that anyone signing a membership agreement could be deemed to have waived any hazard known to relate to the use of the health club facilities, such as the risk of a sprained ankle due to improper exercise or overexertion, a broken toe from a dropped weight, injuries due to malfunctioning exercise or sports equipment, or injuries from slipping in the locker-room shower. No patron, however, could be charged with realistically appreciating the risk of injury from simply reclining on a sauna bench. Because the collapse of a sauna bench, when properly used, is not a "known risk," the court concluded that the plaintiff did not assume the risk of this incident as a matter of law.

Case 9-3 illustrates the successful use of assumption of the risk as a defense. Compare this case to the action against the Family Fitness Center to see whether you agree with the different outcomes in the two cases.

---

[8] *Leon v. Family Fitness Center, Inc.,* 61 Cal. App. 4th 1227 (1998).

CASE 9-3   EX PARTE EMMETTE L. BARRAN III
SUPREME COURT OF ALABAMA
730 SO. 2D 203 (1998)

When Jason Jones enrolled at Auburn University in 1993, he chose to become a pledge of the Kappa Alpha fraternity. Within two days, Jones began to experience hazing by fraternity members. Hazing activities included the following: (1) digging a ditch and jumping into it after it was filled with water, urine, feces, dinner leftovers, and vomit; (2) receiving paddlings to his buttocks; (3) eating foods such as peppers, hot sauce, and butter; (4) being pushed and kicked; (5) doing chores for fraternity members; (6) appearing at 2 a.m. "meetings" where pledges would be hazed for several hours; and (7) "running the gauntlet," in which pledges would run down a hallway and flight of stairs while fraternity members would push, kick, and hit them. Although Jones was aware that 20–40% of the pledges dropped out of the pledge program, Jones remained in the program until he was suspended from the university for poor academic performance. In 1995, Jones sued the national and local Kappa Alpha organization, alleging negligence, assault and battery, negligent supervision, and various other claims. He argued that he suffered "mental and physical injuries" as a result of the hazing. For the negligence claims, the trial court granted summary judgment for Kappa Alpha. The trial court argued that Jones assumed the risk of hazing because he voluntarily entered the organization and could have quit at any time. Jones appealed, and the Court of Civil Appeals reversed the negligence ruling, reasoning that the peer pressure associated with fraternity life prevented Jones from voluntarily withdrawing from the pledge class. Kappa Alpha appealed.

JUSTICE SEE: Assumption of the risk has two subjective elements: (1) the plaintiff's knowledge and appreciation of the risk; and (2) the plaintiff's voluntary exposure to that risk. . . . [I]n order to find, as a matter of law, that Jones assumed the risk, this Court must determine that reasonable persons would agree that Jones knew and appreciated the risks of hazing and that he voluntarily exposed himself to those risks.

First, KA and its members argue that Jones knew and appreciated the risks inherent in hazing. . . . Jones's deposition indicates that before he became a KA pledge he was unfamiliar with the specific hazing practices engaged in at KA, but that the hazing began within two days of his becoming a pledge; that despite the severe and continuing nature of the hazing, Jones remained a pledge and continued to participate in the hazing activities for a full academic year; that Jones knew and appreciated that hazing was both illegal and against school rules; and that he repeatedly helped KA cover up the hazing by lying about its occurrence to school

officials, his doctor, and even his own family. Given Jones's early introduction to the practice of hazing and its hazards, and in light of his own admission that he realized that hazing would continue to occur, the trial court correctly determined that reasonable people would conclude that Jones knew of and appreciated the risks of hazing.

Second, in addition to establishing that Jones both knew of and appreciated the risk, KA and the individual defendants argue that Jones voluntarily exposed himself to the hazing. Jones responds by arguing that a coercive environment hampered his free will to the extent that he could not voluntarily choose to leave the fraternity. The Court of Civil Appeals, in reversing the summary judgment as to KA and the individual defendants, stated that it was not clear that Jones voluntarily assumed the risk of hazing, because, that court stated:

> In today's society, numerous college students are confronted with the great pressures associated with fraternity life and . . . compliance with the initiation requirements places the students in a position of functioning in what may be construed as a coercive environment.

With respect to the facts in this case, we disagree. . . . The record indicates that Jones voluntarily chose to continue his participation in the hazing activities. After numerous hazing events, Jones continued to come back for more two o'clock meetings, more paddlings, and more gauntlet runs, and did so for a full academic year. Auburn University officials, in an effort to help him, asked him if he was being subjected to hazing activities, but he chose not to ask the officials to intervene. Jones's parents, likewise acting in an effort to help him, asked him if he was being subjected to hazing activities, but he chose not to ask his parents for help.

Moreover, we are not convinced by Jones's argument that peer pressure created a coercive environment that prevented him from exercising free choice. Jones had reached the age of majority when he enrolled at Auburn University and pledged the KA fraternity. We have previously noted: "College students and fraternity members are not children. Save for very few legal exceptions, they are adult citizens, ready, able, and willing to be responsible for their own actions." Thus, even for college students, the privileges of liberty are wrapped in the obligations of responsibility.

Jones realized that between 20% and 40% of his fellow pledges voluntarily chose to leave the fraternity and the hazing, but he chose to stay. See Prosser & Keeton, The Law of Torts 491 ("Where there is a reasonably safe alternative open, the plaintiff's choice of the dangerous way is a free one, and may amount to assumption of the risk. . . ."). As a responsible adult in the eyes of the law, Jones cannot be heard to argue that peer pressure prevented him from leaving the very hazing activities that, he admits, several of his peers left.

Jones's own deposition testimony indicates that he believed he was free to leave the hazing activities:

> *Q:* You didn't have to let this [hazing] happen to you, did you?
> *A:* No.
> *Q:* And you could have quit at any time?
> *A:* Yes.
> *Q:* But yet you chose to go through with what you have described here in your complaint with

the aspirations that you were going to become a brother in the Kappa Alpha Order? You were willing to subject yourself to this for the chance to become a member of the brotherhood . . . were you not?

> *A:* Yes.

We conclude that Jones's participation in the hazing activities was of his own volition. The trial court correctly determined that reasonable people could reach no conclusion other than that Jones voluntarily exposed himself to the hazing.

REVERSED and REMANDED.

CRITICAL THINKING

Is there any important missing information that might influence your thinking about the court's conclusion that Jones participated in the hazing activities of his own volition? Why is this missing information important?

ETHICAL DECISION MAKING

Return to the WPH process of ethical decision making. Which stakeholders are affected by the court's decision? Why are these people affected?

Compare the defendant's use of the assumption-of-the-risk defense in Case 9-3 with the Kansas City Royals' attempt to use the defense in the Case Nugget on the next page.

Legal Principle: **If the plaintiff voluntarily and unreasonably encountered the risk of the actual harm the defendant caused, the defendant may raise the defense of assumption of the risk to avoid liability.**

SPECIAL DEFENSES TO NEGLIGENCE

Many states have additional ways to defend against a claim of negligence. For example, laws in some states hold that people in peril who receive voluntary aid from others cannot hold those offering aid liable for negligence. These laws, commonly called Good Samaritan statutes, attempt to encourage selfless and courageous behavior by removing the threat of liability.

The defendant in a negligence suit can also avoid liability by establishing a superseding cause. A *superseding cause* is an unforeseeable event that interrupts the causal chain between the defendant's breach of duty and the damages the plaintiff suffered. For example, suppose Jennifer is improperly storing ammonia in her garage when a meteor strikes her garage, spilling the ammonia into a stream nearby. Will, living downstream, drinks water from the stream and becomes dangerously ill. Because the meteor was unforeseeable, Jennifer is not liable for Will's injuries, even though she breached her duty of care to Will.

Superseding causes allow the defendant to avoid liability because they are evidence that the defendant's breach of duty was not the proximate cause of the plaintiff's injuries. In other words, superseding causes disprove the causation element necessary to sustain a negligence claim.

Strict Liability

Strict liability is liability without fault. The law holds an individual liable without fault when the activity in which she engages satisfies three conditions: (1) It involves a risk of serious harm to people or property; (2) it is so inherently dangerous that it cannot ever be

L04

What are the elements of strict liability?

ASSUMING THE RISK OF A FLYING HOTDOG?

John Coomer v. Kansas City Royals Baseball Team
__S.W.3d ---, 2013 WL 150838 (Mo. App. W.D. 2013)

Coomer and his father were sitting in open seats six rows behind the third-base dugout. Between the third and fourth innings, the Royals had its promotional event, the "Hotdog Launch," during which Shores, the team mascot, shot a number of hot dogs into the stands with an air gun and then began tossing hot dogs into the stands by hand. Shores was in the third-base dugout, in front of Coomer and his father, and people behind them were cheering and yelling for Shores to throw hot dogs to them. Coomer saw Shores turn his back and make a motion with his arm behind his back; Coomer then looked away to the scoreboard and "a split second later" felt something hit him in the face and knock off his hat. Coomer assumed he had been hit with a line drive.

Two mornings later, Coomer had difficulty seeing, and he was subsequently diagnosed with a tearing and detached retina, requiring surgery. He lost vision for three weeks, and he developed a cataract, for which he had surgery, and now has an artificial lens in his eye.

Coomer sued the baseball team for negligence, but the jury found the plaintiff 100 percent at fault, applying jury instructions including the defense of primary assumption of the risk. Coomer appealed on grounds (among others) that a "mascot throwing hotdogs directly at business invitees is not an inherent or unavoidable risk of the game of baseball," which was the basis for the primary-assumption-of-risk defense.

To prove a claim for negligence, Coomer was required to show that (1) the Royals had a duty to conform to a standard of conduct to protect him from unreasonable risks, (2) that duty was breached, (3) the breach resulted in proximately causing him injury, and (4) he suffered damages.

The defendant raised the defense of assumption of the risk, which was successful at the trial court level. On appeal, however, the court overturned the trial court decision, ruling that the jury had been improperly instructed on the assumption-of-the-risk defense. The appellate judge stated that everyone who attends a baseball game assumes the risk of being hit by a ball, making that a risk inherent in the game. However, being hit by a hotdog is not a well-known incidental risk of attending a baseball game, even though the "Hotdog Launch" promotion had been a long-running event. Consequently, it could not be said that the plaintiff had consented to, and voluntarily assumed, the risk merely by attending the game. That tossing out promotional items is a customary activity does not equate to a fan's consent to the risk of being hit by a promotional item. According to the court, inherent risks are those that inure in the nature of the sport itself, not the general experience of enjoying the game.

safely undertaken; and (3) it is not usually performed in the immediate community. Instead of banning these activities, the law allows people to engage in such activities but holds them liable for all resulting harm.

Inherently dangerous activities include dynamite blasting in a populated area and keeping animals that have not been domesticated. If an animal has shown a "vicious propensity," strict liability applies and the owner of the animal is responsible for any injuries suffered in an attack by the animal.[9] If an individual keeps an animal that has not shown vicious propensity, he has a duty to warn and protect individuals who come into contact with the animal. As you will see in the next chapter, in today's society, strict liability has had an enormous impact on cases involving unreasonably dangerous products.

BUT WHAT IF. . .
WHAT IF THE FACTS OF THE CASE OPENER WERE DIFFERENT?

Let's say, in the Case Opener, that the farm owners spend a little time each day trying to knock down the dock so that they can be rid of it. Eventually the dock is extremely unsafe, but they leave it up, deciding to completely take it apart at a later time. What three conditions would this situation have to satisfy to result in strict liability? Does this situation meet the three conditions?

---

[9] *Schwartz v. Armand ERPF Estate*, 688 N.Y.S.2d 55 (Sup. Ct., App. Div., N.Y. 1999).

CASE OPENER WRAP-UP

The Case of the Collapsing Dock

The appellate court affirmed the decision of the trial court, which claimed that the doctrine of *res ipsa loquitur* did not apply. The plaintiff then sought review of the appellate court's decision. On review the court ruled that the plaintiff could in fact rely on the doctrine of *res ipsa loquitur* to fill the evidentiary gaps of the case. According to the court, the plaintiff showed all the necessary elements to rely on the doctrine to prove negligence: (1) the accident would not ordinarily happen in the absence of negligence because properly maintained wooden docks do not give way under foot; (2) there was no evidence before the court that the dock was not in the exclusive control of the defendants; and (3) the plaintiff herself did not contribute in any way to the accident.

In conclusion, the court reversed the appellate court's ruling that the doctrine of *res ipsa loquitur* did not apply and remanded the case to trial by jury. Whether the plaintiff's injury was caused by negligence on the part of the defendants is to be decided by the future jury.

KEY TERMS

actual cause 219

assumption of the risk 227

compensatory
    damages 221

contributory negligence 226

dram shop acts 225

Good Samaritan
    statutes 229

gross negligence 221

last-clear-chance
    doctrine 226

modified comparative
    negligence 227

negligence 215

negligence per se 224

proximate cause 219

punitive damages 221

pure comparative
    negligence 226

reasonable person
    standard 216

res ipsa loquitur 221

strict liability 229

unfortunate accident 215

SUMMARY OF KEY TOPICS

When an individual fails to maintain a duty of care to protect other individuals, negligence and strict liability may occur.

Introduction to Negligence and Strict Liability

Duty: The standard of care that the defendant (i.e., a reasonable person) owes the plaintiff.

Elements of Negligence

Breach of duty: The defendant's lack of maintaining the standard of care a reasonable person would owe the plaintiff.

Causation: The defendant's conduct (breach of duty) that led to the plaintiff's injury.

Damages: Compensable injuries suffered by the plaintiff.

Res ipsa loquitur: Doctrine that permits the judge or jury to *infer* that the defendant's negligence was the cause of the plaintiff's harm in cases in which there is no direct evidence of the defendant's lack of due care.

Plaintiff's Doctrines

Negligence per se: Doctrine that permits a plaintiff to prove negligence by offering evidence of the defendant's violation of a statute that has been enacted to prevent a certain type of harm.

Defenses to Negligence   *Contributory negligence:* A defense that allows the defendant to entirely escape liability by demonstrating any degree of negligence on the part of the plaintiff that contributed to the plaintiff's harm.

Comparative negligence: A defense that allows the liability to be apportioned between plaintiff and defendant in accordance with the degree of responsibility each bears for the harm suffered by the plaintiff.

Assumption of the risk: A defense that allows the defendant to escape liability by establishing that the plaintiff engaged in an activity fully aware that the type of harm he or she suffered was a possible consequence of engaging in that activity.

Strict Liability   Persons who engage in activities that are so inherently dangerous that no amount of due care can make them safe are strictly liable, regardless of the degree of care they used when undertaking the activity.

POINT / COUNTERPOINT

Should Negligence Law Hold All Individuals to the Reasonable Person Standard?

NO	YES
One major problem with the reasonable person standard is that it fails to set up clear rules to which individuals can conform their behavior. "Reasonableness" varies tremendously from one person to another; what one person considers reasonable, another considers unnecessary. Unclear laws also discourage efficiency because both the plaintiff and the defendant may believe they are likely to be victorious in court and thus have little incentive to settle. When the law is clear, individuals have a better idea of the strength of their case, and those with poor chances of victory have an incentive to settle and thereby avoid costly litigation expenses.	The law should certainly concern itself with fairness to defendants, but that concern is only half the story. The law also ought to concern itself with fairness to plaintiffs. A plaintiff who gets run over by a high school dropout is no less injured than a plaintiff who gets run over by a professor. Yet an individualized negligence standard might allow the second plaintiff to recover but not the first. Civil society requires a certain absolute level of care from all its members, regardless of their individual predispositions.
In addition, the reasonable person standard holds all individuals to the same duty of care, regardless of their individual characteristics. This standard is unfair to individuals who exercise all the possible care of which they are capable yet whose level of care still does not meet the reasonable person standard. Alternatively, individuals can exercise levels of care that they know create a substantial likelihood of harm to others yet the care satisfies the reasonable person standard. Thus, the reasonable person standard functions like a regressive tax. To promote fairness to all defendants, tort law ought to take into account individualized factors. Instead of asking whether the defendant has behaved reasonably, the law ought to ask whether the defendant has behaved reasonably given his or her individual characteristics, including age, education, gender, wealth, and so on.	Moreover, a more individualized standard in negligence law would tend to decrease, not increase, the clarity of the law. An injured defendant would have to ascertain the plaintiff's individual characteristics to determine the likelihood of victory in court, and more variables mean more uncertainty. Who owes a higher standard of care: a college-educated yet poor defendant or a high school–educated yet rich defendant? If the law wants to promote uniformity, consistency, and stability, it ought to use a uniform standard, not a more individualized one.
	Finally, it is not clear how individualized characteristics of a defendant would count. How does a defendant's gender affect the standard of care to which the law will hold him or her? If women are held to a different standard of care than men, is the law making a statement about the relative reasonableness of men and women?

QUESTIONS & PROBLEMS

1. Explain the differences between contributory and comparative negligence.

2. Explain the relationship between negligence per se and *res ipsa loquitur.*

3. Explain the purpose of Good Samaritan statutes.

4. List and describe the elements that must be proved for a successful strict-liability claim.

5. The plaintiff's father collapsed near the racquetball courts of a Bally's health club. While an ambulance was being called, a Bally's employee trained in cardiopulmonary resuscitation and the use of the club's automatic external defibrillator (AED) assessed the man's medical condition. The employee decided that neither life-saving measure was appropriate given that the heart attack victim was breathing and had a pulse. He left the man to check on the status of the 911 response, and when he returned to the plaintiff's father, two club members, a doctor and a medical student, were administering CPR.

   Upon arrival, the paramedics shocked the father with an AED, but he never recovered. The plaintiff submitted the affidavit of a board-certified cardiologist, who opined that the father's "chances of survival would have been significantly higher if the AED had been used within the first few minutes after his collapse" rather than upon arrival of the ambulance.

   At the time of the incident, the state had a law that required all health clubs in the state to provide on the premises an AED and a person in attendance at the club who was properly certified to operate an AED and perform CPR.

   The trial court initially dismissed the case on grounds that the state law requiring health clubs to have AEDs on the premises did not impose a duty on health clubs to use the devices in cardio emergencies. On appeal, the court overturned the dismissal, saying that the plaintiff should have an opportunity to present his case not based on the statutory duty of defendants but based on a different duty. What duty do you think that, according to the court, the plaintiff should have a chance to prove the defendant breached? *Miglino v. Bally Total Fitness of Greater New York,* [New York State Court of Appeals No. 10. Feb. 7, 2013. Lawyers USA No. 993–3800.]

6. Mary Dobsa owned a home in Biloxi, Mississippi, in which she and Neil Paul resided. Countrywide Home Loans, Inc., was the mortgage lender on the home. Before financing and in accordance with the National Flood Insurance Act, Countrywide selected Landsafe to determine whether Dobsa's home was located in a federal flood zone. Dobsa paid for Landsafe's services. Landsafe indicated that the home was not situated in a flood-hazard area. Accordingly, Countrywide provided financing without requiring Dobsa to obtain flood insurance through the National Flood Insurance Program. Unfortunately, Hurricane Katrina struck and caused substantial damage to this residence for which no flood insurance coverage existed. It was then learned that the home was actually located in a flood-hazard area. Dobsa and Paul sued Landsafe, alleging negligence and negligent misrepresentation. The district court granted Landsafe's motion for summary judgment. Dobsa appealed. How did the court rule on appeal? Why? [*Paul v. Landsafe Flood Determination, Inc.,* 550 F.3d 511 (5th Cir. 2008).]

7. Plaintiff Caruso was gambling at the Foxwoods Casino, which was owned by defendant Mashantucket Pequot Gaming Enterprise. When he went to use the restroom, Caruso noticed an attendant holding a mop in his hand. Almost immediately thereafter, Caruso slipped and fell on the floor in an area that had just been mopped. To gain compensation for the injuries he suffered from the fall, he sued the casino for negligence for failing to place warning signs or cones around the just-mopped area. The casino argued that contributory negligence on the part of Caruso in failing to pay attention to his surroundings in light of the obviousness of the danger should bar him from recovering. How do you believe the court ruled in this case and why? [*Caruso v. Mashantucket Pequot Gaming Enterprise,* 2010 WL 323079 (Mash. Pequot Tribal Ct. 2010).]

8. Mashantucket Pequot Gaming Enterprise owned a casino that Scanlon was patronizing. Scanlon was viewed on a security camera standing on a box on a balcony. Two security guards went to investigate because they were concerned for the customer's safety. Scanlon told the guards that he was fine and had just talked another patron out of

committing suicide on that very spot. The guards still did not want him standing on the box, so they walked Scanlon out of that area and into the main mall area of the casino. After they left him, Scanlon evidently went back to where he had been and jumped, killing himself. His heirs sued the casino for negligently causing the death of Scanlon by not taking steps to prevent him from committing suicide. The casino filed a motion to dismiss. How do you think the court ruled in this case and why? [*Scanlon v. Mashantucket Pequot Gaming Enterprise,* 2009 WL 4188488 (Mash. Pequot Tribal Ct. 2009).]

9. David Glenn Koch and Roderick Cook were employees of International Tentnology Corporation (InTents), a company that provides and installs equipment for events and parties. InTents set up a tent for the Chile Pepper Festival that is held in an open field at the University of Arkansas. Koch and Cook, as well as four other employees of InTents, were moving a large, fully assembled hexagonal tent across the field. To avoid a temporary mesh fence in their path, they attempted to lift the tent over it. The aluminum center support pole of the tent hit an energized overhead power line and three of the men, including Koch and Cook, were fatally electrocuted. Three others were severely injured. The administrators of the estates of Koch and Cook sued Southwestern Electric Power Company (SWEPCO). SWEPCO maintains and operates the power line traversing the field. The line is at least 25 feet above the ground and complies with National Electric Safety Code clearance requirements. The line was installed at a time when the area was much more rural than it is today, and the estates contend that SWEPCO was negligent in not elevating, burying, or insulating the line now that the field is occasionally used for major public events. The district court granted SWEPCO's motion for summary judgment on the ground that it had had no legal duty because it had not received written notification that work would be occurring near the power line. The estates appealed, conceding that no notification was sent to the utility but arguing that SWEPCO owed the decedents a duty of care. Did SWEPCO owe any duty of care to anyone using the field for public events? Was the failure to change the line enough to constitute negligence? Why? [*Koch v. Southwestern Electric Power Co.,* 544 F.3d 906 (8th Cir. 2008).]

Looking for more review materials?

The Online Learning Center at **www.mhhe.com/kubasek3e** contains this chapter's "Assignment on the Internet" and also a list of URLs for more information, entitled "On the Internet." Find both of them in the Student Center portion of the OLC, along with quizzes and other helpful materials.

Product Liability

LEARNING OBJECTIVES

After reading this chapter, you will be able to answer the following questions:

1 What are the theories of liability in product liability cases?

2 What is market share liability?

CASE OPENER

Is Human Sperm Subject to Product Liability Laws?

Many single women and married couples use donated sperm to conceive children each year. Pennsylvania resident Donna Donovan decided to use donated sperm from Idant Laboratories, a New York sperm bank that emphasized (1) its screening process far exceeded mandated standards and (2) its rigorous screening process ensured that donors had a good genetic history. After using sperm from Idant Laboratories, Donovan gave birth to a girl, Brittany. Donovan began noticing abnormalities in Brittany's development, and Brittany was soon diagnosed as a Fragile X baby. Fragile X is a genetic mutation that causes a range of mental and physical impairments, such as learning disabilities, mental retardation, and behavior disorders. A genetic test for Fragile X was developed two years before Donovan used the sperm from Idant Laboratories. Two years after Brittany's birth, genetic tests showed that the sperm from Idant Laboratories was the carrier of the Fragile X defect. Donovan and Brittany brought suit against Idant Laboratories for selling defective sperm.

1. What do you think the outcome of Donovan's case was?
2. Should the sale of sperm be considered the sale of a product?
3. How do product liability issues affect you?

The Wrap-Up at the end of the chapter will answer these questions.

Breast implants, Ford Explorers, cigarettes, pet food, fast food, fingers in fast food—all of these topics have been the subject of product liability suits. According to the U.S. Department of Justice's Bureau of Justice Statistics, approximately 5 percent of state tort trials in 2005 involved product liability issues.[1] Approximately 25 percent of these trials addressed toxic substances, such as asbestos, tobacco, chemicals, and other toxic substances. The median award to plaintiffs in state court product liability cases that went to trial was $500,000. Each year, juries award hundreds of millions of dollars to plaintiffs bringing suit against companies offering products. If a company manufactures or sells a product, it should expect to be a party to a product liability lawsuit.

In this chapter, we examine the legal theories commonly used by plaintiffs in product liability cases, along with some of the defenses that are used against these cases. By understanding the law of product liability, you may be less likely to take actions that would lead you and your company into costly litigation.

Theories of Liability for Defective Products

L01

What are the theories of liability in product liability cases?

Product liability law is based primarily on tort law. There are three commonly used theories of recovery in product liability cases: negligence, strict product liability, and breach of warranty. A plaintiff may bring a lawsuit based on as many of these theories of liability as apply to the plaintiff's factual situation. While a plaintiff must establish different elements under each of these theories, the plaintiff must generally show two common elements: (1) that the product is defective, and (2) that the defect existed when the product left the defendant's control.

How might a product be defective? Suppose you select a glass bottle of Diet Coke at the grocery store. When you grab the bottle, it shatters in your hand and severely cuts your thumb. Most bottles of soda do not shatter when touched; thus, there must have been a problem in the manufacture of this particular bottle. When an individual product (e.g., the shattered Diet Coke bottle) has a defect making it more dangerous than other identical products (the 200 other Diet Coke bottles at the grocery store), this individual product has a manufacturing defect.

Given your severe cut from the Diet Coke bottle, you get into your car to drive to the hospital. Unfortunately, someone rear-ends your car; the crash causes your driver's seat to bend backward such that you hit your head on the backseat and suffer a serious neck injury. The design of the driver's seat allowed the seat to bend backward, and all driver's seats in this type of car have the same design. When all products of a particular design are defective and dangerous, these products have a design defect.

Because of the pain associated with your neck injury and lacerated thumb, you take a new over-the-counter pain reliever. You read and follow the instructions on the box and take two pills. However, you begin to feel incredibly ill. You rush to the hospital and discover that you are experiencing negative side effects from the pain reliever because it has interacted with some of your other medications. You had carefully read the instructions and warnings, but you did not see anything about drug interactions. A product may be defective as a result of the manufacturer's failure to provide adequate warnings about potential dangers associated with the product.

The product examples above (Diet Coke bottle, driver's seat in a car, pain reliever) are tangible items. However, can an intangible "product" be subject to product liability claims? See the Case Nugget "What Is a Product?"

[1] Bureau of Justice Statistics, "Civil Justice Survey of State Courts: Tort Breach and Jury Trials in State Courts, 2005," November 2009, http://bjs.ojp.usdoj.gov/content/pub/pdf/tbjtsc05.pdf.

Radford v. Wells Fargo Bank
2011 WL 1833020 (D. Haw. 2011)

Plaintiff Richard Radford brought a suit against Wells Fargo Bank alleging that he was enticed into purchasing a defective product and claiming an intentional or negligent failure to warn of a defective product (i.e., his mortgage loan). The district court held that a mortgage is not a "product" that can be subject to product liability claims for at least three reasons. First, "[p]roducts liability covers products that are reasonably certain to place life and limb in peril and may cause bodily harm if defective. The language of products liability law reflects its focus on tangible items." Second, the Restatement (Second) of Torts provides examples of items covered by product liability claims, and a mortgage loan does not appear on the list. Finally, there was no case law in Hawaii supporting Radford's contention that a loan is a product.

In summary, a product may be defective because of a manufacturing defect, a design defect, or inadequate warnings. As you read the chapter, think about how these types of defects fit in with the three theories of liability: negligence, strict liability, and breach of warranty.

NEGLIGENCE

To win a case based on negligence, the plaintiff must prove the four elements of negligence explained in Chapter 9: (1) The defendant manufacturer or seller owed a duty of care to the plaintiff; (2) the defendant breached that duty of care by supplying a defective product; (3) this breach of duty caused the plaintiff's injury; and (4) the plaintiff suffered actual injury.

Prior to the landmark 1916 case of *MacPherson v. Buick Motor Co.,* negligence was rarely used as a theory of recovery for an injury caused by a defective product because of the difficulty of establishing the element of duty. Until that case, the courts said that a plaintiff who was not the purchaser of the defective product could not establish a duty of care, because one could not owe a duty to someone with whom one was not "in privity of contract." Being *in privity of contract* means being a party to a contract. Because most consumers do not purchase goods directly from the manufacturers, product liability cases against manufacturers were rare before the *MacPherson* case.

Following *MacPherson,* any foreseeable plaintiff can sue a manufacturer for its breach of duty of care. Foreseeable plaintiffs include users, consumers, and bystanders. Moreover, foreseeable plaintiffs can bring a case against retailers, wholesalers, and manufacturers. However, retailers and wholesalers can satisfy their duty of care by making a cursory reasonable inspection of a product when they receive it from the manufacturer.

Negligent Failure to Warn. To bring a successful case based on negligent failure to warn, the plaintiff must demonstrate that the defendant knew or should have known that without a warning, the product would be dangerous in its ordinary use, or in any *reasonably foreseeable* use, yet the defendant still failed to provide a warning. For example, the 10th Circuit recently affirmed a trial court decision in which a smoker was awarded approximately $200,000 from R. J. Reynolds Tobacco, which before 1969 had negligently failed to warn smokers of the harm associated with smoking cigarettes. No duty to warn exists for dangers arising either from unforeseeable misuses of a product or from obvious dangers. A producer of razor blades, for example, need not give a warning that a razor

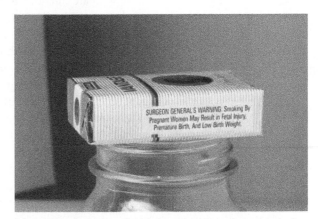

Prior to these required warning labels on cigarette packages, one basis for suing the tobacco industry was failure to warn.

blade may cut someone. For example, in *Ward v. Arm & Hammer*,[2] after being convicted on criminal charges for distribution of crack cocaine, the plaintiff brought suit against Arm & Hammer, arguing that the company should have included a warning on its package of baking soda of the criminal consequences of using the baking soda to make cocaine. The court emphasized that the manufacturer of a raw component that is not in itself dangerous has no duty to warn the public of the dangers associated with combining that component in a dangerous or criminal manner. Courts often consider the likelihood of the injury, the seriousness of the injury, and the ease of warning when deciding whether a manufacturer was negligent in failing to warn. To the extent that a company is aware of potential harm associated with reasonably foreseeable uses of its products, the safest course of action for the company is to identify this harm to the consumers as a warning.

When providing a warning, the manufacturer must ensure that the warning will reach those who are intended to use the product. For example, if parties other than the original purchaser will be likely to use the product, the warning should be placed directly on the product itself, not just in a manual that comes with the product. Picture warnings may be required if children, or those who are illiterate, are likely to come into contact with the product and risk harm from its use.

Products such as drugs and cosmetics are often the basis for actions based on negligent failure to warn because the use of these products frequently causes adverse reactions. When the user of a cosmetic or an over-the-counter drug has a reaction to that product, many courts find that there is no duty to warn unless the plaintiff proves that (1) the product contained an ingredient to which an appreciable number of people would have an adverse reaction; (2) the defendant knew or should have known, in the exercise of ordinary care, about the existence of this group; and (3) the plaintiff's reaction was due to his or her membership in this abnormal group.

[2] 341 F. Supp. 2d (D.N.J. 2004).

FAILURE TO WARN ABOUT FOOD

Pelman v. McDonald's
237 F. Supp. 2d 512 (S.D.N.Y 2003)

Consumers have recently been bringing cases that attempt to hold others liable for their health problems allegedly caused by unhealthy food. In *Pelman v. McDonald's,* the plaintiffs alleged that McDonald's failed to warn customers of the "ingredients, quantity, qualities and levels of cholesterol, fat, salt and sugar content and other ingredients in those products, and that a diet high in fat, salt, sugar and cholesterol could lead to obesity and health problems." Judge Sweet originally dismissed the plaintiffs' claims, stating his decision was guided by the principle that legal consequences should not attach to the consumption of hamburgers and other fast-food fare unless consumers are unaware of the dangers of eating such food. He determined that consumers know, or should reasonably know, the potential negative health effects associated with eating fast food. The plaintiffs filed an amended complaint, asserting that McDonald's engaged in a scheme of deceptive advertising that in effect created the impression that McDonald's food products were nutritionally beneficial and part of a healthy lifestyle. In September 2006, Judge Sweet refused to dismiss the plaintiffs' claims, and as of February 2010, the case was still moving forward as a class action.

Similarly, in *Gorran v. Atkins Nutritionals, Inc.,* Jody Gorran argued that he developed heart disease by following the Atkins diet, which encourages dieters to limit carbohydrates such as bread, rice, and pasta while increasing meat, cheese, eggs, and other high-protein (and high-fat) foods.* According to Gorran's complaint, Atkins Nutritionals promoted the health benefits of its diet while knowing that some people were "fat-sensitive" and subject to adverse health effects, yet Atkins failed to warn the public. The court determined that as long as the food was sold in a condition anticipated by the consumer, it was not a defective product simply because it could negatively affect the consumer's health.

* "Judge Rebuffs Atkins' Second Bid to Dismiss Dieter's Lawsuit," Andrews Product Liability Litigation Reporter 16, no. 1 (2005), p. 2.

Other courts, however, use a balancing test to determine negligence in such cases. They weigh the degree of danger to be avoided with the ease of warning. For example, in 1994, a jury awarded over $8.8 million to a man who suffered permanent liver damage as a result of drinking a glass of wine with a Tylenol capsule (the award was reduced to $350,000 due to a statutory cap). As early as 1977, the company knew that combining a normal dose of Tylenol with a small amount of wine could cause massive liver damage in some people, but the company failed to put a warning to that effect on the label because such a reaction was rare. Through the balancing test, the court found that the degree of potential harm was substantial and that it would have been relatively easy to place a warning on the product label.

Furthermore, some courts have permitted a "sophisticated-user" defense, which acts as a complete defense to failure-to-warn claims. For example, in a 2008 case, the Supreme Court of California adopted the sophisticated-user defense, noting that a user's knowledge of certain dangers is equivalent to notice. In that case, the plaintiff was a trained and certified heating, ventilation, and air-conditioning (HVAC) technician who alleged that he suffered harm from exposure to a certain gas frequently used in air-conditioning systems. Because the training and certification for HVAC taught about the harm related to this gas, the court determined that the technician, as a sophisticated or educated user, could not recover.

Negligence Per Se.   As you know from Chapter 9, a statute violation that causes the harm that the statute was enacted to prevent constitutes *negligence per se.* This doctrine is also applicable to product liability cases based on negligence. When a law establishes labeling, design, or content requirements for products, the manufacturer has a duty to meet these requirements. Failure by the manufacturer to meet those standards means that the manufacturer has breached its duty of reasonable care. If the plaintiff can establish that the failure to meet such a standard caused injury, the plaintiff can recover under negligence per se.

Damages.   Damages that are recoverable in negligence-based product liability cases are the same as those in any action based on negligence: compensatory damages and punitive damages. As you should recall from Chapter 8, *compensatory damages* are those designed to make the plaintiff whole again; they cover items such as medical bills, lost wages, and compensation for pain and suffering. While this list of recoverable harms may seem "obvious" to us, not all countries allow such extensive recovery. For example, in German product liability cases, consumers do not have a right to recover damages for pain and suffering or for emotional distress. *Punitive damages* are meant to punish the defendant for extremely harmful conduct. The amount of the punitive-damage award is determined by the wealth of the defendant and the maliciousness of the action.

In 2009–2011, Toyota announced that millions of its cars would be recalled due to acceleration and braking problems. As of February 2010, dozens of product liability lawsuits had been filed against Toyota. In many of these cases, plaintiffs were seeking damages for personal injuries or wrongful death due to the alleged acceleration and braking problems. Some of these cases were claims against Toyota to recover damages for the reduced value of their cars. Specifically, before the recall, Toyota owners claim that they could resell their cars at a certain price; after the recall, this price was several thousand dollars lower. In fact, the *Kelley Blue Book* reported that the resale value of Toyota models fell 1 to 3 percent in just one week following certain recalls.[3]

In December 2012, Toyota agreed to pay over $1 billion to settle the class action litigation regarding the loss-of-economic-value claims related to the recalls.[4] The National Highway Traffic Safety Administration fined Toyota more than $60 million for failing to inform regulators of internal information Toyota had regarding the sudden acceleration.

Legal Principle: **The plaintiff in a product liability case may recover compensatory damages, designed to provide compensation for provable losses, and punitive damages, an amount awarded to punish the defendant.**

Defenses to a Negligence-Based Product Liability Action.   The defenses to negligence discussed in the previous chapter are available in product liability cases based on negligence. A common defense in such cases is that the plaintiff's own failure to act reasonably contributed to the plaintiff's own harm. This negligence on the part of the plaintiff allows the defendant to raise the defense of *contributory, comparative,* or *modified comparative negligence,* depending on which defense is accepted by the state where the case arose. Remember, in a state that allows the contributory negligence defense, proof of any negligence by the plaintiff is an absolute bar to recovery. In a state where the defense of pure comparative negligence is allowed, the plaintiff can recover for only that portion of the harm attributable to the defendant's negligence. In a modified comparative negligence state, the plaintiff can recover the percentage of harm caused by the defendant as long as the jury finds the plaintiff's negligence responsible for less than 50 percent of the harm.

A closely related defense is *assumption of the risk.* This defense arises when a consumer knows that a defect exists but still proceeds unreasonably to make use of the product, creating a situation in which the consumer has voluntarily assumed the risk of injury from the defect and thus cannot recover. To decide whether the plaintiff did indeed assume the risk, the trier of fact may consider such factors as the plaintiff's age, experience, knowledge, and understanding, as well as the obviousness of the defect and the danger it poses. When a plaintiff knows of a danger but does not fully appreciate the magnitude of the risk, the applicability of the defense is a question for the jury to determine.

Another common defense is *misuse* of the product. The misuse must be unreasonable or unforeseeable. When a defendant raises the defense of product misuse, the defendant is really arguing that the harm was caused not by the defendant's negligence but by the plaintiff's failure to properly use the product.

[3] Nick Bunkley, "Some Toyota Owners Voice an Eroding Loyalty," *The New York Times,* February 7, 2010.

[4] Bill Vlasic, "Toyota Agrees to Settle Lawsuit Tied to Accelerations," *New York Times,* December 26, 2012.

PRODUCT MISUSE IN JAPAN

Like the United States, Japan also addresses situations in which the consumer misuses a defective product. In Japan, such a situation is called *comparative negligence*. The negligence of both the defendant and the plaintiff is taken into account when determining the distribution of damages. The leading case of comparative negligence is that of *Miyahara v. Matsumoto Gas Company.* In this case, the defendant purchased a gas stove from Matsumoto.

A faulty rubber nose valve caused the stove to start a fire, resulting in extensive damage to Miyahara's home. An investigation after the fire, however, showed that Miyahara had failed to close the valve before going to sleep the evening of the fire. Consequently, both he and the gas company were found negligent. The cost of the damages was split between the two parties.

The *state-of-the-art defense* is used by a defendant to demonstrate that his alleged negligent behavior was reasonable, given the available scientific knowledge existing at the time the product was sold or produced. If a case is based on the defendant's negligent defective design of a product, the state-of-the-art defense refers to the technological feasibility of producing a safer product at the time the product was manufactured. In cases of negligent failure to warn, the state-of-the-art defense refers to the scientific knowability of a risk associated with a product at the time of its production. This is a valid defense in a negligence case because the focus is on the reasonableness of the defendant's conduct. However, the state of scientific knowledge at the time of production, and the lack of a feasible way to make a safer product, does not always preclude liability. The court may find that the defendant's conduct was still unreasonable because even in its technologically safest form, the risks posed by the defect in the design so outweighed the benefits of the product that the reasonable person would not have produced a product of that design.

Suppose a defendant designs a product to comply with federal safety regulations regarding that product. That defendant may attempt to argue that *compliance with federal laws* is a defense to state tort law because the state tort law is preempted by a federal statute designed to ensure the safety of a particular class of products. The Supreme Court recently issued a ruling on whether a state tort claim was preempted because the FDA had approved the drug label (see Case 10-1).

Each preemption case requires careful scrutiny of the purpose of the statute. For example, in *Tebbetts v. Ford Motor Co.,* the plaintiff argued that the 1988 Ford Escort was defectively designed because it did not have a driver's side air bag. Ford raised the preemption defense, arguing that it had complied with federal safety regulations under the National Traffic and Motor Vehicle Safety Act (NTMVSA). Consequently, Ford argued that its compliance preempted recovery under state product liability laws. After considering the legislative history and the law, the court discovered a clause in the law stating that "[c]ompliance with any Federal motor vehicle safety standard issued under this act does not exempt any person from any liability under common law." Thus, the court ruled that the Tebbetts were not preempted from bringing their product liability action.

Similarly, oil companies have argued that their compliance with the Clean Air Act should not subject them to tort liability for MTBE contamination in groundwater. Through the Clean Air Act, Congress required that oil companies include an oxygenate in gasoline to allow the gasoline to burn more cleanly and thus to improve air quality. MTBE, or methyl tertiary butyl ether, is one type of oxygenate. While everyone expected MTBE to help improve air quality, widespread use of this oxygenate had a negative consequence: It contaminated water. A very small amount of MTBE affects the smell and taste of water. Given these extreme negative consequences, numerous states banned MTBE. Moreover, cities and individuals have sued oil companies to pay for the costs, in the millions of dollars, that will be incurred to clean the drinking water. While a few courts have agreed with

CASE 10-1   WYETH v. LEVINE
UNITED STATES SUPREME COURT
555 U.S. 555, 2009, 129 S. CT. 1187 (2009)

Diana Levine, a professional musician, sought treatment for her migraine headaches and was given an injection of Wyeth's antinausea drug, Phenergan. While the drug was supposed to be injected directly into Levine's vein through a method called the IV-push method, the drug entered an artery instead. Consequently, Levine developed gangrene and had to have her right hand and entire forearm amputated. She incurred substantial medical expenses and could no longer perform as a professional musician. At trial, Levine argued that Wyeth's labeling was defective because although it warned of the danger of gangrene and amputation following inadvertent intra-arterial injection, it failed to instruct clinicians to use the IV-drip method of intravenous administration instead of the higher-risk IV-push method. The jury agreed with Levine. Wyeth argued that the judge should overturn the jury verdict because Levine's claim was preempted because the drug's label had been approved by the Food and Drug Administration. The judge rejected Wyeth's argument, and the Vermont Supreme Court upheld that ruling, holding that the federal regulations created a floor and not a ceiling and Wyeth could have warned against IV-push administration. Wyeth appealed to the U.S. Supreme Court, making 2 arguments: (1) it was impossible to comply with both its state and federal law obligations and (2) Levine's common-law claims stand as an obstacle to the accomplishment of Congress' purposes in the Food, Drug and Cosmetic Act (FDCA).

JUSTICE STEVENS: The . . . question presented is whether federal law preempts Levine's claim that Phenergan's label did not contain an adequate warning about using the IV-push method of administration. Wyeth first argues that Levine's state-law claims are preempted because it is impossible for it to comply with both the state-law duties underlying those claims and its federal labeling duties. The FDA's premarket approval of a new drug application includes the approval of the exact text in the proposed label. Generally speaking, a manufacturer may only change a drug label after the FDA approves a supplemental application. There is, however, an FDA regulation that permits a manufacturer to make certain changes to its label before receiving the agency's approval. Among other things, this "changes being effected" (CBE) regulation provides that if a manufacturer is changing a label to "add or strengthen a contraindication, warning, precaution, or adverse reaction" or to "add or strengthen an instruction about dosage and administration that is intended to increase the safe use of the drug product," it may make the labeling change upon filing its supplemental application with the FDA; it need not wait for FDA approval.

Wyeth argues that the CBE regulation is not implicated in this case because a 2008 amendment provides that a manufacturer may only change its label "to reflect newly acquired information." Resting on this language, Wyeth contends that it could have changed Phenergan's label only in response to new information that the FDA had not considered.

Wyeth could have revised Phenergan's label even in accordance with the amended regulation. As the FDA explained in its notice of the final rule, "newly acquired information" is not limited to new data, but also encompasses "new analyses of previously submitted data." The rule accounts for the fact that risk information accumulates over time and that the same data may take on a different meaning in light of subsequent developments. Levine . . . present[ed] evidence of at least 20 incidents prior to her injury in which a Phenergan injection resulted in gangrene and an amputation. After the first such incident came to Wyeth's attention in 1967, it notified the FDA and worked with the agency to change Phenergan's label. In later years, as amputations continued to occur, Wyeth could have analyzed the accumulating data and added a stronger warning about IV-push administration of the drug.

[A]bsent clear evidence that the FDA would not have approved a change to Phenergan's label, we will not conclude that it was impossible for Wyeth to comply with both federal and state requirements.

Impossibility preemption is a demanding defense. On the record before us, Wyeth has failed to demonstrate that it was impossible for it to comply with both federal and state requirements. The CBE regulation permitted Wyeth to unilaterally strengthen its warning, and the mere fact that the FDA approved Phenergan's label does not establish that it would have prohibited such a change.

Wyeth also argues that requiring it to comply with a state-law duty to provide a stronger warning about IV-push administration would obstruct the purposes and objectives of federal drug labeling regulation. Levine's tort claims, it maintains, are preempted because they interfere with "Congress's purpose to entrust an expert agency to make drug labeling decisions that strike a balance between competing objectives." We find no merit in this argument, which relies on an untenable interpretation of congressional intent and an overbroad view of an agency's power to preempt state law.

Wyeth contends that the FDCA establishes both a floor and a ceiling for drug regulation. Wyeth relies . . . on the preamble to a 2006 FDA regulation governing the content and format of prescription drug labels. In that preamble, the FDA declared that the FDCA establishes "both a 'floor' and a 'ceiling,'" so that "FDA approval of labeling . . . preempts conflicting or contrary State law." It further stated that certain state-law actions, such as those involving failure-to-warn claims, "threaten FDA's statutorily prescribed role as the expert Federal agency responsible for evaluating and regulating drugs." . . .

[T]he FDA's 2006 preamble does not merit deference. When the FDA issued its notice of proposed rulemaking in December 2000, it explained that the rule would "not contain policies that have federalism implications or that preempt State law." In 2006, the agency finalized the rule and, without offering States or other interested parties notice or opportunity for comment, articulated a sweeping position on the FDCA's preemptive effect in the regulatory preamble. The agency's views on state law are inherently suspect in light of this procedural failure.

In short, Wyeth has not persuaded us that failure-to-warn claims like Levine's obstruct the federal regulation of drug labeling. Congress has repeatedly declined to preempt state law, and the FDA's recently adopted position that state tort suits interfere with its statutory mandate is entitled to no weight. Although we recognize that some state-law claims might well frustrate the achievement of congressional objectives, this is not such a case.

We conclude that it is not impossible for Wyeth to comply with its state and federal law obligations and that Levine's common-law claims do not stand as an obstacle to the accomplishment of Congress' purposes in the FDCA. Accordingly, the judgment of the Vermont Supreme Court is affirmed.

AFFIRMED.

CRITICAL THINKING

What are the reasons for the Court's conclusion that Levine's product liability claims are not preempted?

ETHICAL DECISION MAKING

Recall the WPH process for ethical decision making. Who are the relevant stakeholders affected by this decision?

the oil companies, most cases have held that the Clean Air Act does not preempt tort cases because the oil companies had a choice of oxygenates to use. Moreover, the courts state that the problem of water contamination is too far removed from the problem that Congress was trying to address through the Clean Air Act regulations; thus, there is no preemption.

Certain statutory defenses are also available in negligence-based product liability cases. To ensure that there will be sufficient evidence from which a trier of fact can make a decision, states have *statutes of limitations* that limit the time within which all types of civil actions may be brought. In most states, the statute of limitations for tort actions, and thus for negligence-based product liability cases, varies between one and four years from the date of injury.

Statutes of repose provide an additional statutory defense by barring actions arising more than a specified number of years after the product was purchased. Statutes of repose are usually much longer than statutes of limitations, generally running at least 10 years.

STRICT PRODUCT LIABILITY

The requirements for proving strict product liability can be found in Section 402A of the Restatement (Second) of Torts. This section reads as follows:

1. One who sells any product in a defective condition, unreasonably dangerous to the user or consumer or his family is subject to liability for physical harm, thereby, caused to the ultimate user or consumer, or to this property, if

    a. the seller is engaged in the business of selling such a product, and

    b. it is expected to and does reach the consumer or user without substantial change in the condition in which it was sold.

2. The rule stated in Subsection (1) applies although

    a. the seller has exercised all possible care in the preparation and sale of his product, and

    b. the user or consumer has not bought the product from or entered into any contractual relation with the seller.

Under **strict product liability,** courts may hold liable the manufacturer, distributor, or retailer to any reasonably foreseeable injured party. Any reasonably foreseeable injured party includes the buyer; the buyer's family, guests, and friends; and foreseeable bystanders. The actions of the manufacturer or seller are not relevant; rather, strict product liability focuses on the *product.* Thus, duty is irrelevant. Courts focus on whether the product was in a "defective condition, unreasonably dangerous" when sold. To succeed in a strict-liability action, the plaintiff must prove three things:

1. The product was defective when sold.
2. The product was so defective that the product was unreasonably dangerous.
3. The product was the cause of the plaintiff's injury.

As stated earlier, a product may be defective because of (1) a flaw in its manufacturing that led to its being more dangerous; (2) a defective design; or (3) missing or inadequate instructions or warnings that could have reduced or eliminated foreseeable risks posed by the product.

Plaintiffs usually prove that a defect exists by means of (1) experts who testify as to the type of flaw in the product that led to the plaintiff's injury and/or (2) evidence of the circumstances surrounding the accident that would lead the jury to infer that the accident must have been caused by a defect in the product. Exhibit 10-1 describes how expert opinion is used in product liability cases. Case 10-2 illustrates how circumstances can provide a reasonable basis for such an inference.

Exhibit 10-1

The Battle of the Experts

EXPERT OPINION IN PRODUCT LIABILITY CASES

Plaintiffs use experts in product liability cases to show the existence of a flaw or to show that a flaw caused the plaintiff's injuries. To rebut the plaintiff's expert opinion, the defense usually hires an expert to show that there is no defect or that the product did not cause the plaintiff's injuries. These experts frequently battle over the scientific evidence regarding causation.

Expert testimony is used in various types of litigation: drugs, breast implants, automobile accidents, and pollution. Expert opinion is generally admissible in a trial if two conditions are met:
1. The subject matter is one in which scientific, technical, or other specialized knowledge would help the finder of fact, and the knowledge is relevant and reliable.
2. The expert offering the testimony is qualified as an expert.

Juries, or even judges, have sometimes been persuaded by an "expert" advocating "junk science." Junk science may be "biased data, spurious inferences, and logical legerdemain, patched together by researchers whose enthusiasm for discovery and diagnosis outstrips their skill. It is a catalog of every conceivable kind of error: data dredging, wishful thinking, truculent dogmatism, and now and again, outright fraud."* In an attempt to reduce the use of junk science in the courtroom, the Supreme Court, in *Daubert v. Merrell Dow Pharmaceutical,* determined that judges are responsible for assessing expert opinion. It identified four considerations for relevant and reliable opinions:
1. Did the expert use the scientific method?
2. Has the expert's theory or technique been subjected to peer review and publication?
3. Does the particular technique have a significant rate of error?
4. Is the methodology generally accepted in the scientific community?

Expert-witness fees may range from $100 to $1,000 an hour. Experts are usually deposed during litigation, so their time preparing for depositions and trial can easily run into hundreds of hours, which can be quite costly for clients.

* Peter Huber, *Galileo's Revenge: Junk Science in the Courtroom* (New York: Basic Books, 1991).

CASE 10-2   WELGE v. PLANTERS LIFESAVERS CO.
COURT OF APPEALS FOR THE SEVENTH CIRCUIT

17 F.3D 209 (7TH CIR. 1994)

Richard Welge, who boarded with Karen Godfrey, liked peanuts on his ice cream sundaes. Godfrey bought a 24-ounce vacuum-sealed plastic-capped jar of Planters peanuts for Welge at K-Mart. To obtain a $2 rebate, Godfrey needed proof of her purchase from the jar of peanuts. She used an Exacto knife to remove the part of the label that contained the bar code and placed the jar on top of the refrigerator for Welge. A week later, Welge removed the plastic seal from the jar, uncapped it, took some peanuts, replaced the cap, and returned the jar to the top of the refrigerator. A week after that, he took down the jar, removed the plastic cap, spilled some peanuts into his left hand to put on his sundae, and replaced the cap with his right hand. As he pushed the cap down on the open jar, the jar shattered. His hand was severely cut, and became permanently impaired.

Welge filed product liability actions against K-Mart, the seller of the product; Planters, the manufacturer of the peanuts; and Brockway, the manufacturer of the glass jar. Defendants filed a motion for summary judgment after discovery. The district judge granted the motion on the ground that the plaintiff had failed to exclude possible causes of the accident other than a defect introduced during the manufacturing process. The plaintiff appealed.

JUSTICE POSNER: No doubt there are men strong enough to shatter a thick glass jar with one blow. But Welge's testimony stands uncontradicted that he used no more than the normal force that one exerts in snapping a plastic lid onto a jar. So the jar must have been defective. No expert testimony and no fancy doctrine are required for such a conclusion. A nondefective jar does not shatter when normal force is used to clamp its plastic lid on. The question is when the defect was introduced. It could have been at any time from the manufacture of the glass jar by Brockway (for no one suggests that the defect might have been caused by something in the raw materials out of which the jar was made) to moments before the accident. But testimony by Welge and Godfrey . . . excludes all reasonable possibility that the defect was introduced into the jar after Godfrey plucked it from a shelf in the K-Mart store. From the shelf she put it in her shopping cart. The checker at the check out counter scanned the bar code without banging the jar. She then placed the jar in a plastic bag. Godfrey carried the bag to her car and put it on the floor. She drove directly home, without incident. After the bar code portion of the label was removed, the jar sat on top of the refrigerator except for the two times Welge removed it to take peanuts out of it. Throughout this process it was not, so far as anyone knows, jostled, dropped, bumped, or otherwise subjected to stress beyond what is to be expected in the ordinary use of the product. Chicago is not Los Angeles; there were no earthquakes. Chicago is not Amityville either; no supernatural interventions are alleged. So the defect must have been introduced earlier, when the jar was in the hands of the defendants.

. . . [I]t is always possible that the jar was damaged while it was sitting unattended on the top of the refrigerator, in which event they are not responsible. Only if it had been securely under lock and key when not being used could the plaintiff and Karen Godfrey be certain that nothing happened to damage it after she brought it home. That is true—there are no metaphysical certainties—but it leads nowhere. Elves may have played ninepins with the jar of peanuts while Welge and Godfrey were sleeping; but elves could remove a jar of peanuts from a locked cupboard. The plaintiff in a product liability suit is not required to exclude every possibility, however fantastic or remote, that the defect which led to the accident was caused by someone other than one of the defendants. The doctrine of *res ipsa loquitur* teaches that an accident that is unlikely to occur, unless the defendant was negligent, is itself circumstantial evidence that the defendant was negligent. The doctrine is not strictly applicable to a product liability case because, unlike an ordinary accident case, the defendant in a products case has parted with possession and control of the harmful object before the accident occurs. . . . But the doctrine merely instantiates the broader principle, which is as applicable to a products case as to any other tort case, that an accident can itself be evidence of liability. . . . If it is the kind of accident that would not have occurred but for a defect in the product, and if it is reasonably plain that the defect was not introduced after the product was sold, the accident is evidence that the product was defective when sold. The second condition (as well as the first) has been established here, at least to a probability sufficient to defeat a motion for summary judgment. Normal people do not lock up their jars and cans lest something happens to damage these containers while no one is looking. The probability of such damage is too remote. It is not only too remote to make a rational person take measures to prevent it; it is too remote to defeat a product liability suit should a container prove dangerously defective.

. . . [I]f the probability that the defect which caused the accident arose after Karen Godfrey bought the jar of Planters peanuts is very small—and on the present state of the record we are required to assume that it is—then the probability that the defect was introduced by one of the defendants is very high.

. . . The strict-liability element in modern product liability law comes precisely from the fact that a seller, subject to that law, is liable for defects in his product even if those defects were introduced, without the slightest fault of his own for failing to discover them, at some anterior stage of production. . . . So the fact that K-Mart sold a defective jar of peanuts to Karen Godfrey would be conclusive of K-Mart's

[continued]

liability, and since it is a large and solvent firm there would be no need for the plaintiff to look further for a tortfeasor.

. . . Here we know to a virtual certainty (always assuming that the plaintiff's evidence is believed, which is a matter for the jury) that the accident was not due to mishandling after purchase, but to a defect that had been introduced earlier.

REVERSED and REMANDED in favor of the plaintiff.

CRITICAL THINKING

What are Justice Posner's reasons for reversing the decision? Do you find his reasons compelling?

ETHICAL DECISION MAKING

Suppose that the defect had been introduced by Brockway and that corporate management had been aware of the defect but believed the chances of someone's being hurt were small enough to be negligible. Therefore, Brockway did not inform Planters of the defect. Should it have informed Planters?

In Case 10-2, the product had a manufacturing defect, which was fairly straightforward to prove. However, it is sometimes more difficult to prove that a design is defective. States are not in agreement as to how to establish a design defect, and two different tests have evolved to determine when a product is so defective as to be unreasonably dangerous. The first test, set out in the Restatement (Second) of Torts, is the *consumer expectations test:* Did the product meet the standards that would be expected by the reasonable consumer? This test relies on the experiences and expectations of the ordinary consumer, and thus it is not answered by the use of expert testimony about the merits of the design. See Exhibit 10-2 for an analysis of the difference between the second and third Restatement of Torts.

Exhibit 10-2

Impact of the Restatement (Third) of Torts

Section 402A of the Restatement (Second) of Torts is generally the foundation of modern product liability law, but that section has been subject to considerable criticism. In 1998, the criticisms led the American Law Institute to adopt the "Restatement of the Law (Third), Torts: Product Liability," which is intended to replace Section 402A.

Under the Restatement (Third):

[O]ne engaged in the business of selling or otherwise distributing products who sells or distributes a defective product is subject to liability for harm to persons or property caused by the defect.

The section departs from the Restatement (Second) by holding the seller to a different standard of liability, depending on whether the defect in question is a manufacturing defect, a design defect, or a defective warning.

It is only a manufacturing defect that results in strict liability. A manufacturing defect arises when "the product departs from its intended design," and liability is imposed regardless of the care taken by the manufacturer.

The Restatement (Third) applies a reasonableness standard to design defects, stating:

[A] product is defective in design when the foreseeable risks of the harm posed by the product could have been reduced or avoided by the adoption of a reasonable alternative design by the seller . . . and the omission of the alternative design renders the product not reasonably safe.

Comments in the Restatement (Third) list a number of factors the court can use to determine whether a reasonable alternative design renders the product not reasonably safe, including:

(continued)

Exhibit 10-2
Continued

the magnitude and probability of the foreseeable risks of harm, the instructions and warnings accompanying the product, and the nature and strength of consumer expectations regarding the product, including expectations arising from product portrayal and marketing, . . . the relative advantage and disadvantages of the product as designed and as it alternatively could have been designed, . . . the likely effects of the alternative design on product longevity, maintenance, repair and esthetics, and the range of consumer choice among products.

Thus, the Restatement (Third) has in effect shifted to a risk-utility test.

The Restatement (Third) has likewise adopted a reasonableness standard for defective warnings:

A product is defective because of inadequate instructions or warnings when the foreseeable risks of harm posed by the product could have been reduced or avoided by the provision of reasonable instructions or warnings by the seller . . . and the omission of the warnings renders the product not reasonably safe.

The potential effects of changes brought about by the newest Restatement have yet to be fully felt. As of 2001, the Restatement (Third) had not been widely adopted by the states.

The second is the *feasible alternatives test,* sometimes referred to as the *risk-utility test.* In applying this test, the court focuses on the usefulness and safety of the design and compares it to an alternative design. The exact factors that the court examines are detailed in Case 10-3, which makes explicit the differences between the two tests.

CASE 10-3   **SPERRY–NEW HOLLAND, A DIVISION OF SPERRY CORPORATION v. JOHN PAUL PRESTAGE AND PAM PRESTAGE**
SUPREME COURT OF MISSISSIPPI
617 SO. 2D 248 (1993)

Mr. Prestage's foot and lower leg were caught in a combine manufactured by defendant Sperry–New Holland. He and his wife sued defendant for damages arising out of the accident. Their first cause of action was based on the theory of strict product liability. A jury awarded John $1,425,000 for his injuries and Pam $218,750 for loss of consortium (the ability to engage in sexual relations with one's spouse). Defendant appealed.

JUDGE PRATHER: . . . Two competing theories of strict liability in tort can be extrapolated from our case law. While our older decisions applied a "consumer expectations" analysis in products cases, recent decisions have turned on an analysis under "risk-utility." We today apply a "risk-utility" analysis and write to clarify our reasons for the adoption for that test.

Section 402A is still the law in Mississippi. How this Court defines the phrases "defective conditions" and "unreasonably dangerous" used in 402A dictates whether a "consumer expectations" analysis or a "risk-utility" analysis will prevail. Problems have arisen because our past decisions have been unclear and have been misinterpreted in some instances.

"Consumer Expectations" Analysis

. . . In a "consumer expectations" analysis, "ordinarily the phrase 'defective condition' means that the article has something wrong with it, that it did not function as expected." Comment g of Section 402A defines "defective condition" as "a condition not contemplated by the ultimate consumer, which will be unreasonably dangerous to him." Thus, in a "consumer expectations" analysis, for a plaintiff to recover, the defect in a product which causes his injuries must not be one which the plaintiff, as an ordinary consumer, would know to be unreasonably dangerous to him. In other words, if the plaintiff, applying the knowledge of an ordinary consumer, sees a danger and can appreciate that danger, then he cannot recover for any injury resulting from that appreciated danger.

"Risk-Utility" Analysis

In a "risk-utility" analysis, a product is "unreasonably dangerous" if a reasonable person would conclude that the danger-in-fact, whether foreseeable or not, outweighs the utility of the product. Thus, even if a plaintiff appreciates the danger of a product, he can still recover for any injury resulting from the danger, provided that the utility of the product is outweighed by the danger that the product creates. Under the "risk-utility" test, either the judge or the jury can balance the utility and danger-in-fact, or risk, of the product.

A "risk-utility" analysis best protects both the manufacturer and the consumer. It does not create a duty on the manufacturer to create a completely safe product. Creating such a product is often impossible or prohibitively expensive. Instead, a manufacturer is charged with the duty to make its product reasonably safe, regardless of whether the plaintiff is aware of the product's dangerousness. . . . In balancing the utility of the product against the risk it creates, an ordinary person's ability to avoid the danger by exercising care is also weighed.

Having here reiterated this Court's adoption of a "risk-utility" analysis for product liability cases, we hold, necessarily, that the "patent danger" bar is no longer applicable in Mississippi. Under a "risk-utility" analysis, the "patent danger" rule does not apply. In "risk-utility," the openness and obviousness of a product's design is simply a factor to consider in determining whether a product is unreasonably dangerous.

There is sufficient evidence to show that Prestage tried his case under a "risk-utility" analysis. It is also clear from the record that the trial court understood "risk-utility" to be the law in Mississippi and applied that test correctly.

AFFIRMED in favor of plaintiff.

CRITICAL THINKING

Why was the risk-utility test viewed as the best method of evaluating this case?

ETHICAL DECISION MAKING

The risk-utility test allows products to pose a danger to consumers as long as they are reasonably safe. Under which ethical theory would producing such a product be ethical? Under which theory would such production not be ethical?

Some states require that one of these tests must be used. For example, in South Carolina, the risk utility test is the exclusive test.[5] Other states permit use of either the consumer expectations test or the risk utility test (e.g., Illinois).[6]

Legal Principle: **A product liability case based on the theory of strict product liability may be brought when a person is injured by a product with a manufacturing defect that caused that product to be unreasonably dangerous.**

Liability to Bystanders. We have been looking thus far at liability to those who are in lawful possession of the defective product. The question arises as to whether strict product liability can be used by someone other than the owner or user of the product. The Bystanders Case Nugget provides the rationale of one court that chose to allow recovery by a bystander.

Various companies involved in manufacturing and selling products may be named as defendants in product liability cases. However, some states restrict which companies may be named as defendants. See the Case Nugget "Who Is the Proper Defendant?"

Defenses to a Strict–Product Liability Action. Most of the defenses to a negligence-based product liability claim are available in a strict–product liability case. These defenses include product misuse, assumption of the risk, and the lapse of time under statutes of limitations and statutes of repose.

One defense that may not be available in all states, however, is the state-of-the-art defense. Courts have rejected the use of this defense in most strict-liability cases, reasoning

---

[5] *Peters-Martin v. Navistar Intern. Transp. Corp.*, 2011 WL 462657 (4th Cir. 2011).
[6] 659 F.3d 584 (7th Cir. 2011).

STRICT LIABILITY FOR BYSTANDERS

James A. Peterson, Adm'r of the Estate of Maradean Peterson et al. v. Lou Backrodt Chevrolet Co.
Appellate Court of Illinois
307 N.E.3d 729 (1974)

A car dealer sold an automobile with a defective brake system. When the defective brakes failed, the driver struck two minors, killing one and injuring the other. The deceased minor's estate brought a product liability action against the car dealer. The court relied on a statement by the California Supreme Court in *Elmore v. American Motors Corp.* to allow recovery by bystanders:

If anything, bystanders should be entitled to greater protection than the consumer or user where injury to bystanders from the defect is reasonably foreseeable. Consumers and users, at least, have the opportunity to inspect for defects and to limit their purchases to articles manufactured by reputable manufacturers and sold by reputable retailers, whereas the bystander ordinarily has no such opportunities. In short, the bystander is in greater need of protection from defective products which are dangerous, and if any distinction should be made between bystanders and users, it should be made . . . to extend greater liability in favor of the bystanders.

that the issue in such cases is not what the producers knew at the time the products were produced but whether the product was defective and whether the defect caused it to be unreasonably dangerous. For example, the supreme court of Missouri, in a case involving an asbestos claim, said that the state of the art has no bearing on the outcome of a strict-liability claim because the issue is the defective condition of the product, not the manufacturer's knowledge, negligence, or fault.

The refusal of most courts to allow the state-of-the-art defense in strict-liability cases is consistent with the social policy reasons for imposing strict liability. A reason for imposing strict liability is that the manufacturers or producers are best able to spread the cost of the risk; this risk-spreading function does not change with the availability of scientific knowledge. The counterargument is that if the manufacturer has indeed done everything as safely and carefully as available data allow, it seems unfair to impose liability on the defendant. After all, how else could the company have manufactured the product?

WARRANTY

Another theory of liability for defective products is *breach of warranty*. Unlike negligence and strict-liability theories, breach of warranty stems from contract theory rather than tort theory. This theory of liability is established through the Uniform Commercial Code (UCC). A warranty is a guarantee or a binding promise regarding a product. Generally, the product (or the product's performance) does not meet the manufacturer's or seller's promises.

Warranties may be either *express* (clearly stated by the seller or manufacturer) or *implied* (automatically arising out of a transaction). Either type may give rise to liability. Two types of implied warranties may provide the basis for a product liability action: warranty of merchantability and warranty of fitness for a particular purpose.

Express Warranty. When a seller makes an affirmative representation about a product, this representation—an express warranty—becomes part of the bargain. The representation may be a written or verbal guarantee about the product. For example, a car dealer may make an express statement that the car will work perfectly for the first 30,000 miles. In contrast, a car dealer may engage in vague sales talk (e.g., "This car runs well") that does not constitute an express warranty.

Determining whether a statement is a warranty may be a difficult task. In one case, for example, the court considered whether advertising statements constituted a warranty:

> To see how total quality management relates to prevention of product liability cases, please see the **Connecting to the Core** activity on the text website at www.mhhe.com/kubasek3e.

Block v. Toyota Motor Corporation
2011 WL 6306689 (8th Cir. 2011)

Angela Block filed a strict-liability suit after her son was killed and her daughter was seriously injured in a collision with a Toyota vehicle that allegedly improperly suddenly accelerated. Block filed suit in Minnesota state court against Toyota (the manufacturer of the vehicle), its affiliates, and Brooklyn Park Motors, the automobile dealership that had originally sold the Toyota vehicle 10 years earlier. The defendants removed the case to federal court, and the plaintiff argued that removal of the case to federal court was improper because the automobile dealership was a Minnesota resident. Minnesota has a "seller's exception statute" that requires the dismissal of strict-liability claims against nonmanufacturers when the nonmanufacturer provides the identity of the manufacturer unless the plaintiff shows that the nonmanufacturer falls into one of three exceptions:

1. The defendant has exercised some significant control over the design or manufacture of the product or provided instruction or warnings to the manufacturer.
2. The defendant had actual knowledge of the defect in the product that caused the injury, death, or damage.
3. The defendant created the defect in the product that caused the injury, death, or damage. The district court concluded that the auto dealership fell under the seller's exception statute and dismissed all claims with prejudice against the dealership. On appeal, the Eighth Circuit upheld the dismissal.

When a consumer was deciding whether to buy a luxury yacht, the seller gave him a brochure with a picture of the yacht along with the following caption: "Offering the best performance and cruising accommodations in its class, the 3375 Esprit offers a choice of either stern drive or inboard power, superb handling and sleeping accommodations for six." The buyer argued that on the basis of express representations about the yacht in this brochure, he chose to purchase the $150,000 yacht. Later, the yacht had mechanical and electrical problems. The supreme court of Utah concluded that an express warranty is a promise or affirmation of fact. "[T]he photograph and caption contained in Cruisers' brochure are not objective or specific enough to qualify as either facts or promises; the statements made in the caption are merely opinions, and the photograph makes no additional assertions with regard to the problems of which Boud has complained." Thus, the court ruled there was no express warranty.

To establish a claim for breach of express warranty, the plaintiff must show that (1) the representation was the basis of the bargain and (2) there was a breach of the representation. Generally, the plaintiff simply has to demonstrate a breach of warranty; she does not have to prove that the occurrence of the breach was the defendant's fault.

Implied Warranty of Merchantability. When a seller sells a particular kind of goods, there is an implied warranty of merchantability. *Merchantability* means that the particular goods would be accepted by others who deal in similar goods. Thus, an implied warranty of merchantability means that the goods are fit for the purpose for which they are sold and used. This warranty is found in Article 2, Section 314(2), of the UCC. Under the UCC, for goods to be merchantable, they must meet six conditions:

a. Pass without objection in the trade under the contract description.
b. In the case of fungible goods, be of fair average quality within the description.
c. Be fit for the ordinary purposes for which such goods are used.
d. Run, within the variations permitted by the agreement, of even kind, quality and quantity within each unit and among all units involved.
e. Be adequately contained, packaged, and labeled as the agreement may require.
f. Conform to the promises or affirmations of fact made on the container or label, if any.

In a footnote in the Sperry–New Holland case, the court relied on Professor John Wade's article "On the Nature of Strict Tort Liability for Products"* to list seven factors a trial court may find helpful when balancing a product's utility against the risk the product creates:

1. The usefulness and desirability of the product—its utility to the user and to the public as a whole.

2. The safety aspects of the product—the likelihood that it will cause injury and the probable seriousness of the injury.

3. The availability of a substitute product that would meet the same need and not be as unsafe.

4. The manufacturer's ability to eliminate the unsafe character of the product without impairing its usefulness or making it too expensive to maintain its utility.

5. The user's ability to avoid danger by the exercise of care in the use of the product.

6. The user's anticipated awareness of the dangers inherent in the product and their avoidability, because of general public knowledge of the obvious condition of the product or of the existence of suitable warnings or instructions.

7. The feasibility, on the part of the manufacturer, of spreading the loss by setting the price of the product or carrying liability insurance.

With regard to factor 6, the court's analysis considered whether warnings included in an owner's manual were suitable to warn Prestage of the danger of the combine. One of Sperry's expert witnesses testified: "Warnings are a third-rate way of preventing accidents. . . . [W]arnings are something that . . . operators read once, and forget."

Query: Is it possible that as owner's and user's manuals become available online, judges and experts will be less sympathetic to the owner or user who says he read the warnings once but then forgot about them? Have you ever misplaced an owner's or user's manual and later looked for it online when you needed information about a product? If so, are you more likely to review safety information than you may have been in the past, when it was easy to misplace manuals?

* *Mississippi Law Journal* 44 (1973), p. 825.

For example, a consumer purchased an "unbreakable" baseball bat that developed cracks after the repeated use of hitting baseballs. The consumer brought suit against the retailer that sold the bat. Given that the bat could not be used for the purpose for which it was intended (i.e., hitting baseballs), the judge relied on the implied warranty of merchantability to determine that the consumer was entitled to a refund.[7]

One of the requirements of this provision is that the seller of the good must be a "merchant with respect to goods of that kind" [UCC Section 2–314(1)]. Thus, the seller must deal with the goods in question on a regular or continuous basis. For example, a private individual who places an advertisement in the paper to sell her personal car is not a seller of goods under this section of the UCC.

Contracts for sales of goods frequently contain numerous disclaimers, and one of these disclaimers includes the implied warranty of merchantability. If the disclaimer uses the word *merchantability*, the disclaimer will be upheld for economic losses but not personal injuries.

stus.com

Here's a dilemma. Should the disclaimer for our client's new sleeping pill read, "May cause drowsiness" or "May not cause drowsiness"?

Implied Warranty of Fitness for a Particular Purpose. When a customer purchases a product for a particular purpose and the seller is aware of this purpose, an implied warranty of fitness for a particular purpose arises. This warranty is found in Article 2, Section

---

[7] *Dudzik v. Klein's All Sports,* 158 Misc. 2d 72 (N.Y. Just. Ct. 1993).

WHEN MIGHT YOUR COMPANY UNEXPECTEDLY BE CONSIDERED A SELLER OF GOODS?

Nutting v. Ford Motor Company
180 A.D.2d 122 (N.Y.A.D. 1992)

Catherine Nutting was driving her 1984 Mercury Marquis station wagon when the engine stalled, and the car collided with another vehicle. Nutting brought suit against Ford Motor Company, the car manufacturer, and Hewlett-Packard (HP), a manufacturer and seller of computer products. Why HP? HP had purchased the car at issue in this case from Ford through a program where HP purchased approximately 3,200 cars for use by HP employees. After about one and a half years, HP disposed of the cars through an auction conducted by its agent. Hi-Way Motors, a used-car dealership owned by Nutting's father, purchased the car at auction and transferred titled to Nutting. When Nutting brought suit against HP for breach of implied warranty of merchantability, HP argued that it was an occasional seller of surplus vehicles. The court disagreed, finding that HP was in the regular business of a used-car dealer and thus was a seller and merchant within the meaning of UCC Section 2-314. You may want to examine the way that your business regularly disposes of surplus equipment or other products to consider whether you could unexpectedly be considered a seller of goods.

315, of the UCC. The buyer is relying on the seller's skill and judgment to select the particular goods. Thus, to succeed on a claim for breach of implied warranty of fitness for a particular purpose, the plaintiff would need to show (1) knowledge—the seller had knowledge of the customer's specific purpose; and (2) reliance—the customer relied on the seller's skill and judgment. Unlike the implied warranty of merchantability, which requires that the seller be a merchant of the goods involved, the implied warranty of fitness for a particular purpose applies to a sale of goods regardless of whether the seller qualifies as a merchant.

Exhibit 10-3 summarizes the three theories of product liability.

Exhibit 10-3 Summary of Product Liability Theories

THEORIES OF LIABILITY	WHO CAN SUE	WHO CAN BE LIABLE	DEFENSES	DAMAGES
Negligence	Any foreseeable plaintiff	Any commercial supplier in the distribution chain (Retailers and sellers can satisfy their duty by a cursory reasonable inspection.)	Assumption of the risk Comparative/contributory negligence	Personal injuries Property damages No recovery solely for economic damages
Strict liability	Anyone harmed (buyer, user, bystander)	Any commercial supplier in the distribution chain	Assumption of the risk Product misuse	Personal injuries Property damages No recovery solely for economic damages
Warranty	Privity required (Injured party must be the buyer, the buyer's family, or the buyer's guest.)	Any seller	Assumption of the risk Product misuse Disclaimer	Recovery solely for economic damage

Market Share Liability

L02

What is market share liability?

In most cases, the plaintiff can identify the manufacturer of a defective product that caused the injury at issue. Sometimes, however, some plaintiffs may not learn of their injuries until years after the injury occurs. By this time, plaintiffs cannot trace the product to any particular manufacturer. Often, a number of manufacturers produced the same product, and the plaintiff would have no idea whose product had been used. A plaintiff may have even used more than one manufacturer's product.

Before the 1980s, plaintiffs in this situation would have been unable to gain any sort of recovery for their injuries. However, recovery may be possible today because of the market share theory, created by the California Supreme Court in the case of *Sindell v. Abbott Laboratories.*

In *Sindell,* the plaintiffs' mothers had all taken a drug known as diethylstilbestrol (DES) during pregnancies that had occurred before the drug was banned in 1973. Because DES had been produced 20 years before the plaintiffs suffered any effects from the drug their mothers had taken, it was impossible to trace the defective drug back to each manufacturer that had produced the drug causing each individual's problems. To balance the competing interests of the victims, who had suffered injury from the drug, and the defendants, who did not want to be held liable for a drug they did not produce, the court allowed the plaintiffs to sue all the manufacturers that had produced the drug at the time that the plaintiffs' mothers had used the drug. Then the judge apportioned liability among the defendant-manufacturers on the basis of the share of the market they had held at the time that the drug had been produced.

This theory has since been used by some other courts, primarily in drug cases. Courts using the market share theory generally require that the plaintiff prove that (1) all defendants are tortfeasors; (2) the allegedly harmful products are identical and share the same defective qualities; (3) the plaintiff is unable to identify which defendant caused her injury, through no fault of her own; and (4) the manufacturers of substantially all the defective products in the relevant area and during the relevant time are named as defendants.

Some states have modified the approach of *Sindell.* At least one court has held that the plaintiff need sue only one maker of the allegedly defective drug. If the plaintiff can prove that the defendant manufactured a drug of the type taken by the plaintiff's mother at the time of the mother's pregnancy, that defendant can be held liable for all damages. However, the defendant may join other defendants, and the jury may apportion liability among all defendants.

While the utility of this theory for drug cases is evident, plaintiffs have not been as successful in extending the theory to products other than drugs. For example, in 2001, plaintiffs who were unable to identify the maker of the guns that were used to kill their family members were unsuccessful in their attempt to sue a group of manufacturers for negligent marketing under the theory of market share liability. However, at least one court has extended the theory to lead carbonate to permit market share liability for lead poisoning.

A related issue is product liability insurance. Start-up companies often have difficulty obtaining product liability insurance because they frequently cannot meet the insurance company's requirements, such as sales totaling a certain amount per year. The cost of the insurance will depend on the purpose of the product. If the product is related to safety or product performance, the product will be more expensive to insure than a product related to a decorative function. Insurance premiums for start-up products could range from $2,500 to $10,000 per year.[8]

---

[8] Karen Klein, "When You Can't Secure Product Liability Insurance," *BusinessWeek,* June 9, 2009, www.businessweek.com/smallbiz/content/jun2009/sb2009069_307233.htm.

COMPARING THE LAW OF OTHER COUNTRIES

COLLECTIVE INSURANCE IN SCANDINAVIA

The Scandinavian countries of Sweden, Finland, Denmark, and Norway share a unique feature: the role of collective insurance groups in product liability. Manufacturers, producers, and importers of similar products form cooperative groups and obtain an insurance policy. For example, in Finland, a voluntary insurance policy group headed by the Finnish Pharmaceutical Insurance Pool enlists pharmaceutical companies as members. To hear the appeals of those seeking damages, the pool appoints a board. The board follows the basic liability principle of insurance groups, which is that causation, rather than fault or defectiveness, determines compensation.

Pharmaceutical companies find this principle especially appealing because they can admit liability without damaging the name of their products as a whole. Supporters of the insurance system also point out that elimination of the defectiveness requirement enables product developers to concentrate on improving their products, as opposed to being tied up with product liability cases.

CASE OPENER WRAP-UP

Is Human Sperm Subject to Product Liability Laws?

Donovan's case was the first decision to hold that a sperm bank could be sued under product liability theories for the sperm it provides.[9] One of the issues was whether Pennsylvania or New York law applied to the sale of the sperm. (Donovan and Brittany were Pennsylvania residents, and the sperm came from New York.) Many states, including Pennsylvania and New York, have enacted "blood shield" statutes that prohibit product liability suits based on donated blood. Pennsylvania's blood shield statute included human tissue other than blood, but New York's statute shielded blood and its derivatives only. Therefore, Donovan could have a product liability claim in New York but not in Pennsylvania. The court decided that because the screening of the sperm and the formation of the contract occurred in New York, New York law would apply in Donovan's case and thus, under New York law, the suit could move forward. Another issue was whether Idant provided a service or a product. The court again referred to the blood shield statute and stated that "[u]nder New York law, the sale of sperm is a product and is subject to strict liability."

The court's decision did not find that the sperm actually was defective; it simply found that a New York sperm bank could be sued under product liability laws. However, the case raises some interesting questions: Should a laboratory be held responsible for genetic diseases for which there are no tests? Do the same standards apply to donated eggs? Suppose Brittany Donovan had children who had the same genetic effects. Would they have any claim against the sperm bank?

[9] *Donovan v. Idant Laboratories,* Case No. 08-4075, Memorandum and Order (E.D. Pa., Mar. 31, 2009).

KEY TERMS

design defect 236
express warranty 249
failure to provide adequate
  warnings 236

implied warranty of fitness for
  a particular purpose 251
implied warranty of
  merchantability 250

manufacturing defect 236
market share theory 253

strict product liability 244
warranty 249

SUMMARY OF KEY TOPICS

Negligence: Plaintiff must show that (1) the defendant manufacturer or seller owed a duty of care to the plaintiff; (2) the defendant breached that duty of care by supplying a defective product; (3) this breach of duty caused the plaintiff's injury; and (4) the plaintiff suffered actual injury.

Theories of Liability For Defective Products

Strict product liability: Plaintiff must show that (1) the product was defective when sold; (2) the product was so defective that the product was unreasonably dangerous; and (3) the product was the cause of the plaintiff's injury.

Express warranty: The plaintiff must show that (1) the representation was the basis of the bargain and (2) there was a breach of the representation.

Implied warranty of merchantability: The plaintiff must show that the goods are fit for the purpose for which they are sold and used.

Implied warranty of fitness for a particular purpose: The plaintiff must show that the customer purchased a product for a particular purpose and the seller was aware of this purpose.

When plaintiffs cannot trace a product to any particular manufacturer and a number of manufacturers produced the same product, a court may use the theory of market share liability to impose a portion of fault on a number of manufacturers.

Market Share Liability

POINT / COUNTERPOINT

Should Companies Be Held Strictly Liable for Their Products?	
YES	NO
Companies, rather than individual consumers, are in the best position to absorb the risk of their products. The manufacturer is in the best position to anticipate the harm the product might cause and has more information regarding the product. If a company manufactures and sells a product that seriously harms large numbers of individuals (both consumers and bystanders), the company, rather than the individuals should be responsible for these costs. The company receives all the rewards of selling the product (i.e., the profit) and should thus bear the risks associated with selling the product.	The cost of product liability insurance is so high that companies need to add this cost to the price of the product. Consequently, consumers have to pay unnecessarily higher prices for products, and this creates inefficiency in the market. Similarly, manufacturers waste time and resources creating unnecessary warnings on labels (e.g., "Do not eat" warnings on nonfood products). Furthermore, strict liability discourages companies from developing and testing new products because of the fear that the product could be faulty. Finally, strict–product liability law incentivizes consumers to improperly use products.

QUESTIONS & PROBLEMS

1. Explain the elements one would have to prove to bring a successful product liability case based on negligence, and identify the available defense.

2. Why would a defendant prefer to be found to have produced a product that was defectively manufactured rather than defectively designed?

3. Explain the defenses available in a case based on a theory of strict product liability.

4. The plaintiff suffered a carotid artery tear that left him partially paralyzed after being tackled during a high school football scrimmage. While he was on the field, his coaches removed his helmet, which was then lost. The plaintiff's mother filed suit against the helmet manufacturers, alleging that the helmet's liner and foam padding were defectively designed. The district court granted summary judgment to the defendants because the plaintiff could not produce the specific helmet at issue and thus could not prove the helmet was defective. The plaintiff appealed, arguing that the fact that she could not produce the specific helmet was irrelevant as she was arguing that all of the helmets were defective due to their design. Do you think the appellate court agreed that the specific helmet need not be produced?

[*A.K.W. v. Easton-Bell Sports, Inc., et al.,* No. 11-60293, 2011 U.S. App. LEXIS 21108 (5th Cir. 2011).]

5. The plaintiff's son was given St. Joseph's Aspirin for Children when he had the flu. The aspirin triggered Reye's syndrome, leaving the child a quadriplegic, blind, and mentally retarded. The aspirin contained a warning, approved by the Food and Drug Administration, about the dangers of giving aspirin to children with the flu. The product was advertised in Spanish in the Los Angeles area, but the warning was not in Spanish. The child's guardians could not read English. Do you believe the court imposed liability on the company for failure of its duty to warn? Why or why not? [*Ramirez v. Plough, Inc.,* 25 Cal. Rptr. 2d (1993).]

6. Plaintiff Darren Traub was playing a pickup game of basketball on his college campus and tried to dunk the ball, but his hand hit the rim and he fell down, hurting both wrists. He sued the basketball hoop manufacturer and the university, claiming that the rigid rim caused his injury or made it worse. The defendants filed a motion for summary judgment. Do you think it should have been granted? [*Traub v. Cornell,* 1998 WL 187401 (N.D.N.Y. 1998).]

7. In 1991, three-year-old Douglas Moore was playing with one of BIC's lighters. While playing with the lighter, he started a fire that severely injured his 17-month-old brother. BIC Manufacturers Inc. included several child-safety warning labels on their lighters. These labels identified the risk of fire or injury as a result of misusing the product. The lighter provided warnings to adults to "keep out of reach of children" or "keep away from children." The BIC Corporation had knowledge that its lighters could be manipulated by children, but it felt that including safety features would significantly increase the cost of the lighter. The Moore family brought a strict-liability suit against BIC. Explain why strict liability should or should not be applicable in this case. [*Price v. BIC Corp.,* 702 A.2d 330 (Sup. Ct. N.H. 1997).]

8. The federal Organic Foods Production Act and National Organic Program create uniform federal standards for organic labeling. Under these federal programs, producers of products can become certified as organic.

Aurora's Milk, sold by Aurora Dairy Corp., was certified as organic under these programs. In 2007, the USDA produced a report regarding alleged violations in Aurora's organic operations, but Aurora's organic certification was not revoked. The plaintiffs brought suit against Aurora Dairy Corp. for false certification. The defendants argued that the plaintiffs' claims were preempted. Do you think the defendants were successful in their preemption argument? [*Aurora Dairy Corp. Organic Milk Marketing and Sales Practices Litigation,* Case No. 08-md-01907 (E.D. Mo. 2009).]

9. Three men were riding in a pickup truck when the tire tread separated on a rear wheel. The driver lost control of the truck, which rolled over. The two passengers in the truck were killed, and the estate of one of the passengers brought suit against Cooper Tire, the manufacturer of the tire. The plaintiff argued that the tire was defective in design and had a manufacturing defect. During the discovery portion of the case, the plaintiff sought information regarding all tires manufactured by the defendant; specifically, the plaintiff was seeking information to show that Cooper Tire had notice of a tread separation problem in its other tires. Cooper Tire refused to produce that information, arguing that information regarding other tires that it manufactured but were not at issue in the case was irrelevant. What arguments, if any, could the plaintiff use to establish that the information regarding other tires is relevant? [*Mario Alvarez v. Cooper Tire & Rubber Co.,* 75 So. 3d 789 (Fla. Dist. Ct. App., 4th Dist. 2011).]

10. Chris Hill ran a red light while talking on his cell phone. He crashed into a car driven by Linda Doyle, who was killed in the collision. Doyle's estate brought suit against Sprint/Nextel Corp., arguing that Sprint was negligent in failing to warn Hill that it was dangerous to use a cell phone while driving. Sprint moved to dismiss the case, arguing that it had no duty to noncustomer automobile drivers to warn customers of the dangers of talking on the phone while driving. Do you think the court agreed with Sprint? [*Estate of Doyle v. Sprint/Nextel Corp.,* 248 P.3d 947 (Okla. Civ. App. 2010).]

Looking for more review materials?

The Online Learning Center at **www.mhhe.com/kubasek3e** contains this chapter's "Assignment on the Internet" and also a list of URLs for more information, entitled "On the Internet." Find both of them in the Student Center portion of the OLC, along with quizzes and other helpful materials.

Introduction to Contracts

LEARNING OBJECTIVES

After reading this chapter, you will be able to answer the following questions:

1 What is a contract?

2 What are the sources of contract law?

3 How can we classify contracts?

4 What are the rules that guide the interpretation of contracts?

CASE OPENER

A Questionable Contract

Mary Kay Morrow began working for Hallmark in 1982. At the beginning of 2002, Hallmark adopted the "Hallmark Dispute Resolution Program," which required, among other things, that claims against the company be resolved in binding arbitration rather than litigation. Hallmark assumed that employees who remained at Hallmark after the policy became effective were bound by the new company policy. Additionally, Hallmark reserved the right to modify the program at any time and excluded claims it brought from the arbitration requirement.

Fifteen months after the policy became effective, Hallmark terminated Morrow's employment. Morrow filed a claim against Hallmark, claiming that she had not been fired for just cause but, rather, had been terminated because of age discrimination and retaliation resulting from her earlier complaints about company policies. In response to the suit, which was filed in the circuit court of Jackson County, Hallmark filed a motion to stay the litigation and compel arbitration in accordance with its Dispute Resolution Program. The court granted Hallmark's motion.

After several additional failed attempts to get the circuit court to hear the case, Morrow proceeded with the only route she had left—arbitration. The arbitrator dismissed Morrow's claims for lack of timeliness and ruled that the program constituted a valid contract and was not unconscionable. In yet another effort to have the case heard, Morrow went back to the trial court with a motion to vacate the arbitrator's ruling. The motion was denied. Morrow appealed the case to the Missouri Court of Appeals on the grounds that the Dispute Resolution Program did not constitute an enforceable contract.

1. By what standard would the courts determine whether a contract existed?
2. Did each party to the supposed contract make a valid promise that would support the existence of the contract?

The Wrap-Up at the end of the chapter will answer these questions.

The Definition of a Contract

L01

What is a contract?

This part of the text focuses on contracts, but what is a contract? The Restatement (Second) of Contracts defines a contract as "a promise or set of promises for the breach of which the law gives a remedy or the performance of which the law in some way recognizes a duty."[1] Another way to think of a contract is as a set of legally enforceable promises. Contracts play a fundamental role in business; after all, almost all business relationships are created by contracts.

One of the most important business relationships, the relationship that exists between employers and employees, is often created through contracts. Typically, during the hiring process, an employer will establish an employment contract, which lists the terms and obligations a new employee must agree to before starting work. One particular type of employment contract is a covenant not to compete. Covenants not to compete restrict what an employee may do after leaving a company, and they often dictate where, when, and with whom an employee may work. Employers justify the use of covenants not to compete by saying they are necessary to protect their trade secrets, talent, and proprietary information.

Noncompete contracts are especially common in industries such as technology and sales, where possession of cutting-edge information or client lists can greatly affect the competition between companies. For example, in 2008, IBM and Apple found themselves in a court battle over employee Mark Papermaster. Apple had hired Papermaster away from his high-level position at IBM and wished to put him in charge of Apple's iPhone and iPod division. In turn, IBM argued that Papermaster's move to Apple violated his covenant not to compete, which stated that he would not work for a competitor during the year after he left IBM. Former employer IBM also argued that because Papermaster had been a top executive at IBM, he was in possession of confidential and proprietary information that could be valuable to Apple. The court agreed with IBM and thus issued an injunction barring Papermaster from starting work at Apple until after a trial had taken place. Apple and IBM opted to reach an agreement out of court, and Papermaster was cleared to start work at his new position in April 2009.[2] Covenants not to compete are discussed in greater detail in Chapter 16 of this text.

ELEMENTS OF A CONTRACT

We can flesh out the definition of a contract by examining the four elements that are necessary for it to exist. These elements are the agreement, the consideration, contractual capacity, and a legal object. The agreement consists of an offer by one party, called the *offeror,* to enter into a contract and an acceptance of the terms of the offer by the other party, called the *offeree* (see Exhibit 13-1). This first element is discussed in detail in Chapter 14.

The second element of the contract is the consideration, the bargained-for exchange or what each party gets in exchange for his or her promise under the contract. We discuss consideration in Chapter 15.

[1] Restatement (Second) of Contracts, sec. 1.
[2] See www.networkworld.com/community/node/37835 and http://library.findlaw.com/2003/Feb/5/132530.html.

BUT WHAT IF . . .

WHAT IF THE FACTS OF THE CASE OPENER WERE DIFFERENT?

To fulfill the element of consideration, both parties to a contract must make promises to the other. Recall that, in the Case Opener, Hallmark made no promises to the employees who had to agree to the program. In fact, Hallmark stipulated that it could "modify or discontinue" the program at any time. But what if Hallmark promised raises to each employee who agreed to abide by the rules of the program? Do you see any potential problems with such an agreement?

Exhibit 13-1   The Formation of a Contract

This exhibit illustrates the first element of the contract, the agreement. For a contract to exist, the parties also must have legal capacity to enter into a contract, exchange valid consideration, and be entering into a contract with a legal purpose. The contract is formed as soon as the second party makes his or her promise.

The offer and acceptance together constitute the agreement, which is the first element of the contract.

This is an offer because it is being communicated to the offeree, contains all the material terms, and conveys an intent to be bound by an acceptance.

This is an acceptance because it is being communicated to the offeror, reflects an intent to be bound to the contract, and complies with the mirror image rule.

"I will tutor you every Tuesday from 6 to 7 p.m. for the rest of the semester for $50 an hour."

"I agree to pay you $50 an hour to tutor me every Tuesday from 6 to 7 p.m. for the rest of the semester."

Contract law operates on the Internet, with adjustments for special issues that range from jurisdiction to payment. Which state's or country's laws apply if the parties to an e-contract end up in a dispute? What happens if an online company engages in fraud by using a customer's credit card information in ways the customer never intended?

Contract formation via the Internet is especially important. Issues regarding contract formation range from timing to contract terms. For instance, given the speed with which e-mails go back and forth between parties, it is sometimes difficult to know when the parties have created a contract. Once a contract is formed, additional questions arise: What specific terms does the contract include? Can a company post standard terms on a website rather than in a document or on a ticket?

Fortunately, legislators have drafted and implemented key pieces of legislation that clarify issues related to contract formation and e-commerce. Two examples of e-commerce legislation are the Electronic Signatures in Global and National Commerce (ESIGN) Act and the Uniform Electronic Transactions Act (UETA).

Congress passed ESIGN to facilitate the use of electronic records and signatures in e-commerce. The federal law affirms e-contracts as legally valid. This law makes it clear that documents produced electronically are as valid as documents produced on paper. Congress did not write or pass UETA. Instead, the National Conference of Commissioners on Uniform State Laws proposed this piece of legislation, which almost every state has adopted. UETA's intent was similar to Congress's intent regarding ESIGN. In addition to affirming electronic contracts as legally valid, UETA attempts to make state laws consistent regarding topics such as the validity of signatures created online.

The third element is contractual capacity. Capacity is the legal ability to enter into a binding agreement. Most adults over the age of majority have capacity; those under the age of majority, people suffering from mental illness, and intoxicated persons do not. Chapter 16 explains further cases that limit or prohibit capacity.

Chapter 16 also discusses the fourth element of a binding legal contract, legal object. This means that to be enforceable, the contract cannot be either illegal or against public policy.

Legal Principle: **A legally binding contract requires four elements: agreement, consideration, capacity, and legal object.**

DEFENSES TO THE ENFORCEMENT OF A CONTRACT

Sometimes a contract appears to be legally binding because all four elements of a contract are present, but one of the parties may have a defense to its enforcement. Such defenses fall into two categories. The first is a lack of genuine assent (Chapter 17). A contract is supposed to be entered into freely by both parties, but sometimes the *offeror* (the party proposing the contract) secures acceptance of the agreement through improper means such as fraud, duress, undue influence, or misrepresentation. In these situations, there is no genuine assent to the contract, and the *offeree* (the person who agreed to or accepted the contract) may be able to raise that lack of genuine assent as a defense to enforcement of the agreement.

BUT WHAT IF . . .

WHAT IF THE FACTS OF THE CASE OPENER WERE DIFFERENT?

Recall that, in the Case Opener, Hallmark made it company policy for employees to participate in the dispute Resolution Program when a dispute arose. Employees were bound to the program through employment documents. But what if the facts were different? Let's say that company managers told employees they would be immediately terminated if they did not sign a contract agreeing to the program. Would the contract be valid? If not, on what grounds would the contract be invalid?

The second defense, discussed in Chapter 18, is that the contract lacks the *proper form,* which typically means it lacks a writing. As Chapter 18 will explain, the contract itself does not have to be in writing, but a writing meeting certain criteria that confirms the existence of the contract must exist.

Exhibit 13-2 summarizes the requirements of an enforceable contract.

Legal Principle: **Two defenses to the enforcement of a contract are lack of genuine assent and lack of proper form.**

THE OBJECTIVE THEORY OF CONTRACTS

Contract law is based on an *objective theory of contracts,* which means we base the existence of a contract on the parties' outward manifestations of intent and we base its interpretation on how a reasonable person would interpret it. Thus, the subjective intent of the parties is not usually relevant; what matters is how they represented their intent through their actions and words.

The subjective intent may be relevant, however, under a limited number of circumstances. As Chapter 17 explains in its discussion of mistake, if a mutual misunderstanding between the parties exists, and if as a result they did not really come to a meeting of the minds, there is no contract. The courts may then look at how each party subjectively interpreted the situation to determine whether the parties really reached an agreement.

Legal Principle: **In determining whether parties intended to enter into a contract, the courts look at their objective words and behavior and do not try to figure out what they might have been secretly intending.**

Sources of Contract Law

The two most important sources of contract law are case law and the Uniform Commercial code (UCC). A third source of law, which has become more important with increasing globalization, is the Convention on Contracts for International Sales of Goods (CISG). In this part of the book we focus primarily on the law of contracts as established by common law. (Part Three, "Domestic and International Sales Law," focuses more on the law as set out by the UCC and CISG.)

L02

What are the sources of contract law?

COMMON LAW

Today's law of contracts actually originated in judicial decisions in England, later modified by early courts in the United States. Since then, contract law has been further modified by U.S. legislatures and court rulings. The law of contracts is primarily common law. Therefore, to find out what the law is, we could go to the Reporters and read the decisions,

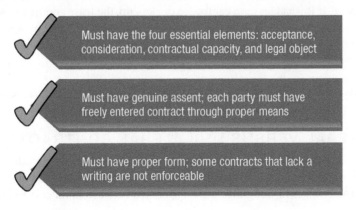

Exhibit 13-2

Requirements of an Enforceable Contract

Must have the four essential elements: acceptance, consideration, contractual capacity, and legal object

Must have genuine assent; each party must have freely entered contract through proper means

Must have proper form; some contracts that lack a writing are not enforceable

Countries outside the United States have slightly different laws for different types of contracts. China, for example, has seven chapters of general provisions for contracts but also has chapters with special provisions for 15 different types of contracts governing sales, leases, loans, donations, construction projects, storage, and transportation.

but it is easier to go to the Restatement (Second) of the Law of Contracts. Prominent legal scholars, recruited by the American Law Institute, organized the principles of the common law of contracts into the original *Restatement of the Law, Contracts*. The compilation has been revised and published as *Restatement of the Law Second, Contracts*. The case in the opening scenario is governed by common law.

The Restatement (Second) is not actually the law itself, although judges frequently cite it because it is an authoritative statement of what the law is. As the common law of contracts evolved, not all states interpreted all aspects of it in the same way, so while we can make generalizations about the law of contracts, you will always want to know exactly what the law at issue is in your own state. In the Restatement (Second), the drafters often explain what the law about a particular matter is in the majority of states and then provide alternative approaches other states have adopted.

UNIFORM COMMERCIAL CODE

Having different laws governing contracts in different states did not make interstate commerce flow smoothly. To remedy some of the difficulties created by a patchwork of different laws governing commercial transactions, the National Conference of Commissioners on Uniform State Laws and the American Law Institute drafted a set of commercial laws that could be applicable to all states. This effort was called the Uniform Commercial Code (UCC). The UCC became law in each state that adopted it in whole or in part as an element of its state code. Thus, if a firm enters into a contract governed by the Uniform Commercial Code in Ohio, it will be operating under the Ohio Uniform Commercial Code.

Legal Principle: **All contracts are governed by either common law or the Uniform Commercial Code (UCC). If the contract is for the sale of a good, it falls under Article 2 of the UCC; if it is for anything else, it falls under common law.**

The part of the Uniform Commercial Code relevant to contracts is Article 2, which governs contracts for the sale (exchange for a price) of goods (tangible, movable objects). In this part of the book we will sometimes point out important differences between the UCC and common law, but we discuss contracts governed by the UCC primarily in Part Three. Also relevant to contract law is UCC Article 2A, which governs contracts for the lease of goods. For instance, if Rashad leases a car from a dealership, the lease contract is governed by Article 2A. If Rashad purchases the car, the purchase contract is governed by Article 2 of the UCC.

Classification of Contracts

L03

How can we classify contracts?

Contracts are classified in a number of different ways. Different classifications are useful for different purposes. This section describes the primary ways by which we classify contracts.

BILATERAL VERSUS UNILATERAL CONTRACTS

All contracts are either unilateral or bilateral. Knowing whether a contract is unilateral or bilateral is important because that classification determines when the offeree is legally bound to perform. Exhibit 13-3 highlights the difference between unilateral and bilateral contracts.

| A PROMISE + A PROMISE = A *BILATERAL* CONTRACT |
| A PROMISE + A REQUESTED ACTION = A *UNILATERAL* CONTRACT |

Exhibit 13-3
Bilateral vs. Unilateral
Contracts

If the offeror wants a promise from the offeree to form a binding contract, the contract is a bilateral contract, commonly defined as a promise in exchange for a promise. As soon as the promises are exchanged, a contract is formed and the parties' legal obligations arise. When Shannon promises to pay Gary $1,000 in exchange for his promise to paint her car on July 1, they have a bilateral contract. If either party fails to perform, the other may sue for breach. In the opening scenario, Hallmark wanted its employees to promise to submit any claims against it to arbitration rather than litigation. At issue in this case is, among other things, the question of whether Hallmark promised anything in return.

Another example of a bilateral contract can be found in the bidding process used by eBay. When an auction on eBay's website has closed, a bilateral contract exists between the seller and the individual who made the highest bid. The seller has promised to send the item (which needs to be comparable to the item described in the listing) to the bidder. The bidder has promised to make payment to the seller in the full amount of his or her bid. Should either party fail to perform, the other party may seek legal remedy according to the terms and conditions set forth by eBay's seller-bidder agreements.

In a bilateral contract, it is crucial that both parties are in fact making binding promises. In Case 13-1, you can see that one party wanted to argue that there was a bilateral agreement, when in fact that party was not binding itself to anything.

CASE 13-1   **IN RE ZAPPOS.COM INC., CUSTOMER DATA SECURITY BREACH LITIGATION**
2012 WL 4466660 (D. NEV., SEPT. 27, 2012)

Zappos.com is a popular website known mainly for its discounted shoe sales. In 2012, a hacker hacked into the Zappos website in an effort to obtain the personal account information of Zappos shoppers. After releasing news of the breach, Zappos faced numerous lawsuits from unhappy customers. Subsequently, Zappos moved to compel arbitration as mandated in its terms of use listed on its website. Zappos argued that it and its customers were in a bilateral agreement stating that arbitration must be used in the event of a dispute between the two parties, as supported by its customer terms of use. However, also in the terms of use, Zappos stipulated that it could change its terms of use and all of its agreements anytime at its own discretion. Hence, customers argued that the agreement was not bilateral and was in fact unfairly unilateral. Specifically, customers argued that Zappos was not actually agreeing to anything and made no promise to its customers regarding dispute resolution. Therefore, customers argued that they should not have to use arbitration and instead should be able to file their class action lawsuit against Zappos.

JUDGE JAMES: . . . The first paragraph of the Terms of Use provides [a] relevant part: "We reserve the right to change this Site and these terms and conditions at any time." The Priera Plaintiffs argue that because the Terms of Use grants Zappos the unilateral right to revise the Arbitration Clause, the contract is illusory and therefore unenforceable. In other words, Plaintiffs argue that the Arbitration Clause is illusory because Zappos can avoid the promise to arbitrate simply by amending the provision, while Zappos.com users are simultaneously bound to arbitration.

Most federal courts that have considered this issue have held that if a party retains the unilateral, unrestricted right to terminate the arbitration agreement, it is illusory and unenforceable, especially where there is no obligation to receive consent from, or even notify, the other parties to the contract.

. . .The Terms of Use gives Zappos the right to change the Terms of Use, including the Arbitration Clause, at any time without notice to the consumer. On one side, the Terms of Use purportedly binds any user of the Zappos.com website to mandatory arbitration. However, if a consumer sought to invoke arbitration pursuant to the Terms of Use, nothing would prevent Zappos from unilaterally changing the Terms and making those changes applicable to that pending dispute if it determined that arbitration was no longer in its interest. In effect, the agreement allows Zappos to hold its customers and users to the promise to arbitrate while reserving its own escape hatch. By the terms of the Terms of Use, Zappos is free at any time to require a consumer to arbitrate and/or litigate anywhere it sees fit, while consumers are required to submit to arbitration in Las Vegas, Nevada. Because the Terms of Use binds consumers to arbitration while leaving Zappos free to litigate or arbitrate wherever it sees fit, there exists no mutuality of obligation. We join those other federal courts that find such arbitration agreements illusory and therefore unenforceable.

A court cannot compel a party to arbitrate where that party has not previously agreed to arbitrate. The arbitration provision found in the Zappos.com Terms of Use purportedly binds all users of the website by virtue of their browsing.

However, the advent of the Internet has not changed the basic requirements of a contract, and there is no agreement where there is no acceptance, no meeting of the minds, and no manifestation of assent. A party cannot assent to terms of which it has no knowledge or constructive notice, and a highly inconspicuous hyper link buried among a sea of links does not provide such notice. Because Plaintiffs did not assent to the terms, no contract exists, and they cannot be compelled to arbitrate. In any event, even if Plaintiffs could be said to have consented to the terms, the Terms of Use constitutes an illusory contract because it allows Zappos to avoid arbitration by unilaterally changing the Terms at any time, while binding any consumer to mandatory arbitration in Las Vegas, Nevada. We therefore decline to enforce the arbitration provision on two grounds: there is no contract, and even if there was, it would be illusory and therefore unenforceable.

IT IS, THEREFORE, HEREBY ORDERED that Defendant Zappos.com, Inc.'s Motion to Compel Arbitration and Stay Action (#3) is DENIED.

CRITICAL THINKING

Is there enough ambiguity with the word *agreement* that Zappos could argue that it had an agreement with its customers? If Zappos could change any rule or promise it made to a customer at any time, how could Zappos argue that it was agreeing to anything?

ETHICAL DECISION MAKING

When a court makes a decision in a contract case, what values is it elevating? In other words, the court is anchoring its reasoning on a preference for a particular value or set of values. What is that value or set of values in a contract case?

In a **unilateral contract,** the offeror wants the offeree to *do* something, not to promise to do something. Perhaps the most common kind of unilateral offer is a reward. If Jim loses his dog, he may post a sign saying, "$50 reward for the safe return of my Poodle, Frenchie." When Michiko calls Jim and says, "Don't worry, I'll find your dog," she is not making a contract because the unilateral offer calls for an action, not a promise.

Just as the offeree is under no obligation to actually perform the act called for by the offeror, the offeror may revoke the offer at any time before performance. Initially this situation created problems because a person could be halfway through the performance and the offeror could revoke the offer. Because of the unfairness of such a scenario, today the courts hold that once an offeree begins performance, the offeror must hold the offer open for a reasonable time to allow the offeree to complete it.

? BUT WHAT IF . . .

WHAT IF THE FACTS OF THE CASE OPENER WERE DIFFERENT?

Recall that, in the Case Opener, Hallmark's contract with its employees involved an employee promise to settle disputes with the company through arbitration. What if, instead, the contract said that if employees settled disputes with the company through arbitration, all fees resulting from the dispute would be covered by Hallmark? Which scenario is bilateral? Which is unilateral?

EXPRESS VERSUS IMPLIED CONTRACTS

We can classify contracts as express or implied depending on how they are created. The terms of express contracts are all clearly set forth in either written or spoken words. In the opening scenario, Hallmark contended that the Dispute Resolution Program constituted an express contract because it had laid out the terms for the contract in a writing received by its employees. Implied contracts, in contrast, arise not from words but from the conduct of the parties. If you have a dental emergency and the dentist pulls your severely infected tooth without prior negotiation about payment, or even any mention of payment, you have an implied contract for payment for her services. However, if you go to the dentist's office, ask how much it will cost to whiten your teeth, and sign a written agreement that stipulates exactly what the process will entail and how much you will pay, you have an express contract.

Apple's iTunes store provides another example of express contracts. Apple has several express contracts with music labels and television stations to sell music and television shows online. As a result of each sale, Apple retains a percentage of the profit and submits the remainder to the music label or television station. Should Apple, or the label, not receive the appropriate percentage of the sale, a breach-of-contract suit could be filed.

As a general rule, three conditions must be met for the courts to find an implied, or *implied-in-fact,* contract. First, the plaintiff provided some property or service to the defendant. Second, the plaintiff expected to be paid for such property or service, and a reasonable person in the position of the defendant would have expected to pay for it. Third, the defendant had an opportunity to reject the property or service but did not. In Case 13-2, the court had to decide whether the facts gave rise to an implied-in-fact contract.

CASE 13-2   **PACHE v. AVIATION VOLUNTEER FIRE CO.**
**SUPREME COURT OF NEW YORK, APPELLATE DIVISION,
THIRD DEPARTMENT
20 A.D.3D 731, 800 N.Y.S.2D 228 (2005)**

Mr. Pache was the fire chief of the Aviation Volunteer Fire Company, which serves several neighborhoods in the Bronx. Mr. Pache suffered a fatal heart attack at the scene of a fire. His widow applied for Workers' Compensation, and was ultimately granted benefits by the Workers' Compensation Board. The decision was based on a finding that there was an implied contract between Aviation and the City of New York giving rise to the City's liability pursuant to the Volunteer Fireman's Benefit Law. The City appealed.

MERCURE, J.: . . . The City initially contended that claimant was not a covered employee within the meaning of Volunteer Firefighters' Benefit Law because the City had no written contract with Aviation. In relevant part, Volunteer Firefighters' Benefit Law § 30(2) provides:

If at the time of injury the volunteer fire[fighter] was a member of [an incorporated] fire company . . . and located in a city, . . . protected under a contract by the fire department or fire company of which the volunteer fire[fighter] was a member, any benefit under this chapter shall be a city . . . charge.

Having conceded at oral argument that an implied contract against the City is a legal possibility, the City argues that it was error to find an implied contract in this case because there was no evidence that the Commissioner of the Fire Department of the City of New York (hereinafter FDNY) ever approved such a contract and there was insufficient proof of the elements of formation of an implied contract. We find both contentions to be unavailing.

In general, "it is well settled that a contract may be implied in fact where inferences may be drawn from the facts and circumstances of the case and the intention of the parties as indicated by their conduct." . . . However, there cannot be a valid implied contract with a municipality when the Legislature has assigned the authority to enter into contracts to a specific municipal officer or body or has prescribed the manner in which the contract must be approved, and there is no proof that the statutory requirements have been satisfied.

Here, the City relies on several provisions of the City Charter for the proposition that the Commissioner of the FDNY has the exclusive authority to enter into contracts on behalf of the FDNY (New York City Charter §§ 16-389, 17-394, 19-487). To the extent that this argument—explicitly

[continued]

asserted for the first time before this Court—is properly before us, it is unpersuasive because these provisions, individually and in conjunction, do not include an express assignment of exclusive contracting authority to the Commissioner.

The City further contends that there was insufficient evidence to support the Board's finding of an implied-in-fact contract because there was no evidence of assent by the City to the alleged contract. While acknowledging the absence of direct evidence on the issue of assent, we conclude that the Board's finding of an implied contract between the City and Aviation should not be disturbed. The Board was presented with evidence that Aviation had been in existence since 1923, and that it worked "hand in hand" with the local FDNY company to fight fires. There was evidence that the local fire company occasionally called Aviation to request its assistance. A representative of the City provided evidence that the City was aware of Aviation, and knew that it fought

fires in conjunction with the FDNY. If Aviation arrived at the scene of a fire before the local FDNY company, Aviation would be in charge of a fire scene until the FDNY company arrived and would thereafter continue working under its supervision. There was no evidence that City officials or the local fire company ever objected to or rejected the services of Aviation. Moreover, although the City was directed to produce an employee from the local FDNY company with knowledge of the relationship between the local fire company and Aviation as well as other facts relevant to the implied contract issue, it failed to do so. . . . Inasmuch as the Board was entitled to draw reasonable and adverse inferences from the City's failure to produce a knowledgeable employee, we are satisfied that substantial evidence supports the Board's determination that an implied-in-fact contract existed between the City and Aviation.

AFFIRMED in favor of Plaintiff.

CRITICAL THINKING

Do you agree that enough evidence has been considered in establishing an implied-in-fact contract? If so, what makes the evidence strong; and if not, what further evidence do you feel is necessary to make a confident claim?

Can you find an appreciable body of evidence in this case in support of an opposite contention? What is it?

ETHICAL DECISION MAKING

Justify the decision reached by the court by using different guidelines for ethical decision making. Which guideline fits most strongly with the case data? Why?

What values might the court be attempting to uphold with this ruling? What values are necessarily sacrificed to these interests? Can you justify this preference, and if so how?

QUASI-CONTRACTS

Quasi-contracts are sometimes called *implied-in-law contracts,* but they are not actually contracts. Rather, in order to prevent one party from being unjustly enriched at the expense of another, the courts impose contractual obligations on one of the parties *as if* that party had entered into a contract.

Assume Diego hears a noise in his driveway. He looks out and sees a group of workers apparently getting ready to resurface it. The doorbell rings, but he does not answer it. He goes down to his basement office and stays there until the workers have gone and he has a resurfaced driveway. When he receives a bill from the paving company, Diego refuses to pay on the grounds that he did not ask to have the driveway paved. In such a case, where the defendant knew the company was getting ready to bestow on him a benefit to which he was not entitled, the court will probably impose a quasi-contract, requiring that Diego pay the paving company the fair market value of the resurfacing. Imposing such a duty prevents him from being unjustly enriched at the expense of the paving company.

There are limits to the doctrine, however; specifically, the enrichment must be unjust. Sometimes a benefit may be conferred on you simply because of a mistake by the other party, and the courts will not make people pay for others' mistakes. Had Diego been out of town when his driveway was repaved, he would have just gotten lucky. The courts are not going to make him pay for the pavers' mistake when he could have done nothing to prevent the benefit from being bestowed on him.

A defendant, however, does not need to acknowledge the subcontractor's role, as was the case in Case 13-3, for a quasi-contract to exist.

CASE 13-3   REISENFELD & CO. v. THE NETWORK GROUP, INC.; BUILDERS SQUARE, INC.; KMART CORP.
U.S. COURT OF APPEALS FOR THE SIXTH CIRCUIT
277 F.3D 856 U.S. APP. (2002)

Network Group ("Network") was contracted by BSI to assist in selling or subleasing closed Kmart stores in Ohio. A few years later, Network entered into a commission agreement with Reisenfeld, a real estate broker for Dick's Clothing and Sporting Goods ("Dicks"). Dicks then subleased two stores from BSI. According to executed assignment and assumption agreements signed in November of 1994, BSI was to pay a commission to Network. Network was then responsible, pursuant to the commission agreement with Reisenfeld, to pay a commission of $1 per square foot to Reisenfeld. There was no direct agreement made between BSI and Reisenfeld.

During this time, Network's sole shareholder was defrauding BSI. This shareholder was convicted of several criminal charges stemming from his fraudulent acts. Network was ordered by the district court to disgorge any commissions received from BSI, and BSI was relieved of any duty to pay additional commissions to Network. As such, Reisenfeld never received his commission related to the Dicks sublease.

Reisenfeld sued in state court for the $160,320 in commissions he had not been paid. In addition to suing Network, Reisenfeld also named BSI as a defendant. The suit alleged, among other things, that based on a theory of quasi-contracts, BSI was jointly and severally liable for the commission.

JUDGE BOOGS: . . . A contract implied-in-law, or "quasi-contract," is not a true contract, but instead a liability imposed by courts in order to prevent unjust enrichment. . . . Under Ohio law, there are three elements for a quasi-contract claim. There must be: (1) a benefit conferred by the plaintiff upon the defendant; (2) knowledge by the defendant of the benefit; and (3) retention of the benefit by the defendant under circumstances where it would be unjust to do so without payment. . . .

There is no disagreement as to the first two requirements. It is clear that Reisenfeld's work as broker benefited BSI and that BSI was aware of the work Reisenfeld was doing. The disagreement rests on the third requirement—whether it would be unjust for BSI to retain the benefit it received without paying Reisenfeld for it. . . . Unreported Ohio Court of Appeals cases support the proposition that, in the contractor/subcontractor context, when the subcontractor is not paid by the contractor and the owner has not paid the contractor for the aspect of the job at issue, the subcontractor can look to the owner for payment under a theory of unjust enrichment. . . . Further, another Ohio case, in dicta, supports the proposition that nonpayment by the owner would make payment on an unjust enrichment theory appropriate. . . .

[H]ere, BSI has not paid Network on this contract, and the losses suffered by BSI at Network's hands were "soft" losses of additional profits Network might have made, rather than quantifiable losses (due, for example, to theft) that might be held to constitute payment. . . . Therefore, though not controlling of this matter, the Ohio contractor/subcontractor cases involving property owners who have not paid the contractors provide persuasive support for the proposition that Reisenfeld may hold BSI accountable on a theory of quasi-contract for the benefits it provided to BSI, and for which it was not compensated by Network. . . .

Of course, liability under quasi-contract does not necessarily imply liability for the amount of money promised Reisenfeld under its contract with Network. Instead, the proper measure of liability is the reasonable value of the services Reisenfeld provided to BSI. We must therefore vacate the district court's order and remand the case for a determination of value.

REMANDED for consideration of damages.

CRITICAL THINKING

What words or phrases important to the reasoning of this decision might be ambiguous? What alternate definitions are possible? How does this ruling appear to be defining the words or phrases? Would another choice affect the acceptability of the conclusion?

Provide an example of one piece of new evidence that might lead Judge Boggs to a different conclusion, and explain how this information changes the consideration.

ETHICAL DECISION MAKING

Does this ruling establish a positive precedent in terms of the potential effect on future participants in disputes of this sort?

Does this decision appear to follow the Golden Rule guideline? Why or why not? How is this question particularly relative to the person making the judgment, and what sorts of interpersonal differences might lead to a variety of responses?

Legal Principle: **Recovery in quasi-contract may be obtained when (1) a benefit is conferred by the plaintiff upon the defendant; (2) the defendant has knowledge of the benefit that is being bestowed upon her; and (3) the defendant retains the benefit under circumstances in which it would be unjust to do so without payment.**

VALID, VOID, VOIDABLE, AND UNENFORCEABLE CONTRACTS

What everyone hopes to enter into, of course, is a valid contract, one that contains all the legal elements set forth in the beginning of this chapter. As a general rule, a valid contract is one that will be enforced. However, sometimes a contract may be valid yet unenforceable when a law prohibits the courts from enforcing it. The statute of frauds (Chapter 18) requires that certain contracts must be evidenced by a writing before they can be enforced. Similarly, the statute of limitations mandates that an action for breach of contract must be brought within a set period of time, thereby limiting enforceability.

A void contract is in effect not a contract at all. Either its object is illegal or it has some defect so serious that it is not a contract. If you entered into a contract with an assassin to kill your business law professor, that contract would be void because it is obviously illegal to carry out its terms.

A contract is voidable if one or both parties has the ability to either withdraw from the contract or enforce it. If the parties discover the contract is voidable after one or both have partially performed, and one party chooses to have the contract terminated, both parties must return anything they had already exchanged under the agreement so that they will be restored to the condition they were in at the time they entered into it.

Certain types of errors in the formation of a contract can make it voidable. Typically, the person who can void the contract is the person the court is attempting to protect, or the party the court believes might be taken advantage of by the other. For example, contracts by minors are usually voidable by the minor (Chapter 16). Contracts entered into as a result of fraud, duress, or undue influence, as described in Chapter 17, may be voided by the innocent party. In the opening scenario, Morrow attempted to prove that the Dispute Resolution Program was a voidable contract because it did not include mutual promises, could be changed at any time without approval, and lacked genuine assent from the employees.

EXECUTED VERSUS EXECUTORY CONTRACTS

Once all the terms of the contract have been fully performed, the contract has been executed. As long as some of the terms have not yet been performed, the contract is executory. If Randolph hires Carmine to paint his garage on Saturday for $800, with $200 paid as a down payment and the balance due on completion of the job, the contract becomes executory as soon as they reach agreement. When Randolph makes the down payment and Carmine's work is half complete, it is still executory. Once the painting has been finished and the final payment made, the contract is an executed contract. In the opening scenario, Hallmark assumed that any employee who remained at the company had executed the contract.

FORMAL VERSUS INFORMAL CONTRACTS

Contracts can be formal or informal. Formal contracts have a special form or must be created in a specific manner. The Restatement (Second) of Contracts identifies the following

A SPECIAL KIND OF CONTRACT IN IRAQ

While most foreign states recognize the marriage contract, a different kind of marriage contract, sanctioned by Shiite clerics, is legal in Iraq. Called *muta'a* ("contract for a pleasure marriage"), it can last anywhere from an hour to 10 years and is renewable. Under the contract, the male typically receives sexual intimacy, in exchange for which the woman receives money. For a one-hour contract, she can generally expect the equivalent of $100; for a longer-term arrangement, $200 a month is typical, although she might receive more. The couple agrees to not have children, and if the woman does get pregnant, she can have an abortion but then must pay a fine to a cleric. The male can usually void the contract before the term ends, but the female can do so only if such a provision is negotiated when the contract is formed.

Muta'as originally developed as a way for widows and divorced women to earn a living and for couples whose parents would not allow a permanent marriage to be together. Many women's rights advocates, however, see these contracts as exploiting women and are opposed to their increased popularity after the fall of Saddam Hussein in 2003. But as the aftermath of the war in Iraq continues to produce greater numbers of widows, increasing numbers of them are turning to this method of putting food on the table for themselves and their children.

Source: Rick Jervic, "'Pleasure Marriages' Regain Popularity in Iraq," *USA Today,* May 5, 2005, p. 8A; Bobby Caina Calvin, "In Shiite Iraq, Temporary Marriage May Be Rising," *McClatchy News,* www.mcclatchydc.com/103/story/21584.html (accessed June 9, 2009).

four types of formal contracts: (1) contracts under seal, (2) recognizances, (3) letters of credit, and (4) negotiable instruments.

When people hear the term *formal contract,* what often comes to mind is a *contract under seal,* named in the days when contracts were sealed with a piece of soft wax into which an impression was made. Today, sealed contracts may still be sealed with wax or some other soft substance, but they are more likely to be simply identified with the word *seal* or the letters *L.S.* (an abbreviation for *locus sigilli,* which means "the place for the seal") at the end. Preprinted contract forms with a printed seal can be purchased today, and parties using them are presumed, without evidence to the contrary, to be adopting the seal for the contract.

U.S. states today do not require that contracts be under seal. However, 10 states still allow a contract without consideration to be enforced if it is under seal.

A recognizance arises when a person acknowledges in court that he or she will perform some specified act or pay a price upon failure to do so. A bond used as bail in a criminal case is a recognizance. The person agrees to return to court for trial or forfeit the bond.

A letter of credit is an agreement by the issuer to pay another party a sum of money on receipt of an invoice and other documents. The Uniform Commercial Code governs letters of credit.

Negotiable instruments (discussed in detail in Chapters 26 and 27) are unconditional written promises to pay the holder a specific sum of money on demand or at a certain time. The most common negotiable instruments are checks, notes, drafts, and certificates of deposit. They are governed primarily by the UCC.

Any contract that is not a formal contract is an informal contract, also called a simple contract. Informal contracts may in fact be quite complex, but they are called "simple" because no formalities are required in making them. Even though informal, or simple, contracts may appear less official, they are just as important and legally binding as their more formal counterparts. One particular case, *Baum v. Helget Gas Products, Inc.,* proved that something as basic as handwritten notes can be considered an enforceable employment contract in a court of law.

In *Baum v. Helget Gas Products, Inc.,*[3] Robert Baum alleged that a series of handwritten notes, which were compiled during his interview with Helget Gas Products, constituted a three-year employment contract with the company. The notes Baum took during the interview process outlined three years' worth of salary, bonuses, benefits, and vacation time as discussed in the meetings. After being hired by the company, Baum also added "contract with Helget Gas Products St. Louis Mo. Market" to the top of the notes and had a Helget executive sign the document. Helget countered by saying that Baum, a salesman for the company, knew that he must meet certain performance goals each month or risk being fired. Thus, Helget's decision to fire Baum, based on his poor performance only a year after being hired, was legitimate. Helget further said that the itemizations produced by Baum in his notes were simply specifications of what Baum would receive if he remained employed by the company for the duration of three years and were not the components of an employment contract.

BUT WHAT IF . . .

In 2012, a hospital in Pennsylvania communicated with Republic Bank through e-mails about purchasing medical equipment from the bank. In the series of e-mails, the hospital agreed to purchase the equipment for stipulated prices. The bank agreed to the terms. However, the hospital never followed through with the deal. The bank sued the hospital, claiming there was a breach of contract. What kind of contract could the e-mails be labeled as?

Initially, the district court agreed with Helget Gas Products and ruled against Baum on his breach-of-contract claim. However, Baum appealed, and the U.S Court of Appeals for the Eighth Circuit reversed the district court's judgment on the breach-of-contract claim. For business students, *Baum v. Helget Gas Products, Inc.,* demonstrates the importance of being aware of what you are agreeing to when you sign a document, regardless of how informal, or simple, it may seem.

For a summary of contract classification, see Exhibit 13-4.

Interpretation of Contracts

L04

What are the rules that guide the interpretation of contracts?

Perhaps the best-known rule of interpretation is the plain-meaning rule, which states that if a writing, or a term in question, appears to be plain and unambiguous on its face, we must determine its meaning from just "the four corners" of the document, without resorting to outside evidence, and give the words their ordinary meaning.

Although parties try to draft contracts as clearly as possible, sometimes they disagree about exactly what their obligations are under the agreement. Over time, the courts have developed some general guidelines to aid them in interpreting contracts and ascertaining the intentions of the parties:

- A judge should interpret a contract so as to give effect to the parties' intentions at the time they entered into the contract and to ensure the agreement makes sense as a whole. If possible, the court should ascertain the parties' intentions from the writing.

[3] 440 F.3d 1019; 2006 U.S. App. (accessed on Lexis Nexis, April 4, 2009).

Exhibit 13-4   Classification of Contracts

BILATERAL	or	UNILATERAL
Consists of a promise in exchange for a promise		Requires a performance by the offeree to form a contract

EXPRESS	or	IMPLIED
The terms of the contract are clearly formed either in written or spoken words		Arises from the conduct of the parties rather than their words

EXECUTED	or	EXECUTORY
A contract whose terms have been fully performed		A contract in which not all the duties have been performed

FORMAL	or	INFORMAL
Contracts created in a specific manner: contracts under seal, recognizances, letters of credit, and negotiable instruments		Simple contracts that require no formalities in making them; payment can be demanded by the payee at any time (e.g., checks)

VALID	or	VOID	or	UNENFORCEABLE	or	VOIDABLE
A contract that has all the legal elements of a contract and thus can be enforced		Not a contract because either its object is illegal or it has a serious defect		A valid contract that can't be enforced because some law prohibits it		A contract in which one or both parties has the ability to either withdraw from or enforce the contract

- If multiple interpretations are possible, the court should adopt the interpretation that makes the contract lawful, operative, definite, reasonable, and capable of being carried out.
- If the contract contains ambiguity, the judge should interpret it against the interests of the drafter. After all, the drafter is the one who could have prevented the ambiguity in the first place.
- If there is a conflict between preprinted and handwritten terms, the handwritten ones prevail. If numerals and numbers written out in words conflict, the written words prevail. If there is a conflict between general terms and specific ones, the specific terms apply.
- The court should interpret technical words in a contract as they are usually understood by persons in the profession or business to which they relate, unless clearly used in a different sense.

The Case Nugget on page 320 illustrates how some of these principles can be important in determining the outcome of a case.

Davco Holding Co. v. Wendy's International
2008 U.S. Dist. LEXIS 27108

Plaintiff Davco Holding Co., a franchisee of Wendy's, sued the company for breach of the franchise agreement for refusing to allow Davco to sell Pepsi from an unapproved supplier. The franchise agreement permits franchisees desiring to purchase products from an unapproved supplier to submit a written request to Wendy's for approval to do so. In response to Davco's written request to obtain beverage syrup from unapproved Pepsi, Wendy's informed Davco that CCF was the only approved supplier for fountain beverages and, further, that Pepsi syrup was not even an equivalent to Coke syrup because the drinks were made from two different secret formulas. The plaintiff alleged that Wendy's failed to adequately consider its request to solicit bids from Pepsi or to investigate Pepsi as a potential supplier and that this failure resulted in a breach by Wendy's of the franchise agreement.

The paragraph discussing the request for using an unapproved supplier contained the following language:

> Franchisor shall have the right to require that Franchisor be permitted to inspect the supplier's facilities, and that samples from the supplier be delivered, either to Franchisor or to an independent laboratory designated by Franchisor for testing. . . . Franchisor reserves the right to reinspect the facilities and products of any such approved supplier and to revoke its approval upon the supplier's failure to continue to meet any of Franchisor's then-current criteria. Nothing in the foregoing shall be construed to require Franchisor to approve any particular supplier, nor to require Franchisor to make available to prospective suppliers, standards and specifications for formulas that Franchisor, in its sole discretion, deems confidential.

The plaintiff claimed that Wendy's breached the agreement because it didn't inspect the facilities of Pepsi, request samples, or make its criteria available to Pepsi.

In interpreting the contract, the court said that where the terms of an existing contract are clear and unambiguous, the court "cannot create a new contract by finding an intent not expressed in the clear and unambiguous language of the written contract," and that a written agreement that appears complete and unambiguous on its face will not be given a construction other than that which the plain language of the contract provides.

As the court pointed out in dismissing the plaintiff's claims, the clause gives Wendy's the right to inspect a potential supplier, but giving someone a right to do something is not imposing a duty to do so. Thus, Wendy's failure to inspect cannot be a breach. Likewise, the terms of the clause clearly state that approval of another supplier lies within the sole discretion of Wendy's and that Wendy's does not have to share its criteria with the potential supplier.

CASE OPENER WRAP-UP

A Questionable Contract

The main issue in the Hallmark case was whether a valid contract existed. Hallmark argued that by staying with the company beyond the effective date of the program, employees were agreeing to the terms of the contract. To Hallmark, the bargained-for exchange was continued employment in exchange for a promise to submit to arbitration in lieu of litigation. The circuit court sent the case to arbitration, where the arbitrator found that the program constituted a valid contract.

The appellate court, however, using the objective standard for determining whether a contract existed, found that there was not a valid contract. For a valid, bilateral contract to exist, both sides would have to be making a valid promise. Hallmark was not binding itself to anything. The program did not require Hallmark to submit its claims to arbitration or in any way bind the company to keep any other promise mentioned in the Dispute Resolution Program (DRP). Further, Hallmark had reserved the right to "modify or discontinue the DRP at any time."

In response to the claim that continued employment was given to the employees in exchange for their promise to submit all disputes to arbitration, the court found that no such promise had been made by Hallmark. The employees to be bound by the program were at-will employees. As such, employment could be terminated at any time by Hallmark. Thus, the employees were receiving no rights in regard to employment that they did not already have. Because no mutually binding promises were exchanged, the appellate court ruled that the trial court had erred in accepting the arbitrator's award. In other words, because there was no consideration from Hallmark, there was no binding contract to submit disputes to arbitration. The case was remanded for further proceedings on Morrow's discrimination and retaliation claims.[4]

KEY TERMS

acceptance   306

agreement   306

bilateral contract   311

consideration   306

contract   306

contractual capacity   308

covenant not to compete   306

executed   316

executory   316

express contracts   313

formal contracts   317

implied contracts   313

informal contract   317

lack of genuine assent   308

letter of credit   317

negotiable instruments   317

offer   306

plain-meaning rule   318

quasi-contracts   313

recognizance   317

simple contract   317

unenforceable   316

Uniform Commercial Code (UCC)   310

unilateral contract   311

valid   316

void   316

voidable   316

SUMMARY OF KEY TOPICS

Contracts at their simplest level are legally enforceable agreements. A *valid contract* is generally one that has the following elements:

The Definition of a Contract

- *Agreement,* which is made up of the offer and the acceptance.
- *Consideration,* which is the bargained-for exchange.
- *Legal object,* which means that the subject matter does not violate the law or public policy.
- *Parties with contractual capacity,* which means they are at least the age of majority and do not suffer from any defect that renders them unable to understand the nature of the contract or their obligations under it.

The two most important sources of contract law are state common law and the Uniform Commercial Code. The Uniform Commercial Code, in Article 2, governs contracts for the sale of goods. All other contracts are also governed by the UCC.

Sources of Contract Law

Contracts may be classified in a number of ways. Every contract is either unilateral or bilateral; express or implied; valid, voidable, void, or enforceable; executed or executory; and formal or informal.

Classification of Contracts

- A *unilateral contract* requires a performance in order to form a contract.
- A *bilateral contract* consists of a promise in exchange for a promise.
- An *express contract* has all the terms clearly set forth in either written or spoken words.
- An *implied contract* arises from the conduct of the parties rather than their words.

[4] *Mary Kaye Morrow v. Hallmark Cards,* 273 S.W.3d 15, 2008 Mo. App. LEXIS 908.

- A *valid contract* is one that contains *all* the legal elements of a contract (agreement, consideration, contractual capacity, and legal object).
- A contract is *void* when either its object is illegal or it has some defect so serious that it is not actually a contract.
- A contract is *unenforceable* when some law prohibits the court from enforcing an otherwise valid contract.
- A contract is *voidable* if one or both of the parties has the ability to withdraw from the contract or to enforce it.
- *Executed contracts* are those whose terms have been fully performed.
- A contract is considered *executory* when some of the duties have not yet been performed.

Interpretation of Contracts

Courts have established rules to help interpret contracts so that they can ascertain and enforce the intent of the agreement.

The *plain-meaning rule* requires that if a writing, or a term in question, appears to be plain and ambiguous, its meaning must be determined from the instrument itself, with the words given their ordinary meaning.

POINT / COUNTERPOINT

Should the Distinction between Sealed and Unsealed Contracts Be Abolished?

NO	YES
The distinction between sealed and unsealed contracts was drawn for several reasons, many of which are still relevant. As such, the distinction should remain intact despite the many attempts to have it abolished.	Advocates of abolishing the distinction between sealed and unsealed contracts argue that the distinction has become unnecessary and outdated. Sealed contracts can be dated back to medieval England when a substantial portion of the population was illiterate and many people were unable to sign their own names. As a result, each party to a sealed contract was responsible for impressing on the physical document a wax seal or some other mark bearing his or her individual sign of identification. The seals, in place of signatures, became proof of the parties' identities as well as the authenticity of the document.
Sealed contracts, at common law, did not require consideration. In many instances today, consideration is not a necessary part of the agreement. These instances include releases, modifications and discharges, promises to keep offers open, promises based on past consideration, and promises to make gifts. In these instances, one party is offering to give something without consideration. For example, an individual wishing to make a charitable donation could enter into a binding agreement to make the donation without receiving any consideration in return. By sealing the contract, the charitable organization receiving the donation would be protected against lawsuits arising from a lack of consideration. In this instance, the distinction between a sealed and unsealed contract would be the difference between a judgment in favor of the charitable organization despite the lack of consideration and an outright dismissal.	The practice of actually affixing a seal to a document is no longer necessary. Today, the parties to a sealed contract need only write the words "under seal" or "sealed" or the letters "L.S" (*locus sigilli*) for the document to be given the privileged status of a sealed document.
Additionally, sealed contracts are often accompanied by an increased statute of limitations. In instances when there are potentially long-term ramifications tied to the signing of a contract, a sealed contract would provide a much longer period in which the parties could sue than would be the case if the contract were left unsealed.	In response to those who argue that sealed contracts are necessary to bind contracts that do not contain consideration, abolishment advocates argue that there are other, and perhaps more meaningful, methods of accomplishing this. Instead of sealing a contract, one could (1) require that the promise without consideration be explicitly referenced and agreed to in the text itself; or (2) require that witnesses be present at the signing of the contract (as is the practice with regard to wills); or (3) simply rewrite the contract to provide for consideration.

(Continued)

Given the protections offered by sealed contracts, abolishing them would be irresponsible. Moreover, the elimination of the sealed-unsealed distinction would necessarily result in the creation of another method of enforcement. Why should we abolish a technique that provides protection to the parties involved in the making of a contract only to turn around and create a similar distinction under a different name?

The practice of sealing contracts is outdated and irrelevant. Parties to contracts lacking consideration could be more protected from lawsuits by using different methods of enforcement. The sealed contract should be abolished in all states (as has already been done in several states).

QUESTIONS & PROBLEMS

1. What are the elements of a valid contract?

2. What is the difference between an offer for a unilateral contract and an offer for a bilateral contract? Why might that difference be important to understand?

3. Explain how a valid contract differs from one that is void or voidable.

4. What is the objective theory of contracts?

5. What must a party prove to recover under the theory of quasi-contract?

6. What is the difference between a formal and an informal contract?

7. What is the plain-meaning rule?

8. AES was formed in 1996 and hired eight employees. At a meeting in 1997, these employees expressed concern that the company might not survive as it was using outdated equipment. At that meeting, a company executive asked the employees to remain with the firm and stated that the company was likely to merge with another firm and, if it did, the original eight employees would receive 5 percent of the value of the sale or merger as a reward for staying. In 2001, the firm was bought by another firm, and the seven employees who had stayed sought to collect their 5 percent. The company refused to pay on grounds there was no contract. Did the company and employees have a bilateral or a unilateral contract? Explain. [*Vanegas v. American Energy Services,* 302 S.W.3d 299, 2009 WL 4877734 (Sup. Ct. Tex., 2009).]

9. R.J. Reynolds Tobacco Company (RJR) operated a customer rewards program, called Camel Cash, from 1991 to 2007. Under the terms of the program, RJR urged consumers to purchase Camel cigarettes, to save Camel Cash certificates included in packages of Camel cigarettes, to enroll in the program, and, ultimately, to redeem their certificates for merchandise featured in catalogs distributed by RJR.

The plaintiffs were 10 individuals who joined the Camel Cash program by purchasing RJR's products and filling out and submitting signed registration forms to RJR. RJR sent each plaintiff a unique enrollment number that was used in communications between the parties. These communications included catalogs RJR distributed to the plaintiffs containing merchandise that could be obtained by redeeming Camel Cash certificates.

From time to time, RJR issued a new catalog of merchandise offered in exchange for Camel Cash, which it either sent on request or mailed to consumers enrolled in the program. The number of Camel Cash certificates needed to obtain merchandise varied from as few as 100 to many thousands, and this encouraged consumers to buy more packages of Camel cigarettes and also to save Camel Cash certificates to redeem them for more valuable items.

RJR honored the program from 1991 to 2006, and during that time Camel's share of the cigarette market nearly doubled, from approximately 4 percent to more than 7 percent. In October 2006, however, RJR mailed a notice to program members announcing that the program would terminate on March 31, 2007. The termination notice stated: "As a loyal Camel smoker, we wanted to tell you our Camel Cash program is expiring. C–Notes will no longer be included on packs, which means whatever Camel Cash you have is among the last of its kind. Now this isn't happening overnight—there'll be plenty of time to redeem your C–Notes before the program ends. In fact, you'll have from OCTOBER '06 though MARCH '07 to go to camelsmokes. com to redeem your C–Notes. Supplies will be limited, so it won't hurt to get there before the rush."

Beginning in October 2006, however, RJR stopped printing and issuing catalogs and told consumers that it did not have any merchandise available for redemption. Several of the plaintiffs attempted, without success, to redeem C–Notes or obtain a catalog during the final six months of the program. The plaintiffs had saved hundreds or thousands of Camel Cash certificates that they were unable to redeem.

In November 2009, the plaintiffs filed a class action complaint against RJR. They alleged breach of contract and promissory estoppel, among other claims, because RJR's actions had made the plaintiffs' unredeemed certificates worthless.

The Defendant argued that it had no bilateral contract to breach because the plaintiffs had not promised to do anything. The trial court agreed and dismissed the complaint. The plaintiffs appealed.

How do you think the appellate court ruled, and why? [*Sateriale v. R.J. Reynolds Tobacco Co., 697 F.3d 777, C.A.9 (Cal. 2012).*]

10. An oral agreement was made among multiple parties to put together some money and open a bar and restaurant. The men had to first create a joint company. However, one potential owner was not able to provide his share of the funding at the time of the company formation and was subsequently pushed out of the deal by the other owners, who formed the company without him. The man then sued the owners. In response, the defendants argued that the plaintiff had no documentation to support a cause of action. The court had to decide whether the plaintiff's complaint and statement of fact could support a breach-of-contract claim when no contract seemed to exist. Furthermore, the court considered the idea that a theory of quasi-contract could maintain a cause of action that could consist of the theft of ownership opportunity and/or breach of fiduciary duty. How do you think the court ultimately decided? [*Don v. Broger,* Index No. 6826/12 (Sup. Ct. Kings Cnty., Oct. 10, 2012).]

Looking for more review materials?

The Online Learning Center at **www.mhhe.com/kubasek3e** contains this chapter's "Assignment on the Internet" and also a list of URLs for more information, entitled "On the Internet." Find both of them in the Student Center portion of the OLC, along with quizzes and other helpful materials.

Agreement

14

LEARNING OBJECTIVES

After reading this chapter, you will be able to answer the following questions:

1 What are the elements of a valid offer?

2 How may an offer terminate?

3 What are the elements of an acceptance?

CASE OPENER

The Problematic Promotion

A Pepsi promotion encouraged consumers to collect "Pepsi points" and redeem them for merchandise. If they did not have quite enough points for the prize they wanted, they could buy additional points for 10 cents each; however, at least 15 original Pepsi points had to accompany each order.

In an early commercial for the promotion, which can be viewed on the web at www.youtube.com/watch?v=U_n5SNrMaL8, three young boys are sitting in front of a high school, one reading his Pepsi Stuff catalog while the others drink Pepsi. All look up in awe at an object rushing overhead as the military march in the background builds to a crescendo. A Harrier Jet swings into view and lands by the side of the school building, next to a bicycle rack. Several students run for cover, and the velocity of the wind strips one hapless faculty member down to his underwear. The voice-over announces: "Now, the more Pepsi you drink, the more great stuff you're gonna get."

A teenager opens the cockpit of the fighter and can be seen, without a helmet, holding a Pepsi. He exclaims, "Sure beats the bus," and chortles. The military drumroll sounds a final time as the following words appear: "Harrier Fighter 7,000,000 Pepsi Points." A few seconds later, the following appears in more stylized script: "Drink Pepsi—Get Stuff."

A 21-year-old student named John Leonard decided to accept what he believed was Pepsi's offer of the Harrier fighter jet for 7 million Pepsi points. He quickly realized it would be easier to raise the money to buy points than to collect 7 million points. In early March 1996, he filled out an order form requesting the jet and submitted it to Pepsi, along with 15 Pepsi points and a check for $700,000.

The plaintiff in the opening scenario hoped to obtain a jet like this one.

In response, Pepsi sent him a letter saying, "The item that you have requested is not part of the Pepsi Stuff collection. It is not included in the catalogue or on the order form, and only catalogue merchandise can be redeemed under this program." Leonard sued for breach of contract.

1. Did Pepsi offer to sell the Harrier jet for 7 million points?
2. Did Leonard's submission of the order form constitute an acceptance of an offer?

The Wrap-Up at the end of the chapter will answer these questions.

Elements of the Offer

L01

What are the elements of a valid offer?

The first element of a contract is the agreement, which is made up of an offer and an acceptance, as shown in Exhibit 14-1. Formation of the agreement begins when the party initiating the contract, called the *offeror,* makes an offer to another party, called the *offeree.* The elements of an offer are (1) serious intent by the offeror to be bound to an agreement, (2) reasonably definite terms, and (3) communication to the offeree. Remember, this chapter focuses on the elements of a contract under the common law. Some of these elements have been modified under the UCC for contracts for the sale of goods, and we discuss these changes in Chapter 21.

? BUT WHAT IF . . .
WHAT IF THE FACTS OF THE CASE OPENER WERE DIFFERENT?

Recall that, in the Case Opener, the Pepsi commercial shows a fighter jet jokingly dropping a boy off at school. But what if the Pepsi commercial featured a man fully capable of owning and operating a fighter jet who turned in an appropriate and realistic number of Pepsi points and Pepsi Company officials subsequently handed him the keys and deeds to such a prize? What if the commercial announcer turned to the viewers and seriously announced that such a prize was included in the prize catalog and could be theirs? Do both scenarios constitute a realistic offer, or does neither scenario, or only the second scenario constitute such an offer?

INTENT

The first element of the offer is intent. The offeror must show intent to be bound by the offeree's acceptance. As explained in Chapter 13, we interpret contracts using an objective standard, meaning the courts are concerned only with the party's outward manifestations of intent, not internal thought processes. The courts interpret the parties' words and actions the way a reasonable person would interpret them.

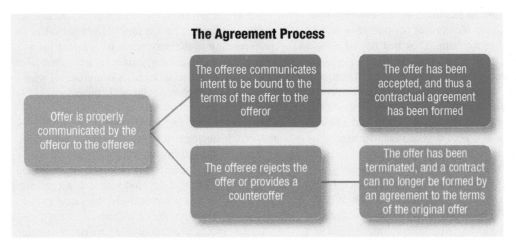

Exhibit 14-1

The Formation of an Agreement

Thus, if Jude is clearly joking or speaking in anger, a reasonable person would not think Jude seriously intended to make an offer and the courts will not treat his words as an offer. If someone tries to accept Jude's offer, the courts will find a contract has not been made.

Sometimes an offeror may try to avoid being bound to a contract by later claiming she was only joking when she made the offer, but the courts are not interested in her hidden intent. As Case 14-1 demonstrates, if you joke too well, you may find yourself in an unwanted contract.

CASE 14-1   LUCY v. ZEHMER
SUPREME COURT OF APPEALS OF VIRGINIA
196 VA. 493, 84 S.E.2D 516 (1954)

Plaintiffs W. O. and J. C. Lucy had wanted to purchase Ferguson Farm from the Zehmers for at least eight years. One night, Lucy stopped by the establishment the Zehmers operated and said that he bet Zehmer wouldn't accept $50,000 for the place. Zehmer replied that he would, but he bet that Lucy wouldn't pay $50,000 for it. Over the course of the evening, the parties drank whiskey and engaged in casual conversation, with the talk repeatedly returning to the sale of Ferguson Farm. Eventually Lucy got Zehmer to draw up a contract for the sale of the farm for $50,000.

When Lucy later attempted to enforce the agreement, Zehmer refused to complete the sale, arguing that he had been drunk, and that the agreement to sell the property had been made in jest. Lucy sued to enforce the agreement. The trial court found for the defendants and the plaintiffs appealed.

JUSTICE BUCHANAN: If it be assumed, contrary to what we think the evidence shows, that Zehmer was jesting about selling his farm to Lucy and that the transaction was intended by him to be a joke, nevertheless the evidence

shows that Lucy did not so understand it but considered it to be a serious business transaction and the contract to be binding on the Zehmers as well as on himself. The very next day he arranged with his brother to put up half the money and take a half interest in the land. The day after that he employed an attorney to examine the title. The next night, Tuesday, he was back at Zehmer's place and there Zehmer told him for the first time, Lucy said, that he wasn't going to sell, and he told Zehmer, "You know you sold that place fair and square." After receiving the report from his attorney that the title was good, he wrote to Zehmer that he was ready to close the deal.

Not only did Lucy actually believe, but the evidence shows he was warranted in believing, that the contract represented a serious business transaction and a good faith sale and purchase of the farm.

In the field of contracts, as generally elsewhere, "We must look to the outward expression of a person as manifesting his intention rather than to his secret and unexpressed intention. 'The law imputes to a person an intention corresponding to the reasonable meaning of his words and acts.'"

At no time prior to the execution of the contract had Zehmer indicated to Lucy by word or act that he was not in earnest about selling the farm. They had argued about it and discussed its terms, as Zehmer admitted, for a long time. Lucy testified that if there was any jesting it was about paying $50,000 that night. The contract and the evidence show that he was not expected to pay the money that night. Zehmer said that after the writing was signed he laid it down on the counter in front of Lucy. Lucy said Zehmer handed it to him. In any event there had been what appeared to be a good faith offer and a good faith acceptance, followed by the execution and apparent delivery of a written contract. Both said that Lucy put the writing in his pocket and then offered Zehmer $5 to seal the bargain. Not until then, even under the defendants' evidence, was anything said or done to indicate that the matter was a joke. Both of the Zehmers testified that when Zehmer asked his wife to sign he whispered that it was a joke so Lucy wouldn't hear and that it was not intended that he should hear.

The mental assent of the parties is not requisite for the formation of a contract. If the words or other acts of one of the parties have but one reasonable meaning, his undisclosed intention is immaterial except when an unreasonable meaning which he attaches to his manifestations is known to the other party.

The law, therefore, judges of an agreement between two persons exclusively from those expressions of their intentions which are communicated between them.

An agreement or mutual assent is of course essential to a valid contract but the law imputes to a person an intention corresponding to the reasonable meaning of his words and acts. If his words and acts, judged by a reasonable standard, manifest an intention to agree, it is immaterial what may be the real but unexpressed state of his mind.

So a person cannot set up that he was merely jesting when his conduct and words would warrant a reasonable person in believing that he intended a real agreement. . . .

Whether the writing signed by the defendants and now sought to be enforced by the complainants was the result of a serious offer by Lucy and a serious acceptance by the defendants, or was a serious offer by Lucy and an acceptance in secret jest by the defendants, in either event it constituted a binding contract of sale between the parties.

Defendants contend further, however, that even though a contract was made, equity should decline to enforce it under the circumstances. These circumstances have been set forth in detail above. They disclose some drinking by the two parties but not to an extent that they were unable to understand fully what they were doing. There was no fraud, no misrepresentation, no sharp practice and no dealing between unequal parties. The farm had been bought for $11,000 and was assessed for taxation at $6,300. The purchase price was $50,000. Zehmer admitted that it was a good price. There is in fact present in this case none of the grounds usually urged against specific performance.

REVERSED and REMANDED in favor of Plaintiff.

CRITICAL THINKING

How can someone be held to have made a contract when the necessary acceptance was "in secret jest"? In other words, why must a joke be visibly a joke to a reasonable observer for there to be no acceptance?

ETHICAL DECISION MAKING

What stakeholders are being protected by this ruling? What value is playing the largest role in shaping this ruling?

Legal Principle: **In determining intent to enter into a contract, the court looks at the person's objective manifestation of intent and does not try to interpret what the person may have been secretly thinking.**

Preliminary Negotiations. An invitation to negotiate or an expression of possible interest in an exchange is not an offer because it does not express any willingness to be bound by an acceptance. For example, if Rachael asked Bill whether he would sell his car for $5,000, she is not making an offer; she is just inquiring about his potential willingness to sell. Likewise, when a firm or government entity requests bids for a construction project, the request is just an invitation for contractors to make offers. The bids, however, would be offers.

While it may seem easy to distinguish an offer from an invitation to negotiate, whether an offer in fact existed is a question of fact and sometimes ends up being litigated. When

WHEN IS AN AD AN OFFER?

Lefkowitz v. Great Minneapolis Surplus Store, Inc.
251 Minn. 188, 86 N.W.2d 689 (1957)

Great Minneapolis Surplus Store published a newspaper announcement stating: "Saturday 9 AM Sharp, 3 Brand New Fur Coats, Worth up to $1,000.00, First Come First Served $1 Each." Morris Lefkowitz arrived at the store, dollar in hand, but was informed that under the defendant's "house rules," the offer was open to ladies but not gentlemen. The court ruled that because the plaintiff had fulfilled all the terms of the advertisement, and the advertisement was specific and left nothing open for negotiation, a contract had been formed.

From this case came the often-quoted exception to the rule that advertisements do not create any power of acceptance in potential offerees: an advertisement that is "clear, definite, and explicit, and leaves nothing open for negotiation." In that circumstance, "it constitutes an offer, acceptance of which will complete the contract." Unlike the illustration of the invitation for an offer in the text (below), where the store obviously could not give every person who came to the store a rocking chair, in the Lefkowitz case, it was very clear that there were three new fur coats and the first three people who showed up with $1 would receive them. There was nothing indefinite or unclear about how to accept the offer.

you are either making an offer or attempting to begin negotiations about a possible contract, you should use very precise language that clearly expresses your intent.

Advertisements.   Another illustration of an offer to make an offer is the advertisement. If a custom furniture maker places an advertisement in the paper that reads, "Old-fashioned, hand-crafted cedar rocking chairs only $250 the first week in May," the store is merely inviting potential customers to come to the store and offer $250 for a rocker. Because no reasonable person would expect the store to be able to sell a rocking chair to every person who might see the ad, the court will interpret the intent of the store as being to invite readers to make an offer.

Under limited circumstances, however, an ad can be treated as an offer. If it appears from the wording that the store did, in fact, intend to make an offer, that is, the ad specifies a limited quantity and provides a specific means by which the offer can be accepted, the courts will treat the ad as an offer, as demonstrated by the Case Nugget at top of this page.

John Leonard, the plaintiff in the case described in the opening scenario, tried to rely on the *Lefkowitz* decision to argue that the Pepsi commercial was an offer because it was "clear, definite, explicit, and left nothing to negotiation." After all, the commercial clearly stated that 7 million points earned a Harrier jet, and the catalog provided an additional means of buying the points for cash.

The court, however, found that the commercial could not be regarded as sufficiently definite because it specifically reserved the details of the offer to a separate writing, the catalog. Also, the commercial itself made no mention of the steps a potential offeree would be required to take to accept the alleged offer of a Harrier jet.

The court further found that the only offer in this scenario was the plaintiff's letter of March 27, 1996, along with the order form and appropriate number of Pepsi points. Since Pepsi rejected this offer with its letter, there is no contract.

Sometimes, however, unlike in the opening scenario, the advertiser's intent does appear to be to enter into a contract, even though that is not what the advertiser subjectively had in mind. A good example of such a situation occurred when Cathy McGowan called in to a U.K. radio station to enter a contest and win the advertised prize: a brand new car. The radio DJ told McGowan that to win the new car, a Renault Clio, she would have to identify a scrambled version of a song. McGowan did correctly identify the song and was told that she could come down to the radio station to collect her prize. It was not until she arrived at the radio station that McGowan became aware that she was going to receive not an actual new car but, instead, a toy version of the Renault Clio.

An upset McGowan took her case to court and argued that the radio station broadcasters gave no indication to their listeners that the contest prize was actually a toy version of the car. A Derby crown court judge agreed with McGowan and ruled that the radio station had a legal contract to provide the contest winner with a new car. The judge further said that after reviewing the broadcast, he saw nothing that suggested the radio DJ was joking or intended to award contest winners with toy cars. Cathy McGowan was thus awarded £8,000, the cost of a new Renault Clio. The case, although from the United Kingdom, still has important implications for U.S. business students. In many respects U.K. contract laws are very similar to those of the United States, and had this case occurred on U.S. soil, a similar outcome would have been reached.[1]

To prevent possible "bait-and-switch" advertising that would appear as offers, some states have consumer protection laws requiring advertisers to state in their ads either that quantities of the item are limited to the first X number of people or that rain checks will be available if the item sells out.

Auctions.   Another situation in which what seems to be an offer may not be is the auction. When Janine places a good with an auctioneer for sale by auction, is she making an offer, or is Kevin, who bids on it? It depends on what kind of auction is taking place.

If nothing is stated to the contrary in the terms of the auction, an auction is presumed to be *with reserve,* which means that the seller is merely expressing intent to receive offers. The auctioneer may withdraw the item from auction at any time before the hammer falls, signaling the acceptance of the bid. The bidder may also revoke the bid before that point.

In an auction *without reserve,* the seller is treated as making an offer to accept the highest bid and therefore must accept it. Not surprisingly, very few auctions are without reserve.

Legal Principle: **If an auction is without reserve, the auctioneer must accept the lowest bid; if it is with reserve, the auctioneer may refuse to sell the item if he or she is not satisfied with the size of the highest bid.**

DEFINITE AND CERTAIN TERMS

Under the common law, the terms of the offer must be definite and certain. In other words, all the material terms must be included.[2] The material terms allow a court to determine damages in the event that one of the parties breaches the contract. They include the subject matter, price, quantity, quality, and parties.

Sometimes an offer contains not the material term itself but a method for determining it. For example, Hampton's Construction Company is building a new garage for Jones, and the parties want to make it possible for Jones to pay one-third of the price of the garage in advance, one-third upon completion, and one-third in 12 monthly payments, with interest, beginning a month after completion. Rather than stipulating an interest rate to be charged on the monthly payments, the contract might specify an external standard according to which the interest rate would be set through the course of the 12-month payment period.

The question of whether the terms of an alleged offer were adequate for the formation of a valid contract often arises when one party believes a contract has been formed and the other believes the terms were not definite enough. That issue is the focus of Case 14-2.

[1] www.dailymail.co.uk/news/article-40153/8-000-Clio-winner-handed-toy.html.

[2] See UCC § 2-204 or Chapter 21 of this text for the modification of this element for sale-of-goods contracts.

CASE 14-2 ANDRUS v. STATE, DEPARTMENT OF TRANSPORTATION, AND CITY OF OLYMPIA
WASHINGTON STATE APPELLATE COURT
117 P.3D 1152 (WASH. APP. 2005)

Scott Andrus applied for a position as a building inspector with the city of Olympia. He received a call from Tom Hill, an engineering supervisor with the city. Hill stated, "You're our number one choice, and I'm offering you the job." Andrus responded "Great" and "Yes." Hill did not discuss the specifics of the job, so Andrus asked Hill to fax him those details. The city never sent such a fax or a written job offer and request for acceptance.

On the same day that Andrus received the call from Hill, the city checked Andrus's employment references, including his current employer (the Washington Department of Transportation), which proved unsatisfactory. Hill called Andrus the next day, informing him that the city had withdrawn the job offer because of further reference checks.

Andrus sued the city and the DOT, claiming wrongful discharge and arguing that the phone call from Hill offering the position was an employment contract. He also alleged the

DOT was liable for defamation for providing a bad employment reference to the city. The superior court granted the city's request to dismiss his claims without a trial, and he appealed only the breach of contract claim against the city.

JUSTICE QUINN-BRINTNALL: An enforceable contract requires, among other things, an offer with *reasonably certain* terms. Restatement (Second) of Contracts §33 (1979) ("The fact that one or more terms of a proposed bargain are left open or uncertain may show that a manifestation of intention is not intended to be understood as an offer or as an acceptance"). Hill's "job offer" contained no starting date, salary, or benefit information. Moreover, it was to be followed by a written offer and request for acceptance. Under these facts, the July 13 phone conversation did not form an employment contract.

AFFIRMED in favor of the city.

CRITICAL THINKING

How could the original phone call from Hill be considered an employment contract? What would have to be included in the conversation? What could be left out? How different do you think the call would have needed to be to qualify as an employment contract between the plaintiff and the city? Why?

ETHICAL DECISION MAKING

How well does this decision hold up under examinations of ethicality, such as the public disclosure test and the universalization test? Do you think Justice Quinn-Brintnall took such examinations into account in reaching this decision? Why or why not?

COMMUNICATION TO THE OFFEREE

The third element of the offer is communication. The offer must be communicated to the offeree or the offeree's agent. Only the offeree (or his agent acting on his behalf) can accept the offer. If Bill overhears Sam offer to sell his car to Helen for $5,000, Bill cannot walk over and form a contract with Sam by accepting the offer to Helen. If he says to Sam, "I'll give you $5,000 for your car," he is not accepting the offer but, rather, is making a new offer.

Legal Principle: **To have a valid offer under the common law, you need (1) the intent to be bound by an acceptance, (2) definite and certain terms, and (3) communication to the offeree.**

Termination of the Offer

Offers, once made, do not last forever. At some point in time they terminate. When an offer is terminated, the offeree can no longer accept it to form a binding contract. Termination of an offer can occur in one of five ways: revocation by the offeror, rejection or counteroffer

L02

How may an offer terminate?

by the offeree, death or incapacity of the offeror, destruction or subsequent illegality of the subject matter of the offer, or lapse of time or failure of other conditions stated in the offer. Each method is discussed below and summarized in Exhibit 14-2.

REVOCATION BY THE OFFEROR

> To see how the six components of communication relate to the making of an agreement, please see the **Connecting to the Core** activity on the text website at www.mhhe.com/kubasek3e.

The offeror is said to be the "master of his or her offer" and, as such, can revoke it at any time, even if the offer states it will be open for a specified period of time. If Jim sends Carol a letter offering to mow her yard every week during the summer for the price of $20 per week as long as she responds to his offer within the next month, he can still change his mind and tell her at any time before she responds that he is no longer interested in working for her, thereby revoking his offer.

As a general rule, a revocation is effective when the offeree receives it. If it is really important to the offeror that the offeree know the offer has been revoked, the offeror should deliver the revocation personally.

Exceptions to the Revocability of the Offer.   An offeree who wishes to ensure that an offer will in fact be held open for a set period of time may do so by entering into an option contract with the offeror. In an option contract the offeree gives the offeror a piece of consideration in exchange for holding the offer open for the specified period of time.

There is no requirement as to the value of the consideration. If it is money, the parties may agree that if the offer is eventually accepted and a contract is formed, the consideration will become part of the offeree's payment under the contract. This situation frequently arises in real estate contracts. Jose may be considering opening a restaurant and would like to have the option of purchasing a lot owned by Simone, so he gives her $1,000 for a 30-day option to purchase, with the provision that she will deduct the $1,000 from the purchase price if Jose purchases the property. If he does not, Simone will keep the $1,000.

Detrimental reliance on the offer may also form the basis for the court's not allowing the offeror to revoke an offer. If the offeree had reasonably relied on the offeror's promise to hold the offer open and had taken action in reliance on the offer, the courts may use the doctrine of promissory estoppel to estop, or prevent, the offeror from revoking his offer.

Detrimental reliance also comes into play to prevent a party who made a unilateral offer from revoking the offer once the offeree has begun performance of the action necessary to accept the unilateral offer. While the contract cannot be considered formed until the action requested has been completed, most courts recognize that to allow the offeror to revoke her offer after the offeree has expended significant amounts of time or money in

Exhibit 14-2

Ways an Offer Can Be Terminated

Revocation	The offeror can revoke the offer at any time unless the offeree entered into an option contract with the offeror.
Rejection	The offeree can reject the offer.
Counteroffer	If the offeree offers a counteroffer, the original offer is terminated.
Death or incapacity	If the offeror becomes incapacitated or dies, the offer immediately terminates.
Illegality	If the subject matter of the offer becomes illegal, the offer immediately terminates.
Lapse of time	The offer will expire after a reasonable amount of time, which depends on the subject matter of the offer, unless a specific time condition is given.

reliance on the offer would be to allow an unjustifiable injustice to occur. Therefore, once significant partial performance in reliance has begun, most courts require that the offeror give the offeree a reasonable amount of time to complete performance.

BUT WHAT IF . . .

In 1985, two New York couples went to court over an adopted two-year-old girl. The girl's adopted parents had reared the girl since she was five days old, yet when the girl was 15 weeks old her biological parents decided they wanted her back. In other words, the biological parents wanted to revoke their offer for their baby to be adopted. The biological parents argued that a revocation time frame for revocation had not been made sufficiently clear. However, New York State adoption law clearly stipulates that parents have only 30 days to revoke their consent for adoption, and the parents in this case had signed an "irrevocable consent" form. Would the parents be able to get their biological daughter back? Why or why not?

REJECTION OR COUNTEROFFER BY THE OFFEREE

The second means by which an offer can be terminated is rejection by the offeree. Regardless of how long the offer was stated to be open, once the offeree rejects it, it is terminated. In our earlier illustration, if Carol calls Jim and says she is not interested in his working for her this summer or any summer because of the poor quality of his work but then she calls him back an hour later to say she has changed her mind and would like to hire him in accordance with his proposed terms, it is too late. There is no offer for her to accept because her rejection terminated it.

In the same illustration, if Carol tells Jim she would indeed like him to cut her grass every week this summer but will pay him only $15 each week, she has made a counteroffer, defined by the Restatement as "an offer made by an offeree to his offeror relating to the same matter as the original offer and proposing a substituted bargain differing from that proposed by the original offer."[3] A counteroffer terminates the original offer, and so Carol's counteroffer terminates Jim's original offer. Thus, if you receive an offer that you might want to accept but you are wondering whether you can get better terms, you should inquire about how set the offeror is on the terms proposed before you make a counteroffer. For example, Carol might have simply asked Jim whether he would consider doing the job at any other price.

DEATH OR INCAPACITY OF THE OFFEROR

An offer terminates immediately if the offeror dies or loses the legal capacity to enter into the contract, even if the offeree does not know of the terminating event. If the parties had already entered into an option contract to hold the offer open for a set period of time, however, the administrator of the offeror's estate or the guardian of the offeror must hold the offer open until it expires in accordance with the option contract.

DESTRUCTION OR SUBSEQUENT ILLEGALITY OF THE SUBJECT MATTER

If the subject matter of the offer is destroyed or becomes illegal, the offer immediately terminates. For example, if Jamie offers Mercedes a job managing the riverboat casino he plans to open on January 1 but, before Mercedes accepts the offer, the state decides to no longer allow riverboat casinos to operate, the offer of employment terminates.

[3] Restatement (Second) of Contracts, sec. 39 (1981).

LAPSE OF TIME OR FAILURE OF ANOTHER CONDITION SPECIFIED IN THE OFFER

We've noted that the offeror has the power to revoke the offer at any time, even if the offer states that it will be held open for a set period. But if the offer states that it will be held open for only a certain time, it terminates when that time expires. In the absence of such a time condition, the offer will expire after the lapse of a reasonable amount of time. What constitutes a reasonable amount of time varies, depending on the subject matter of the offer. An offer by a retailer to purchase seasonal goods from a wholesaler would lapse sooner than an offer to purchase goods that could be easily sold all year long. The Case Nugget above illustrates the consequences of not paying attention to the time or other limiting conditions specified in an offer, and see again a summary of the ways a contract can be terminated can be found in Exhibit 14-2.

The Acceptance

L03

What are the elements of an acceptance?

Once an offer has been made, the offeree has the power to accept that offer and form a contract. Under the common law, the basic requirements for a valid acceptance parallel those for a valid offer. There should be a manifestation of intent to be bound by the acceptance to the contract, agreement to the definite and certain terms of the offer, and communication to the offeror.

MANIFESTATION OF INTENT TO BE BOUND TO THE CONTRACT

In general, there are two ways an offeree can manifest intent to enter into the contract: by performance or by a return promise. The offeree must either do or say something to form the contract.

Recall, from Chapter 12, the distinction between a bilateral and a unilateral contract. If the offer is for a unilateral contract, the offeree can accept only by providing the requested performance. If Bill offered to pay $500 to anyone who returned his lost dog to him, Mary could accept the offer only by returning the dog. Bill did not want her promise, and if she called and promised to return the dog to him, that promise would have no legal effect because the only way to accept a unilateral offer is by performance.

BUT WHAT IF . . .

WHAT IF THE FACTS OF THE CASE OPENER WERE DIFFERENT?

Recall that, in the Case Opener, PepsiCo required that a customer mail in Pepsi points before the company would mail the customer a prize. But what if the Pepsi-points contract required that the customer only send in a signed statement that they had the requisite number of points and would be subsequently sending in the Pepsi points on a certain date and that PepsiCo would send the prize upon receipt of the statement? Would this scenario create a unilateral or a bilateral contract?

Remember from the previous section that the offeror has the right to revoke the offer at any time before it has been accepted. This rule is slightly modified with respect to unilateral offers so that if one party has begun performance, the offeror must give the offeree a reasonable time to complete it.

In a bilateral contract, what the offeror wants is not performance but, rather, a return promise. Sometimes, however, it is not clear what the offeror wants. Then the offeree has the option of either performing or making a return promise.

Silence as a Form of Acceptance.   Silence, as a general rule, cannot be used to form a contract. Lisa and Marie both work at a local diner where the manager is very flexible about their hours and lets them trade shifts. Marie leaves Lisa a voice-mail message saying, "I can't work my three night shifts this week. If you can cover them for me, I'll pay you an extra $40 on top of the money you'll receive from the boss for working my shifts. If I don't hear from you by 7 p.m. tomorrow, I'll assume we have a deal. Thanks so much!" If Lisa does not call back, no contract has been formed because silence under these circumstances will not constitute acceptance.

There are, however, a few situations in which silence *can* mean acceptance. In the most common, the parties, by their previous course of dealing with each other, have established a pattern of behavior whereby it is reasonable to assume silence communicates acceptance. If a wholesaler and a retailer have a long-standing relationship in which the retailer will reject a shipment that does not meet his needs, when a shipment is not sent back it is reasonable for the wholesaler to assume that the retailer means to accept it.

Silence can also be acceptance when the offeree receives the benefits of the offered services with reasonable opportunity to reject them and knowledge that some form of compensation is expected yet remains silent. In this case, an implied-in-fact contract is created. Because many unscrupulous businesspersons once took advantage of this rule and sent unordered merchandise to people, stating the goods could be returned or be kept on payment of a set price, most states have passed laws providing that unsolicited merchandise does not have to be returned and the recipient may keep it as a gift, with no contract being formed.

A third situation occurs when the parties agree that silence will be an acceptance. For example, a person may join a book club whose contract provides that a new book will be sent every month if the member does not send notification rejecting the month's selection.

The Japanese tend to view contracts as ongoing relationships in which parties work with each other to smooth out any problems that arise in performance of the contract. Often suspicious of long, detailed contracts, they have a distinct preference for short, flexible agreements that leave a number of terms to be decided later.

ACCEPTANCE OF DEFINITE AND CERTAIN TERMS: THE MIRROR-IMAGE RULE

When a bilateral contract is being formed under the common law, the mirror-image rule applies to the acceptance. The mirror-image rule says that the terms of the acceptance must mirror the terms of the offer. If they do not, no contract is formed. Instead, the attempted acceptance is a counteroffer.[4]

COMMUNICATION TO THE OFFEROR

An offeror has the power to control the means by which the acceptance is communicated, so if the offeror specifies that only a certain means of communication will be accepted, then only an acceptance by that means forms a valid contract. Suppose Jennifer offers to paint Rashad's car for $500 but says he must accept the offer by telephone before midnight on Thursday. If Rashad sends Jennifer an e-mail Thursday morning accepting her offer, there is no contract. Even though e-mail might be a valid means of accepting a contract offer if no means is specified, when the offer is limited to a specific means of communicating the acceptance, only that means results in a valid contract. Thus, Rashad's attempted acceptance was simply a new offer.

? BUT WHAT IF . . .
WHAT IF THE FACTS OF THE CASE OPENER WERE DIFFERENT?
Recall that, in the Case Opener, PepsiCo stipulated that customers must mail in Pepsi points. What if, instead, the company required that contestants fax in photos of their collected Pepsi points. If Leonard mailed his Pepsi points to the company, would that count as a valid acceptance of the offer?

If no means of communicating the acceptance is specified, any reasonable means is generally acceptable. Telephone, mail, fax, and e-mail are all valid means of accepting an offer, as is accepting it in person. When drafting an offer, if a person wishes acceptance to be only by a particular means, the offer must make it clear that only certain means are allowed. As Case 14-3 illustrates, courts will carefully interpret provisions specifying the means of acceptance.

The Mailbox Rule. Because not all acceptances are made in person, the courts needed a rule to determine the point at which an acceptance made through the mail became effective. They settled on the mailbox rule, which provides that an acceptance is valid when the offeree places it in the mailbox, whereas a revocation is effective only when the offeree receives it. The mailbox rule is not applicable when there is instantaneous communication, such as over the phone, in person, or by telex.

---

[4] See UCC § 2-207 and Chapter 21 for an explanation of how the UCC modifies the mirror-image rule for contracts for the sale of goods.

CASE 14-3   ALEXANDER v. LAFAYETTE CRIME STOPPERS, INC.
COURT OF APPEALS OF LOUISIANA, THIRD CIRCUIT
28 SO. 3D 1253 (LA. APP. 3 CIR., 2010)

In the summer of 2002, after several South Louisiana women had been murdered, the Multi Agency Homicide Task Force (Task Force) was established to investigate these murders, which they believed were being committed by the individual referred to as the South Louisiana Serial Killer. In April 2003, the Baton Rouge Crime Stoppers (BRCS) began publicizing a reward offer in newspapers, television stations, and billboards around the Baton Rouge area regarding the South Louisiana Serial Killer. A short time later, Lafayette Crime Stoppers (LCS) also publicized a reward offer. Both reward offers included an expiration date of August 1, 2003.

On July 9, 2002, Dianne Alexander was attacked in her home in St. Martin Parish. Her son came home during the attack and chased the attacker away. Ms. Alexander reported the attack to local police, and, later, both Ms. Alexander and her son described the attacker to the St. Martin Sheriff's Department.

The lead investigator on Ms. Alexander's attack began to suspect that Ms. Alexander's attacker could be the South Louisiana Serial Killer, so in May 2003, he shared information regarding Ms. Alexander's attack with the Lafayette Sheriff's Department, which then shared it with the Task Force.

On May 22, 2003, Ms. Alexander was interviewed by an FBI agent assisting the Task Force. Based upon that interview, a composite sketch was drawn and released to the public on May 23, 2003. Investigators believed the composite sketch matched the description of a possible suspect in an investigation being handled by the Louisiana Attorney General's Office and the Zachary Police Department. On May 25, 2003, Ms. Alexander, in a photo lineup, identified her attacker as the same man suspected in the Zachary investigation.

Around August 14, 2003, Ms. Alexander contacted LCS and sought to collect the advertised award, but was told she was ineligible to receive the award. In 2006, Ms. Alexander and her son sued BRCS and LCS, alleging that the defendants owed them $100,000 and $50,000, respectively, for the information they provided to the defendants. The defendants filed motions for summary judgment asserting there was no genuine issue of material fact because the plaintiffs would be unable to prove that a contract ever existed between the parties. The trial court granted the motions. The plaintiffs appealed, asserting that there is a genuine issue of material fact over whether LCS and BRCS offers contained a requirement that acceptance of the reward must be done through the Crime Stoppers' tip line.

JUDGE AMY: . . . The defendants filed motions for summary judgment asserting that a valid contract never existed between the parties. Specifically, the defendants argued that the plaintiffs never provided information to Crime Stoppers via the tipster hotline and thus did not comply with the "form, terms, or conditions required by the Crime Stoppers offers[.]" The trial court granted the defendants' motions for summary judgment, finding that the offer from Crime Stoppers was conditioned on the information being provided to the defendant entities rather than law enforcement. . . .

Louisiana Civil Code Article 1927 provides:

A contract is formed by the consent of the parties established through offer and acceptance.

Unless the law prescribes a certain formality for the intended contract, offer and acceptance may be made orally, in writing, or by action or inaction that under the circumstances is clearly indicative of consent.

Unless otherwise specified in the offer, there need not be conformity between the manner in which the offer is made and the manner in which the acceptance is made.

"Louisiana jurisprudence has recognized that an advertisement may constitute an offer susceptible of giving rise to a binding contract upon acceptance in instances where a prize is offered or where the terms of a contest are announced." . . . Once a plaintiff performs all of the requirements of the offer in accordance with the published terms, it creates a valid and binding contract, under which one is entitled to the promised rewards. . . . '68 So. 2d (1953)

The offer made by LCS in a May 14, 2003, press release, reads as follows:

The Greater Lafayette Chamber of Commerce has joined with Lafayette Crime Stoppers to offer a reward of $50,000 for information relating to the murders of five south Louisiana women. A $25,000 reward offer by Lafayette Crime Stoppers has been matched through commitments from Chamber members.

In order to qualify for the reward, the tipster must provide information which leads to the arrest, DNA match, and the formal filing of charges against a suspect through grand jury indictment or Bill of Information. In addition, the qualifying tip must be received prior to midnight, August 1, 2003. Investigators with the Serial Killer Task Force have expressed optimism that a large enough reward might provide the impetus for someone with knowledge of the killings to come forward. By stipulating a deadline, investigators hope to expedite receipt of the information.

All callers the Crime Stoppers Tips line remain anonymous. A code number is issued as the only means of identification. Tips can be submitted 24 hours a day at 232–TIPS or toll free at 1–800–805–TIPS.

The offer from BRCS, as published in the *Morning Advocate,* reads as follows:

> Crime Stoppers, Inc. $100,000 reward for information on the South Louisiana Serial Killer. A $100,000 reward will be given for information leading to the arrest and indictment of the South Louisiana Serial Killer. Call today and help make Baton Rouge a safer place for you and your family. All calls remain anonymous. 334–STOP or 1–877–723–7867. Reward expires August 1, 2003.

Both LCS and BRCS offers were irrevocable offers because they specified a period of time for acceptance. La. Civil Code Article 1934 provides that "acceptance of an irrevocable offer is effective when received by the offeror." Acceptance is received when it comes into the possession of a person authorized by the offeror to receive it, or when it is deposited in a place the offeror has indicated as the place where communications of that kind are to be deposited for him.

The plaintiffs argue that there is a genuine issue of material fact as to whether they accepted the Crime Stoppers' reward offers; however, the plaintiffs admit that they did not contact either Crime Stopper organization before August 1, 2003. The plaintiffs argue that they accepted the offers by performance when they provided information about the serial killer to law enforcement. Further, the plaintiffs contend that this performance is a customary manner of accepting reward offers from Crime Stopper organization.

In the present matter, the plaintiffs' acceptance of the reward offers must have been received by the defendants (offerors) by the time prescribed in the offer (August 1, 2003) in the place where communications of that kind were to be deposited (the phone number cited in the offers). The record contains no evidence indicating the defendants were notified by the plaintiffs in the time and manner indicated in the offer. While the plaintiffs may have provided information related to the arrest or indictment of Derrick Todd Lee to local law enforcement and the Task Force, there is no indication in the offer that either of those parties were the offerors of the reward or persons authorized to receive acceptance on their behalf.

The plaintiffs argue that they accepted the offers by performance when they provided information about the serial killer to law enforcement. Further, the plaintiffs contend that this performance is a customary manner of accepting reward offers from Crime Stopper organization. While acceptance may be valid if customary in similar transactions, according to La.Civ.Code art. 1936, it must be "customary in similar transactions at the time and place the offer is *received*." As indicated above, there is no evidence in the record that the defendants received any acceptance of the offer. Accordingly, no contract was formed between the parties.

Summary Judgment in favor of Defendants, AFFIRMED.

CRITICAL THINKING

What is ambiguous about the concept of acceptance? How does the law act to clarify the potential liability?

ETHICAL DECISION MAKING

How might the public disclosure test give false guidance to the ethics of this decision? Do you think that the public's attitude toward the interaction between Crime Stoppers and the people who helped solve a crime might have resulted in a different decision had the public disclosure principle been used to resolve the case?

Since the mailbox rule does not apply to instantaneous communications, when are faxes, text messages, and e-mail effective? Are these instantaneous forms of communication? Text messages seem the easiest to answer yes to. There is still some disagreement among jurisdictions as to whether faxes and e-mail should be effective on dispatch or receipt. The majority rule with respect to faxes appears to be that faxes are instantaneous transmissions and therefore effective on receipt, but some jurisdictions have applied the mailbox rule to them. There seems to be greater split among the jurisdictions over how to treat e-mail transmissions. The Uniform Electronic Transactions Act seems to create an electronic version of the mailbox rule, providing that an e-mail is sent when properly addressed to an information processing system designated by the recipient, in a form capable of being processed by that system, and enters an information processing system out of

Many people would like to know what sort of terms they are going to be held to when buying a product. Unfortunately, many people aren't aware of the importance of receiving prior disclosures and also don't realize that online businesses commonly refrain from giving full disclosure of terms about a product until they receive the customer's payment information. If e-businesses do happen to provide these certain terms before a customer agrees to buy a product, the link to the terms themselves may be hard to find. Another aspect of the terms (if given) is that the language in which the contract is written is dense legal language, which may be hard for the ordinary person to understand fully. These e-business practices in regard to disclosure of terms can be very deceptive. A customer may inadvertently agree to a contract when the customer is only given some information about it. This situation would be similar to one in which a student were given a page of text that appeared to be whole and complete, and the student had completed an entire report on the text before being given an additional 50 pages that were also a part of the text. Customers who shop online should be aware of the potential for deception with online sellers and should use caution when making purchases.

Source: http://digitalcorpora.org/corp/nps/files/govdocs1/021/021056.pdf.

the control of the sender. It is considered received when it enters the information processing system designated by the recipient.

Authorized Means of Acceptance.   The means by which the offeree can communicate acceptance to the offeror may either be expressly stated in the offer, which is called an *express authorization,* or be implied from the facts and circumstances surrounding the communication of the offer to the offeree. If the offer specifies that acceptance must be communicated by a specific mode, that mode is the only means for accepting the offer, and once the acceptance is dispatched, the contract has been formed. If any other attempted means of acceptance is used, there is no valid contract. For example, if the offer says acceptance must be by certified mail, then as soon as the acceptance is taken to the post office, there is a valid contract. If the offeree instead faxes an acceptance, there is no contract.

According to the Restatement, if no mode of communication is specified in the offer, any reasonable means of acceptance is valid. To determine the reasonableness of the means, courts look at such factors as the means by which the offer was communicated and the surrounding circumstances.

Effect of an Unauthorized Means of Acceptance.   As noted above, when an offer specifies that acceptance must be communicated by a particular mode, no other form of acceptance is valid. However, if the offer merely authorizes certain modes of acceptance but does not condition acceptance on the use of those modes, use of an unauthorized means of acceptance is acceptable but the contract is not formed until the acceptance is received by the offeror. For example, if Beth sends an offer to Joe via a fax, saying in the offer that acceptance may be via fax or e-mail, and Joe accepts her offer by overnight mail, his acceptance is valid but it is effective only on receipt.

If the offeree makes a mistake and sends the acceptance to the wrong address, there is no acceptance on dispatch. However, if a correction is made and the letter eventually reaches the offeror, the acceptance is valid on receipt, assuming the offer was still open.

The Effect of an Acceptance after a Rejection.   We've seen that if an acceptance is received after a rejection, the acceptance is not valid because the rejection terminated the offer. However, sometimes a rejection is dispatched, but before it is received, the acceptance is communicated to the offeror. In that case, a valid contract has been formed because the rejection is not effective until it is received. Suppose Brenda e-mails an offer to Harry, and he puts a rejection in the mail; then, before it is received, Harry calls Brenda and tells her he accepts. A valid contract has been formed, and the rejection will have no effect when Brenda receives it. However, if Harry telephoned after Brenda had received the rejection, there could be no contract.

BUT WHAT IF . . .

WHAT IF THE FACTS OF THE CASE OPENER WERE DIFFERENT?

What if Leonard had sent in a certain number of Pepsi points to receive a corresponding prize but at the last minute e-mailed the company to reject the prize because he wanted to save his points for a bigger prize. If the company receives his mailed points before his e-mailed rejection, is his rejection valid?

CASE OPENER WRAP-UP

The Problematic Promotion

Much to the plaintiff's dismay, the court in the Pepsi case found that the commercial could not be regarded as sufficiently definite to be an offer, because it specifically reserved the details of the offer to a separate writing, the catalog.[5] Also, the commercial itself made no mention of the steps a potential offeree would be required to take to accept the alleged offer of a Harrier jet. As in most cases where a consumer attempts to place an order for an advertised item, the court regarded the plaintiff's purported acceptance as an offer. And it was an offer that Pepsi obviously rejected. And while the court did not specifically mention this factor, common sense should have indicated to the plaintiff and his family that Pepsi did not really intend to give a harrier jet as one of the promotional prizes.

KEY TERMS

acceptance 334	definite and certain terms 330	material terms 330	rejection 333
communication 331	intent 326	mirror-image rule 336	revocation 332
counteroffer 333	mailbox rule 336	option contract 332	termination 331

SUMMARY OF KEY TOPICS

Elements of the Offer   A valid offer requires (1) the manifestation of the offeror's intent to be bound, (2) definite and certain terms, and (3) communication to an offeree.

Termination of the Offer   An offer can be terminated by revocation by the offeror; rejection or counteroffer by the offeree; death or incapacity of the offeror; destruction or subsequent illegality of the subject matter of the offer; or lapse of time or failure of other conditions stated in the offer.

The Acceptance   An acceptance is valid when a manifestation of intent to be bound to the terms of the offer is communicated to the offeror by the offeree.

[5] *Leonard v. Pepsico,* 210 F.3d 88, 2000 U.S. App. LEXIS 6855.

POINT / COUNTERPOINT

Should Internet Click-Wrap and Browse-Wrap Agreements Be Treated as Legally Binding Contacts?	
YES	**NO**
Nearly all computer users have, at some point, encountered form contracts while browsing the Internet. Whether they pertain to downloading software, signing up for a free e-mail service, or making an online purchase, many online forms are designed to protect the host company or retail store's interests. To protect these companies and ensure continued online commerce, these contracts *must* be viewed as legally binding. The two types of Internet contracts are click-wrap and browse-wrap contracts. A click-wrap contract requires that users read all terms and conditions before clicking an "I Agree" button. Such contracts give users the ability to *choose* whether to accept the conditions and proceed or decline and withdraw. This process includes an offer by the offeror (the terms and conditions as listed) and acceptance by the offeree (clicking the "I Agree" button). The contract includes a clear manifestation of the offeree's intent to be bound when he or she clicks the accept button. In the second type of Internet contract, the browse-wrap agreement, the user is not required by the site to click any button but is seen under the law as having accepted the terms by viewing the website. In such instances, the site provides its terms and conditions via a hyperlink at the top of a web page. By posting the link, the website has provided users with notice that there are terms and conditions associated with the site and that users who continue making use of the site should be bound by those terms. By viewing the site (the performance), the user is bound to the terms (the offer). Given the large quantity of transactions occurring over the Internet, browse-wrap and click-wrap agreements offer an efficient means for governance. In an effort to protect companies and ensure compliance by consumers, these agreements *must* be treated as legally binding contracts.	Nearly all computer users have agreed to and proceeded beyond click-wrap agreements. Many of these computers users have used websites that have browse-wrap agreements embedded within their pages. But the mere existence of these agreements does not mean that they are valid contracts under existing contract laws; they should not. In both click-wrap and browse-wrap agreements, the terms are decided prior to the user even installing the software or visiting the site. The user is not given an opportunity to negotiate the terms; in essence, there is no meeting of the minds. If the user wishes to use the website, software, or e-mail system, he or she must accept the prewritten terms. Click-wrap agreements have become so prevalent throughout recent years that Internet users often ignore the text of the agreement and simply click the "I Agree" box. Without reading and understanding the terms of the agreement, lawyers, consumers, and companies are left to wonder whether the user lacked genuine assent. Browse-wrap agreements, unlike click-wrap agreements, are not even located on the general web page. In order to view the terms and conditions of use, the user must find the hyperlink on a page, click on it, read the terms, and then decide whether or not to continue reading the web page. The site owners cannot be certain that users will find, read, or understand the terms and conditions of use before they browse the site. Without knowledge, Internet users should not be bound to the terms and conditions. Finally, when paper contracts are signed, one can be certain whom the relevant parties are. With electronic contracts, that certainty quickly dissipates. Even though a click-wrap agreement is offered and accepted, without proper verification, one cannot be certain who was using the computer at the time the contract was formed. If, for example, a friend uses your computer while visiting your dorm room and enters into a click-wrap agreement, which you later violate unknowingly, who is accountable? Can you prove you were not the one who agreed to the terms? Identifying the parties associated with electronic contracts would be more difficult than identifying those associated with paper contracts.

QUESTIONS & PROBLEMS

1. What is the mirror-image rule?

2. What is the mailbox rule?

3. In July 2012, the six adult cast members of the hit television show *Modern Family* filed a joint lawsuit against Twentieth Century Fox Television in an attempt to void their contracts. The lawsuit claimed that their contracts were illegal, in that the contracts broke California's "7-year rule." The 7-year rule stipulates that contracts regarding personal services may not span longer than seven years. Yet the actors' contracts guaranteed their services from 2009 to 2016. A big incentive for the actors to file the lawsuit was to increase the amount they each were paid per episode, which for most of them was $65,000 an episode. If a contract is illegal, may it be voided even if the actors knowingly signed to the terms of the contract? How do you think the judge should have decided this case, and why? [*Vergara et al. v. Twentieth Century Fox International Television, Inc.* BC488786 (Sup. Ct. L.A. 2012).]

4. Michael and Laurie Montgomery negotiated with Norma English with regard to the potential sale of the Montgomerys' home. English submitted a bid for $272,000, but she included a request to purchase some of the Montgomerys' personal property and expressed that an "as-is" provision was not applicable to the sale. When the Montgomerys received the offer, they deleted the personal property provision, deleted provisions related to latent defects and a building inspection, and added a specific as-is rider. English's agent then delivered the counteroffer to English, who initialed many, but not all, of the Montgomerys' modifications, such as the deletion of the personal property provision. The Montgomerys refused to proceed with the sale, so English filed suit for specific performance of the contract. Under the mirror-image rule, did a contract exist between the Montgomerys and English? Why or why not? [*Montgomery v. English*, 2005 Fla. App. LEXIS 4704.]

5. Nutritional Sciences LLC sponsored the "Quarter Million Dollar Challenge," a contest requiring contestants to use the company's nutritional products and training plans to lose weight and get in shape during a 13-week period. A panel of judges would select a number of winners based on their success in the program. Contest rules stipulated that "all winners must agree to the regulations outlined specifically for winners before claiming championship or money." Next to this statement was an asterisk. The note linked to the asterisk reserved the right of Nutritional Sciences to cancel the contest or alter its terms at any time. Donna Englert learned that she was chosen female runner-up in her age group, and she expected to receive the advertised prize of $1,500 cash and $500 worth of products. When she went to sign the agreement to claim her prize, she found that the company had changed the cash prize to $250, so she refused to sign and sued for breach of contract. The trial court initially dismissed her case, and she appealed. How do you think the court of appeals decided the case and why? [*Englert v. Nutritional Sciences, LLC*, 2008 WL 44 4416597 (Ohio App. 2008).]

6. The Pennsylvania Department of Transportation (PennDOT) issued a Request for Bid Proposal for Vending Machine Services for rest areas on highways in the state. ATI submitted the lowest bid for the sites. PennDOT selected ATI for a contract for 35 vending sites. Enclosed with the notice of award sent to ATI was a service purchase contract to be executed by ATI, by PennDOT, by the commonwealth comptroller, and by PennDOT's attorney. Also, "if required," signature lines for the Office of General Counsel and the Attorney General's Office were provided. The award notice indicated that the contract would become effective "after all approvals have been received from the administrative and fiscal personnel in Harrisburg" and further stated that no activities may be performed until the contract is fully executed. ATI returned an executed contract to PennDOT. PennDOT's director of the Bureau of Maintenance and Operations and a representative from its legal department executed the agreement. The comptroller and Office of General Counsel subsequently signed the contract; however, the Attorney General's Office refused to execute the agreement. The Attorney General's Office subsequently filed criminal charges, related to sales tax issues, against ATI's president. As a result, the Attorney General's Office notified PennDOT it would not approve the contract.

PennDOT never returned an executed contract to ATI or provided a notice-to-proceed to ATI. Instead, PennDOT notified ATI it would not enter into the contract because it determined ATI is not a responsible contractor. ATI filed a complaint alleging PennDOT breached a valid contract. After the hearing, the board determined that PennDOT never delivered an acceptance of the offer to ATI and, as a result, a contract was never formed. ATI appealed, arguing that the board erred in finding a contract did not exist because PennDOT's representatives, who signed the contract, intended to bind PennDOT to the terms of the contract. How did the court rule on appeal? Did the documents contain a proper acceptance? [*Makoroff v. DOT*, 938 A.2d 470 (Pa. Commw. Ct. 2007).]

7. Plaintiff Business Systems Engineering, Inc., was one of several subcontractors that agreed to provide technical consultants for defendant IBM's work on a transit project. In a "plan of utilization" provided by IBM to the transit authority, IBM had listed Business Systems as one of its intended subcontractors, with $3.6 million listed on that document under the heading "contract amount." The terms of the arrangement between IBM and its subcontractors for the job were that when IBM needed technical consultants for a part of the project, the subs would submit bids and when the subcontractor's bid was accepted, the subcontractor would receive a specific statement of work detailing the scope of the specific project, the time frame, the conditions under which the task would be deemed complete, and the hourly wage, followed by a work authorization. The transit authority retained the authority to reject any individual consultant who was selected by the subcontractor, and the contract between the subcontractors and IBM incorporated by reference the contract between IBM and the transit authority. Work was not to begin until a final work authorization was issued. At the end of the project, 38 work authorizations had been issued to the plaintiff by the defendant for a total of $2.2 million, rather than the $3.6 million that had been projected in the original estimate IBM had provided to the transit authority. IBM had paid the plaintiff the $2.2 million for the work done on the work authorizations, but the plaintiff argued that it should have been entitled to the full $3.6 million contained in the estimate that was incorporated by reference in the contracts between IBM and the subcontractors. The plaintiff argued that it had a contract with IBM for the full $3.6 million. The district court granted summary judgment for the defendant. What do you think the plaintiff's argument was on appeal? What do think the outcome of the appeal was and why? [*Business Systems Engineering, Inc. v. International Business Machines Corp.*, 547 F.3d 883, 2008 U.S. App LEXIS 23682.]

8. Plaintiff VanHierden injured his thumb and finger at work and had it surgically repaired. He later developed a persistent pain at the base of his thumb. He went to see the defendant about having a sympathectomy to alleviate his pain. The defendant told the plaintiff, "We're going to get rid of your pain and get you back to work." The plaintiff then signed a written consent form to have the surgery, which included the following:

The procedure listed under paragraph 1 has been fully explained to me by Dr. Swelstad and I completely understand the nature and consequences of the procedure(s). I have further had explained to me and discussed available alternatives and possible outcomes, and understand the risk of complications, serious injury or even death that may result from both known and unknown causes. I have been informed that there are other risks that are adherent to the performance of any surgical procedure. I am aware that the practice of medicine and surgery is not an exact science and I acknowledge that no guarantees have been made to me concerning the results of the operation or procedure(s).

The defendant performed the sympathectomy, but it did not alleviate the plaintiff's pain; nor was he able to return to work, so he sued the defendant for breach of a contract to cure the pain. The district court granted summary judgment for the defendant, finding that no contract had been formed as a matter of law. On appeal, do you believe the court found a valid agreement between the parties? Why or why not? [*Ronald VanHierden v. Jack Swelstad, MD*, 2010 Wis. App. 16, 2009 Wis. App. LEXIS 1013.]

9. In 2008, a lawyer for Mutual Life Insurance e-mailed Dr. Miles regarding the settlement of a lawsuit that he had filed against the insurance company. The e-mail that the attorney sent contained proposed settlement terms. Dr. Miles's attorney sent an e-mail back explicitly stating that Dr. Miles accepted the terms the company was offering. After

the trial was canceled in light of the settlement, the company's attorney sent Dr. Miles a written settlement that was different from the terms contained in the e-mail. Thus, Dr. Miles rejected the offer, and the company subsequently claimed that there was no settlement. Dr. Miles then took the company to court a second time regarding whether a contract was created through the e-mail that proposed specific settlement terms. If the e-mail seemed to contain all the essential terms of an offer, how do you think the judge decided? [*Miles v. Northwestern Mutual Life Insurance Company,* 677 F. Supp. 2d 1312, U.S. Dist. LEXIS 123597 (2009).]

10. Sarah and Eddie Hogan wanted to sell 2.5 acres of land through their real estate agent, Darita Richardson. On December 10, 2001, Warren Kent offered to purchase the land for $52,500. An "Agreement to Buy or Sell" was created, which Kent signed right away. One term of the agreement was that the offer would expire on December 11, 2001, at 3 p.m., and it stated additionally, "Time is of the essence and all deadlines are final except where modifications, changes, or extensions are made in writing and signed by all parties." Although Richardson scheduled a meeting on December 11, 2001, at 2 p.m. with the Hogans, the Hogans failed to appear. However, the parties agreed to a two-day extension, lasting until December 13, 2001, at 3 p.m., and the extension was binding and irrevocable according to the "Addendum to Agreement to Purchase or Sell." The Hogans signed both documents at 9 a.m. on December 13, 2001. At about 11 a.m., Kent also signed the addendum. However, neither Kent's agent nor Richardson contacted the Hogans before 3 p.m. about Kent's acceptance. After 3 p.m., Richardson realized that the Hogans had not placed the date and time next to their signatures. When she met with the Hogans, the Hogans placed the date and the time as 4:48 p.m., informing Richardson that they, the Hogans, had changed their minds about the sale. Kent sued for specific performance of the contract. What effect, if any, did the failure to communicate the acceptance of the offer before 3 p.m. have in terms of whether a contract was formed? What was the appellate court's reasoning? [*Kent v. Hogan,* 2004 La. App. LEXIS 2539.]

Looking for more review material?

The Online Learning Center at **www.mhhe.com/kubasek3e** contains this chapter's "Assignment on the Internet" and also a list of URLs for more information, entitled "On the Internet." Find both of them in the Student Center portion of the OLC, along with quizzes and other helpful materials.

Consideration

LEARNING OBJECTIVES

After reading this chapter, you will be able to answer the following questions:

1 What is consideration?

2 What are the rules regarding consideration?

3 What is promissory estoppel, and when can it be used?

4 What is an illusory promise?

5 What is the difference between a liquidated debt and an unliquidated debt?

6 What is an accord and satisfaction?

CASE OPENER

Upper Deck—Contract Liability or Gift?

In 1988 the Upper Deck Company was a company with an idea for a better baseball card: one that had a hologram on it. By the 1990s the firm was a major corporation worth at least a quarter of a billion dollars.

In 1988, however, its outlook hadn't been so bright. Upper Deck lacked the funds for a $100,000 deposit it needed to buy some special paper by August 1. Without that deposit its contract with the Major League Baseball Players Association would have been jeopardized.

Upper Deck's corporate attorney, Anthony Passante, Jr., loaned the company the money. That evening, the directors of the company accepted the loan and, in gratitude, agreed to give Passante 3 percent of the firm's stock. Passante never sought to collect the stock, and later the company reneged on its promise. Passante sued for breach of oral contract.[1]

1. If you were on the jury, how would you decide the case? Was the offer of 3 percent of the firm's stock legal consideration for the loan? Or was it a mere gift?

2. Does Upper Deck have a moral obligation to give Passante the stock? If so, is this obligation legally enforceable?

The Wrap-Up at the end of the chapter will answer these questions.

[1] *Passante v. McWilliam,* 53 Cal. App. 4th 1240 (1997).

What is Consideration?

L01

What is consideration?

Consideration is required in every contract. It is what a person will receive in return for performing a contract obligation. Suppose Dan agrees to purchase Marty's car for $1,000. Dan's payment of $1,000 is the consideration Marty will receive for the car. Title to and possession of the car are the consideration Dan will receive in exchange. Consideration can be anything, as long as it is the product of a bargained-for exchange. In a business context it is often (but not always) money. Exhibit 15-1 provides other examples of consideration.

Rules of Consideration

L02

What are the rules regarding consideration?

The key to understanding consideration is understanding the rules that govern it and their exceptions. We explore them below.

LACK OF CONSIDERATION

A court will enforce one party's promise only if the other party promised some consideration in exchange. For example, in a bilateral contract (a promise for a promise), the consideration for each promise is a return promise. Suppose Nicole promises to pay Mike $2,000 tomorrow for his car. Mike promises to sell Nicole his car tomorrow for $2,000. There is an oral contract between them. Nicole's promise is her consideration to Mike. Mike's promise is his consideration to Nicole. There has been a mutual exchange of something of value.

An example of a bilateral contract, or a promise for a promise, occurred when the U.S. government seized control of insurance giant American International Group (AIG). The government agreed to lend AIG up to $85 billion in exchange for nearly 80 percent of AIG's stock. The consideration AIG received was the promise of up to $85 billion in U.S. government loans. The consideration the government received was a promise of almost 80 percent of AIG's stock.[2]

In a unilateral contract (a promise for an act), one party's consideration is the promise and the other party's consideration is the act. Suppose your professor made the following statement in class: "If any student shows up at my house on Saturday and does the gardening, I will pay that student $100." You show up and do the gardening. The professor's consideration to you is the promise of the payment of $100 on completion of the gardening, and your consideration to the professor is the act of completing the gardening. Once again, there has been a mutual exchange of something of value.

Exhibit 15-1

Examples of Consideration

TYPE OF CONSIDERATION	EXAMPLE
A benefit to the promisee	A promise to stay in a job until a particular project is complete (this is a benefit to the employer)
A detriment to the promisor	A promise to your football coach to refrain from riding your motorcycle during football season even though you love riding it
A promise to do something	A promise to cook dinner for your roommate for the next six months
A promise to refrain from doing something	A promise to stop staying out late at night during exam week

[2] "U.S. Seizes Control of AIG with $85 Billion Emergency Loan," *Washington Post,* September 17, 2008, www.washingtonpost.com/wp-dyn/content/article/2008/09/16/AR2008091602174 (accessed May 25, 2009).

TYPE OF CONTRACT	PROMISOR	PROMISEE
Bilateral	A promise	A promise
Unilateral	A promise	An act

Exhibit 15-2
Type of Consideration
Based on Type of
Contract

See Exhibit 15-2 for an explanation of bilateral and unilateral contracts.

Legal Principle: **For a promise to be enforced by the courts, there must be consideration.**

One exception to the rule requiring consideration is promissory estoppel. Promissory estoppel occurs when three conditions are met:

- One party makes a promise and either knows or should know that the other party will reasonably rely on it.
- The other party does reasonably rely on the promise.
- The only way to avoid injustice is to enforce the promise.

L03

What is promissory estoppel, and when can it be used?

How does promissory estoppel work? Suppose upon graduation from college, Amanda receives a job offer across the country. She gives up her apartment, cancels all her other job interviews, and moves all her possessions. Upon arriving, she rents a new apartment and shows up for work. Amanda is then told there is no job! May she sue the employer? The answer in most states is yes, under the theory of promissory estoppel. Amanda may be able to recover her *reliance damages* (money she spent in "reliance" on the job offer). Promissory estoppel is not awarded regularly, but in the right case it can provide a remedy where no other remedy exists.

In a recent case, the Ninth Circuit Court of Appeals held that Yahoo's promise to remove a nude photo from its website was subject to a claim of promissory estoppel. In that case, the plaintiff learned that her ex-boyfriend, pretending to be her, had posted nude photos of her on Yahoo. He also included all her contact information and an invitation for men to contact her for sexual purposes.[3] The plaintiff contacted Yahoo (in accordance with its established policies) and requested that the photo be removed. Yahoo agreed but, despite repeated requests, did not remove the photo for six months. The court held that Yahoo's promise to depost the profile meant that Yahoo had a duty to the plaintiff. As such, the plaintiff's claim of promissory estoppel could be maintained. If the plaintiff is able to prove that she reasonably relied on Yahoo's promise to her detriment, she may well prevail on her claim for damages.

BUT WHAT IF . . .
WHAT IF THE FACTS OF THE CASE OPENER WERE DIFFERENT?

Recall, in the Case Opener, that the attorney for the Upper Deck Company was a very wealthy attorney who invested $100,000 in the company for a 3 percent share. But what if the attorney was not very wealthy, invested in the company at extreme financial risk to himself, and was promised a quick return on the money, which did not get returned. If the attorney could prove that he reasonably relied on the promise of the company to his detriment, could promissory estoppel be awarded?

---

[3] "Do Interactive Websites Have a Legal Duty to Remove Malicious Content?" http://writ.news.findlaw.com/scripts/printer_friendly.pl?page5/ramasastry/20090519.html (accessed May 25, 2009) [discussing *Barnes v. Yahoo, Inc.,* 2009 U.S. App. LEXIS 10940 (9th Cir. 2009)].

Double AA Builders, Ltd. v. Grand State Construction L.L.C.
114 P.3d 835 (Ariz. Ct. App. 2005)

In anticipation of submitting a bid for the construction of a Home Depot Store in Mesa, Arizona, Double AA solicited bids from subcontractors for various portions of the work. Grand State faxed a written but unsigned bid to Double AA in the amount of $115,000 for installation of the exterior insulation finish system (EIFS) on the project. The proposal stated: "Our price is good for 30 days." Double AA relied on several subcontractor bids, including Grand State's, in preparing its overall price for the project.

On December 21, 2001, Home Depot advised Double AA it was the successful bidder for the project. On January 11, 2002, within the 30-day "price is good" period, Double AA sent a subcontract for the EIFS work to Grand State to be signed and returned. Grand State advised Double AA it would not sign the subcontract or perform on the project. Double AA subsequently entered into a subcontract with a replacement subcontractor to install the EIFS at a cost of $131,449, which exceeded Grand State's quoted price by $16,449. Double AA demanded that Grand State pay the difference between its bid and Double AA's ultimate cost to perform the same work. After Grand State refused, Double AA filed suit based on promissory estoppel.

When a general contractor prepares an overall bid for a competitively bid construction project, it receives bids and quotes from subcontractors for portions of the work. The general contractor uses the bids in preparing its overall price for the project. A subcontractor's refusal to honor its bid can be financially disastrous for the general contractor, because the general contractor will typically be bound by the bid price it submitted to the project owner.

Promissory estoppel may be used to require that the subcontractor perform according to the terms of its bid to the contractor if the contractor receives the contract award, because the contractor has detrimentally relied on the subcontractor's bid and must perform for a price based on that reliance. Double AA prevailed. Nonperformance by the subcontractor resulted in damages equal to the difference between what the contractor had to pay and what it would have paid had the subcontractor performed.

A second exception to the rule requiring consideration is a *contract under seal*. In the past, contracts were sealed with a piece of soft wax into which an impression was made. Today, sealed contracts are typically identified with the word *seal* or the letters *L.S.* (an abbreviation for *locus sigilli,* which means "the place for the seal") at the end. Consumers may also purchase contract forms with a preprinted seal. The parties using them are presumed, without evidence to the contrary, to be adopting the seal for the contract. States in the U.S. no longer require that contracts be under seal. However, 10 states still allow a contract without consideration to be enforced if it is under seal.

Legal Principle: **Promissory estoppel and contracts under seal are two exceptions to the common law rule requiring consideration.**

ADEQUACY OF CONSIDERATION

The court does not weigh whether you made a good bargain. Suppose Donna purchases a flat-screen TV from Celia, a friend in her business law class. Donna pays $500 for the TV but later realizes it is worth less than $100! May Donna sue Celia? Typically, the answer is no. It is Donna's responsibility to do her research and determine what price she should pay. The court will not set aside the sale because she made a bad deal. Conversely, if the court believes fraud or undue influence occurred, the court may look at adequacy of consideration. (For example, suppose a person divests himself of all his assets for pennies on the dollar and then declares bankruptcy—the court would likely review the consideration paid to determine whether there was fraud by the debtor against the creditors.)

BUT WHAT IF . . .

WHAT IF THE FACTS OF THE CASE OPENER WERE DIFFERENT?

Recall, in the Case Opener, that the company attorney Passante invested $100,000 into the Upper Deck Company so that it could produce hologram baseball cards. In return, Passante received a 3 percent share of the company. What if the hologram baseball cards were not successful and the company filed for bankruptcy? If Passante made a bad investment and did not receive a return on his money, could he sue the company for damages?

Legal Principle: **The court seldom considers adequacy of consideration.**

Is a promise to refrain from something you are legally entitled to do appropriate consideration for a contract? See Case 15-1.

CASE 15-1   HAMER V. SIDWAY
COURT OF APPEALS OF NEW YORK
124 N.Y. 538 (1891)

Plaintiff sought to enforce against the defendant estate a promise made by his now-deceased uncle to pay plaintiff a sum of money if plaintiff refrained from the use of alcohol and tobacco for a period of years. Plaintiff so refrained and sought recovery of the sum promised.

J. PARKER: In 1869, William Story, 2d, promised his nephew that if he refrained from drinking liquor, using tobacco, swearing, and playing cards or billiards for money until he was 21 years of age, then he would pay him the sum of $5,000. William Story, the nephew, agreed and fully performed.

The defendant (the deceased uncle's estate) now contends that the contract was without consideration to support it, and, therefore, invalid. He asserts that the nephew, by refraining from the use of liquor and tobacco, was not harmed but benefited; that that which he did was best for him to do independently of his uncle's promise, and insists that it follows that unless the nephew was benefited, the contract was without consideration. This contention, if well founded, would seem to leave open for controversy in many cases whether that which the promisee did or omitted to do was, in fact, of such benefit to him as to leave no consideration to support the enforcement of the promisor's agreement.

Such a rule could not be tolerated, and is without foundation in the law. Consideration means not so much that one party is profiting as that the other abandons some legal right in the present or limits his legal freedom of action in the future. Now, applying this rule to the facts before us, the promisee used tobacco, occasionally drank liquor, and he had a legal right to do so. He abandoned that right for a period of years based upon the promise of his uncle that for such forbearance he would give him $5,000. We need not speculate on the effort which may have been required to give up the use of those stimulants. It is sufficient that he restricted his lawful freedom of action within certain prescribed limits upon the faith of his uncle's agreement. Now, having fully performed the conditions imposed, it makes no difference whether such performance was actually a benefit to the promisor, and the court will not inquire into it. Even if it were a proper subject of inquiry, we see nothing in this record that would permit a determination that the uncle was not benefited in a legal sense. It is deemed established for the purposes of this appeal, that on January 31, 1875, defendant's testator was indebted to William E. Story, 2d, in the sum of $5,000. All concur.

The order reversing the trial court judgment in favor of plaintiff is reversed on the grounds that plaintiff's promise to abandon his legal right to use tobacco and alcohol was sufficient consideration to enforce the contract.

CRITICAL THINKING

What difference would it have made in this case had the nephew not had the legal right to drink or smoke? Why is this question crucial to the decision?

ETHICAL DECISION MAKING

William Story, 2d, may well have thought that he should win the case on moral grounds. He is applauding his nephew's behavior in recognition that the behavior the nephew stopped was behavior that was harming his nephew. So, since his nephew is now in better condition than he was before their exchange of views, why does the court put itself in the position of requiring William Story, 2d, to pay the $5,000?

In Case 15-2, the court had to consider whether $1 plus "love and affection" was adequate consideration for the transfer of property.

CASE 15-2   THELMA AGNES SMITH V. DAVID PHILLIP RILEY
**COURT OF APPEALS OF TENNESSEE,
EASTERN SECTION, AT KNOXVILLE
2002 TENN. APP. LEXIS 65 (2002)**

The plaintiff, Thelma Agnes Smith, lived with the defendant out of wedlock for several years. When the relationship ended, she sued the defendant, seeking to enforce two written agreements with him regarding the sale and assignment of property to her. The trial court enforced the agreements and divided the parties' property. The defendant appealed, arguing the agreements lacked consideration and were void as against public policy.

JUDGE CHARLES D. SUSANO: . . . Thelma Agnes Smith and David Phillip Riley, both of whom then resided in Florida, separated from their respective spouses in 1997 and began a romantic relationship. In early 1998, the two moved to Tennessee and began cohabitating. . . . Smith and Riley opened a joint checking account in March, 1998. Over time, Smith deposited into that account $9,500—the proceeds from an insurance settlement and monies received when her divorce later became final; she also deposited her monthly social security check of $337 into the same account. Smith continued to deposit her social security check in the joint account until December, 1998, when she opened her own checking account. Riley also contributed to the joint account. He placed a settlement of $84,000 from the Veteran's Administration into the account. In addition, he deposited his monthly pension check of $2,036 into the same account. . . .

On July 31, 1998, Riley entered into a lease with Jerry Strickland and Wanda Strickland with respect to a residence owned by them; the lease was accompanied by an option to purchase. Almost four months later, on November 20, 1998, Smith and Riley returned to their attorney's office, at which time the attorney prepared a bill of sale and an assignment. In the bill of sale, Riley transferred [to Smith] a one-half undivided interest in seven items of personal property. . . . Riley also assigned to Smith a one-half undivided interest in the lease and option to purchase with the Stricklands, which interest included a right of survivorship in the one-half interest retained by Riley as well. The property Riley sold and assigned to Smith in the two agreements was stated in each to be "for and in consideration of the sum of One Dollar ($1.00) and other and good and valuable consideration, the sufficiency of which is hereby acknowledged. . . ."

When Smith and Riley separated in April, 1999, Smith filed suit against Riley in the trial court, seeking the dissolution of their "domestic partnership." Smith alleged that she and Riley had been living together for several years without the benefit of marriage and had acquired both real and personal property, some of which Riley had assigned to her. As a result, she asked the court to award her 50 percent of the "partnership" assets, leaving the other 50 percent to Riley. . . . [The trial court ruled in favor of Smith and Riley appealed.]

Riley first argues that the trial court erred in finding that the bill of sale and assignment are supported by valid consideration. Specifically, Riley relies on Smith's statements at trial that she considered their pending engagement and the funds she deposited into their joint account to be consideration for their agreements.

It is a well-settled principle of contract law that in order for a contract to be binding, it must, among other things, be supported by sufficient consideration. [Citations omitted.] In expounding on the adequacy of consideration, the Tennessee Supreme Court has stated that it is not necessary that the benefit conferred or the detriment suffered by the promisee shall be equal to the responsibility assumed. Any consideration, however small, will support a promise. In the absence of fraud, the courts will not undertake to regulate the amount of the consideration. The parties are left to contract for themselves, taking for granted that the consideration is one valuable in the eyes of the law. . . .

Quoting the United States Supreme Court, the Tennessee Supreme Court went on to state that "[a] stipulation in consideration of $1 is just as effectual and valuable a consideration as a larger sum stipulated for or paid." [Citations omitted.] Indeed, the consideration of love and affection has been deemed sufficient to support a conveyance. . . .

Both the bill of sale and the assignment recite that they are undertaken "for and in consideration of the sum of One Dollar ($1.00) and other and good and valuable consideration, the sufficiency of which is hereby acknowledged. . . ." Facially, the documents are therefore supported by sufficient consideration, as clearly recognized by the Supreme Court. . . . Moreover, Smith's "society and consortium"—a concept comparable to the love and affection . . . is further evidence of sufficient consideration to support these conveyances.

Riley calls our attention to Smith's statement at trial that she considered the funds she deposited into their joint account to be consideration for the conveyances. If this were the only consideration involved in this case, Riley's argument regarding past consideration supporting a present transaction might have some merit. However, the recitals of nominal consideration that are present in both agreements, as well as the consideration of Smith's love and affection, are adequate consideration and will support the conveyances represented by the assignment and bill of sale. . . .

Judgment affirmed in favor of Plaintiff.

CRITICAL THINKING

What is the reasoning of the appellant in terms of why the consideration was not adequate to cause the contracts to be enforceable? What key rule of law did this reasoning overlook?

ETHICAL DECISION MAKING

What values are being advanced by the logic of the relevant rule of law in this case? In other words, what values prevent the rule of law from being that "consideration must be in an amount similar in value to the item or services being transferred in order for the contract to be enforceable"?

ILLUSORY PROMISE

L04
What is an illusory promise?

What is an illusory promise? Suppose Shawn offers to sell Molly his skis for $300. Molly responds, "I'll look at them in the morning, and if I like them, I'll pay you." At this point, Molly has not committed to doing anything. The law considers this an illusory promise— it is not a promise at all.

Legal Principle: **An illusory promise is not consideration.**

BUT WHAT IF . . .
WHAT IF THE FACTS OF THE CASE OPENER WERE DIFFERENT?
Let's say that, in the Case Opener, Passante was approached by executives of the Upper Deck Company and they asked him to invest money into their company so that they could purchase hologram baseball cards. In response, Passante told them, "That sounds like a good idea. I'll have my financial adviser call you for more details." Is Passante making a contractual promise to the company? What is the term for his type of response in this situation?

PAST CONSIDERATION

For a court to enforce a promise, both sides must offer consideration. Imagine you graduate from college and get a great job. After five years, your boss says to you, "Because you have done such a great job the last five years, I am going to give you 5 percent of the company stock." Six months later, you still have not received the stock. May you sue your boss to enforce the promise? The answer is no. For a promise to be enforceable, there must be bargaining and an exchange. Because your work has already been performed, you have given nothing in exchange, and the court will not enforce the promise. A promise cannot be based on consideration provided before the promise was made. You are at the mercy of your boss's goodwill.

Legal Principle: **Past consideration is no consideration at all.**

As you have probably guessed by now, there is an exception to this rule. Under the Restatement (Second) of Contracts (a persuasive, though not binding, authority), promises

COMPARING THE LAW OF OTHER COUNTRIES

CONTRACT ENFORCEMENT IN CHINA

Every year the World Bank publishes its Doing Business rankings, which rate 181 countries by ease of doing business (the rankings can be found at **www.doingbusiness.org/rankings**). In the category "Enforcing Contracts," China is rated number 10. This means that China has one of the best systems in the world for enforcement of contracts. Compare that with India, which is rated 180 out of 181 countries, or Brazil, which is rated at 100. China is actually rated better than the United Kingdom, which comes in at 23, and better than Japan, which comes in at 21. It is therefore a serious mistake to place China in the same category as some of its developing country competitors.

Source: Dan Harris, "Enforcing Contracts in China: Way, Way Better Than You Think," July 13, 2009, www.chinalawblog.com/2009/07/enforcing_contracts_in_china_w.html.

based on past consideration may be enforceable "to the extent necessary to avoid injustice." In some cases, if past consideration was given with expectation of future payment, the court may enforce the promise.

In Case 15-3, the court must decide whether the promise to pay a friend for coming up with a merchandising idea is compensable when the promise to pay was made after the idea was given.

CASE 15-3   JAMIL BLACKMON V. ALLEN IVERSON
U.S. DISTRICT COURT FOR THE EASTERN DISTRICT OF PENNSYLVANIA
324 F. SUPP. 2D 602 (2003)

The defendant, Allen Iverson, was a professional basketball player. The plaintiff, Jamil Blackmon, was a family friend. In July of 1994, Mr. Blackmon suggested that Mr. Iverson use "The Answer" as a nickname in the summer league basketball tournaments in which Mr. Iverson would be playing. Mr. Blackmon told Mr. Iverson that Mr. Iverson would be "The Answer" to all of the National Basketball Association's ("NBA's") woes. Mr. Blackmon and Mr. Iverson also discussed the fact that the nickname "The Answer" had immediate applications as a label, brand name, or other type of marketing slogan for use in connection with clothing, sports apparel, and sneakers. The parties also discussed using "The Answer" as a logo. Later that evening, Mr. Iverson promised to give Mr. Blackmon twenty-five percent of all proceeds from the merchandising of products sold in connection with the term "The Answer." The parties understood that in order to "effectuate Mr. Iverson's agreement to compensate" Mr. Blackmon, Mr. Iverson would have to be drafted by the NBA.

Mr. Blackmon thereafter began to invest significant time, money, and effort in the refinement of the concept of "The Answer." Mr. Blackmon continued to develop and refine the marketing strategy for the sale of merchandise, such as athletic wear and sneakers, in connection with the term "The Answer." He retained a graphic designer to develop logos bearing "The Answer" as well as conceptual drawings for sleeveless T-shirts, adjustable hats, and letterman jackets for sale in connection with "The Answer." In 1994 and 1995, during Mr. Iverson's freshman year at Georgetown University and the summer thereafter, there were numerous conversations between Mr. Blackmon and Mr. Iverson regarding Mr. Blackmon's progress in refining the marketing concept for "The Answer." In 1996, just prior to the NBA draft, during which Mr. Iverson was drafted by the Philadelphia 76ers, Mr. Iverson advised Mr. Blackmon that Mr. Iverson intended to use the phrase "The Answer" in connection with a contract with Reebok for merchandising of athletic shoes and sports apparel. Mr. Iverson repeated his promise to pay Mr. Blackmon twenty-five percent of all proceeds from merchandising goods that incorporated "The Answer" slogan or logo. . . . Despite repeated requests and demands from Mr. Blackmon, Mr. Iverson has never compensated Mr. Blackmon and continues to deny Mr. Blackmon twenty-five percent of the proceeds from the merchandising of products incorporating "The Answer."

Mr. Blackmon is now suing Mr. Iverson, seeking damages for claims alleging [among others] . . . breach of contract . . . arising out of the basketball player's use of "The Answer," both as a nickname and as a logo or slogan. The defendant filed a motion to dismiss this complaint.

JUDGE MARY A. MCLAUGHLIN: . . . The essence of . . . the plaintiff's claim is that the defendant took and used the plaintiff's ideas without compensating the plaintiff.

. . . The plaintiff claims that he entered into an express contract with the defendant pursuant to which he was to receive twenty-five percent of the proceeds that the defendant received from marketing products with "The Answer" on them. The defendant argues that there was not a valid contract because the claim was not timely filed under the Pennsylvania statute of limitations, the terms of the contract were not sufficiently definite, and there was no consideration alleged. Because the Court has determined that the claim should be dismissed for failure to allege proper consideration, the Court need not address the defendant's other arguments about the statute of limitations and definiteness of terms. . . .

According to the facts alleged by the plaintiff, he made the suggestion that the defendant use "The Answer" as a nickname and for product merchandising one evening in 1994. This was before the defendant first promised to pay; according to the plaintiff, the promise to pay was made later that evening. The disclosure of the idea also occurred before the defendant told the plaintiff that he was going to use the idea in connection with the Reebok contract in 1996, and before the sales of goods bearing "The Answer" actually began in 1997. Regardless of whether the contract was formed in 1994, 1996, or 1997, the disclosure of "The Answer" idea had already occurred and was, therefore, past consideration insufficient to create a binding contract. **Motion granted in favor of Defendant.**

CRITICAL THINKING

What key fact would have had to be different for Mr. Blackmon to have received a favorable ruling in this case?

ETHICAL DECISION MAKING

Most people reading this case probably feel some sympathy for Mr. Blackmon. He put in a lot of time in reliance on a promise he was made by Iverson. He received nothing for that time even though Iverson benefited from some of it. What stakeholders in a contract are being protected by strict adherence to the need for consideration that the court used to form its conclusion?

PREEXISTING DUTY

There are two parts to the preexisting duty rule. *Performance of a duty you are obligated to do under the law is not good consideration.* Part of a police officer's sworn public duty is catching suspected criminals. If someone offers a reward for the capture of a suspect, the police officer may not collect it, as he or she was already obligated to apprehend the suspect. Moreover, *performance of an existing contractual duty is not good consideration.* Gene decides to have a pool built in his backyard. Under the existing contract, the pool is to be completed by June 1, just in time for summer. The pool contractor then explains that due to a shortage of workers, the completion date cannot be met; however, if Gene were to pay an extra $5,000, additional workers could be hired and the pool completed on time. Gene tells the contractor he will pay the $5,000. On June 1, the pool is completed and the contractor asks for the additional payment. Is Gene legally obligated to pay? The answer is no. The pool contractor had a preexisting contractual duty to complete the pool by June 1. Gene is under no obligation to pay the additional money.

Legal Principle: **A promise to do something that you are already obligated to do is not valid consideration.**

BUT WHAT IF . . .

WHAT IF THE FACTS OF THE CASE OPENER WERE DIFFERENT?

Recall that, in the Case Opener, Passante agreed to invest $100,000 in the Upper Deck Company so that he could own 3 percent of it. But what if the company told Passante that its sales were sinking and that if he didn't agree to invest another $50,000, the company would go bankrupt and Passante would receive no return on his investment? Suppose Passante agrees. If a month later the company came to collect the $50,000, does Passante legally have to pay the extra money because he told the company he would?

Exceptions to the Preexisting Duty Rule.   There are exceptions to the preexisting duty rule: unforeseen circumstances, additional work, and UCC Article 2 (sale of goods).

If *unforeseen circumstances* cause a party to make a promise regarding an unfinished project, that promise is valid consideration. Suppose the pool contractor has been building pools in Gene's neighborhood for the last 20 years and has never had any problem with rocks—until now. While bulldozing the hole for the pool in Gene's backyard, the pool contractor hits solid rock. It will cost an additional $5,000 to clear the rock with jackhammers, possibly even dynamite. The contractor says unless Gene agrees to pay the additional money, he will not be able to finish the pool. Gene agrees to pay. When the pool is completed, the contractor asks for the additional $5,000. Will a court enforce Gene's promise? The answer is yes. Even though the contractor is completing only what he was obligated to do under the contract, neither party knew of the solid rock. The contractor has given additional consideration (removal of the rock) and Gene will be held to his promise to pay the additional money.

If a party to a contract agrees to do *additional work* (more than the contract requires), the promise to do it is valid consideration. If the contractor asks Gene for an additional $10,000 but agrees to add a waterfall and a deck to the pool, the promise to do the additional work is consideration. If Gene agrees to pay the $10,000, that is his consideration. Both parties are now bound.

Partial Payment of a Debt

L05

What is the difference between a liquidated debt and an unliquidated debt?

Partial payment of a debt may or may not be valid consideration, depending on whether the debt is liquidated or unliquidated. In a liquidated debt, there is no dispute that money is owed or how much. Natalie calls her credit card company and explains she is a poor student and cannot afford to pay the entire $3,000 she owes. The credit card company agrees to accept $2,000 as payment in full. The following month, Natalie receives her new credit card statement showing she owes the remaining $1,000. May the credit card company collect the additional $1,000? Yes! A creditor's promise to accept less than owed, when the debtor is already obligated to pay the full amount, is not binding.

The exception to the rule regarding liquidated debt occurs when the debtor offers different performance. Suppose Natalie offered the credit card company her car in full settlement of the $3,000 debt. If the credit card company accepts, regardless of the value of the car, the debt is paid in full and the credit card company may not sue Natalie for any additional money.

L06

What is an accord and satisfaction?

In an unliquidated debt, the parties either disagree about whether money is owed or dispute the amount. They can settle for less than the full amount if they enter into an accord and satisfaction, which must meet three requirements to be enforceable:

1. The debt is unliquidated (the amount or existence of the debt is in dispute).
2. The creditor agrees to accept as full payment less than it claims is owed.
3. The debtor pays the amount they have agreed on.

Under these circumstances, the debt is fully discharged. The *accord* is the new agreement to pay less than the creditor claims is owed. The *satisfaction* is the debtor's payment of the reduced amount. It pays to keep your word: If the debtor fails to pay the new amount, the creditor may sue for the full amount of the original debt. Exhibit 15-3 clarifies the accord-and-satisfaction process.

Legal Principle: **When a debt is unliquidated, the parties may enter into an accord and satisfaction.**

Debtors sometimes attempt to create an accord and satisfaction by sending the creditor a check with "paid in full" written on it. Under the common law, in many states this did

Exhibit 15-3   Accord and Satisfaction

DEBT DISPUTED?	STATUS OF DEBT	PAYMENT?	CREATE AN ACCORD?	CREATE A SATISFACTION?
Yes—*amount* of debt in dispute	Unliquidated	Debtor offers to pay less money than creditor believes is owed as full payment, and creditor agrees.	Yes	Yes. Once debtor pays the money agreed to, the debt is satisfied and the creditor may not collect any additional money.
Yes—*existence* of debt in dispute	Unliquidated	Debtor offers to pay a sum of money as full payment when debtor does not believe anything is owed, and creditor agrees.	Yes	Yes. Once the debtor pays the money agreed to, the debt is satisfied and the creditor may not collect any additional money.
No dispute over amount of debt or existence of debt	Liquidated	Debtor offers to pay less money than is owed as full payment, and creditor agrees.	No	No. Even if the debtor pays the money agreed to, the creditor may still sue for the balance it believes is owed.
No dispute over amount of debt or existence of debt	Liquidated	Debtor offers a *different* payment (e.g., her car) as full payment.	Yes	Yes. Once the debtor makes a *different* payment, the debt is satisfied and the creditor may not collect anything else.

create an accord and satisfaction, and if the creditor cashed the check, he or she was bound to accept the lesser amount as payment in full. The UCC (introduced in Chapter 13) has reduced the scope of this rule, however. Under UCC Section 3-311, effective in 30 states, the rule has two major exceptions.

First, business organizations can receive thousands of checks each day. To protect themselves, they may notify their debtors that any offer to settle a claim for less than the amount owed must be sent to a particular address and/or person. If you check the terms printed on your credit card statement, you will likely find language directing you to send such payments to a different address and person than regular payments are sent to. This safeguard protects businesses from inadvertently creating accord-and-satisfaction agreements. Below is a typical clause you might find on any credit statement regarding conditional payments:

> *Conditional Payments:* Any payment check or other form of payment that you send us for less than the full balance that is marked "paid in full" or contains a similar notation, or that you otherwise tender in full satisfaction of a disputed amount, must be sent to [address omitted]. We reserve all rights regarding these payments (e.g., if it is determined that there is no valid dispute or if any such check is received at any other address, we may accept the check and you will still owe any remaining balance).[4]

In the second exception, if a business does inadvertently cash a "paid-in-full" check, it has 90 days to offer the debtor repayment in the same amount. For example, if John owed his credit card company $3,000 and sent a $2,000 check marked "paid in full" to the correct address and person, the credit card company has 90 days to offer to repay John the $2,000. Once the business has made that offer, no accord and satisfaction exists.

To see how an accord and satisfaction relates to income taxation, please see the **Connecting to the Core** activity on the text website at www.mhhe.com/kubasek3e.

[4] From Chase Visa statement.

Thomas v. CitiMortgage, Inc.
2005 U.S. Dist. LEXIS 14641 (Dist. Ct. Ill. 2005)

In November 1979, Thomas assumed an existing mortgage, which CitiMortgage now holds, that required him to make a payment on the first of each month. Beginning in April 1996, his payments became sporadic. On December 16, 1996, Thomas sent a letter to CitiMortgage. He wrote:

> My primary concern is the effect on my credit rating and the fact that I have an application to refinace [*sic*] the mortgage which cannot be finalized, at great cost to me, unless this matter is resolved and my credit cleared up. I have enclosed a check in the amount of the monthly payment on condition that it be applied to tha [*sic*] May payment and that it will allow you to remove the negative material relative to my credit rating.

CitiMortgage cashed the check enclosed with the December 16 letter and credited it to Thomas's account. At CitiMortgage as of 1996, mail was sorted in a central mail room. The persons processing checks lacked the authority either to accept conditions on payments or to change credit reports. In his breach-of-contract claim, Thomas asserted that he and CitiMortgage had entered an agreement whereby he would make a payment on his mortgage in exchange for CitiMortgage's agreement to "remove the negative material" from his credit rating. He further claimed that CitiMortgage accepted the contract when it cashed the check he enclosed with his December 16 letter. Whether Thomas's claim was considered an accord and satisfaction or a simple contract, he could not prevail unless he established that consideration supported the agreement.

Consideration can consist of a promise, an act, or a forbearance. The preexisting duty rule provides, however, that when a party does what it is already legally obligated to do, there is no consideration because there has been no detriment. Thomas claimed that the payment he made with his December 16 letter constituted consideration for the agreement. As of that date, however, he was already two months in arrears on his mortgage payment. Thus, he was already legally obligated—under the terms of the mortgage—to make the payment he enclosed with the letter. Accordingly, that payment could not be consideration for an additional agreement to "remove the negative material" from his credit rating.

CASE OPENER WRAP-UP

Upper Deck—Contract Liability or Gift?

As you know from the Case Opener, Passante sued Upper Deck for breach of oral contract. At trial, the jury awarded him close to $33 million—the value of 3 percent of Upper Deck's stock at the time of the trial in 1993. Upper Deck appealed.

As a matter of law, any claim by Passante for breach of contract is necessarily based on the rule that consideration must result from a bargained-for exchange. In this case, the appellate court held that if the stock promised was truly bargained for, then Passante had an obligation to give Upper Deck the opportunity to have separate counsel represent it in the course of that bargaining. The legal profession has certain rules regarding business transactions with clients. Bargaining between the parties might have resulted in Passante's settling for just a reasonable finder's fee.

All Passante's services in arranging the $100,000 loan for Upper Deck had already been rendered (even though the board had not formally accepted the loan) before the idea of giving him stock came up. There was no evidence he had any expectation of receiving stock in return. If there is no expectation of payment by either party when services are rendered, the promise is a mere promise to make a gift and not enforceable. The promise of 3 percent of the stock represented a moral obligation but was legally unenforceable.

KEY TERMS

accord and satisfaction   354   illusory promise   351   preexisting duty   353   unliquidated debt   354
consideration   346   liquidated debt   354   promissory estoppel   347

SUMMARY OF KEY TOPICS

Consideration is something of value given in exchange for something else of value; it must be the product of a mutually bargained-for exchange. **What Is Consideration?**

The key to understanding consideration is understanding the various rules: **Rules of Consideration**

*   For a promise to be enforced by the courts, there must be consideration.
*   *Exception: Promissory estoppel* occurs when one party makes a promise knowing the other party will rely on it, the other party does rely on it, and the only way to avoid injustice is to enforce the promise even though it is not supported by consideration.
*   The court seldom considers adequacy of consideration.
*   An *illusory promise* is not consideration.
*   Past consideration is no consideration at all.
*   A promise to do something you are already obligated to do is not valid consideration. (This is the *preexisting duty rule*.)

In a *liquidated debt,* there is no dispute that money is owed or the amount. In an *unliquidated debt,* the parties dispute either the fact that money is owed or the amount. **Partial Payment of a Debt**

To be enforceable, an *accord and satisfaction* must meet three requirements: (1) The debt is unliquidated (the amount or existence of the debt is in dispute); (2) the creditor agrees to accept as full payment less than the creditor claims is owed; and (3) the debtor pays the amount they agree on.

POINT / COUNTERPOINT

Should the Courts Require Consideration to Create a Binding Contract?	
YES	NO
The rules of consideration have been established for many years and precedent should be followed. Requiring consideration gives the court a way to distinguish between binding and nonbinding promises, or between a promise made as a gift and a promise made as part of a contract. We have enough exceptions to the rule requiring consideration to make enforcement fair. If a promise was made and there was expectation of economic benefit, some courts will permit enforcement under the moral-obligation exception. If we suddenly did not require consideration to create binding contracts, the courts would fill with civil cases of people trying to enforce all kind of promises.	All promises should be enforced, eliminating the need to distinguish between binding and nonbinding promises. If a person makes a promise, its timing should not make a difference. If Barbara's grandmother promises her $50,000 for "all you have done for me these last five years," why should Barbara be denied the money because it was based on acts she did in the past? The right thing, ethically and morally, is to enforce this promise whether or not Barbara acted with expectation of payment. Under current law, some states can use the moral-obligation exception to reward those who expect something when they do good and punish those who do the right thing with no expectation of reward.

QUESTIONS & PROBLEMS

1. List the four types of consideration described in the text.

2. What is required to prove promissory estoppel when consideration is missing?

3. Can $1 be adequate consideration? Why or why not?

4. List and describe the three exceptions to the preexisting duty rule.

5. List the three elements of accord and satisfaction.

6. The plaintiff is Amir Peleg, a gay Jewish male of Israeli national origin. He worked at the Neiman Marcus store in Beverly Hills from December 28, 2005, to February 21, 2008. The store is owned by the defendant, Neiman Marcus Group, Inc. Peleg worked in the fragrances department and performed his duties in an exemplary manner. Peleg alleges that on February 21, 2008, he was discharged because of his national origin, religion, and sexual orientation in violation of the California Fair Employment and Housing Act (FEHA). Neiman Marcus responded to the complaint with a motion to compel arbitration of the entire case. The company established that, at the time of hire, Peleg was given its "Mandatory Arbitration Agreement." Peleg asserted that the agreement was illusory and unenforceable in light of the following provision:

> This Agreement to arbitrate shall survive the termination of the employer-employee relationship between the Company and any Covered Employee, and shall apply to any covered Claim whether it arises or is asserted during or after termination of the Covered Employee's employment with the Company or the expiration of any benefit plan. This Agreement can be *amended, modified, or revoked in writing by the Company at anytime,* but only upon thirty (30) days' advance notice to the Covered Employee of that amendment, modification, or revocation. However, any amendment, modification, or revocation will have *no effect on any Claim that was filed for arbitration prior to the effective date* of such amendment, modification, or revocation.

Plaintiff alleges that the arbitration agreement is illusory. Do you agree? Why or why not? [*Peleg v. Neiman Marcus Group, Inc.,* 204 Cal. App. 4th 1425 (2012).]

7. Joana Perez began working for Datamark in January 2005. She received two booklets at orientation, the "Non-Staff Employee Handbook" and the "Summary Plan Description." She did not read either one of them. According to the human resource director, Perez also received the "Problem Resolution Program" booklet (the PRP) that described company dispute resolution policies and procedure. Perez denied receiving it, but she did sign the "Receipt and Arbitration Acknowledgment," which was maintained in her personnel file. Her signature acknowledged that she had received and read (or had the opportunity to read) both the "Summary Plan Description" and the PRP. She also acknowledged that an arbitration policy required the submission of all employee-related disputes to an arbitrator in accordance with the procedures described in the PRP. Datamark reserved the right to revoke or modify the PRP in writing at any time as long as the writing was signed by an officer of the company and articulated an intent to revoke or modify a policy. Perez learned she was pregnant in August 2005. While employed fulltime, she began to miss work due to pregnancy difficulties. She was discharged on October 21, 2005, and she filed suit alleging unlawful discrimination because of her gender and/or pregnancy. Perez also alleged that Datamark intentionally or recklessly engaged in extreme and outrageous behavior that caused her severe emotional distress. Datamark filed a motion to compel arbitration. In her response to the motion, Perez alleged that the arbitration agreement was illusory because Datamark could unilaterally change or terminate the agreement without prior notice to the employees. Do you believe the agreement to arbitrate is illusory? Why or why not? [*In re Datamark, Inc., Relator,* 296 S.W.3d 614, 2009 Tex. App. LEXIS 794 (2009).]

8. On February 1, 2004, Zhang entered into a contract to buy former realtor Frank Sorichetti's Las Vegas home for $532,500. The contract listed a March closing date and a few household furnishings as part of the sale. On February 3, Sorichetti told Zhang that he was terminating the sale "to stay in the house a little longer" and that Nevada law allows the rescission of real property purchase agreements within three days of contracting. Sorichetti stated that he would sell the home, however, if Zhang paid more

money. Zhang agreed. Another contract was drafted, reciting a new sales price, $578,000. This contract added to the included household furnishings drapes that were not listed in the February 1 agreement, and it set an April, rather than March, closing date. The primary issue before the court was whether a real property purchase agreement is enforceable when it is executed by the buyer only because the seller would not perform under an earlier purchase agreement for a lesser price. Should the court enforce the second contract? Why or why not? [*Zhang v. The Eighth Judicial District Court of the State of Nevada*, 103 P.3d 20 (Sup. Ct. Nev. 2004).]

9. Charles Houser began working for the appellee, 84 Lumber Company, L.P., in 1985. In 1998, Houser became an outside salesman with 84 Lumber, and his compensation changed from a set salary to commission based on his sales. At that time, Houser signed a noncompete agreement, which prohibited him from engaging in sales activities with a competitor of 84 Lumber within a 25-mile radius of 84 Lumber's Macedonia store for a two-year period following the conclusion of his employment with 84 Lumber. In June 2008, Houser signed a contract providing a set weekly draw and yet another noncompete agreement. In March 2009, Houser left 84 Lumber and, almost immediately thereafter, began working for Carter Lumber, a competitor of 84 Lumber. 84 Lumber filed a lawsuit alleging that Houser had violated the noncompete agreement. The essential question is whether the 2008 noncompete agreement was supported by adequate consideration. "[A] restrictive covenant is enforceable if supported by new consideration, either in the form of an initial employment contract or a change in the conditions of employment." 84 Lumber Company argued that Houser's continued employment was adequate consideration for the new noncompete agreement. Do you agree? Why or why not? [*84 Lumber Co., L.P. v. Houser*, 2011 Ohio 6852 (2011).]

10. Five employees of American Electric Power (AEP) Service Corp. invented a new product. "In consideration of the sum of One Dollar (1.00), and of other good and valuable consideration paid to the undersigned Assignor," each employee signed an agreement giving AEP exclusive patent rights to the invention. Some of the employees sued, alleging that there was no contract because AEP never paid the one dollar. How do you think the court ruled? Explain your reasoning. [*Bennett et al. v. American Electric Power Service Corporation*, 2001 Ohio App. LEXIS 4357 (Ohio Ct. App. 2001).]

Looking for more review materials?

The Online Learning Center at **www.mhhe.com/kubasek3e** contains this chapter's "Assignment on the Internet" and also a list of URLs for more information, entitled "On the Internet." Find both of them in the Student Center portion of the OLC, along with quizzes and other helpful materials.

PART 2

CONTRACTS

LEARNING OBJECTIVES

After reading this chapter, you will be able to answer the following questions:

1 What is the legal effect of a lack of capacity on a person's ability to enter into a contract?

2 Under what circumstances would a party have limited capacity to enter into a contract?

3 What is the legal effect of entering into a contract for an illegal purpose?

CASE OPENER

Apple's Questionable Contracts

Parents of minors took Apple to court in 2012 for supplying game applications, on iPhones, that were "free" but through which users could purchase in-game currencies. Apparently, parents would log on to the games, but within a subsequent 15-minute time frame, the minors using the game would rack up bills ranging from $99.99 to $338.72 "at a time."

Apple stated that while minors were downloading these applications and in-game currency, the contract in question was actually the Terms of Service between the parents and Apple. According to the Terms of Service, any unauthorized log-in on one's account or unauthorized purchases by anyone on the account were the responsibility of the account holder. On the other hand, the parents argued that all in-game purchases made by minors were separate contracts that may be disaffirmed by a parent or guardian. Apple also argued that a "contract" as the parents were describing it could not legally exist in that, as the parents described the scenario, the contractual offer was made to parents in the Terms of Service, yet accepted by the children, and consideration was provided by the parents (the original offerees).[1]

1. Do the individual purchases made by the minors indeed qualify as separate contracts between Apple and the minors?

2. Even if the purchases were contracts between the minors and Apple, could the parents void these contracts?

The Wrap-Up at the end of the chapter will answer these questions.

---

[1] *In re Apple In-App Purchase Litigation*, 5:11-CV-1758 (N.D. Cal., Mar. 31, 2012).

Capacity

L01

What is the legal effect of a lack of capacity on a person's ability to enter into a contract?

Capacity is the third element of a legally binding contract. A person who has legal capacity has the mental ability to understand his or her rights and obligations under a contract and therefore presumably to comply with the terms. *Incapacity,* or *incompetence* as it is sometimes called, is the possession of a mental or physical defect that prevents a natural person from being able to enter into a legally binding contract. Depending on the nature and extent of the defect, a person may have either no capacity, the complete inability to enter into contracts, or limited capacity, the ability to form only voidable contracts.

Historically, people with limited or no capacity included married women, minors, and insane persons. Other categories were added by statutes, such as people for whom guardians had been appointed, including habitual drunkards, narcotic addicts, spendthrifts, the elderly, and convicts. Today, married women have been removed from the category of those lacking contractual capacity, although in a few states their capacity to enter into certain kinds of contracts is still limited. In this section of the chapter, we explain the current law limiting the capacity of some categories of persons to enter into legally binding agreements.

MINORS

L02

Under what circumstances would a party have limited capacity to enter into a contract?

One of the oldest limitations on capacity is the fact that minors may enter into only voidable contracts. Today, in all but three states, a *minor* is someone under the age of 18.[2] In most states, however, a person is given full legal capacity to enter into contracts when he or she becomes emancipated before reaching the age of majority. *Emancipation* occurs when a minor's parents or legal guardians give up their right to exercise legal control over the minor, typically when the minor moves out of the parents' house and begins supporting himself or herself. Often the minor will petition the court for a declaration of emancipation. In most cases, when a minor marries, she or he is considered emancipated.

Legal Principle: **As a general rule, any contract entered into by a minor is voidable by the minor until he or she reaches the age of majority or a reasonable time thereafter.**

Disaffirmance of the Contract.   Because their contracts are voidable, minors have the right, until a reasonable time after reaching the age of majority, to disaffirm or void their contracts. Note that it is only the minor who has the right to disaffirm, never the adult with whom the minor entered into the agreement. No formalities are required to disaffirm the contract; the minor need only show an intention to rescind it, either by words or actions. However, the minor must void the entire contract; he or she cannot choose to disaffirm only a portion of it.

BUT WHAT IF . . .

WHAT IF THE FACTS OF THE CASE OPENER WERE DIFFERENT?

Let's say, in the Case Opener, that the court decided that all of the purchases made by the minors were indeed contracts between the minors and Apple. Let's say that the parents attempted to void the contracts themselves because the parents are technically the minors' legal guardians. Would such a move be effective? Why or why not?

---

[2] In Alabama, Nebraska, and Wyoming, full capacity to contract does not arise until the person reaches the age of 19, which is the age of majority in those states. In Mississippi, the age of majority is still 21.

People in the United States take the idea of an "age of majority" for granted; the only question is whether it should be 18, 19, or 21. Yet in Great Britain there is no magical age at which a young person suddenly acquires the legal capacity to enter into a contract. British courts will not enforce contracts with immature minors. However, they make the decision of whether a person is too immature to enter into a contract on a case-by-case basis. If the courts consider a person under 18 to be able to look out for his or her own interests, the contract will be enforced. If not, it will be void. A key factor is often the fairness of the agreement. If the agreement is one-sided and favors the adult, the young person is usually considered to lack the maturity to enter into it.

The minor's obligations on disaffirmance vary from state to state. Traditionally, most states simply required the minor to notify the competent party and return any consideration received, regardless of its condition. If the consideration had been damaged or destroyed, the other party had no recourse against the minor. For instance, if William, a minor, purchased a flat-screen TV from Sound Systems, Inc., under a six-month contract and dropped the TV a week after he took it home, he could return it in its broken condition and tell the store owner he wished to rescind the contract. He would be entitled to the return of his down payment and would owe no further obligations to the store.

The traditional rule makes sense if we view minors as innocents in need of protection from competent adults who would otherwise take advantage of them. However, it is not going to encourage competent parties to enter into contracts with minors, and some argue that it allows a knowledgeable and unethical minor to take advantage of a competent party. Thus, a number of states have modified the duty of the minor on disaffirmance, holding that the minor has a duty of restitution, requiring that she or he place the competent party back in the position that party was in at the time the contract was made. In these states, William would have a duty of restoration that would require him to compensate the store owner for the difference between the value of the TV when he got it and its value when he returned it.

The disaffirmance must occur before or within a reasonable time of the minor's reaching the age of majority. What constitutes a reasonable time is determined on a case-by-case basis. But even when the courts scrutinize the cases individually, the laws created to protect minors from being victimized by competent adults do not necessarily protect competent adults from being taken advantage of by knowledgeable and unethical minors. Thus, individuals operating or working in businesses subject to laws requiring that their customers be the age of majority or older must familiarize themselves with the laws pertaining to minors, because often the responsibility of making sure that a business is dealing with people who are of legal age falls on the employees and the owner. However, since some minors use false identification or misrepresent themselves as adults, it is difficult for business owners and employees to recognize which customers are truly of age.

For example, as CEO of Girls Gone Wild (GGW), Joe Francis runs a business that requires he be familiar with the laws surrounding minors. In fact, Francis has said that GGW has very specific procedures in place to prevent filming underage girls and even teaches its camera crew ways to ensure that the girls the crew is selecting to appear in GGW spring break videos are of age. During the selection procedure, the GGW camera crew is required to check the IDs of girls wanting to be filmed, obtain signed written

GGW has very specific procedures in place to prevent filming underage girls and even teaches its camera crew ways to ensure that the girls the crew is selecting to appear in GGW spring break videos are of age. During the selection procedure, the GGW camera crew is required to check the IDs of girls wanting to be filmed, obtain signed written release forms in which the girls give their consent to be filmed, and videotape the girls' IDs as well as the actual process of signing the release forms. Regardless of his company's strict policies, Francis found himself in the middle of a heated legal battle in 2003 when seven girls claimed that they were underage when the GGW camera crew filmed them on vacation in Panama City, Florida. Francis fought back, saying that the girls misrepresented themselves, knowingly sought out the GGW crew and wanted to exploit the company in order to obtain a monetary settlement. After four years of court proceedings and intense media coverage, Francis reached an undisclosed settlement with the women, who reportedly wanted a total of $70 million.[3]

Exceptions to the Minor's Right to Disaffirm the Contract. The minor's right to disaffirm is designed to protect the minor from competent parties who might otherwise take advantage of him or her. But primarily for public policy reasons, in most states, courts or state legislatures have determined that the minor should *not* have the right to disaffirm contracts for life insurance, health insurance, psychological counseling, the performance of duties related to stock and bond transfers and bank accounts, education loan contracts, child support contracts, marriage contracts, and enlistment in the armed services.

Most of these exceptions apply in most, but not all, states. Another issue on which the states disagree is what should happen when a minor misrepresents his or her age. While the majority rule is that a minor's misrepresentation of age does not affect the minor's right to disaffirm the contract, some states hold that when a minor who appears to be of the age of majority misrepresents his or her age and a competent party relies on that misrepresentation in good faith, the minor gives up the right to disaffirm the agreement and can be treated as an adult. One justification for this rule is that any minor who is going to misrepresent his or her age does not need the protection that disaffirmance is designed to provide.

Other states have compromised, either by requiring that the minor restore the competent party to that party's precontract position before allowing the disaffirmance or by allowing the minor to disaffirm but then giving the competent party the right to sue the minor in tort and recover damages for fraud.

> To see how marketing research relates to the legal system's protection of minors, please see the **Connecting to the Core** activity on the text website at www.mhhe.com/kubasek3e.

Liability of Minors for Necessaries. A necessary is a basic necessity of life, generally including food, clothing, shelter, and basic medical services. Technically, minors can disaffirm contracts for necessaries, but they will still be held liable for the reasonable value of the necessary. The purpose of this limitation on the minor's right to disaffirm is to ensure that sellers will not be reluctant to provide minors the basic necessities of life when their parents will not provide them.

Food, clothing, shelter, and basic medical services are clearly necessaries, but it is sometimes difficult to determine whether something is in fact a necessary. Some courts define a necessary as what a minor needs to maintain his or her standard of living and financial and social status, but this can lead to a problem when an item considered a necessary for a child of upper-income parents is a luxury to a child of lower-income parents. Whether an item is considered a necessary also depends on whether the minor's parents are

---

[3]www.meetjoefrancis.com/legalstory/; www.associatedcontent.com/article/280397/two_florida_women_sue_girls_gone_wild.html?cat=17; and www.usatoday.com/life/people/2007-06-13-joe-francis_N.htm.

willing to provide it. Clearly, the games in the opening scenario would not be considered necessaries!

Ratification.   Once a person reaches the age of majority, he or she may ratify, or legally affirm, contracts made as a minor. Once ratified, the contract is no longer voidable. Ratification may be either express or implied (see Exhibit 16-1).

An *express ratification* occurs when, after reaching the age of majority, the person states orally or in writing that he or she intends to be bound by the contract entered into as a minor. For example, when she is 17, Marcy enters into an agreement to purchase an automobile from Sam for 10 monthly payments of $1,000. After making the fifth payment, Marcy turns 18 and decides to move out of state. She e-mails Sam and tells him not to worry because even though she is moving, she still intends to make her monthly payments to purchase the car. Marcy has expressly ratified the contract.

An *implied ratification* occurs when the former minor takes some action after reaching the age of majority consistent with intent to ratify the contract. Going back to the previous example, if the day after she turns 18 Marcy enters into an agreement with Joe to sell him the car in six months, that action is obviously consistent with intent to finish purchasing the car, so she has impliedly ratified the contract with Sam. Most courts find that continuing to act in accordance with the contract, such as continuing to make regular payments after reaching the age of majority, constitutes ratification. So, if (without the agreement with Joe) Marcy continued using the car and making payments on it for several months after reaching the age of majority, the courts would probably find that she had ratified the contract.

Parents' Liability for their Children's Contracts, Necessaries, and Torts.   As a general rule, parents are not liable for contracts entered into by their minor children. Thus, merchants are often reluctant to enter into contracts with minors unless some competent person is willing to cosign and become legally bound to perform if the minor no longer wishes to live up to the terms of the contract. Parents do, however, have a legal duty to provide their children with the basic necessities of life, such as food, clothing, and shelter. Thus, they may be held liable in some states for the reasonable value of necessaries for which their children enter into contracts.

In most states, minors, not their parents, are liable for a minor's personal torts. In many states, however, parents may be liable when a child causes harm if it can be proved that the parent failed to properly supervise the child, thereby subjecting others to an unreasonable risk of harm.

Exhibit 16-1
Ratifying a Contract

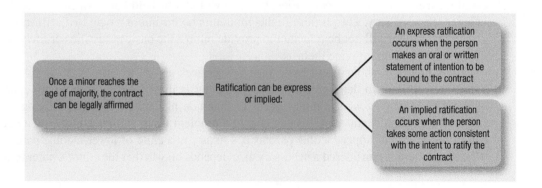

MENTALLY INCAPACITATED PERSONS

Persons suffering from a mental illness or deficiency may have full, limited, or no legal capacity to enter into a binding contract, depending on the nature and extent of their deficiency. If a person suffers from mental problems yet still understands the nature of the contract and the obligations it imposes, that person may enter into a binding, legal agreement. Suppose Gina suffers from the delusion that she is a rock star. When an encyclopedia salesperson comes to her door, she buys a set from him because she believes it is important to be knowledgeable to set a good example for her fans. As long as she understands that she is binding herself through a contract to make monthly payments for two years, Gina is bound to the contract. If, after making a year of payments, she no longer suffers from her delusions and wishes to disaffirm the contract, she will not be able to do so because her delusions had not affected her understanding of what she was legally agreeing to do when she entered into the contract.

However, a person has only limited capacity to enter into a contract if she suffers from a mental illness or deficiency that prevents her from understanding the nature and obligations of the transaction. If, in the above scenario, Gina's delusions persuaded her that she was giving the salesperson her autograph when she signed the contract, the contract is voidable. She may disaffirm it at any time until a reasonable time after she no longer suffers from the mental deficiency. Once the deficiency has been removed, Gina may also choose to ratify the contract.

As with contracts of minors, a contract for necessaries by a person suffering from a mental deficiency can be enforced for the reasonable value of the necessary.

If a person has been adjudicated insane and has a guardian appointed, that person has no capacity to enter into contracts and any contract he does attempt to enter into is void. Guardians may also be appointed for persons who have been adjudicated habitual drunkards and for those whose judgment has been impaired because of a condition such as Alzheimer disease. The guardian has the sole legal capacity to enter into contracts on such a person's behalf.

Legal Principle: **Contracts of a person with limited mental capacity can be valid, voidable, or void, depending on the extent of the mental incapacity. If a person suffers from delusions that may impair his judgment but he can still understand that he is entering into a contract and understand his obligations under the contract, his contract is valid; if his delusions prevent him from understanding that he is entering into a contract or the nature and extent of his obligations under the contract, his contract is voidable; and if he has been adjudicated insane, his contract is void.**

BUT WHAT IF . . .

WHAT IF THE FACTS OF THE CASE OPENER WERE DIFFERENT?

Let's say, in the Case Opener, that it was not children making a purchase but a mentally disabled person named Chloe, who was convinced that she owned a dog even though she didn't. And let's say that instead of purchasing in-game currencies on an iPhone, she ordered $1,000 worth of dog food. How would you describe Chloe's legal capacity? Could she avoid liability under her contract if she were subsequently treated by a therapist, no longer had her delusions, and realized that she had no need for the dog food? What if Chloe had been adjudicated insane and committed to a mental institution, but was staying with her sister on a weekend visitation pass when she made the purchase using her sister's computer?

The degree of intoxication is crucial when determining the capacity to agree to a legal contract.

INTOXICATED PERSONS

For purposes of determining capacity, intoxicated persons include those under the influence of alcohol or drugs. Most states follow the Restatement of Contracts, Section 16, which provides that contracts of an intoxicated person are voidable if the other party had reason to know that intoxication rendered the person unable to understand the nature and consequences of the transaction or unable to act in a reasonable manner in relation to the transaction. If the intoxication merely causes someone to exercise poor judgment, the person's capacity is not affected unless the other party unfairly capitalizes on this impaired judgment. Exhibit 16-2 presents the key points regarding contracts made by intoxicated persons.

Recall the case of *Lucy v. Zehmer*, discussed in Chapter 14. Another argument Zehmer tried to make in that case was that he was "high as a Georgia pine" when he signed the agreement and that the transaction was "just a bunch of two doggoned drunks bluffing to see who could talk the biggest and say the most."[4] Lucy, however, testified that while he felt the drinks, he was not intoxicated and that, from the way Zehmer handled the transaction, he did not think Zehmer was either. Zehmer's discussion of the terms of the agreement made it clear that he did in fact understand the nature of the transaction and thus could not claim a lack of capacity due to intoxication.

Similarly, if one party had no way of knowing that the other was intoxicated and if the agreement is a fair one, most courts will uphold it. Suppose Lisa e-mails Rob and offers to buy his antique car for $8,000. Rob has been drinking all day and immediately responds with a yes. Lisa has no way of knowing Rob is intoxicated, so they would have a valid contract in most states.

Exhibit 16-2
Intoxicated Individuals

Generally, contracts made by intoxicated persons are voidable. However, there are exceptions:

1. If the intoxication just causes the person to exercise poor judgment, the contract is not voidable unless the other party unfairly capitalized on the impaired judgment.

2. When the intoxicated person becomes sober, the contract can be ratified or disaffirmed; however, the courts will fairly liberally interpret behavior that seems like ratifying the contract once the intoxicated person becomes sober.

---

[4] *Lucy v. Zehmer*, 84 S.E.2d 516 (1954).

Once sober, the previously intoxicated person has the ability to either ratify or disaffirm the contract. Because public policy does not favor intoxication, the courts tend to not be sympathetic to intoxicated parties and will fairly liberally interpret behavior that seems like ratification as ratifying the contract. If Jim became intoxicated at a bar one evening and Randi took advantage by getting him to sign a contract to sell her his 2010 SUV for $8,000, any act Jim takes consistent with ratification after becoming sober will result in a binding contract. If Randi appears at his house the next morning with the cash, shows him the contract drafted on a napkin he signed, and asks for the keys and the title, by giving her the keys and saying, "I knew I shouldn't have drunk that much," Jim has entered into a binding contract.

If the contract is disaffirmed on the basis of intoxication, each party must return the other to the condition he or she was in at the time they entered into the contract. And, just as with contracts of minors and mentally incapacitated persons, the courts will enforce an intoxicated person's contract for necessaries for their reasonable value.

Exhibit 16-3 summarizes the general rules on incapacity and contracts.

Exhibit 16-3
The Three *I*'s of Incapacity: General Rules

TYPE OF INCAPACITY	CONSIDERATIONS	IF THE ANSWER IS YES, THE GENERAL RULE IS:
*I*nfancy	Is the person under the age of majority (a minor)?	The contract is voidable.
*I*nsanity	Is the person suffering from mental deficiencies that prevent him from understanding his legal obligations under the contract he is entering into?	The contract is voidable.
	Does the person's mental deficiency simply impair her judgment about the desirability of the contract but not prohibit her from understanding her obligations under it?	The contract is valid.
	Is the person adjudicated insane?	The contract is void.
*I*ntoxication	Is the sober party aware that the intoxicated person is so impaired that he is unable to understand his legal obligations under the contract he is entering into?	The contract is voidable.
	Is the intoxication such that it impairs only the intoxicated person's judgment but not her understanding of her contractual obligations?	The contract is valid.
	Has the intoxicated person been adjudicated a habitual drunkard?	The contract is void.

Legality

LO3

What is the legal effect of entering into a contract for an illegal purpose?

To be enforceable, contracts must have legal subject matter and must be able to be performed legally. They cannot violate either state or federal law. A contract overturned for illegal subject matter or for being illegal to perform is generally declared void. A contract need not be in violation of a statute to be illegal; agreements against generally accepted public policy are also illegal and unenforceable.

Contracts that are made for an illegal purpose or that cannot be carried out by legal means are made void for two main reasons: First, making them void clearly indicates that such agreements are not socially acceptable, and, second, doing so prevents the legal system's being used to promote agreements that are harmful to society.

CONTRACTS THAT VIOLATE STATE OR FEDERAL STATUTES

There are any number of ways in which contracts can violate a state or federal statute. Some of the more common ones are discussed below and summarized in Exhibit 16-4.

Agreements to Commit a Crime or Tort.   Again, contracts cannot be for illegal purposes or require illegal acts for performance. Any agreement to commit a crime or tort is illegal and unenforceable. However, should a legal contract be formed and its subject later become illegal under a new statute, the contract is considered to be discharged by law. Suppose Jim agrees to paint Hiroki's house and, in exchange, Hiroki agrees to be a poker dealer at Jim's casino, starting in two weeks. Before Hiroki can begin work, however, the state amends its gaming statute, making all games of chance other than slot machines illegal. Because it is now illegal for Jim's casino to offer poker, it would be illegal for Hiroki to perform the contract. Because a change in the law has made the subject matter of the contract illegal, both parties are discharged from their obligations under the contract.

Licensing Statutes.   All 50 states have statutes requiring that people in certain professions obtain a license before practicing their craft. For example, doctors of all varieties, plumbers, cosmetologists, lawyers, electricians, teachers, and stockbrokers are all required to obtain a license before practicing. While this list is far from exhaustive, it demonstrates how widespread the licensing requirement can be. For most of these licensed professions, licenses are typically issued only after extensive schooling, training, and/or demonstrating some degree of competence. These requirements reflect the value society places on proper performance of duties in the licensed professions.

Licensing statutes have three main purposes in addition to indicating this value. The first is to give the government some control over which people, and how many people, can perform certain jobs. Second, by charging for licenses, the government can obtain revenue.

Exhibit 16-4

Contracts That Violate State or Federal Statutes

Agreements to commit a crime or tort are illegal in all states.

Agreements made for the purpose of protecting the public's health, safety, or welfare by a party unlicensed to do so are typically illegal in all states.

Agreements regarding usurious loans may be illegal in some states.

Agreements regarding gambling are illegal in most states.

Agreements that violate Sabbath or Sunday laws are illegal in some states.

The third purpose of licensing statutes, the protection of the public's health, safety, and welfare, is related to the public interest. By imposing legal standards on a profession, the government can try to prevent harm to public health, safety, and welfare due to substandard work. For instance, it is not in the public's best interest to allow an unqualified person to perform the delicate and complicated process of medical surgery. To limit the number of people who might be harmed during surgery, the government requires that prospective surgeons, even after extensive schooling, obtain a license.

Given these different reasons for licensing various professionals, different outcomes can result when someone enters into an agreement with a person who is unlawfully unlicensed, depending on the purpose of the licensing statute. The state in which the unlicensed person is practicing is relevant, because many licensing statutes occur at the state level and thus vary from state to state. In some states the rule is "no license, no contract." These states will not enforce any agreement with an unlawfully unlicensed professional.

However, in other states the courts typically consider the purpose of licensing. If it is to provide government control over the profession or generate revenue, most states allow enforcement of the contract. Although the unlicensed professional is acting in violation of the law and is usually required to pay a fine for working without a license, there are no grave reasons the contract should not be carried out.

If the licensing statute is intended to protect the public's health, safety, and welfare, however, the agreement is typically deemed illegal and unenforceable. For example, the public would not be made safer if the government allowed unlicensed people to perform surgery. Therefore, a person cannot enter into a contract for professional service with an unlicensed professional when the law requires a license out of intent to protect the public.

Case 16-1 illustrates how failure to obtain a license can preclude a party from suing to enforce a contract.

CASE 16-1   KING v. RIEDL
ALABAMA CIVIL COURT OF APPEALS
58 SO. 3D 190 (2010)

Roseann and Bryan Riedl entered into a contract with Jim King d/b/a King Home Services to make improvements to the Riedls' house. The improvements entailed work throughout the entire property, including work to the yard and demolition and installation work to the house. The Riedls paid King a total of $14,075 for some, but not all, of the work specified in the contract. King was not at any time a licensee of the Alabama Home Builders Licensure Board.

The Riedls were unsatisfied with the work contracted for and performed by King. Consequently, Roseann filed a small-claims complaint in the small-claims division of the Madison District Court, alleging that King had damaged her house. Roseann sought compensation for repair work performed by other parties. In response, King filed an action in the Madison Circuit Court against the Riedls, alleging a number of claims, including breach of contract. In the district court, King requested that the district-court action be consolidated with the circuit-court action. After the Riedls also requested consolidation, the district-court action was transferred to the circuit court, and the two actions were consolidated.

The Riedls filed a motion for a summary judgment in the circuit court, asserting that King lacked standing to institute the circuit-court action against them because he was an unlicensed home builder. In response, King claimed that he did not need a license in order to enforce his contract with the Riedls. After a hearing, the circuit court entered a summary judgment in favor of the Riedls, dismissing all King's claims against them. King filed an appeal of the summary judgment entered in the circuit-court action.

JUDGE THOMAS:

I. Breach of Contract Claim

Section 34–14A–5, Ala.Code 1975, requires all home builders to be licensed by the Alabama Home Builders Licensure Board. A residential home builder is defined by § 34–14A–2(10), Ala.Code 1975, as follows:

(10) Residential home builder. One who constructs a residence or structure for sale or who, for a fixed price, commission, fee, or wage, undertakes or offers to undertake the construction or superintending of the construction, or who manages,

supervises, assists, or provides consultation to a homeowner regarding the construction or superintending of the construction, of any residence or structure which is not over three floors in height and which does not have more than four units in an apartment complex, or the repair, improvement, or reimprovement thereof, to be used by another as a residence *when the cost of the undertaking exceeds ten thousand dollars ($10,000).* Nothing herein shall prevent any person from performing these acts on his or her own residence or on his or her other real estate holdings. Anyone who engages or offers to engage in such undertaking in this state shall be deemed to have engaged in the business of residential home building.

. . . Thus, whether a license is required depends on the cost of the undertaking.

King argues that the cost of the undertaking in the present case was less than $10,000 because, he contends, work done to the Riedls' porch, "doggie doors," and fence should not be included in calculating the cost of the undertaking. King further argues that the Riedls had full control over the subcontractors and, thus, that he is exempted from obtaining a license by § 34–14A–6(5). Also, King contends that he did not have sufficient control over the subcontractors and materials for the amounts paid to those subcontractors and for those materials to contribute toward the cost of the undertaking. Finally, King argues that he was compensated for his work by periodic payments of less than $10,000 each, and, thus, he argues, he was not required to have a license.

Two of King's arguments are raised for the first time on appeal: King's argument that work done to the porch, "doggie doors," and fence should be considered separately from work performed on the house in calculating the total cost of the undertaking and his argument that he did not have sufficient control over the subcontractors and, thus, falls within an exemption to the licensing scheme. . . . Arguments not presented to the trial court are not proper arguments for appeal. . . . Accordingly, we consider all the work performed by King to be work performed on a house, which requires a license if the cost of the undertaking is greater than $10,000.

King argues that there remains a genuine issue of fact regarding whether the cost of the undertaking was more than $10,000. The Riedls note that King's admission that the costs of the undertaking exceeded $10,000 in his response to an interrogatory is in conflict with his affidavit filed in response to the Riedls' motion for a summary judgment. King's contradictory assertions in his response to an interrogatory and in his affidavit filed in response to the motion for a summary judgment do not create a genuine issue of a material fact regarding the cost of the undertaking. The Riedls' seventh interrogatory to King stated:

Regarding the contract alleged to have been breached by [the Riedls] within [King's] Complaint, provide the total amount to be paid for said work and services under the terms of said contract, including any and all estimated or fixed costs for materials provided.

King answered that the cost of the undertaking, under the terms of the contract, was "[i]n excess of $10,000.00." However, King submitted affidavit testimony in opposition to the motion for a summary judgment that stated that "at no time was I contracted to receive in excess of $10,000.00 as payment for my services." This contradiction cannot be used to create a genuine issue of material fact. . . .

King argues on appeal that payments made through him for the countertop and carpet were ultimately controlled by the Riedls. Contrary to his argument on appeal, however, the evidence submitted in support of and in opposition to the motion for a summary judgment does not indicate that King was hired to install carpet or to install the countertop. King produced no evidence indicating that the payments he received were intended to pay for either of those tasks, or for the materials involved in those tasks. The evidence indicates that King provided "turnkey" construction and supervision to the Riedls for an amount over $10,000.

The Riedls made periodic payments to King as he worked on the property, which, King contends, represent separate transactions. Thus, King argues, the contracted amount never exceeded $10,000. We have rejected this argument before, albeit in a case concerning a licensing statute pertaining to general contractors that is similar to § 34–14A–14. . . . "[A] contrary holding would encourage unscrupulous contractors to avoid the requirements of the licensing statute by designating payments to subcontractors and suppliers incident to 'separate contracts.' ". . . Similarly, allowing King to avoid licensure requirements by classifying a series of periodic payments as pertaining to separate contracts would render the residential home builder licensing statute meaningless. Thus, we conclude that there is no genuine issue of material fact on this issue and that the cost of the undertaking was over $10,000.

King violated § 34–14A–14 because he performed work, under his direct control and supervision, for more than $10,000. A residential home builder who fails to maintain a license with the Alabama Home Builders Licensure Board is statutorily barred from bringing or maintaining "any action to enforce the provisions of any contract for residential home building which he or she entered into in violation of this chapter." . . . King admitted that he was not a licensed residential home builder before, during, or after the construction work on the Riedls' house. Furthermore, the cost of the undertaking was more than $10,000. Therefore, King violated § 34–14A–14, and, thus, he has no standing to bring his breach-of-contract claim.

Summary Judgment affirmed in favor of the Reidls.

CRITICAL THINKING

When a judge or judicial panel makes a decision, the judge or panel must do so on the basis of the information available. What is an illustration of a fact that, were it true, would have caused this case to have provided King standing with respect to his breach-of-contract action? What fact was especially important in moving the decision in the direction of summary judgment?

ETHICAL DECISION MAKING

The statute spelling out the need for a residential home builder license has an exemption for small contracts. What stakeholders are being especially advantaged by the exemption?

Legal Principle: **If the licensing statute is intended simply to generate revenue, then the contract of an unlicensed person is valid; if the purpose of the licensing statute is to protect the public's health, safety, and welfare, however, the agreement of an unlicensed person is typically deemed illegal and unenforceable.**

Usury. Almost as widespread as licensing statutes, statutes prohibiting usury are found on the books of nearly every state. Usury occurs when a party gives a loan at an interest rate exceeding the legal maximum. The legal maximum interest rate varies from state to state, but it is easy to determine the rate of any given state.

While usury statutes act as a ceiling on rates, there are a few legal exceptions whereby loans may exceed the predetermined maximum. To facilitate business transactions and keep the economy healthy, for example, most states with usury statutes allow corporations willing to pay more to lend and borrow at rates exceeding the maximum. The rationale behind the corporation exception is that if a business needs money to expand and is willing to pay the higher interest rate, the corporation should be afforded the opportunity to borrow. The converse is that if a corporation is willing to borrow at a high interest rate, parties should be allowed to lend at that rate for corporations only. The intent is to facilitate business transactions in order to keep the economy in a healthy state.

Many states also allow parties to make small loans at rates above the maximum to parties that cannot obtain a needed loan at the statutory maximum. The belief is that if people need money and the statutory maximum is not inducing others to lend, certain parties will make the necessary loans at a higher rate as long as the loan is "small." This exception allows cash advance institutions to operate.

If no exception allows a usurious loan, the legal outcome varies by state. A few states declare all usurious loans void, which means the lender is not entitled to recover either interest or principal from the borrower. A larger number of states allow lenders to recover the principal but no interest. States most favorable toward lenders allow recovery of the principal as well as interest up to, but not exceeding, the statutory maximum.

Gambling. All states regulate gambling. As used in this chapter, the term gambling refers to agreements in which parties pay consideration (money placed during bets) for the chance, or opportunity, to obtain an amount of money or property. Industry officials, however, prefer to use the term *gaming.*

While gambling is illegal in most states, some allow casino gambling, notably Nevada, New Jersey, and Louisiana. Some allow certain other types of gambling, either intentionally or through legal loopholes. For example, given California's definition of gambling, betting on draw poker is legal. Some states make other exceptions, such as for horse tracks, casinos on Native American reservations, or state-run lotteries, which, although most people do not consider them to be such, are a form of gambling.

Sabbath days stem from the religious traditions that were so widespread in America's early days. Among the religions that still practice observing Sabbath days today is Judaism, which has very strict laws in relation to refraining from conducting business on the Sabbath. This prohibition even extends to the online realm. Not only are those of the Jewish faith told to abstain from conducting online transactions on the day of the Sabbath, but it is also prohibited to make transactions online on the Sabbath even if the individual in question has no awareness of doing so. For example, if an individual schedules to pay for an item when it ships and the item happens to be shipped on the day of the Sabbath, it is considered that the individual has broken Sabbath law. Laws against conducting certain types of business are still active even today, though they may not be rigidly enforced.

Source: http://belogski.blogspot.com/2008/03/must-your-online-shop-shut-on-shabbat.html.

Sabbath Laws.   A large number of states still have *Sabbath, Sunday,* or *blue* laws on the books. Sabbath laws limit the types of business activities in which parties can legally engage on Sundays. In Colonial times, these laws prohibited store operations and all work on the "Lord's day" (Sunday). Today these laws vary by state. Most prohibit the sale of all alcohol, or specific types, either all day or at particular times on Sundays. Some Sabbath laws also make it illegal to enter into any contract on a Sunday. However, an executed, or fully performed, contract created on a Sunday cannot be rescinded.

There are exceptions to Sabbath laws. Most states allow the performance of charity work on Sundays. In addition, the laws typically do not apply to contracts for obtaining "necessities," including prescription medication, food, and anything else related to health or survival.

Regardless of how widespread Sabbath laws are, the vast majority of states do not enforce some or all of their Sabbath laws. In fact, some have been held to violate the First Amendment. If they are on the books, however, they can be applied, and some states do apply them. Prudent businesspersons should always find out whether Sabbath laws exist in their state and whether authorities enforce them.

AGREEMENTS IN CONTRADICTION TO PUBLIC POLICY

Some types of agreements are not illegal per se, as they are not in violation of any statute or legal code, but are nevertheless unenforceable because courts have deemed them to be against public policy. Public policy involves both the government's concern for its citizens and the beliefs people hold regarding the proper subject of business transactions. The focus is what is "in society's best interest."

Contracts in Restraint of Trade.   It is a widely held belief in economics, and in U.S. culture in general, that competition drives down prices, which is good for consumers. Thus, agreements that restrain trade, called *anticompetitive agreements,* are viewed as being harmful to consumers and against public policy. They also frequently violate antitrust laws. See Chapter 47 for an in-depth discussion of antitrust law.

When courts determine a restraint on trade is reasonable, however, and the restraint is part of a subordinate, or ancillary, clause in the contract, the restraint is typically allowed. Such restraints are known as covenants not to compete, or *restrictive covenants.* There are two types.

The first enforceable type of restrictive covenant is one made in conjunction with the sale of an ongoing business. The public policy argument in favor of supporting restrictions regarding the sale of a business involves the fairness of the sale, as illustrated by the following hypothetical: Suppose you purchase a jewelry store from Ann, a well-respected member of the community, whose business has been around for many years. The people in the community know the store, and they trust Ann to provide fair exchanges. As a well-informed businessperson, you know about Ann's good reputation and it made the purchase more appealing.

Now suppose a month later Ann opens another jewelry store a block away. Ann's loyal customers are likely to go to her new store because they still trust her. In the meantime, Ann's good name is no longer associated with your store, and your business suffers accordingly. You entered into the sales agreement thinking you would benefit from Ann's good name, but in the end you overpaid for a business that lacks that benefit, because Ann took her name with her when she went into competition with your store. In the interest of fairness, courts are willing to impose restrictions preventing Ann, or others in her position, from going into immediate competition with you, or others in your position. Public policy requires fairness in business transactions, which does not occur when people profit from the sale of a business and then start a new business that destroys the one they just sold.

Remember, if the covenant not to compete is an integral part of the main agreement, not subordinate, the agreement is typically considered unenforceable and void, because it goes against public policy by creating unreasonable restraints on trade. When the covenant is subordinate, however, the specific noncompetition clause can be removed and the agreement can go forward as planned. In Case 16-2, the court had to determine the reasonableness of a covenant not to compete that was included in a separation agreement.

CASE 16-2   WILLIAM CAVANAUGH v. MARGARET McKENNA
SUPERIOR COURT OF MASSACHUSETTS, AT MIDDLESEX
22 MASS. L. REP. 694; 2007 MASS. SUPER. LEXIS 298

Defendant entered into a separation agreement with the plaintiff at the time of their divorce. The agreement provided in part that defendant would not accept full-time employment or open her own funeral business in Wilmington so long as the plaintiff maintained his funeral business. The trial court found that plaintiff had breached the agreement by competing with defendant by working for, and later owning, Nichols Funeral Home. On appeal, the defendant argued that the covenant not to compete was unenforceable as a restraint of trade that violated public policy.

JUSTICE SMITH: A covenant to not compete must be reasonable in time and scope, serve to protect a party's legitimate business interest, be supported by consideration, and be consonant with the public interest. . . . While most covenants not to compete arise either in the context of an employment relationship or the sale of a business, there are situations which do not "fit neatly into existing standards for reviewing such covenants" which require analogy. *Boulanger v. Dunkin' Donuts, Inc.,* . . . (2004) (finding covenant in franchise agreement akin to that of covenant in sale of business). With the sale of a business, "courts look less critically at covenants not to compete because they do not implicate an individual's right to employment to the same degree as in the employment context." . . . Courts will consider whether the parties were represented by counsel in making the agreement and entered the agreement without compulsion. . . .

The reasonableness of a covenant not to compete must be determined by the facts of each case. . . . Factors considered in determining the reasonableness of a restriction as to time include: 1) the nature of the business; 2) the type of employment involved; 3) the situation of the parties; 4) the legitimate business interests; and 5) a party's right to work and earn a livelihood. . . . Legitimate business interests include trade secrets, confidential business information, and good will. *Id.,* 779–80.

Here, the covenant not to compete contained within the separation agreement is most analogous to the sale of a business. While McKenna worked at Cavanaugh Funeral Home before her divorce, she was not considered to be an employee. Her relinquishment of the right to operate a competing funeral home is akin to her sale of an asset. As such, the covenant not to compete should be construed more liberally. Also important in this consideration is the fact that McKenna was represented by counsel when she agreed to the noncompete provision, and there is no allegation that she was in any way coerced.

The Court finds that her covenant not to compete in the funeral business in the town of Wilmington for as long as Cavanaugh operates his funeral home there is reasonable in time and space. The restriction only applies to the town of Wilmington. Nothing prevents McKenna from entering the funeral business in another town (in fact, she worked for a funeral business in the town of Newton previously). In addition, it is important to note that there are only two funeral homes in Wilmington, Cavanaugh's and Nichols Funeral Home, and the defendant's utilization of the personal relationships forged while working at the plaintiff's funeral home would, in effect, misappropriate the good will of the plaintiff's business.

As part of the separation agreement, Cavanaugh gave up his right to the marital home and assumed the mortgage, and, in the modification, agreed to make weekly support payments, obtaining protection for the good will of his business in return. Allowing McKenna to compete in the same town while soliciting his clientele can be expected to eviscerate the good will of his business, the protection of which he received in return for his contractual undertakings.

In these circumstances, the Court finds that her covenant not to compete is enforceable. . . . Accordingly, the Court grants summary judgment to the plaintiff on Count I, leaving the issue of damages for trial.

AFFIRMED in favor of Plaintiffs.

CRITICAL THINKING

Provide an example of a piece of evidence that the defendant could have provided to indicate the unreasonableness of the scope of the covenant in this case. How does your example weigh in comparison to the evidence provided to the contrary? Do you think it would or should be sufficient to change the conclusion of the court? Defend your answer.

ETHICAL DECISION MAKING

What values are in conflict in this case? Which are supported by the ruling, and which are not? How well can the ethical stance taken by the court in this area be defended, and what ethical guidelines might be used in the effort to do so?

Legal Principle: **Covenants not to compete in conjunction with the sale of a business are generally enforceable if they are for a reasonable length of time and involve a reasonable location.**

The second category of permissible restraints on trade is covenants not to compete in employment contracts. The employee is agreeing, in the event of her leaving, not to compete with her boss (by starting her own company or working for competitors) for a designated period of time within a designated geographic area. These covenants are not unusual. In fact, many middle or upper-level managers enter into them.

Covenants not to compete in employment contracts are legal in most states, but they must protect a legitimate business interest. They must also apply to a period of time and geographic area that are reasonable for that purpose and not unlawfully impinge on the employee's rights. Not surprisingly, the enforceability of covenants not to compete in employment contracts varies from state to state. California does not allow any covenants not to compete. Texas requires that the employee gain or be given a specific benefit beyond employment before its courts will enforce even a reasonable covenant not to compete.

Employers and employees may therefore attempt to file suit or have their cases heard in the location that can provide them with the most favorable legal environment given their situation. Thus, business owners who create covenants not to compete may prefer to file suit in a location that is more tolerant of covenants not to compete, and employees may wish to have their cases heard in a location, such as California, that generally prohibits the enforceability of covenants not to compete.

For example, when executive Kai-Fu Lee left his job with Microsoft to join rival Google, Microsoft filed suit in the state of Washington, alleging that Lee's decision was in violation of his noncompete contract. Google fought back by filing suit against Microsoft in California, the state where Google is based, saying that under California laws Lee's noncompete contract was unenforceable. Both companies fought one another in court to have the case heard in the state where one or the other had the best chance of winning. In the end, a district court judge ruled that the case would first be tried in Washington, and if Google wanted to pursue the case further in California, it could do so after the trial. Early decisions made by the judge in Washington state court seemed to fall in Microsoft's favor, and Lee was initially barred from doing certain tasks for Google until after the trial. However, before the trial could end, the two companies reached a private settlement agreement.[5]

Unconscionable Contracts or Clauses. When courts are asked to review contracts, fairness is not usually high on their list of things to look for. Instead, they typically assume that the contracting parties are intelligent, responsible adults who enter into contracts because they want to. Nevertheless, some agreements are so one-sided that the courts will not make the innocent party be harmed by fulfilling his or her contractual duties. These heavily one-sided agreements are known as unconscionable agreements. The term *unconscionable* refers to the fact that the agreement in question is so unfair that it is void of conscience.

The common law would not enforce contracts the courts deemed unconscionable. Now rules against unconscionable contracts exist in both the Restatement (Second) of Contracts and the Uniform Commercial Code. UCC Section 2-302 states:

> (1) If the court as a matter of law finds the contract or any clause of the contract to have been unconscionable at the time it was made, the court may refuse to enforce the contract, or it may enforce the remainder of the contract without the clause, or it may so limit the application of any unconscionable clause as to avoid any unconscionable result; (2) When it is claimed or appears to the court that the contract or any clause thereof may be unconscionable, the parties shall be afforded a reasonable opportunity to present evidence as to its commercial setting, purpose, and effect to aid the court in making the determination.

Every state except California and Louisiana has incorporated this section into its UCC. Section 208 of the Restatement also incorporates the above section.

There are two main types of unconscionable agreements, procedural and substantive. Procedural unconscionability describes conditions that impair one party's understanding of a contract, as well as the integration of terms into a contract. These conditions can be anything from tiny, hard-to-read print on the back of an agreement to excessive use of legalese (unnecessarily technical legal language) or even a person's inability to fully read a contract and ask questions before being required to sign.

Procedural unconscionability usually arises in an adhesion contract, an agreement presented on a take-it-or-leave-it basis or as the only chance the presented party (the *adhering party*) will have to enter into it. While adhesion contracts are legal, they do raise red flags for courts, which will try to determine how voluntary the agreement really was.

[5] http://news.cnet.com/Kai-Fu-Lees-California-case-put-on-hold/2100-1022_3-5918672.html; www.forbes.com/2005/12/23/gates-microsoft-google-cx_cn_1223autofacescan02.html; and http://news.cnet.com/Microsoft-sues-over-Google-hire/2100-1014_3-5795051.html.

Substantive unconscionability occurs when an agreement is overly harsh or lopsided. Courts would find the following, for example, to be substantively unconscionable: large differences between cost and price in a sales agreement; agreements in which one party gains vastly more than the other; agreements in which one party is prevented from having equal benefit or has little to no legal recourse; and portions of an agreement unrelated to either party's business risk.

Exculpatory Clauses.   An exculpatory clause releases one of the contracting parties from all liability, regardless of who is at fault or what injury is suffered. Because tort law attempts to return the wronged party to a state he or she was in before the wrong occurred, anything preventing this corrective mechanism is against public policy. It does not benefit society to allow some parties to get away with not having to pay for wrongs they commit simply because they state they will not be liable in various contracts. In fact, the patently unfair nature of an exculpatory clause is closely tied to the idea of unconscionable contracts.

Exculpatory clauses frequently show up in rental agreements for commercial or residential property. It does not serve the public's interest to allow landlords, especially of residential property, to disavow in advance all liabilities for injuries due to carelessness, negligence, or other wrongdoing. If they were allowed to do so, nothing would require them to fix problems in their rental units, including potentially lethal problems like faulty wiring or the presence of lead-based paint.

A basic test to determine whether an exculpatory clause is enforceable is to see whether the enforcing party engages in a business directly related to the public interest, as does a bank, transportation provider, or public utility. Courts believe it is against the public interest to allow businesses engaging in work in the public's interest *not* to be held accountable to the public they are serving.

Businesses serving the public interest can also possess unfair bargaining power in negotiating a contract; they could simply demand that all customers accept the exculpatory clause, thereby escaping all liability. Worse, there would then be no financial motive for them to conduct operations carefully, and the potential for increased accidents would be great. Obviously, it is not in the public's interest to have unsafe businesses not be accountable to the public. Thus, these businesses cannot enforce exculpatory clauses.

Case 16-3 details a court's determination that an illegal exculpatory clause existed.

CASE 16-3   ERIC LUCIER AND KAREN A. HALEY v. ANGELA AND JAMES WILLIAMS, CAMBRIDGE ASSOCIATES, LTD., AND AL VASYS

SUPERIOR COURT OF NEW JERSEY, APPELLATE DIVISION
841 A.2D 907 (2004)

Eric Lucier and Karen A. Haley, a young married couple, were first-time home buyers. They contracted with the Williamses to purchase a single-family residence. Lucier and Haley engaged the services of Cambridge Associates, Ltd. (CAL), to perform a home inspection. Al Vasys had formed CAL and was its president. Lucier dealt directly with Vasys, and Vasys performed the inspection and issued the home inspection report on behalf of CAL.

The home inspection agreement contains a provision limiting CAL's liability to "$500, or 50% of fees actually paid to CAL by Client, whichever sum is smaller." This provision,

like several others in the form agreement prepared by CAL, was followed by a line for the clients' initials. Lucier initialed this provision. The fee for the home inspection contract was $385, which Lucier paid to CAL.

Lucier claims when he began to read the agreement, in Vasys' presence, he felt some of the language was unfair and confusing. According to Lucier, Vasys stated he would not change any provisions, that it was a standard contract based upon home inspections done in New Jersey, and Lucier would have to sign the agreement "as is" or not at all. Vasys does not dispute this but relies upon Lucier's signing the agreement and initialing the limitation of liability clause. Likewise, Lucier does not deny signing the contract or initialing that clause.

Lucier and Haley obtained title to the property from the Williamses. Shortly after, they noticed leaks in the house. They engaged the services of a roofing contractor and found the roof was defective. Lucier and Haley argue Vasys should have observed and reported the problem to them. The cost of repair was about $8,000 to $10,000.

Lucier and Haley brought suit against the Williamses, CAL, and Vasys, seeking damages to compensate them for the loss occasioned by the alleged defect. CAL and Vasys moved for partial summary judgment seeking a declaration that the limit of their liability in the action, if any, was one-half the contract price, or $192.50. The motion for partial summary judgment was granted. Lucier and Haley then filed this appeal, seeking review of the partial summary judgment order.

JUDGE LISA: There is no hard and fast definition of unconscionability. As the Supreme Court explained in *Kugler v. Romain,* unconscionability is "an amorphous concept obviously designed to establish a broad business ethic." The standard of conduct that the term implies is a lack of "good faith, honesty in fact and observance of fair dealing."

In determining whether to enforce the terms of a contract, we look not only to its adhesive nature, but also to "the subject matter of the contract, the parties' relative bargaining positions, the degree of economic compulsion motivating the 'adhering' party, and the public interests affected by the contract." Where the provision limits a party's liability, we pay particular attention to any inequality in the bargaining power and status of the parties, as well as the substance of the contract.

We also focus our inquiry on whether the limitation is a reasonable allocation of risk between the parties or whether it runs afoul of the public policy disfavoring clauses which effectively immunize parties from liability for their own negligent actions. To be enforceable, the amount of the cap on a party's liability must be sufficient to provide a realistic incentive to act diligently.

Applying these principles to the home inspection contract before us, we find the limitation of liability provision unconscionable. We do not hesitate to hold it unenforceable for the following reasons: (1) the contract, prepared by the home inspector, is one of adhesion; (2) the parties, one a consumer and the other a professional expert, have grossly unequal bargaining status; and (3) the substance of the provision eviscerates the contract and its fundamental purpose because the potential damage level is so nominal that it has the practical effect of avoiding almost all responsibility for the professional's negligence. Additionally, the provision is contrary to our state's public policy of effectuating the purpose of a home inspection contract to render reliable evaluation of a home's fitness for purchase and holding professionals to certain industry standards.

This is a classic contract of adhesion. There were no negotiations leading up to its preparation. The contract was presented to Lucier on a standardized preprinted form, prepared by CAL, on a take-it-or-leave-it basis, without any opportunity for him to negotiate or modify any of its terms.

The bargaining position between the parties was grossly disparate. Vasys has been in the home inspection business for twenty years. He has inspected thousands of homes. He has an engineering degree. He has served as an expert witness in construction matters. He holds various designations in the building and construction field. He advertises his company and holds it and himself out as possessing expertise in the home inspection field. Lucier and Haley, on the other hand, are unknowledgeable and unsophisticated in matters of home construction. They are consumers. They placed their trust in this expert. They had every reason to expect he would act with diligence and competence in inspecting the home they desired to purchase and discover and report major defects. The disparity in the positions of these parties is clear and substantial.

The foisting of a contract of this type in this setting on an inexperienced consumer clearly demonstrates a lack of fair dealing by the professional. The cost of homes in New Jersey is substantial.

The limitation of liability clause here is also against public policy. First, it allows the home inspector to circumvent the state's public policy of holding professional service providers to certain industry standards. Second, it contravenes the stated public policy of New Jersey regarding home inspectors.

With professional services, exculpation clauses are particularly disfavored. The very nature of a professional service is one in which the person receiving the service relies upon the expertise, training, knowledge and stature of the professional. Exculpation provisions are antithetical to such a relationship.

In summary, the limitation of liability provision in this contract is unconscionable and violates the public policy of our State. The contract is one of adhesion, the bargaining power of the parties is unequal, the impact of the liability clause is negligible to the home inspector while potentially severe to the home buyer, and the provision conflicts with the purpose of home inspection contracts and our Legislature's requirement of accountability by home inspectors for their errors and omissions.

REVERSED and REMANDED.

CRITICAL THINKING

In this decision, does Judge Lisa make any assumptions regarding the facts of the case without proper evidence to support them as a reasoning step? For instance, what evidence supports her characterization of Lucier? Is it possible he is significantly different from the way he has been presented? How might such differences affect the acceptability of the conclusion? Can you locate any other assumptions in this ruling? How do they affect the reasoning?

ETHICAL DECISION MAKING

Examine the actions of each party leading up to this dispute. Who behaved in a blameworthy fashion, and who in a praiseworthy fashion? What facts from the case and what ethical theories or guidelines support your claim?

Now consider each party's stance in the legal dispute. Does either one appear more or less ethical, relative to that party's earlier actions? Why or why not?

While businesses closely linked to the public interest cannot enforce exculpatory clauses, not all such clauses are unlawful. To prevail, the party seeking enforcement must be a private business or individual *not* important to the public interest. These private businesses or individuals provide nonessential services and thus do not have the same bargaining power as the previously discussed groups, such as banks, utilities, or airlines. Given their lack of huge bargaining power, courts assume such businesses and individuals will enter a contract voluntarily and on relatively equal terms.

Private businesses that *can* enforce exculpatory clauses thus include skiing facilities such as resorts or rental places, private gyms or health clubs, any business offering sky diving or bungee jumping, and amusement parks, to name a few. Because their services and those of others in this category are not related to the public interest and are not activities in which people *must* engage, these parties are allowed to deny liability if the other party agrees to the exculpatory clause. Just because these parties *might* be able to enforce an exculpatory clause, however, does not mean the clause is always automatically enforceable.

EFFECT OF ILLEGAL AGREEMENTS

When an agreement is deemed illegal, courts will usually label it void. The reason is the legal principle of *in pari delicto,* which means both parties are equally responsible for the illegal agreement. In that case, it does not make sense for the courts to attempt to salvage the agreement or reward either party. Therefore, neither party can enforce the agreement, and neither is entitled to recovery.

But what if both parties are *not* at fault? What if one is significantly more culpable? Then it sometimes makes sense to allow one party to an illegal agreement to recover various damages.

The first exception to the general rule occurs when a member of a protected class is party to an agreement that contradicts a statute intended to protect the specific class. That party is allowed to sue for performance. The reasoning is that a statute intended to protect a specific class should not be allowed to harm those in the class.

For example, a work agreement between Diego and his employer may specify that Diego gets paid for the number of hours he works as a truck driver. Yet certain statutes limit the number of hours truck drivers may drive in a given time period. If Diego accidentally drives more than the allowable hours, he has technically violated a statute. However, this violation does not allow his employer to refuse to pay him for the extra hours. Rather, Diego may sue his employer to enforce the work agreement.

The second exception to the voiding of illegal agreements occurs when *justifiable ignorance of facts* leaves one party unaware of a provision of the agreement that would

DETERMINING THE LEGALITY OF AN ARBITRATION CLAUSE

Buckeye Check Cashing, Inc. v. Cardegna et al.
United States Supreme Court
126 S. Ct. 1204, 163 L. Ed. 2d 1038 (2006)

The respondents, Cardegna et al., entered into a number of deferred-payment transactions with Buckeye Check Cashing. Each agreement they signed contained a provision requiring binding arbitration to resolve disputes arising out of the agreement. The respondents filed a class action suit against Buckeye in Florida state court, alleging that Buckeye charged usurious interest rates and that the agreement violated various Florida laws, rendering it illegal on its face. The trial court denied Buckeye's motion to compel arbitration, holding that a court rather than an arbitrator should resolve a claim that a contract is illegal and void *ab initio*. A state appellate court reversed, but its decision was in turn reversed by the Florida Supreme Court, which reasoned that enforcing an arbitration agreement in a contract challenged as unlawful would violate state public policy and contract law. The case was appealed to the U.S. Supreme Court to determine whether the courts or an arbitrator should determine the legality of a potentially illegal contract containing a binding arbitration clause.

The Court answered this question by relying on three established propositions. First, as a matter of substantive federal arbitration law, an arbitration provision is severable from the remainder of the contract. Second, unless the challenge is to the arbitration clause itself, the issue of the contract's validity is considered by the arbitrator in the first instance. Third, this arbitration law applies in state as well as federal courts. Applying these propositions to the case, the high court concluded that when an agreement as a whole, but not specifically its arbitration provisions, is challenged, the arbitration provisions are enforceable apart from the remainder of the contract. The challenge to the legality of the contract itself should therefore be considered by an arbitrator, not a court.

make it illegal. While ignorance of the law does not excuse illegal behavior, not knowing that the other party intended to fulfill the agreement through illegal means does function as an excuse.

When one party is relatively innocent, the court may give back any consideration that party gave or may require exchange for partial performance such that both parties can be returned to the positions they were in before they entered into the agreement. If one party is completely innocent of any illegality and has completed his or her portion of the contract, then—depending on the reason the contract is considered illegal and which state's laws are in question—the court might enforce the entire agreement.

A third exception to the general rule occurs when one of the parties withdraws from an illegal agreement. The key to any recovery is that the party must have withdrawn before any illegality occurred. The party may then recover value for whatever partial or full performance has been completed. However, a party involved in the illegal activity in any way cannot recover at all.

Severable Contracts.

Severable contracts, also known as *divisible contracts,* contain multiple parts that can each be performed separately and for which separate consideration is offered. In essence, a severable contract

What happened to you?!?!

stus.com

The court severed my illegal provision. Man, it hurts.

is like numerous contracts in one. An indivisible contract, on the other hand, requires complete performance by both parties, even if it appears to contain multiple parts.

With respect to illegality, severable contracts have a huge advantage: If they have both legal and illegal portions, the court can void only the illegal sections and enforce the rest as long as they represent the main purpose of the original agreement. Indivisible contracts must be enforced or rejected in their entirety. If declaring parts of a contract void substantially alters it, the court is not likely to enforce the remaining portions. Courts ultimately want to facilitate business transactions and enforce the legal wishes of parties, and severable contracts enable them to do so.

Legal Principle: **If the court can sever the illegal part of a contract from the legal part, it will generally do so and enforce only the legal part; if the contract is indivisible, then it generally will be unenforceable.**

CASE OPENER WRAP-UP

Apple's Questionable Contract

The U.S. District Court for the Northern District of California denied Apple's motion to dismiss the lawsuit. The court stated that the complaint could not be dismissed because no case law was provided to prove that Apple's Terms of Service served as a contract for all subsequent transactions. Apple then constructed a settlement with all the plaintiffs in the class action lawsuit that had to be court-approved.

First, Apple would have to immediately send notices to 23 million customers with iTunes accounts, notifying the customers of parental controls that can block extra purchases. Second, customers in the lawsuit were to receive a $5 credit for use at the iTunes store. Customers whose children spent $30 or more would be entitled to a cash refund instead of credits. Finally, Apple would pay $1.3 million in attorney fees.

KEY TERMS

adhesion contract 375	exculpatory clause 376	procedural unconscionability 375	substantive unconscionability 376
capacity 361	gambling 371	Sabbath laws 372	unconscionable 375
covenants not to compete 372	*in pari delicto* 378	severable contracts 379	usury 371
	indivisible contract 380		

SUMMARY OF KEY TOPICS

Capacity

Natural persons over the age of majority are presumed to have the full legal capacity to enter into binding legal contracts.

A person has only limited capacity to enter into a legally binding contract, and therefore can enter into only voidable contracts, if the person is either:

- A minor.
- Suffering from a mental deficiency that prevents the person from understanding the nature and obligations of contracts.
- Intoxicated.

A person has no capacity to enter into a contract if the person either:

- Has been adjudicated insane.
- Has been adjudicated a habitual drunkard.
- Has had a legal guardian appointed to enter into contracts on his or her behalf.

Necessaries: Even if a party has the ability to disaffirm a contract, if the contract is for a necessary—something like food, clothing, or shelter—the party cannot completely disaffirm the contract; she will be held liable for the reasonable value of the necessary.

Legality

Contracts that do not have a legal object are not valid.

Contracts that lack a legal object because they violate a statute or violate public policy are not valid.

When a contract is partly legal and partly illegal, if the illegal part can be severed, then the legal part will still be enforced, but if the contract is indivisible, it will be void and not enforced.

POINT / COUNTERPOINT

Should the Age at Which Minors Have Full Capacity to Enter into Binding Contracts Be Lowered to 16?	
YES	**NO**
Given the rights and responsibilities currently granted to 16-year-olds, lowering the age at which minors can enter into legally binding contracts seems logical.	Under the law, teenagers are not viewed as adults until they have reached the age of majority. In nearly every state, the age of majority is at least 18. The age at which teenagers can enter into binding contracts should *not* be lower than the age of majority.
One of the most widely argued reasons given against lowering the age requirement pertains to a teenager's ability to fully understand a contract and comprehend the consequences associated with it. In response, proponents argue that society has already given children responsibilities and rights that are associated with long-term consequences; 16-year-olds are viewed, in the eyes of the law, as being able to consent to a sexual relationship. Along with this right comes the responsibility of understanding the potential for pregnancy and/or disease (which are *extremely* long-term consequences).	At the age of 16, teenagers are still in the process of completing high school. They have not taken courses in financial management and have not been adequately introduced to contracts through life experiences. As such, these youths lack the ability to fully understand or comprehend the nature of or consequences associated with entering into contracts.

Perhaps as a result of their ability to consent to sexual relationships, 16-year-olds are often able to marry if the female is pregnant. Marriage is, by definition, a contract. These teenagers are already able, albeit in a limited fashion, to enter into binding contracts.

Furthermore, at the age of 16, a teenager can request a work permit and begin employment. As a result of this employment, the teenager is able to earn an income and make purchases. By maintaining the current age at which teenagers are seen as having the legal capacity to enter into a contract, society is, in effect, limiting the teenager's ability to make transactions he or she would otherwise be able to make. This limitation not only restricts teenagers' freedoms but also reduces commerce in this country. Society *should* lower the age requirement to 16.

Additionally, at the age of 16, nearly all teenagers are still residing within the home of a parent and/or guardian. Parents are held liable for many actions and decisions of their children. To cite but one potential example, if a child under the age of majority entered into a cell phone contract and was eventually unable to pay the related bills, it is possible that under parental liability law the parents will be held responsible for the funds owed. In short, society could prevent this undue burden from being placed on parents by keeping the age at which youths have the capacity to enter into contracts equal to, or greater than, the age of majority. Parents should have the ability to decide whether or not they wish to sign a contract on their child's behalf if it is potentially they who will ultimately be held responsible.

QUESTIONS & PROBLEMS

1. How does the concept of the age of majority differ in Great Britain from that in the United States?

2. Explain the obligations of a minor who chooses to disaffirm a contract.

3. Go back to the discussion of contracts that cannot be disaffirmed by minors, and explain the policy reasons that support each of the exceptions. Can you make an argument for any additional kinds of contracts that should not be subject to disaffirmance by minors?

4. If all you know about a man is that his neighbors think he is crazy, you do not know whether the contract he entered into was valid, voidable, or void. Why not?

5. What factors determine whether a covenant not to compete is legal or illegal?

6. What is the relationship between contracts in restraint of trade and unconscionable contracts?

7. Three salesmen worked for Sentient Jet, a small luxury airline charter service. They signed a noncompete agreement, promising to not go to work for a competing employer within a year after working for Sentient and also agreeing to not take any confidential information with them when they left the firm. When there was a change in the CEO of their firm, and talk of the company's possibly being bought out, the employees left the firm and went to work for Apollo Jets, a competitor, and allegedly took proprietary information with them that allowed them to solicit former Sentient clients. The plaintiff sought an injunction to ban the employees from working for a competitor for a year and also sought damages. The defendants argued that material changes in circumstances should have made the agreement not to compete unenforceable. How do

you think the jury decided in this case? [*Sentient Jet v. MacKenzie,* Massachusetts Superior Court, January 2013 non-reported case. Discussed at http://www.hrwlawyers.com/pdfs/MLW-Non-Compete-Article-1-21-2013-(A121154).pdf.]

8. Paul Stewart and Ellen Chalk bought a wireless LAN PC card, manufactured by Sony, to connect wirelessly to the Internet through service provided by T-Mobile. Stewart and Chalk also signed a one-year service agreement with T-Mobile. The service agreement mandated arbitration and prohibited class action lawsuits. For approximately three weeks after the purchase of the card, Stewart and Chalk were able to insert it into their IBM ThinkPad laptop and connect to the Internet without any difficulty. They then did not attempt to use the card again for a few months, at which time they were unable to insert the card into their ThinkPad. They contacted T-Mobile technical support several times and received refurbished cards on three separate occasions. None of the refurbished cards fit into the ThinkPad. After Stewart and Chalk were unable to insert the third card, staff from T-Mobile technical support informed them that they would have to pursue the issue at the T-Mobile store where they purchased the original card. At the store, a Sony representative attempted to insert the card, but he failed as well. He then promised to contact them about how to solve the problem. They never heard back from him, despite multiple e-mail inquiries.

Ultimately, Stewart and Chalk filed a class action lawsuit against T-Mobile and Sony. The complaint alleged that Sony and T-Mobile knew or should have known that the card "was not compatible and/or did not fit into the IBM ThinkPad laptop" computers and that Sony and T-Mobile allowed customers to purchase cards and enter into long-term service contracts from which consumers would receive no benefit without a compatible card. Sony and T-Mobile filed a motion to compel arbitration. Stewart and Chalk opposed the motion, contending that the arbitration clause was unconscionable and therefore unenforceable. The district court ruled in favor of Sony and T-Mobile. Stewart and Chalk appealed. Is the arbitration agreement unconscionable? If you were an attorney for Stewart and Chalk, would you argue that the arbitration clause was procedurally unconscionable, substantively unconscionable, or both? Why? [*Chalk v. T-Mobile, USA, Inc.,* 560 F.3d 1087 (2009).]

9. Washington State resident Patty Gandee entered into a debt adjustment contract with Freedom Enterprises. She subsequently sought to file a class action against Freedom for violations of the state debt adjusting act and the Consumer Protection Act. The company sought to compel arbitration based on a binding arbitration clause she had signed. The clause provided that any disputes under the contract were to be submitted to arbitration that would take place in Orange County, California, under American Arbitration Association rules, and the prevailing party would be entitled to reasonable legal fees and costs, including attorney fees. Both the trial court and the Washington Supreme Court refused to enforce the binding arbitration clause. Explain why they would not enforce the clause. [*Patty J. Gandee v. LDL Freedom Enterprises,* Case No. 87674-6 (Wash. Sup. Ct., Feb. 7, 2013) (available at http://lawyersusaonline.com/wp-files/pdfs-5/gandee-v-ldl-freedom-enterprises.pdf).]

10. The Finches hired Inspectech to perform a home inspection of property they were purchasing. The contract they signed included a clause that read:

It is understood and agreed that the COMPANY [Inspectech] is not an insurer and that the inspection and report are not intended to be construed as a guarantee or warranty of the adequacy, performance or condition of any structure, item or system at the property address. The CLIENT [the Finches] hereby releases and exempts the COMPANY and its agents and employees of and from all liability and responsibility for the cost of repairing or replacing any unreported defect or deficiency and for any consequential damage, property damage or personal injury of any nature. In the event the COMPANY and/or its agents or employees are found liable due to breach of contract, breach of warranty, negligence, negligent misrepresentation, negligent hiring or any other theory of liability, then the liability of the COMPANY and its agents and employees shall be limited to a sum equal to the amount of the fee paid by the CLIENT for the inspection and report.

After the inspection, which reported no significant defects, the Finches purchased the house. Within one week of closing, the Finches discovered water damage; prior repairs to correct the water damage; and water infiltration in the basement of their new home, as well as structural problems affecting the house's foundation. The Finches alleged that these defects were not obviously visible because of the location of a workbench owned by the sellers. They sued to recover the $39,000 they had to spend to repair the water and structural damage.

On the basis of the contractual language, the circuit court awarded summary judgment to Inspectech, concluding that the release prohibited the Finches from asserting their claims against Inspectech for damages they claimed were occasioned by Inspectech's failure to identify and disclose various defects in their new home. The court concluded that the clause was unambiguous and conspicuously placed in the contract and that the Finches had specifically agreed to its terms and its inclusion in the parties' Inspection Agreement contract. On what grounds do you think the West Virginia Supreme Court overturned the granting of summary judgment to Inspectech? [*David Finch and Shirley Finch v. Inspectech, LLC,* Case No. 11-0278 (W. Va. Sup. Ct. App., May 24, 2012) (available at http://lawyersusaonline.com/wp-files/pdfs-4/finch-v-inspectech.pdf).]

Looking for more review materials?

The Online Learning Center at **www.mhhe.com/kubasek3e** contains this chapter's "Assignment on the Internet" and also a list of URLs for more information, entitled "On the Internet." Find both of them in the Student Center portion of the OLC, along with quizzes and other helpful materials.

CHAPTER

17 Legal Assent

LEARNING OBJECTIVES

After reading this chapter, you will be able to answer the following questions:

1 Why is legal assent important?

2 What are the elements of mistake?

3 What are the elements of misrepresentation?

4 What are the elements of undue influence?

5 What are the elements of duress?

6 What are the elements of unconscionability?

CASE OPENER

A Disagreement over an Agreement

In spring 1989, Michael Jordan and the Chicago Bulls were in Indianapolis, Indiana, to play against the Indiana Pacers. At the same time, Karla Knafel was singing with a band at a hotel in Indianapolis. After Knafel's performance, a National Basketball Association referee approached her and introduced her to Jordan via telephone. Knafel and Jordan began a long-distance telephone relationship that continued for several months.

In December 1989, Knafel traveled to Chicago to meet with Jordan, where the couple had unprotected sex for the first time. In November 1990, the couple had unprotected sex again while in Phoenix, Arizona. Shortly after this second meeting, Knafel learned that she was pregnant. Knafel was "convinced that she was carrying Jordan's baby" despite having had sex with other male partners. Later, during spring 1991, Knafel informed Jordan "she was pregnant with his child."

As a result of several conversations about the baby, Knafel alleged that the two had agreed that Jordan would pay her $5 million when he retired from professional basketball. In return, Knafel promised she would not file a paternity suit against him and would keep their relationship a secret.

In July 1991, the baby was born. Jordan paid some hospital bills and medical costs, and he paid Knafel $250,000 for "her mental pain and anguish arising from her relationship with him." Knafel continued to keep the relationship and paternity a secret.

After Jordan retired from professional basketball, a lawsuit arose between the parties in 2000. Jordan sought declaratory judgment and an injunction against Knafel, who had been approaching him for the $5 million. Knafel filed a counterclaim for Jordan's alleged breach of contract. The trial court dismissed all claims, but the appellate court remanded Knafel's claim for breach of contract. Although Jordan had originally denied the existence of the agreement, on remand he did not contest the existence of the alleged settlement agreement. Instead, Jordan argued that the alleged agreement was not enforceable because it either was fraudulently induced or was based on a mutual mistake of fact. In support of his argument, Jordan produced the affidavit of Dr. Storm, who, after DNA testing, concluded that Jordan was not the child's father.

In response to Jordan's argument, Knafel claimed that the paternity of the child was irrelevant to the enforceability of the alleged agreement. An obstetrician had told Knafel that the baby was conceived on November 19 or 20, 1990 (while she was in Phoenix with Jordan). As a result of this information, Knafel believed that the baby was Jordan's. Additionally, Knafel asserted that the paternity was irrelevant because Jordan entered into the agreement knowing that she had been having sex with other men.

The trial court ruled in favor of Jordan, finding that "as a result of Knafel's fraudulent misrepresentation to Jordan that he was the child's father or, alternatively, as a result of a mutual mistake of fact, the alleged settlement contract is voidable and is therefore unenforceable against Jordan." Knafel appealed.

1. Imagine you are the judge in this case. Do you think that both parties were able to legally assent to the agreement?

2. Under which ethical system, if any, should Knafel be able to recover the $5 million for breach of contract?

The Wrap-Up at the end of the chapter will answer these questions.

The Importance of Legal Assent

L01

Why is legal assent important?

When two people talk in the hope that an exchange will take place between them, all kinds of things can go wrong. Yet global business needs dependability. Imagine what transactions would be like if "Yes" meant "Maybe"! Deals would be closed only to be reopened again and again. The costs of all purchases would soar. Businesses would be forced to charge extra to pay for all the extra time they had to spend to finally get to the point where "Yes" really meant "Yes."

To make business transactions smoother and more dependable, courts have developed rules about when an assent to do something is a legal assent, that is, a promise the courts will require the parties to obey.

The courts see some forms of assent as more genuine or real than others. It is important for businesspeople to know the differences among the various kinds of assent. Why do the differences matter? Jamal may think he has sold his tutoring services to Harrison. However, without legal assent the contract may be voidable, a circumstance that can cost a business large profits when the transaction is significant. A voidable contract can be rescinded, or canceled, permitting the person who canceled the contract to require the return of everything she gave the other party. She must herself return whatever she has received. An enormous waste of time and an unnecessary cost of doing business may be the result.

The major theme of this chapter is that *best-practice firms aim for legal assent in their contracts*. This chapter shows you how to achieve legal assent. It explains the major obstacles to legal assent: mistake, misrepresentation, undue influence, duress, and unconscionability. By knowing about these potential problems, you will be in a good position to avoid them.

Mistake

L02

What are the elements of mistake?

When people agree to buy or sell, they do so with a particular understanding about the nature of the good or service they are about to exchange. However, one or both parties may think they consented to exchange a particular thing only to find out later that no meeting of the minds had occurred. People may misunderstand either some fact about the deal or the value of what is being exchanged. We focus on misunderstandings about facts, because they are the only issues that raise the potential of rescission (the rescinding of a contract) in U.S. courts. Mistaken beliefs about the subjective value of an item do not affect the validity of the contract.

In contract law a mistake of fact is an erroneous belief about the facts of the contract *at the time the contract is concluded.* Legal assent is absent when a mistake of fact occurs. Later in this chapter, when we discuss misrepresentation, our focus will be on incorrect beliefs about the facts of the contract caused by the other party's untrue statements. Mistakes in contract law do *not* result from these untrue statements.

Mistakes can be unilateral, the result of an error by *one* party about a material fact, that is, a fact that is important in the context of the particular contract. Or mistakes can be mutual, shared by both parties to the agreement. As we see next, this distinction is important in determining which contracts are voidable.

The insurance companies are fighting about "mutual mistake." I thought they were talking about the accident, but it's actually about the wording of the insurance documents.

stus.com

THE EUROPEAN VIEW ABOUT MISTAKES ABOUT VALUE

European courts take a different approach to mistakes about the *value of performance* of the contract. In general, they agree with the reluctance of U.S. courts to interfere with a contract just because the value of the item in question has changed since the agreement. The parties are assumed to have accepted the risk that the value might change after they made the contract. However, European courts permit rescission of the contract for a mistake of value when the mistake involves more than 50 percent of the value at the time of the contract.

UNILATERAL MISTAKE

Because courts are hesitant to interfere when one of the parties has a correct understanding of the material facts of the agreement, a unilateral mistake does not generally void a contract. For instance, a widow seeking to rescind her and her husband's election to have his retirement benefits paid out over *his* life was not permitted to receive survivor's pension benefits. The court held that representatives of the retirement system had provided sufficient information to the plaintiff and her husband before they elected that particular form of payout.[1] The Case Nugget on the next page provides another illustration of a failed attempt to argue that a unilateral mistake was present.

On rare occasions, however, rescission *is* permitted for unilateral mistakes. Because our economic well-being depends so heavily on reliable contracts, we want to be fully aware of the circumstances under which unilateral mistakes permit rescission. Any of the following conditions would permit a court to invalidate a contract on grounds of unilateral mistake:

1. One party made a mistake about a material fact, and the other party knew or had reason to know about the mistake.

2. The mistake was caused by a clerical error that was accidental and did not result from gross negligence.

3. The mistake was so serious that the contract is unconscionable, that is, so unreasonable that it is outrageous.

These situations are rare, but it is important to be aware of them because any rescission can be costly in terms of time and lost opportunities.

MUTUAL MISTAKE

When both parties are mistaken about a current or past material fact, either can choose to rescind the contract. Rescission is fair because any agreement was an illusion: Ambiguity prevented a true meeting of the minds.

The famous story of the ship *Peerless*[2] has taught generations of students the importance of being very clear in defining material facts in any contract. The parties in the case had agreed that the vessel *Peerless* would deliver the cotton they were exchanging. Unfortunately for them, there were two ships named *Peerless*. So when the deal was made, one party had one *Peerless* in mind while the other meant the second. The times the ships sailed were materially different, so the court rescinded the contract. *Warning:* Anticipate ambiguity in material facts, and clarify them in advance to save yourself headaches later.

[1] *Ricks v. Missouri Local Government Employees Retirement System,* 1999 WL 663217 (Mo. App. WD).
[2] *Raffles v. Wichelhaus,* 159 Eng. Rep. 375 (1864).

Mary W. Scott (Respondent-Appellant) v. Mid-Carolina Homes, Inc. (Appellant-Respondent)
Court of Appeals of South Carolina
293 S.C. 191 (1987)

Mary Scott signed a contract to purchase a repossessed 1984 mobile home from Mid-Carolina Homes, Inc., for $5,644 to be paid in full before delivery. Scott gave the salesperson a check for $2,913.71, and agreed to pay the balance before the end of the month. Within the next week, the salesman called Scott and told her that according to the standards of the South Carolina Manufactured Housing Board he could not sell her the home because it had a bent frame. Scott offered to buy it as is and sign a waiver, but the salesman said that would not be legal. A few weeks later, Mid-Carolina sold the mobile home to another couple for $9,220. Scott sued and was awarded $3,600 actual damages, $6,400 punitive

damages for breach of contract accompanied by a fraudulent act, and $3,000 actual damages for violation of a state consumer protection law. The appeals court upheld the award.

On appeal, Mid-Carolina argued that it was entitled to rescind the contract because the salesperson was acting under a mistake of fact when he gave Scott the sales price. In upholding the award, the state supreme court explained that a contract may be rescinded for unilateral mistake only when the mistake has been induced by fraud, deceit, misrepresentation, concealment, or imposition of the party opposed to the rescission, without negligence on the part of the party claiming rescission, or when the mistake is accompanied by very strong and extraordinary circumstances that would make it a great wrong to enforce the agreement. Mid-Carolina had not demonstrated the presence of any of these. The salesperson was in the superior bargaining position to know the price, and the buyer's reliance on a salesperson's representation of the price was reasonable.

For a mutual mistake to interfere with legal consent, all the following must be present:

1. A basic assumption about the subject matter of the contract.
2. A material effect on the agreement.
3. An adverse effect on a party who did not agree to bear the risk of mistake at the time of the agreement.

Courts will not void contracts for reason of mutual mistake if even one of these conditions is missing. (See Exhibit 17-1.) Let's see why they matter.

To rise to the level of a basic assumption, a mistake must be about the existence, quality, or quantity of the items to be exchanged. To be material, condition 2, the mistake must affect the essence of the agreement. A fact is material when it provides a basis for a person's agreeing to enter into the contract. Neither party can void the contract simply by falsely claiming that the item to be exchanged is not the one he intended.

The third condition protects those who bargain with someone who agreed, at the time of the agreement, to bear the risk of mistake but then later wishes to avoid that risk when the contract does not work out as well as he or she had planned. This situation might arise, for instance, if the adversely affected party had agreed in the contract to accept items "as is" but later felt they were not worth the price paid. In the opening scenario, had Jordan agreed to pay Knafel the $5 million regardless of the outcome of any future paternity tests, the

Exhibit 17-1

Enforceability of a Mutual Mistake

Before a contract can be voided for a mutual mistake, you must answer each of the following questions with a yes:

1. Is the mistake about a basic assumption that affects the subject matter of the contract?
2. Does the mistake have a material effect on the agreement?
3. Would enforcement of the contract have an adverse effect on the party who did not agree to bear the risk of mistake at the time of the agreement?

outcome of the case would have been very different. Instead, Jordan had allegedly agreed to pay Knafel the money on the basis of misinformation that the child was definitely his. Upon learning that the child was not his, Jordan wanted to have the contract rescinded on the basis, partly, of the mutual mistake made between himself and Knafel. Case 17-1 provides an illustration of an unsuccessful attempt to avoid a contract on the basis of mutual mistake.

CASE 17-1   SIMKIN v. BLANK
COURT OF APPEALS OF NEW YORK
19 N.Y.3D 46 (2012)

When Steven Simkin and Laura Blank divorced in 2006, they split their $13.5 million in assets. Most of Simkin's $5.4 million share of the settlement was invested in Bernie Madoff's Ponzi scheme, whereas Blank received a cash settlement. Then, in 2008, Simkin thought the terms of the divorce contract should be renegotiated because he lost almost all of his divorce proceeds when it came to light that his investment in Madoff's business turned out to be a fraud and Madoff's business turned out to be a huge Ponzi scheme. Simkin argued that both he and his ex-wife had shared in the mistake of investing funds into Madoff's project, yet only Simkin received the invested funds in the divorce settlement and Blank received cash. Simkin also argued that because his funds never existed as an "investment" as they had already vanished in the Ponzi scheme, he never really received an equal share of their existing assets. Thus, he asked Ms. Blank if the two could renegotiate the contract. When she refused, he sued. A lower court granted Simkin the right to sue, but the case moved on to the Court of Appeals of New York.

JUDGE GRAFFEO: Marital settlement agreements are judicially favored and are not to be easily set aside. Nevertheless, in the proper case, an agreement may be subject to rescission or reformation based on a mutual mistake by the parties. Similarly, a release of claims may be avoided due to mutual mistake. Based on these contract principles, the parties here agree that this appeal turns on whether husband's amended complaint states a claim for relief under a theory of mutual mistake.

We have explained that the mutual mistake must exist at the time the contract is entered into and must be substantial. Put differently, the mistake must be "so material that . . . it goes to the foundation of the agreement" ["The parties must have been mistaken as to a basic assumption of the contract. . . . Basic assumption means the mistake must vitally affect the basis upon which the parties contract"]. Court-ordered relief is therefore reserved only for "exceptional situations." The premise underlying the doctrine of mutual mistake is that "the agreement as expressed, in some material respect, does not represent the meeting of the minds of the parties."

Although we have not addressed mutual mistake claims in the context of marital settlement agreements, the parties cite a number of Appellate Division cases that have analyzed this issue. Husband relies on True v True . . . where the settlement agreement provided that the husband's stock awards from his employer would be "divided 50-50 in kind" and recited that 3,655 shares were available for division between the parties. After the wife redeemed her half of the shares, the husband learned that only 150 shares remained and brought an action to reform the agreement, arguing that the parties mistakenly specified the gross number of shares (3,655) rather than the net number that was actually available for distribution. The Second Department agreed and reformed the agreement to effectuate the parties' intent to divide the shares equally, holding that the husband had established "that the parties' use of 3,655 gross shares was a mutual mistake because it undermined their intent to divide the net shares available for division, 50-50 in kind."

Other cases relied on by husband involve marital settlement agreements that were set aside or reformed because a mutual mistake rendered a portion of the agreement impossible to perform. In Banker v Banker . . . the Third Department reformed a provision of a marital settlement that required the subdivision of a parcel of real property because the parties were unaware of a restrictive covenant against further subdivision.

Applying these legal principles, we are of the view that the amended complaint fails to adequately state a cause of action based on mutual mistake. As an initial matter, husband's claim that the alleged mutual mistake undermined the foundation of the settlement agreement, a precondition to relief under our precedents, is belied by the terms of the agreement itself. Unlike the settlement agreement in True that expressly incorporated a "50-50" division of a stated number of stock shares, the settlement agreement here, on its face, does not mention the Madoff account, much less evince an intent to divide the account in equal or other proportionate shares. To the contrary, the agreement provides that the $6,250,000 payment to wife was "in satisfaction of [her] support and marital property rights," along with her release of various claims and inheritance rights. Despite the fact that the agreement permitted husband to retain title to his "bank, brokerage and similar financial accounts" and enumerated two such accounts, his alleged $5.4 million Madoff investment account is neither identified nor valued. Given the extensive and carefully negotiated nature of the settlement agreement, we do not believe that this presents one of those "exceptional situations" warranting reformation or rescission of a divorce settlement after all marital assets have been distributed.

Even putting the language of the agreement aside, the core allegation underpinning husband's mutual mistake claim— that the Madoff account was "nonexistent" when the parties executed their settlement agreement in June 2006—does not amount to a "material" mistake of fact as required by our case law. The premise of husband's argument is that the parties mistakenly believed that they had an investment account with Bernard Madoff when, in fact, no account ever existed. In husband's view, this case is no different from one

in which parties are under a misimpression that they own a piece of real or personal property but later discover that they never obtained rightful ownership, such that a distribution would not have been possible at the time of the agreement. But that analogy is not apt here. Husband does not dispute that, until the Ponzi scheme began to unravel in late 2008—more than two years after the property division was completed—it would have been possible for him to redeem all or part of the investment. In fact, the amended complaint contains an admission that husband was able to withdraw funds (the amount is undisclosed) from the account in 2006 to partially pay his distributive payment to wife. Given that the mutual mistake must have existed at the time the agreement was executed in 2006, the fact that husband could no longer withdraw funds years later is not determinative.

REVERSED in favor of defendant Blank.

CRITICAL THINKING

When Simkin claimed that the contract terms should be altered on the basis of a "mutual mistake" when the two entered into the divorce contract, he referenced their "mistake" being that the settlement terms allocated to him were nonexistent due to the Ponzi scheme. Should Simkin have defined his use of "nonexistent" according to a time frame? The funds were nonexistent two years after the divorce settlement, but the funds were existent in 2006 during the divorce.

ETHICAL DECISION MAKING

Could a decision in favor of Simkin's altering the terms of the marriage contract create copycat suits? Courts typically leave divorce terms intact except in rare circumstances, but many couples could attempt to claim that an outside force affected their divorce settlement assets.

Misrepresentation

L03

What are the elements of misrepresentation?

Misrepresentations are similar to mistakes in that at least one of the parties is in error about a fact material to the agreement. But a misrepresentation is an untruthful assertion by one of the parties about that material fact; it prevents the parties from having the mental agreement necessary for a legal contract. They only *appeared* to agree, so their contract lacked legal assent.

The courts insist on a meeting of the minds for a valid contract. Thus, they might rescind a contract even though the person making the false assertion was entirely innocent of any intentional deception.

The topic of misrepresentation should be particularly important to future business professionals, especially those interested in marketing or advertising careers, as it may one day be your job to develop promotional materials for a company's products. Marketing and advertising professionals must exercise special care when developing product labels, packaging, and advertisements because consumers often depend on the information provided by a company when deciding whether to purchase a product. Thus, if the marketing materials created by a company are seen as being inaccurate or appear to misrepresent what a product truly is or what benefits the product offers, consumers may attempt to take legal action.

For example, in 1991 a Michigan man, Richard Overton, filed suit against Anheuser-Busch, claiming that the company's commercials made untrue statements and misrepresentations that caused him to continually buy and consume the company's beer. More specifically, Overton alleged that Anheuser-Busch was liable for creating advertisements that falsely suggested drinking its beer would result in fantasies coming to life (tropical settings, beautiful women, and happiness). Overton sought to recover $10,000 in damages from Anheuser-Busch for causing him physical and mental injury as well as emotional distress and financial loss. A circuit court granted summary judgment in favor of the defendant. Richard Overton appealed, and the Michigan Court of Appeals affirmed the lower court's ruling.[3] While the company won the case, it still had the expense of defending its actions. It is always better to try to avoid being sued in the first place.

INNOCENT MISREPRESENTATION

An innocent misrepresentation results from a false statement about a fact material to an agreement that the person making it believed to be true. The person had no knowledge of the claim's falsity. We say he or she lacked scienter (from the Latin root of the word meaning "knowledge").

Innocent misrepresentations permit the misled party to rescind the contract. However, because the other party had no intent to mislead, the aggrieved party cannot sue for damages. The reasoning in these cases resembles the arguments in a mutual mistake case, as you might expect.

BUT WHAT IF . . .
WHAT IF THE FACTS OF THE CASE OPENER WERE DIFFERENT?

Let's say that, in the Case Opener, Knafel was incorrectly told by her doctor that the baby was Jordan's. She then told Jordan that she indeed was carrying his baby. Thus, Jordan signed the contract and paid Knafel a large sum of money. Later, the two found out the baby was not Jordan's. What kind of misrepresentation occurred? Can Jordan sue for damages?

NEGLIGENT MISREPRESENTATION

In some contract negotiations, one party makes a statement of material fact that he thinks is true. If he could have known the truth by using reasonable care to discover or reveal it, his statement is a negligent misrepresentation.

Even though he had no intent to deceive, in contract law the party is treated as if he did. If this standard seems unfair to you, remember that the courts find negligent misrepresentation only when the party making the false statement should have known the truth using the skills and competence required of a person in his position or profession. The impact of negligent misrepresentation is identical to that of fraudulent misrepresentation, discussed next.

FRAUDULENT MISREPRESENTATION

Any fraud on the part of a party to a contract provides a basis for rescission. The parties cannot be said to have assented when one of the parties was tricked into the "agreement"

[3] 205 Mich. App. 259, 517 N.W.2d 308 (case summary accessed on Lexis Nexis May 25, 2009).

by a fraudulent misrepresentation. Thus, the agreement was not voluntary and can be rescinded on the ground that there was no meeting of the minds.

Even in countries trying to encourage joint ventures and global commercial activity, such as the People's Republic of China, fraudulent claims can end the country's hospitality to agreements with outsiders.[4] In China, accusations of outsiders' fraudulent misrepresentation have resulted in heavy fines and even refusals to allow the fraudulent party to enter into any more agreements with Chinese firms. In most, if not all, cultures, little judicial sympathy exists for those who consciously mislead others in commercial activities.

A **fraudulent misrepresentation** is a consciously false representation of a material fact intended to mislead the other party. It is also referred to as **intentional misrepresentation.** Here scienter is clear: The party making the misrepresentation either knows or believes that the factual claim is false or knows there is no basis for it.

To understand the requirements for a finding of fraudulent misrepresentation, start with the two elements from the definition:

1. *A false statement about a past or existing fact that is material to the contract.*
2. *Intent to deceive,* which can be inferred from the particular circumstances.

Then add a third necessary element:

3. *Justifiable reliance on the false statement by the innocent party to the agreement:* Justifiable reliance is generally present unless the injured party knew, or should have known by the extravagance of the claim, that the false statement was indeed false. For example, a homeowner could not justifiably rely on a claim by a gardener that if she will pay him to apply a special fertilizer to her trees once a week, the trees would never die.

Finally, if damages are sought, the defrauded party must have been injured by the misrepresentation.

In the opening scenario, Jordan claimed that he had been the victim of a fraudulent misrepresentation made by Knafel. To meet the three requirements, Jordan argued that Knafel told him that he was definitely the child's father despite her knowledge that she had been having sexual relationships with other men during the same time period. According to Jordan, Knafel had reason to believe that her representation could be false and still made it with certainty in an effort to deceive him. Finally, it was based on the assertion that he was the father that Jordan allegedly agreed to pay Knafel $5 million. Hence, according to Jordan, he had proved that the statement qualified as a fraudulent misrepresentation. Does Knafel's representation that Jordan was the child's father amount to a fraudulent misrepresentation?

Each of the three aforementioned elements can become a source of debate in any attempt to rescind a contract on grounds of fraudulent misrepresentation. Thus, it is your responsibility as a person who will be involved with dozens of contracts in your business activities to know these elements. A rescinded contract is a time-consuming and expensive business opportunity that has gone wrong. And don't forget that you can collect damages only from parties you can locate.

Before we go into greater detail about the elements of fraudulent misrepresentation, please consider Case 17-2. Follow the court's reasoning as it works through the elements of the attempt to rescind a contract.

---

[4] Charles D. Paglee, "Contracts and Agreements in the People's Republic of China," www.qis.net/chinalaw/explan1.htm, updated March 6, 1998.

CASE 17-2 GARY W. CRUSE AND VENITA R. CRUSE v. COLDWELL BANKER/ GRABEN REAL ESTATE, INC.
SUPREME COURT OF ALABAMA
667 SO. 2D 714 (1995)

Mr. and Mrs. Cruse sued Mr. and Mrs. Harris, Coldwell Banker, and Graben Real Estate, Inc., alleging defective workmanship in the construction of a house they had bought from the Harrises and fraudulent misrepresentation and/or suppressed material facts about the condition of the house.

When the Cruses began looking for a home, they contacted Graben Real Estate, and a Graben agent took them to see the Harrises' house. Randy Harris, a building contractor, had built the house for sale, and he and his wife were occupying it at that time. Graben listed the house as "new" in its advertisements, and the agent told the Cruses it was new. She also told them it was comparable to, or even better than, other houses in the neighborhood, that it was a good buy, and that if they purchased it they could look forward to years of convenient, trouble-free living.

The Cruses signed a contract on November 11, 1992, to purchase the house from the Harrises. When they told the agent they wanted to hire an independent contractor to assess its condition, she told them it was not really necessary to do so because Randy Harris was a contractor and the house was well-built.

The Cruses signed an "Acceptance Inspection Contract," which stated that they had inspected the property or waived the right to do so, accepted it in "as-is" condition, and based their decision to purchase on their own inspection and not on any representations by the broker.

Plaintiffs took possession of the residence in mid-December 1992 and soon began noticing many defects in the structure and electrical wiring. They contacted Graben Real Estate, which sent an agent to remedy the problems. The defects continued and multiplied, so the Cruses sued. At the trial, defendants moved for summary judgment, which was granted. Plaintiffs appealed.

JUSTICE BUTTS: To establish fraudulent misrepresentations, the Cruses are required to show that Graben Real Estate made a false representation concerning a material fact and that they relied upon that representation, to their detriment. The Cruses contend that Graben Real Estate represented to them that the house was new; that, in reliance on that representation, they decided not to hire a contractor to inspect the house and discover its defects; and that reliance resulted in damage to them.

The unequivocal term "new," when applied to real estate, is not merely descriptive. It is a definite legal term that carries with it the implied warranty of habitability and prevents the realtor from invoking the protection of the doctrine of caveat emptor. Graben Real Estate marketed the house as "new," both in print and in direct response to the Cruses' queries. In so doing, Graben Real Estate made statements that went beyond the patter of sales talk and became representations of material fact. Moreover, Gary Cruse testified . . . that he relied upon this representation in failing to hire a contractor to inspect the house before he bought it.

Graben Real Estate argues that even if it did misrepresent the newness of the house, the Cruses could not have justifiably believed the misrepresentation and relied upon it to the point that they would not closely inspect the house before buying it. Graben Real Estate relies heavily on the fact that the Cruses knew that the house was being occupied by the Harrises at the time of the sale, and concludes that this alone should have proved to the Cruses that the house was not actually new. . . . We do not agree that the mere knowledge of the Harrises' prior occupancy so wholly contradicted the printed and spoken representations of Graben Real Estate that the Cruses could not, as a matter of law, have justifiably relied upon them.

Graben Real Estate also argues that, regardless of whether the house was new or was used, the Cruses cannot recover because they signed an "as-is" agreement at the time of the sale, thereby, Graben Real Estate says, accepting the condition of the house without a prior inspection. Graben Real Estate relies on Hope v. Brannan, wherein this Court held that buyers of a 58-year-old house who signed a statement accepting the house "as-is," without independently inspecting it for defects, could not maintain an action for fraud arising from the seller's statements concerning the condition of the house.

Graben Real Estate's reliance on Hope is misplaced; in Hope, the house was not new, nor was it represented to be new. A buyer's failure to inspect the premises of a 58-year-old house before signing an "as-is" agreement is hardly the equivalent of the Cruses' failure to inspect the premises of a house that their realtor had represented to be new.

The evidence establishes that Graben Real Estate misrepresented a material fact and creates a jury question as to whether the Cruses could have justifiably relied upon this misrepresentation in deciding not to closely inspect the house before buying it. The fact that the Cruses knew the house was occupied by a third party before they bought it, along with the fact that they signed an "as-is" agreement, separate from the purchase contract, for a house they claim to have regarded as new, are elements for the jury to consider.

REVERSED and REMANDED.

[continued]

CRITICAL THINKING

Several key points in the reasoning of this decision rely on personal testimony. On the basis of your life experience and any knowledge you may have accumulated through your educational career, how reliable do you think witness testimony is as a form of evidence in legal disputes? What are some of the ways that this testimonial evidence might be flawed? What are its particular strengths? In this case, do you think the testimonies are valid? Why or why not?

ETHICAL DECISION MAKING

What general values might the court be interested in protecting in this ruling? How are they similar to values upheld by other cases in this chapter? How are they different? What opposing values are less important in these rulings?

The elements of fraudulent misrepresentation become more complicated in the context of actual disagreements. Let's revisit them for more insight.

False Assertion of Fact. For fraudulent misrepresentation to be the basis for a contract rescission, the statement of fact need not be an actual assertion. It can also be an act of concealment or nondisclosure. Concealment is the *active* hiding of the truth about a material fact, for example, removing 20,000 miles from the odometer on your car before selling it. Nondisclosure is a failure to provide pertinent information about the projected contract. The courts have until recently been hesitant to use nondisclosure as a basis for rescinding a contract because it is a passive form of misleading conduct. Under ordinary situations associated with a legal bargain, it is not the obligation of one party to bring up any and all facts he or she might possess. Each individual is, to a large extent, treated as a responsible decision maker.

However, courts will now find nondisclosure as having the same legal effect as an actual false assertion under certain conditions:

1. *A relationship of trust exists between the parties to the contract.* In this situation the relationship provides a reasonable basis for one person's expectation that the other would never act to defraud him or her.

2. *There is failure to correct assertions of fact that are no longer true.* Caroline's failure to inform Vito of the recent outbreak of rust on her "rust-free" car that Vito agreed to purchase next month is nondisclosure.

3. *A statute requires the disclosure,* such as mandatory disclosures under residential real estate sales laws.

4. *The nondisclosure involves a dangerous defect,* such as bad brakes in a car that is being sold.

Nondisclosure is especially likely to provide the basis for rescission when one party has information about a basic assumption of the deal that is unavailable to the other party. Sellers thus have a special duty to disclose because they know more about the structural makeup of the item being purchased.

BUT WHAT IF . . .
WHAT IF THE FACTS OF THE CASE OPENER WERE DIFFERENT?

Let's say that, in the Case Opener, Knafel had Jordan sign a contract that stipulated he must make monthly payments to her for the baby they both believed was genetically theirs together. Then, after signing, Knafel discovered the baby was not in fact Jordan's but did not relay the information to him. What kind of misrepresentation occurred here?

FRAUDULENT MISREPRESENTATION IN SOCIAL MEDIA

Online social media create a prime opportunity for individuals to create false identities. In some cases, these false identities are then used to communicate with unsuspecting individuals, often causing the real individuals who communicate with the misrepresented identities to experience financial or emotional harm. A tragic example of this is the case of *United States v. Lori Drew*, in which Drew created the false identity of a boy on the networking site MySpace. Megan Meier, a young girl, was lured by Drew and Drew's daughter to strike up a relationship with the false identity. When the "boy" broke up with Meier, Meier unfortunately committed suicide. The prosecution of Drew was unsuccessful. A major issue with the prosecution was that there was no federal statute against cyberbullying, and the judge did not feel comfortable relying on a breach-of-contract premise that would make this case of fraudulent misrepresentation equivalent to a case of computer hacking. As the likelihood of fraudulently misrepresenting an individual increases, misrepresentation must be addressed in such a way that all possible aspects in which fraudulent misrepresentation could occur are covered by statutes.

Source: www.wired.com/threatlevel/2009/07/drew_court/.

Intent to Deceive. *Scienter* is present when the party making the fraudulent assertion believed it was false or had no regard for whether it was true or false. *Intent to deceive* occurs when the party making the false statement claims to have or implies having personal knowledge of its accuracy. Any resulting assent is not legal because the injured party was not allowed to join the mind of the deceiving party. The party with scienter or intent to deceive wanted the contract to be fulfilled on the basis of a falsehood.

Justifiable Reliance on the False Assertion. What responsibilities does the injured party have in a case of false assertion? As we've said, the injured party has no justifiable claim of fraud after relying on assertions whose falsity should have been obvious. Anyone who pays for a house in reliance on the claim that it was "built before the founding of our country" cannot later rescind the contract on grounds of fraudulent misrepresentation.

Nor can parties successfully claim they justifiably relied on a false assertion when its falsity would have been clear to anyone who inspected the item. However, the duty to inspect is declining in modern contract law, and courts are giving increasing responsibility to the person who made the erroneous assertion.

As you might infer from the foregoing discussion, the process of determining whether intentional misrepresentation has occurred can be an extremely difficult task. This process can become even more complex when the defendant believes that the other party was never misled in the first place. Such was the case when several individuals involved in the movie *Borat* filed suit against Sacha Baron Cohen and Twentieth Century Fox for fraudulent and negligent misrepresentation as well as other various claims. The plaintiffs in the case were lawyers who represented the locals of the Romanian village of Glod, where the opening scenes of the movie were filmed. In their suit, the villagers alleged that Cohen and Twentieth Century Fox convinced them that they were taking part in a documentary film about poverty in Romania, not a blockbuster movie set in Kazakhstan. Further, the lawsuit asserted that Cohen and Twentieth Century Fox "used their superior educational background, stature, influence and economic position" to exploit the villagers and that the company also encouraged villagers to sign documents that they did not understand and that had not been fully explained.

Twentieth Century Fox defended its film and claimed that the villagers of Glod knew they were participating in a movie and not a documentary. The company further defended its position by stating that the villagers were paid more than the average going wage for movie extras. Eventually, the lawsuit was thrown out by a U.S district court judge who stated that the allegations against Sacha Baron Cohen and Twentieth Century Fox needed to be more specific. The lawyers of the Glod villagers said that they intended to file a new suit in the future.[5]

[5] http://news.bbc.co.uk/2/hi/europe/7686885.stm; and http://74.125.113.132/search?q=cache:jQ0M5aR16wUJ:www.courthouse-news.com/onpoint/borat_NY.pdf+Twentieth+century+fox+v+michael+witti+and+ed+fagan&cd=1&hl=en&ct=clnk&gl=us.

In 1997, after studying the application of civil law in the country, the Japanese Social Policy Council, an advisory body to the prime minister, recognized that the consumer environment was growing more diversified and that a significant gap existed between consumers and businesses in their access to information and knowledge and their negotiating power. Because it cannot honestly be said that consumers and businesses are equal, as contracting parties are presumed to be under the country's Civil Code, the council developed a special Consumer Contracts Law. This legislation is considered to place consumers and businesses on a more equal footing in transactions.

Under the Consumer Contracts Law, a consumer may cancel the contract whenever a business (1) fails to provide information about the contents of the contract, (2) fails to provide information necessary for the consumer to decide to enter into the contract, or (3) makes misrepresentations. In many such cases, the consumer would not have been entitled to relief under the Civil Code because of its strict requirements for the application of fraud.

To see how certain aspects of marketing relate to misrepresentation, please see the **Connecting to the Core** activity on the text website at www.mhhe.com/kubasek3e.

Before we conclude this section about misrepresentation, consider what would have happened if Karla Knafel, in the opening scenario, had told Jordan there was a strong probability that the child was his. Would Jordan have been able to claim that their contract lacked assent because of Knafel's misrepresentation?

Legal Principle: **The effect of both a negligent misrepresentation and a fraudulent misrepresentation is that the victim can either rescind the contract or keep the contract and sue for damages, whereas if the mistake is innocent, the victim can seek only rescission.**

Undue Influence

L04

What are the elements of undue influence?

When legal assent is present, the courts assume both parties have made their own choices based on complete freedom to accept or reject the terms of the bargain. However, many factors can work to make our choices anything but free. Undue influence refers to those special relationships in which one person takes advantage of a dominant position in a relationship to unfairly persuade the other and interfere with that person's ability to make his or her own decision. When people bargain with their attorney, doctor, guardian, relative, or anyone else in a relationship that includes a high degree of trust, they are susceptible to being persuaded by unusual pressures unique to that relationship. Consequently, the assent that results may not be legal consent. The courts may see the undue influence of the relationship as interfering with the free choice required for an enforceable contract. Whatever contracts result from undue influence are voidable.

Are all contracts in which undue influence might arise likely to be rescinded? Not necessarily. The courts look to the mental condition of the person relying on the guidance of the dominant person. Courts look to the extent to which the dominant person used the persuasive powers of his or her dominance to secure assent.

Factors that enter into the finding of undue influence are the following:

1. Was the dominant party rushing the other party to consent?
2. Did the dominant party gain undue enrichment from the agreement?
3. Was the nondominant party isolated from other advisers at the time of the agreement?
4. Is the contract unreasonable because it overwhelmingly benefits the dominant party?

The more of these factors present, the more likely a court is to rescind the contract on grounds of undue influence. The Case Nugget on the next page provides an illustration of undue influence.

Evan Rothberg v. Walt Disney Pictures
1999 U.S. App. 1472

Robert Jahn was a senior executive at Walt Disney Pictures until he died of complications from AIDS. Within days before his death, a Disney official visited him at the hospital and convinced him to sign a release that waived his rights to approximately $2 million in employee benefits, including life insurance, stock options, bonuses, and deferred compensation. After his death, his estate sued to recover the benefits waived in the release. Disney received a motion for summary judgment, and the plaintiff appealed. In reversing the motion for summary judgment, the court ruled that the question of whether the release had been procured by undue influence was a question for a jury. The court pointed out that undue influence requires (1) undue susceptibility on the part of the weaker party and (2) application of excessive pressure by the stronger party. In this case, the first fact was self-evident. The defendant was in the hospital and was fearful that Disney would expose information that would destroy his reputation. Regarding the second element, however, the court noted that in most undue-influence cases, and this case was no exception, direct evidence is rarely obtainable and thus the jury must decide the issue on the basis of inferences drawn from all the facts and circumstances. Thus, the court said that summary judgment was improper.

Legal Principle: **The essential element of undue influence is the existence of a dominant-subservient relationship, so if you are going to enter into a contract with someone with whom you have such a relationship, to ensure that the agreement will be enforced in the future, make sure that the person in the subservient position has independent advice before entering into the contract.**

BUT WHAT IF . . .
WHAT IF THE FACTS OF THE CASE OPENER WERE DIFFERENT?

Let's say that, in the Case Opener, Jordan was married at the time of his affair with Knafel and he did not want his wife or the public to know about the affair or the baby. Furthermore, let's say that Knafel threatened to make the information public (among other information about Jordan) if he did not sign her contract. Would such a scenario constitute undue influence?

Duress

Duress is a much more visible and active interference with free will than is undue influence. Duress occurs when one party is forced into the agreement by the wrongful act of another.

The wrongful act may come in various forms. Any of the following would trigger a successful request for rescission on grounds of duress:

L05

What are the elements of duress?

- One party threatens physical harm or extortion to gain consent to a contract.
- One party threatens to file a criminal lawsuit unless consent is given to the terms of the contract. (Threats to bring civil cases against a party to a lawsuit do not constitute duress unless the suit is frivolous.)
- One party threatens the other's economic interests (this is known as *economic duress*). For instance, a person refuses to perform according to a contract unless the other person either signs another contract with the one making the threat or pays that person a higher price than specified in the original agreement.

DURESS IN AUSTRALIA

Australia recognizes a special category called *duress of goods,* which occurs whenever one party makes an illegitimate threat to hold goods unless another party makes payment or enters into an agreement. Note that this is different from a situation in which someone legitimately holds goods when money is owed on them or the goods have been used as security for a loan.

Australia also recognizes economic duress, which is the unacceptable use of economic power to leave someone with no practical alternative but to submit to the accompanying demand.

To prove economic duress, a plaintiff must establish that (1) pressure was used to procure his or her assent to an agreement or to the payment of money, (2) the pressure was illegitimate in the circumstance, (3) the pressure in fact contributed to the person's assenting to the transaction, and (4) the person's assent to the transaction was reasonable in the circumstances.

Just as with economic duress in the United States, it is often unclear when pressure is illegitimate. A threat to do something unlawful is almost always undue pressure. A threat to use the civil legal process is usually considered lawful, unless the contemplated legal action would clearly be an abuse of process. "Driving a hard bargain" or refusing to do any more business with someone in the future is generally not regarded as economic duress.

The injured party makes the case for duress by demonstrating that the threat left no reasonable alternatives and that the free will necessary for legal consent was removed by the specifics of the threat.

Legal Principle: **When one party is forced to enter into a contract by the wrongful threat of another, the contract is voidable by the innocent party due to duress.**

BUT WHAT IF . . .

In 2009, a humane society officer named William Sandstrom confiscated Miles Thomas's dog due to certain violations of the state's animal cruelty laws. Thomas signed a release form for the humane society to take ownership of the dog. Later, Thomas claimed the release form was unenforceable because he was under duress when he signed it. Specifically, he claimed he was under duress at the time because he was sad about his dog. Does Thomas's account of his signing the release form actually fulfill the requirements of duress? Is the release form unenforceable?

Unconscionability

L06

What are the elements of unconscionability?

A final way to question the appropriateness of consent arises when one of the parties has so much more bargaining power than the other that he or she dictates the terms of the agreement. Such an agreement can be rescinded on grounds of unconscionability (as discussed in Chapter 4). The disproportionate amount of power possessed by one party to the contract has made a mockery of the idea of free will, a necessity for legal consent. The resulting contract is called an adhesion contract.

Although unconscionability has traditionally been limited to the sale of goods under the Uniform Commercial Code, many courts have not followed that tradition. When they see contracts written by one party and presented to the other with the threat to "take it or leave it," they sometimes extend the idea of unconscionability beyond the sale of goods.

Follow the judge's reasoning in Case 17-3 to review the type of reasoning that makes up a claim for unconscionability.

CASE 17-3   ORVILLE ARNOLD AND MAXINE ARNOLD, PLAINTIFFS v.
UNITED COMPANIES LENDING CORPORATION,
A CORPORATION, AND MICHAEL T. SEARLS,
AN INDIVIDUAL, DEFENDANTS
SUPREME COURT OF APPEALS OF WEST VIRGINIA
1998 WL 8651015

*On September 17, 1996, Michael Searls came to the resi-
dence of Orville and Maxine Arnold, an elderly couple, and
offered to arrange a loan for them, acting as a loan broker. He procured a loan for them. From the loan proceeds,
a mortgage broker fee of $940.00 was paid to Searls and/or
Accent Financial Services, with which Searls was affiliated.*

*At the loan closing, United Lending had the benefit of
legal counsel, while the Arnolds apparently did not. During the course of the transaction, the Arnolds were presented with more than twenty-five documents to sign.
Among these were a promissory note, reflecting a principal
sum of $19,300.00 and a yearly interest rate of 12.990%;
a Deed of Trust, giving United Lending a security interest
in the Arnolds' real estate; and a two-page form labeled
"Acknowledgment and Agreement to Mediate or Arbitrate,"
which stated that all legal controversies arising from the
loan would be resolved through nonappealable, confidential arbitration, and that all damages would be direct damages, with no punitive damages available. However, this
agreement not to arbitrate did not limit the lender's right to
pursue legal actions in a court of law relating to collection
of the loan.*

*On July 10, 1997, the Arnolds filed suit against United
Lending and Searls, seeking a declaratory judgment adjudg-
ing the arbitration agreement to be void and unenforceable.
On August 11, 1997, United Lending moved to dismiss the
entire action on the basis of the compulsory arbitration
agreement. The circuit court certified three questions to the
state supreme court.*

JUSTICE McCUSKEY: We reformulate the question as
follows: Whether an arbitration agreement entered into as
part of a consumer loan transaction containing a substantial waiver of the consumer's rights, including access to the
courts, while preserving for all practical purposes the lender's right to a judicial forum, is void as a matter of law.

The drafters of the Uniform Consumer Credit Code
explained that the [basic test] of unconscionability is
whether . . . the conduct involved is, or the contract or
clauses involved are, so one-sided as to be unconscionable
under the circumstances existing at the time the conduct
occurs or is threatened or at the time of the making of the
contract. . . . [T]his Court stated:

["W]here a party alleges that the arbitration
provision was unconscionable, or was thrust upon

him because he was unwary and taken advantage
of, or that the contract was one of adhesion, the
question of whether an arbitration provision was
bargained for and valid is a matter of law for
the court to determine by reference to the entire
contract. . . ." A determination of unconscionability
must focus on the relative positions of the parties,
the adequacy of the bargaining position, the
meaningful alternatives available to the plaintiff,
and "the existence of unfair terms in the contract."

Applying the rule . . . leads us to the inescapable
conclusion that the arbitration agreement between the
Arnolds and United Lending is "void for unconscionability" as a matter of law. . . . The relative positions of
the parties, a national corporate lender on one side and
elderly, unsophisticated consumers on the other, were
"grossly unequal." In addition, there is no evidence that
the loan broker made any other loan option available to
the Arnolds. In fact, the record does not indicate that the
Arnolds were seeking a loan, but rather were solicited by
defendant Searls. Thus, the element of "a comparable,
meaningful alternative" to the loan from United Lending
is lacking. Because the Arnolds had no meaningful alternative to obtaining the loan from United Lending, and also
did not have the benefit of legal counsel during the transaction, their bargaining position was clearly inadequate
when compared to that of United Lending.

Given the nature of this arbitration agreement, combined
with the great disparity in bargaining power, one can safely
infer that the terms were not bargained for and that allowing
such a one-sided agreement to stand would unfairly defeat
the Arnolds' legitimate expectations.

Finally, the terms of the agreement are "unreasonably favorable" to United Lending. United Lending's acts
or omissions could seriously damage the Arnolds, yet the
Arnolds' only recourse would be to submit the matter to
binding arbitration. At the same time, United Lending's
access to the courts is wholly preserved in every conceivable situation where United Lending would want to secure
judicial relief against the Arnolds. The wholesale waiver of
the Arnolds' rights together with the complete preservation
of United Lending's rights "is inherently inequitable and
unconscionable because in a way it nullifies all the other
provisions of the contract."

Judgment in favor of Plaintiffs.

[continued]

CRITICAL THINKING

This case highlights the importance of language in the legal system. Phrases quoted from the law are subject to significant judicial discretion, which allows rulings like this to be possible. Using the contextual clues found in the information given, choose two descriptions in quotes and write your idea of how the judge must be defining the relevant phrase. Then come up with some other ways these phrases could have been defined. Would the use of your alternatives significantly affect the reasonableness of the conclusion?

ETHICAL DECISION MAKING

Does this case lend itself very well to considerations of ethicality? What sort of theoretical approach do you see the court taking with this ruling?

On the basis of other decisions you have encountered in this book, what do you think is probably the most common ethical framework U.S. courts use in guiding their rulings? How well does this case fit with larger trends? Support your answer.

CASE OPENER WRAP-UP

A Disagreement over an Agreement

The trial court agreed with Michael Jordan's argument regarding a mutual mistake or fraudulent misrepresentation in the contract. Knafel appealed, and the court affirmed the lower court's decision. The court held that Knafel's representation to Jordan that he was the father met the requirements of being (1) a material fact, (2) made for the purpose of inducing Jordan to act, (3) that either was known by Knafel to be false or was not actually believed by her on reasonable grounds to be true, but Jordan reasonably believed it to be true, and (4) that was relied on by Jordan to his own detriment. Thus, the appellate court found that Knafel's representation that Jordan *was* the father constituted fraud. The agreement can be rescinded because Jordan would not have entered into the agreement but for the fraudulent representation made by Knafel. Even if Knafel did not act fraudulently, at the time the agreement was created both parties believed that the child was Jordan's. After the paternity tests revealed that the baby was *not* Jordan's, the agreement could still be rescinded based on a mutual mistake of fact.

KEY TERMS

adhesion contract 398
concealment 394
duress 397
fraudulent
   misrepresentation 392
innocent
   misrepresentation 391

intentional
   misrepresentation 392
legal assent 385
misrepresentation 390
mistake
   of fact 386
mutual 386

negligent
   misrepresentation 391
nondisclosure 394
rescinded 385
scienter 391
unconscionability 398
undue influence 396

unilateral 386
voidable 385

400

SUMMARY OF KEY TOPICS

If assent is not genuine, or legal, a contract may be voidable.

The Importance of Legal Assent

Mistakes are erroneous beliefs about the material facts of a contract at the time the agreement is made. They may be either unilateral or mutual. Only under certain rare conditions are unilateral mistakes a basis for rescinding a contract. However, if both parties to a contract are mistaken about a material fact, either can opt to rescind it. The agreement was not based on a meeting of the minds, a basic criterion for a legal assent.

Mistake

Misrepresentation is an intentional untruthful assertion by one of the parties about a material fact. An innocent misrepresentation occurs when the party making the false assertion believes it to be true. The misled party may then rescind the contract. When a misrepresentation is fraudulent, any assent is gained by deceit and the courts permit rescission. In addition to requiring a false assertion and intent to deceive, fraudulent misrepresentation also requires the innocent party's justifiable reliance on the assertion.

Misrepresentation

Undue influence is the persuasive efforts of a dominant party who uses a special relationship with another party to interfere with the other's free choice of the terms of a contract. Any relationship in which one party has an unusual degree of trust in the other can trigger concern about undue influence.

Undue Influence

Duress occurs when one party threatens the other with a wrongful act unless assent is given. Such assent is not legal assent because coercion interferes with the party's free will. For the courts to rescind the agreement, the injured party must demonstrate that the duress left no reasonable alternatives to agreeing to the contract.

Duress

Unconscionability may be a basis for avoiding a contract if one party has so much relative bargaining power that he or she in effect dictates the terms. The resulting agreement is an adhesion contract.

Unconscionability

POINT / COUNTERPOINT

Are Payday Loans, and the Accompanying Interests Rates, Unconscionable?	
YES	NO
The consumers who take out payday loans are often desperate and lack other methods of obtaining a loan. For these consumers, getting a loan from a bank is impossible due to their poor credit ratings or lack of necessary collateral. The companies that offer these consumers payday loans are preying on a vulnerable population by exploiting their lack of bargaining power. Payday loans are unconscionable.	The companies that supply payday loans offer short-term solutions to difficult financial situations. For consumers who find themselves strapped and in dire need of cash, payday loans provide a means to repair a broken-down car, pay the rent, or pay other accumulating bills. Although the interest rates are high, these loans do not violate any laws and the consumers' loan agreements are not unconscionable.
Regardless of the amount of advertising a lender may provide, consumers who find themselves in need of payday loans lack the necessary bargaining power to make these loans conscionable. For a loan to be unconscionable, one of the parties has to have so much more bargaining power than the other that he or she dictates the terms of the agreement; in payday loans it is the lender that has the power to dictate the terms. Desperate consumers often feel that they are left with no choice but accepting the terms offered by the payday lenders.	When consumers approach a payday lender for a loan, they are greeted by a plethora of signs indicating relevant interest rates. Before signing the loan documents, the consumer is given numerous documents containing the interest rates. Additionally, many states require that the lender verbally state the interest rates to consumers. These consumers have numerous opportunities to walk away from the lender if they are unwilling to accept the high interest rates.

Additionally, payday loans exploit the financial hardships experienced by consumers and often result in increased hardship. A typical bank loan is usually capped at an APR of 35 percent; payday loans average an APR of 530 percent. The consumers' ability to pay back the loans is often limited by the individuals' impoverished situation, and, as a result, these loans will often roll over, making it impossible for consumers to recover. As a result of the consumers' limited bargaining power, payday loans trap disadvantaged populations in high–interest rate loans they cannot afford. Thus, payday loans are *inherently unconscionable*.

In response to those who argue that these loans are unconscionable, supporters argue that consumers still have the free will to choose whether or not to enter into the loan agreement. These loans do not involve any coercion or enticing.

Furthermore, the high interest rates tied to payday loans are the reason these lenders are able to make small (often between $100 and $500) loans to otherwise risky consumers. Without the ability to raise interest rates, these companies would not be able to offset their own risk in providing the loans. Therefore, these loans are *not unconscionable*.

QUESTIONS & PROBLEMS

1. Explain the difference between a unilateral mistake and a mutual mistake.

2. Explain when a unilateral mistake can lead to a contract's being voidable.

3. Distinguish innocent misrepresentation from fraudulent misrepresentation.

4. Explain how nondisclosure can be treated as misrepresentation.

5. Explain the primary differences between duress and undue influence.

6. After a collision involving Alston and Alexander, Alston was diagnosed with chest problems and was prescribed a number of medications. During the time of her treatment and release on the day of the accident, she did not make note of any pain in her neck or back. Instead, she argued that she developed neck and back pain between one and two days after her original treatment. Later, Alston signed a release for her injury compensation check, which is standard insurer procedure. However, Alston later testified that she did not read the insurance release and her compensatory check and that the check from the insurance company did not contain compensation for her injuries that occurred later. Alston sued on the grounds of mutual mistake. Specifically, the check did not make light of all of her injuries, and she did not read the check release. Thus, she claimed the release was invalidated. The superior court upheld the validity of a general release signed by Alston and granted summary judgment in Alexander's favor on that basis. Alston appealed. With whom do you think the state's supreme court agreed and why? [*Alston v. Alexander*, Del. Sup. Ct. LEXIS 384 (2012).]

7. Audrey Vokes was a 51-year-old widow who wanted to become an "accomplished dancer." She was invited to attend a "dance party" at J. P. Davenports' School of Dancing, an Arthur Murray franchise. She subsequently signed up for dance classes, at which she received elaborate praise. Her instructor initially sold her eight half-hour dance lessons for $14.50 each, to be used one each month. Eventually, after being continually told that she had excellent potential and that she was developing into a beautiful dancer—when, in fact, she was not developing her dance ability and had no aptitude for dance—she ended up purchasing a total of 2,302 hours' worth of dance lessons for a total of $31,090.45. When it finally became clear to Vokes that she was not developing her dance skills, in part because she had trouble even hearing the musical beat, she sued Arthur Murray. What would be the basis of her argument? Her case was initially dismissed by the trial court. What do you think the result of her appeal was? [*Okes v. Arthur Murray*, 212 So. 2d 906 (1968).]

8. In 1998, the governor of New York, George Pataki, formulated a $185 million plan to update old Amtrak trains. The purpose of the project was to make the old trains faster than the more current Amtrak trains. Such a reconstruction would allow for a high-speed rail system between Albany and New York City. Unfortunately, Amtrak produced only one train, and although millions of dollars were poured into the company to fund the project, auditing showed that the company showed little spending on the trains. Problems stemmed in part from the lack of engineering expertise of the Steel Company that was picked to work on the

trains. Also, the state's Department of Transportation was not experienced in overseeing projects of this type, so little oversight was given to Amtrak. Additionally, unforeseen problems arose such as air-conditioning malfunctions and the removal of asbestos from train cabins. After the plan seemed as though it would never be successful and Amtrak was extremely low on money due to normal operations, the company tried to settle with the state to escape the project. However, the state filed a lawsuit against Amtrak. Amtrak's defense was that both parties made a unilateral mistake because neither party foresaw the problems or extra costs associated with the project that made it unrealistic. How do you think the court decided? [*New York v. Amtrak*, 2007 U.S. Dist. LEXIS 13045 (N.D.N.Y, Feb. 23, 2007).]

9. The Winklers were interested in purchasing a home in the Valleyview Farms housing development. They contacted the developer, Galehouse, and selected a lot that cost $57,000. They asked the developer to show them plans for houses for which the construction costs would range from $180,000 to $190,000, indicating this was the price they would be willing to spend for construction only and wasn't to include the lot price. The developer gave them several books and plans to look at.

   After the Winklers had several conversations with Galehouse, the developer drafted plans for a 2,261-square-foot house and gave the Winklers a quote of $198,000 for construction. The lot price was not included. After several months of adding options and upgrades to the plan, the cost rose to $242,000, excluding the lot. The parties then engaged in a couple of weeks of negotiations regarding the price of the construction and lot. Eventually they reached a compromise price of $291,000 ($243,000 for the construction and $48,000 for the lot).

   Galehouse prepared a written contract to reflect the parties' agreement, but the developer forgot to include the lot price. The Winklers paid Galehouse $48,000, the lot price, as a deposit on the contract. When the construction was completed, and the Winklers were finalizing their loan from the bank, the parties discovered the drafting error. Galehouse sued to have the contract reformed to reflect the agreed-on price. Should the contract be reformed? Why or why not? [*Galehouse v. Winkler*, 1998 WL 312527.]

10. Vincent Concepcion sued AT&T mobile in 2006, claiming that the company had deceptively advertised a free phone with a wireless plan. After the suit evolved into a class action suit, the company claimed that in accordance with their contracts, the plaintiffs must settle through individual arbitration processes. Yet the district court ruled that California law banned parties from creating contracts that excused them from an infraction based on certain clauses—specifically, clauses like the AT&T clause disallowing class action suits although the damages to the individual are small and not worth the time or money required to engage in an individual arbitration process. Thus, the district court refused to dismiss the suit. The company then appealed to the Ninth Circuit Court of Appeals and finally the Supreme Court, arguing that the Federal Arbitration Act should trump state law. However, unconscionability doctrines and substantial consumer protection laws are created under state law. Thus, the justices questioned, "Are we going to tell the State of California what it has to consider unconscionable?" How do you think the justices decided? [*AT&T Mobility LLC v. Concepcion*, 2011 U.S. LEXIS 3367.]

Looking for more review materials?

The Online Learning Center at **www.mhhe.com/kubasek3e** contains this chapter's "Assignment on the Internet" and also a list of URLs for more information, entitled "On the Internet." Find both of them in the Student Center portion of the OLC, along with quizzes and other helpful materials.

LEARNING OBJECTIVES

After reading this chapter, you will be able to answer the following questions:

1 What is the purpose of the statute of frauds?

2 Which kinds of contracts require a writing to satisfy the statute of frauds?

3 What must a writing contain to be sufficient to satisfy the statute of frauds?

4 What is the purpose of the parol evidence rule?

CASE OPENER

Admissibility of an Oral Contract in Court

Monroe Bradstad borrowed $100,000 from his aunt, Jeanne Garland, to purchase farmland. Both parties subsequently signed a promissory note stipulating that interest would be accrued prior to or on January 1, 1992. After that, payments and interest would be made on January 1 of each following year, with the final balance due on January 1, 2010. The land was used as security for the note; thus Branstad executed a mortgage. Branstad paid a total of $33,000 from 1993 to 1997. In 1998, Branstad and Garland had a falling out, and Garland served Branstad with a notice to pay $43,998 in past-due interest. However, Branstad and his wife claimed that they had made a subsequent oral agreement with Garland that they would manage and spend money on her other properties in lieu of paying interest. Garland argued that there was no oral agreement and that any oral evidence would be inadmissible in court due to the parol evidence rule. Branstad argued that the oral agreement was made after the written contract was created, not before or during, and thus the oral contract was a separate contract and not subject to the parol evidence rule.

1. Does it matter when the oral contract was made in relation to when the written contract was created?

2. Why might it be ethically important for the court to hear the subsequent oral agreement made between Branstad and Garland?

The Wrap-Up at the end of the chapter will answer these questions.

Written contracts provide certain advantages oral contracts lack. Disputes about the specifics of the terms in an oral contract are easier to settle when the terms are solidified in writing. The moment of writing also allows both parties to reconsider their terms and ensure that they are advocating what they desire in the contract. In general, written contracts smooth the conduct of business transactions. Some contracts thus require a writing.

This idea actually comes from an English law, the Act for the Prevention of Frauds and Perjuries passed by Parliament in 1677. To correct a problem in the common law, the act required that specific types of contracts be in writing and be signed by both parties to ensure enforceability.

Although the law frequently references the *statute of frauds,* the term is somewhat misleading. There is no federal legislation entitled "Statute of Frauds." Rather, the statute exists as legislation at the state level. In fact, almost every state has created its own version of the 1677 English act, adopting it in total or in part. The exceptions are Louisiana, which has no such legislation, and New Mexico and Maryland, which follow statutes of frauds

Before entering into a contract one needs to know whether its subject matter requires a writing.

created by judicial decision and not the legislature. Interestingly enough, the English have repealed almost all their requirements for writing, while U.S. states and courts are still expanding the requirements for what falls within the statute of frauds.

In addition to the statute's not being a unitary government act, the name "statute of frauds" is misleading in another way. It does not relate to fraudulent contracts, nor does it address the issue of illegal contracts. Rather, it addresses the enforceability of contracts that fail to meet the requirements set forth in it. Furthermore, the statute serves to protect promisors from poorly considered oral contracts by requiring that certain contracts be in writing.

This chapter addresses some commonalities of the statutes of frauds of different states; in it, we refer to the "statute of frauds" as if it were a unitary law. We examine which contracts need to be in writing, as well as exceptions to the rule. Then we look at the parol evidence rule, which discusses which types of oral evidence are admissible and when, as related to contracts within the scope of the statute of frauds.

Statute of Frauds

LO1

What is the purpose of the statute of frauds?

The **statute of frauds** has three main purposes. First, it attempts to ease contractual negotiations by requiring sufficiently reliable evidence to prove the existence and specific terms of a contract. When a contract is deemed important enough that being in writing is required under the statute of frauds, the statute specifies what is considered reliable evidence.

The second main purpose of the statute of frauds is to prevent unreliable oral evidence from interfering with a contractual relationship. By requiring that a contract be in writing, the statute precludes the admittance of oral evidence denying the existence of a contract or claiming additional terms that would substantially alter the contract from its agreed-on written form. This chapter further discusses the admissibility or denial of oral evidence later, in the section on the parol evidence rule.

The third main purpose of the statute of frauds is to prevent parties from entering into contracts with which they do not agree. That is, it provides some degree of cautionary protection for the parties, who must carefully consider the terms, agree to them, write them out, and finally sign the contract. The law assumes that these steps will allow time for careful consideration. Thus, the statute works to prevent hasty, improperly considered contracts.

Contracts Falling within the Statute of Frauds

As previously mentioned, only specific types of contracts are within the scope of the statute of frauds and thus required to be evidenced by a writing. They are (1) contracts whose terms prevent possible performance within one year, (2) promises made in consideration of marriage, (3) contracts for one party to pay the debt of another if the initial party fails to pay, and (4) contracts related to an interest in land. Although required to be in writing under the Uniform Commercial Code (UCC), and not the statute of frauds, a related fifth category is contracts for the sale of goods totaling more than $500.[1]

CONTRACTS WHOSE TERMS PREVENT POSSIBLE PERFORMANCE WITHIN ONE YEAR

Contracts whose performance, based on the terms of the contract, could not possibly occur within one year fall within the statute of frauds and therefore must be in writing.[2] Note that the one-year period begins the day after the contract is created, *not* when it is scheduled to begin.

For example, Roberto enters into a contract with Elise to work for her for one year starting October 1. If the contract is created on the preceding September 15, it cannot be completed in one year from September 16; therefore, it must be in writing. However, if the contract is scheduled to start immediately, it *can* be completed in one year and need not be in writing because it is not within the statute of frauds.

It's technically possible that you could finish this deal within a year, so let's just shake on it.

The test for compliance with the one-year rule does not consider the likelihood of completing the contract within one year. Rather, it considers the *possibility* of completing the contract in one year. While Roberto and Elise's contract is within the statute because, according to its terms, it cannot be performed within one year, a contract for lifetime employment does not need to be in writing.

If Roberto contracts with Elise for lifetime employment, they do not have to write and sign the agreement because it is possible for the contract to be completed within one year: Robert *could* die after two days of work. Moreover, if oral, their contract would be enforceable, because it is not within the statute of frauds. The possibility that a contract's terms could be performed within one year removes the contract from the statute's written requirements.

[1] UCC § 2-201.

[2] Restatement (Second) of Contracts, sec. 130.

AURIGEMMA V. NEW CASTLE CARE, LLC

2006 Del. Super. LEXIS 337, June 12, 2006

Dr. Ralph M. Aurigemma filed suit against New Castle Care, LLC, alleging breach of an oral contract. New Castle Care operated the Arbors Rehabilitation Center, the facility where Aurigemma worked. Aurigemma claimed that after the medical director for the Arbors unexpectedly died, he and many other doctors expressed an interest in filling the newly vacant position. Aurigemma stated that individuals from New Castle Care made him interim medical director and, on September 4, 2003, created an oral contract under which he agreed to serve as permanent medical director from October 1, 2003, until October 1, 2004.

New Castle Care claimed that it made no such oral contract with Aurigemma and stated that even if it had, Aurigemma's oral contract would not be enforceable because the terms of the contract, which was created on September 4, 2003, and intended to go until October 1, 2004, could not possibly be completed within a year. Therefore, New Castle Care claimed that Aurigemma's alleged oral contract fell within the statue of frauds and thus required a writing to be enforceable. Additionally, New Castle Care claimed it had been clear that the company had not intended to have Aurigemma act as permanent medical director, and it cited a written contract it had created with another doctor on September 15, 2003, as proof that no oral contract existed.

Aurigemma countered by saying that because he began to assume the duties of medical director, he had already partially performed the terms of the contract. Thus, because partial performance sometimes creates an exception to the statue of frauds, Aurigemma argued that the oral contract did not need to be in writing.

On June 15, 2006, New Castle Care filed a motion for summary judgment; shortly after, a Delaware superior court granted summary judgment in favor of the company on both counts. In conclusion, the court stated that New Castle Care was correct in its argument. Because the terms of the oral contract were for a time period of more than a year, the oral contract would have had to have been in writing in order to have been valid. The court also pointed out that in Delaware the partial-performance exception to the statute of frauds does not apply to oral contracts incapable of being performed within a year. Therefore, Aurigemma's alleged oral contract was not included in the partial-performance exception to the statute of frauds and was accordingly unenforceable.

Similarly, contracts for complex construction projects need not be in writing because, theoretically, they can be completed within one year if a sufficiently large crew works around the clock every day, even if the scenario is highly unlikely.

Legal Principle: **If a contract can possibly be performed within a year, even if such performance is highly unlikely, then the contract does not need a writing to be enforceable.**

BUT WHAT IF . . .

WHAT IF THE FACTS OF THE CASE OPENER WERE DIFFERENT?

Let's say, in the Case Opener, that the promissory note was issued when Branstad had purchased a tractor for a price of $475 from Garland and both parties agreed on April 15, 2012, that Branstad would pay Garland back in full on or before March 30, 2013. Would such an agreement require a writing according to the statute of frauds?

The above Case Nugget illustrates how important the facts are when ascertaining whether a contract cannot be performed within a year.

PROMISES MADE IN CONSIDERATION OF MARRIAGE

Agreements regarding marriage in which one party is gaining something other than a return on his or her promise to marry are within the statute of frauds and must be in writing.[3] In other words, when one party promises something to the other as part of an offer of marriage, the contract must be in writing to be enforceable.

[3] Ibid., sec. 124.

For example, Ed and Jeanie want to get married. Ed promises Jeanie he will buy her a new car every other year if she will marry him. To be enforceable, Ed and Jeanie's agreement must be in writing because Jeanie stands to benefit, by way of new cars, if she marries Ed.

Mutual promises to marry do not fall within the statute of frauds. If Ed and Jeanie promise each other they will get married, this agreement does not need to be in writing because neither party is gaining anything other than a return on his or her promise to marry; thus the agreement does not fall within the statute.

While mutual promises to marry do not fall within the statute of frauds, prenuptial agreements do. A **prenuptial agreement** is an agreement two parties enter into before marriage that clearly states the ownership rights each party enjoys in the other party's property. For these agreements, writing is required, although not sufficient, to establish enforceability. Furthermore, although consideration is *not* legally required, courts tend to privilege prenuptial agreements that include it. Consideration offers evidence that both parties understand and agree to all the terms of the agreement and that the agreement is not biased in favor of one party.

Legal Principle: **Contracts in which one party promises something in exchange for another's promise to marry must have a writing to be enforceable, but mutual promises to marry do not require a writing.**

CONTRACTS FOR ONE PARTY TO PAY THE DEBT OF ANOTHER IF THE INITIAL PARTY FAILS TO PAY

The contracts within the statute of frauds that concern promises to pay a debt are of a very limited kind. Known as *secondary obligations,* they are also called *secondary promises, collateral promises,* or *suretyship promises.* A secondary obligation occurs when a party outside a primary agreement promises to fulfill one of the original party's (primary debtor's) obligations if the original party fails to fulfill it. For example, Helen enters into a contract with Tomas to sell him her car. Subsequently, Rina agrees to pay Tomas's debt if he fails to pay Helen the money he owes her. To be enforceable, Rina's promise needs to be in writing because it is a secondary obligation and therefore falls within the statute.

The distinction between primary and secondary obligations determines when the statute requires a written agreement. *Primary obligations* are debts incurred in an initial contract. Using our car-sale example, the primary obligation is Tomas's promise to pay Helen for the car. Primary obligations are not within the statute of frauds and, therefore, need not be in writing to be enforceable. Secondary obligations, as we've seen, are within the statute and need to be in writing.

A specific instance of a secondary obligation involves the administrator or executor of an estate. Administrators and executors of estates are responsible for paying off the debts of an estate and then dividing the remaining assets appropriately among the heirs. While an agreement to pay the estate's debts with these funds need not be in writing, promises the administrator or executor makes to do so personally are within the statute of frauds and must be in writing. Because the administrator or executor is promising to pay with his or her own money, and not the estate's, the promise must be in writing to be enforceable; the administrator or executor has assumed a secondary obligation.

There is an exception under which a secondary obligation need *not* be in writing: the *main-purpose rule.* If the main purpose for incurring a secondary obligation is to obtain a personal benefit, the promise does not fall within the statute and does not have to be in writing.[4] The assumption is that a party attempting to achieve a personal benefit will not

---

[4] Ibid., sec. 116.

back out of the promise, therefore eliminating the need of a written record of the promise. The court's job is to use the context surrounding the agreement to determine the third party's main purpose for entering the agreement, which will determine whether a writing is required for the agreement to be enforceable.

Legal Principle: **Primary obligations do not require a writing, but secondary obligations do unless the main reason a person makes a secondary promise is to obtain a personal benefit.**

BUT WHAT IF . . .

WHAT IF THE FACTS OF THE CASE OPENER WERE DIFFERENT?

Let's say that Branstad buys a tractor from Garland. Branstad makes an agreement to pay Garland back in full, but his father makes a promise to pay for the tractor in case Branstad fails to complete his payments. Garland says that there needs to be a written contract explaining the father's promise according to the statute of frauds. Is Garland correct?

Case 18-1 is an example of a court's consideration of a suretyship promise in its attempt to determine whether the promise falls within the statute of frauds.

CASE 18-1   POWER ENTERTAINMENT, INC., ET AL. v. NATIONAL FOOTBALL LEAGUE PROPERTIES, INC.
U.S. COURT OF APPEALS FOR THE FIFTH CIRCUIT 151 F.3D 247 (1998)

Pro Set had a licensing agreement with NFLP, which allowed Pro Set to market NFL cards bearing the statement "official card of the National Football League." Pro Set filed for bankruptcy owing NFLP approximately $800,000 in unpaid royalties from card sales. Representatives of Power Entertainment met with NFLP to discuss taking over the licensing agreement between NFLP and Pro Set. Power Entertainment alleges NFLP orally agreed to transfer Pro Set's license to Power Entertainment in return for Power Entertainment's agreement to assume Pro Set's debt to NFLP. NFLP subsequently refused to transfer the licensing agreement to Power Entertainment.

Power Entertainment then brought a breach of contract suit against NFLP seeking damages for amounts spent in reliance on the alleged agreement and for lost profits. The district court granted NFLP's motion to dismiss, holding Power Entertainment's contract claim failed as a matter of law because it was not in writing and Power Entertainment had failed to plead facts sufficient to support an estoppel claim. Power Entertainment filed timely notice of appeal.

JUDGE BENAVIDES: In granting NFLP's motion to dismiss, the district court concluded the "suretyship" statute of frauds rendered the alleged oral agreement between NFLP and Power Entertainment unenforceable because Power

Entertainment promised to assume Pro Set's debt to NFLP as part of the alleged oral agreement. The relevant statute of frauds provision under Texas law provides "a promise by one person to answer for the debt, default, or miscarriage of another person" must be in writing. As the Supreme Court of Texas has explained, the suretyship statute of frauds serves an evidentiary function:

Probably the basic reason for requiring a promise to answer for the debt of another to be in writing is the promisor has received no direct benefit from the transaction. When the promisor receives something, this is subject to proof and tends to corroborate the making of the promise. Perjury is thus more likely in the case of a guaranty where nothing but the promise is of evidentiary value. The lack of any benefit received by the promisor not only increases the hardship of his being called upon to pay but also increases the importance of being sure that he is justly charged.

These evidentiary concerns do not pertain, however, if "the promise is made for the promisor's own benefit and not at all for the benefit of the third person. . . ." Consistent with this common-sense approach, the Texas courts have adopted the "main purpose doctrine," which, broadly speaking, removes an oral agreement to pay the debt of another from the statute of frauds "wherever the main purpose and object of the promisor is not to answer for another, but to subserve some purpose of his own. . . ."

In applying the main purpose doctrine under Texas law, this court has articulated the three factors used by Texas courts to determine whether the main purpose doctrine applies:

(1) [Whether the] promisor intended to become primarily liable for the debt, in effect making it his original obligation, rather than to become a surety for another;

(2) [Whether there] was consideration for the promise; and

(3) [Whether the] receipt of the consideration was the promisor's main purpose or leading object in making the promise; that is, the consideration given for the promise was primarily for the promisor's use and benefit.

Applying these factors to the facts alleged by Power Entertainment, it is apparent Power Entertainment may be able to show the alleged oral agreement falls outside of the statute of frauds. Consistent with the allegations in its complaint, Power Entertainment may be able to adduce facts that would prove Power Entertainment intended to create primary responsibility on its part to pay Pro Set's $800,000 debt to NFLP, rather than merely acting as a surety for Pro Set's obligation. According to Power Entertainment's complaint, Pro Set had already declared bankruptcy and defaulted on its royalty obligations to NFLP, and there is no indication Pro Set was involved in any way in the negotiations between NFLP and Power Entertainment.

Further, the licensing agreement constituted valuable consideration for Power Entertainment's agreement to pay Pro Set's debt. Finally, Power Entertainment apparently agreed to pay Pro Set's debt to NFLP not to aid Pro Set, but to induce NFLP to transfer Pro Set's licensing agreement to Power Entertainment for Power Entertainment's use and benefit. Under these circumstances, we conclude Power Entertainment may be able to prove a set of facts that would allow a jury to find the alleged oral agreement is not barred by the statute of frauds. Thus, the district court erred in dismissing Power Entertainment's complaint based on the statute of frauds.

REVERSED and REMANDED.

CRITICAL THINKING

Why do you think that the judge describes a certain approach to verbal contracts as "common sense," and what is that approach? How strong is the argument for the commonsense approach? What assumptions are probably shared by most people who accept this argument as common sense?

ETHICAL DECISION MAKING

The judge seems to think that in some circumstances a verbal agreement could facilitate unethical behavior. What ethical theory does the judge seem to assume most people use in ethical decision making? Why might it be wise to use the judge's assumption when making business decisions?

CONTRACTS RELATED TO AN INTEREST IN LAND

Within the statute of frauds, "land" encompasses not only the land and soil itself but anything attached to the land, such as trees or buildings. Because the statute requires a writing as evidence of the contract, a claim to an oral contract for the sale of land is not enough to prove such a contract existed.

Contracts transferring other interests in land are also within the statute of frauds. Mortgages and leases are within the statute because they are considered transfers of interest in land.

Determining exactly what constitutes an "interest in land" within the statute of frauds is difficult. A number of things that seem as if they are interests in land do not fall within the statute. For example, promises to sell crops annually, agreements between parties for profit sharing from the sale of real property, and boundary disputes that have been settled through the use of land are all outside the statute of frauds and, therefore, do not require evidence in writing. The nearby Case Nugget presents a case related to land in which the parties disagreed as to whether a writing was needed.

WHAT IS AN "INTEREST IN LAND"?

Shelby's, Inc. v. Sierra Bravo, Inc. 68 S.W.3d 604 (2002)

Shelby's, Inc., and Sierra Bravo entered into a written agreement that granted Sierra permission to use Shelby's land as a disposal site for waste and debris Sierra removed as part of the construction of a new highway. Shelby's claimed the parties also entered into an oral contract for Sierra to construct a waterway and building pad on Shelby's property. Sierra never completed the construction and denied that an oral contract existed. Shelby's sued, and the jury found in its favor.

Sierra appealed on the basis that the oral agreement was within the statute of frauds and therefore unenforceable. Sierra saw the alleged oral agreement as specifying a sale of an interest in land, which is within the statute of frauds. Therefore, the agreement, to be enforceable, would have had to be in writing. The court firmly disagreed with Sierra's argument, stating:

We agree with the well-reasoned argument of Respondent [Shelby's]. The contract in this case was not a "sale," much less a sale of an interest in lands. . . . Here, there was no transfer of ownership or title. The written agreement gave Appellant [Sierra] permission to deposit debris and soil on Respondent's land, not the right to do so. The oral contract was for the construction of a waterway and building pad and passed no interest in the land. . . . We decline to create a new category to which the statute of frauds applies, that of a contract for services for the deposit of dirt and soil on land. The trial court did not err in denying Appellant's motion for judgment notwithstanding the verdict. Appellant's point is denied and the judgment of the trial court is affirmed.

CONTRACTS FOR THE SALE OF GOODS TOTALING MORE THAN $500

Agreements for a sale in which the total price is $500 or more are required by the UCC, Section 2-201, to be recorded in a written contract or a memorandum. This writing need only state the quantity to be sold; buyer, seller, price, and method of payment do not need to be included. In fact, terms other than quantity can be inexact or left out of the writing as long as what is written does not contradict the parties' agreement about them. The contract will be enforceable for the stated quantity and not a unit more. Furthermore, for the contract to be enforceable, both the UCC and the statute of frauds require that the party against whom action is sought must have signed the written document.

Suppose Donnie and Gretchen enter into a sales contract. Donnie wrote the agreement, and Gretchen was the only party to sign. Later, Donnie attempts to enforce the agreement against Gretchen for the agreed-to quantity. Because Gretchen signed it, Donnie can bring suit against her. However, because Donnie did not sign the agreement, Gretchen can neither sue nor countersue him.

Other situations under the UCC that require contracts in writing are the lease of goods and the sale of securities[5] and personal property[6] if the price is greater than $5,000.

FURTHER REQUIREMENTS SPECIFIC TO CERTAIN STATES

Because the statute of frauds is actually state law, certain states have various requirements not found in others. In some states, under the equal dignity rule contracts that would normally fall under the statute and need a writing if negotiated by the principal must be in writing even if negotiated by an agent. For example, Luke appoints Sanjeev to act as his agent. Sanjeev enters into an agreement for Luke with Carrie that cannot be completed within one year according to the contractual terms. Had Luke contracted directly with Carrie, the agreement would be within the statute and require a writing. Therefore, Sanjeev's contract, which is on behalf of Luke, must also be in writing according to the equal dignity rule.

[5] UCC § 8-319.
[6] UCC § 81-206.

While the United States and other Western countries have adopted versions of the 1677 English act that gave birth to the statute of frauds, the English have gone in the opposite direction. Instead of expanding the powers and use of the 1677 act, they have severely limited the number of cases falling within their statute of frauds.

Although formal complaints were levied against the English statute of frauds as early as 1937, no action was taken until 1953. In that year, the Law Reform Committee addressed numerous 1937 arguments in favor of repeal. The 1953 committee recommended that Parliament repeal Section 4 of the 1677 act, which identifies specific types of contracts as required to be in writing. The Law Reform Act of 1954 subsequently repealed Section 4, with one cautionary exception. The 1954 act still required that promises to pay for the debt of others, what we call *suretyship* or *collateral promises,* be in writing.

A few states have special provisions in matters related to promises to pay debt. To be enforceable, a promise to pay a debt that has already been discharged because of bankruptcy must be in writing, to prevent the promisor from hiding behind the fact that the debt has been discharged. Another example is a promise to pay a debt when collection is barred by a statute of limitations. The logic here is the same as that in the first example. If the agreement is not in writing, the promisor can easily claim he or she does not need to pay. Therefore, the statute of frauds in certain states requires that both of these types of promises be in writing to be enforceable.

One last example of rules that hold only in some states occurs when the contract cannot be performed in the promisor's lifetime. For example, Heather promises to give $10,000 to Misha's charity on Heather's death. According to the terms of the promise, the agreement cannot be carried out within Heather's lifetime. In some states, Heather's promise would fall within the statute of frauds and would therefore have to be in writing. The intent here is to offer estates some protection from claims made on the basis of alleged oral contracts.

Exhibit 18-1 summarizes the contracts that fall within the statute of frauds and presents a mnemonic for remembering them.

Exhibit 18-1

A Mnemonic for Remembering Which Contracts Fall within the Statute of Frauds

Circumstances in Which the Statute of Frauds Applies (MY LEGS)		
M	Marriage	Contracts made in consideration of marriage
Y	Year	Contracts whose terms prevent possible performance within one year
L	Land	Contracts related to an interest in land
E	Executor	Contracts in which the executor promises to pay the debt of an estate with the executor's own money
G	Goods	Contracts for the sale of goods totaling more than $500
S	Suretyship	Contracts involving secondary obligations or suretyships

LO3

What must a writing contain to be sufficient to satisfy the statute of frauds?

Sufficiency of the Writing

There are no specific requirements for the form of a written contract under the statute of frauds. In fact, one or several documents can together make up the written agreement under the statute, although certain elements need to be present for a writing to constitute proper evidence of a written contract under the statute (see Exhibit 18-2).

Required elements include the identification of the parties to the contract, the subject matter of the agreement, the consideration (if any), and any pertinent terms. The contract

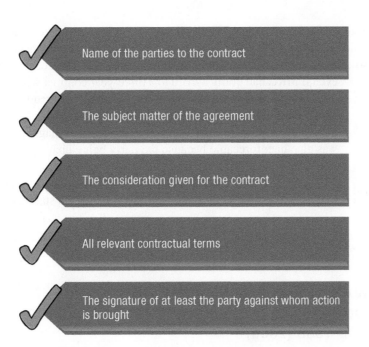

must be signed, but the signature need not be at the end. In fact, it need not be a full signature; a mark, such as an initial, is permissible as long as it is intended as a signature. While it is standard for both parties to sign the agreement, because the writing is being offered as proof of an agreement, only the party against whom action is sought needs to have signed it. If only one party signed, it is possible to have an agreement enforceable against that party but not the other. In some states oral testimony regarding an invoice for products sold is enough to meet the requirements under the statute if an actual invoice is not produced. The required elements in a writing can be contained in a memorandum, a document, or a compilation of several documents.

As you might gather from the information provided above, the statute of frauds can be particularly helpful to individuals involved in business transactions because it requires that certain important elements be present when a contract is in writing. In a way, the statute of frauds may help eliminate, or reduce, the ambiguity involved with contracts by requiring that certain conditions be met for a written document to constitute an enforceable contract. For example, when Medical Research Consultants (MRC) hired Michael Gallagher as a sales representative, the company required that he sign an employee handbook that outlined the terms of his employment. In signing the employee handbook, Gallagher acknowledged that he was an at-will employee of the company and could potentially be let go by MRC at any time. After Gallagher signed the handbook, a human resource representative for MRC faxed him a draft of an employment agreement which stated that Gallagher would work for a period of three years. Over the next several months, while Gallagher was working for MRC, he altered the draft that was faxed to him by MRC; Gallagher changed the number of years under the noncompete clause from two years to one year, and he wrote "3 weeks paid vacation" in a blank space on the draft (even after being told on more than one occasion that he was to receive two weeks' unpaid vacation). Then, after being employed by MRC for approximately four months, Gallagher faxed the draft with his signature back to the company. An attorney for MRC promptly responded to Gallagher and stated in an e-mail that "the draft sent to you . . . was for discussion purposes only. MRC never agreed to an employment contract with you and will not enter into one." Soon after, Gallagher was terminated from employment at MRC.

Gallagher filed suit against MRC, alleging breach of his three-year employment contract, which he maintained was created both orally during his early negotiations with MRC and also through the signed employment agreement draft. The court, however, found that even if MRC had orally agreed to a three-year contract with Gallagher, it would not have been enforceable because the statute of frauds dictates that agreements incapable of being completed within a year must be in writing. Further, according to the statute of frauds, the draft that Gallagher faxed back to MRC was also unenforceable because the party being charged must have signed the document and MRC clearly had not.[7]

Case 18-2 demonstrates how judges go about determining what constitutes a writing and when a writing is sufficient under the statute of frauds.

> To see how effective writing principles relate to contracts under the statute of frauds, please see the **Connecting to the Core** activity on the text website at www.mhhe.com/kubasek3e.

[7] *Michael J. Gallagher v. Medical Research Consultants, LLP,* Civil Action No. 04-236 (case summary accessed on LexisNexis May 26, 2009).

CASE 18-2   STEWART LAMLE v. MATTEL, INC.
U.S. COURT OF APPEALS FOR THE FEDERAL CIRCUIT
394 F.3D 1355 (2005)

Steward Lamle is the inventor of Farook, a board game. Lamle obtained two patents for Farook from the United States Patent and Trademark Office and negotiated with Mattel, Inc., regarding the licensing of Farook by Mattel. Early in these negotiations, Lamle signed Mattel's standard Product Disclosure Form, which contained the following provision:

> *I understand that . . . no obligation is assumed by [Mattel] unless and until a formal written contract is agreed to and entered into, and then the obligation shall be only that which is expressed in the formal, written contract.*

The negotiations advanced, and a meeting was held on June 11 where the parties discussed the terms of a licensing agreement. Mattel and Lamle there agreed on many terms of a license including a three-year term, the geographic scope, the schedule for payment, and the percentage royalty. Mattel asked Lamle to "draft a formal document memorializing 'The Deal'" and "promised [that] it would sign a formal, written contract before January 1, 1998."

Mattel employee Mike Bucher sent Lamle an email entitled "Farook Deal" on June 26 that substantially repeated terms agreed to at the June 11 meeting. The email stated the terms "have been agreed in principal [sic] by . . . Mattel subject to contract." The salutation "Best regards Mike Bucher" appeared at the end of the email.

On October 8, Mattel notified Lamle of its decision not to go ahead with the production of Farook. Lamle filed action asserting, among other things, a claim of breach of contract. The district court granted summary judgment in favor of Mattel on all claims. The Court of Appeals vacated that grant of summary judgment and remanded the case to the district court. The district court on remand again granted summary judgment in favor of Mattel on all claims. Lamle appealed again.

JUDGE DYK: Mattel contends, and the district court held, any oral agreement made during the June 11 meeting cannot be enforced because of the California Statute of Frauds.

There is no question the alleged oral agreement for a three year license was one that, by its terms, could not be "performed within a year from the making thereof." The only question, therefore, is whether there is a writing to evidence the agreement or an applicable exception to the Statute of Frauds. To satisfy the Statute of Frauds, a writing must contain all the material terms of the contract. The writing must also be signed by the party against whom enforcement is sought. Lamle argues the June 26 email from Bucher satisfied both requirements.

The June 26 email specified the term of the license, the geographic scope, the percentage royalty, and the total advance and minimum amount to be paid under the contract. Bucher stated these terms had "been agreed in principal [sic] by [his] superiors at Mattel subject to contract" and the email message "covers the basic points."

California law is clear that "a note or memorandum under the statute of frauds need not contain all of the details of an agreement between the parties." Rather, the statute only requires "every material term of an agreement within its provisions be reduced to written form." "If the court, after acquiring knowledge of all the facts concerning the transaction which the parties themselves possessed at the time the agreement was made, can plainly determine from the memorandum the identity of the parties to the contract, the nature of its subject matter, and its essential terms, the memorandum will be held to be adequate." What is an essential term "depends on the agreement and its context and also on the subsequent conduct of the parties."

Mattel correctly points out the June 26 email does not contain all the terms that Lamle asserts are part of the oral contract. In particular, Mattel correctly notes Lamle alleges Mattel (1) guaranteed to sell 200,000 units of Farook each year; (2) promised to sell Farook units to Lamle at cost; and (3) promised Lamle the right to approve or disapprove the design and packaging of Farook units. None of these terms appears in the June 26 email. Again, we think there is a genuine issue of material fact as to the materiality of these terms. The Ninth Circuit, interpreting California law, has stated "the subject matter, the price, and the party against whom enforcement is sought" are the "few terms deemed essential as a matter of law by California courts." A jury could well conclude these omitted terms allegedly agreed to at the meeting but not reflected in the writing were not material.

There also remains the issue of whether an email is a writing "subscribed by the party to be charged or by the party's agent." The party to be charged in this case is Mattel, and the June 26 email was written by Bucher, an employee of Mattel, and his name appears at the end of the email, which concludes with "Best regards Mike Bucher." Mattel has not disputed the agency authority of Bucher to bind it. Therefore, the only question is whether Bucher's name on an email is a valid writing and signature to satisfy the Statute of Frauds.

California law does provide, however, typed names appearing on the end of telegrams are sufficient to be writings under the Statute of Frauds. California law also provides that a typewritten name is sufficient to be a signature. We can see no meaningful difference between a typewritten signature on a telegram and an email. Therefore, we conclude under California law the June 26 email satisfies the Statute of Frauds, assuming there was a binding oral agreement on June 11 and the email includes all the material terms of that agreement.

To prove a contract with Mattel, Lamle must prove the parties objectively intended to be immediately bound by an oral contract on June 11; the June 26 email contains the material terms of that oral contract; and Bucher had actual or apparent authority to sign for Mattel. Reviewing the record, Lamle has presented sufficient evidence to create genuine issues of material fact on these points. This is not to say Lamle should prevail at trial. Indeed, among other things, Lamle faces a difficult burden persuading the jury, despite Mattel's stating it would sign a formal contract later, the objective intention of both parties was to be immediately bound by the oral contract, and to abrogate a prior written agreement to the contrary.

Therefore, we vacate the grant of summary judgment with respect to the breach of contract claim and remand for further proceedings consistent with this opinion.

VACATED-IN-PART and REMANDED.

CRITICAL THINKING

The judge makes an argument about what constitutes a signature by referring to precedent and drawing an analogy between e-mails and telegrams. How strong is this analogy? Outline an argument against it. Explain.

ETHICAL DECISION MAKING

When Mattel's agents in charge of buying or rejecting games were negotiating with Lamle, they may have considered the ethical aspects of their decisions. If you were Mattel's agent, what ethical guidelines and values would you want to consider while evaluating the ethicality of terminating Mattel's relationship with Lamle? What ethical considerations would you find the most important?

Exceptions to the Statute of Frauds

Like most legal rules, the statute of frauds allows certain exceptions. These exceptions are (1) admission, (2) partial performance, and (3) promissory estoppel. There are also exceptions under the UCC. All these exceptions are summarized in Exhibit 18-3.

ADMISSION

An admission is a statement made in court, under oath, or at some stage during a legal proceeding in which a party against whom charges have been brought admits that an oral contract existed, even though the contract was required to be in writing.[8]

---

[8] Restatement (Second) of Contracts, sec. 133.

Exhibit 18-3

Exceptions to the
Statute of Frauds

Admission	The party against whom charges have been brought admits during legal proceedings that an oral contract existed, even though the contract was supposed to be in writing.
Partial performance	A buyer of land, in alleged contract, has paid a portion of the sales price, has begun permanently improving the land, or has taken possession of it; these actions prove the existence of a contract.
Promissory estoppel	One party was detrimentally reliant on the contract, and this reliance was for seeable by the other party.
Exceptions under the UCC	1. Oral contracts between merchants selling goods to one another need not be in writing.
	2. Oral contracts for customized goods are enforceable, even if they would normally have to be in writing.

Sinead enters into an agreement with Jin for the sale of a plot of land. The parties fail to write down their agreement but proceed as if it were finalized. Jin changes his mind and does not go through with the transaction. Sinead then sues him. If Jin admits during trial that there was an oral contract between him and Sinead, the courts would uphold the contract for the sale of land. Without this admission, the agreement between Sinead and Jin for the sale of interest in land would need to be in writing to be enforceable.

All states except Louisiana and California allow the admission exception. To the extent that the statute of frauds is intended to require proper evidence of agreements, the admission exception is well reasoned. However, to the extent that the statute is intended to encourage care and caution in establishing the specific details of agreements, the admission exception seems to unnecessarily punish honest parties while rewarding dishonest ones.

Like the statute of frauds, the UCC makes an exception when parties admit to the existence of an oral contract. However, it provides that a contract required to be in writing but admitted to in court will be enforceable only for the quantity admitted.[9]

BUT WHAT IF . . .
WHAT IF THE FACTS OF THE CASE OPENER WERE DIFFERENT?
Let's say that Branstad buys $1,000 worth of products from Garland. Such an agreement requires a writing, yet the two parties never made a written contract for the agreement. In court, both parties admit to making an oral agreement encompassing the same terms. Would the court be able to view such an agreement as being a valid contract?

PARTIAL PERFORMANCE

Although the statute of frauds requires a writing for sales of interests in land, under the partial-performance exception, if the buyer in an alleged contract for the sale of land has paid any portion of the sale price, has begun to permanently improve the land, or has taken possession of it, the courts will consider the contract partially performed and this partial performance will amount to proof of the contract.

---

[9] UCC § 2-201(3)(b).

Accordingly, partial performance can override the statute's requirement for a written agreement. The logic here is that the actions of both parties demonstrate the existence of their agreement, so the agreement no longer needs to be in writing to be enforceable. Under similar sections of the UCC, an oral contract is enforceable by the buyer or seller to the extent that he or she accepts payment or delivery of the goods in question.[10]

BUT WHAT IF . . .

WHAT IF THE FACTS OF THE CASE OPENER WERE DIFFERENT?

Let's say that Branstad bought land from Garland. Although such an agreement requires a writing, the two parties made only an oral agreement. Shortly after the agreement, Branstad began making payments and fixing up the land. Garland subsequently denied any agreement being made. Could some of Branstad's actions following the agreement be proof of the agreement? Could the court recognize the oral agreement as a valid contract?

PROMISSORY ESTOPPEL

Under certain circumstances, when a party relies on an oral contract that within the statute of frauds is required to be in writing, the reliance can create a situation in which the contract is nevertheless enforceable. Promissory estoppel is the legal enforcement of an otherwise unenforceable contract due to a party's detrimental reliance on the contract.

For promissory estoppel to be in effect, the party's reliance must be to her own detriment. Furthermore, the reliance must have been reasonably foreseeable; that is, the party who did not rely on the contract should have known the other party was going to rely on it.[11]

Suppose you enter into a contract to buy a house after having accepted an offer on your current house. The new house costs more than the price you are getting for your old house, and the person from whom you are buying knows about the sale of your old house and the difference in prices. To come up with the price difference, you sell your collection of rare coins. Unfortunately, however, you forget to create a written contract for your purchase of the new house, and the other person refuses to sell it to you. You are now homeless and have sold off your only real assets. Because the other person reasonably should have known you were relying on the contract, and because you did so to your own detriment, under promissory estoppel you could win performance of the sales contract.

This argument is not an easy one to make, however. For example, when Cheesecake Factory tried to argue that it should have been entitled to rely on a bank's oral representation that a loan would be approved, the court said that the firm's reliance on such representations was not reasonable. Further, the time between the representation and the firm's discovery that it would not receive the loan was so brief that the reliance could not have been that detrimental.[12]

EXCEPTIONS UNDER THE UCC

Exceptions also exist under the UCC. For instance, oral contracts between merchants need not be in writing to be enforceable. If one merchant agrees to sell goods to another, the contract is enforceable even if it is not in writing.

[10] UCC § 2-201(3)(c).

[11] Restatement (Second) of Contracts, sec. 139.

[12] *Classic Cheesecake Company, Inc., et al., v. JPMorgan Chase Bank, N.A.*, 546 F.3d 839, 2008 U.S. App. LEXIS 21632.

An issue that comes up again and again in e-commerce is the lack of precedents or statutes applicable to situations arising in the new environment. Until rather recently, there weren't any statutes that specifically addressed the nature of electronic transactions. This situation requires that judges rely on their good judgment when interpreting traditional contract law and applying it to e-commerce. For some transactions to be viewed as legally valid under the statute of frauds, there must be written copies of the contract that are then signed by at least one of the parties. In 2000, the Uniform Electronic Transactions Act was proposed by the National Conference of Commissioners on Uniform State Laws. It was subsequently adopted as law in 49 states plus the District of Columbia, Puerto Rico and the U.S. Virgin Islands. This act circumvents the former requirements of the statute of frauds regarding the validity of online transactions. The act reflects the decision that particular electronic transactions may constitute a "written copy" and therefore have legal significance, despite the fact that the electronic transaction is not technically a written document. These statutory changes ensure that business owners are assured of the validity of an online contract.

Source: Uniform Electronic Transactions Act, National Conference of State Legislatures, http://www.ncsl.org/issues-research/telecom/uniform-electronic-transactions-acts.aspx.

Likewise, oral contracts for customized goods are enforceable even if they would normally have to be in writing. The reasoning is that customized goods are not likely to be salable to a general audience, so the party that did not back out of the agreement probably incurred unreasonable costs under the contract.

Parol Evidence Rule

L04

What is the purpose of the parol evidence rule?

A problem arises with written contracts when a party asserts that the writing is in some way deficient. To smooth transactions by limiting the types of evidence admissible in such claims, the courts rely heavily on the parol evidence rule. This common law rule makes oral evidence of an agreement inadmissible if it is made before or at the same time as a writing that the parties intend to be the complete and final version of their agreement.[13] *Parol* in "parol evidence rule" means speech or words, specifically words outside the original writing.

The purpose of the parol evidence rule is to prevent evidence that substantially contradicts the agreement in its written form. Therefore, evidence of prior agreements and negotiations, as well as contemporaneous agreements and negotiations, is typically excluded under the parol evidence rule. A written agreement is assumed to be complete, and evidence contradicting it usually impedes business transactions, which is why the rule exists.

However, when a court determines that the written agreement does *not* represent a complete and final version of the agreement, evidence to further the court's understanding may be admissible. The additional evidence is limited to elements missing from the writing but consistent with it. These may be terms typically included in similar transactions or separate agreements in which consideration had been offered.

Note, however, that parol evidence applies first and foremost to spoken and written words extrinsic to the original writing. The parol evidence rule is also *not* a rule of evidence; rather, it relates to the substantive legal issue of what constitutes a legally binding agreement and how we know what that agreement is. Finally, the parol evidence rule is not a unitary concept or rule but an amalgamation of different rules and conditions.

Although the parol evidence rule applies to writings created at the same time as the written agreement, these writings tend to be treated differently than prior or contemporaneous oral agreements. That is, the writings are more readily admitted as part of the written agreement than is oral evidence regarding conditions or terms in the final agreement. As long as contemporaneous written documents do not substantially contradict what is in the final

---

[13] Restatement (Second) of Contracts, sec. 213.

writing, judges can use their discretion to deem these other writings part of that agreement. Consequently, the parol evidence rule does not usually exclude extrinsic written evidence.

Sometimes parties take the initiative and, in a merger clause, attempt to signal to judges that the written contract is intended to be the final and complete statement of their agreement. In essence, a merger clause seeks to blend other agreements either into the final agreement or into something explicitly identified as being outside the final agreement. Not all courts consider merger clauses to be conclusive proof of a contract. Where they are accepted, however, merger clauses greatly reduce the amount of guesswork courts must do in determining what is the final statement of the agreement.

Legal Principle: **Once a fully integrated agreement has been written, no oral evidence of any prior or contemporaneous agreement can be admitted in court to change the terms of the agreement.**

BUT WHAT IF . . .
WHAT IF THE FACTS OF THE CASE OPENER WERE DIFFERENT?
Recall that, in the Case Opener, Garland and Branstad's alleged oral agreement regarding interest payments was made after the completion of the written agreement. What if the oral agreement had been made before the two parties completed the written agreement? Would the oral agreement be admissible in court under the parole evidence rule?

Exceptions to the Parol Evidence Rule

Like the statute of frauds, the parol evidence rule admits some exceptions in which parol evidence, normally excluded, may be admissible in court. These exceptions are (1) contracts that have been subsequently modified, (2) contracts conditioned on orally agreed-on terms, (3) contracts that are not final as they are part written and part oral, (4) contracts with ambiguous terms, (5) incomplete contracts, (6) contracts with obvious typographical errors, (7) voidable or void contracts, and (8) evidence of prior dealings or usage of trade. (See Exhibit 18-4.)

Exhibit 18-4
Summary of Parol
Evidence Rule

Parol Evidence Rule

Oral evidence of an agreement is inadmissible if it is made before or at the same time as a writing that the parties intend to be the complete and final version of the agreement.

Exceptions to the Rule

- Contract has been subsequently modified.
- Written agreement was based on an orally agreed-on condition.
- Contract is nonfinalized in that it is partly written and partly oral.
- Contract contains ambiguous terms that significantly affect its interpretation.
- Contract is incomplete in that it is missing critical information.
- Contract contains obvious typographical errors.
- Contract is void or voidable.
- Evidence about past business transactions will clarify missing information or ambiguities in the contract.

CONTRACTS THAT HAVE BEEN SUBSEQUENTLY MODIFIED

Although parol evidence contradictory to the final terms is inadmissible, evidence regarding a contract's subsequent modification *is* admissible. The modification must have been made after the writing, and the evidence must clearly indicate this later modification.

Despite the allowance of evidence to demonstrate modifications, not all evidence of modification is admissible. If the agreement is required to be in writing because it is within the statute of frauds, oral modifications are unenforceable. However, oral evidence of a subsequent written agreement is admissible. In addition, if the contract's terms require that modification be in writing, oral modifications are inadmissible and unenforceable.[14]

CONTRACTS CONDITIONED ON ORALLY AGREED-ON TERMS

The parol evidence rule does not prevent parties from introducing evidence proving the written agreement was conditioned on terms agreed to orally. The reason is that the evidence being elicited does not substantially modify the written agreement. Rather, what is at issue with such evidence is the enforceability of the contract as written. No terms are altered, so the parol evidence rule does not apply.

When an entire contract is conditioned on something else's occurring first, that first event is known as a condition precedent. Evidence of the existence of a condition precedent agreed to orally is admissible, as stated previously, because the contract is not modified by such evidence; rather, its enforceability is called into question. Since the statute of frauds is concerned primarily with the enforceability of agreements, it logically follows that the parol evidence rule does not apply to evidence of condition precedents.

NONFINALIZED, PARTIALLY WRITTEN AND PARTIALLY ORAL CONTRACTS

When a contract consists of both written and oral elements, judges tend to treat it as nonfinalized and assume that the parties do not intend to have the written part represent the entire agreement. Therefore, oral evidence related to the contract is admissible because the written document is not the complete and final representation of the agreement.

CONTRACTS CONTAINING AMBIGUOUS TERMS

A contract that contains what the court deems to be ambiguous terms presents a dilemma in interpretation. To reach the most accurate interpretation of the original agreement, the

[14] UCC § 2-209(2),(3).

court allows evidence, even if it is oral, for the sole purpose of clarifying, *not* changing, ambiguous contractual terms. As with the evidence regarding orally agreed-on condition precedents, evidence used to clarify ambiguity is believed not to modify the contract but, rather, to clarify, and therefore it is admissible.

INCOMPLETE CONTRACTS

When a contract is fundamentally flawed because it is missing critical information, typically related to essential terms, courts can allow parol evidence to fill in the missing parts while not modifying the written agreement in any substantial way. Parol evidence is here used to facilitate business transactions, not to force the parties to enter into a new, complete agreement.

CONTRACTS WITH OBVIOUS TYPOGRAPHICAL ERRORS

Whenever a written agreement under the statute of frauds contains a serious, and obvious, typographical error (typo), parol evidence is admissible to demonstrate that it was a typo, as well as to set forth the proper term. This admission does not fundamentally alter the written agreement because the typo is not an accurate reflection of the parties' agreement.

VOID OR VOIDABLE CONTRACTS

Certain conditions can make an otherwise valid contract void or voidable. (Refer to Chapter 13 for an in-depth discussion of what makes a contract void or voidable.) While the contract does not list these conditions, the courts allow parol evidence to demonstrate them. Like most exceptions to the parol evidence rule, this one does not fundamentally alter the terms of the contract but, rather, addresses its enforceability. Furthermore, evidence of a defense against a contract (discussed in Chapter 16) is admissible to prove a contract is void or voidable.

EVIDENCE OF PRIOR DEALINGS OR USAGE OF TRADE (UCC)

This final exception actually falls under the UCC and not the statute of frauds. According to the UCC, parol evidence is admissible for the sake of clarification if it addresses prior dealings between the parties or usages of trade in the business they are in.[15] Evidence related to past dealings can help clarify missing or ambiguous terms by demonstrating how the parties have previously interacted; the assumption is that they will continue to interact in a similar manner. Therefore, if a term is missing or ambiguous, the courts rely on evidence of what the parties did in the past to gauge what they intended in the contract in question.

Similarly, when a contract is ambiguous or incomplete, the courts examine standard practices in the business, assuming the parties intend to engage in these practices even if they are not included in the agreement. Once again, an exception is made to allow parol evidence to clarify a contract, as opposed to changing any material terms.

Integrated Contracts

Integrated contracts are written contracts intended to be the complete and final representation of the parties' agreement. When the courts deem a contract integrated, with the exception of the above exceptions, parol evidence is inadmissible. In partially integrated contracts, parol evidence is admissible to the extent that it clarifies part of the contract or

---

[15] UCC §§ 1-205 and 2-202.

addresses its enforceability.[16] Therefore, the easiest test to determine the admissibility of parol evidence is to check whether the written contract, within the statute of frauds, is an integrated contract.

We've seen that one way parties can indicate their desire to create an integrated contract is through the use of a merger clause. A merger clause explicitly states that the written contract is intended to be the complete and final version of the contract between the parties and that other possible agreements between the parties, besides the one in question, are not part of the final written agreement. Most states will allow a merger clause to constitute the stated intent of the parties unless one party offers proof of a personal defense against the contract. However, some states consider merger clauses to be recommendations, not necessarily binding on the parties.

CASE OPENER WRAP-UP

Admissibility of an Oral Contract in Court

The district court found for Branstad after seeing evidence that Branstad and his wife had not only managed Garland's other properties until 1998 but had spent their own money on the properties' upkeep. Additionally, in accordance with Branstad's account of the oral agreement, the payments Branstad had made to Garland were listed in payment and tax records as noninterest payments. Such information showed that Garland had made no attempt to collect interest payments until the two had a falling out in 1998. Furthermore, the court determined that the parol evidence rule did not apply to the oral agreement in question because the agreement was made after the completion of the written contract, not before or during. Ultimately, the court determined that the oral contract existed as a separate agreement and not as part of the original written agreement.[17]

[16] Restatement (Second) of Contracts, sec. 216.

[17] *Garland v. Brandstad*, 648 NW 2d 65 (2002).

KEY TERMS

admission   415

condition precedent   420

equal dignity rule   411

integrated contracts   421

merger clause   419

parol evidence rule   418

partial performance   416

prenuptial agreement   408

promissory estoppel   417

statute
of frauds   405

SUMMARY OF KEY TOPICS

The term *statute of frauds* refers to various state laws modeled after the 1677 English Act for the Prevention of Frauds and Perjuries. These state laws are intended to (1) ease contractual negotiations by requiring sufficient reliable evidence to prove the existence and specific terms of a contract, (2) prevent unreliable oral evidence from interfering with a contractual relationship, and (3) prevent parties from entering into contracts with which they do not agree.

Statute of Frauds

Contracts falling within the statute of frauds:

Contracts Falling within the Statute of Frauds

1. Contracts whose terms prevent possible performance within one year.
2. Promises made in consideration of marriage.
3. Contracts for one party to pay the debt of another if the initial party fails to pay.
4. Contracts related to an interest in land.
5. Under the Uniform Commercial Code, contracts for the sale of goods totaling more than $500.

A sufficient writing under the statute of frauds must clearly indicate (1) the parties to the contract, (2) the subject matter of the agreement, (3) the consideration given for the contract, (4) all relevant contractual terms, and (5) the signature of at least the party against whom action is brought.

Sufficiency of the Writing

Under the UCC, writing must clearly indicate (1) the quantity to be sold and (2) the signature of the party being sued.

Under both the statute of frauds and the UCC, a writing may consist of multiple documents as long as they explicitly reference one another.

Exceptions to the requirement of a writing under the statute of frauds:

Exceptions to the Statute of Frauds

1. Admission that an oral agreement exists.
2. Partial performance of the contract.
3. Promissory estoppel (legal enforcement due to a party's detrimental reliance on the contract).
4. Various exceptions under the UCC.

The *parol evidence rule* is a common law rule stating that oral evidence of an agreement made prior to or contemporaneously with the written agreement is inadmissible when the parties intend to have a written agreement be the complete and final version of their agreement.

Parol Evidence Rule

Exceptions to the parol evidence rule:

Exceptions to the Parol Evidence Rule

1. Contracts that are subsequently modified.
2. Contracts conditioned on orally agreed-on terms.
3. Contracts that are not final because they are partly written and partly oral.
4. Contracts with ambiguous terms.
5. Incomplete contracts.

6. Contracts with obvious typographical errors.

7. Voidable or void contracts.

8. Evidence of prior dealings or usage of trade.

Integrated Contracts *Integrated contracts* are written contracts within the statute of frauds intended to be the complete and final representation of the parties' agreement, thus precluding the admissibility of parol evidence other than in the exceptions listed above.

POINT / COUNTERPOINT

Does the United States Still Benefit from Having a Statute of Frauds?	
YES	NO
The statute of frauds provides great benefit as a social lubricant aiding U.S. business transactions. By requiring that certain types of contracts be in writing, we ensure that they either will have enough evidence to prove the existence and terms of the contract or will be unenforceable. Because only certain contracts are required to be in writing, the rule does not preclude oral contracts, but it ensures that the most important contracts can be enacted without complications.	The statute of frauds acts as an impediment to contractual agreements, and the states should repeal the relevant sections of their laws.
Another way in which the statute of frauds benefits U.S. business is by preventing unreliable evidence from being used in court. Human memories are notoriously weak and faulty, and it does not make sense to base important legal decisions on what someone says he or she remembers. Furthermore, people with a vested interest can change their testimony on the basis of changed circumstances in pursuit of personal gain. However, with the requirement that certain contracts be in writing, the parties are bound by what they wrote.	When parties agree, why should they be subjected to unnecessary formalities? The written requirements of the statute of frauds get in the way of business transactions more often than they help.
Finally, the act of writing gives people time to pause for reflection. No one benefits when parties hastily rush into an agreement they later regret. Thoughtful reflection prevents parties from entering into contracts with which they do not agree, and this means fewer cases are brought due to one party's entering an unfair, or otherwise defective, agreement.	Furthermore, the required writing frequently imposes additional costs on the parties. When even simple agreements in which neither party contests the terms must be written, more time is spent *not* conducting other business. Frequently, the parties have to hire attorneys to write their contracts, imposing still more costs and helping decrease whatever benefit the parties might have gained from the original agreement before the writing took place.
	In addition, although most parties enter agreements in good faith, it is not uncommon for parties to seek a way out of contracts they cannot perform. The writing requirements are not always accurately fulfilled, and unethical parties can exploit minor technicalities to have a contract declared void. In the end, the innocent party is harmed by the writing requirement, and the unethical party escapes a bad situation with little to no harm.

QUESTIONS & PROBLEMS

1. Describe the contents of a writing that would be sufficient to satisfy the statute of frauds under the common law.

2. List the kinds of contracts that require a writing under the statute of frauds.

3. Identify the exceptions to the parol evidence rule, and explain why some people might argue that the rule is not very effective.

4. The McCartheys controlled Salt Lake City's largest daily newspaper, *The Salt Lake Tribune,* through their

collective ownership of shares in the Kearns-Tribune (KT) Corporation, a holding company for the newspaper. In 1997, KT merged with Tele-Communications, Inc. (TCI). The McCartheys originally opposed the merger but later agreed to it. In 1999, TCI and AT&T merged, and AT&T sold the *Tribune* to MediaNews in 2001. The McCartheys argue that according to an oral agreement reached in 1997, at the time of the original merger that they opposed, the McCartheys have the opportunity to buy back the *Tribune* after five years (in 2002) for a fair market price but that MediaNews tried to block any attempt at a sale. The McCartheys filed suit to enforce the oral agreement. MediaNews moved for a declaratory judgment that the McCartheys have no independent rights in the *Tribune.* The district court granted the defendant's motions as to all claims. The McCartheys appealed. Under what conditions would the McCartheys' claim be successful? As a judge, what evidence would help you decide whether the oral agreement constituted a valid contract? [*MediaNews Group, Inc. v. McCarthey,* 494 F.3d 1254 (2007).]

5. Antwun Echols, a professional boxer, signed a promotional agreement with Banner Promotions Inc. The agreement gave Banner the right to be Echols's sole representative in negotiations for all fights. Banner's major obligation under the agreement was to "secure, arrange and promote" not less than three bouts for Echols during each year of the contract. Banner was to pay Echols not less than a contractually stated minimum amount for each bout in which he appeared, with the amount of the minimum depending on where the bout was televised and whether Echols appeared as a champion. However, Banner had the option to renegotiate the amounts if Echols lost a fight, which he did one month into the contract; afterward, Banner chose to negotiate Echols's compensation on a bout-by-bout basis. After several fights under the new agreement, Echols became dissatisfied with the situation, arguing that Banner had made him "take it or leave it" offers for what he believed was below-market compensation. Echols sued Banner, arguing that the variable amounts made the contract vague and therefore unenforceable. Did the agreement constitute a valid contract? Why or why not? [*Echols v. Pelullo,* 377 F.3d 272 (2004).]

6. Sunkist Growers Inc. brought Nabisco to court, claiming that under the companies' mutually agreed-on license agreement, Nabisco was causing Sunkist to engage in improper practices. Nabisco claimed that, under the license agreement, the companies had to settle the dispute through arbitration. However, Sunkist claimed that it was a nonsignatory to the contract and thus did not have to settle through arbitration. Nabisco claimed that Sunkist was legally compelled to settle through arbitration, even though Sunkist had not signed the document, because the two parties admitted to the license agreement being an agreement between them and both companies' actions had been based on the agreement. How do you think the court decided? [10 F. 3d 753 (Ga. CA 11, 1993).]

7. The plaintiff investor sued the defendant investment company for breach of an oral agreement on the part of the defendant to recommend hedge funds for the plaintiff and exercise due diligence with respect to the recommendations, in exchange for which the plaintiff would pay a 1 percent fee for every year the defendant held the fund. The suit arose when the plaintiff found out that the hedge fund the company recommended was a ponzi scheme. The district court dismissed the case on the grounds that the contract was an ongoing one that would not be completed within a year and therefore required a writing to be enforceable. The plaintiff appealed. How do you think the appellate court ruled on this issue, and why? [*South Cherry Street, LLC v. Hennessee Group LLC,* 573 F.3d 98, 2009 U.S. App. LEXIS 15467.]

8. In 1995, Schaefer was in a car accident, and his vehicle was damaged. His insurance company looked at his vehicle and gave him money to repair it. However, even with the repairs, Schaefer's vehicle's overall value dropped almost $3,000 due to the accident. Schaefer's interpretation of the insurance company's written policy was that the company would return the vehicle to its original value before the accident. On the other hand, the insurance company interpreted the written policy as meaning that the company would pay the lesser option of either replacing the vehicle with one of a similar value or paying for repairs. How do courts usually resolve cases of ambiguity in contracts? How did the court decide this case? [*Am. Mfrs. Mut. Ins. Co. v. Schaefer,* 124 S.W.3d 154, 2003 Tex. LEXIS 472, 47 Tex. Sup. Ct. J. 40 (Tex. 2003).]

9. In 2004, real estate broker Richard Davis called an A&E television executive about partnering on a

new reality show called *Flip This House*. Davis said he would undertake the financial risks of purchasing and later reselling the real estate and he and the network would split the net profits. Davis received confirmation from the network director over the phone and later with three other executives. The network never paid Davis and claimed no agreement was made. The district court found on behalf of Davis, and the network appealed. The appellate court stipulated that two facts must be true to find on behalf of Davis: first, that Davis reasonably believed that an agreement was made during the phone conversations and, second, that such a belief would be made by an objectively reasonable person. How do you think the court decided? [*Davis v. A&E Television,* 422 Fed. Appx. 199, 2011 U.S. App. LEXIS 7382.]

10. Benito Brino owned real property that he leased to Salvatore and Linda Gabriele. During the lease, the Gabrieles attempted to purchase the property from Brino. Both parties agreed on a purchase price of $565,000 with a closing date of September 15, 2001. However, the Gabrieles were not able to obtain the full amount in loan financing from the bank, so they made a counteroffer to purchase for $450,000, which Brino rejected. The Gabrieles later obtained the full $565,000 from another lending institution and drafted an addendum to the July sales agreement that altered the closing date to May 5, 2002. Brino orally accepted the terms of the agreement, but the document was not signed until May 16, 2002, after the closing date. Consequently, the bank refused to acknowledge the addendum's validity. Thereafter, the Gabrieles drafted a second sales agreement with the same terms as the July agreement, except that the second agreement did not include a closing date but stated that the effective date would be the signing date. Both parties signed the agreement on June 16, 2002, and the bank accepted the agreement and agreed to provide the loan. The Gabrieles informed Brino that they were ready to close, but Brino did not convey title of the property to the Gabrieles. The Gabrieles brought suit against Brino, seeking specific performance, but Brino argued that the agreement was not enforceable as it did not satisfy the statute of frauds, primarily because the agreement did not designate the seller. In response, the Gabrieles claimed that their obtaining financing was partial performance of the agreement. How did the court resolve this issue with regard to the statute of frauds? [*Gabriele v. Brino,* 2004 Conn. App. LEXIS 428.]

Looking for more review materials?

The Online Learning Center at **www.mhhe.com/kubasek3e** contains this chapter's "Assignment on the Internet" and also a list of URLs for more information, entitled "On the Internet." Find both of them in the Student Center portion of the OLC, along with quizzes and other helpful materials.

Third-Party Rights to Contracts

LEARNING OBJECTIVES

After reading this chapter, you will be able to answer the following questions:

1 What is an assignment?

2 What are the rights and duties of an assignor?

3 What are the rights and duties of an assignee?

4 What is a third-party beneficiary contract?

5 What are the differences among donee beneficiaries, creditor beneficiaries, and incidental beneficiaries?

CASE OPENER

Fallout from a Unforgettable Fight

On June 28, 1997, in Las Vegas, heavyweight boxers Mike Tyson and Evander Holyfield met for what proved to be a night to remember. During the third round of the fight, a desperate Tyson illegally bit off a piece of Holyfield's ear and, moments later, bit the other ear too.[1] Tyson was disqualified. Some fans were so outraged that they decided to sue Tyson, the fight promoters, and the telecasters, seeking a refund.[2] Among other things, they claimed to be third-party beneficiaries to various contracts into which the defendants had entered.

1. Are fans entitled to refunds on the basis of third-party beneficiary rights? What type of beneficiaries would fans have to be to enforce contractual rights?

2. If you were one of the fight promoters, what sorts of contractual duties would you have to the viewers?

The Wrap-Up at the end of the chapter will answer these questions.

---

[1] CNN/SI, "Year in Review 1997," http://sportsillustrated.cnn.com/features/1997/yearinreview/topstories.

[2] *Castillo v. Tyson*, 268 A.D.2d 336 (2000).

As you read in Chapter 13, contracts are agreements between two parties who each agree to give to or do something for the other party. Contracts are typically private agreements in that they bind the two parties and no one else. Thus, parties not in *privity of contract* (anyone other than the contracting parties) usually do not have rights to a contract. However, as is frequently the case in the law, there are exceptions to the general rule.

A third party gains rights to a contract to which she or he is not a party in two situations. In the first, one of the contracting parties transfers rights or duties to the third party. In the second, the third party is a direct beneficiary of a contract between two other parties. This chapter examines both situations.

Assignments and Delegations

Both parties to a contract are both obligors (contractual parties who agreed to do something for the other party) and obligees (contractual parties who agreed to receive something from the other party). Contracts thus create a situation in which both parties have a duty to perform the agreed-on action and a right to be the recipient of the other party's duty. These rights and duties can be transferred to third parties. This section discusses both the transfer of rights—assignment—and the transfer of duties—delegation.

ASSIGNMENT

L01

What is an assignment?

Assignment occurs when a party to a contract—an assignor—transfers her rights to receive something under the contract to a third party—an assignee (see Exhibit 19-1). For example, Bina agrees to sell her car to José for $8,000. She then assigns her right to receive José's payment to Kelly. Kelly, who was not part of the original contract between Bina and José, is an assignee and now has the right to receive payment from José for Bina's car.

L02

What are the rights and duties of an assignor?

When an assignor transfers her rights to an assignee, the assignor legally gives up all rights she had to collect on the contract.[3] Now the assignee may legally demand performance from the other party to the original contract. Returning to our example, once Bina transfers her right to Kelly, Bina can no longer require that José pay her for her car; Kelly, however, can request that José pay her for Bina's car.

Exhibit 19-1

Assignment of Rights

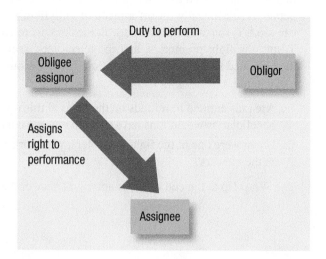

---

[3] Restatement (Second) of Contracts, sec. 317.

Legal Principle: **A person who transfers his or her rights under a third party is an assignor, and the person who receives the transfer and is now entitled to enforce the rights is the assignee.**

An assignee essentially fills in for the assignor as the legal recipient of the contractual duties and thereby acquires the same rights the assignor had. The assignee is offered no additional protections, however, and the obligor (the other party to the contract, who owes a duty to the assignee) may raise any of the same defenses for nonperformance to the assignee that he would have been able to raise against the assignor. Returning to our earlier example, if Bina failed to deliver her car to José, he can legally refuse to pay Kelly on the basis of Bina's breach of contract. It does not matter that Kelly had no duty in the original contract; she is subject to the same defense José has against Bina and therefore would not be paid in this situation.

L03

What are the rights and duties of an assignee?

Although assignments require no special wording or forms to be valid, certain restrictions exist. First, assignments covered by the statute of frauds must be in writing.[4] Because it is difficult to prove the existence of assignments given orally, it is usually suggested they all be in writing.

Second, an assignee must agree to accept the assigned rights. An assignee may decline an assignment if he has not legally agreed to it and if he declines in a timely fashion after learning about the assignment and its terms.[5] There is no protocol for rejecting an assignment, but once rejected, it is considered rejected from the time it was first offered. Third, in some situations contractual rights cannot be assigned.[6]

Case 19-1 demonstrates the problems that can arise in business transactions when it is not clear whether something is a sale or an assignment of rights. Pay close attention to the court's discussion of assignment of rights as opposed to the transfer of business property.

---

[4] The UCC requires that assignments be in writing when the amount assigned is greater than $5,000.

[5] Restatement (Second) of Contracts, sec. 327.

[6] Ibid., sec. 317(2).

Most countries do not grant third-party rights to contracts. Rather, most countries require that a party be a direct party to a contract before he or she can recover under the contract. The logic of the doctrine of privity is that a person who is not a party to a contract does not have the right to enforce it because no consideration was offered to him or her under the contract.

One notable exception is Australia, where a third party can sue for breach of contract. In most other countries, privity must be established before a party may sue.

However, privity requirements are beginning to be relaxed in the United Kingdom, expanding third-party rights. U.K. solicitors (lawyers) who have been negligent in the creation of a will have been held liable to the will's intended beneficiaries. Privity is still required in most situations in Australia and the United Kingdom, but the number of exceptions continues to grow.

CASE 19-1   GENERAL MILLS, INC. v. KRAFT FOODS GLOBAL, INC.
U.S. COURT OF APPEALS FOR THE FEDERAL CIRCUIT
487 F.3D 1368 (2007)

General Mills sells rolled food items under the brand name Fruit by the Foot, and it owns two U.S. patents on the rolled food item. In 1995, General Mills sued Farley for infringement of these patents, a dispute that General Mills and Farley resolved through a settlement agreement. The Settlement Agreement required Farley to pay General Mills a lump sum in exchange for the grants by General Mills of a release of its patent claims and a covenant not to sue Farley for past, current, or future infringement. The Settlement Agreement includes as "Farley" any and all parent companies, subsidiaries, predecessors, and successors. The covenant not to sue also contains language defining the "Releasee" as including Farley and its "successors." The Settlement Agreement also contains two provisions that define limiting conditions to the assignment or transfer of rights under the Agreement to another party by Farley (or its successors).

Kraft became the successor to Farley. General Mills agrees that Kraft became Farley's successor. In 2002, Kraft "sold and transferred Farley assets, including the Farley trademark and goodwill, to a subsidiary of Catterton Partners." It is undisputed that Kraft retained at least some portion of the original Farley assets and of Farley's rolled food business. After a few years of what General Mills alleges to be infringing activity, Kraft sold the remainder of its rolled food business and purported to transfer whatever rights it had under the Settlement Agreement to Kellogg Company. General Mills does not claim that Kraft engaged in infringing activities after the Kellogg transaction. General Mills sued Kraft alleging infringement of the two patents in the period between the Catterton transaction and the Kellogg transaction. Kraft argues that General Mills breached the Settlement Agreement by filing suit. The district court granted Kraft's motion to dismiss. General Mills appealed.

JUDGE LINN:

II. Discussion

B. Kraft's Status as Successor to Farley

As mentioned above, General Mills concedes that Kraft became Farley's successor by virtue of the Farley transaction. General Mills does not allege infringement prior to the Farley transaction or between the Farley transaction and the Catterton transaction. Rather, General Mills argues that "[t]he Catterton Transaction divested Kraft of any rights it might have had under the Settlement Agreement, because without the Farley assets that were sold to Catterton Partners, Kraft cannot be 'Farley' under the Settlement Agreement."

The part of the Settlement Agreement from which General Mills derives this argument is Article 8.4, which requires that Farley (including its successors, under Article 1.6) "must transfer its entire rolled food business" if it wishes to assign its rights under the Settlement Agreement without General Mills' consent. Article 8.4, General Mills argues, "makes certain that the Farley Agreement remains with Farley's entire rolled-food business." However, as the district court correctly recognized, the Settlement Agreement speaks only to the assignment of rights: "[n]either article [8.3 or 8.4] addresses Farley's retention of the Settlement Agreement and sale of other assets." Because the Catterton transaction did not purport to assign Kraft's rights under the Settlement Agreement, the restrictions imposed by Article 8.4 simply do not apply.

Nor does any other provision of the Settlement Agreement bar Farley from retaining its rights under the agreement when it transfers parts of its rolled food business. As mentioned, General Mills does not dispute that pursuant to Article 8.4, Kraft became Farley's successor before the Catterton transaction. Accordingly, the question is not whether Kraft complied with the conditions necessary for it to become

Farley's successor. The question is whether the Settlement Agreement imposed conditions on Kraft's continuing entitlement to the covenant not to sue. Although General Mills and Farley could have agreed to impose on Farley or Farley's successor ongoing obligations such as the retention of specified assets, they did not do so. There is simply nothing in the contract that requires Kraft to retain all or any particular assets of the Farley business to preserve Kraft's status as successor.

General Mills nonetheless argues that general principles of successorship prevent Kraft from continuing as "Farley" or a "successor" once it had sold off assets that were part of the original Farley business in the Catterton transaction. For General Mills to prevail, Kraft's rights under the agreement must have either (1) terminated by operation of law at the time of the Catterton transaction, or (2) been transferred from Kraft to Catterton by operation of law or by the terms of the Catterton transaction. We are not persuaded that either of these eventualities has occurred. . . .

As to the second possibility—that Catterton became Farley's successor after the Catterton transaction and divested Kraft of that status—General Mills does not even make this argument. The record contains no allegations as to what law controls the Catterton transaction or what assets, aside from Farley's goodwill and trademarks, Kraft transferred to Catterton. However, we note that the general rule of corporate law is that a transaction involving a transfer of property "from one corporation to another without consolidation or merger, does not include a transfer of all the powers or immunities of the selling corporation." Here, not only did the Catterton

transaction not involve a merger or consolidation, but there is not even an allegation that Catterton acquired the entirety of Farley. Indeed, had Kraft not retained at least some part of Farley's rolled food business after the transaction, General Mills could not have alleged infringement. There is simply no basis from which we might conclude that anyone other than Kraft succeeded to Farley's rights under the Settlement Agreement, at least until the Kellogg transaction.

There is also no merit to General Mills' argument that the Catterton transaction excused General Mills' obligation to perform under the Settlement Agreement pursuant to the doctrine of impossibility. It is true that after the Catterton transaction, Kraft no longer owned the Farley name and all of Farley's assets. But this fact did not prevent General Mills from affording Kraft the same rights under the Settlement Agreement that it had possessed since the Farley transaction. In the other direction, Kraft's only obligation that the Catterton transaction might possibly interfere with—the requirement in Article 8.4 that Farley "transfer its entire rolled food product business"—applies only when Farley or its successor purports to assign its rights under the Settlement Agreement. At the time of the Catterton transaction, no one alleges that this occurred.

Accordingly, we hold that at least until the Kellogg transaction, Kraft was entitled to the protection of Farley's covenant not to sue, and the district court properly dismissed General Mills' patent infringement claim against Kraft. . . .

AFFIRMED.

CRITICAL THINKING

Notice that one of the keys to the decision is whether the deal between Kraft and Catterton involved a sale of a part of a business or involved an assignment of contractual rights. In business, specific definitions can be important for determining which laws apply in a given situation. Besides the transaction between Kraft and Catterton, are there significant ambiguous words or phrases in the decision that would lead to possible confusion regarding the ruling? In what way do these ambiguities affect the ruling?

ETHICAL DECISION MAKING

Two critical events led up to this case: (1) the transaction between Kraft and Catterton and (2) General Mills' decision to sue Kraft. What ethical implications exist in each of these decisions? Can the behavior of one side or the other be deemed more ethically defensible? If so, which side, and why? What ethical theories or guidelines support your claim? Does the decision of the court reflect an agreement with your view?

Rights That Cannot Be Assigned. Exhibit 19-2 lists the four situations in which contractual rights cannot be assigned to a third party. We discuss each of them below.

First, the rights to a contract cannot be assigned when the contract is personal in nature, meaning the obligor has promised something specific to the person receiving it. Third parties cannot legally become the recipient in such situations unless the only part of a contract left to be fulfilled is the payment,[7] because rights to payment can always be assigned.

[7] Ibid., secs. 317 and 318.

Almost all developed market economies permit the free assignability of contract rights. Assignments play a crucial role in business financing because they enable banks and businesses to make loans and pay debts. Almost all developed market economies thus permit the free assignability of contract rights, while most centrally planned economies, such as China, permit only limited assignability. When a contract is with the state, approval by the proper state authority must first be obtained unless the contract allows for assignments. If the contract is with a private party, the assignor must first get the obligor's approval before an assignment can be made.

For example, when Burkhart went to work for NES, a company that rented and sold trenching equipment to Las Vegas–area contractors, he received $10,000 to sign an agreement not to compete for one year if he left the company's employ. NES was subsequently sold to Traffic Control Services. Burkhart refused to sign a noncompete agreement with the new firm and subsequently quit and went to work for a competitor. When Traffic Control Services sued to enforce the noncompete agreement Burkhard had signed with NES, the court ultimately found that the agreement could not be assigned.[8]

Second, rights cannot be assigned when the assignment increases the risk or duties the obligor would face in fulfilling the original contract. For example, Ben agrees to replace the siding on Erin's two-bedroom ranch. Erin cannot assign her right to Ben's services to Chris, who lives in a three-story, five-bedroom house, because Ben's duties would be greatly increased by the change.

Third, rights cannot be assigned when the contract expressly forbids assignments. When parties include an *antiassignment clause* in their contract, the parties are attempting to limit their ability to assign their rights under the contract. However, the wording of the antiassignment clause is determinative regarding the effectiveness of the clause. That is, if worded improperly or ambiguously, the clause does not effectively limit assignments.

Most courts consider antiassignment clauses as promises. Assignments made despite such clauses are effective, but the party who makes the assignment will still be liable for breaching the terms of the contract. Moreover, unless the clause is very specific, courts generally consider that it prevents delegation of duties, not assignment of rights.[9] A clause stating "All assignments are void under this contract" will be considered effective in prohibiting the assignment of rights. In contrast, when a contract includes a clause explicitly permitting assignments, the parties may assign rights, even when assignments would normally be considered improper because of an increased duty, risk, or burden to the obligor.[10]

Even in the presence of an antiassignment clause, there are exceptions in which assignments can still be made. For instance, antiassignment clauses do not affect assignments made by operation of law. If a law necessitates an assignment, such as in bankruptcy cases, the assignment is effective regardless of any contractual agreement to the contrary.

Exhibit 19-2

Contractual Rights That Cannot Be Assigned

1. Rights that are personal in nature.
2. Rights whose assignment would increase the obligor's risk or duties.
3. Rights whose assignment is prohibited by contract.
4. Rights whose assignment is prohibited by law or public policy.

---

[8] *Traffic Control Services v. United Rentals Northwest*, 87 P.3d 1054 (Sup. Ct. Nev. 2004).

[9] Restatement (Second) of Contracts, sec. 322(1) and UCC § 2-210(3).

[10] Ibid., sec. 323(1).

Likewise, as we've said above, the right to assign monetary payments cannot be denied. Therefore, even when a contract has an antiassignment clause, either party may still assign his or her right to receive payment.[11] One reason the law does not bar the right to receive payment is that companies often transfer rights to payments in the regular course of business. Preventing these transfers would have a negative impact on the business community. Also, one's duty to pay is not affected when the party receiving payment changes; that is, no added burden is placed on the obligor.

BUT WHAT IF . . .

WHAT IF THE FACTS OF THE CASE OPENER WERE DIFFERENT?

Let's say, in the Case Opener, that Tyson was performing in the match for a large sum of money. He wanted to assign his monetary rights to his mother. However, there was an antiassignment clause in the contract. Would Tyson still be able to assign his financial rights to his mother?

In addition, assignments of the right to receive damages for a breach of contract to sell goods or services are unaffected by antiassignment clauses.[12] If one party breaches the contract, the other can sue and transfer the right to recovery to a third party.

Finally, when law or public policy forbids assignments, the forbidden rights cannot be assigned. Various state and federal statutes prohibit the assigning of specific rights. If the assignment is determined to be against public policy, it is also deemed ineffective. Except as outlined in this section, all other rights are presumed assignable. Once it has been established that an assignment is valid, notice should be given to the obligor regarding the assignment.

Notice of Assignment.   Although notice need not be given for a valid assignment, it is usually a good idea for the assignor or the assignee to notify the obligor. Assignments are effective immediately regardless of notice, but by providing notice the assignor can help avoid two serious complications.

The first possible complication occurs if the obligor fulfills the contract as written. Because fulfilling the contract discharges the obligor's duties, the act also discharges the assignee's claim on the assignor's right. However, once given notice, the obligor can discharge his contractual obligations only by fulfilling the contract for the assignee.

For example, suppose Stefan contracts with Latoya to purchase her speedboat. Latoya assigns her right to collect Stefan's money to Meghan. Neither Latoya nor Meghan notifies Stefan of the assignment. Accordingly, Stefan pays Latoya for the boat. His contractual duties have been discharged, and Meghan cannot request performance from him. Had Stefan been notified about the assignment, the only way he could fulfill his contractual obligations would be by paying Meghan the money owed to Latoya. If, after receiving notice, Stefan pays Latoya, Meghan may still legally request that he pay her. Giving the obligor proper notice avoids such problems with performance.

Legal Principle: **The assignee should always give notice to the obligor as soon as possible after receiving the assignment, because the obligor may satisfy his or her obligations by performing for the assignor until receiving notice of the assignment from the assignee.**

[11] UCC § 9-318(4).

[12] UCC § 2-210(2).

Exhibit 19-3

Assignment of the Same
Right to Two Parties

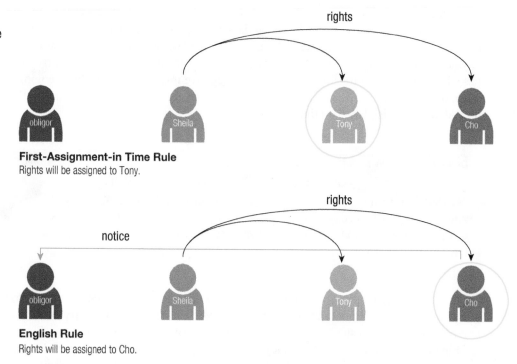

First-Assignment-in Time Rule
Rights will be assigned to Tony.

English Rule
Rights will be assigned to Cho.

The second complication occurs when an assignor assigns two or more parties the same right, and confusion arises as to which party has the right to the contract. Most states use the first-assignment-in-time rule, which gives the contractual right to the first party granted the assignment. Giving proper notice can ensure that there is no confusion over when the assignment was made. Furthermore, a minority of states have adopted the English rule, which states that the first assignee to give notice of assignment to the obligor is the party with rights to the contract. Especially in a state using the English rule, parties are well advised to give notice of assignments to ensure that they maintain their assigned rights.

Suppose Sheila assigns her contractual rights to Tony. A week later, she assigns the same rights to Cho. As shown in Exhibit 19-3, under the first-assignment-in-time rule, Tony legally has Sheila's rights to the contract. However, if Cho gives notice first and the state in question uses the English rule, although Sheila assigned her rights to Tony first, legally Cho possesses them.

The Restatement (Second) of Contracts takes a position between the first-assignment-in-time rule and the English rule.[13] It grants legal right to the first assignee in most situations. However, if the first assignment is legally voidable or revocable by the assignor, subsequent assignments are considered evidence of the voiding or revocation of the first assignment and the later assignee has legal right to the contract. Also, the later assignee is considered the legal owner of the contractual right if she offers something to the assignor as consideration and then obtains (1) performance by the obligor on his duty, (2) judgment requiring performance by the obligor, (3) a new contract with the obligor, or (4) evidence frequently used to signify a contractual right (a writing indicating a contractual obligation).

DELEGATION

A delegation occurs when a party to a contract—a delegator—transfers her duty to perform to a third party—a delegatee—who is not part of the original contract. Whereas

---

[13] Sec. 342.

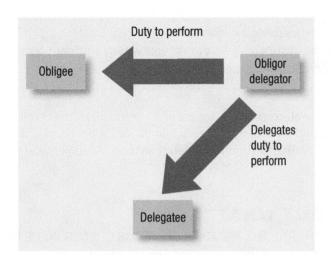

Exhibit 19-4
Delegation of Duties

assignments transfer rights to a contract, delegations transfer *duties*. (See Exhibit 19-4.) Instead of receiving something, as in an assignment, the delegatee must fulfill the delegator's contractual obligation to the obligee—the party to the contract to whom a duty is owed. For example, Johann contracts with Teresa to have her deliver machinery to his factory. Teresa then delegates her duty to Bill, who delivers the machinery to John.

One important distinction between assignments and delegations is apparent in the rights of the transferring party. After making an assignment, the assignor has no right left to the original contract. After making a delegation, however, the delegator is not relieved of his duty to perform. If the delegatee fails to fulfill the contract, the delegator is still liable to the obligee for fulfillment. Using the previous example, if Bill fails to deliver the machinery to John, Teresa is liable to Johann for damages.

Legal Principle: **A party transferring her or his duties under the contract is the delegator, and the one receiving the transfer is the delegatee. After the delegation, although the delegatee is bound to perform, the delegator remains liable if the delegatee fails to perform.**

Duties That Cannot Be Delegated.

As with assignments, the starting assumption is that duties to a contract can be delegated. However, courts tend to examine delegations more closely than assignments. The reasoning is that assignments usually do not affect the party to the contract who is not involved in the assignment (the obligor), whereas a delegation forces the uninvolved party (the obligee) to receive performance from a party with whom he or she did not directly contract.

Also, just as with assignments, certain duties cannot be delegated (see Exhibit 19-5).[14] The first is any duty of a personal nature that requires the specific talents, skills, or expertise of the obligor. Victorine contracts with Michael, a famous artist, to paint her portrait using his skill and expertise. Michael cannot delegate his duty to paint Victorine's portrait to anyone else, not even someone of equal skill or talent.

An interesting situation arises when the initial contract bears an implicit assumption that work will be performed by others. In such situations, if supervision is important to the task, the supervision could be considered a personal duty the obligor may not delegate. Suppose you are planning to have a new office building built to specifications you have personally created. You contract

To see how delegation of duties relates to business management, please see the **Connecting to the Core** activity on the text website at www.mhhe.com/kubasek3e.

---

[14] Restatement (Second) of Contracts, sec. 318, and UCC § 2-210.

Exhibit 19-5

Duties That Cannot Be
Delegated

1. Duties that are personal in nature.
2. Duties for which the delegatee's performance will vary significantly from the delegator's.
3. Duties in contracts that forbid delegations.

with Ian, the well-respected manager of a construction firm. Both you and Ian know that he will not build the office building single-handedly, but because he was sought out for his management skills, his contractual duties are considered personal and therefore cannot be delegated.

? BUT WHAT IF . . .

WHAT IF THE FACTS OF THE CASE OPENER WERE DIFFERENT?

Assume that Mike Tyson had been hired for the match because of his fame and his enhanced skills. If Tyson tried to delegate his duties to another athlete who was neither famous nor highly skilled, would such a delegation of duties be lawful?

Delegation of personal duties is permissible where otherwise not allowed when there is an explicit contractual agreement to allow delegations. Usually, for a delegation of personal duties to be effective, the contract must state that delegations are permitted.

Any nonpersonal duties in a contract can be delegated. For example, delivering goods, mowing a lawn, paying money, and painting a house are all considered nonpersonal duties because they do not require particular skill or expertise and most people could complete them. Thus, they can all be delegated.

The second type of duty that cannot be delegated is one whose performance would vary significantly from what the obligee has a contractual right to if the performance were done by the delegatee. To protect the obligee, who is a part of the original contract, when performance would differ substantially from what the obligee contractually has the right to, courts will rule that the delegation is ineffective. The focus here is the skill or abilities of the delegatee. If the delegatee cannot perform the contract at a level comparable to that of the delegator, the obligee would be unnecessarily harmed, and thus the delegation is deemed ineffective.

The third situation in which delegations are prohibited occurs when the contract prohibits them. The courts typically treat included agreements not to delegate as indicating the parties' desire to consider the contractual obligations personal and will find otherwise-allowable delegations inappropriate. However, even if a clause prohibiting delegations exists, the courts will probably allow delegations if they are impersonal, such as the payment of money.

Case 19-2 demonstrates the problems arising from a party's failure to acknowledge a nondelegation agreement. Although the case discusses assignments of obligations, the court is treating the term *assignment* as a synonym for *delegation of duties*. Some courts use the term *assignment* to refer to a transfer of either rights *or* duties.

Assignment of the Contract

Contracts often use ambiguous language that makes it unclear what is being assigned or delegated. Examples are "I assign the contract" or "I assign all my rights under the contract," which fail to specify what is being transferred. When a court cannot clearly tell what

CASE 19-2   FOREST COMMODITY CORP. ("FCC") v. LONE STAR INDUSTRIES, INC., ET AL.
COURT OF APPEALS OF GEORGIA, THIRD DIVISION
255 GA. APP. 244 (2002)

CAL and FCC entered into a three-year contract for the "thru-putting" of aggregate stone. In the contract, FCC agreed to provide terminal space for unloading aggregate stone, which FCC would then store, reload onto trucks, and weigh for transshipment. CAL promised to unload a minimum of 150,000 tons per year, for a total of 450,000 tons over the three-year contract period. The agreement also contained a provision prohibiting the assignment or subcontracting of any portion of the obligations without the written consent of the other party.

During the contract period, CAL unloaded a total of 198,170 tons of aggregate. Soon thereafter, CAL entered into negotiations with Martin Marietta Materials, Inc., for the sale of CAL's assets. Martin Marietta agreed to accept CAL's rights and obligations under the agreement with FCC, and CAL requested FCC accept an assignment of the thru-put agreement to Martin Marietta. FCC refused. FCC and Martin Marietta eventually entered into a substantially similar contract for the thru-putting of aggregate. It is undisputed that after Martin Marietta's acquisition of CAL and its assets, and pursuant to the new contract with FCC, Martin Marietta thru-put 286,698 tons of aggregate stone at the FCC terminal during the remainder of the original contract period for the CAL thru-put agreement. When combined with the 198,170 tons shipped by CAL, a total of 484,868 tons of aggregate stone was shipped through the FCC facility, 34,868 tons more than the guaranteed minimum under the original agreement.

FCC sued CAL for breach of contract, alleging CAL failed to ship the minimum amount of aggregate stone under the contract. CAL filed a motion for summary judgment as to the breach of contract claim. The trial court granted the motion for summary judgment, finding FCC was precluded from enforcing the contract because it failed to comply with the nonassignability clause. FCC appealed.

JUDGE JOHNSON: FCC contends the trial court erred in granting summary judgment to CAL because there are genuine issues of material fact regarding whether FCC assigned the contract. However, the irrefutable evidence, even when construed in a light most favorable to FCC, points inevitably to the conclusion an assignment of the CAL thru-put agreement was effected. The numerous items of undisputed facts in this case show FCC's interests and obligations in the CAL thru-put agreement were transferred to Woodchips Export Corporation ("WEC") without the written consent of CAL, thereby violating the nonassignability clause of the agreement and extinguishing any right to recovery which FCC may have had.

The thru-put agreement obligated FCC to provide a marine terminal facility for the off-loading of aggregate and to perform both the reloading of the aggregate onto trucks and the weighing of such trucks. Yet, the evidence in the record shows the terminal facility where the CAL aggregate was off-loaded was leased by FCC to WEC. In addition, it is undisputed FCC had no employees and no equipment to perform the obligations under the CAL agreement. FCC's vice-president admits FCC had no employees and FCC entered into an unwritten agreement with WEC under which WEC agreed to perform FCC's obligations as its operations agent.

Moreover, FCC's tax returns for the years covered by the thru-put agreement show the only income received by FCC during this time period was rental income. These tax returns do not show any income for aggregate thru-putting, nor do they include any expenses for employee wages, equipment rental or maintenance, or fuel expenditures necessary to carry out its obligations under the CAL thru-put agreement. On the other hand, WEC's income statements and tax returns reveal WEC deducted the expenses incurred in conjunction with aggregate thru-putting and received income for the thru-put of aggregate in amounts that correspond to the amounts generated by the CAL thru-put agreement.

Indeed, FCC's own accountants testified such debiting and crediting could not have occurred between these two parties since FCC files separate tax returns from the tax returns of WEC and other related companies. Furthermore, the same accountants testified even if such funds had, in fact, been debited and credited between these two companies, the income would first have appeared on the company actually earning it, which in this case was WEC. As a final note, FCC has offered no documentary evidence supporting this accounting practice, such as documents memorializing such inter-company adjustments through debits and credits.

FCC next argues no assignment can be found in this case since there is no written assignment document or any other document indicating an intent to assign. However, an assignment can be inferred from the totality of the circumstances and need not be reduced to writing. In addition, Georgia courts may look to tax returns as probative evidence in ascertaining the existence of an assignment. The affirmative decision to declare the thru-put income on the tax returns of WEC and not on the tax returns of FCC is certainly evidence of an intent to assign. Moreover, FCC's vice-president testified oral agreements between FCC and WEC were entered into under his direction and supervision, showing yet another intent to assign. The trial court properly found FCC had assigned the CAL thru-put agreement to WEC.

AFFIRMED.

CRITICAL THINKING

Do you agree with the reasoning of this decision? Is the evidence as strongly in support of the court's conclusion as the judge states? Are any pieces of evidence given unfair weight or insufficient weight?

Further, what evidence that might not be included in this decision could affect the court's conclusion? Come up with at least one fact, not included in the ruling but possible given the information provided above, that would have a significant impact on the acceptability of this reasoning.

ETHICAL DECISION MAKING

How do you think this decision would hold up under the public disclosure test? Who might react favorably, and who unfavorably? What differences in ethical standards could explain contradictory reactions? What reaction do you think the majority of the U.S. public would have? Why?

the parties intended, it usually considers the assignment to be of both rights and duties. (See Exhibit 19-6.) This interpretation removes any right the assignor had to collect under the contract, but he or she is still liable to the obligee for any duties the delegatee, who is also the assignee, fails to perform.

Third-Party Beneficiary Contracts

LO4

What is a third-party beneficiary contract?

We've seen that one way third parties may obtain rights or duties to a contract is through assignments or delegations. We now move on to the other way, which is through being an intended beneficiary of the contract. A third-party beneficiary is created when two parties enter into a contract with the purpose of benefiting a third party, called the *intended beneficiary.* The beneficiary need not be named in the contract, as long as the terms of the contract or events occurring after its creation make it clear who he or she is.

INTENDED BENEFICIARIES

Early in the common law, courts had difficulty when contracts were written to benefit third parties, and they usually deemed that third parties had no rights to contracts to which they were not in privity. Now, however, third parties who are intended beneficiaries have the right to enforce contracts. An intended beneficiary is a third party to a contract whom the contracting parties intended to benefit directly from their contract. In determining whether

Exhibit 19-6

Assignment of the Contract

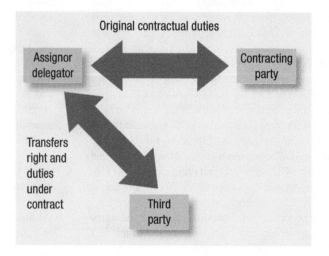

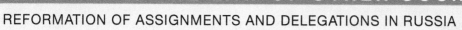

Many industrialized nations have fairly similar laws regarding assignments and delegations. Part of this similarity is attributable to the similarity of their market-based economies. Russia, which was centrally planned under the Soviet Union, is attempting to join the industrialized nations by developing a market-based economy.

To aid the transition, it has modified its Civil Code to allow the same freedom of assignments of rights and duties found in the German code, a change that may prove critical to Russia's potential for success as a market-based economy.

a third party is an intended beneficiary, courts ask whether the contracting parties intended that the third party be the "direct," "primary," or "express" beneficiary of the contract.

The promisor in a third-party beneficiary contract is the party who makes the promise that benefits the third party. The promisee is the party who owes the promisor something in exchange for the promise made to the third-party beneficiary. For example, Marissa contracts with Alex to clean his house. In exchange, Alex will pay Marissa's credit card debt. The credit card company is the third-party beneficiary, because the contract is created to benefit the company. Alex is the promisor, for he made the promise to pay the third-party beneficiary. Marissa is the promisee, because she owes a duty to the promisor, Alex.

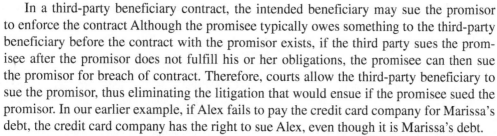

BUT WHAT IF . . .

WHAT IF THE FACTS OF THE CASE OPENER WERE DIFFERENT?

Let's say that a venue owner contacted Tyson about performing in a match at his venue. Tyson will compete in the match for free, and all of the money from the ticket sales will go to charity. Is there a third-party beneficiary in this scenario? Also, who is the promisor, and who is the promisee?

In a third-party beneficiary contract, the intended beneficiary may sue the promisor to enforce the contract Although the promisee typically owes something to the third-party beneficiary before the contract with the promisor exists, if the third party sues the promisee after the promisor does not fulfill his or her obligations, the promisee can then sue the promisor for breach of contract. Therefore, courts allow the third-party beneficiary to sue the promisor, thus eliminating the litigation that would ensue if the promisee sued the promisor. In our earlier example, if Alex fails to pay the credit card company for Marissa's debt, the credit card company has the right to sue Alex, even though it is Marissa's debt.

Let us return to the opening scenario. The fans of the Tyson fight argued that they were third-party beneficiaries and therefore had rights under several contracts that were violated when Tyson was disqualified early in the fight. Boxing matches are widely viewed events, arguably organized for the enjoyment of fans. Does the idea of boxing matches' being organized for the fans make the fans the "direct," "primary," or "express" beneficiaries of contracts involved in the fight? In other words, are the fans of the Tyson fight intended (i.e., direct, primary, or express) beneficiaries to the contracts Tyson entered into when agreeing to the fight? What else do we need to know before we can determine whether the fans have a legal right to a refund?

There are two types of intended beneficiaries: creditor beneficiaries and donee beneficiaries.

Creditor Beneficiaries. A creditor beneficiary is a third party that benefits from a contract in which the promisor agrees to pay the promisee's debt. In our previous example, because Alex (the promisor) agreed to pay the debt of Marissa (the promisee), Marissa's credit card company is a creditor beneficiary.

Case 19-3 illustrates the importance of being a creditor beneficiary as opposed to a donee beneficiary if you want to enforce a contract.

CASE 19-3   ALLAN v. NERSESOVA
COURT OF APPEALS OF TEXAS, DALLAS 307 S.W.3D 564, 2010 TEX. APP. LEXIS 1662

Allan and Koraev both owned condominiums in the same building. Koraev's unit was directly above Allan's. While Allan lived in her own unit, Koraev leased his. The leasing of Koraev's unit was managed by Nersesova. Between 2005 and 2007 plumbing problems in Koraev's unit damaged Allan's unit eight different times. Thus, Allan sued Nersesova and Koraev, among other building executives. The terms of the lawsuit included breach of contract and negligence. All defendants excluding Koraev and Nersesova settled with Allan before the trial. The jury found on behalf of Allan for the negligence of both Koraev and Nersesova and, additionally, breach of contract of Koraev. Both parties were found responsible for damages as third parties. However, Koraev moved for judgment notwithstanding the verdict, arguing that there was no contract between Allan and Koraev that made Koraev a third party.

JUSTICE SMITH: Having concluded a contract existed between Koraev and the Association, we next consider whether Allan could bring suit for breach of that contract. To have standing to bring a suit for breach of contract, the plaintiff must either be in privity of contract with the defendant or be a third-party beneficiary entitled to enforce the contract.

Allan's contract claim was based on the text of the governing documents. Paragraph 1 of the Declaration provided that its terms apply to "any person acquiring or owning an interest in the property." Paragraph 11 stated, "All present and future Unit Owners, tenants and occupants of Units shall be subject to and shall comply with the provisions of this Second Amended Declaration, the Amended Bylaws, and the Rules and Regulations, as they may be amended from time to time."

Privity of contract is established by proving that the defendant was a party to an enforceable contract with either the plaintiff or a party who assigned its cause of action to the plaintiff. Allan was not a party to nor an assignee of the contract between Koraev and the Association. Accordingly, Koraev and Allan were not in privity of contract. Because Allan was not in privity of contract with Koraev, she has standing to bring a breach of contract claim only if she demonstrated she was a third-party beneficiary.

A third party, such as Allan, may sue to enforce a contract as a third-party beneficiary only if the contracting parties entered into the contract directly and primarily for the third party's benefit. There is a presumption against conferring third-party-beneficiary status. There are three types of third-party beneficiaries—donee, creditor, and incidental. Donee and creditor beneficiaries may bring suit to enforce a contract; incidental beneficiaries may not. A person is a donee beneficiary if the performance of the contract inures to his benefit as a gift. A person is a donee beneficiary only if a donative intent expressly or impliedly appears in the contract. A party is a creditor beneficiary if no intent to make a gift appears from the contract, but performance will satisfy an actual or asserted duty of the promisee to the beneficiary, such as an indebtedness, contractual obligation, or other legally enforceable commitment to the third party, and the promisee must intend that the beneficiary will have the right to enforce the contract. "The intent to confer a direct benefit upon a third party 'must be clearly and fully spelled out or enforcement by the third party must be denied.' " "Incidental benefits that may flow from a contract to a third party do not confer the right to enforce the contract."

Paragraph 1 of the Declaration stated, "The Association does hereby publish and declare that the covenants, limitations, and obligations contained herein shall be deemed to run with the land and shall be a burden and a benefit to the Association and any person acquiring or owning an interest in the property." Paragraph 19 of the Declaration stated, "Each Owner shall comply strictly with the provisions of the Second Amended Declaration, the Amended Bylaws, Rules and Regulations, policies, and the decisions and resolutions of the Association adopted pursuant to the Second Amended Declaration or Amended Bylaws as the same may be lawfully amended from time to time. Failure to comply with any of the same shall be grounds for an action to recover sums due, for damages or injunctive relief or both, and for reimbursement of all attorney's fees incurred in connection therewith, which action shall be maintainable by the Managing Agent or Board of Directors in the name of the Association, in behalf of the Owners or, in a proper case, by an aggrieved owner."

Paragraph 38 of the Rules and Regulations required a unit owner to repair at his own expense any damage he (or his tenants) may cause to the condominium. Allan's testimony about the damages she suffered as a result of Koraev and his tenants' breach of the governing documents established that she was an aggrieved owner. But there must be some evidence that this is a "proper case" under Paragraph 19 of the

[continued]

Declaration for Allan as an aggrieved owner to maintain an action to recover damages and be reimbursed for attorney's fees. After reading paragraph 19 to his client, Allan's attorney elicited the following testimony from his client at trial:

Q. Did your homeowners' association take any action to recover the damages for your unit from the owner of Unit 234?

A. No.

Q. And based on their failure to act, did you have to act on your behalf?

A. Yes.

Allan then testified about having to hire attorneys to represent her in this case and stated that she had agreed to pay them a reasonable fee for their services. The Association's failure to act is some evidence that this is a proper case for the aggrieved owner herself to bring suit for damages and for reimbursement of attorney's fees, as authorized under Paragraph 19 of the Declaration.

Paragraph 1 imposed a contractual duty on Koraev to follow the requirements of the Declaration, Bylaws, and Rules and Regulations for the "benefit of the Association and any person acquiring or owning an interest in the property." Allan was such a person. The contract between the Association and Koraev "clearly and fully express[ed] an intent to confer a direct benefit to" Allan and others owning an interest in the property. Thus, Koraev's "performance will come to [Allan] in satisfaction of a legal duty owed to [her] by [Koraev]." Paragraph 19 gave authority to Allan as an aggrieved owner to bring an action against Koraev for his failure to follow the Declaration, Bylaws, and Rules and Regulations "in a proper case." Therefore, Koraev's failure to perform the contract between himself and the Association was a breach of his duty not to cause damage to Allan's unit. As an intended creditor beneficiary, Allan had standing to bring suit against Koraev for his breach of the governing documents.

We conclude the governing documents made Allan an intended creditor beneficiary of the contract between Koraev and the Association and granted her authority to bring suit for Koraev's breach of those documents. Accordingly, we conclude the trial court erred by granting Koraev's motion for judgment notwithstanding the verdict on Allan's claim for breach of contract. We sustain Allan's first issue.

AFFIRMED IN PART, REVERSED IN PART AND REMANDED

CRITICAL THINKING

Was there ambiguity in the relevant portions of the declaration quoted in the opinion that made unit owners' duties to other owners as a third party unclear? Or did Koraev simply not read the document carefully?

ETHICAL DECISION MAKING

Should each condominium owner have a duty to the other owners who own adjacent properties? Why would Koraev feel he was not liable for the damage his property caused to another?

Donee Beneficiaries. The other type of intended beneficiaries is donee beneficiaries, third parties who benefit from a contract in which a promisor agrees to give a gift to the third party. The most common form of donee beneficiary contract is life insurance policies. The promisee pays premiums on a life insurance plan to have the insurer (the promisor) pay a third party (the donee beneficiary) on the promisee's death.

The fans in the Tyson case argued that they are intended beneficiaries. If the fans are correct, and we know Tyson did not have a debt to them, then they must be donee beneficiaries. Does an agreement to perform create a situation in which the audience becomes the intended beneficiaries of the performance?

Vesting of Rights. Although an intended beneficiary can enforce her rights to a contract, she cannot do so until her rights to the contract vest, or mature such that she can legally act on them. Before a third party's rights have vested, the original contracting parties can make changes to the original contract without her permission. For example, third-party rights in a life insurance policy do not vest until the promisee's death. Consequently, Jane (the promisee) can change the intended beneficiary of her life insurance policy from

L05

What are the differences among donee beneficiaries, creditor beneficiaries, and incidental beneficiaries?

441

Mercedes to Peter. Jane does not need Mercedes' permission, and Mercedes cannot sue Jane, because her rights have not vested.

Generally, one of three things must occur for a third party's right to a contract to vest.[15] First, under certain circumstances, third-party rights vest immediately even if the beneficiary does not know about the contract. When rights vest immediately, the third party can enforce the contract at any time. These rights take effect instantaneously, even if the beneficiary does not know about the contract.

Second, rights may vest when the beneficiary decides to accept them, which must sometimes be done by notifying the contracting parties of acceptance. However, in the absence of an overt act rejecting the rights to a contract, acceptance is assumed when the beneficiary becomes aware of the contract.

Third, the beneficiary must change his position based on a reliance on the contractual rights. In other words, the beneficiary must take some action he would not have otherwise taken because he is expecting to benefit from the contract. For example, when Vince finds out he is a third-party beneficiary to a contract, he decides to lease a new car because he is expecting to benefit from the contract. Obtaining the lease causes his rights to vest because doing so demonstrates a change in position based on reliance on the contract.

If a contract specifies that the original contracting parties maintain the right to alter or rescind the contract, vesting of the third party's rights does not prevent the promisor or the promisee from doing so. For instance, all life insurance policies allow the promisee to change the beneficiary.

Many states hold that donee beneficiary rights vest before creditor beneficiary rights. The rationale is that even if the contract is altered, the creditor beneficiary maintains her rights against the debtor (the promisee). Suppose your friend owes you $1,000 and enters a contract with Dagmar in which you are a creditor beneficiary. If your friend and Dagmar change the contract before your rights vest, you still have a right to the money your friend owes you, even if you cannot enforce this right against Dagmar. Donee beneficiaries do not have the same option as creditor beneficiaries, and thus many states allow their rights to vest more quickly than those of creditor beneficiaries.

Creditor versus Donee Beneficiaries.   There are two main distinctions between creditor beneficiaries and donee beneficiaries (see Exhibit 19-7). The first is based on the reason the third-party beneficiary contract was created. If the promise in the contract is intended to release a party from an obligation to a third party, such as the paying of a debt, the contract creates a creditor beneficiary. Conversely, if the contract intends to grant a gift to a third party, the third party is a donee beneficiary.

Exhibit 19-7

Creditor versus Donee Beneficiaries

CREDITOR BENEFICIARY	DONEE BENEFICIARY
Purpose of the Contract	
Contractual performance fulfills an obligation to a third party.	Contractual performance gives a gift to a third party.
Enforcement of Rights	
Beneficiary can enforce rights to a contract if the contract is valid and the rights have vested.	Beneficiary has limited ability to enforce contracts, depending on the jurisdiction.
Beneficiary can enforce rights against the promisor or the promisee.	Beneficiary can enforce rights against the promisor.

[15] Restatement (Second) of Contracts, sec. 311.

The second distinction occurs when an intended beneficiary can enforce his or her rights under a contract. Creditor beneficiaries can enforce their rights under a contract whenever the contract is valid. Donee beneficiaries can enforce their rights to most contracts. However, some jurisdictions do not allow donee beneficiaries to enforce their contractual rights in all situations. For example, the state of New York does not grant them the right to enforce a contract unless they have a familial relationship to the promisee.

When a donee beneficiary may enforce rights under a contract, he or she may do so only against the promisor, because the promisee has no duty to the donee beneficiary. Conversely, creditor beneficiaries may sue the promisor or the promisee for performance, because both these parties owe him or her a duty. A creditor beneficiary who wins a judgment against one party may not seek judgment against the other party, however. In addition, if a creditor beneficiary wins judgment against the promisee, the promisee may sue the promisor to recover under a theory of breach of contract.[16]

As you might have guessed, it is not always easy to determine when someone is a creditor or a donee beneficiary. Sometimes a contract is created for reasons that are intended both to be charitable and to pay a debt. Given the lack of clear distinction, the Restatement (Second) of Contracts takes a different approach,[17] focusing on the difference between intended and incidental beneficiaries.

Legal Principle: **Both a donee beneficiary and a creditor beneficiary are intended beneficiaries of a contract and can therefore sue to enforce its performance.**

BUT WHAT IF . . .
WHAT IF THE FACTS OF THE CASE OPENER WERE DIFFERENT?
Let's say that the owner of the Las Vegas venue hosting Mike Tyson's match forms a contract with Tyson which specifies that if customers pay for the match the first night, Mike Tyson will come back to the venue a week later so that the same customers can go to a second match for free. However, Mike Tyson gets disqualified from the rest of the season during the first match. Could the fans file lawsuits as third-party beneficiaries?

INCIDENTAL BENEFICIARIES

Creditor and donee beneficiaries are both intended beneficiaries, and according to the Restatement, intended beneficiaries have the right to enforce a contract. When it is clear that the contract was created for the benefit of a third party, and performance of the contractual duties will pay off the payee's debt or give a gift as the payee intended, the third party is an intended beneficiary. When the contracting parties do not *intend* to benefit someone but unintentionally do so, that third party is an incidental beneficiary. (See Exhibit 19-8.)

For example, Cassandra contracts with Garrett to have him build a well-financed private high school on property she owns. The new school will raise the property values of the houses surrounding it. Although neither Cassandra nor Garrett intended to benefit these local homeowners with their contract, the homeowners did benefit. Accordingly, the local homeowners are incidental beneficiaries to Cassandra and Garrett's contract.

One significant difference between intended and incidental beneficiaries is that incidental beneficiaries maintain no rights to enforce other people's contracts. In the previous

---

[16] Ibid., sec. 310.

[17] Ibid., sec. 302.

Exhibit 19-8

Intended versus
Incidental Beneficiaries

INTENDED BENEFICIARIES	INCIDENTAL BENEFICIARIES
Contracting parties intended to benefit the third party with their contract.	Contracting parties did not intend to benefit the third party with their contract.
Beneficiary has the right to enforce the contract.	Beneficiary does not have the right to enforce the contract.
Beneficiary benefits from direct reception of contractual performance.	Beneficiary benefits from indirect circumstances created by contractual performance.

example, if Cassandra and Garrett decide to rescind their contract, the local homeowners cannot sue to enforce it, because it was never Cassandra or Garrett's intent to benefit them.

In determining whether a party is an incidental beneficiary, the courts will take a reasonable person approach and ask whether a reasonable person in the position of the party in question would believe the contracting parties intended to benefit him or her. If so, the courts consider the party an intended beneficiary. If not, the third party is an incidental beneficiary.

Let's consider the reasonable person test in the context of the Tyson case in the opening scenario. For fans to receive refunds, a reasonable person in their position would have to believe Tyson intended to benefit his fans by entering into his contract to fight. Do the fans meet the reasonable person test? Contrast the Tyson case with the one described in the Case Nugget on the next page, in which the court found sufficient evidence that the plaintiff was an intended beneficiary.

Another thing the court considers when deciding whether a party is an incidental beneficiary is whether performance of the contract is done directly for or to the third party. For example, performance of Cassandra and Garrett's contract—payment and the building of the school—is contained wholly within the contracting parties. Nothing is explicitly done for or given to a third party, and therefore the homeowners are incidental beneficiaries.

The court also examines the third party's ability to control the specifics of performance. If a third party can provide input regarding how the contractual duties are fulfilled, he or she is probably an intended beneficiary. Suppose Dianne (the promisee) agrees to pay Charles (the promisor) to paint Hector's (the third party's) house. Hector tells Charles what color he wants the house, as well as when Charles should be there to paint. Hector's ability to control how Charles paints the house demonstrates his status as an intended beneficiary. In addition, Charles renders performance directly to Hector, so by this test also Hector is an intended beneficiary.

A third factor the courts examine in determining the type of third-party beneficiary is whether the contract directly states that the third party is the benefiting party. In the previous example, because Charles agreed in the contract to paint Hector's house, the contract lists Hector as the beneficiary. Consequently, he is an intended beneficiary. In fact Hector meets all three additional tests besides the reasonable person test, although it is not necessary to meet all three. A third party who meets at least one of the last three tests is usually an intended beneficiary.

Legal Principle: **The third-party beneficiary who is in the strongest legal position is the creditor beneficiary because he can sue both the person who made the contract on his behalf and the person who was supposed to perform for him. The donee beneficiary is in the second-strongest position because she can sue the person who is supposed to perform the contract for her. The incidental beneficiary is in the worst legal position because he cannot sue anyone.**

INTENDED OR INCIDENTAL BENEFICIARY?

Wesley Locke v. Ozark City Board of Education
910 So. 2d 1247 (Ala. 2005)

Wesley Locke, a physical education teacher employed by the Dale County Department of Education, served as an umpire for high school baseball games. Locke was a member of the Southeast Alabama Umpires Association, which provides officials to athletic events sponsored by the Alabama High School Athletic Association (AHSAA).

One evening, Locke was serving as head umpire in a baseball game between Carroll High School and George W. Long High School. Carroll High School, where the game was being held, did not provide police protection or other security personnel for the game. After the game, the parent of one of Carroll High's baseball players attacked Locke, punching him three times in the face and causing him to sustain physical injuries to his neck and face that subjected him to pain, discomfort, scarring, and blurred vision. Locke sued the Ozark City Board of Education, alleging that the board breached its contract with the AHSAA by failing to provide police protection at the baseball game and that Locke was an intended third-party beneficiary under the contract.

While the trial court found that Locke was not an intended beneficiary and awarded summary judgment to the Board of Education,

the court of appeals disagreed. It found evidence that the parties anticipated the existence of third parties by contract language stating that the purpose of the words "adequate police protection" was to provide good game administration and supervision. The court reasoned that game administration and supervision necessarily included umpires. It found further evidence of the AHSAA's and the board's intent for police protection to directly benefit the umpires in a letter from the AHSAA sanctioning one of the high schools for the incident.

The state supreme court reiterated that to recover under a third-party beneficiary theory, a complainant must show (1) that the contracting parties intended, at the time the contract was created, to bestow a direct benefit on a third party; (2) that the complainant was the intended beneficiary of the contract; and (3) that the contract was breached. Applying this standard to the facts, the court found that Locke had presented substantial evidence indicating that the board and the AHSAA intended to provide a direct benefit to umpires, that he was an intended direct beneficiary of the contract, and that the board breached the contract. It therefore overturned the summary judgment and remanded the case to the trial court for hearing on the issue of whether the board had provided adequate protection at the game.

Exhibit 19-9 summarizes third-party benefiaries' ability to sue.

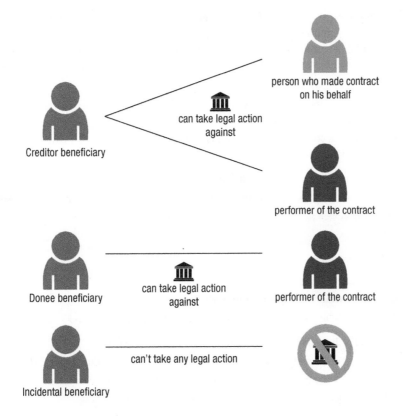

Exhibit 19-9

Legal Recourse of Third-Party Beneficiaries

CASE OPENER WRAP-UP

Fallout from a Unforgettable Fight

The court hearing the Tyson case quickly dismissed the claims. It held that the fans were in no way third-party beneficiaries to any contract into which Tyson, the promoters, or the telecasters had entered. The fans cannot meet any of the tests for an intended beneficiary. Simply put, they are incidental beneficiaries.

KEY TERMS

assignee 428	delegation 434	first-assignment- in-time	obligors 428
assignment 428	delegator 434	rule 434	promisee 439
assignor 428	donee beneficiaries 441	incidental beneficiary 443	promisor 439
creditor beneficiary 439	English rule 434	intended beneficiary 438	third-party beneficiary 438
delegatee 434		obligees 428	vest 441

SUMMARY OF KEY TOPICS

Assignments and Delegations

A contract is typically an agreement between two parties. When a right or duty under that contract is transferred to a third party, we need a way to talk about the party who is not directly involved in the transfer but is one of the original parties to the contract who is now going to either perform for a third party (when there is an assignment) or receive a performance from a third party (when there is a delegation).

An *obligor* is a contractual party who owes a duty to the other party in privity of the contract and now must instead perform for a third party.

An *obligee* is a contractual party who is owed a duty from the other party in privity of the contract and now will receive performance from a third party.

An *assignment* is the transfer of rights under a contract to a third party.

The assignor is the party to a contract who transfers his or her rights to a third party.

The *assignee* is a party not in privity to a contract who is the recipient of a transfer of rights to a contract.

Contractual rights that cannot be assigned:

1. Rights that are personal in nature.
2. Rights that would increase the obligor's risks or duties.
3. Rights in a contract that expressly forbids assignment.

A *delegation* is the transfer of a duty under a contract to a third party.

A *delegator* is the party to a contract who transfers his or her duty to a third party.

A *delegatee* is the party not in privity to a contract who is the recipient of a transfer of duty to a contract.

Contractual duties that cannot be assigned:

1. Duties personal in nature.

2. Duties resulting in performance substantially different from that which the obligee originally contracted.

3. Duties in a contract that expressly forbids delegation.

When ambiguous language is used, courts interpret the transfer to consist of an assignment of rights and a delegation of duties.

Assignment of the Contract

An *intended beneficiary* is a third party to a contract whom the contracting parties intended to benefit directly from their contract.

Third-Party Beneficiary Contracts

   A *promisor* is the party to a contract who made the promise that benefits the third party.

   A *promisee* is the party to the contract who owes something to the promisor in exchange for the promise made to the third-party beneficiary.

   A *creditor beneficiary* is a third party who benefits from a contract in which the promisor agrees to pay the promisee's debt.

   A *donee beneficiary* is a third party who benefits from a contract in which a promisor agrees to give a gift to the third party.

   Vesting is the maturing of rights such that a party can legally act on the rights.

An *incidental beneficiary* is a third party who unintentionally gains a benefit from a contract between other parties. That is, it was never the conscious objective of the contracting parties to benefit the third party.

POINT / COUNTERPOINT

Should Incidental Beneficiaries Be Allowed to Sue to Enforce a Contract?	
YES	NO

Suppose a major buyer places a large order for widgets from a manufacturer that employs its workers *at will* (at-will employment is discussed in Chapter 10). Suppose further that the buyer breaches its contract with the manufacturer before the manufacturer makes the widgets for the order. Because of the late notice of the buyer's breach, the manufacturer is unable to find a replacement buyer. As a result, the manufacturer is forced to lay off some workers, many of whom are unable to find replacement work. These workers are *incidental beneficiaries* of the manufacturer's contract with the buyer, and under current law they cannot sue to enforce the contract.
 	
   A number of legal scholars find this result unfair. The manufacturer's workers relied on the promises of the buyer when they made important financial decisions, such as how many hours to work and whether to look for additional employment opportunities. Moreover, at-will workers tend to have very little bargaining power. They also usually lack the resources to relocate in response to job openings in other cities, states, or countries or to obtain
	The difficulties facing the at-will employees in the widget manufacturing example may be compelling, but contract law is not the ideal way to address the problem. Such an approach would be expensive and slow because incidental beneficiaries could recover a remedy only after a series of lawsuits with many expensive lawyers. Instead, we ought to use the social welfare system—tax redistribution and unemployment benefits—to aid vulnerable workers.
	
	   Moreover, it is not clear that at-will workers are enormously susceptible to exploitation. A number of econometric studies have attempted to determine whether at-will employees receive higher wages than "secure" employees who provide equivalent labor. Although it is not entirely conclusive, significant evidence suggests that at-will workers receive a "bonus" for taking the risks of at-will employment (economists call these bonuses *compensating differentials*).
	
	   Permitting incidental beneficiaries to sue to enforce a contract would also establish perverse incentives. At-will employees laid off when a third party breaches a contract with their employer would know they can recover damages

additional training to prepare them for other job markets. As a result, at-will employees often have difficulty finding replacement employment when buyers breach contracts with their employer. In such cases, the law fails to help the most vulnerable.

if they do not find replacement work. If they do find replacement work, however, they can recover only the difference between what they would have earned if the breach had not occurred and what they actually earned in their replacement work. This incentive would encourage them to avoid finding replacement work. (Economists call perverse incentive structures like this one *moral hazards.*)

QUESTIONS & PROBLEMS

1. Integrate the concept of assignments with the concept of delegations.

2. Explain the difference between an assignor's liability and a delegator's liability after rights have been transferred to a third party.

3. Why is it that incidental beneficiaries cannot enforce rights under a contract? Should they be able to enforce such rights?

4. Why are courts stricter with interpretations of anti-delegation clauses in contracts than of antiassignment clauses?

5. An investor brought suit against an architect after the investor lost $600,000 in a failed project. To develop the real estate project in Chicago, Burnham Station, an LLC, was created by JDL. The investor arranged to buy shares of Burnham that totaled $600,000. JDL managed Burnham Station. JDL hired the architectural firm Tigerman McCurry Architects (TMA) to develop the real estate. After the investor filed suit to recover the money he had lost in the project, TMA claimed that the investor could not file that suit because the contract at issue was between TMA and JDL. TMA claimed that Burnham was never envisioned as a third party or beneficiary of the contract. If Burnham was not included in the written contract but was involved with JDL and Burnham's money was lost in the project, does this mean the investor is automatically a third party to the contract? How did the court decide? [*F. H. Paschen/S. N. Nielsen, Inc. v. Burnham Station, L.L.C.* (2007 WL 837240, 2007 Ill. App. LEXIS 245).]

6. The farmers are former customers of Ron Kaufman, the owner and operator of Southeast Implements, Inc., a Case International Harvester equipment dealership. Between 1996 and 1998, they agreed to purchase or lease various items of farm equipment from Southeast. In each instance, the farmers and Kaufman orally negotiated the terms of the purchase or lease, and Kaufman then prepared a written purchase agreement for each transaction, assigning his rights thereunder to Case. Case, in turn, after approving the assignments and agreeing to finance the purchases and leases, paid Kaufman for the equipment and looked to the farmers, as debtors, for payment. The written purchase agreements, however, were prepared and assigned without the farmers' knowledge and did not reflect the terms of the oral contracts. Kaufman inflated the purchase and lease prices and forged the farmers' signatures, thereby obtaining thousands of dollars in overpayments from Case. When Case became aware of Kaufman's fraud, it sent representatives to meet with the individual farmers. After verifying that the farmers were in possession of equipment covered by the forged purchase agreements, Case attempted to enforce the terms of the forged contracts. The farmers allege that Case's assignment was improper because the rights assigned were not the ones to which the farmers agreed. The farmers filed suit against Case and Southeast. The court found in favor of Case, and the farmers appealed. Is Kaufman's assignment made to Case binding? What defenses might the farmers have against Case? [*Day v. Case Credit Corp.,* 427 F.3d 1148 (2005).]

7. Prime Finish paints and finishes plastic parts. In 2004, Herbert–Jones became an independent sales representative responsible for developing sales for Prime Finish and formed Cameo to serve this purpose. ITW supplies automotive parts to automakers. After being contacted by Cameo, ITW expressed interest in contracting with Prime Finish

to paint and decorate ITW's automotive parts. During negotiations between Prime Finish and ITW, in which Herbert–Jones was a participant, Prime Finish explained that its financial position was not strong and its facilities were currently not capable of handling the volume of production needed by ITW. ITW, Cameo, and Prime Finish decided that ITW would guarantee a sufficient volume of business to justify the installation of a new Prime Finish paint line. Cameo offered to provide the capital for the line to facilitate this arrangement. The parties then entered into two different contracts.

The first was the Supply Agreement between ITW and Prime Finish, in which Prime Finish agreed to paint and decorate parts provided by ITW. It recognized that Prime Finish "will be investing in a new paint line to meet [ITW's] requirements," and ITW agreed to provide a sufficient number of parts to sustain certain revenue levels for Prime Finish. The Supply Agreement was to last four years and stated that ITW would have to pay a penalty if it terminated the contract early. Cameo was not a party to and is not mentioned in the Supply Agreement between Prime Finish and ITW.

The second contract was the Production Service Agreement between Prime Finish and Cameo, which stated that "Cameo will fund and place in service at Prime Finish a 2-booth paint-line and fixture painting equipment," which were both to be operated by Prime Finish. The paint line would enable Prime Finish to complete ITW's orders, and the Production Agreement stated that "all ITW projects are to run through this line." Prime Finish agreed to "pay Cameo a royalty of 7% of Prime Finish invoiced parts that are base-coated and/or clear-coated through this line." ITW was not a party to the Production Agreement, but the contract stated that "Cameo hereby agrees and acknowledges that Cameo drafted and agrees to the terms and conditions set forth in the Product Supply Agreement between Prime Finish and ITW." Herbert-Jones obtained loans on behalf of Cameo and invested his own money to arrange the $1.6 million needed to fund the new paint line.

Several months after signing the Production Agreement, Cameo and Prime Finish executed a Modification Agreement, which stated that any penalty payment received by Prime Finish pursuant to the Production Supply Agreement between Prime Finish and ITW would be paid to Cameo.

ITW terminated the Supply Agreement early. Prime Finish sued ITW, and Cameo intervened, asserting its rights under the contract to the early termination penalty. Prime Finish and ITW then moved for summary judgment against Cameo, arguing that Cameo lacked standing because it was not a party to the Supply Agreement and was not an intended creditor beneficiary. The district court agreed that Cameo lacked standing and granted summary judgment for ITW. Cameo appealed. Explain what you believe happened on appeal and why. [*Prime Finish, LLC v. Cameo, LLC,* 487 Fed. Appx. 956 (C.A.6, KY. 2012).]

8. CEI and NU were planning a multibillion-dollar merger. Among the terms and conditions of the underlying merger agreement, CEI agreed to purchase all of NU's outstanding shares for $3.6 billion to $1.2 billion over the prevailing market price. Shortly before the scheduled closing, CEI declared that NU had suffered a material adverse change that "dramatically lowered" NU's valuation, and CEI declined to proceed with the merger unless NU would agree to a lower share price. NU rejected the share price reduction, treated CEI's demand as an anticipatory repudiation and breach of the agreement, and declared that the merger was "effectively terminated." Both parties brought suit. The district court ruled that NU could sue on behalf of its shareholders for $1.2 billion. The court reasoned that the merger agreement expressly designated NU's shareholders as intended third-party beneficiaries. Due to subsequent legal actions, both parties appealed. The appellate court then decided the issue of whether any of NU's shareholders were intended third-party beneficiaries. If you were on the court, how would you have ruled? Why? [*Consol. Edison, Inc. v. Northeast Utils.,* 426 F.3d 524 (2005).]

9. Physical Distribution places long-haul and over-the-road truck drivers with parcel and freight delivery companies. Donnelley is a large printing company that purchased CTC Distribution Services and CTC's subsidiary company, Parcel Shippers Express. CTC and Parcel Shippers became subsidiary corporations of Donnelley. Parcel Shippers solicited Physical Distribution to provide drivers. Parcel Shippers and Physical Distribution entered into an agreement that included a nonassignment clause. The parties never executed a written contract, but Physical Distribution began

supplying drivers to Parcel Shippers. Physical Distribution sent invoices for its services to Parcel Shippers, and Donnelley made payments on behalf of Parcel Shippers. Donnelley then sold CTC and Parcel Shippers to American Package Express. Physical Distribution continued, without complaint, to supply drivers to American Package, and American Package paid its bills. However, American Package eventually went through a period of not paying its bills before filing for bankruptcy. Physical Distribution filed suit against Donnelley, alleging breach of contract. According to Physical Distribution, it contracted with Donnelley to provide drivers to Parcel Shippers, and the sale of Parcel Shippers to American Package resulted in an assignment of the contract in violation of the antiassignment provision. Donnelley argued that the contract was between Physical Distribution and Parcel Shippers, a subsidiary corporation of CTC, which was in turn a subsidiary of Donnelley. Thus, Physical Distribution contracted with an entirely separate legal entity, and Donnelley's sale of Parcel Shippers did not result in an assignment of the contract. The district court concluded that the sale of Parcel Shippers did not breach the anti-assignment language of the contract. Was Physical Distribution successful on appeal in convincing the court that Donnelley violated the antiassignment agreement? Why? [*Physical Distribution Services, Inc. v. R.R. Donnelley & Sons Co.,* 561 F.3d 792 (2009).]

10. Potential expert witnesses made an oral agreement with a plaintiff's attorney to testify on behalf of the plaintiff for $60,000. However, after receiving the money, the witnesses backed out of the agreement and said they would not testify in court or pay back the money. The witnesses claimed that the plaintiff could not sue them because their oral contract was with the attorney and not the plaintiff. Yet the plaintiff claimed she could sue because she was a third-party beneficiary to the contract. The court made a landmark decision regarding expert witnesses and third-party beneficiary case law. What was the rationale for such a surprising decision? [*Isbell v. Friedman,* U.S. App. No. 11-2113. (4th Cir. 2012).]

Looking for more review materials?

The Online Learning Center at **www.mhhe.com/kubasek3e** contains this chapter's "Assignment on the Internet" and also a list of URLs for more information, entitled "On the Internet." Find both of them in the Student Center portion of the OLC, along with quizzes and other helpful materials.

Discharge and Remedies

LEARNING OBJECTIVES

After reading this chapter, you will be able to answer the following questions:

1 What are the primary methods of discharging a contract?

2 What are the primary legal remedies available for a breach of contract?

3 What are the primary equitable remedies available for a breach of contract?

CASE OPENER

Impossible Wine Bottles

The Anchor Glass Container Corporation and its parent company, Consumers Packaging, Inc. (CPI), entered into a series of agreements with Encore Glass, Inc., to supply glass containers of a specific type and quality for the wine industry. On June 24, 1999, Encore entered into an amended agreement with Anchor and CPI. In the amended agreement, the parties agreed that the products would be manufactured at CPI's Lavington plant. Additionally, the amended agreement gave Encore a generous rebate schedule ranging from 1 to 2.5 percent and a new discount schedule.

In May 2001, CPI filed for bankruptcy. As a result of the bankruptcy proceedings, the Lavington plant was sold in August 2001. The new owners of the Lavington plant did not assume CPI's obligations under the amended agreement. The Lavington plant could no longer be used to supply the glass containers to Encore. As a result of the sale, Anchor notified Encore on October 12, 2001, that it considered itself relieved of its obligations under the agreement due to its impossibility to perform. Encore took its business to another company, which did not offer the same rebates and discounts as had Anchor.

When Anchor filed for bankruptcy in 2002, Encore filed a claim to recover the $6,102,912.60 it lost when Anchor stopped providing it with rebates and discounts under the contract. The bankruptcy court ruled against Encore, finding that it was impossible for Anchor to perform after the Lavington plant was sold. Encore appealed.

1. Should Anchor be required to honor the contract despite the loss of the Lavington plant? Why or why not?

2. What ethical system, if any, would permit Encore to recover the lost rebates and discounts?

The Wrap-Up at the end of the chapter will answer these questions.

Methods of Discharging a Contract

L01

What are the primary methods of discharging a contract?

The previous seven chapters focus primarily on how parties enter into a legally binding agreement. Once a party has entered into a binding agreement, how does the party terminate his or her obligation under the contract? That question is the focus of this chapter. When a party's obligations under a contract are terminated, the party is said to be discharged. There are a number of ways by which a party's contractual obligations can be terminated and the party thereby discharged. The first, and the one most parties hope to secure from the other when they enter into an agreement, is performance. The others are the happening of a condition or its failure to occur, material breach by one or both parties, agreement of the parties, and operation of law. This chapter explains each of these methods.

CONDITIONS

Under ordinary circumstances, a party's duty to perform the promise agreed to in a contract is absolute. Sometimes, however, a party's duty to perform may be affected by whether a certain condition occurs. Contracts containing conditions affecting the performance obligations of the parties are called conditional contracts. The conditions may be either implied by law or expressly inserted into the contract by the parties.

Discharge by Conditions Precedent, Subsequent, and Concurrent. There are three types of conditions: condition precedent, condition subsequent, and concurrent conditions (see Exhibit 20-1). A condition precedent is a particular event that must occur in order for a party's duty to arise. If the event does not occur, the party's duty to perform does not arise. Frequently, real estate contracts are conditioned on an event such as the buyer's being able to sell his current home by a certain date. If the home does not sell, the condition does not arise. Thus, the parties have no duty to perform and are discharged from the contract.

We're suing for breach of contract because we almost fulfilled our end of the bargain.

Come back if you can get rid of the "almost."

stus.com

Another common example of a contract containing a condition precedent is an insurance contract. If Bill purchases a life insurance contract, he is obligated to pay the monthly premiums specified in the contract but the insurance company's obligation to perform arises only when he dies. His death is the condition that triggers the company's duty to pay his beneficiary.

A condition subsequent is a future event that terminates the obligations of the parties when it occurs. For example, Joan may enter into an agreement to lease an apartment for five years, conditioned on her not being called to active duty in the National Guard. If she is called to serve, her obligation to be bound by the lease is discharged.

Exhibit 20-1

Conditional Contracts:
Types of Conditions

Condition precedent	The party's duty to perform arises after a particular event occurs; if the event never occurs, the party's duty to perform never arises and the parties are thus discharged from the contract.
Condition subsequent	The party has a duty to perform until a future event occurs that discharges the party from the obligation.
Condition concurrent	The party's duty to perform requires that each party perform for the other at the same time. If one party offers to perform his duty and the other party does not, he can sue the other for nonperformance.
Express conditions	Conditions in the contract that are usually preceded by words such as *provided that, if,* or *when.* If these conditions are not met, a party could be discharged from the contract.
Implied conditions	Conditions that are inferred from the nature and language of the contract and are not explicitly stated. If the implied conditions are met, the party could be discharged from the contract.

Legal Principle: A condition precedent exists when a condition must occur before a party's duty to perform arises, whereas a condition subsequent exists when the occurrence of the condition extinguishes a party's duty to perform.

Concurrent conditions occur when each party's performance is conditioned on the performance of the other. They occur only when the parties are required to perform for each other simultaneously. For example, when a buyer is supposed to pay for goods on delivery, the buyer's duty to pay is impliedly conditioned on the seller's duty to deliver the goods, and the seller's duty to deliver the goods is impliedly conditioned on the buyer's duty to pay for the goods. The legal effect of a contract's being concurrently conditioned is that each party must offer to perform before being able to sue the other for nonperformance.

Legal Principle: Concurrent conditions exist when the parties are to perform their obligations for each other simultaneously.

Express and Implied Conditions.   Conditions in contracts are also described as being express or implied. Express conditions are explicitly stated in the contract and are usually preceded by words such as *conditioned on, if, provided that,* or *when.* For example, in a situation involving a potential sale of a house, the offer expressly required that the buyer make a deposit of $1,000 "on acceptance." The buyer wrote "accepted" on the offer and returned it but did not include the deposit. No deposit of money was ever made. The seller then canceled the transaction. Several weeks later, the buyer attempted to tender payment to the seller. The court found that under the terms of the contract, payment of the $1,000 was an express condition of acceptance and since the acceptance was incomplete, there was no contract.[1]

Implied conditions are those that are not explicitly stated but are inferred from the nature and language of the contract. For example, if one enters into a contract with a builder to replace the windows in one's house, there is an implied condition that the builder will be given access to the home so that she may fulfill her obligations under the contract.

---

[1] *Smith v. Holmwood,* 231 Cal. App. 2d 549 (1965).

Legal Principle: **An express condition is clearly stated, whereas an implied condition is not stated but can be inferred from the nature and language of the contract.**

BUT WHAT IF . . .
WHAT IF THE FACTS OF THE CASE OPENER WERE DIFFERENT?

Let's say, in the Case Opener, that the contract between Encore and Anchor included a clause that stated that the two companies would owe duties to each other as long as CPI was not bankrupt and was involved in the relationship. What kind of a condition would that be? Would Encore have been able to sue Anchor?

DISCHARGE BY PERFORMANCE

In most situations, parties discharge their obligations by doing what they respectively agreed to do under the terms of the contract; this is called *discharge by performance*. Parties also discharge their duty by making an offer to perform and being ready, willing, and able to perform. This offer of performance is known as a tender. If a painter shows up at Sam's house with his paint and ladders and is ready to start painting the garage, he has tendered performance. If Sam refuses to let him start, the painter has now discharged his duties under the contract by his tender of performance and he may sue Sam for material breach (discussed later in this chapter).

Types of Performance.   There are two primary kinds of performance: complete performance and substantial performance. Performance may also be conditioned on the satisfaction of a party to the contract or of a third party.

Complete performance occurs when all aspects of the parties' duties under the contract are carried out perfectly. In many instances, complete performance is difficult, if not impossible, to attain, and courts today generally require only substantial performance.

Substantial performance occurs when the following conditions have been met: (1) completion of nearly all the terms of the agreement, (2) an honest effort to complete all the terms, and (3) no willful departure from the terms of the agreement. Substantial performance discharges the party's responsibilities under the contract, although the court may require that the party compensate the other party for any loss in value caused by the failure to meet all the standards set forth in the contract. For example, if a contract called for all bedrooms of a house to be painted blue but one was inadvertently painted green, the court may require that the contractor compensate the buyer by the amount that it will cost the buyer to have that room repainted. Of course, it is sometimes difficult to determine whether in fact there has been substantial performance, which is why there is litigation over this issue.

Performance Subject to Satisfaction of a Contracting Party.   Sometimes the performance of the contract is subject to the satisfaction of one of the contracting parties. In such a case, a party is not discharged from the contract until the other party is satisfied. Satisfaction is considered an express condition that must be met before the other party's obligation to pay for the performance arises.

Satisfaction may be judged according to either a subjective or an objective standard. When the judgment involved is a matter of personal taste, such as when a woman is having a dress custom made for her, the courts apply a subjective satisfaction standard. As long as the person, in good faith, is not satisfied, the other party is deemed to have not met the condition.

If the performance is one related to a mechanical or utility standard, the objective satisfaction standard applies. Also, if the contract does not clearly specify that the satisfaction is to be personal, the objective standard applies. When an objective standard is used, the courts ask whether a reasonable person would be satisfied with the performance.

Sometimes the contract is conditioned on the satisfaction of a third party. Usually, such provisions arise in construction contracts specifying that before a buyer accepts a building, an architect must provide a certificate stating that the building was constructed according to the plans and specifications.

DISCHARGE BY MATERIAL BREACH

A *breach* occurs whenever a party fails to perform her obligations under the contract. If the breach is a minor one, it may entitle the nonbreaching party to damages but it does not discharge the nonbreaching party from the contract.

A material breach, however, discharges the nonbreaching party from his obligations under the contract. A material breach occurs when a party unjustifiably fails to substantially perform his obligations under the contract. It is often difficult to know when the court is going to determine that a breach is material. For example, auto racing fans thought that a contract between them and Formula One and the Indianapolis Speedway, created by their purchase of tickets to a recent car race, had been materially breached when a race that was scheduled to feature 20 cars ended up having only 6. The reduction in the number of cars occurred when it was discovered that a flaw in the tires of a number of cars made it too dangerous for those cars to be in the race and there was not enough time to find replacement vehicles. Regulations explicitly provide that races may be canceled when fewer than 12 cars are available, but the organizers chose to go ahead and hold the race. The court found that the contract was for the event and that no fan would reasonably expect that organizers were specifically guaranteeing a set number of participants.[2] Case 20-1 demonstrates the analysis a court may use to determine whether a defendant's behavior constitutes material breach.

[2] *Larry Bowers, Alan G. Symons, Carey Johnson, et al., v. Federation Internationale de l'Automobile, Formula One Administration Limited, Indianapolis Motor Speedway Corporation, et al.,* 489 F.3d 316 (2007).

CASE 20-1   **HAMILTON v. STATE FARM FIRE & CASUALTY INSURANCE COMPANY**
U.S. COURT OF APPEALS FOR THE FIFTH CIRCUIT
2012 U.S. APP. LEXIS 8744

When the Hamiltons' home was ruined by a hurricane, the couple moved out of the home to other residences. The couple provided their insurance company with several documents and submitted an insurance claim. However, the couple refused to allow representatives from the insurance agency to inspect their other homes and refused to give the company other vital documents proving the damage of certain assets. Thus, the insurance company denied the Hamiltons' insurance claim, saying that the couple materially breached the contract because they did not comply with the terms of the policy. The appellate court found that the couple could not recover under the insurance policy because they materially breached the contract by not complying with the cooperation clause.

JUDGES BENAVIDES, STEWART, AND HIGGINSON:
Louisiana law provides that an insurance policy is a contract between the parties and should be construed by using the general rules of interpretation of contracts set forth in the Louisiana Civil Code. "If the policy wording at issue is clear and unambiguously expresses the parties' intent, the insurance contract must be enforced as written."

"In an insurance contract, the insured's duty to provide information ordinarily arises only under the express policy obligations." Cooperation clauses in insurance contracts "fulfill the reasonable purpose of enabling the insurer to obtain relevant information concerning the loss while the information is fresh." "Compliance with insurance policy provisions are conditions precedent to recovery under that policy, which must be fulfilled before an insured may proceed with a lawsuit." "[F]ailure of an insured to cooperate with the insurer has been held to be a material breach of the contract and a defense to suit on the policy." Such failure may be "manifested by a refusal to submit to an examination under oath or a refusal to produce documents."

"[T]he purpose of the oral examination of the insured is to protect the insurer against fraud, by permitting it to probe into the circumstances of the loss, including an examination of the insured[.]" The defendant must also show that it has been prejudiced by the failure of the plaintiffs to submit to examinations under oath. "The burden is on the insurer to show actual prejudice."

In this case, the Hamiltons reported the alleged theft to local law enforcement, submitted their claim to State Farm, and returned the PPIFs to State Farm as requested; the Hamiltons failed to provide most of the supporting documentation of their loss as requested by State Farm, with the exception of a few duplicate receipts. When asked for the additional documentation, the Hamiltons simply provided their sworn statements as to the losses claimed, without providing the additional supporting documentation requested.

The Hamiltons' failure to comply with State Farm's request to examine the separate residences in which they lived, while not expressly required under the policy's cooperation clause, appears from the record to have been the event which prompted State Farm to request the examinations under oath. The Hamiltons, however, failed to respond to State Farm's multiple verbal and written requests for examinations under oath. Their failure to do so was in direct violation of the policy's cooperation clause provision, Section 1 - Conditions, (2)(d)(3)(b), and is thus considered a "material breach of the contract." The Hamiltons concede in their brief that they failed to respond to State Farm's request for their examinations under oath but submit that State Farm was not prejudiced by their refusals because they would have consented to depositions to be taken later in the litigation. This argument is not persuasive. The underlying purpose of a cooperation clause is to allow the insurer to obtain the material information it needs from the insured to adequately investigate a claim of loss prior to the commencement of litigation proceedings.

Without the additional requested documentation in support of their loss or their sworn statements under oath, State Farm had nothing but the Hamiltons' original recorded statements, which often conflicted with each other factually, and several duplicated receipts to process their claim of over $120,000 in losses. Consequently, it is clear that State Farm's investigation into the claim was prejudiced from the Hamiltons' failure to comply with the terms of the cooperation clause.

Because the Hamiltons materially breached the terms of the policy by failing to comply with the terms of the cooperation clause, they were precluded from recovering under the policy. Additionally, considering that State Farm's denial of the claim was due to the Hamiltons' material breach of the policy, the Hamiltons are also precluded from recovering penalties and attorney fees.

AFFIRMED in favor of State Farm.

CRITICAL THINKING

What kind of evidence would have persuaded State Farm that the Hamiltons had a legitimate insurance claim? What is the reasoning of the court in supporting State Farm's expectations under the cooperation clause in the policy?

ETHICAL DECISION MAKING

How would the universalization principle have aided the Hamiltons in understanding the logic being used by State Farm?

BUT WHAT IF . . .

WHAT IF THE FACTS OF THE CASE OPENER WERE DIFFERENT?

Recall, in the Case Opener, that CPI manufactured Encore's products in its factory. Let's say that CPI simply stopped allowing the products in the factory. Would Encore be able to be discharged from the contract, or would Encore have to stay in the contract and find some sort of resolution?

Anticipatory Repudiation. Sometimes a contracting party may decide not to complete the contract before the actual time of performance. This situation often arises when market conditions change and one party realizes that it will not be profitable to carry out the terms of the contract. The breaching party may convey the anticipatory breach to the nonbreaching party either by making an express indication of her intent to no longer perform or by taking an action that would be inconsistent with her ability to carry out the contract when performance was due.

Once the contract has been anticipatorily repudiated, the nonbreaching party is discharged from his obligations under the contract. He is free to go ahead and sue for breach, as well as find another similar contract elsewhere. However, if the nonbreaching party wishes, he may decide to give the party who repudiated the opportunity to change her mind and still perform.

DISCHARGE BY MUTUAL AGREEMENT

Sometimes the parties to a contract agree to discharge each other from their obligations. They may do so through four primary means: discharge by mutual rescission, discharge by a substituted contract, discharge by accord and satisfaction, or discharge by novation. (See Exhibit 20-2.)

Mutual Rescission.   Parties may agree that they simply wish to discharge each other from their mutual obligations and therefore rescind or cancel the contract. For example, if James had agreed to cater a graduation reception for Bill's son but it appeared that the child was not going to graduate when planned, James could agree to no longer hold Bill responsible for paying him the agreed-on cost for the catering in exchange for Bill's agreement to no longer expect James to cater a reception.

> To see how techniques of group problem solving relate to mutual rescission, please see the **Connecting to the Core** activity on the text website at www.mhhe.com/kubasek3e.

Substituted Contract.   Sometimes, instead of canceling the contract and terminating their relationship, the parties wish to substitute a new agreement in place of the original. The substituted contract immediately discharges the parties from their obligations under the old contract and replaces those obligations with the new obligations imposed by the substituted contract.

In the opening scenario, the amended agreement between Anchor and Encore is a substituted contract. In their original contract, the parties were silent about where the wine bottles would be produced and Anchor provided Encore with a rebate discount schedule ranging from 1 to 2.5 percent. Their substituted contract (the amended agreement) discharged the parties from the previous requirements, specified the Lavington facility as the production location, and increased the rates associated with the discount schedule.

		Exhibit 20-2
Mutual rescission	Parties mutually agree to discharge each other from the contract.	Ways to Discharge by Mutual Agreement
Substituted contract	Parties mutually agree to discharge each other from the contract by substituting a new agreement.	
Accord and satisfaction	Parties agree that one party will perform her or his duty differently from the performance specified in the original agreement; after the new duty is performed, the party's duty under the original contract becomes discharged.	
Novation	The original parties and a third party all agree that the third party will replace one of the original parties and that the original party will then be discharged.	

Accord and Satisfaction.   An accord and satisfaction is used when one of the parties wishes to substitute a different performance for his or her original duty under the contract. The promise to perform the new duty is called the *accord,* and the actual performance of that new duty is called the *satisfaction.* The party's duty under the contract is not discharged until the new duty is actually performed. Thus, it is the satisfaction that discharges the party.

Novation.   Sometimes the parties to the agreement want to replace one of the parties with a third party. This substitution of a party is called a novation. The original duties remain the same under the contract, but one party is discharged and the third party now takes that original party's place. All three parties must agree to the novation for it to be valid.

DISCHARGE BY OPERATION OF LAW

Sometimes a contract may be discharged not by anything the parties do but, rather, by operation of law. Alteration of the contract, bankruptcy, tolling of the statute of limitations, impossibility, commercial impracticability, and frustration of purpose are all situations in which a contract may be discharged by operation of law.

Alteration of the Contract.   The courts wish to uphold the sanctity of contracts. Therefore, if one of the parties materially alters a written contract without the knowledge of the other party, the courts have held that such alteration allows the innocent party to be discharged from the contract. For example, if a seller, without knowledge of the buyer, changes the price of the contract, the buyer can treat the contract as terminated.

Bankruptcy.   When a party files bankruptcy, the court allocates the assets of the bankrupt among the bankrupt's creditors and then issues the party a discharge in bankruptcy. Once the assets have been distributed, all of the bankrupt's debts are discharged. (Bankruptcy is discussed in detail in Chapter 32.)

Tolling of the Statute of Limitations.   The tolling of the statute of limitations does not technically discharge a party's obligations under a contract. However, once the statute of limitations has tolled, neither party can any longer sue the other for breach, so for all practical purposes the parties are no longer bound to perform.

Impossibility of Performance.   Sometimes an unforeseen event occurs that makes it physically or legally impossible for a party to carry out the terms of the contract. In such a situation, the party will be discharged on grounds of impossibility of performance. Courts distinguish between objective impossibility, meaning it is in fact not possible to lawfully carry out one's contractual obligations, and subjective impossibility, meaning it would be very difficult to carry out the contract. Objective impossibility, but not subjective impossibility, discharges the parties' obligations under the contract.

For example, if farmer Gray has a contract with the Hunts Corporation to provide it with 100 bushels of tomatoes on August 30 and a flood wipes out Gray's crop, it is not physically impossible for him to comply with the agreement. He has to go out on the market and purchase 100 bushels of tomatoes to ship to the Hunts Corporation. It may be inconvenient, and perhaps subjectively impossible, but it is not objectively impossible.

In contrast, suppose farmer Jones owns a historic farmhouse built in 1827 and he agrees to sell it to Smith, but the night before the parties are to exchange money for the title, lightning strikes the farmhouse and the building burns to the ground. It is now objectively impossible to comply with the terms of the contract, so the parties are discharged from their obligations. The historic farmhouse is not like tomatoes; the subject matter of the contract is forever destroyed and cannot be re-created.

There are three main situations in which the courts find objective impossibility. The first is *destruction of the subject matter,* as in the example of the historic farmhouse destroyed by fire. If we go back to the example of the tomatoes, note that we said the farmer still had to perform because it was still possible for him to obtain tomatoes elsewhere. To protect himself in the event that his crop was destroyed, farmer Gray could have drafted the contract to identify the subject matter as 100 bushels of tomatoes grown on the Gray family farm. In that case, if Gray's fields were flooded, it would be objectively impossible to comply with the contract because there would be no tomatoes from the Gray farm in existence.

The second situation of objective impossibility is the *death or incapacity of a party whose personal services are necessary* to fulfill the terms of the contract. For example, if a famous artist is commissioned to paint a portrait and the artist dies, the contract is discharged. The artist's style is unique, and there is no way for anyone to take over the artist's role.

The third situation is *subsequent illegality.* If the law changes after the contract is made, rendering the performance of the contract illegal, then the contract is discharged. For example, Bill orders a case of a nutritional supplement from Osco Drugs and Supplements. Before his order can be filled, the nutritional supplement is banned because of recently discovered harmful side effects. The parties are now discharged from their duties because to sell the banned substance would be to violate the law.

The opening scenario provides another example of impossibility of performance. The parties in the opening scenario do not dispute that the contract provided that "[t]he parties contemplate that the products (as hereinafter defined) shall be manufactured at CPI's Lavington facility" (the Lavington plant). When the Lavington plant was no longer available for production, it became impossible for Anchor to fulfill the terms of the contract. Ultimately, Anchor informed Encore that it considered itself discharged from the contract.

Legal Principle: **A contract is objectively impossible, and therefore parties are discharged from their obligations under it, when the subject matter is destroyed, one of the parties whose personal services are required dies or becomes incapacitated, or the law changes, rendering performance of the contract illegal.**

Commercial Impracticability.   Commercial impracticability can be seen as a response to what some might interpret as a somewhat unfair harshness of the objective-impossibility standard. Commercial impracticability is used when performance is still objectively possible but would be extraordinarily injurious or expensive to one party. Commercial impracticability arises when, because of an unforeseeable event, one party would incur unreasonable expense, injury, or loss if that party were forced to carry out the terms of the agreement.

According to the Restatement (Second) of Contracts, Section 261 (1981), discharge by reason of impracticability requires that the party claiming discharge prove the following three elements:

1. That an event occurred whose nonoccurrence was a basic assumption of the contract.
2. That there is commercial impracticability of continued performance.
3. That the party claiming discharge did not expressly or impliedly agree to performance in spite of impracticability that would otherwise justify nonperformance.

It is sometimes difficult to know whether the potential harm to the party seeking to avoid the contract is sufficient to give rise to the use of commercial impracticability. The doctrine is most commonly used in situations in which raw materials needed for manufacturing goods under the contract become extraordinarily expensive or difficult to obtain because of an embargo, war, crop failure, or unexpected closure of a plant. Case 20-2 illustrates how the courts sometimes struggle to determine whether to apply the doctrine of commercial impracticability to discharge a contract.

CASE 20-2   THRIFTY RENT-A-CAR SYSTEM v. SOUTH FLORIDA TRANSPORT
U.S. DISTRICT COURT FOR THE NORTHERN DISTRICT OF OKLAHOMA
2005 U.S. DIST. LEXIS 38489

The plaintiffs, Thrifty Rent-A-Car System and its affiliates DTG and Rental Car Finance Corp., allowed South Florida Transport (SFT), the defendant, to establish a Thrifty franchise. In 2003, Thrifty and SFT entered into four agreements, which provided SFT the right to use Thrifty's trademark and business methods in exchange for payment to Thrifty of licensing and administrative fees. The agreements also provided that SFT would maintain a fleet of automobiles for rental.

In July 2004, SFT provided DTG with a check as payment, but the check was returned for insufficient funds. SFT continued to make delinquent payments, and by August, SFT owed Thrifty and DTG $1,134,819.40. Due to SFT's failure to make payments, Thrifty and DTG informed SFT that they were going to terminate the licensing agreements and repossess the vehicles, to which DTG had legal title. However, DTG agreed to postpone repossession due to predictions of severe weather, and allowed SFT to continue renting vehicles until repossession was completed.

When DTG repossessed the vehicles, DTG noticed that numerous cars were missing. In response, SFT notified DTG that it had sold 51 vehicles without authorization. By August 2005, SFT owed Thrifty and DTG $4,238,249.53. SFT claimed that several hurricanes rendered their business operations commercially impracticable. The plaintiffs filed a motion for summary judgment, seeking full reimbursement for the debts owed by SFT.

JUDGE EAGAN: Performance may become impracticable due to extreme and unreasonable difficulty, expense, injury, or loss to one of the parties involved. Impracticability does not equate to impracticality, however. "A mere change in the degree of difficulty or expense . . . unless well beyond the normal range does not amount to impracticability since it is this sort of risk that a fixed-price contract is intended to cover." The law also imposes an objective standard on the duty to perform for those seeking to invoke the defense of impracticability. A party to a contract is not discharged

from his duty to perform merely by demonstrating that a supervening event prevented him from performing; he must also demonstrate that similarly situated parties were also deprived of the ability to perform.

The undisputed facts relevant to Greenstein's claim of impracticability are as follows: In August and September 2004, Hurricanes Charley, Frances, Ivan, and Jeanne hit the state of Florida. One of those storms, Hurricane Ivan, also affected the state of Alabama. Although some of SFT's rental car business locations incurred damage during the course of the storm, it is undisputed that the locations remained substantially intact, and the vehicles leased from DTG were not destroyed.

The hurricanes in late summer 2004 clearly constitute supervening events for the purposes of impracticability doctrine. However, the record suggests that the nonoccurrence of those hurricanes was not an assumption upon which the parties grounded their agreement. Hardy testified that he lived in Florida approximately ten years, during which time severe weather, including hurricanes, had hit the coast of Florida.

The doctrine of commercial impracticability is typically invoked in cases involving the sale of goods. Codified in section 2-615 of the Uniform Commercial Code (UCC), which has been adopted by the Oklahoma legislature, the doctrine of commercial impracticability provides a defense to a seller for a delay in delivery or nondelivery of promised goods if performance has been made impracticable by a contingency, the nonoccurrence of which is an assumption of the contract.

Commercial impracticability may excuse a party from performance of his obligations under a contract where performance has become commercially impracticable because of unforeseen supervening circumstances not within the contemplation of the parties at the time of contracting. UCC commentary provides that a party pleading commercial impracticability must demonstrate the "basic assumption" prong of the test also found in the impracticability of performance context, that is, that the nonoccurrence of the

[continued]

supervening event was a basic assumption of the parties at the time of contracting. A rise or a collapse in the market standing alone does not constitute a justification for failure to perform. A contract is deemed commercially impracticable when, due to unforeseen events, performance may only be obtained at "an excessive and unreasonable cost . . . or when all means of performance are commercially senseless." In applying the doctrine of commercial impracticability, the crucial question is "whether the cost of performance has in fact become so excessive and unreasonable that failure to excuse performance would result in grave injustice."

For many of the reasons already discussed, defendant is not entitled to the defense of commercial impracticability.

The evidence strongly suggests that the nonoccurrence of hurricanes was not a basic assumption of the parties' agreements. Moreover, defendant provides no evidence to support a suggestion that the event of the hurricanes made the cost of performance of the terms of the agreements unduly burdensome, or even remotely more expensive. Finally, the Court observes, again, that SFT was behind on its payments to Thrifty and DTG before the arrival of the hurricanes in August 2004. No genuine issue of material fact exists, and the Court holds that the defense of commercial impracticability is unavailable to defendant.

Plaintiff's motion for summary judgment granted.

CRITICAL THINKING

What are the implications of the court's decision that commercial impracticability is not constituted by the significant hurricane damages imposed on Florida in 2004? Especially given the increased rates of severe weather and natural disasters witnessed recently around the world, to what extent can parties entering into contracts reasonably be expected to plan for the effects of a rapidly changing global climate?

ETHICAL DECISION MAKING

How might ethical theories founded in deontology and in ethics of care differ in their interpretation of the behaviors examined in this case? Which interpretation do you think is more ethically defensible? Which interpretation does Judge Eagan appear to favor? Justify your response.

What purpose does this ruling appear to support? Is there a larger ethical end implied by Judge Eagan's decision? Why or why not?

BUT WHAT IF . . .

WHAT IF THE FACTS OF THE CASE OPENER WERE DIFFERENT?

Let's say that CPI left its factory to Anchor so that Anchor could still manufacture products for Encore as stated in the contract. However, manufacturing the products as CPI did would be outrageously expensive for Anchor. Does Anchor still have to remain in the contract with Encore?

Frustration of Purpose. Closely related to impracticability is frustration of purpose. Sometimes, when a contract is entered into, both parties recognize that the contract is to fulfill a particular purpose, and the happening of that purpose is said to be a basic assumption on which the contract is made. If, due to factors beyond the control of the parties, the event does not occur, and neither party had assumed the risk of the event's nonoccurrence, the contract may be discharged.

This doctrine arose from the so-called coronation cases in England. Numerous parties had contracted for rooms along the parade route for the king's coronation, but the king became ill and the coronation was canceled. The courts held that the parties' duties under the room contracts should be discharged and that any payments made in advance should be returned as the essential purposes of the contracts could no longer be fulfilled, through no fault of any of the parties.

461

? BUT WHAT IF . . .

WHAT IF THE FACTS OF THE CASE OPENER WERE DIFFERENT?

Let's say that Anchor and Encore had entered into the contract with the purpose of creating a certain kind of bottle that was better for the environment than normal bottles. However, the two companies tried but could not produce such a bottle. Can the contract be discharged?

This doctrine is not frequently used. For example, if you contract for an organist to play at your daughter's wedding but the groom gets cold feet at the last moment and the wedding is canceled, you cannot use frustration of purpose to discharge the contract because the groom's changing his mind was a foreseeable event, even though it was unlikely. The Case Nugget on the next page illustrates another unsuccessful attempted use of this doctrine.

Exhibit 20-3 summarizes the five methods of discharging a contract.

Exhibit 20-3

Methods of Discharging a Contract

Discharge by conditions	If precedent, concurrent, implied, and express conditions are not met or subsequent condition occurs.
Discharge by performance	If a party performs the terms of the contract or makes a tender (an offer to perform), or if the party performs to the satisfaction of the contracting party.
Discharge by material breach	If a party fails to substantially perform his obligations, thereby justifying that the nonbreaching party be discharged from the contract.
Discharge by mutual agreement	If the parties mutually agree to discharge one another, substitute a new contract, substitute a party, or substitute a different performance.
Discharge by operation of the law	If one of the following occurs: alteration of the contract, bankruptcy, tolling of the statute of limitations, impossibility, commercial impracticability, or frustration of purpose.

L02

What are the primary legal remedies available for a breach of contract?

Remedies

The fact that one party has breached a contract does not necessarily mean that the non breaching party will sue. A number of factors go into the decision of whether or not it makes sense to file suit (see Exhibit 20-4). Some of those considerations include (1) the likelihood of success, (2) the desire or need to maintain an ongoing relationship with the potential defendant, (3) the possibility of getting a better or faster resolution through some form of alternative dispute resolution, and (4) the cost of litigation or some form of ADR as compared to the value of the likely remedy.

Exhibit 20-4

Things to Consider before Filing Suit

1. The likelihood of success.
2. The desire or need to maintain an ongoing relationship with the potential defendant.
3. The possibility of getting a better or faster resolution through some form of alternative dispute resolution.
4. The cost of litigation or some form of ADR as compared to the value of the likely remedy.

Liggett Restaurant Group, Inc. v. City of Pontiac
260 Mich. App. 127, 676 N.W.2d 633 (Mich. App. 2003)

Elias Brothers Restaurants, Inc., had a contract with the defendant, City of Pontiac Stadium Building Authority, to provide concessions at the Silverdome until 2000. The parties renegotiated the contract in 1990, and Elias Brothers agreed to pay additional consideration for the option to extend the contract until 2005 to coordinate with the end of the Detroit Lions' sublease. The additional consideration involved paying the city a higher percentage on profits from sales. This option was exercised on December 1, 1998, and the Detroit Lions prematurely discontinued playing in the Silverdome after the 2001 football season.

The plaintiff sought to use the frustration-of-purpose doctrine to discharge its obligations under the contract extension and therefore have returned to it the additional consideration it had paid under the extension. The plaintiff argued that the contract was made on the assumption that the Lions would play in the Silverdome until their lease ran out and thus their early departure frustrated the purpose of the extension.

The court said the doctrine was inapplicable in this case. The court first set forth the conditions under which the doctrine applied: (1) The contract must be at least partially executory; (2) the frustrated party's purpose in making the contract must have been known to both parties when the contract was made; (3) this purpose must have been basically frustrated by an event not reasonably foreseeable at the time the contract was made, the occurrence of which has not been due to the fault of the frustrated party and the risk of which was not assumed by him. Then the court noted that the situation clearly did not meet the third criterion. Far from being an unforeseeable event, the Lions' leaving prematurely was expressly addressed in the original contract by a paragraph specifying a reduction in the guaranteed minimum annual payment for each year in which the Lions did not play a minimum of eight games in the stadium.

The remedies the potential plaintiff will be thinking about can generally be classified as either *legal remedies* (also known as *monetary damages*) or *equitable remedies,* some form of court-ordered action. The distinction between legal and equitable remedies can be traced back to a time in our legal system's English roots when, instead of one unitary legal system, there were two separate courts, a court of law and a court of equity. When parties were seeking money damages, they went to the court of law; but when parties needed any remedy other than money damages, they went to the High Court of Chancery, which was a court of equity. When the United States was establishing its legal system, it combined both these types of powers in a unitary system. The reasons for this joinder are not known, but it seems likely that the primary reason was that the early colonists simply did not have the resources to support two separate systems. The courts did, however, still maintain the distinction between legal and equitable remedies. However, unlike judges in the old English courts, judges in the U.S. system have the power to award both legal and equitable remedies in the same case. This section discusses these various remedies.

LEGAL REMEDIES (MONETARY DAMAGES)

Monetary damages are also referred to as *legal damages* or *legal remedies,* and they include compensatory, punitive, nominal, and liquidated damages. Whenever possible, courts award monetary damages rather than some form of equitable relief.

Compensatory Damages. The most frequently awarded damages are compensatory damages, damages designed to put the plaintiff in the position he would have been in had the contract been fully performed. These damages are said to compensate the plaintiff for his loss of the benefit of the bargain. He can recover, however, only for those provable losses that were foreseeable at the time the contract was entered into. Sometimes, the plaintiff actually may have no losses. Suppose, for example, that Dr. Wilcox hires Jeremy to work exclusively as his research assistant during the fall semester, for a salary of $2,000 per month. If Wilcox breaches the contract and terminates Jeremy for no reason with two months left on the contract, and the only job Jeremy can get as a substitute

463

pays only $500 per month, Jeremy would be entitled to compensatory damages of $3,000. However, if Jeremy gets a new job that pays $2,500 per month, he is actually better off, so no compensatory damages would be awarded. Sometimes these damages are referred to as *expectation damages* because they compensate a person for the benefit she or he expected to gain as a result of entering into the contract.

In addition to losing the benefit of the bargain, the plaintiff may suffer other losses directly caused by the breach. These losses may be compensated for as *incidental damages*. For example, because Jeremy was unfairly terminated before his contractual term was over, he may have to spend money to find another job. His job search expenditures would be considered incidental damages.

BUT WHAT IF . . .
WHAT IF THE FACTS OF THE CASE OPENER WERE DIFFERENT?

Let's say that after Anchor and Encore stopped doing business together, Encore entered into an agreement with another company whereby it received bigger discounts than those it received from Anchor. Could Encore still sue Anchor for compensatory damages for breaching the contract?

Some kinds of contracts have special rules for determining compensatory damages, namely, contracts for the sale of goods or land and construction contracts. Each of these is discussed in a little more detail below.

Contracts for the sale of goods are governed today by the Uniform Commercial Code. If the seller breaches the contract, compensatory damages are generally calculated as the difference between the contract price and the market price on the day the goods were supposed to be delivered,[3] plus any incidental damages resulting from the breach. In other words, this measure of damages is the difference between what the buyer would have paid for the goods under the contract and what he or she is now going to have to pay to obtain the goods from another seller. Occasionally, however, the buyer may have no damages because the market price of the goods is lower than the parties had anticipated it would be at the date of delivery and so the buyer can now actually purchase the goods at a lower price than the contract price.

If the buyer breaches before accepting the goods, the seller would be able to resell the goods and recover as compensatory damages the difference between the price he sold the goods for and the contract price, plus any incidental expenses associated with the sale.[4] If the seller is unable to sell the goods to another buyer, as might be the case, for example, with shirts embroidered with a company's monogram, then the seller may be entitled to the contract price as damages. If the buyer breaches before the goods are even manufactured, the seller's damages would typically be based on the profits that would have been made from the sale.

In construction contracts, contracts whereby an owner enters into an agreement to have a building constructed, damages are calculated differently depending on who the breaching party is and what stage the construction is in when the breach occurs. If the contract is breached by the owner before the construction is begun, damages are simply lost profits, which are calculated by subtracting the projected costs of construction from the contract

---

[3] UCC §§ 2-708 and 2-713.

[4] UCC §§ 2-706 and 2-710.

price. For example, if Cameron Construction Company anticipates building a warehouse for the Johnson Corporation with a contract price of $500,000 and the cost of raw materials and labor is $420,000, Cameron could recover $80,000 in lost profits if the Johnson Corporation were to breach the contract before performance had begun.

If, however, Cameron Construction had already expended $20,000 in materials and labor on the job when the breach occurred, the company would be able to recover $100,000 in damages because the amount of damages when construction is in progress is measured by the lost profits plus any money already invested in the project. If the breach by the owner had occurred after construction was completed, the construction company would be entitled to recover the entire contract price, plus interest from the time payment for the project was due.

If the construction company or contractor breaches the contract before or during the construction, the owner's damages are generally measured by the cost of hiring another company to complete the project, plus any incidental costs associated with obtaining a new contractor, as well as any costs arising from delays in the construction project. If the contractor completes the job but finishes after the date for completion, the owner is entitled to damages for the loss of the use of the building that she would have had if the contract had been completed in a timely manner.

Consequential Damages.   It should be apparent by now that contract law requires greater certainty in the proof of damages than does tort law. Damages are not recoverable for breach of contract unless they can be proved with a high degree of certainty. One type of damages in contract cases that is often especially difficult to prove is what are called consequential or special damages. Consequential damages are foreseeable damages that result from special facts and circumstances arising outside the contract itself. These damages must be within the contemplation of the parties at the time the breach occurs.

In Case 20-3, a classic case, the court distinguishes consequential damages from the damages that arise naturally from a breach of contract.

CASE 20-3   HADLEY v. BAXENDALE
COURT OF EXCHEQUER
156 ENG. REP. 145 (1854)

Plaintiffs were millers in Gloucester. On May 11, their mill was stopped when the crank shaft of the mill broke. They had to send the shaft to Greenwich to be used as a model for a new crank to be molded. The plaintiffs' servant took the shaft to the defendant, a common carrier, and told the defendant's clerk that the mill was stopped, and that the shaft must be sent immediately. The clerk said it would be delivered at Greenwich on the following day. The defendant's clerk was told that a special entry, if required, should be made to hasten the shaft's delivery. The delivery of the shaft at Greenwich was delayed by some neglect, and consequently, the plaintiffs did not receive the new shaft for several days after they would otherwise have received it. During that time the mill was shut down, and the plaintiffs thereby lost the profits they would otherwise have received had the shaft been delivered on time. They sought to recover damages for lost profits during that time. The defendant argued that the lost profits were "too

remote." The court decided for the plaintiffs and allowed the jury to consider the lost profits in awarding damages. The defendant appealed.

JUSTICE ALDERSON: We think that there ought to be a new trial in this case; but, in so doing, we deem it to be expedient and necessary to state explicitly the rule which the Judge, at the next trial, ought, in our opinion, to direct the jury to be governed by when they estimate the damages. . . .

Now we think the proper rule in such a case as the present is this: Where two parties have made a contract which one of them has broken, the damages which the other party ought to receive in respect of such breach of contract should be such as may fairly and reasonably be considered either arising naturally, i.e., according to the usual course of things, from such breach of contract itself, or such as may reasonably be supposed to have been in the contemplation of both parties, at the time they made the contract, as the probable result of the breach of it. Now, if the special circumstances under which the contract was actually made were communicated by the plaintiffs to the defendants, and thus known to both parties, the damages resulting from the breach of such a contract, which they would reasonably contemplate, would be the amount of injury which would ordinarily follow from a breach of contract under these special circumstances so known and communicated. But, on the other hand, if these special circumstances were wholly unknown to the party breaking the contract, he, at the most, could only be supposed to have had in his contemplation the amount of injury which would arise generally, and in the great multitude of cases not affected by any special circumstances, from such a breach of contract. For, had the special circumstances been known, the parties might have specially provided for the breach of contract by special terms as to the damages in that case; and of this advantage it would be very unjust to deprive them. . . . Now, in the present case, if we are to apply the principles above laid down, we find that the only circumstances here communicated by the plaintiffs to the defendants at the time the contract was made, were, that the article to be carried was the broken shaft of a mill, and that the plaintiffs were the millers of the mill.

But how do these circumstances show reasonably that the profits of the mill must be stopped by an unreasonable delay in the delivery of the broken shaft by the carrier to the third person? . . . But it is obvious that, in the great multitude of cases of millers sending off broken shafts to third persons by a carrier under ordinary circumstances, such consequences would not, in all probability, have occurred; and these special circumstances were here never communicated by the plaintiffs to the defendants. It follows therefore, that the loss of profits here cannot reasonably be considered such a consequence of the breach of contract as could have been fairly and reasonably contemplated by both the parties when they made this contract. For such loss would neither have flowed naturally from the breach of this contract in the great multitude of such cases occurring under ordinary circumstances, nor were the special circumstances, which, perhaps, would have made it a reasonable and natural consequence of such breach of contract, communicated to or known by the defendants.

Judgment for defendant for a new trial.

CRITICAL THINKING

What are the key terms essential to this argument? Are alternative definitions of important words or phrases possible? If so, how could the acceptability of this argument be affected by the use of these alternative meanings?

What additional information would be useful in deciding the acceptability of this argument? For instance, what do we really know about the proposed loss of profit? Does this missing information have a significant impact on the reasoning?

ETHICAL DECISION MAKING

What value preferences can be discovered in Judge Alderson's ruling? Are they properly justified? What ethical theories or guidelines might aid in their justification? Why?

Punitive Damages.   Just as in tort law, punitive damages in contract law are designed to punish the defendant and deter him and others from engaging in similar behavior in the future. Because the primary objective of contract law, however, is to ensure that parties' expectations are met, punitive, or exemplary, damages are rarely awarded. Most jurisdictions award them only when the defendant has engaged in reprehensible conduct such as fraud. The primary factor in determining the amount of punitive damages is how much is necessary to "punish" the defendant; thus the amount depends on matters such as the wealth and income of the defendant.

Nominal Damages.   In a case where no actual damages resulted from the breach of contract, the court may award the plaintiff nominal damages. The award is typically for $1 or $5, but it serves to signify that the plaintiff has been wronged by the defendant.

Liquidated Damages.   Typically, the court determines the amount of damages to which a nonbreaching party is entitled. Sometimes, however, the parties recognize that if there is a breach of contract, it will probably be somewhat difficult for the court to determine exactly what the damages are. To prevent a difficult court battle, the parties specify in advance what the liquidated damages will be if there is a particular kind of breach. The parties specify these damages in what is called a *liquidated* or *stipulated-damage clause* in the contract. The damages may be specified as either a fixed amount or a formula for determining how much money is due. Such clauses are frequently used in construction contracts when the buyer needs to know the property is going to be available by a specific date so that she can make her plans for moving in. In such a case, the parties may estimate in advance what it will cost the buyer for storage and temporary housing if the property is not ready by the specified date. The courts generally enforce these clauses as long as they appear to bear a reasonable relationship to what the actual costs will be. If the amount specified is so unreasonable as to not seem to bear any logical relationship to foreseeable costs, the courts declare the clause a penalty clause and do not enforce it.

Mitigation of Damages.   When a contract has been breached, the nonbreaching party is often angry at the breaching party and may want to make the breaching party "pay through the nose." However, the courts do not allow a nonbreaching party to intentionally increase his damages. In fact, to recover damages in a breach-of-contract case, the plaintiff must demonstrate that he used reasonable efforts to minimize the damage resulting from the breach. This obligation is referred to as the *duty to mitigate one's damages.*

Thus, if you are the manager of a hotel and a person who had booked 10 rooms for the week calls to cancel all the reservations, you have a duty to attempt to rent the rooms to minimize the damages. The mitigation must be reasonable, however, and no one is expected to settle for something less than what was contemplated under the contract in order to mitigate the damages.

One area where interesting mitigation issues arise is cases in which an employee is wrongfully discharged and must seek new employment to mitigate her damages. If the employee does not seek alternative employment, the amount of lost wages recovered as damages will be reduced by the amount the employee reasonably could have earned in another job. If the employee does not find another job, the court must decide whether the employee could have found comparable alternative employment with reasonable effort.

EQUITABLE REMEDIES

As noted earlier, equitable remedies grew out of the English court's authority to fashion remedies when the existing laws did not provide any adequate ones. These remedies were typically unique solutions specifically crafted to the demands of the situations. Today, the most common equitable remedies include rescission and restitution, orders for specific performance, and injunctions.

As a carryover from the days of the English courts of law and equity, a party seeking equitable relief must meet five requirements. The party must prove that (1) there is no adequate legal remedy available; (2) irreparable harm to the plaintiff may result if the equitable remedy is not granted; (3) the contract is legally valid (except when seeking relief in quasi-contract); (4) the contract terms are clear and unambiguous; and (5) the plaintiff has "clean hands," that is, has not been deceitful or done anything in breach of the contract.

Rescission and Restitution.   Sometimes the parties simply want to be returned to their precontract status; they want to have the contract terminated and to have any

L03

What are the primary equitable remedies available for a breach of contract?

Article 114 of Chapter 7, "Liability for Breach of Contracts," of the Contract Law of the People's Republic of China provides for the equivalent of the liquidated-damage clause recognized under U.S. law. The first part of the Chinese law is almost identical to our law. It provides that the parties to a contract may agree that one party shall, when violating the contract, pay breach-of-contract damages of a certain amount in light of the breach or they may agree on the calculating method of compensation for losses resulting from the breach of contract.

However, the Chinese law has an interesting twist for circumstances in which the projected damages end up being different from what the actual damages are. If the agreed breach-of-contract damages are lower than the losses caused, any party may request that the people's court or an arbitration institution increase it; if it is excessively higher than the losses caused, any party may request that the people's court or an arbitration institution make an appropriate reduction.

transferred property returned to its original owner. That is, they want rescission and restitution. Rescission is the termination of the contract, and restitution is the return of any property given up under the contract.

Restitution and rescission are most frequently awarded in situations in which there is a lack of genuine assent (discussed in Chapter 17). When a party enters into a contract because of fraud, duress, undue influence, or a bilateral mistake, the contract is voidable and the party who wants out may seek to avoid the contract or, in other words, may seek rescission and restitution.

Specific Performance. Specific performance is sometimes called *specific enforcement*. It is an order requiring that the breaching party fulfill the terms of the agreement. Courts are very reluctant to grant specific performance and will do so only when monetary damages simply are not adequate, typically because the subject matter of the contract is unique. If the subject matter is unique, then even if the nonbreaching party is given compensation, he cannot go elsewhere to buy the item from someone else, so this renders any kind of money damages inadequate.

Primarily for historical reasons, every piece of real property is considered unique. Therefore, an order for specific performance would often be the appropriate remedy for the breach of a contract for the sale of a piece of real estate.

Injunction. An injunction is an order either forcing a person to do something or prohibiting a person from doing something. Most commonly, injunctions are prohibitions against actions. Such an injunction might be used, for example, as a remedy in a contract case involving a personal service. Mandy is a lounge singer, and she has a contract to perform at JZ's Lounge every weekend night from January through June. Two months into her contract she decides to work for Bally's Lounge instead because Bally's will pay her twice as much. There is no way to adequately calculate the damages that would arise from the singer's going over to the other club to perform, so money damages would not really be an adequate remedy. Instead, the owner of JZ's may obtain an injunction prohibiting Mandy from performing in any lounge until the end of June, when her term of performance under the contract will have been completed.

Sometimes, when a party is suing another for breach of contract, one of the parties is concerned that before the court has had a chance to decide the case, the other party will do something to make it impossible for the concerned party to get the relief he would be entitled to. In such a situation, the concerned party may ask for a preliminary injunction to prohibit the other party from taking any action during the course of the lawsuit that would cause irreparable harm to any of the parties to the contract. For example, Jim agrees to sell Bob a very rare antique car for $15,000 but then says he is not going to comply with the terms of the agreement. Bob sues Jim for breach of contract, but before the case goes to trial, Bob finds out that Sara has told Jim that she would be willing to pay him $20,000 for the car. Bob may seek a preliminary injunction to prohibit Jim from selling the car to anyone else until the court decides whether Bob is entitled to an order for specific performance forcing Jim to sell the car to him. Thus, the preliminary injunction fulfills the purpose of maintaining the status quo until the case can be finally decided.

It is not always easy to predict when a court will issue a preliminary injunction, however, as Bear, Stearns & Co. recently discovered when the court refused to issue a preliminary injunction to enforce a contractual provision requiring that an employee provide 90 days' notice of termination of employment (a so-called garden-leave provision). The court's refusal was based in part on public policy concerns.[5] The company's executive director of private client services submitted his notice of resignation, effective immediately, and began working for Morgan Stanley the next day. Bear, Stearns & Co. sought to enjoin the former director from working for a competitor during the contractually specified 90-day notice period. In denying the injunction, despite a stated belief that the company would ultimately win the breach-of-contract claim, the court provided three reasons. First, the company could not establish that it would suffer irreparable harm, because its harm could be recompensed by money damages. Second, any hardship to Bear Stearns due to permitting the defendant to resume his employment with Morgan Stanley in violation of the 90-day restriction was outweighed by the risk to his "professional standing and the inability to advise his clients in times of economic turmoil." Third, the court could not order the requested relief because doing so would require the defendant to continue an at-will employment relationship against his will.[6]

Reformation.   Sometimes a written contract does not reflect the parties' actual agreement, or there are inconsistencies in the contract, such as the price being listed as "$200,000 (twenty thousand dollars)." In such a case, the written document may be rewritten to reflect what the parties had agreed on.

Recovery Based on Quasi-Contract.   When an enforceable contract does not in fact exist, the court may grant a recovery based on quasi-contract; that is, the court may impose a contractlike obligation on a party to prevent an injustice from occurring. Recovery in quasi-contract is often sought when a party thought a valid contract existed and thus gave up something of value in relying on the existence of a contract. To justify recovery under a theory of quasi-contract, sometimes referred to as *recovery in quantum meriut,* a plaintiff must prove that (1) the plaintiff conferred a benefit on the defendant; (2) the plaintiff had reasonably expected to be compensated for the benefit conferred on the defendant; and (3) the defendant would be unjustly enriched from receiving the benefit without compensating the plaintiff for it.

[5] "Court Declines to Issue Preliminary Injunction to Enforce Garden Leave Provision," *Labor and Employment Alert,* www.goodwinprocter.com/~/media/208D97723AA140B58BE5D0622EFEC428.ashx (accessed June 2, 2009).

[6] Ibid.

CASE OPENER WRAP-UP

Impossible Wine Bottles

Under the amended agreement between Anchor and Encore, the production of bottles was to take place at the Lavington plant. The Lavington plant was the only facility owned by CPI that was capable of producing the specific type and quality of glass container that is required by the wine industry. According to the court's ruling, when the Lavington plant was sold and the new owners did not take over CPI's obligations, the terms of the contract became impossible for Anchor to meet. As a result of the impossibility of performance, Anchor was discharged from the contract.

KEY TERMS

compensatory damages   463
complete performance   454
concurrent conditions   453
condition precedent   452
condition subsequent   452
conditional contracts   452

consequential damages   465
express conditions   453
implied conditions   453
injunction   468
liquidated damages   467
material breach   455

monetary damages   463
nominal damages   466
novation   458
objective impossibility   458
punitive damages   466
rescission   468

restitution   468
special damages   465
specific performance   468
subjective impossibility   458
substantial performance   454
tender   454

SUMMARY OF KEY TOPICS

Methods of Discharging a Contract

Contracts may be discharged in a number of different ways, including:

- The occurrence or nonoccurrence of a condition.
- Complete performance.
- Substantial performance.
- Material breach.
- Mutual agreement.
- Operation of law.

Remedies

Courts may grant parties in a breach-of-contract action legal or equitable remedies. *Legal remedies,* or money damages, include:

- *Compensatory damages:* Damages designed to put the plaintiff in the position he or she would have been in had the contract been fully performed.
- *Nominal damages:* Token damages that merely recognize that the plaintiff had been wronged.
- *Punitive damages:* Damages designed to punish the defendant.
- *Liquidated damages:* Damages specified in advance in the contract.

Equitable remedies, which are granted only when legal remedies are inadequate, include:

- *Rescission and restitution:* The termination of the contract and the return of the parties to their precontract status.
- *Specific performance:* An order requiring the defendant to perform some act.
- *Injunction:* An order prohibiting the defendant from performing some act.

POINT / COUNTERPOINT

Should Nonbreaching Parties Be Required to Mitigate Damages?	
NO	**YES**
Courts' requiring nonbreaching parties to mitigate damages is unfair.	Courts' requiring nonbreaching parties to mitigate damages provides the most equitable solution when a contract is breached.

<table>
<tr>
<td>

Contract law is designed to reward both parties for the agreement that they have reached. If one party is irresponsible and cannot perform as agreed, why should courts then punish the nonbreaching party by requiring him or her to mitigate damages? After all, the nonbreaching party likely made decisions subsequent to the contract on the assumption that the contract terms would be carried out, and mitigating damages introduces stress regarding those decisions. For instance, if a hotel owner entered a contract with a person who agreed to rent 50 hotel rooms and a conference room for a weekend, the hotel owner would focus his time and energy on advertising for other weekends. But to require the hotel owner, after learning that the person no longer wanted the rooms, to mitigate damages places stress on the owner that he would not have otherwise experienced. Instead of completely focusing on booking rooms for other weekends, the hotel owner must now take time away from advertising those rooms so that he can try to fill the 50 vacant rooms and conference room, even if he wants to sue for breach of contract.

In addition, requiring nonbreaching parties to mitigate damages encourages irresponsible behavior on the part of contracting parties. If a party knows she can breach a contract as long as she provides enough notice, she may be able to avoid most, if not all, liability. Returning to the hotel example, if the person who contracted to rent the 50 rooms notifies the hotel owner of the breach two months before the weekend she contracted for, the hotel owner could fill the rooms and the breaching party would likely not be liable for any damages, even though the hotel owner incurred greater expense and spent additional time filling the rooms with other guests. "Mitigating damages," therefore, is just a fancy way of saying that the burden shifts back to the nonbreaching parties, rewarding the very people who should bear the costs of breaching a contract.

</td>
<td>

Although a nonbreaching party could understandably be frustrated with the breaching party, such a breach does not license the nonbreaching party to force the breaching party to provide full payment for the contract, especially when many costs could have been avoided. For example, if a city contracts with a company to construct a bridge across a river and the city later learns that the roads that would connect to the bridge would disrupt a nesting bald eagle, the company should not be permitted to still build the bridge and demand full payment. The city would then have to pay for a useless bridge, even though the company could have avoided the costs of building the bridge.

In this example and similar contexts, the breaching parties would have an incentive to do nothing and still demand payment, even though damages could have been reduced. For instance, if a person entered a two-year employment contract to work for a company but the company could not honor the contract, the nonbreaching party should not be entitled to sit at home for two years and still receive compensation.

In other words, if nonbreaching parties were not required to mitigate damages—either by discontinuing performance, as in the bridge example, or by finding a reasonable replacement, such as a different job in the employment example—nonbreaching parties would run up the costs by completing performance under the contract or doing nothing. In the context of finding a reasonable alternative, nonbreaching parties would actually have an incentive to do nothing.

Finally, mitigating damages promotes better relationships between contracting parties, making both parties more willing to contract again in the future.

</td>
</tr>
</table>

QUESTIONS & PROBLEMS

1. Explain the difference between legal and equitable remedies.

2. Explain how the existence of conditions subsequent and precedent affects the discharge of a contract.

3. Explain the relationship between commercial impracticability and frustration of purpose.

4. List the conditions that must be met for a court to impose a quasi-contract.

5. The Thompsons intended to buy a pickup truck from Lithia Dodge. They signed a retail installment contract which listed the annual interest rate as 3.9 percent and which stated that the contract was not binding until financing was completed and that any disputes arising under the contract would be resolved through arbitration. The Thompsons took their new truck home and left their trade-in vehicle with Lithia Dodge. A week later, the financing manager called the Thompsons and informed them that the financing rate of 3.9 had not been accepted and they would have to come in and sign a contract at a 4.9 percent rate. The Thompsons filed suit against Lithia Dodge, which by this time had already sold their trade-in vehicle. Lithia Dodge filed a motion to dismiss, arguing that the case had to go to arbitration because of the binding arbitration clause. The district court agreed. How do you believe the appellate court ruled, and why? [*Thompson v. Lithia Chrysler Jeep Dodge of Great Falls,* 185 P.3d 332 (Sup. Ct. Mt. 2008).]

6. Turner Construction entered into a contract to provide general construction of Granby Towers. Turner then entered into a subcontract with Universal to install precast concrete floors in the Granby Towers construction project. The general construction contract was incorporated by reference into the subcontract. The contract between Turner and Universal contained a "pay-when-paid provision" that conditioned any payments to Universal on Turner's first receiving payment from Universal. Due to the economic downturn, financing for the project fell through. Universal had substantially completed all its work by that time, and it sought payment of $885,507 from Turner, which refused to pay because it had not received any payment from the owner of the project. Turner asked the court for summary judgment on Universal's breach-of-contract claim. Should the court's grant of summary judgment be upheld? Why or why not? [*Universal Concrete Products v. Turner Construction Co.,* 4th Cir. Case No. 09-1569 (2010).]

7. Mantz worked for TruGreen, a lawn care company. He, along with other TruGreen employees, signed the company's noncompete, nonsolicitation, and nondisclosure agreements. Mantz quit and went to work for Mower Brothers, a competitor. Other TruGreen employees followed Mantz to Mower Brothers. TruGreen sued Mantz and the other employees for breach of the agreements and Mower Brothers for tortuous interference with contract. What do you think the Utah high court said was the proper measure of damages in such a case? [*TruGreen Companies v. Mower Brothers, Inc.,* 2008 Utah LEXIS 193 (2008).]

8. On November 7, 2005, Briarwood signed an agreement to sell Toll Brothers a planned 66-acre, 41-lot subdivision property in the Village of Pomona, New York, for $13,325,000. The agreement expressly conditioned Toll's payment obligations on Briarwood's delivery, at its sole cost and expense, of final, unappealable subdivision approval of the property in accordance with the subdivision plan and the satisfaction by Briarwood of any conditions of the final approval, such that on posting of customary security and payment of application and inspection fees by Toll Brothers, the company would be able to file the plat and commence infrastructure improvements and apply for and obtain building permits.

The agreement stated that the conditions set forth in the approval shall be subject only to "such conditions as Toll may approve at its sole discretion, which approval shall not be unreasonably withheld with respect to those modifications which do not have a material adverse effect on the proposed development." Closing was to take place 30 days following the date on which all conditions to closing set forth in the approval have been satisfied and, "[i]f on or before the date of closing all contingencies and conditions specified herein are not or cannot be satisfied, then Toll shall have the option of . . . cancelling this Agreement."

On January 12, 2006, Briarwood obtained preliminary subdivision approval of the property from the Pomona Planning Board. Final subdivision approval of the property, however, was subject to a number of conditions. By letter dated December 22, 2006, Toll notified Briarwood that five of the conditions would have a material adverse effect on the proposed development and that it would not accept them.

Toll Brothers claimed that Briarwood's December 28, 2006, response to Toll's December 22, 2006, letter was an anticipatory repudiation of the agreement.

In response to Toll's five objections, Briarwood (1) offered to post a bond to cover the potential cost of repaving Klinger Court; (2) pointed out that the steep slope condition restated the Village Code requirement to secure a site development plan permit for each lot within a subdivision; (3) agreed to pay any cost differential resulting from use of a 4 percent rather than a 10 percent grade for the cul-de-sac; (4) proposed two alternative solutions to the drainage system problem; and (5) pointed out that the landscaping plan condition, like the steep slope condition, restated a Village Code requirement.

Toll Brothers treated the letter from Briarwood as an anticipatory repudiation of the contract and refused to complete the transaction, so Briarwood sued for breach of contract. Both parties filed motions for summary judgment.

The district found that no reasonable reader could construe Briarwood's response as a positive and unequivocal repudiation of the agreement and that it did not signal that Briarwood was unwilling to comply with paragraph 16(a)(iii) or any other provision of the agreement. The court therefore granted summary judgment to Briarwood. Toll Brothers appealed. How do you believe the court of appeals ruled, and why? [*Briarwood Farms, Inc. v. Toll Bros., Inc.,* 452 Fed. Appx. 59, 2011 WL 6415185 (C.A.2, N.Y. 2011).]

9. Two companies had an agreement in which Sunrich was providing a food product to Nutrisoya. However, Sunrich allegedly did not deliver the products covered in the contract, and Nutrisoya took the company to court for material breach of contract. The seller wanted the district court to instruct the jury on the difference between a breach of a single installment and a breach of an entire installment contract, arguing that a single-installment breach did not disregard the value of the whole contract. However, the district court did not give such an instruction and left the defendant to argue the point. How do you think the jury decided? [*Nutrisoya v. Sunrich,* 641 F.3d 282, 2011 U.S. App. LEXIS 11561.]

10. The opera company was hired to perform in the outside pavilion of the Wolf Trap Foundation. The company performed the three performances without problem. Then, right before the last performance, a severe thunderstorm moved into the area and created an electrical storm. The storm cut the power on the pavilion where the performance was to have taken place. The Wolf Trap Foundation never paid the opera company for the last performance. Thus, the company took the foundation to court, demanding payment because the performers were ready and willing to perform at the event for which the company was scheduled. The foundation argued that it was dismissed from the contract due to impossibility to perform. The first court found in favor of the opera company, and the foundation appealed. How do you think the appellate court decided? [*The Opera Company of Boston, Inc., v. the Wolf Trap Foundation for the Performing Arts,* 817 F.2d 1094 (1987).]

Looking for more review materials?

The Online Learning Center at **www.mhhe.com/kubasek3e** contains this chapter's "Assignment on the Internet" and also a list of URLs for more information, entitled "On the Internet." Find both of them in the Student Center portion of the OLC, along with quizzes and other helpful materials.

Introduction to Sales and Lease Contracts

LEARNING OBJECTIVES

After reading this chapter, you will be able to answer the following questions:

1 What is the UCC?

2 What is a sales contract?

3 What kinds of contracts fall under the UCC interpretations?

4 What is a merchant, and why is that designation significant?

5 What is a lease contract?

6 What is the CISG?

 CASE OPENER

Dropped Calls, or More Appropriately, Dropped Towers: Are Cell Towers Goods or Services?

Crown Castle purchased a number of assets from a variety of cell phone providers in upstate New York between 1995 and 2000. These providers had earlier contracted with the Fred A. Nudd Corporation for the construction and placement of monopoles, more commonly known as "cell towers." However, after some time the monopoles began to collapse structurally. In fact, problems began to develop as early as 2001. In 2003, two cell towers actually collapsed. Crown Castle brought suit in 2005,[1] more than four years after the first of the monopoles began failing. This is an important timing issue: Under common law, a breach-of-contract lawsuit must be brought within six years; but, under the UCC, the lawsuit must be brought within four years. Thus, the first major legal question is whether the lawsuit can stand and not be dismissed under the statute of limitations. To decide this, the court must rule, as a matter of law, on whether the contract for the construction and placement of the monopoles was a contract created under common law or under the UCC.

1. Is the sale of monopoles a contract for the sale of goods when the contract also included installation and initial maintenance? Does this contract fall under UCC Article 2 or under common law?

[1] *Crown Castle Inc. et al. v. Fred A. Nudd Corporation et al.*, 2008 U.S. Dist. LEXIS 3416, 64 U.C.C. Rep. Serv. 2d (Callaghan) 871.

2. If this is a contract for both goods (the monopoles) and services (the installation and initial maintenance), how is the contract determined to fall under either common law or the UCC?

The Wrap-Up at the end of the chapter will answer these questions.

Businesses and organizations that purchase products need to be aware of which laws govern their purchases because the laws can differ. Three sources of laws that interpret sales contracts exist: state common law, the Uniform Commercial Code, and state statutory law. There is very little, if any, federal law that governs contracts for the buying and selling of items, and when such law does exist, it is highly specialized (e.g., the buying and selling of stock under laws created by the Securities and Exchange Commission).

This chapter introduces the Uniform Commercial Code. It explains the scope and significance of the UCC, discusses sections of the UCC that govern both sales and lease contracts, reviews how these contracts are formed, and provides a summary of the legislation that governs international sales contracts.

The Uniform Commercial Code

THE SCOPE OF THE UCC

In some areas of law, federal statutes ensure that the same law applies in all the states. Federal statutes do not govern the formation of sales and lease contracts. Instead, each state passes its own laws to outline rules in this area. Consequently, laws vary from state to state. While all states (except Louisiana) follow the English common law, over 200 years of legal precedent that has developed in each separate state can create differences in contract interpretation and application. With the development of interstate commercial activities, these differences began to pose problems for parties from different states entering into a contract with each other. What was needed was some kind of uniform law for business transactions that all the states could adopt.

In some areas of law, lawyers and law school professors have worked together to pass *uniform,* or model, state laws that states may consider adopting. Two important groups of lawyers and law school professors are the National Conference of Commissioners on Uniform State Laws (NCCUSL) and the American Law Institute (ALI), which worked together to create the Uniform Commercial Code (UCC). The UCC was created in 1952 and has been adopted by all 50 states, the District of Columbia, and the Virgin Islands. When a state adopts the UCC, that code becomes part of the law of that particular state; it becomes the commercial code for that state. Each state is allowed to rewrite parts of the UCC to reflect the wishes of its state legislature.

L01

What is the UCC?

The UCC is divided into sections known as *articles*. These articles cover a wide range of topics, from sales contracts to secured transactions (see Exhibit 21-1). This book explains all the articles of the UCC, starting in this chapter and ending with Chapter 29, which explains the law that governs secured transactions. The NCCUSL and ALI work to revise the UCC as business practices change. Because, as we will learn, goods are movable from state to state, UCC Article 2 applies only to the sale of goods. Land and services contracts are still governed by common law. Therefore, the first question in any sales contract is whether common law or the UCC applies.

THE SIGNIFICANCE OF THE UCC

The UCC is significant because it clarifies sales law and makes this area of law more predictable for businesses that engage in transactions in more than one state. Essentially, the UCC facilitates commercial transactions.

Exhibit 21-1

An Outline of the UCC

ARTICLE	TOPIC
1	General provisions
2	Sales
2(A)	Leases
3	Negotiable instruments
4	Bank deposits and collections
4(A)	Wire transfers
5	Letters of credit
6	Bulk transfers
7	Documents of title
8	Investment securities
9	Secured transactions

However, it is important to emphasize that the UCC does not pertain to all business transactions. Under UCC Article 2, the subject matter of this chapter, the UCC explains the creation and interpretation of sales contracts.

Articles 2 and 2(A) of the UCC

Article 2 of the UCC governs sales contracts, while Article 2(A) governs lease contracts. Specifically, Article 2 focuses on contracts for the sale of goods; Article 2(A) focuses on contracts for the lease of goods. For the purpose of "selling something," the UCC divides all the items that can be bought and sold into three categories: goods, realty, and services (including intangible goods such as securities). Article 2 pertains only to the sale of goods. Nonetheless, Article 2 is not a comprehensive guide to sales contract formation. When Article 2 is silent on an issue of sales contract formation or interpretation, the common law rules apply. Of course, if a state has passed statutory law regarding contracts, that law always supersedes the common law. Additionally, it is important to note that under the UCC the rules for transactions involving merchants differ from those for transactions involving regular buyers and sellers. Merchants will generally be held to a higher standard of care and behavior than nonmerchants. Every state except Louisiana[2] has adopted Article 2 of the UCC.

If you are not sure whether a contract falls under common law or under the UCC, the decision-tree rubric in Exhibit 21-2 can help you make a determination. To use this rubric, consider the definitions presented in the discussion that follows of many of its terms.

BUT WHAT IF . . .

WHAT IF THE FACTS OF THE CASE OPENER WERE DIFFERENT?

Suppose that, in the Case Opener, the contract involved only the transmission of electricity. Would that fact alter the approach the court would have taken?

---

[2] Louisiana's civil tradition is based on the Code Napoleon, or the French Civil Code.

ARE TRADE NAMES "GOODS" UNDER UCC ARTICLE 2?

**Eureka Water Company v. Nestle Waters
North America, Inc.
U.S. Court of Appeals for the 10th Circuit
690 F.3d 1139, 2012 U.S. App. LEXIS 16149,
78 U.C.C. Rep. Serv. 2d (Callaghan)
363 (Aug. 3, 2012, Filed)**

In a 1975 contract Eureka was given the exclusive right to sell spring water and other products under the Ozarka trade name in 60 Oklahoma counties in exchange for $9,000 paid to Arrowhead, which owned the trade name. In 1987 Arrowhead was acquired by Perrier Group of America, which was subsequently purchased in 1992 by Nestle, making Nestle the owner of the trade name Ozarka. Nestle then began delivering spring water under the Ozarka name within Eureka's territorial claim. In 1997 this became known to Eureka, and Nestle agreed to pay Eureka royalties of 30 cents a case and 50 cents a case for bulk purchases. Eureka would receive from Nestle 67 checks totaling about $2.5 million over the next 10 years. In late 2003 Nestle unilaterally reduced the payment to 25 cents a case. Eureka invoiced Nestle for the difference but was never paid. On October 15, 2007, Eureka received a letter which stated that Nestle would no longer pay royalties.

One important legal principle here is the principle of what is a good. Goods have been defined in various legal cases as anything that was movable at the time of the contract. If a contract involves both goods and nongoods, Oklahoma uses the predominant factor to decide whether it is covered under UCC Article 2. This contract had both a right to sell under a trade name and a right to buy water at cost plus freight. A trade name has been judged by many courts to be a good, but this court said that a trade name is not movable at the time of the contract and is therefore not a good. The predominant-factor test was used, but since Eureka still has to purchase the water at cost plus freight or, if Eureka can find a different supplier, the intellectual property (i.e. the trade name) can be given to that supplier, it is a matter of financial indifference to Nestle. Therefore, the predominant factor in the $9,000 contract was the trade name. Thus the UCC was not applicable to this ruling, and Oklahoma common law was used to decide the case.

ARTICLE 2 OF THE UCC

Sale.   Section 2-106(1) of the UCC states that a sale "consists of the passing of title from the seller to the buyer for a price." Thus, in the transaction involving Crown Castle and Fred Nudd, the sale consisted of the passing of title (right of ownership) of the monopoles to the original buyers (the various cell phone companies) and then to Crown Castle.

L02

What is a sales contract?

Goods.   Section 2-105 of the UCC defines goods as "all [tangible] things . . . which are movable at the time of identification to the contract for sale." Items are tangible if they exist physically. The issue in our opening case is whether the delivery of "electricity" is a "good," and under the contractual interpretation of the UCC, or whether it is a "service," and under the

1. Does the transaction involve a sale or lease (as opposed to, let's say, a gift)?

   If yes → go to question 2.

   If no → apply the appropriate area of common or statutory law.

2. Is the transaction for the sale or lease of a good?

   If yes → go to question 3.

   If no → apply common law.

3. If the contract is for the sale or lease of both goods and nongoods, which type of item is predominant in the contract?

   If goods → UCC Article 2 applies; go to question 4.

   If nongoods (real estate or services) → common law applies.

4. If this is a UCC Article 2 transaction, is either party a merchant?

   If yes → pay close attention to when the special rules on merchants apply.

   If no → then only "reasonable" care applies to the parties; no "special" or heightened duty of care will apply to a party deemed to be a merchant.

Exhibit 21-2
Common Law or UCC?

contractual interpretation of the common law. Note that Section 2-105 reads "at the time of identification to the contract." Some items are not goods under Article 2. For example, corporate stocks and copyrights are not tangible, so they are not goods. Real estate cannot be moved, so it is not a good. Yet items attached to real estate that are used for business activities are known as *trade fixtures* and are treated as goods under the UCC.

BUT WHAT IF . . .

WHAT IF THE FACTS OF THE CASE OPENER WERE DIFFERENT?

Let's say, in the Case Opener, that Crown Castle had purchased an office from the New York cell phone providers. The office was poorly built and began to fall apart. Castle brought suit for breach of contract, and the court needed to determine whether common law or the UCC was applicable. If the court looked into Article 2 of the UCC, would this article be applicable to the sale of the office building? Why or why not?

Items taken from real estate may be treated as goods. Minerals, clay, and soil can all be treated as goods, with their sales contract governed by Article 2, if the owner takes these items out of the ground and then sells them to the buyer. Should the owner sell the buyer the right to come and remove the items, the contract would be governed not by the UCC but by common law for the sale of an interest in realty, in this case, an interest known as a "profit." Crops that are sold while still growing in the field are also considered goods, and their sale contracts are subject to UCC interpretation.

> To see how the definition of a good relates to marketing issues, please see the **Connecting to the Core** activity on the text website at www.mhhe.com/kubasek3e.

Mixed Goods and Services Contracts.   Sometimes, it is not easy to tell whether something is a good because a tangible item is tied to or mixed with something intangible, such as a service. A contract that combines a good with a service is a mixed sale. Article 2 applies to mixed sales if the goods are the predominant part of the transaction. This is the test that the court needed to apply to the Crown Castle case. Did the sale, installation, and initial maintenance of the monopoles constitute a contract predominantly for the sale of goods or predominantly for the sale of services? Consider Case 21-1 to determine the standard to be applied.

L03

What kinds of contracts fall under the UCC interpretations?

In Case 21-1, the court had to decide whether a particular contract (a settlement agreement) was a contract for the sale of goods (foot-pump slippers) or a contract for something intangible (a settlement to resolve a lawsuit). The distinction was especially important to the plaintiff, Novamedix, because if the contract was for the sale of goods, the company could take advantage of other provisions of the UCC, especially implied warranties that the foot-pump slippers would serve the purpose for which they were designed.

To resolve contract issues in cases in which a tangible good is mixed with something intangible (e.g., a service or a legal settlement), most states employ some variation of the *predominant-purpose test* discussed in Case 21-1. In the Novamedix case, the court determined that the case should not be governed by Article 2 of the UCC because the settlement agreement was not predominantly a sale of goods. The predominant purpose of the agreement was to settle the patent infringement suit, not to transfer foot-pump slippers. The reader can infer from the court's analysis that the settlement agreement was more of a service contract than a goods contract, with the service component focusing on the terms of the settlement.

L04

What is a merchant, and why is that designation significant?

Legal Principle: **When determining whether a contract falls under the UCC, first determine if the sale is for goods and then determine if the contract is predominantly for the sale of goods.**

CASE 21-1   NOVAMEDIX, LIMITED, PLAINTIFF-APPELLANT v. NDM ACQUISITION CORPORATION AND VESTA HEALTHCARE, INC., DEFENDANTS-APPELLEES
U.S. COURT OF APPEALS, FEDERAL CIRCUIT
166 F.3D 1177 (1999)

This case shows that even when a lawsuit ends through settlement, the dispute is not necessarily over. In this case, Novamedix and a competitor, NDM, resolved a patent infringement lawsuit by entering into a settlement agreement. At issue in the patent infringement lawsuit was a particular medical device—a foot-pump slipper, designed to aid in blood circulation from the feet to the heart of bedridden patients. Prior to the patent infringement lawsuit, both companies manufactured this particular foot-pump slipper. As a consequence of the patent infringement suit, NDM agreed to admit that it had infringed on Novamedix's patents, cease infringing on the patents, deliver its entire inventory of foot-pump slippers to Novamedix, grant Novamedix an exclusive license under NDM's own patents, and pay Novamedix $47,500.

When Novamedix received the inventory of foot-pump slippers, the company claimed that the slippers could not be sold because they did not meet FDA requirements for this particular medical device. Novamedix had wanted to sell NDM's inventory to NDM's former customers, but could not do so because the product failed to meet FDA requirements. Novamedix then filed suit against NDM, arguing that the settlement agreement was a contract for the sale of goods and therefore subject to the implied warranties of merchantability and fitness of New York's version of the UCC. In essence, Novamedix asked the court to declare the settlement agreement a contract for the sale of goods so it could take advantage of warranties outlined in the UCC. Novamedix asked the court to interpret the settlement agreement for NDM's inventory under Article 2 of the UCC because the foot-pump slippers were a "good" and title had passed for them from NDM to Novamedix. NDM contended that the agreement should not be interpreted under UCC Article 2. A lower court agreed with NDM, and Novamedix appealed.

SENIOR CIRCUIT JUDGE EDWARD S. SMITH: . . .
Appellant [Novamedix] argues that under New York law, a "contract for the sale of goods" requires only that there be a sale (i.e., the "passing of title from the seller to the buyer for a price") . . . and that the subject of the sale be goods rather than services. Here, the argument goes, the settlement agreement was a contract for the sale of the defective slippers, because NDM passed title of the slippers (the goods) to Novamedix in exchange for a release for its patent infringement claim (the price).

We disagree. The world of commercial transactions is not limited to the binary world presented by Appellant, a world in which an agreement that passes title to Article 2 goods must either be a contract for the sale of goods or a contract for the sale of services. Many commercial transactions are not governed by Article 2 of the UCC: sale of land or securities, assignment of a contract right, or granting a license under a patent or copyright, just to name a few. The mere fact that title to Article 2 goods changed hands during one of these transactions does not by that fact alone make the transaction a sale of goods. . . . Here the mere fact that the parties' settlement agreement includes the transfer of personal property in its provisions does not make it a simple sale of goods (slippers) for a price (release of a legal claim). The settlement agreement between NDM and Novamedix is an agreement to release a legal claim for (1) binding admissions, (2) money damages of $47,500, (3) patent license rights, and (4) transfer of NDM's existing inventory to Novamedix. To elevate the inventory term over the other elements of consideration given by NDM is to distort the entire agreement through the lens of Novamedix's asserted purpose of selling the inventory when it entered into the agreement. The settlement agreement is no more a contract for the sale of slippers than it is a licensing agreement for NDM's patents. In fact, it is neither exclusively; it is a mixed contract, similar to a mixed contract for the provision of both goods and services. It should therefore be analyzed as a mixed contract.

To determine whether the UCC's implied warranties apply in a mixed goods/services contract, New York courts apply the "predominant purpose" test; if the predominant purpose of the contract was to sell goods, the contract falls within the UCC. However, "[i]f service predominates and the transfer of title to personal property is an incidental feature of the transaction, the contract does not fall within the ambit of the Code."

. . . Although the present settlement agreement is not a mixed goods/services contract, the same analysis is applicable to determine whether it should be treated as a contract for the sale of goods. Thus, the UCC's implied warranties of merchantability and fitness apply to the settlement agreement only if its predominant purpose was for the sale of slippers. We hold that it was not. The essential nature of the settlement agreement was to settle a patent infringement lawsuit. The agreement arose out of a patent infringement suit. The agreement contained multiple provisions relating to patent rights held by Novamedix and NDM. . . . Perhaps the inventory-related provisions were essential elements of the overall agreement, at least to

[continued]

Novamedix; perhaps they even support Novamedix's professed intent to sell the slippers to NDM's former customers. But those factors are simply not relevant to the question of whether the "essential nature" of the agreement was the exchange of slippers for the release of a legal claim. It was not, and cannot be construed as such with the benefit of hindsight. Therefore, the agreement was not a contract for the sale of goods, and the implied warranties of the UCC do not apply to it. . . .

AFFIRMED.

CRITICAL THINKING

Novamedix asks the court to simplify the case. How so? What rule does the court choose instead of a simple rule? Why do you suppose the court chooses a more complicated analysis than the one Novamedix prefers?

ETHICAL DECISION MAKING

In Chapter 2, you learned about the WPH framework for business ethics, which asks you to consider three questions: *Whom* would this decision affect? What is the *purpose* of the business decision? *How* should managers make decisions? When you are thinking about the purpose of a decision, it is helpful to consider values. Which value does this federal court show it prefers by ruling in NDM's favor?

Merchants. UCC Article 2 pertains to anyone buying and selling goods. However, the UCC distinguishes merchants from regular buyers and sellers (see Exhibit 21-3); thus it contains provisions that either (1) apply only to merchants or (2) impose greater duties on merchants. The drafters of the UCC assumed that merchants have a greater ability to look out for themselves than do ordinary buyers and sellers.

UCC Section 2-104(1) defines a merchant as "a person who deals in goods of the kind, or otherwise by his occupation, holds himself out as having knowledge or skill peculiar to the practices or goods involved in the transaction, or to whom such knowledge or skill may be attributed by his employment of an agent or broker or other intermediary who, by his occupation, holds himself out as having such knowledge or skill."

Legal Principle: **Merchants will be held to a higher standard of behavior under the UCC than will nonmerchants.**

? BUT WHAT IF . . .

WHAT IF THE FACTS OF THE CASE OPENER WERE DIFFERENT?

Let's say, in the Case Opener, that Crown Castle bought land from a private citizen and the land happened to have a cell phone tower on it from the previous landowner. This private citizen didn't know anything about the cell tower and sold the land with no contract for a large cash payment from Crown Castle. Would this seller be a merchant? Depending on the answer to that question, how would he be treated by the law?

Exhibit 21-3
Determining Merchant Status under UCC Article 2

A buyer or seller is a merchant if the answer to any of these three questions is yes:

- Does the buyer or seller in question deal in goods of the kind involved in the sales contract?
- Does the buyer or seller in question, by occupation, hold himself or herself out as having knowledge and skill unique to the practices or goods involved in the transaction?
- Has the buyer or seller in question employed a merchant as a broker, an agent, or some other intermediary?

THE UCC AND THE INTERNET

The Uniform Commercial Code was designed to address the sale of tangible goods such as scooters, electric power tools, and jeans. Because the UCC was written long before the Internet and e-commerce boom, this legislation was not designed for transactions related to less tangible things, such as software and information. Not surprisingly, the UCC does not respond well to certain legal issues that arise in today's marketplace. For example, the UCC does not tell us the answers to these questions: What rules should govern computer software, which is likely to be licensed rather than sold as a good? What about downloadable software files? What rules should govern information providers like America Online (AOL), which provides a continuing service? What rules should govern the exchange of information, such as stock quotes? What rules cover travel reservations a person makes online?

The National Conference of Commissioners on Uniform State Laws (NCCUSL) has adopted the Uniform Commercial Information Transactions Act (UCITA), which answers the questions above and many more. This law promises to do for electronic contracting what the UCC did for transactions in physical goods: protect consumers by providing predictability, uniformity, and clear rules. As with the UCC, states will choose whether to adopt UCITA. In 2001, Virginia became the first state to enact UCITA, probably because major Internet-related companies (e.g., AOL, UUNET Technologies) are headquartered in northern Virginia.

Source: Robert Holleyman, "Updating Contract Law for the Digital Age," *USA Today* (magazine), March 1, 2000; and Scott W. Burt, "Controversial New Rules for Computer Contracts," *Metropolitan Corporate Counsel*, June 2000, p. 8.

Case 21-2 considers the questions of whether a particular person is a merchant and, if so, what impact this merchant status has on a dispute about who owns certain goods. In this case, the goods in question were paintings.

In Case 21-2, we see another feature of merchant status. Felix DeWeldon was a merchant because, by his occupation as an artist, he held himself out as having knowledge or skill peculiar to the paintings. Under Rhode Island's commercial code, one who entrusts goods to a merchant (DeWeldon, Ltd., entrusted the paintings to Felix DeWeldon) assumes the risk that the merchant will act unscrupulously and sell the goods to an innocent third party (McKean). The result of this entrustment was that McKean got to keep the paintings. If Felix DeWeldon had not been a merchant, DeWeldon, Ltd., would have won the case.

At this point, be thinking of questions about merchants as they relate to the transaction between Crown Castle and Fred A. Nudd. Both are businesses. Crown Castle owns and operates wireless telephone services, while Fred A. Nudd manufactures steel fabrications. There is no question, it seems, that both are merchants under any test defined by the UCC.

ARTICLE 2(A) OF THE UCC

Every state except Louisiana has adopted Article 2 of the UCC. Article 2(A) covers contracts for the lease of goods. This section of the UCC is increasingly important, as consumers (both individuals and businesses) are more likely to lease goods today than ever before. Consumers lease cars, equipment, and machines. This article does not cover leases related to real property.

Leases. UCC Section 2A-103(j) defines a lease as "a transfer of the right to possession and use of goods for a term in return for consideration." A lessor is "a person who transfers the right to possession and use of goods under a lease."[3] A lessee is "a person who acquires the right to possession and use of goods under a lease."[4] Thus, if you lease a car, the company that leases the car to you (the lessor) transfers the right of possession and use of the car to you (the lessee) in return for consideration (money).

L05

What is a lease contract?

Special Kinds of Leases. Two special kinds of leases are consumer and finance leases. A consumer lease is a lease (1) that has a value of $25,000 or less and (2) that exists

[3] UCC § 2A-103(p).
[4] UCC § 2A-103(o).

CASE 21-2   DEWELDON, LTD. v. MCKEAN
U.S. DISTRICT COURT FOR THE DISTRICT OF RHODE ISLAND
125 F.3D 24 (1997)

This case arose after Felix DeWeldon, a well-known sculptor and art collector, sold three paintings to Robert McKean in 1994.

Felix DeWeldon declared bankruptcy in 1991. In 1992, DeWeldon, Ltd., purchased all Felix DeWeldon's personal property from the bankruptcy trustee. After this purchase, the director of DeWeldon, Ltd., entrusted the paintings to Felix DeWeldon as custodian. DeWeldon, Ltd., did nothing to make it clear Felix DeWeldon did not own the paintings. For example, DeWeldon, Ltd., did not put a sign on the premises of Beacon Rock, Felix DeWeldon's home in Newport, Rhode Island, nor did DeWeldon, Ltd., tag or label the paintings themselves.

In 1993, Nancy Wardell, the sole shareholder of DeWeldon, Ltd., sold all of her DeWeldon, Ltd., stock to the Byron Preservation Trust. This trust sold Felix DeWeldon an option to repurchase the paintings and a contractual right to continue to retain possession of the paintings until the option expired.

In 1993, DeWeldon, Ltd., sued Felix DeWeldon, seeking possession of the paintings, but was unsuccessful because of the option to repurchase and right of possession. The court enjoined Felix DeWeldon from transferring or removing the paintings from Beacon Rock. The paintings that became the subject of this lawsuit never left Beacon Rock until McKean bought them in 1994.

The question in this case is whether DeWeldon, Ltd., can recover the three paintings it had entrusted to Felix DeWeldon, or, alternatively, whether the district court correctly ruled in favor of McKean, the buyer.

SENIOR CIRCUIT JUDGE HILL: As a general rule, a seller [in this case Felix DeWeldon] cannot pass better title than he has himself. Nevertheless, the Uniform Commercial Cole (UCC) as adopted by Rhode Island provides that an owner [in this case DeWeldon, Ltd.] who entrusts items to a merchant who deals in goods of that kind gives him or her the power to transfer all rights of the entruster to a buyer in the ordinary course of business. . . .

In order for McKean to be protected . . ., DeWeldon, Ltd. must have allowed Felix DeWeldon to retain possession of the paintings. McKean must have bought the paintings in the ordinary course of business. He must have given value for the paintings, without actual or constructive notice of DeWeldon Ltd.'s claim of ownership to them. Finally, Felix DeWeldon must have been a merchant as defined by R.I. Gen. Laws Sec. 6A-2-104. Under this section, a merchant is one who has special knowledge or skill and deals in goods of the kind or "otherwise by his or her occupation holds himself out as having knowledge or skill peculiar to the practices or goods involved in the transaction. . . ." . . . [The court then resolves the preceding factual issues in McKean's favor before looking at the merchant issue.]

. . . Felix DeWeldon acted as a merchant within the meaning of the Rhode Island Commercial Code. Under the Code, "merchant" is given an expansive definition. . . . The Code provides that a merchant is "one who . . . by his occupation holds himself out as having knowledge or skill peculiar to the practices . . . involved in the transaction . . ." R.I. Gen. Laws Sec. 6A-2-104. Comment 2 to this section notes that "almost every person in the business world would, therefore, be deemed to be a 'merchant.' " . . .

The entrustment provision of the UCC is designed to enhance the reliability of commercial sales by merchants who deal in the kind of goods sold. . . . It shifts the risk of resale to the one who leaves his property with the merchant. . . . The district court found that Felix DeWeldon was a "well-known" artist whose work was for sale commercially and a "collector." There was art work all over Felix DeWeldson's home. He had recently sold paintings to a European buyer. By his occupation he held himself out as having knowledge and skill peculiar to art and the art trade. McKean viewed him as an art dealer.

We conclude from these facts that Felix DeWeldon was a "merchant" within the meaning of the entrustment provision of the UCC as adopted by the Rhode Island Commercial Code.

When a person knowingly delivers his property into the possession of a merchant dealing in goods of that kind, that person assumes the risk of the merchant's acting unscrupulously by selling the property to an innocent purchaser. The entrustment provision places the loss upon the party who vested the merchant with the ability to transfer the property with apparently good title. The entrustor in this case, DeWeldon, Ltd., took that risk and bears the consequences.

DeWeldon, Ltd. entrusted three paintings to the care of Felix DeWeldon. Felix DeWeldon was a merchant who bought and sold paintings. Robert McKean was a purchaser in the ordinary course of business who paid value for the paintings without notice of any claim of ownership by another. Under the law of Rhode Island, McKean took good title to the paintings. . . .

AFFIRMED.

[continued]

CRITICAL THINKING

In Chapter 1, you learned of the importance of a particular set of facts in determining the outcome of a case. If you could change one fact in this case to make it more likely that the judge would rule in favor of DeWeldon, Ltd., which fact would you change? Explain.

ETHICAL DECISION MAKING

Apply the universalization test to the outcome of this case. Does the universalization test support Judge Hill's decision?

between a lessor regularly engaged in the business of leasing or selling and a lessee who leases the goods primarily for a personal, family, or household purpose.[5] The UCC offers protections to consumers who sign lease agreements. For example, in some situations consumers may recover attorney fees if the lessor subjects them to an unconscionable lease.

A finance lease is complicated by the addition of a third person—a supplier or vendor who plays a separate role from that of the lessor. In a finance lease, the lessor does not select, manufacture, or supply the goods. Rather, the lessor acquires title to the goods or the right to their possession and use in connection with the terms of the lease.[6] The UCC outlines the specific duties and rights of all three parties to finance leases.

How Sales and Lease Contracts Are Formed under the UCC

In Part Two of this textbook, you studied the common law of contracts, from the rules for agreements to the remedies for breaches. Sales and lease contracts require the same components as general contracts, but some UCC provisions that govern contracts for the sale or lease of goods are not identical to the common law requirements you learned about in Part Two. This section highlights the most important provisions of the UCC with regard to the formation of sales and lease contracts.

FORMATION IN GENERAL

Contracts for the sale or lease of goods may be made in any manner sufficient to show agreement.[7] Courts are willing to consider the conduct of the parties to determine whether a contract exists. Contracts for the sale or lease of goods may also be formed even though some terms of the contract or lease are left open.[8] A court will uphold a contract for the sale or lease of goods as long as the parties intended to make a contract and there is a reasonably certain basis for giving an appropriate remedy.[9]

OFFER AND ACCEPTANCE

Offer. Under the UCC, if certain contract terms are left open, it is acceptable to fill them in. Exhibit 21-4 indicates what generally happens under the UCC when certain terms of a contract or lease are left open. The UCC also creates a new category of offers: the firm offer. Under UCC Section 2-205, offers made by merchants are considered firm offers if the offer (1) is made in writing and (2) gives assurances that it will be irrevocable for up to three months despite a lack of consideration for the irrevocability. If a firm offer is silent as to time, the UCC assumes a three-month irrevocability period. This contrasts sharply with the

---

[5] UCC § 2A-103(1)(e).
[6] UCC § 2A-103(1)(g).
[7] UCC §§ 2-204(1) and 2A-204(1).
[8] UCC §§ 2-204(3) and 2A-204(3).
[9] Ibid.

In recent years, China's legislators have worked to enhance and clarify the country's commercial code. Currently, China has legislation that covers the sale of goods and the supply of services. The country does not, however, have legislation that covers leases.

Recently, China's Law Reform Commission has recommended that China regulate leasing companies. This commission believes that a statute delineating the obligations of lessors and lessees involved in lease agreements will protect Chinese consumers, who currently seek remedies through the country's common law. Legal costs in China prohibit many consumers from filing complaints.

The proposed law covers a range of business services, including home decoration and rentals of videos, cars, dinner jackets, wedding dresses, and machinery. The committee is especially concerned about the number of consumer complaints related to home renovation and wedding dress rentals.

Source: Quinton Chan, "Increased Consumer Protection Considered," *South China Morning Post,* December 18, 2000.

Exhibit 21-4

The UCC and Open Terms

TERM LEFT OPEN	INTERPRETATION UNDER UCC
Price	A "reasonable price" is supplied at the time of delivery.
Payment	Payment is due at the time and place at which the buyer is to receive the goods.
Delivery	The place for delivery is the seller's place of business.
Time	The contract must be performed within a reasonable time.
Duration	The party that wants to terminate an ongoing contract must use good faith and give reasonable notification.
Quantity	Courts generally have no basis for determining a remedy.

common law, under which an offer is revocable at any time before acceptance unless a period of irrevocability (also known as an *option*) is supported by some kind of consideration.

Acceptance.   Under the UCC, an acceptance may be made by any reasonable means of communication,[10] and it is effective when dispatched. It is also important to note that the mirror-image rule that applies under common law does not apply under the UCC. Recall that the mirror-image rule states that an offeree's acceptance must be on the exact terms of the offer. If the acceptance includes additional terms, the acceptance becomes a counteroffer instead of an acceptance.

Under the UCC, additional terms are permitted in contracts for the sale or lease of goods. Under UCC Section 2-207(1), additional terms will not negate acceptance unless acceptance is made expressly conditional on assent to the additional terms.

Legal Principle: **The intent of the parties to be bound by the contract is the overriding focus of the UCC in determining contract formation.**

CONSIDERATION

Sales and lease contracts require consideration. Under the common law, when a contract is modified, it must be supported by new consideration. As explained in Chapter 15, the UCC eliminates that requirement for the modification of sales and lease contracts.[11] The UCC requires only that modifications be made in good faith.[12]

[10] UCC §§ 2-206(1) and 2A-206(1).
[11] UCC §§ 2-209(1) and 2A-208(1).
[12] UCC § 1-203.

WHEN IS A QUOTE AN OFFER UNDER THE UCC?

Reilly Foam Corp., Plaintiff v. Rubbermaid Corp., Defendant
U.S. District Court for the Eastern District of Pennsylvania
206 F. Supp. 2d 643, 2002 U.S. Dist. LEXIS 9273, 48 U.C.C. Rep. Serv. 2d (Callaghan) 81 (May 28, 2002, Decided)

In the U.C.C. context, courts have encountered difficulty determining whether a document that quotes a seller's prices constitutes an offer. Generally, price quotes are not considered offers but rather, "mere invitations to enter into negotiations or to submit offers." The buyer's purchase order—which sets such terms as product choice, quantity, price, and terms of delivery—is usually the offer.

However, some price quotes are sufficiently detailed to be deemed offers, which turn a subsequent document containing a positive response from a buyer into an acceptance.

Reviewing Reilly Foam's March 26 correspondence and its treatment by Rubbermaid, both parties treated the price quote as an offer and not merely a price quote. First, the March 26 letter did not merely list price. The letter refers to itself as a "proposal" in its opening paragraph. The attached list also includes a number of specific terms including the identification of products, their quantities, the licensing of needed technology, and details for the special manufacture of the sponges. Rubbermaid treated the letter as an offer at least with respect to quantities and prices of "other affected products." Thus, with such an understanding the quote constitutes an offer.

REQUIREMENTS UNDER THE STATUTE OF FRAUDS

Under common law, the statute of frauds requires that all material terms to a contract be in writing. Under the UCC, contracts for the sale of goods must be in writing if they are valued at $500 or more;[13] lease contracts that require payments of $1,000 or more must be in writing to be enforceable.[14] There is a significant difference between the statute of frauds and the UCC as to what constitutes a writing that satisfies the statute. Common law requires some kind of writing created or signed by the party who is contesting the enforceability of the contract. This rule holds true under the UCC unless the parties are merchants. If two merchants have an oral agreement, a written memo from either party to the other is deemed to satisfy the statute of frauds, even if it is not acknowledged by the receiving party. If the memo is not objected to within 10 days of receipt, the oral agreement, memorialized by the memo, is binding.

The UCC outlines three exceptions to the statute of fraud's writing requirements.[15] First, the UCC recognizes an exception for *specifically manufactured* goods. If a buyer or lessee has ordered goods made to meet her specific needs, the buyer or lessee may not assert the statute of frauds if (1) the goods are not suitable for sale or lease to others in the ordinary course of the seller's or lessor's business and (2) the seller or lessor has either substantially begun the manufacture of the goods or made commitments for their procurement. Second, the UCC recognizes an exception when parties *admit* that a sales or lease contract was made. Specifically, if a party to an oral sales or lease contract admits in pleadings, testimony, or court that he agreed to a contract or lease, that party cannot assert the statute of frauds against the enforcement of the oral contract. The lease or sales contract is not enforceable beyond the quantity of goods admitted. Third, the UCC includes a *partial-performance* exception. An oral sales or lease contract is enforceable to the extent that payment has been made and accepted or goods have been received and accepted.

Legal Principle: **Any kind of documentation is usually sufficient to satisfy the writing requirement of the statute of frauds.**

[13] UCC § 2-201(1).
[14] UCC § 2A-201(1).
[15] UCC §§ 2-201(3) and 2A-201(4).

BUT WHAT IF . . .

WHAT IF THE FACTS OF THE CASE OPENER WERE DIFFERENT?

Let's say, in the Case Opener, that Crown Castle had a written contract with the New York cell phone providers regarding the cell towers that Castle was purchasing. The contract did not mention a price that Castle would pay for the towers or the quantity of towers that Castle would be acquiring. What are the necessary components of a contract? Do they include price and quantity?

THE PAROL EVIDENCE RULE

The parol evidence rule is a legal concept that aims to protect sales or lease contracts that the parties intended to be the final expression of their agreement. The UCC states that when a written agreement exists that is intended to be a final expression, neither party can provide additional evidence that alters or contradicts the written contract.[16] Courts, however, allow the parties to explain or supplement the written contract with either (1) additional terms that are consistent with the terms in the agreement or (2) evidence that helps the court interpret the agreement, including previous conduct of the parties regarding the contract in question (course of performance),[17] the way the parties have interacted in past transactions (course of dealings),[18] and the way others in a specific place, vocation, trade, or industry usually conduct business (usage of trade).[19]

When courts interpret sales and lease contracts, they look at a combination of four factors: (1) express terms, (2) course of performance, (3) course of dealing, and (4) usage of trade. If they must, courts prioritize these factors as listed. Consider the Case Nugget.

UNCONSCIONABILITY

You learned about the concept of unconscionability in Part Two. A contract or contract provision is *unconscionable* if it is so unfair that a court would be unreasonable if it enforced the contract. The UCC outlines actions a court can take if it discovers that a contract or lease provision or the contract or lease as a whole is unconscionable.[20] If a court finds that a contract or lease provision or the contract or lease as a whole was unconscionable when it was made, the court either can refuse to enforce the contract or lease or can enforce the parts of the contract or lease that are fair.

Contracts for the International Sale of Goods

L06

What is the CISG?

THE SCOPE OF THE CISG

You read at the beginning of this chapter that lawyers and legal scholars drafted the UCC in part to facilitate increased commercial transactions across state lines. By the 1970s, it became clear that, increasingly, businesses planned to conduct commercial transactions not only across state lines but also across country borders. In 1980, the United Nations Convention on Contracts for the International Sale of Goods (CISG) was offered as a treaty that countries could sign, indicating their willingness to allow this treaty to govern international business-to-business sales contracts. The United Nations CISG

[16] UCC §§ 2-202 and 2A-202.

[17] UCC §§ 2-208(10) and 2A-207(1).

[18] UCC § 1-205(1).

[19] UCC § 1-205(4).

[20] UCC §§ 2-302 and 2A-108.

COURSE OF DEALING AND USAGE OF TRADE

Loizeaux Builders Supply Co. v. Donald B. Ludwig Company

366 A.2D 721 (N.J. 1976)

When the defendant building contractor phoned the supply company about the stated price of concrete, the supply company informed the builder that the price would be "adhered to for the year." The builder then put a continuing order in that resulted in concrete being shipped to the builder from February of that year through March of the following year. The phone call had been placed in February. The supply company did not deny any of the facts stated by the builder.

On January 1 in this time period, the stated price of the concrete was increased; the builder was notified of this but did not believe the increase applied to it in light of the phone conversation from the previous February. The builder paid only the "phone call" price, and the supply company sued for the difference. The question was whether the higher price of January 1 applied to the transaction in light of the phone call stating that the lower price would be "adhered to for the year."

In finding for the supply house and awarding the higher price for deliveries after January 1, the court relied on (1) the plain meaning of "adhered to for *the* year" as opposed to "adhered to for *a* year"; (2) the customary practice in the trade for building supply products to be increased on January 1 if they were to be increased at all; and (3) the fact that the builder had had actual notice of the January 1 price increase before the deliveries after January 1.

---

treaty provides the legal structure for international sales. Many major trading nations, including the North American Free Trade Agreement (NAFTA) nations (Canada, the United States, and Mexico), have signed the CISG. Additionally, many South American and European countries have signed or are considering signing this treaty.

THE SIGNIFICANCE OF THE CISG

The CISG is important because if a problem arises with an international sale and a party to the transaction initiates litigation, the UCC does not provide guidance in the litigation; instead, the CISG preempts the UCC. The CISG covers the same general topics as the UCC. For instance, the CISG covers offers, acceptances, and other contract topics. However, specific provisions of the CISG differ from the UCC. For example, the CISG requirements related to the statute of frauds are more lenient than those under the UCC. In particular, the CISG does not require that contracts be in writing. Case 21-3 deals, in part, specifically with this issue.

Businesses that have chosen to operate globally see the CISG as providing the same benefits as the UCC: clarity, predictability, and uniformity. Businesses that create international contracts are increasingly careful to consider the unique context in which they operate. Exhibit 21-5 lists key questions businesses ask as they try to minimize disputes when they transact business in the global economy. However, with the United States' adopting the UCC, the question still remains as to how to apply conflicting provisions of the CISG and UCC in contract disputes between U.S. companies and companies in nations having adopted the CISG. Consider Case 21-3, regarding a contract dispute between a U.S. company and a Canadian company.

Exhibit 21-5

Conflict Avoidance in the Global Economy

Businesses that operate in the global economy try to avoid conflict by asking the following key questions as they form contracts:

- If our business ends up in a dispute with a trading partner, what *language* should govern the dispute?

- In what *forum* should our dispute be resolved?

- Which country's *laws* should apply to the dispute?

After thinking about these questions, businesses create what are known as choice-of-language, forum-selection, and choice-of-law clauses.

ISRAEL ADOPTS THE CISG AS INTERNAL ISRAELI LAW—IS THIS THE WAY TO GO?

On February 1, 2003, Israel became a signatory to the CISG, which became a part of Israeli internal law. To date, 78 nations are signatories to the CISG. The United Kingdom is not a signatory of the CISG and instead applies English common law. A debate exists in the United States as to whether the CISG should be a substitute for the UCC or remain complementary to the UCC. It is currently complementary, as the United States applies both the UCC and the CISG. The debate is a crucial one, and it is argued in the Point / Counterpoint feature at the end of this chapter. An excellent resource for following this extremely pertinent and relevant issue is the website of the United Nations Commission on International Trade Law (UNCITRAL): www.uncitral.org/uncitral/en/index.html.

CASE 21-3 THE TRAVELERS PROPERTY CASUALTY COMPANY OF AMERICA AND HELLMUTH OBATA & KASSABAUM, INC., PLAINTIFFS v. SAINT-GOBAIN TECHNICAL FABRICS CANADA LIMITED, FORMERLY KNOWN AS BAY MILLS, DEFENDANT

U.S. DISTRICT COURT FOR THE DISTRICT OF MINNESOTA
474 F. SUPP. 2D 1075 (2007)

In this case, the plaintiff Hellmuth, Obata and Kassabaum designed and oversaw the construction of an arena. Plaintiff Travelers is the Hellmuth et al. insurer. The Canadian company defendant, Saint-Gobain, provided industrial mesh for use in the construction of the arena. That mesh allegedly was not suitable for the purpose for which it was used and plaintiffs sued for breach of contract in that the mesh was defective.

Two of the issues before the trial court were:

1. *Since the contract referred to provisions in the UCC, then the CISG was preempted and the UCC would prevail.*

2. *If the UCC prevailed over the CISG, then because the contract had not been reduced to writing, it was unenforceable under the Statute of Frauds and the breach of contract suit must be dismissed pursuant to a summary judgment motion by the defendant.*

JUDGE ANN D. MONTGOMERY: . . . [U]nder the *Supremacy Clause,* the law in every state is that "the CISG is applicable to contracts where the contracting parties are from different countries that have adopted the CISG." Id. Thus, absent an express statement that the CISG does not apply, merely referring to a particular state's law does not opt out of the CISG. As the Fifth Circuit stated, "[a]n affirmative opt-out requirement promotes uniformity and the observance of good faith in international trade, two principles that guide interpretation of the CISG." *BP Oil Int'l, 332 F.3d at 337,* citing CISG art. 7(1). The Court adopts the majority position on applicability of the CISG. Therefore, the CISG governs "the formation of the contract of sale and the rights and obligations of the seller . . . and the buyer . . . arising from such a contract." CISG art. 4(a).

. . . The parties seem to assume that only their writings could have formed a contract; the CISG, however, explicitly states that "[a] contract of sale need not be concluded in or evidenced by writing and is not subject to any other requirement as to form. It may be proved by any means, including witnesses." CISG art. 11. Under the CISG, a proposal for concluding a contract is sufficiently definite . . . to constitute an offer "if it indicates the goods and expressly or implicitly fixes or makes provision for determining the quantity and price." CISG art. 14(1). Thus, oral discussions between the parties agreeing to the goods, quantity, and price may have formed a contract before any purchase orders and invoices were exchanged.

Motion by defendant for summary judgment denied on this issue.

CRITICAL THINKING

Think back to the very strict requirements of the statute of frauds, discussed in Part 2 of this text. Does the CISG approach to writing requirements in contract formation as illustrated above make more sense than the common law approach? Why or why not?

ETHICAL DECISION MAKING

Do you find it a bit odd that the Canadian company argues that the CISG should not apply while the U.S. company argues that the CISG should apply in these situations? Is this just legalistic argumentation for the purpose of "winning the case"?

CASE OPENER WRAP-UP

Dropped Calls, or More Appropriately, Dropped Towers: Are Cell Towers Goods or Services?

This case illustrates two classic issues that one has to consider when first addressing a potential UCC Article 2 case. One issue is the type of item involved. First of all, is this a contract for the sale of goods? The key concept to remember when answering this question is whether, *at the time of the contract creation,* the items being bought and sold had physical or tangible properties and were able to be moved. Then the second question is, Is the contract *predominantly* for the sale of these goods, as opposed to services and/or real estate? If the answers to these questions are yes, the case falls under Article 2 of the Uniform Commercial Code as opposed to purely common law.

In this case, the answers to these two questions are fairly clear. Yes, the purchase of cell towers or monopoles constitutes a purchase of goods. These towers have physical property and can be moved, even though once put in place they will remain stationary. Moreover, it is the monopoles that were the items being bought and sold at the time that the contract was executed. Since the monopoles were the items bought and sold under the contract and since the court found that the invoice for these items was separate and distinct from the invoice for any kind of service or maintenance, the contract was predominantly for the sale of goods, not real estate or services.

KEY TERMS

consumer lease   481
finance lease   483
firm offers   483
goods   477
lease   481

lessee   481
lessor   481
merchant   480
mirror-image rule   484
mixed sale   478

parol evidence rule   486
sale   477
Uniform Commercial Code (UCC)   475

United Nations Convention on Contracts for the International Sale of Goods (CISG)   486
writing   485

SUMMARY OF KEY TOPICS

Scope of the UCC: The UCC is a uniform or model law that governs commercial transactions, from the sale of goods to secured transactions.

Significance of the UCC: The UCC adds clarity and predictability to sales law.

The Uniform Commercial Code

Article 2 (Sales) covers contracts for the sale of goods.

Articles 2 and 2(A) of the UCC

- *Sale:* The passing of title from the seller to the buyer for a price.

- *Goods:* Tangible things that can be moved.

- *Mixed goods and services contracts:* Contracts that include both goods and services. Courts apply Article 2 if the goods are the predominant part of the transaction.

- *Merchants:* Buyers or sellers who (1) deal in goods of the kind, (2) by occupation, hold themselves out as having knowledge and skill unique to the practices or goods involved in the transaction, or (3) employ a merchant as a broker, an agent, or some other intermediary. Various provisions of the UCC distinguish merchants from ordinary buyers and sellers.

Article 2(A)(Leases) covers contracts for the lease of goods.

- *Leases:* Transfers of the right to possession and use of goods for a term in return for consideration.
- *Special kinds of leases:* Two special kinds are consumer leases and finance leases.

The UCC outlines special rules and protections for each kind of lease.

How Sales and Lease Contracts Are Formed under the UCC

Formation in general: The UCC is more lenient than common law regarding contract formation. Courts look at the intent of the parties to a sales or lease contract.

Offer and acceptance: Offers are valid even if terms are left open. The common law mirror-image rule does not apply to contracts for the sale or lease of goods. Courts look on a case-by-case basis to determine whether to allow additional terms.

Consideration: When sales and lease contracts are modified, these modifications do not need to be supported by new consideration.

Statute of frauds: Contracts for the sale of goods must be in writing if the goods are valued at $500 or more. Lease contracts that require payments of $1,000 or more must be in writing. Exceptions exist for:

- Specifically manufactured goods.
- Contracts that parties admit exist.
- Situations in which partial performance has occurred.

Parol evidence: Courts try to enforce sales and lease contracts as written. Sometimes courts will allow parties to introduce:

- Additional terms that are consistent with contract terms.
- Information that helps interpret the agreement, including course of performance, course of dealing, and/or usage of trade.

Unconscionability: Under the UCC, a court can refuse to enforce the parts of a contract or lease that are unfair or one-sided.

Contracts for the International Sale of Goods

Scope of the CISG: The CISG is a treaty that countries can sign to allow it to govern international business-to-business sales contracts. Many major trading nations have signed the CISG.

Significance of the CISG: The CISG is important because it, rather than the UCC, governs international sales contracts. The CISG provides clarity, predictability, and uniformity for businesses that operate in the global economy.

POINT / COUNTERPOINT

Should the U.S. Adopt the CISG as a Substitute for the UCC?	
YES	NO
Most global companies that do business with U.S. companies are in countries that have adopted the CISG. While similar to the UCC, the CISG does have some material differences and is not, unlike the UCC, based on common law rules of contract. For example, the CISG does not recognize the parol evidence rule, and the CISG	The common law rules of contract have a solid history and evolved for specific reasons and rationales. These rules, such as the parol evidence rule, evolved for reasons germane to the history and context of the common law. They are necessary in the context of American transactional activity. It seems that the two sets of rules are

recognizes only international trade usages, not national or local ones. However, with commercial activity becoming more and more globalized, the United States needs to "join" the rest of the world so that the rules governing transactional activities will be uniform. At the very least, the UCC should be modified to conform with the CISG.

indeed justified: When the contractual parties are from the United States, the UCC should apply as the UCC principles are relevant to domestic transactions; the CISG, with its differences, should apply to international contracts as the context is different, thus requiring a different set of rules.

QUESTIONS & PROBLEMS

1. Consider the status of being a merchant under the UCC. Should the UCC differentiate between merchants and nonmerchants?

2. In a foreclosure case involving a diner, the creditors went after the business's "real estate." However, the diner itself was a prefabricated building. The business owner claimed that the building was not realty subject to the creditors' claims but was, instead, a trade fixture. Please discuss. [*J.K.S.P Restaurant v. County of Nassau,* 513 N.Y.S. 2d 716 (N.Y. App. Div. 1987).]

3. Thomas Helvey is suing the Wabash County Rural Electrical Company for breach of contract. The electric company caused 135-volt electricity to enter Helvey's home, damaging 110-volt appliances. Helvey brought suit claiming his contract with the electric company falls under UCC Article 2 for the sale of a good. Construct an argument for the plaintiff positing that electricity is a good. Why would this position be beneficial to the plaintiff? Next, construct an argument on behalf of the defendant positing that electricity is not a good under UCC Article 2. Which argument seems more persuasive to you? [*Helvey v. Wabash County REMC,* 278 N.E.2d 608 (1972).]

4. The plaintiff, Betty Epstein, visited a beauty parlor to get her hair dyed. In the dying process, the beautician used a prebleach solution manufactured by Clairol, Inc., and then a commercial dye manufactured by Sales Affiliate, Inc. The treatment went awry, and the plaintiff suffered severe hair loss, injuries to both hair and scalp, and some disfigurement. She sued the beauty salon, Clairol, and Sales Affiliate under Article 2 of the UCC. The defendants claimed that the contract was predominantly for services rather than for the sale of a good. How would you construct arguments supporting each side? What difference does it make whether the beauty treatment is a good or a service? [*Epstein v. Giannattasio,* 197 A.2d 342 (1963).]

5. Anthony J. Ruzzo, Sr., entered into an agreement with LaRose Enterprises, which engages in business under the name Taylor Rental Center, for the use of a plumbing tool known as a "power snake." While Ruzzo was using the power snake, it malfunctioned and he was shocked severely and suffered serious personal injuries. What kind of agreement exists between Ruzzo and Taylor, and how might the kind of agreement affect the case? [*Ruzzo v. LaRose Enterprises,* 748 A.2d 261 (2000).]

6. Consider a transaction that has three parties: (1) JWCJR Corp. (JWCJR) and its owner, John W. Cumberledge, Jr., (2) Bottomline Systems, Inc., and (3) Colonial Pacific Leasing Corp. JWCJR/Cumberledge, an autobody shop and its owner, sought a computer and software package that would allow the shop to generate estimates for insurance companies and improve the way the shop was managed. Bottomline demonstrated a computer and software system to JWCJR/Cumberledge. JWCJR/Cumberledge decided to obtain the system Bottomline demonstrated and subsequently entered into an agreement with Colonial Leasing. Colonial Leasing then purchased equipment from Bottomline. JWCJR/Cumberledge agreed to make payments to Colonial Leasing. What kind of lease do these facts indicate? If the computer system does not work, why does it matter what kind of lease exists? [*Colonial Pacific Leasing Corp. v. JWCJR Corp.,* 977 P.2d 541 (1999).]

7. The purchaser, American Parts, Inc., negotiated with the seller, Deering Milliken, for the purchase of fabric. After oral negotiations, Deering Milliken forwarded to the purchaser a written confirmation of the order stating a price of $1.75 per yard. American Parts responded with a written memo

stating that it could not agree to anything more than $1.50 per yard. The seller did not respond. The seller began shipping goods to the purchaser, who accepted them. The dispute in the case is whether the contract is for $1.75 or $1.50 per yard. How could you construct an argument for each party? [*American Parts, Inc. v. American Arbitration Association*, 154 N.W.2d 5 (1967).]

8. Wisconsin Knife Works, having some unused manufacturing capacity, decided to try to manufacture spade bits for sale to its parent, Black & Decker, a large producer of tools, including drills. A spade bit is made out of a chunk of metal called a *spade bit blank*, and Wisconsin Knife Works had to find a source of supply for these blanks. National Metal Crafters was eager to supply the spade bit blanks. After some negotiating, Wisconsin Knife Works sent National Metal Crafters a series of purchase orders. On the back of each purchase order was printed "Acceptance of this Order, either by acknowledgement or performance, constitutes an unqualified agreement to the following." A list of "Conditions of Purchase" followed, of which the first was "No modification of this contract shall be binding upon Buyer [Wisconsin Knife Works] unless made in writing and signed by Buyer's authorized representative. Buyer shall have the right to make changes in the Order by a notice, in writing, to Seller." The seller met the terms of the first two purchase orders from Wisconsin Knife Works. After the first two orders, National Metal Crafters was late with the deliveries. No delivery date had been specified on the purchase orders, but the delivery dates had been communicated orally between the two parties to the contract. Wisconsin Knife Works claimed that National Metal Crafters breached the contract. National Metal Crafters claimed that it had modified the dates for delivery and that Wisconsin had accepted these dates. What could constitute a binding modification after this contract was formed? [*Wisconsin Knife Works v. National Metal Crafters*, 781 F.2d 1280 (1986).]

9. Utah International, a mining company, entered into a 35-year requirements contract with Colorado-Ute Electric Association, Inc., for the sale of coal. Utah International was to provide all the coal that Colorado-Ute would need in the operation of new electricity generators. Utah International claims that Colorado-Ute built generators that will use far more coal than Utah International is willing to supply and that this breached the contract. Utah International is asking to be released from the contract due to Colorado-Ute's alleged breach. A requirements contract is a contract in which the buyer agrees to purchase and the seller agrees to sell all or up to a stated amount of what the buyer requires. What are the limits placed on a requirements contract? Should this contract be terminated? [*Utah International v. Colorado-Ute Electric Association, Inc.*, 426 F. Supp 1093 (1976).]

10. A company contracted with a marketing firm to construct software and create a business website. A quote was requested and accepted. Sometime later the business asked for updates and revisions but failed to request a quote. The business subsequently refused to pay for the changes, claiming no contract had been formed under the requirements of the offer under the UCC. The marketing firm then took the website down because of nonpayment and subsequently sued for nonpayment of its invoice. The company countersued on the tort of conversion for the loss of the website. This intriguing case raises several questions First, does this dispute fall under UCC subject matter? Second, will the company prevail on the tort of conversion based on the improper use or interference with someone else's property? [*Dennis Conwell et al. v. Gray Look Outdoor Marketing Group, Inc.*, 906 N.E.2d 805, 2009 Ind. LEXIS 465, 69 U.C.C. Rep. Serv. 2d (Callaghan) 71 (Ind. Sup. Ct. 2009).]

Looking for more review materials?

The Online Learning Center at **www.mhhe.com/kubasek3e** contains this chapter's "Assignment on the Internet" and also a list of URLs for more information, entitled "On the Internet." Find both of them in the Student Center portion of the OLC, along with quizzes and other helpful materials.

Title, Risk of Loss, and Insurable Interest

LEARNING OBJECTIVES

After reading this chapter, you will be able to answer the following questions:

1 What is the concept of title? How does it pass?

2 What is insurable interest?

3 What are the different kinds of sales contracts, and how does each type affect title passing, risk of loss, and insurable interest?

CASE OPENER

Keyboards Gone Astray

Silitek is a Taiwanese company. It entered into a contract FOB Taiwan with Burlington Air Express to deliver 1,000 cartons of computer keyboards to the Silitek subsidiary Lite-On in the United States. The bill of lading incorrectly stated that the goods were to be delivered to Reveal Computer Products, a California company. The mix-up occurred because once the goods were to be delivered to Lite-On, Lite-On was then going to check on Reveal Computer Products' creditworthiness and decide whether to deliver the goods to Reveal Computer Products.

The goods were delivered to Reveal Computer Products, and subsequently Reveal could not pay for them due to insolvency, thereby causing Lite-On to lose more than $100,000. Now, the catch in the whole thing is that under the delivery contract, Burlington was to collect a shipment order called a "Combined Express Bill of Lading" from Reveal Computer Products for the goods before delivery was made. Reveal did not have that bill of lading since delivery was supposed to be made to Silitek, if not for the mistake in the original bill of lading. Burlington made the delivery anyway to Reveal Computer Products. Silitek assigned its right to sue to Lite-On, which then brought a lawsuit against Burlington.

The legal question posed in light of the plaintiff's motion for summary judgment is this: Since the contract was FOB Taiwan and the seller, Silitek, is a Taiwanese firm, what kind of contract is this and what are the implications of that determination? That is, did title already pass to the buyer, Reveal, thus prohibiting Silitek's assignee, Lite-On, from suing, since it did not have title?[1]

---

[1] *Lite-On Peripherals, Inc. v. Burlington Air Express,* 255 F.3d 1189 (9th Cir. 2001).

1. What kind of sales contract is the one between Silitek and Burlington Air Express, and what obligations does it create between the parties?
2. What do shipping terms such as "FOB Taiwan" mean?
3. When does title pass for the computer keyboards, and what effect, if any, does that have on the transaction?

The Wrap-Up at the end of the chapter will answer these questions.

When businesses such as Burlington Air Express ship goods pursuant to UCC Article 2 sales contracts the business needs to know its rights and responsibilities. In particular, Silitek and Burlington need to know the UCC's rules regarding title, risk of loss, and insurable interest. This chapter explains these three concepts. It does so in the context of different kinds of sales contracts, including simple delivery, common-carrier delivery, goods-in-bailment, and conditional sales contracts.

The Concept of Title

L01

What is the concept of title? How does it pass?

The UCC defines a sale as the passing of title from the seller to the buyer for a price. However, this definition does not indicate the relationship between *passing title* and *ownership*. Suppose, for example, that you are the owner of a computer store that wants to buy 50 keyboards from Silitek in Taiwan. The deal includes a list of keyboards with descriptions and a price for each kind of keyboard. Delivery is to be within one month.

This looks like a pretty straightforward deal—description of goods, quantity, price, time of delivery—but it is not. It does not tell the parties:

- When the buyer can resell the goods to a third party.
- When insurance on the goods can be purchased.
- When the goods become part of the buyer's inventory and can serve as collateral for a loan.

In addition, there is no indication of who takes the loss if the goods are damaged before delivery, during possession by the seller, or in transit.

Each of these issues needs to be considered before the owner of the goods can be established. Generally, the party with "good title" to the goods has ownership: You cannot own goods unless you have good title to them. This chapter discusses acquiring good title as well as the other topics listed above.

THREE KINDS OF TITLE

There are three kinds of title: good title, void title, and voidable title. First, good title is title that is acquired from someone who already owns the goods free and clear. Next, void title is not true title. Someone who purchases stolen goods, knowingly or unknowingly, has void title. Finally, voidable title occurs in certain situations where the contract between the original parties would be void but the goods have already been sold to a third party. The next few sections of the chapter discuss these types of title in detail.

Acquiring Good Title

The most obvious way of attaining good title is acquiring it from someone who has good title, that is, the person who owns it free and clear, without any qualifications. In contrast, someone who has come into possession of stolen goods never has good title and can never pass a good title. A person in possession of stolen goods has void title.

However, problems may arise when someone thinks he or she has good title but actually has void title. Consider Case 22-1, which concerns a large donation of goods to a charity followed by the subsequent sale of those donated items to a third party. Does that third party have a good title? Did the donee of the charitable gift have a void or voidable title? The case also talks about why that is important.

CASE 22-1

TEMPUR-PEDIC INTERNATIONAL, INC., PLAINTIFF v. WASTE TO CHARITY, INC.; BROCO SUPPLY, INC.; JACK FITZGERALD; ERIC VOLOVIC; HOWARD HIRSCH; THOMAS SCARELLO; NELSON SILVA; CLOSE OUT SURPLUS AND SAVINGS, INC.; AND ERNEST PEIA, DEFENDANTS

U.S. DISTRICT COURT FOR THE WESTERN DISTRICT OF ARKANSAS, FORT SMITH DIVISION

483 F. SUPP. 2D 766, 2007 U.S. DIST. LEXIS 54787

Tempur-Pedic International (TP) manufactures and sells mattresses, pillow cases and other bedding material. In the wake of the Hurricane Katrina disaster, Tempur-Pedic donated 15 million dollars' worth of mattresses and pillows to the Katrina disaster relief effort. It made the donation to Waste To Charity, Inc., (WTC) for distributing the mattresses to victims of the hurricane.

Waste To Charity, Inc., however, sold the donated mattresses to third parties (the other defendants named in this lawsuit). Tempur-Pedic brought this action for a temporary restraining order to stop the further sales of the mattresses and to recover the donated mattresses from the third parties. The issues are these:

1. *Did Waste To Charity, Inc., have a void title to the mattresses? If so, then any third-party purchaser has a void title, regardless of good faith.*

2. *Did Waste To Charity, Inc., have a voidable title to the mattresses? If so, then a good faith third-party purchaser would get good title to the mattresses.*

HON. JAMES R. MARSCHEWSKI, U.S. MAGISTRATE:
[The UCC] . . . "recognizes a legal distinction between a sale of stolen goods and a sale of goods procured through fraud." Midway Auto Sales, Inc. v. Clarkson, 71 Ark. App. 316, 318, 29 S.W.3d 788 (2000). As noted by the court in Midway Auto Sales, "[a]bsent exigent circumstances, one who purchases from a thief acquires no title as against the true owner. However, . . . the result is different when property obtained by fraud is conveyed to a bona fide purchaser." Id. [Citation omitted.]
Section 2-403 in applicable part provides as follows:

(1) A purchaser of goods acquires all title which his transferor had or had power to transfer

except that a purchaser of a limited interest acquires rights only to the extent of the interest purchased. A person with voidable title has power to transfer a good title to a good faith purchaser for value. When goods have been delivered under a transaction of purchase the purchaser has such power even though

(a) the transferor was deceived as to the identity of the purchaser; or

(b) the delivery was in exchange for a check which is later dishonored; or

(c) it was agreed that the transaction was to be a "cash sale"; or

(d) the delivery was procured through fraud punishable as larcenous under the criminal law.

The good-faith purchaser exception is designed to "promote finality in commercial transactions and thus encourage purchases and to foster commerce. It does so by protecting the title of a purchaser who acquires property for valuable consideration and who, at the time of the purchase, is without notice that the seller lacks valid and transferable title to the property." United States v. Lavin, 942 F.2d 177, 186 (3d Cir. 1991). [Citation omitted.]
. . . Here, TP voluntarily gave the donated property to WTC. There was no showing that WTC was just a sham operation. From the evidence before the court, the court believes WTC lawfully came into possession of the property. Thus, it appears clear WTC did acquire voidable title to the donated property.
After the donations were made, TP has presented evidence establishing a fair probability that at least a portion

of the donated products were sold at various places around the country rather than put to their intended charitable use. WTC, although it claimed no knowledge of the sales, had sufficient control of the property. . . . With respect to the mattresses purchased by CSS [one of the defendants] . . . the issue therefore becomes whether CSS was a good-faith purchaser. . . . "Good faith" is defined to mean "honesty in fact in the conduct or transaction concerned." The court has given careful consideration to the documentation submitted to the court in connection with the motion for TRO and/or preliminary injunction, the response filed by CSS, the testimony of the witnesses at the hearing, and the arguments of counsel. I conclude TP has shown a probability that it will succeed on the merits of establishing that CSS is not a good faith purchaser for value of the mattresses.

A number of factors lead the court to this conclusion. First, the price of the mattresses was substantially below market value. . . . Second, the terms of the purported sale were suspicious: all tags had been removed; while the mattresses were confirmed to be TP mattresses they could not be sold as such; no sales could be made to TP dealers; and the representation was made that TP has confirmed the mattresses would not have tags on them. Third, the timing of the attempted sales . . . lends support to the conclusion that CSS was not a good faith purchaser for value. Fourth, Peia, the president of CSS, acknowledged that he knew TP did not authorize the sale of used mattresses. . . .

Request for a TRO is granted.

CRITICAL THINKING

Even though the court found that Waste To Charity, Inc., had a voidable title, it still held that no good title was passed. What would have been required to have the purchasers obtain a good title? Could these purchasers with the voidable title have transferred good title to a subsequent party? How?

ETHICAL DECISION MAKING

Should Waste To Charity be subject to any kind of legal sanctions for its behavior in this case? What public policy issues are involved in this case?

The key point to remember, which many people misunderstand, is that good faith is actually irrelevant when passing a void title. If a person has a void title (as in the best, and most frequent, example: a person has possession of stolen goods), then no matter how honorable the intentions of the seller are, that good-faith seller cannot pass anything to the buyer but another void title. The only exception to this is the entrustment situation, which is discussed later in the chapter. A good maxim to remember is that stolen goods *always* remain stolen goods.

Legal Principle: **In a title transfer, good title is passed when there is a good title held by the seller; however, if a void title is held by the seller, then a good title is never passed—a void title always begets a void title.**

? BUT WHAT IF . . .

WHAT IF THE FACTS OF THE CASE OPENER WERE DIFFERENT?

Let's say, in the Case Opener, that Silitek sold the keyboards to Reveal Computer Products. The two companies had a thorough sales contract to uphold their agreement. However, it turned out that Silitek had sold stolen keyboards. What kind of contract is this called?

VOIDABLE TITLE

When a seller transfers goods to a buyer, normally the buyer gets good title. However, the buyer gets only voidable title if any of the following apply:

- The buyer has deceived the seller regarding his or her true identity.
- The buyer has written a bad check for the goods.

Landshire Food Service, Inc. v. Coghill
709 S.W.2d 509 (Mo. App. 1986)

Coghill sold his Rolls Royce to Daniel Bellman, who paid him with a cashiers check for $94,500. Coghill transferred title over to Bellman. Bellman turned around and advertised the sale of the car and sold it to Barry Hyken for $62,000, transferring title to Hyken.

In the meantime, the cashiers check given by Bellman to Coghill turned out to be a forgery and was dishonored by the bank. Coghill then reported the car missing and stolen. Three weeks after Hyken took possession and title to the vehicle, the police arrived and seized the "stolen" car. Coghill and Hyken now both claim title to the car. The issue posed is, What kind of title did Bellman have? Did he have a good, voidable, or void title?

In answering this issue, the court ruled:

[T]he initial question is whether a bona fide purchaser for value takes good title from one who procured the automobile by a fraudulent purchase? The answer is yes. Where the original owner, although induced by fraud, has voluntarily given to another apparent ownership in the motor vehicle, a bona fide purchaser, who has relied upon that person's possession of the certificate of title and of the vehicle, is protected. . . . The person who procures title through fraud receives voidable title and is able to transfer good title to a bona fide purchaser. Although the result may seem harsh, the purpose of this rule is to promote the free transferability of property in commerce.

- The buyer has committed criminal fraud in securing the goods.
- The buyer and seller agreed that title would not pass until some later time.
- The buyer is a minor.

The first four of these situations that can create a voidable title are articulated in Section 2-403 of Article 2 of the UCC; the final one, the buyer is a minor, comes from common law. A seller who discovers any of these situations has the right to cancel the contract and reclaim the goods, even if they have already been delivered to the buyer. That is why the title is called *voidable*. The Case Nugget presents an example of a situation giving rise to a voidable title.

THIRD-PARTY PURCHASERS AND GOOD TITLE

Problems develop when a buyer with the voidable title turns around and sells the goods to a third-party purchaser. If that third-party purchaser made a good-faith purchase for value (as opposed to receiving the goods as a gift), he or she gets good title, not void or voidable title. See Exhibit 22-1.

Betty Buyer purchases a bicycle from Steve Seller; Betty then resells the bike to Terry, the buyer, who purchases it in good faith and for a reasonable price.

Good Title:
If Steve Seller has a good title, then he passes a good title ➔ to Betty, who passes a good title ➔ to Terry

Bad Title:
Let's say that Steve Seller stole the bike. Steve Seller has a bad title ➔ Betty gets a bad title ➔ Terry gets a bad title.
(Who has the good title? The owner from whom the bike was stolen!)

Voidable Title:*
Steve Seller has a good title ➔ passes a voidable title to Betty; if Terry is a good-faith purchaser, then ➔ Terry gets a good title.

Exhibit 22-1

Status of Title Under the UCC: Good, Bad, Voidable

*See the list in the text of the five situations in which a voidable title is created.

Here is an example of how voidable title works: Suppose a seller sells a bicycle to a buyer and the buyer pays with a bad check. Before the seller can reclaim the bike, the buyer sells the bike to a third-party good-faith purchaser for value. The buyer then takes off, never to be seen again. The seller cannot reclaim the bike from the third-party purchaser because that party has good title. Although this result may seem unfair, it upholds the philosophy of the Uniform Commercial Code itself: the facilitation of commercial activity. The code believes that good-faith purchasers should not have to look over their shoulders to determine whether a commercial transaction is valid.

ENTRUSTMENT

If an owner *entrusts* the possession of goods to a merchant who deals in goods of that kind, the merchant can transfer all rights in the goods to a buyer in the ordinary course of business. Recall that in the previous chapter, the case of *DeWeldon v. McKean* presented an example of entrustment. In that case, an owner had entrusted a merchant (a well-known artist) with possession of paintings. If that merchant had sold the paintings to a buyer in the ordinary course of business, then that buyer gets a good title, even though the merchant had *no* title at all. See the Point / Counterpoint at the end of this chapter to explore this issue more fully.

One form of entrustment occurs when someone entrusts the possession of a good (e.g., a car) to a merchant and asks him to repair that good. Suppose the merchant fraudulently or accidentally sells the item as if it were part of his inventory. If the purchaser is a good-faith purchaser (i.e., did not know that the item belonged to someone else and paid a fair market value, not some unreasonable discounted value), then that purchaser gets a good title. (That purchaser is a buyer in the ordinary course of business.) The original owner's only recourse is to bring suit against the merchant. Again, the rationale behind this concept is the facilitation of commercial activity regarding good-faith purchasers in the marketplace.

BUT WHAT IF . . .
WHAT IF THE FACTS OF THE CASE OPENER WERE DIFFERENT?

Let's say, in the Case Opener, that Silitek entrusted Burlington not only to ship the keyboards to Reveal Computer Products but to sell the keyboards too. Burlington drafted a sales contract for Reveal to sign. However, Reveal said that because Burlington had no title for the keyboards, Burlington could not sell them. Which side is correct in this case?

RECOURSE UNDER THE UCC

The determination of who has good title does not always result in the expected and equitable solution to a problem. For example, suppose you purchased a couch at a furniture store. It is pretty safe to say that once you identify the couch and pay for it, you have "title" to it. Now suppose that when the store attempts to deliver the couch to your home, lightning hits the store's delivery truck and destroys the couch. Is the store legally obligated to replace the couch? Most of us would intuitively answer that it is. After all, you never took possession of the couch. However, as previously noted, *you* have title. Under pre-UCC law, this loss could have fallen on whoever had title at that time—and that person would be you. Under the UCC, if the store is a merchant, the risk of loss remains with the seller until the couch is actually delivered to you.

WHEN DOES INSURABLE INTEREST ARISE?

National Compressor Corp. v. Carrow and McGee
417 F.2d 97 (1969)

National Compressor bought a large compressor from Davis, who had bought the compressor from Carrow and McGee. Title to the compressor was not to pass to National Compressor until the compressor was removed from Carrow and McGee's property. Prior to the compressor's being moved (and title passing to National Compressor) a fire broke out at the site, destroying the compressor. National Compressor had already paid the $12,000 purchase price. The issue before the court was whether National Compressor had any kind of insurable interest since clearly title had not yet passed. The defendants claimed that National Compressor had no standing to bring the lawsuit as it had no "interest" in the property since title had yet to pass.

The court ruled otherwise, stating that National Compressor had an insurable and special interest in the good, thus giving it standing to sue. The court ruled:

Where a third party so deals with goods *which have been identified to a contract* for sale as to cause actionable injury to a party to that contract (a) a right of action against the third party is in either party to the contract for sale who has title to or a security interest or a special property or an insurable interest in the goods; and if the goods have been destroyed or converted a right of action is also in the party who either bore the risk of loss under the contract for sale or has since the injury assumed that risk as against the other. . . .

The buyer obtains a special property and an insurable interest in goods by identification of existing goods as goods to which the contract refers even though the goods so identified are nonconforming and he has an option to return or reject them. Such identification can be made at any time and in any manner explicitly agreed to by the parties. In the absence of explicit agreement identification occurs (a) when the contract is made if it is for the sale of goods already existing and identified. . . .

As a result of these kinds of dilemmas, the UCC breaks up the various issues traditionally correlated with title and treats them separately. Several different issues normally are thought of under the concept of title:

- *Ownership:* When does title actually transfer from the seller to the buyer, since the right to transfer ownership of the goods, whether through a subsequent sale or gift, is tied to title?

- *Encumbrance:* The right to encumber goods as collateral for a debt is dependent on who is holding title. When title passes is important because having title means that one can then sell or encumber the goods. In other words, having title means that one can pass title.

- *Loss:* In regard to the right to indemnification if the goods are damaged, when the risk of loss attaches is important. This is because, regardless of title passing, we need to know the seller's and buyer's responsibility to each other in the event that the goods are damaged or destroyed before the buyer takes complete possession of the goods.

- *Insurable interest:* An *insurable interest* is the right to insure the goods against any risk exposure such as damage or destruction. When an insurable interest is created in the goods is important. Both the buyer and the seller can insure themselves for potential loss, in the event that the goods are damaged or destroyed at some point in the transaction. A key point is identifying the earliest time in the transaction that the buyer can claim an insurable interest. The Case Nugget addresses that issue.

L02

What is insurable interest?

One very important point to note is that the parties are always free to create a contract that lays out and defines such issues as when title passes and when risk of loss passes. The UCC's rules are essentially the default rules for contracts that do not clearly spell out such provisions.

Let's look at each one of these issues within the context of the four kinds of sales contracts that Article 2 creates.

Types of Sales Contracts

LO3

What are the different
kinds of sales contracts,
and how does each type
affect title passing, risk
of loss, and insurable
interest?

The UCC lays out essentially four broad factual scenarios for the sale of goods:

1. *Simple delivery contract:* A simple delivery contract occurs when the purchased goods are transferred to the buyer from the seller at either the time of the sale or some time later by the seller's delivery.

2. *Common-carrier delivery contract:* This type of contract occurs when the goods are delivered to the buyer via a common carrier, such as a trucking line.

3. *Goods-in-bailment contract:* This type of contract occurs when the purchased goods are in some kind of storage under the control of a third party, such as a warehouseman.

4. *Conditional sales contract:* A conditional sales contract occurs when the sale itself is contingent on approval, for example.

In the sections that follow, this chapter answers questions about ownership, encumbrance, loss, and insurable interest as they relate to these four types of sales contracts.

SIMPLE DELIVERY CONTRACT

With a simple delivery contract, the buyer and seller typically execute an agreement, and the buyer leaves with the goods. To most of us, it appears that title, risk of loss, and insurable interest all pass to the buyer at the moment the transaction is consummated and the buyer walks out with the goods. However, under the UCC, there are three distinct steps: (1) Title transfers to the buyer on the goods' being identified to the contract, that is, when the contract is executed; (2) risk of loss transfers to the buyer when the buyer takes possession; and (3) insurable interest is created in the buyer when the goods are identified to the contract, in other words, at the same time that title passes.

But what happens if the buyer comes back later to pick up the goods or arranges to have the seller, or an agent of the seller, deliver the goods at a later time? For the purposes of title and insurable interest, nothing really changes. The dilemma occurs with risk of loss.

Let's suppose a buyer and seller execute a contract in which the seller is going to deliver a refrigerator later in the day to the buyer. Through no fault of the seller, the refrigerator is damaged in a fire at the seller's store. Who has the risk of loss if neither party is at fault? In this case, the issue rests on the seller's status. If the seller is a merchant, as in this instance, the risk of loss remains with the seller until the goods are actually delivered to the buyer. If the seller is not a merchant, the risk of loss remains with the buyer under the rule of tender of delivery. Simply put, tender of delivery is the moment the goods were available for the buyer to take. Consider this example: You purchase a dresser at a garage sale, but you want to go home and get your truck so that you can get the dresser home easily. Unfortunately, a car hits the dresser and destroys it. You, the buyer, cannot get your money back because (1) the law does not consider the seller a merchant and (2) you could have taken the dresser with you when you bought it.

Note that the results are different if either party is at fault for the damage. In that case, the responsible person is liable under tort law for the damage caused. Case 22-2 considers who has the risk of loss between an innocent seller and an innocent buyer.

Legal Principle: **A simple delivery contract includes the scenario in which the seller delivers the goods to the buyer via its own delivery truck. The contract becomes a shipment contract when a common carrier, not the seller's agent, is used for delivery.**

With a simple delivery contract, whereby a seller transfers goods to a buyer without the middle-delivery common carrier, the various interests transfer as shown below. (*Note:* Even if the seller has its agent deliver the goods to the buyer, this is still a simple delivery.)

CASE 22-2   EMERY v. WEED
SUPERIOR COURT OF PENNSYLVANIA
343 PA. SUPER. 224, 494 A.2D 438 (1985)

In this case, Emery's son had been making down payments on a Pacer Corvette sports car sold by an automobile dealership owned by Weed Chevrolet (Weed). Emery's son died prior to paying off and taking possession of the car. In the meantime, through no negligence or fault of the automobile dealership, the car was stolen from the dealership. Emery is suing for the return of the monies paid and to cancel the contract. Weed is counterclaiming, stating that it is entitled to keep the down payments, and also to recover damages in the amount of the difference between the purchase price of the Pacer and its market value on the date Emery sought to cancel the agreement. The trial court ruled in favor of Emery, and Weed appeals.

JUDGE SPAETH: . . . With respect to several of these [UCC] provisions, there is no dispute. The parties agree that the Pacer Corvette "suffer[ed] casualty without the fault of either party," . . . and that the casualty was "total" and occurred "before the risk of loss [had] pass[ed] to the buyer" . . . We . . . agree with the trial court that risk of loss had not passed, but we base that conclusion on 13 Pa.C.S. § 2509(c) ("In any case not within subsection (a) or (b), the risk of loss passes to the buyer on his receipt of the goods if the seller is a merchant. . . .")

The item "identified when the contract was made" was the Pacer Corvette identified in the agreement of sale by its serial number. Appellant argues that it was not required by the agreement to deliver that very Pacer because, it asserts, "[e]ach such automobile was identical to all of the others manufactured, down to the details with respect to the paint job and extras." This assertion, however, is not supported by the record, which only shows that all Pacer Corvettes were painted black and silver; as will be recalled, the trial court disallowed testimony as to the effect that all Pacer Corvettes were identical. Quite apart from its identification in the agreement by serial number, the Pacer was identified by being removed from the display showroom, after the agreement was signed, and being covered and locked. From this it may be inferred that there was "a meeting of the minds as to the particular or actual goods designated." This agreement by [seller] and appellee's son that [seller] would deliver the Pacer identified in the contract was in no way affected by the seller's later apparent willingness to provide [buyer] with a different Pacer. [Seller] argues that "the parties . . . did not consider the particular automobile (the Pacer identified in the agreement by its serial number) to be unique. . . ." However, Section 2613 does not require such proof; it only requires that [buyer] establish that the "contract require[d] for its performance [the Pacer Corvette] identified when the contract [was] made." He has done so.

AFFIRMED.

CRITICAL THINKING

Is the court's decision consistent with your commonsense belief about whether risk of loss had passed? Explain how the court used the UCC to reach its conclusion.

ETHICAL DECISION MAKING

Which primary value does the court's decision show it prefers? Which primary value does Weed Chevrolet probably prefer?

Simple delivery: seller → buyer

1. Title transfers on identification of the goods to the contract.

2. If the seller is a merchant, risk of loss transfers on delivery of the goods to the buyer; if the seller is not a merchant, risk of loss transfers when the goods are made available for the buyer to possess (tender of delivery).

3. The parties may buy insurance on their goods if they hold title or have any risk of loss or other economic interest.

But what if simple delivery is not so simple. For example, what about delivery of liquid via a pipeline. Consider the nearby Case Nugget.

City of Richmond v. Petroleum Marketers, Inc.
221 Va. 372, 269 S.E. 2d 389 (1980)

Petroleum Marketers is a wholesaler of petroleum within Henrico County, Virginia. Its offices are there, and it made all of its contracts with customers in Henrico County, not in the city of Richmond. However, the petroleum was delivered to these customers in Richmond. The city of Richmond claimed that Petroleum Marketers was liable for city taxes as a merchant doing business "in the city."

According to the Virginia Supreme Court,

The ultimate question which we must decide is whether Petroleum's "sales" occurred where the contracts for the purchase of the oil were executed (Henrico County) or where the goods were, in fact, delivered (City). Our inquiry is whether there is a sufficient nexus between the activities of Petroleum and the City to justify the City classifying Petroleum as a wholesale merchant subject to the City's license tax.

The relevant portion of the Virginia UCC (comparable to UCC Article 2) says in part that "[a] 'sale' consists in the passing of title from the seller to the buyer for a price" and that "[u]nless otherwise explicitly agreed title passes to the buyer at the time and place at which the seller completes his performance with reference to the physical delivery of the goods."

The court found that the goods were identified to the contract when the petroleum arrived at the buyer's receptacle in the city, not when it was pumped out of the seller's holding tank in Henrico County. The obvious conclusion is that title passed when the product was pumped out of Petroleum's rented tanks and into whatever facility its customer provided.

COMMON-CARRIER DELIVERY CONTRACT

If a buyer and seller execute a contract and the seller subsequently places the goods with a common carrier for delivery to the buyer, the parties have executed a common-carrier delivery contract. Note that a common carrier is an independent contractor and not an agent of the seller. What makes the common carrier an independent contractor, rather than an agent, is that the carrier controls the primary aspects of performance, such as how the goods are actually delivered.

The UCC names two kinds of delivery contracts in this category: origin or shipment contracts and destination contracts. _Shipment contracts_ require that the seller ship the goods to the buyer via a common carrier. The seller is required to make proper shipping arrangements and deliver the goods into the common carrier's hands. Title passes to the buyer at the time and place of shipment. Thus, the buyer bears the risk of loss while the goods are in transit. _Destination contracts_ require that the seller deliver the goods to the destination stipulated in the sales contract. This may be the buyer's place of business or some other location. The seller bears the risk of loss until that time. Case 22-3 discusses the issue of who bears the risk of loss in a case in which the parties disagreed about whether the contract was an origin/shipment contract or a destination contract. See also Exhibit 22-2, which identifies shipping terms that create the conditions of transit and delivery. Remember in the opening case that the shipment term was FOB Taiwan. How is that interpreted from Exhibit 22-2?

Exhibit 22-2

Shipping Terms Specifying Requirements for Delivery

TERM	EXPLANATION
FOB (free on board)	The selling price includes transportation costs, and the seller carries the risk of loss to either the place of shipment or the place of destination.
FAS (free alongside)	The seller, at seller's expense, delivers the goods alongside the ship before the risk passes to the buyer.
CIF or C&F (cost, insurance, and freight; cost and freight)	The seller puts the goods in possession of a carrier before the risk passes to the buyer. Contracts are usually shipment contracts rather than destination contracts.
Delivery ex-ship (delivery from the carrying vessel)	Risk of loss passes to the buyer when the goods leave the ship.

SINGAPORE TAKES STEPS TO HALT PIRACY

Singapore and Indonesia signed an agreement that allows Singapore-registered ships to hire Indonesian sailors. The agreement will benefit both Indonesian sailors (approximately 10,000 are available for work) and Singapore ship owners, who need workers.

This agreement aims to halt piracy, which occurs when sailors are out of work in a deteriorating economy. Indonesian waters are especially crime-ridden. The Straits of Malacca are a prime location for pirate attacks on ships in Indonesian waters. The agreement between Singapore and Indonesia will put Indonesian sailors on Singapore-flagged ships, where the sailors will have new, legal opportunities to support themselves.

Source: Susan Sim, "Maritime Deal Promises to Cut Piracy in Region," *The Straits Times* (Singapore), February 23, 2001.

CASE 22-3	PILERI INDUSTRIES, INC. v. CONSOLIDATED INDUSTRIES, INC.

COURT OF CIVIL APPEALS OF ALABAMA
740 SO. 2D 1108 (1999)

In this case, Pileri Industries, the seller, shipped goods via a common carrier to Consolidated Industries, Inc., the buyer. The goods were subsequently lost prior to actual delivery. Pileri claimed the sales contract was a shipping contract and thus the risk of loss had passed to the buyer, Consolidated Industries.

Consolidated Industries disagreed. Consolidated claimed the sales contract was a destination contract, and that the risk of loss remained with Pileri Industries, the seller. The trial court, through a nonjury trial, held that Pileri could not support this assertion that there was a shipping contract and thus held for Consolidated Industries, Inc.

The Court of Civil Appeals held that Pileri, the seller, was not entitled to judgment in a breach-of-contract action, and that Pileri's delivery of goods to the carrier did not entitle Pileri to recover money for the goods shipped. What follows is a portion of the dissent in the appellate case.

JUDGE CRAWLEY, DISSENTING: . . . I respectfully dissent because I believe that the trial court erred as a matter of law by entering judgment for Consolidated. . . . [E]ven if Consolidated had established that it never received the November 4 shipment, I would not thereby have proved that it was relieved of its contractual duty to pay for the goods. Under . . . the Uniform Commercial Code, a determination of whether the seller or buyer bears the risk of loss of goods in transit depends on whether the agreement of sale is a "shipment" contract or a "destination" contract.

Under [Article 2 of the Uniform Commercial Code] the "shipment" contract is regarded as the normal one and the "destination" contract as the variant type. . . . Both of these types of contracts usually employ mercantile terms or "trade symbols" specifying the requirements for delivery, such as "F.O.B. the place of shipment," . . . or "F.O.B. the place of destination." *Where no such term is employed and there has been no specific agreement otherwise, the contract for the transportation of goods by carrier will be presumed to be a shipping contract.*

Unlike the majority of this court, I believe that Pileri made a prima facie showing that the contract was a shipment contract and that Consolidated presented no evidence to the contrary. As the main opinion points out, I have, in the absence of Alabama case law on the subject, turned to the construction of the relevant UCC sections by some of our sister states.

In interpreting the UCC we must keep in mind the legislative mandate that is to be . . . applied to promote its underlying purposes and policies, one of which is to make uniform the law among various jurisdictions. . . .

At trial, Pileri introduced a bill of lading indicating that it delivered the goods on November 4, 1992, to Roadway Express for shipment to Consolidated. Mr. Pileri testified that the agreement was a "shipping contract" that required Consolidated to pay the shipping costs and to assume the risk of loss once Pileri had delivered the goods to a common carrier. Pileri stated that it made 14 shipments to Consolidated. It introduced 10 shipping invoices, 6 of which were marked "F.O.B. Farmingdale," Pileri's place of business. For the other four shipping invoices, the "F.O.B." term was left blank.

Although those invoices pertained to a prior agreement of the parties, rather than to the parties' new agreement made on March 30, 1992, they are relevant because they indicate a course of dealing between Pileri and Consolidated. . . . In the absence of any evidence from Consolidated indicating that the agreement was a "destination contract," Pileri was entitled to rely on the presumption established in § 7-2-503, Ala. Code 1975 (Comment 5), that the agreement was a "shipping contract." . . . Here, however, Pileri did more than merely rely on the presumption. Mr. Pileri testified that the "standard procedure" among Government contractors was that, unless otherwise agreed between the parties, the contract was "an F.O.B. contract." Consolidated did not object to Mr. Pileri's testimony on this point. . . . Pileri established Consolidated's liability on an account stated; it also established a breach of a shipment contract by Consolidated. . . .

[continued]

Consolidated presented no evidence either challenging the accuracy of the stated account or disputing Pileri's characterization of the agreement as a shipment contract. Consolidated neither pleaded nor proved the affirmative defense of failure of consideration. The judgment for Consolidated is erroneous as a matter of law and is due to be reversed.

The majority had affirmed; the dissent disagrees.

CRITICAL THINKING

From reading the dissent, can you make any inferences about why the majority must have ruled in favor of Consolidated? Does this case illustrate the significance of who bears the burden of proof?

ETHICAL DECISION MAKING

Which primary value does the dissent's argument show it prefers? Identify and explain a value that clashes with this value.

With a shipment contract whereby a seller transfers goods to a buyer with delivery of the goods effected by a common carrier, the various interests transfer as follows:

Shipment contract: seller → common carrier → buyer

1. If the shipment contract is an origin contract (if the contract is vague or ambiguous, an origin contract will be presumed), the title passes to the buyer when the goods are turned over by the seller to the common carrier.
2. If the shipment contract is a destination contract, the title transfers from the seller to the buyer when the common carrier delivers the goods to the buyer.
3. The risk of loss in either situation—origin or destination contract—transfers from the seller to the buyer simultaneously with the title.
4. An insurable interest is created when the buyer and/or seller holds title or retains a risk of loss.

GOODS-IN-BAILMENT CONTRACT

Goods in bailment are simply goods that are in some kind of storage (e.g., in a warehouse or on board a ship), so the seller cannot transfer physical possession of them. Instead, the seller has one of three documents indicating ownership of the goods: a negotiable document of title, a nonnegotiable document of title, or a contract or some other instrument showing ownership that is not a negotiable or nonnegotiable document of title. If the seller has a negotiable document (i.e., a document containing the words "deliver to the order of [seller]"), then both title and risk of loss transfer from the seller to the buyer as soon as that negotiable instrument is endorsed over to the buyer. On the other hand, if the document is nonnegotiable (i.e., a document lacking the words "to the order of"), then the title passes with the instrument of title but the risk of loss does not pass to the buyer until the bailee (the custodian of the goods) is notified of the transfer or a reasonable time has elapsed since the transaction. Finally, if there is neither a negotiable or nonnegotiable document of title, then the title passes at the time the sales contract is executed but the risk does not pass to the buyer until the bailee is notified of the transaction and acknowledges such notification.

Globalization and the development of information technology are changing the way port operators conduct their business. According to Ernst Frankel, a professor of ocean systems at the Massachusetts Institute of Technology, ports and terminals are streamlining their management, automating their business operations and production processes, and viewing themselves as part of an integrated system that includes carrier systems.

In the future, it is likely that changes in technology will include integrated ports and shipping lines that offer door-to-door service.

Frankel believes that regional and global wireless networks will bring ports, carriers, and shippers together to "maximize operating efficiencies." He states that the factor driving this change is customer need. The bottom line is that the customer wants "knowledge, speed, innovation and quality," and changes in technology are making customer wishes come true.

Source: "Technology Carriers and Operators Learn Integration Lessons," *Lloyd's List International* 6 (March 2, 2001).

With goods in bailment, the three interests—title, risk of loss, insurable interest—pass in the following way:

Seller → buyer, but the goods are elsewhere in some kind of storage and in a third party's possession and care

1. Title passes from the seller to the buyer when the document of title (e.g., a warehouse receipt or a bill of lading) is actually endorsed or signed over to the buyer. If there is no document of title, then title passes when the goods are identified to the contract and the contract is executed.

2. Risk of loss passes to the buyer simultaneously with the document of title provided that the document of title is a negotiable one. If it is nonnegotiable, the risk does not pass until the bailee (the possessor or custodian of the goods) is notified or a reasonable time elapses. If there is no document of title, risk passes to the buyer on notification and acknowledgment by the bailee.

3. Insurable interest is created when either party has title, risk of loss, or some other economic interest attached to the goods (e.g., a creditor who secures a loan by taking the goods as collateral).

CONDITIONAL SALES CONTRACT

Conditional sales contracts are either sale-on-approval contracts or sale-or-return contracts. A contract is a sale-on-approval contract if the seller allows the buyer to take possession of the goods before deciding whether to complete the contract by making the purchase. Title and risk of loss remain with the seller until the buyer notifies the seller about the approval of the contract.

A sale-or-return contract occurs when the seller and buyer agree that the buyer may return the goods at a later time. Such contracts usually occur when the buyer is buying inventory to resell. For example, suppose the seller is a dress wholesaler and the buyer is a retailer who is purchasing the dresses to sell in her store. In their sale-or-return agreement, the insurable interest is created in the buyer once the goods are identified in the contract. Title and risk of loss depend on whether the goods are in bailment, delivered by common carrier, or delivered by the seller himself. Without an agreement to the contrary, if the buyer subsequently returns the dresses, she does so at her own expense and risk.

The general international law regarding foreign merchant ships in internal waters has never been codified. Despite the codification efforts made by the League of Nations and the Geneva Convention on the Territorial Sea and the Contiguous Zone of 1958, the question of territorial waters was solved during the Third United Nations Conference on the Law of the Sea (UNCLOS). In addition, the right of innocent passage of foreign ships has been regulated under the 1982 convention in greater detail than ever before. Still, potential conflicts between coastal states and foreign merchant ships in internal waters and the territorial sea may well arise. The United States assisted with the development of the UNCLOS concepts but has refused to ratify the agreement despite the fact that a vast majority of the world's nations have ratified it. The United States is joined by Israel, Eritrea, Peru, Syria, Turkey, and Venezuela in not signing the treaty. For more information, see www.un.org/Depts/los/convention_agreements/convention_historical_perspective.htm.

? BUT WHAT IF . . .

WHAT IF THE FACTS OF THE CASE OPENER WERE DIFFERENT?

Recall that, in the Case Opener, Silitek had Burlington deliver its products to the buyer. But what if Reveal Computer Products had come to Silitek's warehouse to pick up the goods and transport them to its own store? What kind of sales contract would this constitute?

Risk of Loss during a Breach of Contract

WHEN THE SELLER IS IN BREACH

The failure to deliver goods is the most common way a sales contract is breached. If the seller does not provide the goods that were described in the contract, the buyer may either (1) accept the nonconforming goods as is or (2) reject the goods subject to the seller's curing the deficiency in the goods. The buyer may reject the goods if no cure is possible or the seller fails to cure the deficiency within a reasonable time. In all these instances, the risk of loss remains with the seller until either the buyer accepts the goods or the seller cures the deficiency and provides the buyer with conforming goods.

If a cure is not possible or if the seller has failed to cure the deficiency within a reasonable time, the buyer has the option to revoke the contract. (The remedies will be discussed in subsequent chapters.) However, the UCC creates a disincentive for buyers who do so: If the risk of loss would have transferred to the buyer had there not been a breach, the risk transfers to the buyer to the extent of any insurance the buyer has. The loss reverts to the breaching seller only to the extent that the buyer's insurance does not cover it.

WHEN THE BUYER IS IN BREACH

Most buyer breaches occur when a buyer refuses to accept conforming goods from the seller and then the goods are subsequently lost or damaged. With an origin or shipment contract, the risk would have already transferred to the breaching buyer. However, if the contract is a destination contract, the risk remains with the seller. In order to encourage sellers to create origin contracts, the UCC requires that the risk of loss remain with the seller to the extent of the seller's insurance. If the seller does not have insurance or the loss exceeds the seller's insurance, the remainder transfers to the breaching buyer.

BUT WHAT IF . . .

WHAT IF THE FACTS OF THE CASE OPENER WERE DIFFERENT?

Let's say that, in the Case Opener, Reveal Computer Products had formed a sales contract with Silitek stating that Reveal would send its own truck to Silitek's warehouse to pick up the keyboards it had paid for. On the way back from picking up the keyboards, Reveal's truck was in an accident and the keyboards were destroyed. Reveal attempted to sue Silitek, stating that the risk remained with Silitek since Reveal had not received the products in its inventory yet. Is Reveal correct in this case?

CASE OPENER WRAP-UP

Keyboards Gone Astray

In the opening case, Lite-On Peripherals was suing Burlington Air Express for misdelivery of goods under a sales contract. The three questions posed were:

1. What kind of sales contract is the one between Silitek and Burlington Air Express, and what obligations does it create between the parties?
2. What do shipping terms such as "FOB Taiwan" mean?
3. When does title pass for the computer keyboards, and what effect, if any, does that have on the transaction?

Since the fact pattern was that the seller had engaged a common carrier to deliver goods to a buyer, the contract is a shipment contract. Moreover, since the contract terms had FOB Taiwan and the seller was in Taiwan, this is an origin contract, meaning that the title and risk of loss to the goods had transferred to the buyer when the carrier, Burlington Air Express, took possession of the goods for delivery. Burlington then argued that the seller, having neither title nor risk of loss, had no standing to sue Burlington. However, the irony is that although Burlington raised defenses related to the UCC, the court ultimately found that the controlling issue was not a UCC issue but a simple breach of contract. Burlington failed to perform the duties required under the contract, that is, to not deliver the goods until the buyer presented and turned over to Burlington the receipt. Burlington breached the express terms of its delivery obligation and thus is liable for the misdelivery.

KEY TERMS

common-carrier delivery
     contract   502
conditional sales
     contracts   505

entrustment   498
good title   494
goods in bailment   504
sale   494

sale-on-approval
     contract   505
sale-or-return contract   505
simple delivery contract   500

tender of delivery   500
void title   494
voidable title   494

SUMMARY OF KEY TOPICS

The Concept of Title	There are three kinds of title: good title, void title, and voidable title.

- *Good title* is title that is acquired from someone who already owns the goods free and clear.
- *Void title* is not true title. Someone who purchases stolen goods has void title.
- *Voidable title* occurs in certain situations in which the contract between the original parties would be void but the goods have already been sold to a third party.

Acquiring Good Title	Article 2 of the Uniform Commercial Code covers issues related to acquiring good title.

- The most obvious way to attain *good title* is to acquire it from someone who has good title.
- Someone who has come into possession of stolen goods never has title and can pass only *void title.*
- A buyer gets *voidable title* if he or she has deceived the seller regarding his or her true identity, written a bad check for the goods, committed criminal fraud in securing the goods, or is a minor, or if the buyer and seller agreed that title would not pass until some later time.

Third-party purchasers generally get good title. If an owner *entrusts* the possession of goods to a merchant who deals in goods of that kind, the merchant can transfer all rights in the goods to a buyer in the ordinary course of business.

The UCC provides recourse for situations in which good title may not be enough for an equitable result. The UCC responds to issues related to the following:

- *Ownership* refers to transfer of title.
- *Encumbrance* refers to when goods may be used as collateral for a debt.
- *Loss* refers to who has the risk of loss, which matters when someone is seeking indemnification for damaged goods.
- *Insurable interest* refers to the right to insure goods against any risk exposure.

Types of Sales Contracts	A *simple delivery contract* is formed when the buyer and seller execute an agreement and the buyer leaves with the goods. *Title* transfers to the buyer when the contract is executed. *Risk of loss* transfers to the buyer when the buyer takes possession. *Insurable interest* is created in the buyer at the same time title passes.

A *common-carrier delivery contract* exists when a buyer and seller execute a contract and the seller subsequently places the goods with a common carrier. There are two types of common-carrier delivery contracts: origin, or shipment, contracts and destination contracts.

- In *shipment contracts,* title transfers to the buyer at the time and place of shipment. The buyer bears the risk of loss while the goods are in transit.
- In *destination contracts,* the seller bears the risk of loss until the seller delivers the goods to the destination stipulated in the sales contract.

A *goods-in-bailment contract* is one that identifies goods that are in some kind of storage. Rules regarding passage of title, risk of loss, and insurable interest vary depending on whether the seller has a negotiable document of title, a nonnegotiable document of title, or a contract showing ownership that is neither a negotiable nor nonnegotiable document of title.

A *conditional sales contract* is either a sale-on-approval or sale-or-return contract.

- In a *sale-on-approval contract,* title and risk of loss remain with the seller until the buyer notifies the seller about the approval of the contract.
- In a *sale-or-return contract,* the insurable interest is created in the buyer once the goods are identified in the contract. Title and risk of loss depend on whether the goods are in bailment, delivered by common carrier, or delivered by the seller.

Kahr v. Markland
187 Ill. App. 3d 603, 543 N.E.2d 579

Entrustment is recognized in UCC 2-403(3). In this case, Toby Kahr gave Goodwill a bag of clothes; however, the bag also included valuable sterling silver. The court held that there had been no entrustment because Kahr intended to donate the clothes but not the silver. Its reasoning is as follows.

An entrustment requires four essential elements: (1) an actual entrustment of the goods by the delivery of possession of those goods to a merchant; (2) the party receiving the goods must be a merchant who deals in goods of that kind; (3) the merchant must sell the entrusted goods; and (4) the sale must be to a buyer in the ordinary course of business. (*Dan Pilson Auto Center, Inc. v. DeMarco* (1987), 156 Ill. App. 3d 617, 621, 509 N.E.2d 159, 162.) The court found in the Kahr case that there was no intent to transfer the sterling silver because the plaintiffs were unaware of its place in the bag of clothes.

However, the problem in the Kahr case is that Toby Kahr intended to transfer title of the bag of clothes. Usually in entrustment cases, the owner does not intend to give up title but merely possession to the initial recipient.

In light of these two cases, consider the Point / Counterpoint below.

When the seller is in breach by failing to deliver goods, the buyer may either accept the nonconforming goods as is or reject the goods subject to the seller's curing the deficiencies in the goods. Risk of loss remains with the seller until the buyer accepts the goods or the deficiencies are corrected.

Risk of Loss during a Breach of Contract

When the buyer is in breach because he or she has refused to accept conforming goods and then the goods are subsequently lost or damaged, who bears the risk of loss depends on the type of contract that exists between the buyer and the seller.

POINT / COUNTERPOINT

If a merchant (bailee) is holding goods for someone for repair or storage and sells those goods to a good-faith purchaser, that good-faith purchaser gets good title and the previous owner may recover the loss only from the bailee by suing in the tort of conversion.

Is It Right That a Bailee Who Has Only Possession, Not Title, Can Pass a Good Title to a Purchaser?	
YES	**NO**
The primary purpose of the Uniform Commercial Code, in addition to attempting to "uniformize" manners and methods of commercial processes, is to facilitate and enable commercial activity.	The entrustment rule is an example of the Uniform Commercial Code's taking a principle to an illogical and inequitable conclusion.
To put it succinctly, purchasers should not have to look over their shoulders, so to speak, regarding every transaction for fear that the title may not be valid. The facilitation of commercial activity requires that a good-faith purchaser can rely on the sale to validate his or her title to the goods.	There is no question that the focus of the Uniform Commercial Code is the facilitation of commerce, and the example of the buyer in the ordinary course of business that the opposing view makes is valid except that it is misplaced. A merchant who has a voidable title can pass on a good title; a merchant who has a good title can obviously pass on a good title. But a merchant who has a void or bad title or no title at all cannot pass on a good title. This is a fundamental premise regarding the ability to pass title.
We see such a perspective in other areas of the Uniform Commercial Code. As we see in Article 9, on secured transactions, if a buyer in the ordinary course of business purchases an item that is encumbered, the purchaser gets title over the creditor.	

This philosophy puts the greater goal of the Uniform Commercial Code ahead of any individualized inconvenience of losing title to goods in entrustment. The focus of the code is the facilitation of commerce, and, as such, parties who put goods into entrustment must exercise due care in choosing a bailee.

The entrustment rule is the exception to this title rule, and it is misplaced. First, common sense tells us that this situation occurs so infrequently as to negate the need for a special rule. Second, when it does occur, often the goods may be unique and are not replaceable. Thus, the inequity in denying possession to the true owner of unique goods truly outweighs the need to facilitate commercial activity.

QUESTIONS & PROBLEMS

1. Should entrustment apply when the entrustee is not a merchant? [See *Porter v. Wertz*, 53 N.Y.2d 696, 698 (1981), which notes that the UCC entrustment provision is "designed to enhance the reliability of commercial sales by merchants . . . while shifting the risk of loss through fraudulent transfer to the owner of the goods, who can select the merchant to whom he entrusts the property. It protects only those who purchase from the merchant to whom the property was entrusted in the ordinary course of the merchant's business."]

2. Mitchell Coach Manufacturing Company, Inc., produces motor homes and sells them to other retail dealers and directly to customers. Ronny Stephens was a customer. WW, Inc., bought and sold motor homes from Mitchell. Under their agreement, WW would pay Mitchell either a down payment on a motor home before the motor home was purchased or the entire amount due for the completed product. Under the agreement, the title of the motor home remained with WW until Stephens paid in full. WW paid Mitchell a down payment of $10,000 for the construction of the motor home. Upon completion, the motor home was to be picked up by Stephens at Mitchell. WW paid the remaining balance to Mitchell, but the check was returned for lack of sufficient funds. Stephens, through a loan, had paid for the motor home in full, but WW had not paid Mitchell. Both Mitchell and Stephens claim title to the motor home. Whom does title belong to? [*Mitchell Coach Manufacturing Company, Inc. v. Ronny Stephens,* 19 F. Supp. 2d 1277 (1998).]

3. Sture Graffman entered into a contract with Miguel Espel whereby Espel and his company (MTS) became the exclusive agent for the promotion and sale of Graffman's Picasso painting. Espel asked his brother-in-law, Michael Delecea, to help in the sale of the painting. The painting was sent to Delecea in New York, and Delecea contacted the Avanti Gallery. The gallery owners found a buyer for the painting, and the painting was sold for $875,000. Delecea sent Espel $550,000 and used $200,000 of the proceeds to pay off Espel's debts. Graffman never received any of the money. Subsequently, Graffman brought an action seeking the recovery of the painting or sufficient compensatory damages. Is the entrustment rule applicable? Was the buyer's title to the painting void? How do you think the court handled the dispute? [*Graffman v. Espel,* 96 Civ. 8247 (1998).]

4. Marilyn Thomas purchased an installed pool heater from Sunkissed. The pool heater was delivered to Marilyn's residence, but the delivery slip was signed by Nancy Thomas. Marilyn did not know of anyone by that name. She called Sunkissed to advise them to move the heater. The neighborhood was not safe, and she was worried that the heater would be taken. The heater remained in her driveway for approximately four days. When Marilyn noticed that the heater was no longer in her driveway, she again contacted Sunkissed, but she was told "not to worry." Who was responsible for the loss of the heater? Did Sunkissed actually "deliver" the heater to Marilyn? How do you think the court decided? [*In re Marilyn Thomas,* 182 B.R. 347 (1995).]

5. In 1987 R.H. Love Gallery owned the title to a painting entitled *Marlton's Cove.* The gallery sold 50 percent of the painting to Altman Fine Arts, a New York art dealer, and 50 percent to Andre Lopoukhine, a Boston art dealer. In 1989, plaintiff Morgold, Inc., purchased Altman's 50 percent of

the painting. Morgold and Lopoukhine decided to try to sell the painting. In 1990, Lopoukhine sold the painting to Mark Grossman. Lopoukhine did not pay Morgold the 50 percent due for the sale of the painting. Morgold argued that this lack of payment indicated that the title was never officially passed on to Grossman. Through an art dealer, Grossman sold the painting to Fred Keeler. In 1991, Morgold contacted Keeler and claimed to be the sole owner of the painting. Who do you believe owns title to the painting? [*Morgold, Inc. v. Keeler,* 891 F. Supp. 1361 (1995).]

6. MAN Roland agreed to sell Quantum Color Corporation a used press for $405,000. According to the contract, Quantum was supposed to pay $5,000 at the time of the contract, $265,000 at delivery, and the balance of $135,000 before the press was actually used. The first two payments were made, but MAN Roland did not receive the $135,000. MAN Roland alleged that Quantum had been using the press and, therefore, that Quantum was required to pay the balance. Quantum argued that MAN Roland breached the contract by delivering nonconforming goods. Part of the contract indicated that MAN Roland would provide standard equipment and installation, but MAN Roland did not install the equipment or provide Quantum with the standard equipment. How do you think the court settled this case? [*MAN Roland Inc. v. Color Corp.,* 57 F. Supp. 2d 576 (1999).]

7. William and Donna Hardy purchased a motor home in July 1993 for $38,989. The day after purchasing the motor home, the Hardys commenced a cross-country trip. The Hardys had noticed a small crack on the windshield, but the sellers of the motor home promised to fix the problem when the Hardys returned. Once on the road, the Hardys noticed a loud, clanking noise. They stopped at a dealership and were informed that the drive shaft needed to be replaced. The dealer told the Hardys that this replacement could be done after they completed the trip. The Hardys continued their trip but soon noticed a burning smell. They went to another dealership, and the mechanic worked on the drive shaft. The burning smell was no longer present, but the motor home continued to make loud noises. When the Hardys finally reached California, they took the Winnebago to a third dealer. The mechanic declined to perform any repairs on the motor home.

The Hardys called the Winnebago hotline to see whether it was safe to continue driving the motor home. They were told that it was safe to drive the vehicle home. The Hardys returned home after putting 7,500 miles on the motor home. Hardy took the motor home to the original dealer, but he was told that it would take a few months to make the necessary repairs. Hardy demanded a refund from Winnebago. Did Hardy demonstrate revocation of acceptance? How do you think the court decided? [*Hardy v. Winnebago Industries, Inc.,* 706 A.2d 1086 (1998).]

8. Amar entered into a sales contract with the defendant, Karinol, for the purchase of electronic watches. The contract was silent as to shipping terms. However, the contract did have a notation in it stating that the goods were to be delivered to a location in Mexico. Moreover, seller Karinol put the goods into the possession of a common carrier with the instructions to deliver the goods to the plaintiff-buyer in Mexico. When the goods arrived and were opened for customs, the watches were missing. Between the buyer and the seller, who has the risk of loss? In light of these facts, is this a destination or a shipment contract? [*Pestana v. Karinol,* 367 So. 2d 1096 (1979).]

9. SMG was a frozen-poultry wholesaler, and Sanderson was one of the suppliers. SMG contracted to sell 24 containers of frozen poultry to KVADRO, a Russian company. The shipping terms were CIF (cost insurance and freight). In connection with the business, SMG acquired a one-year, open-cargo insurance policy from Lloyd's. SMG arranged for shipment to Russia though P & O Nedlloyd. In April, the Russian government suspended all previously issued permits for the import of poultry into Russia from the United States. Due to this and the change of the city to which the poultry was to be shipped, the shipment violated the 60-day rule and was subsequently seized. After the investigation ended, the shipment was released, but before it was picked up, it was seized again and SMG never received payment. SMG then filed a claim against the insurance policy with Lloyd's, which was rejected. Nedlloyd and SMG then sued each other, seeking freight charges and damages, respectively. Nedlloyd subsequently added Lloyd's to its suit, claiming to be a third-party beneficiary. Lloyd's moved for summary judgment because

Nedlloyd was not an intended third party, SMG had no insurable interest at the time, Lloyd's policy did not cover credit risk, and seizure by customs was excluded from the contract. A summary judgment was issued by the district court, claiming SMG had no insurable interest and Nedlloyd was not an intended beneficiary. The ruling was appealed by SMG. Does SMG have an insurable interest? [*Nedlloyd v. Sanderson Farms, Inc.,* 2006 U.S. App. LEXIS 22227 (2006).]

10. Marion Bottling Company bottled soft-drink beverages in Marion, Virginia, and shipped them to its warehouse in Galax for storage. The beverages were subsequently delivered from the warehouse to retailers on delivery trucks owned and operated by the bottler. Are the goods identified to the sales contract when the soft drinks are bottled in Marion or delivered from the warehouse in Galax? Which city can tax the sale? [*Marion Bottling Co. v. Town of Galax,* 195 Va. 1115, 81 S.E.2d 624 (1954).]

Looking for more review materials?

The Online Learning Center at **www.mhhe.com/kubasek3e** contains this chapter's "Assignment on the Internet" and also a list of URLs for more information, entitled "On the Internet." Find both of them in the Student Center portion of the OLC, along with quizzes and other helpful materials.

Performance and Obligations under Sales and Leases

LEARNING OBJECTIVES

After reading this chapter, you will be able to answer the following questions:

1 What is the perfect tender rule?

2 What is the difference between conforming and nonconforming goods?

3 What is the right to cure?

4 What is a revocation of the contract as compared to rejection of nonconforming goods?

5 What is commercial impracticability?

CASE OPENER

What a Difference a Day Makes!

Founded in 1966 as a trader of oil and oil products, Vitol is a company with no external shareholders. All shareholders are also employees. It is a conglomerate company of energy companies that work in oil transportation, energy market intelligence, refining, distribution, and trading and financing.[1] It is unencumbered by external shareholders and the need to answer to analysts and investment funds. Instead, Vitol is a group of separate companies, each staffed by energy professionals with a true depth of experience in the business of oil transportation, market intelligence, refining, distribution, marketing, trading, and finance.

Vitol entered into a contract on January 13, 2000, for the delivery of oil with the defendant, Koch Petroleum Group, a component of Koch Industries, Inc., a Wichita, Kansas, private company with over $100 billion in worldwide revenues and over 70,000 employees. The sales contract required that Koch deliver 75,000 barrels of heating oil to a barge designated by Vitol within a window of time between February 3 and 5, 2000.[2] Later that January, Vitol sold the oil to a third party, Castle Oil Corporation. Castle Oil and Vitol agreed that the oil would be delivered to Castle Oil's barge on February 3, and they communicated that fact to Koch. Koch agreed. Koch was unable to deliver the oil on February 3 despite being told by Vitol that time was of the essence regarding that date for Castle Oil. Koch did deliver the oil on February 4, but that one-day difference caused

---

[1] See Vitol's web page at www.vitol.com/about.php.

[2] *Vitol S.A., Inc. v. Koch Petroleum Group, LP,* 2005 U.S. Dist. LEXIS 18688, 58 U.C.C. Rep. Serv. 2d (Callaghan) 2005.

Castle Oil to cancel its contract with Vitol. Castle sued Vitol for breach, and was awarded a $1.7 million arbitration judgment. Vitol then sued Koch for recovery of the $1.7 million it had to pay Castle.

The issue here is that of perfect tender. Koch claimed that it substantially complied with the contract as delivery of the oil was to be during the February 3 to 5 time window. Vitol argued that the contract was modified with Koch's acceptance to delivery specifically on February 3.

1. Did Koch's failure to deliver the oil on February 3 constitute something less than "perfect tender" and thus a breach of contract?
2. Did that one-day difference in delivery constitute a breach of the perfect tender rule?

The Wrap-Up at the end of the chapter will answer these questions.

When individuals and/or organizations like Koch Petroleum Group and Vitol enter into sales contracts or leases with others, they need to know their rights and obligations. This chapter explains the performance obligations of sellers and buyers. Additionally, it explains the performance obligations of lessors and lessees, which are similar to those of buyers and sellers. The chapter explains the perfect tender rule and exceptions to this rule. It also explains the buyer's general obligation to inspect, pay for, and accept goods, and it discusses exceptions to this general obligation.

The Basic Performance Obligation

The obligations of sellers/lessors and buyers/lessees are determined by (1) terms the parties outline in agreements, (2) custom, and (3) rules outlined by the Uniform Commercial Code (UCC). This chapter focuses on rules outlined by the UCC.

Under the UCC, sellers and lessors are *obligated to transfer and deliver conforming goods.* Buyers and lessees are *obligated to accept and pay for conforming goods in accordance with the contract.* Courts rely on UCC rules to clarify these obligations when the contract or lease the parties agreed to is unclear. In the Case Opener, Koch is obligated to deliver oil to a barge designated by Vitol. The window for such delivery is February 3 to 5, 2000. Vitol claims that it has the right to indicate within that time frame the exact date of delivery. It notifies Koch that delivery must be made on February 3. Koch does not make the delivery until February 4. Has Koch breached the contract under the perfect tender rule? Is there perhaps some kind of mistake or misunderstanding between Vitol and Koch? If so, is that material to determining breach of contract? Did Koch act in good faith? If so, does that mitigate the delay of one day? Consider the nearby Case Nugget as you think about these issues.

GOOD FAITH

UCC Section 1-203 requires good faith in the performance and enforcement of every contract. Good faith means *honesty in fact.* When the parties are merchants, the UCC imposes a higher standard. Between merchants, the UCC imposes not only honesty in fact but also reasonable commercial standards of fair dealing. This second requirement is often called commercial reasonableness. In the context of good faith, courts decide the specific

Donovan v. RRL Corporation
26 Cal. 4th 261 (2001)

The Donovans showed up at the defendant car dealership. After hearing the sales pitch, Mr. Donovan stated that he'd take the car at the price quoted in the newspaper, $25,995. The horrified salesman said that he could go as low as $37,995 but not $25,995. At that point, Donovan showed the salesman a copy of an ad that had been running in the local newspaper identifying the very same automobile for $25,995. The salesman responded that the advertisement had to be a mistake. Donovan said that he wanted the car at the $25,995 price. He subsequently brought an action in the municipal

court in Orange County. The trial court found for RRL Corp. on mistake. However, the California court of appeals reversed, stating that all the material elements of a contract were clearly stated in the advertisement and that Donovan's acceptance of those terms constituted a good contract.

The California Supreme Court heard the case, reversing it on a combination of mistake and unconscionability. The supreme court found that a contract was indeed created but that the contract could be rescinded since the evidence showed (1) the defendant's unilateral mistake was made in good faith; (2) the defendant did not bear the risk of the mistake; and (3) the enforcement of a contract with an erroneous price would be unconscionable as a matter of law.

---

obligations of sellers/lessors and buyers/lessees. The next few sections of the chapter discuss these specific obligations.

Specific Obligations of Sellers and Lessors

THE PERFECT TENDER RULE

The UCC requires that sellers and lessors tender conforming goods to the buyer or lessee. UCC Sections 2-503(1) and 2A-508(1) state that tender of delivery requires that the seller/lessor have and hold conforming goods at the disposal of the buyer/lessee and give the buyer/lessee reasonable notification to enable him or her to take delivery. Conforming goods are goods that conform to contract specifications.

> **L01**
> What is the perfect tender rule?

A common law rule known as the perfect tender rule required that the seller deliver goods in conformity with the terms of the contract, right down to the last detail. UCC Sections 2-601 and 2A-509 embrace the perfect tender rule. These sections indicate that if goods or tender of delivery fail *in any respect* to conform to the contract, the buyer/lessee has the right to accept the goods, reject the entire shipment, or accept part and reject part. Common law usually substitutes perfect tender with the doctrine of substantial performance. *Substantial performance* occurs when all the material elements of a contract are satisfied even if some nonmaterial requirements may not be satisfied. The perfect tender rule would not recognize the distinction between material and immaterial contractual requirements.

> **L02**
> What is the difference between conforming and nonconforming goods?

Legal Principle: **The UCC and common law differ, with the UCC requiring perfect tender and common law requiring the lesser standard of substantial performance.**

> To see how the concept of customized purchases is especially significant in Internet marketing, please see the **Connecting to the Core** activity on the text website at www.mhhe.com/ kubasek3e.

BUT WHAT IF . . .

WHAT IF THE FACTS OF THE CASE OPENER WERE DIFFERENT?

Let's say, in the Case Opener, that Vitol made a delivery of barrels of oil to Castle and the time and place of the delivery were exactly as stated in the contract. However, the proper packaging that Castle stipulated was not used, even though no barrels were broken. What would the perfect tender rule say about the legality of this situation?

Consider Case 23-1, which provides an illustration of a situation in which the UCC version of the perfect tender rule was relevant when compared to the common law rule of material breach under the doctrine of substantial performance.

EXCEPTIONS TO THE PERFECT TENDER RULE

The perfect tender rule is not as inflexible as it appears. Although the rule itself demands perfection, both courts and UCC drafters have created exceptions that reduce the rule's rigidity. These exceptions limit the seller's obligation to deliver conforming goods and/or limit the buyer's power to reject goods that do not conform. This section of the chapter

---

CASE 23-1   ALASKA PACIFIC TRADING CO. v. EAGON FOREST PRODUCTS INC.
WASHINGTON APPELLATE DIVISION 1
933 P.2D 417 (1997)

Alaska Pacific Trading Company (ALPAC) and Eagon Forest Products, Inc. (Eagon), contracted to buy and sell raw logs. ALPAC and Eagon engaged in months of communications about a shipment of 15,000 cubic meters of logs from Argentina to Korea between the end of July and the end of August 1993. The delivery date passed without ALPAC shipping the logs. Eagon canceled the contract, alleging that ALPAC had breached the agreement by failing to deliver. ALPAC alleged that its failure to deliver was not a material breach and that the parties had modified the delivery date. Alternatively, ALPAC argued that Eagon breached the contract by failing to provide adequate assurances or repudiating the contract. The miscommunication between the parties occurred after the market for logs began to soften, making the contract less attractive to Eagon. ALPAC was reluctant to ship the goods because it was concerned that Eagon might not accept the shipment. However, Eagon never stated that it would not accept the cargo.

In the ruling below, the judge decides whether ALPAC breached the contract. ALPAC wants the court to rely on the common law doctrine of material breach under the doctrine of substantial performance, while Eagon wants the court to rely on the UCC's perfect tender rule. If the court decides to apply UCC rules, and if ALPAC failed to deliver, Eagon would be allowed to "reject the whole."

JUDGE AGID: ALPAC's first contention is that it did not breach the contract by failing to timely deliver the logs because time of delivery was not a material term of the contract. ALPAC relies on common law contract cases to support its position that, when the parties have not indicated that time is of the essence, late delivery is not a material breach which excuses the buyer's duty to accept the goods. . . . However, as a contract for the sale of goods, this contract is governed by the Uniform Commercial Code, Article II (UCC II) which replaced the common law of material breach, on which ALPAC relies, with the "perfect tender" rule. Under this rule, "If the goods or the tender of delivery fail in any respect to conform to the contract, the buyer may . . . reject the whole." . . . Both the plain language of the rule and the official comments clearly state that, if the tender of the goods differs from the terms of the contract in any way, the seller breaches the contract and the buyer is released from its duty to accept the goods. . . . ALPAC does not dispute that the contract specified a date for shipment or that the logs were not shipped by that date. Thus, under the perfect tender rule, ALPAC breached its duty under the contract and released Eagon from its duty to accept the logs.

AFFIRMED.

CRITICAL THINKING

Here, Eagon got lucky. The company got out of a contract that was unfavorable to it, given the softening market for logs. In what way did Judge Agid simplify the case? Is it fair to say the judge oversimplified the case?

ETHICAL DECISION MAKING

What ethical norm or value underlies Judge Agid's decision? Explain.

explains the six most important exceptions to the perfect tender rule. These exceptions allow sellers/lessors and buyers/lessees to ask questions such as:

- What are the norms in the particular industry and/or what past dealings have the parties had with one another?
- What does the parties' agreement say?
- Is it possible for the seller/lessor to cure or correct the problems?
- What if the goods have been destroyed?
- What if nonconformity substantially impairs the value of the goods?
- What if unforeseen circumstances make contract performance commercially impracticable?

Consider the flowchart in Exhibit 23-1 on the next page.

Norms in the Industry and Past Dealings between the Parties.   The perfect tender rule will always be interpreted both in light of what is expected in the industry and within the context of past dealings between the parties. When the buyer alleges that goods failed to conform to contract specifications, the buyer does not automatically have the right to reject the goods. The UCC requires that courts consider norms in a particular trade. Sometimes, the norms for a particular trade do not permit a buyer to reject goods with minor flaws. UCC Section 1-205(2) defines usage of trade as any practice that members of an industry expect to be part of their dealings.

In addition to its requirement on usage of trade, the UCC requires that courts consider the ideas of course of dealing and course of performance. UCC 1-205(1) defines course of dealing as previous commercial transactions between the same parties. Under UCC 208(1), course of performance refers to the history of dealings between the parties in the particular contract at issue. This rule states that when a contract for sale involves repeated occasions for performance by either party with the other's knowledge of the nature of the performance and opportunity for objection to it, any course of performance accepted or acquiesced to without objection is relevant to determine what the parties' agreement means.

BUT WHAT IF . . .
WHAT IF THE FACTS OF THE CASE OPENER WERE DIFFERENT?

Let's say, in the Case Opener, that Castle Oil and Vitol had a long history of working together to deliver oil to various Castle locations. During these interactions Vitol had a history of using Koch to deliver the oil, and Koch was typically a day or two late delivering the oil but Castle never minded. In what way would the perfect tender rule be affected in light of this information?

Exceptions Outlined in the Parties' Agreement.   Sometimes, language in the parties' agreement limits the rigidity of the perfect tender rule. For instance, parties may agree that the seller must have the opportunity to repair or replace nonconforming goods within a particular period of time. Alternatively, parties may agree with a level of performance that is less than perfect. They could indicate, by agreement, the expectation regarding performance.

The Seller's/Lessor's Right to Cure.   Under UCC Sections 2-508 and 2A-513, sellers and lessors have the right to cure or fix problems with nonconforming goods.

L03

What is the right to cure?

E-COMMERCE AND THE LAW

UCITA

The Uniform Computer Information Transactions Act (UCITA) is a proposed model law under review in several states. UCITA outlines a framework to govern software licenses. Software vendors such as Microsoft are generally in favor of UCITA because this model legislation protects software vendors.

One important way in which UCITA protects software vendors is that it makes sure perfect tender rules that generally apply to the sale of goods do not apply to software. UCITA's rules change when and why a consumer of software can reject a defective product. For example, if a software transaction involves a negotiated contract, UCITA eliminates customers' rights to inspect a product on delivery and reject it for any defects that do not conform to the requirements of the contract. Instead, a buyer of software must prove that the defect represents a material breach of the contract.

Source: Ed Foster, "The Gripe Line," *Info World,* July 3, 2000; and Jeff Moad, "If It Works for Microsoft, Does It Work for You?" *Eweek* (from ZD Wire), May 18, 2001.

In particular, sellers and lessors can repair, adjust, or replace defective or nonconforming goods as long as they give prompt notice of the intent to cure and go ahead and cure within the contract time for performance.

Under UCC 2-508(2) and 2A-513(2), the seller or lessor can still exercise the right to cure once the contract time for performance has passed as long as the seller or lessor has reasonable grounds to believe that the nonconforming tender would be acceptable to the buyer or lessee. In Case 23-2, the court decides whether a seller should have been allowed the right to cure and what consequence the court should impose if a buyer fails to give the seller this opportunity.

Legal Principle: **The right to cure is nearly always applicable to nonconforming goods.**

Destroyed Goods. Under UCC Sections 2-613 and 2A-221, if goods are identified at the time the parties entered into a contract and these goods are destroyed through no fault of the parties before risk passes to the buyer or lessee, the parties are excused from performance. If the goods are only partially destroyed, the buyer can inspect the goods and decide whether to (1) treat the contract as void or (2) ask the seller for a reduction of the contract price and then accept the damaged goods.

Exhibit 23-1

When Lack of Perfect Tender Is Not Fatal to the Contract

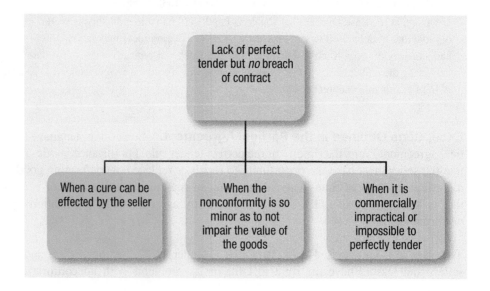

518

CASE 23-2 DEJESUS v. CAT AUTO TECH. CORP.
NEW YORK CITY CIVIL COURT
615 N.Y.S.2D 236 N.Y. CITY CIV. CT. (1994)

Cat Auto Tech. Corp. purchased 10,000 gift certificates from DeJesus. Cat Auto Tech. Corp., an Amoco gasoline station operator, contracted with DeJesus to make 10,000 gift certificates of various denominations, with the Amoco gasoline name and logo on them, stapled together in booklets that included approximately eight gift certificates in each. Delivery was to be within two weeks. Montefiore Hospital had wanted to give these gift certificates to their employees as a Christmas gift.

Michael DiBarro, president of Cat Auto Tech. Corp., stated that the finished product differed from the sample DeJesus had provided in two respects: the paper was different, and the sample contained a decorative border, whereas the finished product did not. Additionally, DiBarro complained that the logo colors were not within the printed borders of the Amoco logo. When the court looked at the certificates, it noted that within a book of gift certificates, two of the eight certificates had colors immediately outside the borders. On one, the problem was slightly noticeable, and on the other, the court could notice the problem only when it inspected closely. DeJesus stated that DiBarro had accepted these minor changes, and that any minor defects were insignificant.

DeJesus delivered the goods to the Cat Auto Tech. Corp. approximately two weeks after the agreed upon delivery date. DiBarro accepted the delivery and paid by check. He did not inspect the certificates at the time of delivery or before he paid. He inspected the certificates a day later, placed a stop payment order on the check without notifying DeJesus, and did not let DeJesus know why he was stopping payment on the check. DeJesus did not know of the stop payment until she eventually received a notice from her bank that she had insufficient funds in her account.

DeJesus wants Cat Auto Tech. Corp. to pay the balance due on the contract, and asks the court to clarify the seller's right to cure defects in nonconforming goods.

JUDGE LUCINDO SUAREZ: . . . UCC 2-601 provides that "if the goods . . . fail in any respect to conform to the contract, the buyer may . . . reject the whole. . . ." . . . New York subscribe[s] to the perfect tender rule, which allows a buyer to reject goods that fail to conform to the contract. UCC 2-602(1) provides the manner to accomplish an effective rejection: Rejection of goods must be within a reasonable time after their delivery or tender. It is ineffective unless the buyer seasonably notifies the seller.

An effective rejection requires the buyer to seasonably notify the seller, even though the delivery is of wholly nonconforming goods. In the case at bar delivery was made two weeks after the date called for in the contract. Defendant buyer paid for the goods by check, inspected them the next day and issued a stop payment order on the check. The time to cure a defective tender, if at all, was immediate. The buyer's notification of its rejection by a stop payment order on its draft was not seasonable, nor within a reasonable time. . . . Indeed, no reasonable attempt on the part of the buyer to notify the seller was undertaken. . . .

The purpose of notification is to afford the seller the opportunity to cure, or to permit the seller to minimize her losses, such as providing a decrease in the price. This opportunity was never afforded to the seller. The perfect tender rule is limited by the seller's ability to cure, which is conditioned upon receipt of notice. UCC 2-508 provides: (1) Where . . . tender . . . by the seller is rejected because nonconforming and the time for performance has not yet expired, the seller may seasonably notify the buyer of his intention to cure and may then, within the contract time, make a conforming delivery. (2) Where the buyer rejects a nonconforming tender which the seller had reasonable grounds to believe would be acceptable with or without the money allowance, the seller may, if he seasonably notifies the buyer, have a further reasonable time to substitute a conforming tender.

Defendant's payment for the goods without inspection on the day of delivery, approximately two weeks after the time called for by the contract, effectively waived the performance provisions of the contract regarding the time of delivery. . . . Therefore, the time within which to perform having expired, subdivision (2) must be referenced. However, subdivision (2) by implication is only applicable if there has been an effective rejection, which is not the case herein.

Defendant's payment by check for the goods upon their delivery provided the plaintiff with a measure of reliance that the same would be acceptable. Defendant's failure to properly notify plaintiff of the nonconformity effectively prevented plaintiff from an opportunity to cure any defects, within the time limitations of this case, and therefore defendant's actions cannot be considered to have effectively rejected the goods herein.

Judgment is awarded in favor of plaintiff in the amount of $1,252.00, representing the balance due and owing under the contract with interest from December 7, 1993.

Judgment for plaintiff.

CRITICAL THINKING

In Chapter 1, you learned of the importance of a particular set of facts in determining the outcome of a case. If you could change one fact in this case to make it more likely the judge would rule in favor of Cat Auto Tech. Corp., which fact would you change? Explain.

ETHICAL DECISION MAKING

Apply the universalization test to the outcome of this case. Does the universalization test support Justice Suarez's decision?

BUT WHAT IF . . .

WHAT IF THE FACTS OF THE CASE OPENER WERE DIFFERENT?

Let's say, in the Case Opener, that Castle Oil was to inspect barrels of oil that were to be shipped to one of Castle's locations by Vitol. A representative inspected the oil purchased by Castle, which was being kept in a warehouse. The morning that the oil was to be shipped to Castle, the warehouse caught fire and the oil that had been purchased was destroyed. Is Vitol still obligated to deliver the same amount of oil to Castle's designated location that day?

L04

What is a revocation of the contract as compared to rejection of nonconforming goods?

Substantial Impairment. Two sections of the UCC use the concept of substantial impairment to modify the perfect tender rule. The first applies when a buyer *revokes acceptance of goods.* UCC Section 2-608 indicates that the buyer who has accepted goods may later revoke the acceptance only if the buyer can show that the defects substantially impair the value of the goods. The second applies when the buyer and seller have entered into an *installment contract.* UCC Sections 2-612(2) and 2A-510(1) indicate that if a buyer/lessee rejects an installment of a particular item, that buyer/lessee may do so only if the defects substantially impair the value of the goods and cannot be cured.

L05

What is commercial impracticability?

Commercial Impracticability. UCC Sections 2-615(a) and 2A-405(a) state that a delay in delivery or nondelivery, in whole or in part, is not a breach in circumstances in which performance has been made impracticable because a contingency has occurred that was not contemplated when the parties reached an agreement. For example, this rule would be relevant if a change in government regulation that neither party contemplated forbids the import or export of a particular item the parties had agreed would be shipped.

Specific Obligations of Buyers and Lessees

THE BASIC OBLIGATION: INSPECTION, PAYMENT, AND ACCEPTANCE

Under UCC Sections 2-301 and 2A-516(1), buyers and lessees are obligated to accept and pay for conforming goods in accordance with the contract. Before paying for and accepting the goods, buyers/lessees ordinarily inspect the goods to make sure they conform to the specifications in the parties' agreement.

EXCEPTIONS TO THE BASIC OBLIGATION

Buyers/lessees do not always end up accepting and paying for goods. Sometimes, on inspection, the buyer or lessee decides to reject the goods and refrain from paying for them. We have already seen that happen in cases earlier in the chapter. In this section, we

PRINCIPLES OF EUROPEAN CONTRACT LAW

For almost a century, U.S. law has been fortunate to find guidance in something known as the Restatements of the Law. The American Law Institute (ALI), created in 1923, has been publishing these "soft-law" books for nearly 100 years. The Restatements are *soft law* because they are not enacted statutorily but nonetheless influence U.S. courts, judges, and practitioners. The Restatement of Contracts has been enormously influential as soft law. "The ALI's aim is to distill the 'black letter law' from cases, to indicate a trend in common law, and, occasionally, to recommend what a rule of law should be. In essence, [the Restatements] restate existing common law into a series of principles or rules."*

In 2000, Europe began crafting its own version of the Restatement of Contracts: the Principles of European Contract Law, or PECL. The PECL aids in the current debate of whether European nations need a comprehensive statutory code beyond the CISG. The debate is ongoing, and the resolution waits to be seen.†

* See http://libguides.law.harvard.edu/content.php?pid=103327&sid=1036651.

† See Ole Lando and Hugh Beale, *Principles of European Contract Law,* Parts I and II (Commission on European Contract Law, 2000), p. xxiv; and Carlo Castronovo, "Contract and the Idea of Codification in the Principles of European Contract Law," in Ole Lando, *Festskrift,* 1997, pp. 109–124.

take a look at exceptions to the buyer's/lessee's basic obligation. These exceptions allow sellers/lessors and buyers/lessees to ask questions such as:

- What forms of payment are allowed under the UCC?
- In what circumstances can a buyer reject goods?
- Is the buyer allowed to accept part but not all of the goods?
- In what circumstances can a buyer revoke acceptance of goods?
- How and when can a buyer reject nonconforming goods?
- Are installment contracts treated differently than other kinds of contracts?

This section of the chapter answers the questions listed above in three subsections that cover (1) problems on inspection, (2) problems with acceptance, and (3) rescission or revocation of acceptance by the buyer or lessee. Note that this section asks these questions from the buyer's perspective.

Problems on Inspection. If all goes well in a transaction over the sale or lease of goods, the buyer or lessee inspects the goods and then pays by any means the parties have agreed on, including payment by cash, check, or credit card. Unless the parties have agreed otherwise, the buyer or lessee typically inspects the goods before paying. Under UCC Sections 2-513(1) and 2A-515(1), the seller or lessor must provide an opportunity for inspection before enforcing payment.

The concept of reasonableness governs the inspection process. For example, inspection must take place at a reasonable time and place, in a reasonable way. Once the buyer or lessee inspects the goods, he or she decides whether to accept the goods. Sometimes, on inspection, the buyer or lessee decides not to accept the goods. (See Exhibit 23-2 on the next page.) For instance, in Case 23-2, Cat Auto Tech. Corp. inspected the gift certificates and decided it did not want to accept the goods. When, on inspection, the buyer or lessee determines that there may be a problem with the goods, he or she wants to know what circumstances allow a buyer or lessee to reject goods. Of course, if the goods are conforming, the buyer or lessee wants to know how to communicate acceptance.

Legal Principle: **The right to inspect is seldom waived or held by courts to have been waived unless the buyer expressly waives the right.**

Problems with Acceptance. When all goes well, UCC Sections 2-606(1) and 2A-515(1b)(a) indicate that the buyer or lessee, after inspecting, signifies agreement to the seller or lessor that the goods are either (1) conforming or (2) acceptable even though they are nonconforming. UCC Sections 2-602(1), 2-606(1), and 2A-515(1)(b) allow the seller

Chicago Prime Packers v. Northam Food Trading
U.S. Court of Appeals for the Seventh Circuit
408 F.3d 894, 2005 U.S. App. LEXIS 9355

Chicago Prime Packers, the seller, sued Northam Food Trading, the buyer, for breach of contract. At the district level, Chicago Prime was awarded the contract price plus interest. Northam appealed. Neither party was arguing that any fact found by the district court was clearly erroneous, and therefore the appeal was one based on law. On April 24, 2001, Northam had the shipping company Brown Brother's Shipping pick up 40,500 pounds of ribs from Chicago Prime. Brown Brother's signed a bill of lading indicating that the goods were in apparent good order. However, the bill of lading did state that the "contents and condition of contents of packages [were] unknown." Upon delivery, Northam signed a second bill of lading, again stating that the goods were in apparent good order, except for other issues not related to the case. The contract stated that payment was to be mailed before or on May 1, 2001. When no payment was received by May 4, Chicago Prime called Northam and demanded payment. The employee who negotiated the contract for Northam was unaware of any reason why payment would not have been made. As a result of an inspection by the U.S. Department of Agriculture, the entire shipment was deemed condemned, with no salvage value. Although this was not done until May 7, 2001, it was the opinion of the federal inspector that the shipment was contaminated when it arrived. When Chicago Prime became aware of this, it continued to demand payment.

The district court had ruled that Northam had to prove not only that the shipment was contaminated at the time it arrived but also that an inspection had been done as soon as commercially reasonable. The district court further ruled that Northam had failed in its obligation to do so and therefore lost the case and was obligated to pay. The contract was governed by CISG due to its international nature. Although CISG governed this contract, CISG is based on UCC Article 2 and therefore, although Article 2 was not per se applicable, the majority opinion still used it for guidance on the case. The appeals court cited case law in saying that the CISG does give the buyer the burden of proof. While this would have been enough to rule in favor of Northam, the court went on to say that Northam had failed to prove that the goods were contaminated at the time of delivery. Therefore, the appeals court upheld the ruling, and Northam was obligated to pay the price of the contract plus prejudgment interest.

or lessor to presume acceptance if the buyer or lessee fails to reject the goods within a reasonable period of time. Sometimes, there is confusion about whether the buyer or lessee has accepted the goods.

Exhibit 23-2

How the Concept of Reasonableness Governs the Inspection Process

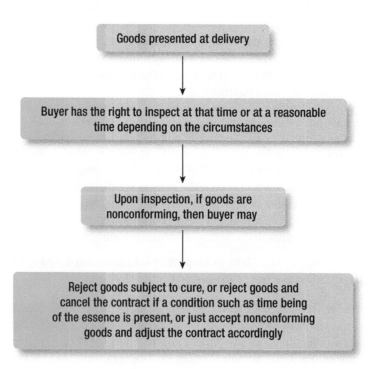

Goods presented at delivery

Buyer has the right to inspect at that time or at a reasonable time depending on the circumstances

Upon inspection, if goods are nonconforming, then buyer may

Reject goods subject to cure, or reject goods and cancel the contract if a condition such as time being of the essence is present, or just accept nonconforming goods and adjust the contract accordingly

BUT WHAT IF . . .

WHAT IF THE FACTS OF THE CASE OPENER WERE DIFFERENT?

Let's say, in the Case Opener, that Castle was trying to plan an inspection of oil it wanted to buy from Vitol. Castle was attempting to plan an inspection, but the two companies could not reach an agreement regarding a time and place for the inspection. If the two companies looked into the laws surrounding inspection, what guiding framework would they come across in regard to scheduling an inspection of goods?

UCC Sections 2-601(c) and 2A-509(1) allow the buyer or lessee to make a partial acceptance when the goods are nonconforming and the seller or lessor has failed to cure the defects. When goods are nonconforming, the buyer or lessee is allowed to revoke or withdraw acceptance of the goods. The previous section on specific obligations of sellers/ lessors discussed this concept under the topic of substantial impairment. From the buyer's/ lessee's perspective, the buyer or lessee may revoke acceptance if the nonconformity substantially impairs the value of the goods but only if he or she had a legitimate reason for the initial acceptance.

Rescission or Revocation of Acceptance by Buyer. Cases in which a buyer decides to assert his or her right to reject nonconforming goods are often categorized under the heading "rescission or revocation of acceptance by buyer." Case 23-3 is one in which a buyer with an installment contract decided to reject nonconforming goods. Rescission or revocation of acceptance by the buyer is the primary subject of the case. The case provides a good review of a wide range of topics that fall under the subject of performance and obligation. Note how the case includes the concept of good faith. This chapter started with the concept of good faith, and it will end with the same topic. It is always good to remember the context in which courts judge the extent to which a buyer or seller has met his or her contractual obligations.

CASE 23-3   HUBBARD v. UTZ QUALITY FOODS, INC.
U.S. DISTRICT COURT (W.D.N.Y.)
903 F. SUPP. 444 (1995)

In this case, a dispute arose between a potato farmer, David Hubbard (Hubbard), and UTZ Quality Foods, Inc. (UTZ), over whether UTZ was within its legal rights when it decided to rescind or revoke acceptance of potatoes supplied by Hubbard. UTZ claims that the potatoes Hubbard supplied failed to meet the quality standards outlined in the parties' agreement.

In particular, UTZ claimed the potatoes did not meet the color standards outlined in the agreement. UTZ did not want dark potato chips, so it demanded that the potatoes had to be the whitest or lightest possible color. Potato color is defined from designation No. 1 (best or lightest) to 5 (the darkest). UTZ's contract indicated that potatoes must meet at least the No. 2 color standards. UTZ contends that the potatoes do not meet this standard, while Hubbard contends that UTZ is arbitrarily refusing to accept his potatoes. The

court states that "this case turns on matters of law relating to the rights of a buyer, such as UTZ, to reject a seller's goods that are deemed to be nonconforming." In the case below, the court explores UTZ's rights.

JUDGE SPAETH: . . . The primary legal issue in this matter is whether UTZ's rejection of Hubbard's potatoes was proper or wrongful. It is clear that this transaction is a sale of goods governed by New York Uniform Commercial Code (UCC) . . . both Hubbard and UTZ are "merchants." . . . It is also clear that the contract between the parties is an "installment contract." . . . [C]oncerning payment, [the contract] states that "[b]uyer agrees to pay for all potatoes accepted within 30 days of acceptance. . . ." This language suggests paying per shipment, since each shipment is subject to inspection (and acceptance). . . .

Clearly this is an "installment" contract as defined in UCC 2-612(1).

As an installment contract, the question of whether UTZ's rejection was wrongful or proper is governed by UCC 2-612(2) and (3). UCC 2-612(2) states that a "buyer may reject any installment which is nonconforming if the nonconformity substantially impairs the value of that installment and cannot be cured. . . ." UCC 2-612(3) states that "whenever nonconformity or default with respect to one or more installments substantially impairs the value of the whole contract there is a breach of the whole."

The purpose of this "substantial impairment" requirement is "to preclude a party from canceling a contract for trivial defects." In this case, UTZ rejected Hubbard's potatoes based upon their failure to satisfy the color standard set forth in paragraph 3(c) of the contract. Thus, the issue for me to decide is whether the failure of Hubbard's potatoes to meet the required #1 or #2 color minimum constitutes a "substantial impairment" of the installments.

Whether goods conform to contract terms is a question of fact. Moreover, in determining whether goods conform to contract terms, a buyer is bound by the "good faith" requirements set forth in NYUCC 1-203—"Every . . . duty within this Act imposes an obligation of good faith in its enforcement or performance." Thus, UTZ's determination that Hubbard's potatoes failed to satisfy the contract terms must be fairly reached.

The UTZ-Hubbard contract contains many specific requirements regarding the quality of the potatoes. In paragraph 1 the contract states that "only specified varieties as stated in contract will be accepted. . . ." Paragraph 3(a) states that "All shipments shall meet the United States Standards for Grades of Potatoes for Chipping, USDA, January 1978 . . ., in addition to other provisions enumerated in this 'Section 3,' loads that do not meet these standards may be subject to rejection. . . ." Paragraph 3(b) sets forth specific size requirements . . .; paragraph 3(c) sets forth specific gravity requirements; paragraph 3(d) contains the color requirements at issue in this case; and paragraph 3(f) sets forth a number of other defects or incidents of improper treatment or handling of the potatoes that provide UTZ with the right to reject the potatoes.

Clearly, the quality standards are of great importance to UTZ. They are the most detailed aspect of the contract—far more so than timing or even quantity specifications.

In a contract of this type, where the quality standards are set forth with great specificity, the failure to satisfy one of the specifically enumerated standards is a "substantial impairment." UTZ obviously cares the most about the specific quality specifications, as is evident from the numerous references throughout the contact.

Additionally, I find that UTZ's determination that the potatoes did not meet the required #2 color standard was made in good faith, as required by UCC 1-203. As noted above, the manner of visual testing utilized by UTZ was reasonable and customary. Further, Smith and DeGroft, the UTZ testers who rejected Hubbard's potatoes, provided credible testimony about their respective experience (Smith—30 years, DeGroft—5–6 years) and method of making such determinations. Accordingly, I find that UTZ fairly and in good faith determined that Hubbard's potatoes were nonconforming.

Thus, I find that Hubbard's failure to meet the proper color standard amounted to a "substantial impairment" of the installments (2-612(2)), substantially impairing the whole contract (2-612(3)). Accordingly, I find that UTZ's rejection of Hubbard's potatoes was proper. . . .

Judgment for defendant.

CRITICAL THINKING

The court tells us that the purpose of the substantial-impairment requirement is to preclude a party from canceling a contract for trivial defects. Then the court considers whether UTZ canceled the contract for trivial defects. Explain the relationship between the court's explanation of the purpose of the substantial-impairment requirement and the concept of good faith.

ETHICAL DECISION MAKING

Both parties probably prefer the ethical norm or value of security. How so? Which facts would each party highlight in explaining how a particular decision would enhance the value of security?

WHAT IS "REASONABLE TIME" FOR ACCEPTANCE OF GOODS?

SCM Group, USA, Inc., v. Custom Designs & Manufacturing Co., Inc.
U.S. Court of Appeals for the Third Circuit
89 Fed. Appx. 779, 2004 U.S. App. LEXIS 2419

The plaintiff, SCM, is the manufacturer and distributor of various woodworking machinery. The defendant, Custom Designs and Manufacturing (CDM) Company, Inc., is in the business of designing and manufacturing custom kitchen cabinetry. SCM and CDM are both sophisticated businesses in the woodworking industry, having peculiar knowledge, skill, and expertise regarding the machinery and equipment attributable to merchants in that industry.

At a point in the summer of 2000, CDM expressed an interest in purchasing a computer-controlled router from SCM that could meet certain criteria. On September 21, 2000, SCM submitted its final proposal. Delivery of the router was forecast during the first half of December, and the order of confirmation was required in writing along with the down payment. The offer to sell was signed on behalf of SCM and dated September 22, 2000. It was signed on behalf of CDM and accepted on September 22, 2000, along with the initial payment of $63,600. The CDM acceptance was faxed to SCM with handwritten changes in the payment terms. The router was delivered at the end of December 2000. At the time, the Cabinet Vision software was not in place, pursuant to a separate contract CDM had with Cabinet Vision. SCM installed the router in January 2001 at CDM. At the time, the second payment of $84,800, due prior to shipment, had not been made by CDM. Thereafter, CDM refused to pay the 40 percent payment and refused to make a final payment of 30 percent that was due, depending on the judicial determination of the contract terms.

On appeal the court held that under Pennsylvania law, a reasonable time for inspection after tender or delivery for rejection or revocation of defective goods

is generally deemed a question of fact to be resolved by the fact finder. Nevertheless, we find here that, as a matter of law, CDM has accepted the goods.

First, CDM clearly had more than a reasonable opportunity to inspect and reject the goods. The Router was delivered in December 2000. By the time of the judgment in this case, CDM had had more than a reasonable amount of time for CDM to determine if the Router was satisfactory. Second, CDM never made an effective rejection of the Router. Thus, as a matter of law, it has accepted the Router and must pay the contractual price for it plus any damages that resulted from its breach of the contract.

CASE OPENER WRAP-UP

What a Difference a Day Makes!

In our opening case, *Vitol v. Koch Petroleum Group,*[3] Vitol had purchased 75,000 barrels of oil from Koch Petroleum to be delivered within the three-day window of February 3 to 5, 2000. The contract also stated that Vitol could designate the date, as long as it was in the three-day window, and location of the delivery. Before delivery of the oil, Vitol sold the oil to Castle Oil. Vitol informed Koch of this and indicated to Koch that delivery must be made on February 3 at Castle's barge in the port. Koch acknowledged this information. It was crucial that Castle receive the oil on February 3. Koch attempted delivery on February 4, but by that time Castle had "covered" its contract with Vitol and procured replacement oil. This cost Castle more than $1 million, and Castle obtained an arbitration judgment against Vitol for that amount. Vitol then sued Koch for its loss due to Koch's breach of contract with Castle. The court found that Koch had indeed violated the perfect tender rule. Since the contract allowed Vitol to set the exact date and location of the delivery, any deviation from the terms designated was indeed a breach of the perfect tender rule and a breach of contract. Koch was liable to Vitol for its loss.

[3] 58 U.C.C. Rep. Serv. 2d (Callaghan) 545 (2005).

KEY TERMS

commercial reasonableness 514	course of dealing 517	cure 517	tender of delivery 515
conforming goods 515	course of performance 517	good faith 514	usage of trade 517
		perfect tender rule 515	

SUMMARY OF KEY TOPICS

The Basic Performance Obligation

Under the UCC, sellers and lessors are obligated to *transfer and deliver conforming goods.*

Buyers and lessees are obligated to *accept and pay for conforming goods* in accordance with the contract.

The UCC requires *good faith* in the performance and enforcement of every contract.

Specific Obligations of Sellers and Lessors

The *perfect tender rule* indicates that if goods or tender of delivery fail in any respect to conform to the contract, the buyer/lessee has the right to accept the goods, reject the entire shipment, or accept part and reject part.

Exceptions to the perfect tender rule allow sellers/lessors and buyers/lessees to consider:

- Norms in the industry and past dealings between the parties.
- Exceptions outlined in the parties' agreement.
- The seller's/lessor's right to cure.
- Excuse from performance when identified goods are destroyed through no fault of the parties.
- The concept of substantial impairment as it relates to revocation of acceptance and installment contracts.
- The concept of commercial impracticability.

Specific Obligations of Buyers and Lessees

If all goes well in a transaction over the sale or lease of goods, the buyer or lessee inspects the goods and then *pays* according to the agreement.

The seller or lessor must provide an opportunity for *inspection.*

- The concept of reasonableness governs the inspection process.
- After inspection, the buyer or lessee decides whether to accept the goods.

After inspecting, the buyer/lessee signifies *acceptance* or partial acceptance.

- Sellers or lessors sometimes presume acceptance.
- Partial acceptance is allowed in some circumstances.
- Buyers or lessees are allowed to revoke or withdraw acceptance of nonconforming goods.
- Buyers or lessees must issue reasonable notice if they decide to reject goods.

Cases in which a buyer decides to assert his or her right to reject nonconforming goods are often categorized under the heading "rescission or revocation of acceptance by buyer."

POINT / COUNTERPOINT

Should "Cure" Be a Required Condition of a UCC Sale?	
YES	NO
Unless there are truly extenuating circumstances, such as time being of the essence, it is accepted that a breaching seller has the right to cure the defect or nonconformity in the goods before the buyer is permitted to revoke the contract. This is consistent with the UCC underlying position that every reasonable means should be taken to protect the integrity of the underlying contract and allow the agreed-on transaction to proceed to fruition. In other words, this rule or practice enforces commercial transactions. This is consistent with the thrust of the UCC in such areas as filling gaps in open contractual terms, utilizing reasonableness when a standard of care is left open, and assuming that the parties intend to be bound, even if the terms are incomplete (in direct contrast to common law). Therefore, in the absence of terms to the contrary, cure should always be allowed when reasonably practical.	When goods are delivered to the buyer and the goods are nonconforming, the option should rest with the non-breaching buyer as to whether cure should be permitted or not. In terms of the UCC's insistence on the perfect tender rule, the UCC requires that ordered goods conform "perfectly" to the requirements of the order or else a breach is declared. If that level of exactitude is required by the UCC, why not give the buyer the option to reject goods and revoke the contract even if cure is possible? Eliminating the "right" to cure would serve as a strong incentive for sellers to get the order right in the first place instead of being able to fall back on the right to cure. Not only would this facilitate commercial activity, but it would serve as an incentive for efficient contract performance and reduce the need for litigation.

QUESTIONS & PROBLEMS

1. Think back to the *Vitol v. Koch* Case Opener. Explain how perfect tender applies not only to the nature of the actual goods themselves but to the entire contractual transaction.

2. Midwest Mobile Diagnostic Imaging (MMDI) brought suit against Ellis & Watts (E&W), a division of Dynamics Corporation of America, for breach of contract. The dispute arose when E&W delivered the first of four trailers equipped with magnetic resonance imaging (MRI) scanners that E&W had agreed to deliver pursuant to a purchase agreement. E&W designs and manufactures trailers for mobile medical uses. MMDI decided to buy the MRI scanners directly from the manufacturer, but it needed assistance from E&W. E&W needed to install the trailers subject to the manufacturer's specifications and approval. MMDI entered into an agreement with E&W for four mobile MRI units. The manufacturer subsequently delivered the first scanner to E&W in September 1995. In November, MMDI paid E&W for the first trailer. The manufacturer then completed its testing of that trailer at the end of November. The first test found that the trailer complied with all technical specifications. A second test failed because it was a "road test," meaning the MRI failed to meet requirements after the trailer was moved and parked. The problem was that the unit's side walls flexed too much, causing unacceptable "ghosting" in the MRI scans. In December, E&W installed a reinforcing brace that solved the wall-flexing problem and satisfied all of the manufacturer's specifications. Consequently, MMDI refused to accept the trailer with the brace and demanded that E&W return the full purchase price. MMDI filed suit, seeking damages. Should MMDI prevail? [*Midwest Mobile Diagnostic Imaging v. Dynamics Corp. of America,* 165 F.3d 27 C.A.6 (Mich.) 1998.]

3. Wilbur Reed operated a small greenhouse in Montana. He ordered most of his plants from McCalif Grower Supplies. Reed often supplied local Kmart and Ernst stores with his products. During the holiday season, he agreed to provide them with poinsettia

plants. Reed ordered the plants from McCalif, and McCalif had growers send the plants to Reed from Colorado. Reed's employee accepted the boxes at the airport and did not note any damages to the packaging. However, when the boxes were opened, the poinsettias appeared damaged. Reed contacted McCalif and notified it that the poinsettias were damaged as a result of poor packing. McCalif advised Reed to report the damages to the carrier, Delta Airlines. Delta paid Reed $924.66 in compensation. McCalif was not able to supply Reed with more poinsettias before the holiday season. As a result, Reed lost accounts to many of the stores. McCalif sued Reed for payment for the poinsettias, $3,223.56. Reed refused to pay and argued that McCalif had failed to deliver according to their contract. Whom did the court agree with? [*McCalif Grower Supplies, Inc. v. Wilbur Reed*, 900 P.2d 880 (1995).]

4. New furniture was delivered to the buyer, and it was badly damaged. The purchaser notified the furniture store of the damage, and the store sent a representative to the buyer. The representative explained that the furniture could be repaired and restored. After hearing the details, the buyer refused and asked for her money back. The store refused, claiming that she had accepted the goods and was required to permit the seller to cure the defects. Who prevailed? [*Clark v. Zaid, Inc.*, 263 Md. 127 (1971).]

5. Rockland Industries agreed to purchase three containers of antimony oxide at $1.80 per pound from Manley-Regan Chemicals. Rockland produces drapes, and antimony oxide is used to fireproof the drapes. A representative from Manley-Regan, David Hess, worked with Conrad Ailstock, Rockland's purchasing agent. Hess informed Ailstock of a slight delay, but he assured Ailstock that the product, which was coming from China, was "on the water." Three months after the two companies had made the agreement, Hess contacted Ailstock to report that the product was not coming. According to Hess, Manley-Regan was considering legal claims against the Chinese supplier or the Chinese government. Rockland was forced to find another supplier, but the price was substantially higher. Rockland brought suit to recover the difference between Manley-Regan's quoted price and the price of the substitute antimony oxide. Is the commercial-impracticability defense appropriate? Explain.

[*Rockland Industries, Inc. v. Manley-Regan Chemicals Division*, 991 F. Supp. 468 (1998).]

6. The buyer contracted with the seller for a customized machine. The seller failed to have the machine ready by the agreed-on deadline. The buyer agreed to two extensions, both of which were not met by the seller. The buyer then terminated the contract. The seller sued for breach, claiming that it had not been given sufficient time to effect a cure. Who prevailed? [Star *Machine, Inc. v. Ford Motor Co.*, 1998 U.S. App. LEXIS 15392 (1998).]

7. David Cooper purchased a computer and software for his supermarket business. He was using a software program recommended and installed by the seller, Contemporary Computer Systems, Inc. The sales contract had a clause that stated that no refunds would be given after the 90-day warranty period. Cooper initially had problems with both the hardware and the software. Contemporary Computer Systems tried to remedy these problems. A pattern of problems and attempts to fix went on for some time, far beyond the 90-day time period expressly described in the contract. When Cooper had had enough, he decided to revoke the contract and demand his money back. Contemporary Computer Systems said the 90-day express clause in the contract precludes this action. Who won? [*David Cooper, Inc. v. Contemporary Computer Systems, Inc.*, 846 S.W.2d 777 (1993).]

8. North American Lighting (NAL) purchased a headlight aiming system from Hopkins Manufacturing Corporation. NAL produces headlamps for most major automobile manufacturers. It is important that NAL produce headlamps that meet government safety requirements, which ensure that drivers can see what they need to see without blinding oncoming motorists. Hopkins tried to sell NAL its Machine Vision System (MVS), which Hopkins believed was appropriate for the kind of testing NAL had to undertake to comply with federal guidelines. NAL decided to purchase the MVS even though it saw problems from the start. NAL based its purchase decision on Hopkins's promises that software could be added to the system to make it meet NAL's needs. After approximately two years of working with Hopkins, and the MVS still failing to meet NAL's needs, NAL informed Hopkins that it was revoking acceptance. The issue in the case is whether NAL can recover the amount

it tendered Hopkins in partial payment. Hopkins wants the unpaid purchase price, as well as an amount that approximates the reasonable rental value of the equipment Hopkins had loaned to NAL. Who gets what? [*North American Lighting, Inc. v. Hopkins Manufacturing Corp.*, 37 F.3d 1253 (1994).]

9. Aubrey Reeves purchased a computer system for his business from Radio Shack Computer Center. Radio Shack is the local retailer for products sold by Tandy, its parent company. During negotiations, it became clear that Reeves needed software that Radio Shack could not provide. A Radio Shack salesperson referred Reeves to a software source book, let Reeves know he could choose compatible software from the source book, and informed him that Tandy does not support or service software from the source book. A disclaimer to this effect appears in the source book. Reeves eventually purchased computers from Tandy, some software from Tandy, and more specialized software from a company called Lizcon. The Lizcon software did not meet Reeves's needs. Reeves subsequently sent a letter to Tandy, asking for rescission of the contract and damages. Can Reeves rescind? [*Aubrey's R.V. Center, Inc. v. Tandy Corporation*, 731 P.2d 1124 (1987).]

10. The defendant, Nwabuoku, purchased $1,500 worth of furniture from the plaintiff, Y&N Furniture. Through an arrangement with the plaintiff, the defendant financed the purchase through a financing company, Beneficial. On receipt of the furniture, the defendant was to notify Beneficial that receipt was effected, and Beneficial would pay Y&N the $1,500 purchase price. Nwabuoku would then begin paying Beneficial the amount due plus interest according to their financing agreement. Nwabuoku refused to acknowledge receipt to Beneficial and eventually rejected the goods, claiming that he did not want the furniture. Is this rejection enforceable? [*Y&N Furniture Inc. v. Nwabuoku*, 734 N.Y.S.2d 392 (2001).]

Looking for more review materials?

The Online Learning Center at **www.mhhe.com/kubasek3e** contains this chapter's "Assignment on the Internet" and also a list of URLs for more information, entitled "On the Internet." Find both of them in the Student Center portion of the OLC, along with quizzes and other helpful materials.

CHAPTER

24 Remedies for Breach of Sales and Lease Contracts

LEARNING OBJECTIVES

After reading this chapter, you will be able to answer the following questions:

1 What constitutes a breach of a sales contract?

2 What is resale?

3 What money damages are available for breach?

4 What are liquidated damages?

5 What is cover?

6 When is specific performance of the contract a remedy?

CASE OPENER

Let's "See" the Damages in Defective Eye Ointment

Abbott Industries is a well-known supplier of pharmaceuticals worldwide. Founded by Dr. Wallace Abbott, the company was incorporated in 1900 after he had been developing and making pharmaceuticals since 1888. Headquartered in the greater Chicago area, Abbott had sales of nearly $30 billion in 2008 and a research and development budget of nearly $8 billion. As a supplier of pharmaceuticals, Abbott contracted with Altana, Inc., later to be purchased by NYCOMED, Inc. The contract required that Abbott provide Altana with the antibiotic erythromycin powder for Altana to use in the manufacture of ophthalmic ointment. Unfortunately, one of the shipment batches of erythromycin was bad. As a result, 1.2 million tubes of the manufactured ointment were unusable.

Abbott actually contacted Altana and admitted to the faulty batch of erythromycin powder. Altana was forced to recall from the market and destroy the 1.2 million tubes and spend a considerable amount of money in employee overtime payments to replace the destroyed tubes. Through a truly herculean effort, Altana was able to satisfy all of its outstanding contracts with buyers of the ophthalmic ointment.[1]

---

[1] *NYCOMED v. Abbott Laboratories,* 542 F.3d 1129 (2008).

The questions that this case raises pertain to the extent of Abbott's liability to Altana. Liability is not an issue, but the extent of the remedies is.

1. Is Abbott responsible for:
   a. The cost of the recall?
   b. The cost of the destruction of the 1.2 million tubes?
   c. The payment of overtime to Altana employees?
   d. The loss of goodwill and future sales that Altana may incur due to this incident?

The Wrap-Up at the end of the chapter will answer these questions.

This chapter explains the remedies available to sales contract parties such as Altana. The first section restates the primary goal of contract remedies. This section helps you understand the range of remedies available to sellers/lessors and buyers/lessees. The next two sections list and explain the remedies available to sellers/lessors and buyers/lessees. The first of these sections focuses on remedies available to sellers/lessors, from the right to cancel the contract to the right to reclaim goods. Then the next section looks at remedies available to buyers/lessees, from the right to recover goods to the right to accept nonconforming goods and then seek damages. The last section of the chapter provides examples of situations in which the parties' agreement modifies or limits remedies available under the UCC.

The Goal of Contract Remedies

The obligations of sellers/lessors and buyers/lessees are determined by (1) terms the parties outline in agreements, (2) custom, and (3) rules outlined by the Uniform Commercial Code (UCC). This chapter focuses primarily on rules outlined by the UCC.

LO1

What constitutes a breach of a sales contract?

The UCC adopts several common law principles, including principles that underlie remedies available under the UCC. A good way to start our analysis is to consider the following reminder of the general purpose of remedies under common law contract rules and the UCC. In *KGM Harvesting Company v. Fresh Network*,[2] the court said:

> The basic premise of contract law is to effectuate the expectations of the parties to the agreement, to give them the "benefit of the bargain" they struck when they entered into the agreement. In its basic premise, contract law therefore differs significantly from tort law. Contract actions are created to enforce the intentions of the parties to the agreement, while tort law is primarily designed to vindicate social policy. The basic object of damages is *compensation,* and in the law of contracts the theory is that the party injured by the breach should receive as nearly as possible the benefits of performance. A compensation system that gives the aggrieved party the benefit of the bargain, and no more, furthers the goal of predictability about the cost of contractual relationships in our commercial system.

Thus, as you think about the range of remedies available to sellers/lessors and buyers/lessees, think about what remedies would give the parties the benefit of the bargain they struck, and nothing more. Of course, the ultimate goal of contractual remedies is the possibility, if not probability, that a system that provides compensation will also function as a system of deterrence in which parties do not breach contracts or, if they do, will be

---

[2] 42 Cal. Rptr. 2d 286, 289. Quotes from and citations to cases the court cites have been omitted from the extract.

amenable to a mutually satisfied settlement. After all, remember the old adage that when disputes turn into litigation, the only winners are often the attorneys. The UCC creates a statute of limitations for bringing a lawsuit arising under a breach of contract for the sale of goods. UCC Section 2-725(1) states that four years is the time frame for a plaintiff to file suit once a cause of action accrues.

Remedies Available to Sellers and Lessors under the UCC

Sellers and lessors have various contract remedies under the UCC. These remedies are discussed below and outlined in Exhibit 24-1.

CANCEL THE CONTRACT

UCC Sections 2-703(f) and 2A-523(1)(a) allow a seller or lessor to cancel the contract if the buyer or lessee is in breach. The UCC requires that sellers/lessors notify buyers/lessees of the cancellation. Then the seller or lessor pursues remedies available under the UCC. Remember, these remedies give the seller/lessor the benefit of the bargain, and nothing more.

Legal Principle: Canceling the contract is the remedy of last resort from the UCC's perspective. Remember: The UCC wants to maintain commercial transactions and provides remedies to keep the contract in force, even when one party has breached.

WITHHOLD DELIVERY

Sometimes a buyer breaches the contract or lease before the seller has delivered the goods. For instance, the buyer or lessee might fail to pay according to the terms of the agreement.

Exhibit 24-1

Possible Remedies for Breach of Contract by Buyer or Lessee

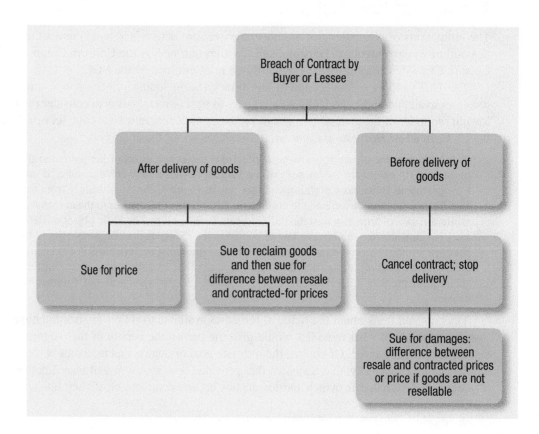

HOW TO COMPUTE "HOT DAMAGES"

Detroit Radiant Products Company v. BSH Home Appliances Corporation
U.S. Court of Appeals for the Sixth Circuit
473 F.3d 623, 2007 U.S. App. LEXIS 300, 2007 FED App. 0005P (6th Cir.), 61 U.C.C. Rep. Serv. 2d (Callaghan) 701 (2007)

Detroit Radiant is a manufacturing company that makes gas-fired infrared heaters that are used for industrial and commercial purposes. BSH requested a price quote based on an estimated annual usage of about 30,000 units. Two purchase orders were sent from BSH to Detroit Radiant on August 10, 2001, and January 8, 2003, for 15,000 and 16,000 units, respectively. Release schedules were provided by BSH to Detroit Radiant for exact timing of the orders. By April 5, 2004, BSH had received 12,886 units, had not contested quality at any point, and had scheduled 6,000 more units to be delivered before February 2005. On April 12 a new schedule was released, slowing production schedules. On June 24 Detroit Radiant filed a suit for the profits relating to 18,114 unsold units and unsellable inventory. BSH contended both that the purchase orders were estimates and that the 2003 order superseded the 2001 order. The 2001 order was a blanket order that BSH claims was an industry standard meaning estimated order. There was an unsigned supplier agreement that stated that all scheduled orders were nonbinding forecasts. On March 1, 2006, a district court ruled in favor of Detroit Radiant, finding that the purchase orders were of a certain quantity and did not contain any language to infer that they were estimates.

Michigan, along with states except Louisiana, has adopted UCC Article 2 to regulate the sale of goods. The default measure of damages under breach of contract is contract price less the market price of items in the time and place plus any incidental damages. However, lost profits are available in two situations: One is "lost volume seller," which Detroit Radiant did not claim to be the case. The other situation is one in which the default measure does not adequately make the seller whole. This could be a result of there being no reliable market price. In this case, the units were a special order for BSH, but that does not in itself make the products unsellable. However, BSH would not have allowed the products to be sold because it considered the units to be proprietary. BSH argued in court that Detroit Radiant did not respect the proprietary nature of the items because it had listed them in a catalog. However, the court found that that did not in itself prove that Detroit Radiant did not consider the units to be proprietary property of BSH. Detroit Radiant may have simply been attempting to show the types of products that it could make. Further, BSH had no proof that Detroit Radiant had actually sold any of these units. Therefore, Detroit Radiant had shown that there was no reliable market value for the units outside BSH. Thus, Detroit Radiant was entitled to lost profits in addition to the value of the unsellable inventory that it now has.

UCC Sections 2-703(a) and 2A-523(1)(c) allow sellers or lessors to withhold delivery of goods when the buyer or lessee is in breach.

BUT WHAT IF . . .

WHAT IF THE FACTS OF THE CASE OPENER WERE DIFFERENT?

Let's say, in the Case Opener, that Abbott was set to deliver a powder to Altana in January. The contract between the two companies stipulated that Altana was supposed to make monthly payments to Abbott from November preceding the shipment to May following the shipment. Altana missed December's payment, which was scheduled right before the shipment. Could Abbott withhold the shipment even though Altana had already been paying for the powder and it had more time within the payment plan time frame?

RESELL OR DISPOSE OF THE GOODS

Sellers or lessors are allowed to sell the goods to another buyer or dispose of the goods when the buyer is in breach and the goods have not yet been delivered. The seller/lessor then holds the buyer/lessee liable for any loss. UCC Section 2-706 allows the seller to recover the difference between the resale price and the contract price, plus incidental damages and minus expenses saved. Although the buyer is liable for these damages, the seller gets to keep any profits it makes on the resale. UCC Section 2A-527(2) outlines a similar rule for lease agreements. The lessor is allowed to lease the goods to another party and

L02

What is resale?

recover unpaid lease payments and any deficiency between the lease payments due under the original lease contract and those due under the new contract. The lessor can also seek incidental damages.

Legal Principle: **Resale is the preferred remedy for nonbreaching sellers (or re-lease for nonbreaching lessors) in that it provides an easy means to determine damages (resale price − contract price + resale costs = damages).**

? BUT WHAT IF . . .

WHAT IF THE FACTS OF THE CASE OPENER WERE DIFFERENT?

Let's say, in the Case Opener, that Abbott and Altana had a contract laying out the terms of Altana's purchase of powder from Abbott and a payment plan for the powder. Altana breached the contract by missing a payment deadline. Because of this one missed payment, is Abbott allowed to sell the merchandise contractually obligated to go to Altana? Or are there other steps that the two companies must go through to remedy their situation?

SUE TO GET THE BENEFIT OF THE BARGAIN

L03

What money damages are available for breach?

In trying to give the seller or lessor the benefit of the bargain, and nothing more, courts often grant damages to recover the purchase price or lease payments due. In some cases, even lost profit will be awarded, especially if the goods cannot be resold in the usual course of business.

LIQUIDATED DAMAGES

L04

What are liquidated damages?

Liquidated damages are damages identified *before* the breach occurs. The parties are free to negotiate, as part of the contract, a liquidated-damage clause in which the parties agree in advance what the damages will be for each party should a breach occur. Generally speaking, a court will enforce a liquidated-damage clause as long as it is not so far out of reasonable range as to be punitive in nature. Liquidated-damage clauses that are deemed to be punitive in nature are not enforceable. For a perspective on the issue of liquidated-damage enforceability, see the Point/Counterpoint at the end of this chapter.

The code provides for liquidated damages if the parties have not expressly negotiated a liquidated-damage clause. UCC Section 2-718 pertains to liquidated damages and allows the nonbreaching seller to claim against a breaching buyer 20 percent of the purchase price or $500, whichever is less, as liquidated damages.

Likewise, although the UCC does not mention the availability of punitive damages, other than in its voiding of liquidated damages that are punitive in nature, an issue that remains unsettled is the awarding of punitive damages against a breaching party who intentionally or egregiously breaches the contract. You will remember from tort law that when a tort is committed either intentionally or recklessly, the court may infer legal malice and instruct a jury that it may consider the awarding of punitive damages in addition to compensatory damages. Although this concept is well settled in tort law, it has never been widely applied in contract law. Yet there are some who argue that it should be, especially to deter intentional breaches of contract.

STOP DELIVERY

UCC Sections 2-705(1) and 2A-526(1) allow a seller or lessor to stop delivery of goods that are in transit. *In transit* means that the seller or lessor has delivered the goods to a carrier or bailee but the carrier or bailee has not yet turned them over to the buyer. Of course, the

CHINA AND LIQUIDATED-DAMAGE CLAUSES

With the enactment in 1999 of the People's Republic of China (PRC) Contract Law legislation, China adopted a Western-style, relatively comprehensive legal approach to contract law. However, some differences occur between the PRC Contract Law, the CISG, and the Anglo-American common law. In Section 114.2 of the PRC Contract Law, Chinese law recognizes the existence and enforceability of liquidated-damage clauses in contracts. However, Chinese judicial interpretation of this section limits liquidated damages to no more than 30 percent above the actual damages incurred by the non-breaching party.

Source: www.wjnco.com/eng/articles show.asp?Articles_id=216.

seller/lessor must give timely notice to the carrier/bailee so that the carrier/bailee is able to stop delivery. Also, the rules are different for insolvent and solvent buyers and lessees. If the buyer/lessee is insolvent, the carrier/bailee can stop delivery regardless of the quantity shipped. If the buyer/lessee is solvent, however, the carrier or bailee can stop delivery only if the quantity shipped is a large shipment (e.g., a carload or truckload).

RECLAIM THE GOODS

Under UCC Sections 2-709(1) and 2A-529(1), if the buyer or lessee has possession of the goods and is in breach, the seller or lessor can sue for the purchase price of the goods or for the lease payments due, plus incidental damages. In some circumstances, the UCC allows the seller or lessee to reclaim the goods. UCC 2-702(2) allows a seller to reclaim goods when it discovers the buyer is insolvent. UCC 2A-525(2) allows a lessor to reclaim goods when the lessee fails to make payments according to the lease terms.

BUT WHAT IF . . .

WHAT IF THE FACTS OF THE CASE OPENER WERE DIFFERENT?

Let's say, in the Case Opener, that Abbott delivered powder to Altana that Altana was still making payments for. Altana missed a payment after already being in possession of the powder. Abbott not only went to Altana to take back the powder but additionally charged Altana for payments due and damages. Altana said that once the goods were physically transferred to Altana, they could not be taken back. Which side is correct in this instance?

Remedies Available to Buyers and Lessees under the UCC

As with sellers and lessors, buyers and lessees also have a number of contract remedies under the UCC. These remedies are explained below and outlined in Exhibit 24-2.

CANCEL THE CONTRACT

Sometimes, sellers or lessors fail to deliver the goods and thus are in breach. UCC Sections 2-711(1) and 2A-508(1)(a) allow buyers and lessees to cancel the contract and then seek remedies that give them the benefit of the bargain. In Case 24-1, a buyer of heating coils had the right to cancel a contract with the seller because the coils did not work according to the buyer's specifications. The buyer subsequently sued for damages.

OBTAIN COVER

Case 24-1 also explains the buyer's right to obtain cover. Under UCC Sections 2-712 and 2A-518, buyers and lessees are allowed to **cover**, or substitute, goods for those due under the sales or lease agreement.

L05

What is cover?

Exhibit 24-2

Remedies for Breach
by Seller or Lessor

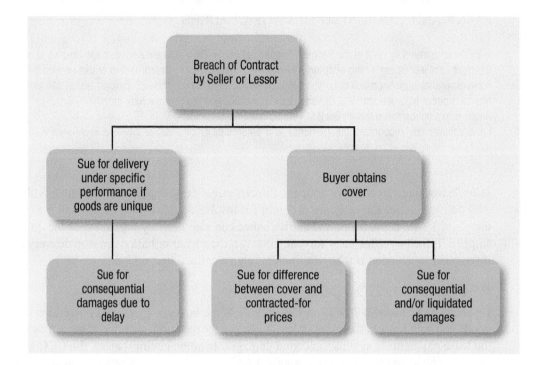

As you read Case 24-1, notice that, in obtaining cover, the buyer must (1) demonstrate good faith in obtaining the substitute goods, (2) pay a reasonable amount for the substitute goods, (3) act without unreasonable delay in purchasing the substitute goods, and (4) purchase goods that are reasonable substitutes.

CASE 24-1   U.S.A. COIL & AIR, INC. v. HODESS BUILDING CO.
WL 66582 R.I. SUPER. (1999)

U.S.A. Coil and Air, Inc. (USA), and Hodess Building Co. (Hodess) were involved in a legal dispute that arose after USA supplied cooling coils for an HVAC system, which was part of a "clean-room" project for Lockheed/Sanders. USA agreed to provide the needed coils to Hodess for $33,156.00. USA did provide the coils, but the coils failed to perform as specified.

USA subsequently sent Hodess replacement coils, but these, too, failed. USA believed the failure was related to Hodess's flawed system, not the coils. Hodess informed USA that it would replace the coils, using a different vendor to supply the coils.

USA requested to have its coils returned, and Hodess agreed, as long as USA paid for shipping or sent someone to pick up the coils. Communication between the parties broke down. Hodess never paid the contract price of $33,156.00. USA brought a breach of contract action to recover this amount. Hodess counterclaimed for breach of contract and asked for its $83,374.95 in replacement costs.

JUDGE. GIBNEY: . . . If a buyer rightfully rejects a tender of goods in a contract such as this one, he is entitled to cancel the contract. UCC 2-711(1). Once the contract is

cancelled, the buyer's obligation to pay the purchase price is discharged. UCC 2-106(3).

USA does not dispute that both sets of coils it provided failed to conform to the performance specifications referenced in the contract purchase order. . . . USA blames the system design for the failure. . . . [T]his court finds that the plaintiff breached the contract purchase order when it failed to provide coils which met the performance specifications. Thus, Hodess was excused from paying the purchase price.

Moreover, with respect to USA's right to cure its breach, Hodess allowed USA the opportunity to do so. Hodess installed USA's replacement coils, carefully following USA's instructions and modifying the system at USA's suggestion. When the replacement coils failed, USA's attempts to cure the breach failed as well. . . . USA is not entitled to recover. . . .

The defendant counterclaims, arguing breach of contract and seeking recovery of the replacement costs incurred due to the breach. Generally, "where a right of action for breach exists, compensatory damages will be given for the net amount of the losses caused and gains prevented by the defendant's breach, in excess of savings made possible." The goal is to place the injured party in as good a position as he would have been if the contract had not been breached. . . . When a buyer justifiably revokes acceptance of goods, the measure of direct damages is the difference between the cost of cover and the contract price, less any expenses saved as a result of the seller's breach. UCC 2-711(1)(b). To cover, a buyer must "in good faith and without reasonable delay" make a "reasonable purchase or contract to purchase . . . goods in substitution for those due from the seller." UCC 2-712(1). Whether the buyer acted in good faith and in a reasonable manner is determined with reference to the conditions at the time and place the buyer attempted to cover. UCC 2-712 at comment 2. It is irrelevant that hindsight may later suggest a cheaper or more effective method. The burden of proof is on the seller of goods to prove that cover was not reasonably obtained. . . .

Having found USA breached the contract, this court also concludes that USA is liable for the resulting damages incurred by Hodess. To replace the defective coils, Hodess incurred substantial expenses for engineering, supervision of, and replacement of the coils. Hodess documented its expenditures with receipts and project expense reports, demonstrating a total reasonable replacement cost of $83,734.95. USA did not present any evidence which would tend to dispute the reasonableness of cover costs. . . . Thus, using the damages formula enunciated in UCC 2-711(1)(b), Hodess is entitled to the replacement costs less the contract price [which was $33,156.00], or $50,578.95. . . .

Judgment for defendant.

CRITICAL THINKING

Hodess appears to have had an advantage in the case because it had better evidence. How so? How could USA have increased its chances of winning?

ETHICAL DECISION MAKING

Suppose Hodess later discovers that its system design was flawed and it was not really USA's fault that the coils did not work. Which ethical test or tests would encourage Hodess's executives to come forward with that information?

Legal Principle: Cover is the preferred remedy for nonbreaching buyers or lessees under the UCC in that it provides an easy, quantifiable means to determine damages (cost of cover − contracted price + incidental costs of cover = damages).

SUE TO RECOVER DAMAGES

In Case 24-1, although Hodess was able to cover, it still incurred damages. Buyers such as Hodess, and lessees, are entitled to incidental and consequential damages. Consequential damages include damages for lost profits as long as these damages are not too speculative. These monetary damages give the injured buyer or lessee the benefit of the bargain. This is one of the contentions being argued by Altana in the Case Opener of this chapter.

RECOVER THE GOODS

UCC Sections 2-502 and 2a-522 allow buyers and lessees to recover the goods identified in the contract if the seller or lessor becomes insolvent within 10 days after receiving the first payment due under the agreement. Buyers or lessees are obligated to pay the remaining balance according to the terms of the agreement.

OBTAIN SPECIFIC PERFORMANCE

UCC Sections 2-716(1) and 2A-521(1) allow buyers and lessees to seek the remedy of specific performance when either (1) the goods are unique or (2) a remedy at law is inadequate. Specific performance usually requires that the seller or lessor deliver the particular goods identified in the contract. In Case 24-2, the court decides what must be shown to apply specific performance as the appropriate remedy.

L06

When is specific performance of the contract a remedy?

WHAT ARE CONSEQUENTIAL DAMAGES?

The Mead Corporation v. McNally-Pittsburg Manufacturing Corporation
U.S. Court of Appeals for the Sixth Circuit
654 F.2d 1197, 1981 U.S. App. LEXIS 11164, 35 U.C.C. Rep. Serv. (Callaghan) 368 (1981)

The Mead Corporation entered into a contract for the McNally-Pittsburg Manufacturing firm to build a coal-washing plant. The McNally did not get the coal-washing machinery delivered in time, and Mead sued for a wide variety of damages incurred due to the delay. The jury awarded Mead slightly over a half million dollars in damages. McNally countersued for the unpaid portion of the contracted purchase price and received a judgment for $1.3 million. McNally is appealing, claiming that the half million dollars awarded to Mead is unsubstantiated consequential damages not covered by the contract.

CASE 24-2

ALMETALS, INC., PLAINTIFF v. WICKEDER WESTFALENSTAHL, GMBH, DEFENDANT
U.S. DISTRICT COURT FOR THE EASTERN DISTRICT OF MICHIGAN
2008 U.S. DIST. LEXIS 87403

Almetals, Inc., a Michigan company, entered into a contract with the German firm Wickeder Westfalenstahl regarding the purchase of "clad metal," a specialty metal used in a variety of industries but primarily the automotive industry. Wickeder is the world's largest manufacturer of "clad metal," a bonded product of layers of different metals. Almetals, Inc., would take the clad metal from Wickeder and process it to specifications for its customers, such as BorgWarner and Dana Corporation. From an initial purchase of just a few hundred thousand dollars of clad metals, Almetals, Inc., became one of the largest suppliers of processed clad metal, a market that took Almetals nearly seven years to cultivate. The contract between Almetals and Wickeder was for seven years with a ten-year add-on for customers that Almetals had under contract. Wickeder, seeing the huge success in North America, attempted to take over Almetals, Inc. In a proposed acquisition, Almetals successfully opposed that attempt. In retaliation, Wickeder refused to renew the contract after the seven years and then demanded that Almetals pay cash for clad metal purchased from Wickeder for the customers under the contract in the ten-year add-on period. The original contract called for payment 60 days after invoicing. Almetals sued for breach of contract and asked for specific performance as the remedy. The trial court granted Almetals' request and analyzed the facts against the UCC requirements for granting specific performance and the subsequent request for a permanent injunction.

JUDGE NANCY EDMUNDS: Almetals is entitled to an order requiring Wickeder to abide by the Court's ruling as to the payment terms (60 days after invoice of the materials in exchange for a .5% price discount) for the duration of the Customer and Order Protection clause for two independent reasons: (1) Almetals has met the test for specific performance under the UCC; and (2) Almetals has met the common-law test for a permanent injunction.

1. Almetals Is Entitled to Specific Performance Under the UCC

The power to grant specific performance rests within the discretion of the court. Under Michigan law, "[t]he remedy of specific performance is an extraordinary one granted only in unusual cases to prevent irreparable harm. It is a matter of grace and not right." . . . The UCC authorizes specific performance of contracts involving unique goods or in other proper circumstances:

(i) Specific performance may be decreed where the goods are unique or in other proper circumstances.

(ii) The decree for specific performance may include such terms and conditions as to payment of the price, damages, or other relief as the court may deem just.

Michigan has also adopted Comment 2 from the 1962 official text to UCC § 2-716, which states that:

> Output and requirements contracts involving a particular or peculiarly available source or market present today the typical commercial specific performance situation. . . . [U]niqueness is not the sole basis of the remedy under this section for the relief may also be granted "in other proper circumstances" and inability to cover is strong evidence of "other proper circumstances."

The UCC is consistent with the common law in which specific performance is well-recognized as an appropriate remedy where goods are unique or scarce. Jaup v. Olmstead, 334 Mich. 614, 55 N.W.2d 119, 120 (Mich. 1952) ("Generally, specific performance is not decreed where the subject-matter of the contract is personalty. However, if the specific property is not obtainable on the market and damages will not provide adequate compensation, equity may take jurisdiction"); In re Smith Trust, 480 Mich. 19, 745 N.W.2d 754, 756

(Mich. 2008) ("Because real property is unique . . . specific performance is the proper remedy"); 71 Am. Jur. 2d Specific Performance § 175 (2008); Bohnsack v. Detroit Trust Co., 292 Mich. 167, 290 N.W. 367 (Mich. 1940) (ordering specific performance of agreement among shareholders to buy life insurance to benefit surviving shareholders).

Indeed, under UCC § 2-716, "a more liberal test in determining entitlement to specific performance has been established than the test one must meet for classic equitable relief." Eastern Air Lines, Inc. v. Gulf Oil Corp., 415 F. Supp. 429, 442–43 (S.D. Fla. 1975) ("In the circumstances, a decree of specific performance becomes the ordinary and natural relief rather than the extraordinary one").

Specific performance under UCC § 2-716 is the appropriate remedy because the varieties of clad metal supplied by Wickeder pursuant to the parties' requirements contract are unique and there are no known alternative sources of supply, but only speculation as to a possible alternative source for .2% or .3% of the product. Sherwin Alumina L.P. v. Aluchem, Inc., 512 F. Supp. 2d 957, 960 n. 2, 970 (S.D. Tex. 2007) (applying UCC § 2-716 and ordering specific performance of a contract to supply calcined alumina, a scarce product, where the supplier had "very few competitors," "there [was] only one other manufacturer of [the product] in North America," and the buyer needed the products for its business to survive). **Order for specific performance granted.**

CRITICAL THINKING

In that the defendant's actions appeared to be retaliatory and the result of an unsuccessful takeover bid, should the court have taken evidence to that effect into consideration. Why or why not?

ETHICAL DECISION MAKING

In this case, Almetals relies heavily on a single supplier for its supply chain. In this case that amount was over 40 percent. Does such an arrangement place some kind of ethical burden on the supplier who is acutely aware that such a one-sided relationship exists?

REJECT NONCONFORMING GOODS

In Chapter 23, and this chapter, several of the cases have focused on what happens when the seller or lessor delivers nonconforming goods. This section and the next two review the buyer's/lessee's remedies when the seller/lessor delivers nonconforming goods. First, UCC Sections 2-601 and 2A-519 allow the buyer or lessee to reject the goods. The buyer or lessee may then obtain cover or cancel the contract.

REVOKE ACCEPTANCE OF NONCONFORMING GOODS

UCC Sections 2-608 and 2A-517 sometimes allow the buyer or lessee to revoke acceptance of nonconforming goods. For instance, in Case 24-1, Hodess rejected acceptance of the nonconforming coils USA provided. Hodess was allowed to reject acceptance because it had made a reasonable assumption that the nonconformity would be cured but then the nonconformity was not cured within a reasonable amount of time.

ACCEPT THE NONCONFORMING GOODS AND SEEK DAMAGES

Under UCC Sections 2-607, 2-714, and 2A-519, buyers or lessees are allowed to accept nonconforming goods and then seek monetary damages to give them the benefit of the bargain. The buyer/lessee must give the seller/lessor reasonable notice of the defect.

Modifications or Limitations to Remedies Otherwise Provided by the UCC

Parties to sales and lease contracts are allowed to modify or limit remedies. Under UCC Sections 2-719 and 2A-503, parties are allowed to create agreements that make it clear the remedies outlined in the agreement are exclusive

> To see how the lawmaking role of government relates to contractual agreements, please see the **Connecting to the Core** activity on the text website at www. mhhe.com/kubasek3e.

COMPARING THE LAW OF OTHER COUNTRIES

CANADA DOES NOT NEED "LEMON LAWS"

In the United States, lemon laws exist to provide remedies for buyers of defective cars when sellers have limited the remedies otherwise provided by the UCC. Lemon laws allow buyers to get a new car, seek replacement of defective parts, or obtain a refund of the consideration they have paid in situations in which a buyer has repeatedly complained about car defects and the seller has been unable to correct the defects after numerous attempts. The buyer who gets a refund of consideration gives the "lemon" back.

Canada does not have lemon laws.* Instead, each province runs an arbitration program through which a buyer can lodge complaints against a carmaker for selling a car that the consumer perceives as being damaged goods. So far, Canadian carmakers have bought back only a few vehicles. For instance, DaimlerChrysler Canada buys "very, very few" lemons, while its U.S. parent has purchased approximately 58,000 in the past eight years.† Dennis DesRosiers, an independent Toronto analyst, says the Canadian car industry does not need a lemon law because "cars are so well built these days that the chances of getting a lemon [in Canada] are very low."‡

* David Steinhart, "'Lemon' Resales Not Happening in Canada," *National Post,* March 20, 2001.

† Ibid.

‡ Ibid.

remedies. Courts uphold modifications or limitations to remedies unless the remedies fail in their essential purpose.

In Case 24-3, the court applies UCC 2-719 to rule on whether a seller could limit the buyer's remedies to repair, replace, or refund. These remedies are standard remedies in the bottling industry. Pay attention to the court's explanation of when remedies outlined in an agreement "failed of their essential purpose."

CASE 24-3   FIGGIE INTERNATIONAL, INC. v. DESTILERIA SERRALLES, INC.

U.S. COURT OF APPEALS, FOURTH CIRCUIT
190 F.3D 252 (1999)

In this case, a dispute arose between Figgie International, Inc. (Figgie), and Destileria Serralles, Inc. (Serralles), over bottle-labeling equipment Figgie sold to Serralles. Serralles is a distributor of rum and other products. It operates a bottling plant in Puerto Rico. When the bottle-labeling equipment failed to place a clear label on a clear bottle of "Cristal" Rum with a raised glass oval, Figgie attempted to repair the equipment. After several attempts to fix the equipment, Figgie returned the purchase price of the equipment and Serralles returned the equipment.

Serralles asked Figgie to pay for alleged losses caused by the equipment's failure to perform as expected. This failure caused a delay in Serralles' production of Cristal Rum. Figgie instituted a declaratory judgment action, asserting that Serralles' remedy for breach was limited to repair, replace, or refund under both the written terms and conditions of the sales agreement (which was lost) and pursuant to usage of trade in the bottle-labeling industry. In this case, the court considered the extent to which usage of trade in the bottling industry makes it clear that Serralles' remedy was limited to repair, replace, or refund. Serralles disputes that usage of trade imposes this limitation. Serralles also argues that because this limited remedy fails of its essential purpose, it is entitled to the full array of remedies the UCC provides.

CIRCUIT JUDGE TRAXLER: ... Because the crux of this appeal centers on whether the agreement between the parties limited Serralles' remedy for breach to repair, replacement, or refund of the purchase price, we begin with the language of S.C.Code Sec. 36-2-719, which governs modifications or limitations to the remedies otherwise provided by the UCC for breach of a sales agreement. Section 36-2-719 provides that:

(1) Subject to the provisions of subsections (2) and (3) of this section and of the preceding section (Sec. 36-2-318) on liquidation of damages,

  (a) the agreement may provide for remedies in addition to or in substitution for those provided in this chapter and may limit or alter the measure of damages recoverable under this chapter, as by limiting the buyer's remedies to return of the goods and repayment of the price, or to repair and replacement of nonconforming goods or parts; and

  (b) resort to a remedy as provided is optional unless the remedy is expressly agreed to be exclusive, in which case it is the sole remedy.

(2) Where circumstances cause an exclusive or limited remedy to fail of its essential purpose, remedy may be had as provided in this act.

[continued]

(3) Consequential damages may be limited or excluded unless the limitation or exclusion is unconscionable. Limitation of consequential damages for injury to the person in the case of consumer goods is prima facie unconscionable, but limitation of damages where the loss is commercial is not.

Under these provisions, parties to a commercial sales agreement may provide for remedies in addition to those provided by the UCC, or limit themselves to specified remedies in lieu of those provided by the UCC. An "[a]greement" for purposes in the UCC is defined as "the bargain of the parties in fact as found in their language or by implication from other circumstances, *including course of dealing or usage of trade. . . .*" . . . (emphasis added). In turn, the Code provides that "[a] course of dealing between parties and any usage of trade in the vocation, or trade in which they are engaged or of which they are or should be aware give particular meaning to and supplement or qualify terms of an agreement." . . . "Usage of trade" is defined as "any practice or method of dealing having such regularity of observance in a place, vocation or trade as to justify an exception that it will be observed with respect to the transaction in question. . . ."

. . . Serralles contends that the district court erred in concluding that usage of trade in the bottle-labeling industry supplemented the agreement between the parties with the limited remedy of repair, replacement, or refund. We disagree.

. . . Figgie submitted several affidavits of persons with extensive experience in the bottle-labeling and packaging industry, attesting that sellers in the industry always limit the available remedies in the event of a breach to repair, replacement, or return, and specifically exclude consequential damages. . . . Serralles offered no evidence to contradict the affidavits submitted by Figgie. Accordingly, the district court correctly concluded that usage of trade would limit Serralles to the exclusive remedy of repair, replacement, or return.

. . . Serralles contends that a limited remedy imposed or implied by trade usage cannot be an exclusive remedy because it is neither "expressly agreed to" nor "explicit." We disagree.

Section 36-2-719 provides that the "agreement" between the parties may limit remedies. Section 36-1-201(3) defines "[a]greement" as including terms "impli[ed] from circumstances including course of dealing or usage of trade." . . . It seems clear to us that . . . usage of trade will supplement agreements and may indeed impose an exclusive remedy in the event of a breach. . . .

Having determined that usage of trade supplemented the agreement of the parties with the exclusive remedy of repair, replacement, or return, we turn to Serralles' contention that the limited remedy "fail[ed] of its essential purpose," entitling it to nevertheless pursue the full array of UCC remedies. *See* S.C.Code Ann. Sec. 36-2-719(2). We conclude that it did not.

Section 36-2-719(1)(a) specifically contemplates that the parties to an agreement may, as they did in this case, limit remedies in the event of a breach to "return of the goods and repayment of the price or to repair and replacement of nonconforming goods or parts." Section 36-2-719(2), however, provides that the general remedies of the UCC will apply, notwithstanding an agreed-upon exclusive remedy, if the "circumstances cause [the remedy] to fail of its essential purpose." Under this provision, "where an apparently fair and reasonable clause because of circumstances fails in its purpose or operates to deprive either party of substantial value of the bargain, it must give way to the general remedy provisions of [the Code]." . . . In the instant case, however, there is no evidence that the limited remedy of repair, replacement, or return has failed of its essential purpose or that the contracting parties have been deprived of the substantial value of the bargain.

Serralles argues that Figgie, by first attempting to repair the equipment, elected to pursue repair as the exclusive remedy and, thereby, forgo enforcement of the remedy and reimbursement. From this premise, Serralles contends that Figgie's failure to repair the machines resulted in the remedy failing of its essential purpose. We find no support in the language of the UCC or in the cases interpreting it for this novel argument, and no evidence that this contemplated remedy of return and refund, once invoked, failed of its essential purpose.

. . . The district court correctly concluded that a limited remedy of repair, replacement, or return did not fail of its essential purpose.

AFFIRMED.

CRITICAL THINKING

Identify a significant ambiguous phrase that affects your ability to accept the court's conclusion. Explain the ambiguity and why it matters.

ETHICAL DECISION MAKING

Both parties probably prefer the ethical norm or value of efficiency. How so? Which facts would each party highlight in explaining how a particular decision would enhance the value of efficiency?

COMPUTER CONTRACTS

Sometimes, computer purchasers are surprised to find out they are bound to agreements that were created when sellers included contracts in the box in which the computer was delivered. Some of these agreements limit the purchaser's remedies. For instance, in *Hill v. Gateway 2000*,* Hill purchased a computer from Gateway 2000 by placing a telephone order. The computer arrived through the mail. Gateway had placed a contract in the computer's shipping box that indicated that the terms sent in the box were binding on the buyer unless the buyer returned the computer within 30 days. One of the terms in this contract was a provision that stated that any disputes between the parties would be resolved through arbitration. The order taker had not read any of the terms of the contract over the telephone when Hill placed the order. When the computer arrived, Hill did not read the contract. In an effort to avoid the arbitration clause, Hill asked the court to determine that Gateway 2000 could not limit buyers' remedies or avenues through which they seek remedies (i.e., through arbitration) by bundling hardware and legal documents. The court ruled that the contract was binding on the parties. The court stated, "A contract need not be read to be effective; people who accept take the risk that the unread terms may in retrospect prove unwelcome."[†]

* 105 F.3d 1147 (1997).
[†] Ibid., p. 1148.

CASE OPENER WRAP-UP

Let's "See" the Damages in Defective Eye Ointment

When Abbott Laboratories contacted Altana about the defective erythromycin powder, the issue of liability was a foregone conclusion. Abbott had manufactured a defective product and thus is liable. But liable for what? To what extent is Abbott responsible? Some no-brainers first: Clearly the purchase price of the erythromycin would be credited back to Altana, and Abbott would be liable to Altana for the cost of manufacturing the defective batch. What about the cost to Altana of the recall and subsequent destruction of 1.2 million ointment tubes? After all, 1.2 million tubes of ointment, regardless of size, is a formidable number. The court found, fairly easily, that had it not been for Abbott's negligence, the cost of the recall and destruction would not have occurred and that it is clearly foreseeable in the pharmaceutical industry that recalls are a result of defective drug manufacture.[3] Abbott was held responsible for the costs incurred by Altana regarding the recall.

The case gets a bit more interesting regarding the last two issues of damages: employee overtime and loss of future sales due to the mistake by Abbott. Employing a test that requires the breaching party (Abbott) to put the nonbreaching party (Altana) in the position it would have been in had there not been a breach, the court found that Abbott was indeed liable to Altana for the overtime payments to employees in order to make up the lost batch and satisfy Altana's contractual customers. However, when the issue of future sales was considered, the court ruled that despite Abbott's breach, Altana was still able to fulfill all of its existing contracts. To award any money to Altana on loss of future sales would be speculative and an unfair windfall to Altana.

[3] *NYCOMED, Inc. v. Abbott Laboratories, Inc.*, 542 F.3d 1129 (2008).

KEY TERMS

consequential damages   537   cover   535   liquidated damages   534   specific performance   537

SUMMARY OF KEY TOPICS

The goal of contract remedies is to give the parties the *benefit of the bargain they struck,* and nothing more.	**The Goal of Contract Remedies**
When the buyer/lessee is in breach, the seller/lessor can: • Cancel the contract. • Withhold delivery. • Sell or dispose of the goods. • Sue to recover the purchase price, lease payments due, or some other measure of damages that gives the seller or lessor the benefit of the bargain. • Claim liquidated damages. • Stop delivery. • Reclaim the goods.	**Remedies Available to Sellers and Lessors under the UCC**
When the seller/lessor is in breach, the buyer/lessee can: • Cancel the contract. • Obtain cover. • Sue to recover damages. • Recover the goods. • Obtain specific performance. • Reject nonconforming goods. • Revoke acceptance of nonconforming goods. • Accept the nonconforming goods and seek damages.	**Remedies Available to Buyers and Lessees under the UCC**
Parties to sales and lease contracts are allowed to *modify or limit remedies.* Courts uphold modifications or limitations to remedies unless the remedies fail in their *essential purpose.*	**Modifications or Limitations to Remedies Otherwise Provided by the UCC**

POINT / COUNTERPOINT

Should a Liquidated-Damage Clause Be Voided for Punitive Results?	
YES	**NO**
The law has generally held that a liquidated-damage clause is enforceable as long as it is not punitive in nature. What is so unusual about a liquidated-damage clause is that it is a lot like a prenuptial agreement in a marriage: The parties agree how the "damages" will be allotted in the event that the relationship falls apart. Liquidated damages mirror the same concept: If the contract is breached, this contractual clause lays out how the nonbreaching party will be compensated, regardless of the actual loss incurred. However, common law throws in one condition: The liquidated damages cannot be so out of kilter with the actual damages that they become punitive in nature. When the liquidated damages are punitive, the clause is unenforceable, presumably under a fairness or public policy doctrine.	The overarching nature of contract formation is that parties may enter the marketplace and freely enter into contracts. Incorporated into this "freedom of contract" is the right and ability to negotiate and agree to liquidated-damage clauses. They are not clauses that are illegal, coerced, fraudulent, or the result of mistake. They are freely entered-into and freely executed contractual clauses. As such, the will of the parties entering into these clauses should be respected. The law negating the results of a duly negotiated liquidated-damage clause under a fairness or public policy doctrine is the kind of contract reformation that puts the entire concept of freedom to contract in doubt.

QUESTIONS & PROBLEMS

1. Define and differentiate between liquidated, consequential, and punitive damages. In your opinion, should punitive damages be permitted in intentional breaches of contracts. Explain your reasoning.

2. Are there limits to the right to cure? Does a breaching party have the right to cure the breach, or can the nonbreaching party proceed directly into a damage claim? (See *Dunleavy v. Paris Ceramics*, 47 Conn. Supp. 565 (2002), for an interesting discussion of the right to cure.)

3. A restaurant called "The Inn Between" entered into a contract to purchase a used restaurant computer system. The contract included installation and training from Remanco Metropolitan, Inc. The contract also required that Remanco keep the computer system in good operating order. The system was delivered and installed on March 29, 1995. The following day the computer malfunctioned and was down for three hours. Between March 30 and July 3, the restaurant contacted Remanco 48 times to report malfunctions. Though Remanco responded to each of the problems, the computer system continued to break down. Inn Between brought an action to revoke its acceptance of the computer system. It viewed the system as a nonconforming good. Remanco counterclaimed, seeking the unpaid price under the system maintenance agreement for nonreturn of the system. Which side gets the remedy it seeks? [*The Inn Between, Inc. v. Remanco Metropolitan, Inc.*, 662 N.Y.S.2d 1011 (1997).]

4. The defendant, Sterile Technologies, Inc., purchased a sterilizer from the plaintiff, Troy Boiler Works, on an installment payment plan. The defendant was to make installment payments charged with 1.5 percent interest per month. The sterilizer was delivered on August 23, 1996. The last payment was received on April 21, 1998. At the time of the last payment, the defendant still owed the plaintiff $112,615 as the balance due on the sterilizer; as of the time of the filing of the lawsuit, the defendant owed an additional $134,214 in finance charges. The plaintiff filed its lawsuit to collect on the account on November 20, 2002. The defendant moved to have the suit dismissed as it was filed after the four-year statute of limitations had run

out (April 21, 1998, to November 20, 2002, is four years, seven months, and one day). Has the statute of limitations run? [*Troy Boiler Works, Inc. v. Sterile Technologies, Inc.*, 777 N.Y.S.2d 574 (2003).]

5. Andy and Melinda Meche purchased a car from Harvey, Inc. The Meches were interested in a low-priced car, and Harvey sold discounted program cars, which are vehicles that were previously owned by rental agencies. The sales representative explained to the Meches that program cars were usually under warranty and had relatively low mileage. The representative added that the cars were well maintained by the rental agencies and were "like new." After a short test drive, the Meches purchased a program car. The representative failed to tell them that the car had been previously wrecked and damaged. The Meches immediately noticed problems with the car and returned to Harvey to have the car inspected. On two occasions the representative told the Meches that the car had never been wrecked. A year later the Meches were involved in an accident, and the repairman noticed that the car had previously been wrecked and repaired. The Meches had put approximately 46,000 miles on the car. They brought an action to demand full rescission of the sale. Harvey, Inc., believed that the proper measure of damages should be reduction of the sales price. The company also believed that the buyers should pay for their use of the automobile. Finally, Harvey, Inc., did not agree with the trial court's finding of bad faith and subsequent award of attorney fees to the Meches. What is the appropriate remedy? [*Meche v. Harvey, Inc.*, 664 So. 2d 855 (1996).]

6. KGM Harvesting Company, the seller, had a contract to deliver 14 loads of lettuce each week to lettuce broker Fresh Network, the buyer, for 9 cents a pound. When the price of lettuce rose, KGM refused to deliver the lettuce it had promised to Fresh Network and instead sold the lettuce to others and made a profit of between $800,000 and $1,100,000. Fresh Network was angry over KGM's breach and subsequently pursued two actions. First, Fresh Network refused to pay KGM $233,000, the amount it owed the supplier for lettuce KGM had already delivered. Second, Fresh

Network purchased lettuce in the open market to fulfill its contractual obligation to Castellini/Club Chef. Fresh Network was forced to spend approximately $700,000 more for lettuce in the open market than it would have paid KGM. Castellini covered all but $70,000 of Fresh Network's extra expense. Castellini passed the extra cost along to Club Chef, which passed at least part of this cost along to its fast-food customers. KGM sought the balance due on its outstanding invoices ($233,000). Fresh Network sought damages for the difference between the price it was forced to pay to buy replacement lettuce and the price it had established through its contract with KGM ($700,000). Who prevails under this issue of cover? [*KGM Harvesting Company v. Fresh Network,* 42 Cal. Rptr. 2d 286 (1995).]

7. Maria Palomo purchased a used car from LeBlanc Hyundai Partnership. She explained to the sales representative that she needed the car to go to work and to take care of her grandchildren. The representative told her that the car would be appropriate for those purposes and that, if she took care of the car, it "would last forever." Palomo believed that this comment meant that the car would last her the rest of her life. She kept up with regular maintenance, but she began to have problems with the car. Palomo's mechanic recommended that she replace the car's engine. Palomo wanted to return the car to LeBlanc and be refunded the purchase price. The trial court awarded her $1,000 for repairs and damages. She appealed the decision. Should Palomo be allowed to revoke acceptance? What is the appropriate remedy? [*Palomo v. LeBlanc,* 665 So. 2d 414 (1996).]

8. Lupofresh, Inc., agreed to sell hops to Pabst Brewing Company. When the hops were processed and ready to be shipped to Pabst, Pabst canceled the order, claiming that the contract's pricing mechanism violated federal antitrust laws. In the subsequent lawsuit by Lupofresh for breach of contract, Pabst claimed that before Lupofresh could maintain a claim for the price, it had to attempt to resell the hops on the market since the goods had not been accepted by Pabst and had been merely identified to the contract. Did Lupofresh make a reasonable effort to resell the goods? Can Lupofresh recover the full purchase price from Pabst? [*Lupofresh, Inc. v. Pabst Brewing Company, Inc.,* 505 A.2d 37 (1985).]

9. Sherman Burrus, a printer, purchased a printing press from Itek Corporation. Itek's salesperson knew that Burrus was a job printer and even suggested various features regarding the printer that would be pertinent to Burrus's business. Burrus had continuing problems with the printer that Itek never corrected. In the subsequent lawsuit, Burrus asked the court to award consequential damages, including an amount to compensate him for lost business. Itek claimed that the defects were due to Burrus's improper maintenance and operation of the machine, but the court disagreed and ruled in favor of Burrus. What is the appropriate measure of damages? [*Burrus v. Itek Corporation,* 360 N.E.2d 1168 (1977).]

10. New Pacific Overseas Group (USA) Inc. alleged that Excal International Development Corp. and its president, Kenneth Shin-Hai King, breached a series of contracts for the sale and installation of concrete-block manufacturing equipment to New Pacific. New Pacific asked the court to issue a preliminary injunction that would require specific performance of the contracts, including the return of a computer unit taken by King from the equipment. Excal claimed that none of the goods identified in the contract were unique and that, consequently, specific performance was an inappropriate remedy. Is Excal correct? [*New Pacific Overseas Group (USA) Inc. v. Excal International Development Corp.,* 2001 WL 40822 (2001).]

Looking for more review materials?

The Online Learning Center at **www.mhhe.com/kubasek3e** contains this chapter's "Assignment on the Internet" and also a list of URLs for more information, entitled "On the Internet." Find both of them in the Student Center portion of the OLC, along with quizzes and other helpful materials.

LEARNING OBJECTIVES

After reading this chapter, you will be able to answer the following questions:

1 What are express warranties?

2 What is the implied warranty of title?

3 What is the implied warranty of merchantability?

4 What is the implied warranty of fitness for a particular purpose?

5 Do warranties apply to third parties?

6 Can warranties be disclaimed?

CASE OPENER

How Much Is That Doggie?

Linda Budd went searching for a new friend . . . and she found one for $400.[1] A brand new puppy. She purchased the puppy from Bernadette Vicidomine, a person who regularly sells puppies. Budd took her new friend home but realized that he was not in the best of health. Already attached to him, she did not return the puppy to Vicidomine, but instead took him to the veterinarian. Nearly $2,400 later, the puppy was medically mended. Budd then sued for the $400 purchase price and nearly $2,400 in vet bills, alleging breach of the implied warranty of merchantability. The questions raised with this simple, initially tragic but ultimately happy tale are:

1. Is this a transaction under UCC Article 2?
2. Is Vicidomine a merchant?
3. If so, does an implied warranty of merchantability attach to this sale?
4. What damages are available if this is a breach of the implied warranty of merchantability?

The Wrap-Up at the end of the chapter will answer these questions.

---

[1] *Linda Budd, Appellant v. Maureen Quinlan et al., Respondents,* 2008 NY Slip Op 28156, 19 Misc. 3d 66, 860 N.Y.S.2d 802, 2008 N.Y. Misc. LEXIS 2472, 66 U.C.C. Rep. Serv. 2d (Callaghan) 358 (2008).

Introduction

Chapters 21 through 24 have illustrated how the Uniform Commercial Code modified common law contract formation and execution to facilitate the ease of contracts for the buying and selling of goods and to reflect certain generally accepted business practices.

This chapter focuses on how the UCC changed the common law of warranties, which are assurances by one party that the other party can rely on its representations of fact. At common law, the only implied warranty is the warranty of assignability. When a party "assigns" a contract to another party, the assignor is impliedly guaranteeing that the rights being assigned are valid. However, the UCC adds to this concept. The warranties discussed in this chapter include both express and implied warranties. *Express warranties* are explicitly stated, whereas *implied warranties* are automatically, as a matter of law, injected into the contract.

After reading this chapter, you will understand what types of warranties arise with the creation of a contract. You will also understand how these warranties can be limited, as well as what role warranty law plays in protecting consumers.

Types of Warranties

Warranties generally arise in conjunction with a sale or lease. They impose certain duties on the seller or lessor, and if the seller or lessor fails to live up to these duties, he or she may be sued for breach of warranty. There are three basic categories of warranties: express warranties, implied warranties of title, and implied warranties of quality. The implied warranties of quality under the UCC include the implied warranty of merchantability, the implied warranty of particular purpose, and the implied warranty of trade usage. Each will be discussed in the following sections.

EXPRESS WARRANTIES

Although the common law does not use the term *express warranty,* the concept and application does exist in the common law. It seems only fair and equitable that promises made by a seller to induce a buyer to execute a sales contract should be enforceable. An express warranty is any description of the good's physical nature or its use, either in general or specific circumstances, that becomes part of the contract. To use common law language, an express warranty is a material term of the sale or lease contract.

L01

What are express warranties?

Express warranties may be found in advertisements or brochures (e.g., "This electric saw comes with a lifetime guarantee"). Such a warranty may also be part of a written sales or lease contract; or it may be a salesperson's oral promise concerning the good, made while attempting to close a deal. A sample or model may also provide an express warranty. Generally speaking, if the buyer relies on representations, those representations become part of the contract in the form of express warranties. Consider Case 25-1, which arose over the issue of whether a federally mandated label constitutes an express warranty.

Sometimes it is difficult to tell the difference between a statement of opinion and an express warranty. Statements of opinion are often salespersons' exaggerations and are known as "puffing." Puffing generally does not create an express warranty because it is not considered a representation of facts. Thus, if a salesperson says, "This is the finest piece of luggage I've ever seen," no one expects the buyer to rely on that as a promise. However, if the statement is "This suitcase is made of real crocodile," an express warranty may be created.

CASE 25-1 DONALD WELCHERT, RICK WELCHERT, JERRY WELCHERT, DEBORAH WELCHERT, APPELLEES v. AMERICAN CYANAMID INC., APPELLANT
U.S. COURT OF APPEALS FOR THE EIGHTH CIRCUIT
59 F.3D 69; 1995 U.S. APP. LEXIS 15719; CCH PROD. LIAB. REP. P14, 246 (1995)

Deborah and Jerry Welchert began commercially growing vegetables in 1989. In 1990, they leased a tract of land southeast of Blair, Nebraska, for this purpose that was also to be farmed by Jerry's brother, Rick Welchert. After they began planting vegetables, the Welcherts noticed that the vegetables were not growing properly. Deborah discovered that the herbicide Pursuit, manufactured by Cyanamid, had been applied to the land. Finding a label for Pursuit Plus, a different product, Deborah, Rick, and Jerry reviewed the label. This label claimed that crops could be planted eighteen months after application of the herbicide. Crops were again planted on the land in 1991, but continued to experience growth problems.

Meanwhile, Rick and another brother, Donald, leased another property in 1991 that had been treated with Pursuit Plus in 1989. Rick never read the Pursuit Plus label, relying on Deborah's account. Donald also did not read the label. The vegetables planted on this land experienced growth problems as well. All four Welcherts filed a suit alleging breach of express warranty for damages caused to their crops by Pursuit and Pursuit Plus.

Pursuit and Pursuit Plus are regulated by the federal government under the Federal Insecticide, Fungicide, and Rodenticide Act (FIFRA), which has specific labeling requirements. The U.S. District Court for the District of Nebraska ruled that the Welcherts' express warranty claims were not preempted by FIFRA. Cyanamid appealed.

JUDGE MCMILLIAN: Section 24 of FIFRA, as amended, provides in part:

(a) In general

A State may regulate the sale or use of any federally registered pesticide or device in the State, but only if and to the extent the regulation does not permit any sale or use prohibited by this subchapter.

(b) Uniformity

Such State shall not impose or continue in effect any requirements for labeling or packaging in addition to or different from those required under this subchapter.

At issue in the present case is the extent to which subsection (b) preempts a state law cause of action for breach of an express warranty. . . .

The express warranty claim of the Welcherts is based entirely on the label's statement with regard to the herbicide's carryover effect. They have not alleged that Cyanamid made any other statements with regard to the product which might serve as the basis for their express warranty claim. . . . [F]ederal regulation requires a pesticide manufacturer to provide labeling information about rotational crop restrictions. . . . Cyanamid's label statement on rotational crop use is thus a mandated disclosure, not a "voluntarily undertaken" promise. See Higgins v. Monsanto Co., 862 F. Supp. 751, 761 (N.D.N.Y. 1994) (Higgins) ("Express warranties have a voluntary quality, which is missing if they are mandated by EPA. The rationale that warrantors should be held to contracts that they voluntarily enter into does not apply when their actions are forced."). The determination that the challenged label statement was required by federal law was essential to the Worm court's [Worm v. American Cyanamid Co., 5 F.3d 744 (4th Cir. 1993)] decision on the preemption of the express warranty claim. The Worm court further rejected the plaintiff's argument that claims of breach of express warranty were not preempted because it "suggested that what was approved by the EPA was inadequate for purposes of establishing a state cause of action."

In the present case, like Worm, the Welcherts' express warranty claim arose solely on the basis of a labeling statement specifically required by federal law and approved by EPA. . . . Where Congress has so clearly put pesticide labeling requirements in the hands of the EPA, the Welcherts' claim challenging the accuracy of the herbicide label's federally-mandated and approved statement cannot survive. See Worm, 5 F.3d at 748 ("Because the language on the label was determined by the EPA to comply with the federal standards, to argue that the warnings on the label are inadequate is to seek to hold the label to a standard different from the federal one."). To hold otherwise would be to allow state courts to sit, in effect, as super-EPA review boards that could question the adequacy of the EPA's determination of whether a pesticide registrant successfully complied with the specific labeling requirements of its own regulations. In such case, state court consideration of the label statement would be an "additional requirement." In light of the extensive federal statutory and regulatory provisions on pesticide registration and labeling requirements, the preemptive language of §24(b) of FIFRA must be read to preclude the Welcherts' claim. Consequently, we hold that their state law claim for breach of an express warranty is preempted by FIFRA.

REVERSED in favor of defendant.

CRITICAL THINKING

If FIFRA did not regulate Pursuit and Pursuit Plus, and Cyanamid had put the label on voluntarily, would the label then have constituted an express warranty? Why or why not?

ETHICAL DECISION MAKING

The continued problems of the Welcherts with the land where Pursuit and Pursuit Plus had been applied perhaps indicate a problem with the pesticide or with the label. Although American Cyanamid won this case, as an ethical company, should it spend money to do more research on its products to determine whether the label should be changed?

BUT WHAT IF . . .

WHAT IF THE FACTS OF THE CASE OPENER WERE DIFFERENT?

Let's say that, in the Case Opener, the breeder of the puppy said that the puppy was so energetic he would probably live forever. What kind of a statement is this? Alternatively, what if the breeder said that the puppy was in perfect health and came from a long line of dogs that never had health problems. What does this statement qualify as? Which statement is an express warranty?

Legal Principle: An express warranty is really just another material term of the contract; it is an oral or written guarantee that is no different from any other descriptive requirement of the good being purchased, such as size, color, or weight.

IMPLIED WARRANTIES OF TITLE

While no warranties automatically arise under the common law, the UCC assumes that the seller:

L02

What is the implied warranty of title?

1. Has good and valid title to the goods.
2. Has the right to transfer title free and clear of any liens, judgments, or infringements of intellectual property rights of which the buyer does not have knowledge.

The UCC specifically permits buyers to recover from sellers who have breached these warranties of title. The only exceptions to title warranties occur if they are disclaimed or modified by specific language in the contract or if the seller is obviously unable to guarantee title, as would be the case, for instance, at a sheriff's sale of seized goods. A buyer knows that goods repossessed and then resold and purchased through a sheriff's sale may have clouds on the title and unresolved liens that may surface.

> To see how providing warranties is a significant marketing tool, please see the **Connecting to the Core** activity on the text website at www.mhhe.com/kubasek3e.

Clearly, if the buyer is aware of any problem with the transfer of goods, the buyer is indeed purchasing them at her own risk. In contrast, if the buyer is unaware that the seller is transferring goods for which no good title passes or on which there are encumbrances or patent claims, the buyer may treat the contract as being in breach. Under such circumstances, the buyer may then avail himself of the remedies available under a breach situation.

IMPLIED WARRANTIES OF QUALITY

Implied warranties arise by operation of law under certain circumstances. Earlier, you read about the implied warranties of title that arise under the UCC. This section focuses on the three warranties of quality that arise under the UCC.

Implied Warranty of Merchantability. Consider the following scenario: You purchase a toaster from a local discount store. When you use the toaster, all you get is either

L03

What is the implied warranty of merchantability?

549

WHEN DOES THE TIME BEGIN TO RUN UNDER THE STATUTE OF LIMITATIONS FOR BREACH OF WARRANTY?

Lucy Mydlach, Appellee v. DaimlerChrysler Corporation, Appellant Supreme Court of Illinois
226 Ill. 2d 307, 875 N.E.2d 1047, 2007 Ill. LEXIS 1162, 314 Ill. Dec. 760, 64 U.C.C. Rep. Serv. 2d (Callaghan) 44

A buyer purchased a used car from a dealer for that brand of cars. The car was still under the car manufacturer's limited warranty. The car buyer, because of problems with the car that she alleged were not fixed, brought her claims under the Magnuson-Moss Warranty–Federal Trade Commission Improvement Act (Magnuson-Moss Act). The circuit court ruled that the claims were time-barred under the four-year statute of limitations in the Illinois Uniform Commercial Code. The state supreme court found that the car buyer could bring a breach-of-written-warranty claim under the Magnuson-Moss Act because the limitations period began to run not when the car was bought but when the repairs under the warranty were not made. However, the car buyer could not bring a revocation of acceptance claim because revocation of acceptance was unavailable under Illinois law against a car manufacturer that was not a party to the sales contract.

burnt toast or bread that is only slightly warm. You take the toaster back to the store and are met with this answer: "Well, we don't guarantee how well the toaster will work. After all, it does toast, either very, very lightly or very, very burnt." This answer, of course, is nonsense. There is a reasonable expectation of how a toaster will perform. That reasonable expectation is codified in the UCC implied warranty of merchantability.

To invoke this implied warranty, the purchaser must have purchased or leased the good from a merchant. Thus, a dirt bike purchased at a bicycle shop is covered by the warranty of merchantability, but a bike that is bought from a neighbor is not, unless the neighbor is a bicycle merchant.

BUT WHAT IF . . .

WHAT IF THE FACTS OF THE CASE OPENER WERE DIFFERENT?

Let's say that a woman goes to an American Kennel Club official dog breeder. She purchases a puppy and goes home. The puppy turns out to have severe physical defects resulting from genetic abnormalities. Is there an implied warranty with the dog? Can this dog be covered by the warranty of merchantability?

Under the UCC, the goods must be *merchantable,* meaning that they must:

1. Be able to pass without objection in the trade or market for similar goods.
2. In the case of fungible goods, be of fair or average quality within the description.
3. Be fit for the ordinary purposes for which such goods are used.
4. Be produced, within the variations permitted by the agreement, of even kind, quality, and quantity within each unit and among all units involved.
5. Be adequately contained, packaged, and labeled as the agreement may require.
6. Conform to the promises or affirmations made on the container or label, if any.

Given the description of the warranty of merchantability, was the puppy in the Case Opener "merchantable" when purchased? Does the implied warranty of merchantability require "good health"?

The quintessential case defining and illustrating the implied warranty of merchantability is that of the Blue Ship Tea Room and Ms. Webster (see Case 25-2). Although it is an older case, from 1964, it is one of the most enjoyable cases to read. If you read the case in its entirety, you'll find the judge giving the actual recipe for New England seafood chowder.

CASE 25-2   PRISCILLA D. WEBSTER v. BLUE SHIP TEA ROOM, INC.
SUPREME JUDICIAL COURT OF MASSACHUSETTS
347 MASS. 421, 198 N.E.2D 309 (1964)

A restaurant patron who ordered seafood chowder and choked on a fishbone brought this case. The plaintiff maintained that she would not have reasonably expected to find a bone in the chowder. At the trial, a jury found for Ms. Webster. The Blue Ship Tea Room, the defendant, appealed the case on the basis of the legal interpretation of the implied warranty of merchantability. The appellate decision below has become a classic in American jurisprudential reasoning.

JUDGE REARDON: . . . On Saturday, April 25, 1959, about 1 p.m., the plaintiff, accompanied by her sister and her aunt, entered the Blue Ship Tea Room operated by the defendant. The group was seated at a table and supplied with menus.

This restaurant, which the plaintiff characterized as "quaint," was located in Boston "on the third floor of an old building on T Wharf which overlooks the ocean."

The plaintiff, who had been born and brought up in New England (a fact of some consequence), ordered clam chowder and crabmeat salad. Within a few minutes she received tidings to the effect that "there was no more clam chowder," whereupon she ordered a cup of fish chowder. Presently, there was set before her "a small bowl of fish chowder." She had previously enjoyed a breakfast about 9 a.m. which had given her no difficulty. "The fish chowder contained haddock, potatoes, milk, water and seasoning. The chowder was milky in color and not clear. The haddock and potatoes were in chunks" (also a fact of consequence). "She agitated it a little with the spoon and observed that it was a fairly full bowl. . . . It was hot when she got it, but she did not tip it with her spoon because it was hot . . . but stirred it in an up and under motion. She denied that she did this because she was looking for something, but it was rather because she wanted an even distribution of fish and potatoes." "She started to eat it, alternating between the chowder and crackers which were on the table with . . . [some] rolls. She ate about 3 or 4 spoonfuls then stopped. She looked at the spoonfuls as she was eating. She saw equal parts of liquid, potato and fish as she spooned it into her mouth. She did not see anything unusual about it. After 3 or 4 spoonfuls she was aware that something had lodged in her throat because she couldn't swallow and couldn't clear her throat by gulping and she could feel it." This misadventure led to two esophagoscopies at the Massachusetts General Hospital, in the second of which, on April 27, 1959, a fish bone was found and removed. The sequence of events produced injury to the plaintiff which was not insubstantial.

We must decide whether a fish bone lurking in a fish chowder, about the ingredients of which there is no other complaint, constitutes a breach of implied warranty under applicable provisions of the Uniform Commercial Code, the annotations to which are not helpful on this point. As the judge put it in his charge, "Was the fish chowder fit to be eaten and wholesome? . . . [N]obody is claiming that the fish itself wasn't wholesome. . . . But the bone of contention here—I don't mean that for a pun—but was this fish bone a foreign substance that made the fish chowder unwholesome or not fit to be eaten?" The plaintiff has vigorously reminded us of the high standards imposed by this court where the sale of food is involved . . . and has made reference to cases involving stones in beans . . . , trichinae in pork . . . , and to certain other cases, here and elsewhere, serving to bolster her contention of breach of warranty.

The defendant asserts that here was a native New Englander eating fish chowder in a "quaint" Boston dining place where she had been before; that "[f]ish chowder, as it is served and enjoyed by New Englanders, is a hearty dish, originally designed to satisfy the appetites of our seamen and fishermen"; that "[t]his court knows well that we are not talking of some insipid broth as is customarily served to convalescents." We are asked to rule in such fashion that no chef is forced "to reduce the pieces of fish in the chowder to minuscule size in an effort to ascertain if they contained any pieces of bone." "In so ruling," we are told (in the defendant's brief), "the court will not only uphold its reputation for legal knowledge and acumen, but will, as loyal sons of Massachusetts, save our world-renowned fish chowder from degenerating into an insipid broth containing the mere essence of its former stature as a culinary masterpiece."

Notwithstanding these passionate entreaties we are bound to examine with detachment the nature of fish chowder and what might happen to it under varying interpretations of the Uniform Commercial Code.

Chowder is an ancient dish preexisting even "the appetites of our seamen and fishermen." It was perhaps the common ancestor of the "more refined cream soups, purees, and bisques." . . . The word "chowder" comes from the French "chaudiere," meaning a "cauldron" or "pot." "In the fishing villages of Brittany . . . 'faire la chaudiere' means to supply a cauldron in which is cooked a mess of fish and biscuit with some savoury condiments, a hodgepodge contributed by the fishermen themselves, each of whom in return receives his share of the prepared dish. The Breton fishermen probably carried the custom to Newfoundland, long famous for its chowder, whence it has spread to Nova Scotia, New

Brunswick, and New England." A New English Dictionary (MacMillan and Co., 1893) p. 386. Our literature over the years abounds in references not only to the delights of chowder but also to its manufacture. A namesake of the plaintiff, Daniel Webster, had a recipe for fish chowder which has survived into a number of modern cookbooks and in which the removal of fish bones is not mentioned at all. One old time recipe recited in the New English Dictionary study defines chowder as "A dish made of fresh fish (esp. cod) or clams, stewed with slices of pork or bacon, onions, and biscuit. 'Cider and champagne are sometimes added.'" Hawthorne, in The House of the Seven Gables . . . , speaks of "[a] codfish of sixty pounds, caught in the bay, [which] had been dissolved into the rich liquid of a chowder."

A chowder variant, cod "Muddle," was made in Plymouth in the 1890s by taking "a three or four pound codfish, head added. Season with salt and pepper and boil in just enough water to keep from burning. When cooked, add milk and piece of butter." The recitation of these ancient formulae suffices to indicate that in the construction of chowders in these parts in other years, worries about fish bones played no role whatsoever. This broad outlook on chowders has persisted in more modern cookbooks. "The chowder of today is much the same as the old chowder. . . ." The American Woman's Cook Book, supra, p. 176. The all embracing Fannie Farmer states in a portion of her recipe, fish chowder is made with a "fish skinned, but head and tail left on. Cut off head and tail and remove fish from backbone. Cut fish in 2-inch pieces and set aside. Put head, tail, and backbone broken in pieces, in stewpan; add 2 cups cold water and bring slowly to boiling point. . . ." The liquor thus produced from the bones is added to the balance of the chowder. . . .

Thus, we consider a dish which for many long years, if well made, has been made generally as outlined above. It is not too much to say that a person sitting down in New England to consume a good New England fish chowder embarks on a gustatory adventure which may entail the removal of some fish bones from his bowl as he proceeds. We are not inclined to tamper with age old recipes by any amendment reflecting the plaintiff's view of the effect of the Uniform Commercial Code upon them. We are aware of the heavy body of case law involving foreign substances in food, but we sense a strong distinction between them and those relative to unwholesomeness of the food itself, e.g., tainted mackerel . . . and a fish bone in a fish chowder. Certain Massachusetts cooks might cavil at the ingredients contained in the chowder in this case in that it lacked the heartening lift of salt pork. In any event, we consider that the joys of life in New England include the ready availability of fresh fish chowder. We should be prepared to cope with the hazards of fish bones, the occasional presence of which in chowders is, it seems to us, to be anticipated, and which, in the light of a hallowed tradition, do not impair their fitness or merchantability. While we are buoyed up in this conclusion by Shapiro v. Hotel Statler Corp. 132 F. Supp. 891 (S. D. Cal.), in which the bone which afflicted the plaintiff appeared in "Hot Barquette of Seafood Mornay," we know that the United States District Court of Southern California, situated as are we upon a coast, might be expected to share our views. We are most impressed, however, by Allen v. Grafton, 170 Ohio St. 249, where in Ohio, the Midwest, in a case where the plaintiff was injured by a piece of oyster shell in an order of friend [sic] oysters, Mr. Justice Taft (now Chief Justice) in a majority opinion held that "the possible presence of a piece of oyster shell in or attached to an oyster is so well known to anyone who eats oysters that we can say as a matter of law that one who eats oysters can reasonably anticipate and guard against eating such a piece of shell. . . ."

Thus, while we sympathize with the plaintiff who has suffered a peculiarly New England injury, the order must be . . . judgment for the defendant.

REVERSED in favor of defendant.

CRITICAL THINKING

As with most legal decisions, the critical-thinking activity that is most obvious is the need to reexamine the analogies used by the court in justifying its conclusion. The plaintiff wished the court to say that fish chowder was like what? What analogy did the defendant want the court to accept? Would the aptness of the analogy depend at all on the size of the bone in the fish chowder?

ETHICAL DECISION MAKING

The judge mainly used assumption of risk to rule against Webster, though she suffered an injury in fact. Should the restaurant have somehow compensated her? What would the WPH framework indicate should be done?

WARRANTIES IN KAZAKHSTAN

What Western law refers to as a *warranty* is called a *pledge* in Kazakhstan. Pledges serve the same function as warranties: They indicate the seller's confidence in the performance of a product and the buyer's right to compensation for nonperformance. Specifically, the Civil Code defines a pledge as "a means of securing the performance of an obligation by virtue of which the creditor (pledgeholder) has the right, in the event of the failure of the debtor to perform the obligation secured by the pledge, to receive satisfaction from the value of the pledged property preferentially before other creditors of the person to whom this property belongs."

A pledge can be given in two instances. First, and most commonly, it can arise from a contract. Second, it can be given because the situation lends itself to legislation that demands a pledge be issued.

When a pledge is violated, the concept of penalties is employed. Penalties are similar to remedies in the U.S. law. Penalties are always issued in monetary form, the amount of which is usually determined by a court. Parties may stipulate penalties for failing to fulfill a pledge in the contract, but this is not necessary for compensation to be collected. Legislation does exist that specifies penalty amounts for particular situations in an attempt to avoid excessive payments.

Implied Warranty of Fitness for a Particular Purpose.   Another important UCC implied warranty is the implied warranty of fitness for a particular purpose. This warranty comes about when a seller or lessor knows or has reason to know (1) why the buyer or lessee is purchasing or leasing the goods in question and (2) that the buyer or lessee is relying on him or her to make the selection. Under this warranty, the seller or lessor does not have to be a merchant.

An implied warranty of fitness for a particular purpose should not be confused with an express warranty. If the buyer walks into a store and the salesclerk says, "This saw will cut through metal," the seller has created an express warranty. However, if the buyer comes into the store and asks the salesclerk for a saw to cut through some copper tubing and the salesclerk refers the customer to a wall of different saws, it is reasonable for the buyer to assume that all the saws on the wall will satisfy the *particular purpose* that the buyer has indicated. Thus, an implied warranty of fitness for a particular purpose has been created.

Implied Warranty of Trade Usage.   The UCC, always diligent in its goal to facilitate the flow and ease of commercial activity, recognizes that a well-accepted course of dealing or trade usage may create implied warranties dependent on the circumstances. For example, if it is generally accepted in the trade that a certain product is always preassembled and shrink-wrapped, the failure of the seller to deliver the goods in that condition would be a breach of the implied warranty of trade usage.

Warranty Rights of Third Parties

The idea of a seller's being in breach of an implied warranty raises an entirely new issue: Is the seller liable to anyone other than the buyer? This question may initially sound peculiar. After all, the seller and the buyer are bound together by contract, and if either breaches, then the breaching party is liable to the nonbreaching party.

Consider this possible scenario: Jane buys a blender from a local store. Before using the blender, she lends it to her cousin Valerie to use at a party. While Valerie is blending drinks at the party, the blades fly off the blender and injure her. What obligation, if any, does the seller have to the injured Valerie? No contractual relationship exists between Valerie and the seller. However, it seems to be patently unfair to conclude that Valerie has no cause of action against the seller. The UCC recognizes this unfairness and clearly states that Valerie may indeed have a cause of action based on breach of warranty against

L04

What is the implied warranty of fitness for a particular purpose?

L05

Do warranties apply to third parties?

IMPLIED WARRANTY OF MERCHANTABILITY: BLUE SHIP TEA ROOM FOLLOW-UP

Jackson v. Bumble Bee Seafoods, Inc.
2003 Mass. App. Div. 6 (2003)

Anthony Jackson ate tuna fish from two cans of tuna canned by the defendant, Bumble Bee Seafoods, Inc. The tuna had been purchased by Canteen Corporation. Small tuna fish bones were in the canned tuna and lodged in Jackson's mouth. Jackson sued Bumble Bee Seafoods, Inc., for breach of the implied warranty of merchantability (and apparently had a Massachusetts attorney who was unaware of Massachusetts case law on this issue).

The trial court granted summary judgment to the defendant, and the plaintiff appealed to the Massachusetts court of appeals.

The court of appeals cited *Phillips v. West Springfield,* which held that a cause of action would lie for the plaintiff if "the

consumer reasonably should not have expected to find the injury-causing substance in the food." Yet, noting that *Phillips* goes on to cite the Blue Ship Tea Room case, the court of appeals stated:

[A]s a matter of law, bones in fish chowder should reasonably be expected. . . . As the Supreme Judicial Court has determined as a matter of law consumers must reasonably expect to find small bones in their chowder, we must find that as a matter of law consumers must reasonably expect to find small ones in canned tuna. Therefore, there are no material facts at issue on plaintiff's claim arising out of the claimed breach of warranty of merchantability; and, the trial court was correct to grant Bumble Bee summary judgment on the portion of plaintiff's case sounding in breach of warranty.

the seller. The states are given the following three choices regarding *third-party beneficiaries of warranties:*

1. Seller's warranties extend to the buyer's household members and guests.
2. Seller's warranties extend to any reasonable and foreseeable user.
3. Seller's warranties extend to anyone injured by the good.

Most states have adopted the second option. Nevertheless, a number of questions remain concerning third-party rights, the nature of privity of contract, and the ability to maintain a lawsuit under the warranty rights of a UCC contract. Note these questions in Case 25-3.

BUT WHAT IF . . .
WHAT IF THE FACTS OF THE CASE OPENER WERE DIFFERENT?

Let's say that, in the Case Opener, the woman purchases a puppy from a registered breeder. It later turns out that the dog has genetic defects due to inbreeding that make the dog extremely aggressive. The dog attacks the owner's neighbor's child. How and why could the breeder be responsible for the attack on the child? Under what law could the neighbor file a breach of warranty against the breeder?

CASE 25-3   MELISSA KAHN v. VOLKSWAGEN OF AMERICA, INC.
SUPERIOR COURT OF CONNECTICUT, JUDICIAL DISTRICT OF STAMFORD-NORWALK AT STAMFORD
2008 CONN. SUPER. LEXIS 376 (2008)

Melissa Khan alleges that on May 27, 2004, she entered into a lease and warranty agreement with Riverbank Motors Corporation, Inc. (the Dealership), for a new, 2004 Volkswagen Toureg (the "Vehicle"), manufactured by the defendant. The Vehicle came with written "factory warranties" for any nonconformities or defects in materials or workmanship.

Ms. Kahn alleges that the defendant, Volkswagen of America, Inc., and the Dealership made various other "express warranties" to the plaintiff regarding the quality of the Vehicle. After delivery, the Vehicle experienced various operating problems and malfunctions on myriad occasions during the period from February 2005 to August 2006, including multiple system monitoring lights coming on, engine stalling, problems with shifting, and the Vehicle lurching forward unexpectedly. The plaintiff returned the Vehicle to the Dealership and other Volkswagen dealerships repeatedly for repairs and service of these problems. Despite multiple attempts and a total of forty-nine days in the repair shop, the problems with the Vehicle were never rectified. She now brings this action under a variety of claims: breach of express warranties, breach of implied warranties, breach of contract, and breach of Connecticut's "lemon law." Her breach of implied warranties pertains to the fact that with all of its defects—which were confirmed—the car was undriveable and thus not merchantable. Here is the court's reasoning regarding her claim of Volkswagen's breach of the implied warranty of merchantability as it applies to the plaintiff, a third-party beneficiary of that implied warranty.

JUDGE DAVID R. TOBIN: . . . In the third count, the plaintiff asserts a claim for breach of implied warranties under the Magnuson-Moss Warranty Act, 15 U.S.C. §2301 et seq., and the Uniform Commercial Code. The defendant has moved to strike the third count on the grounds that plaintiff cannot state a legally sufficient cause of action for breach of implied warranties. The defendant makes two principal arguments in support of its motion to strike: 1) that although it made express warranties, it did not extend implied warranties to the plaintiff; and 2) that the plaintiff may not bring an action for breach of implied warranties sounding in contract against a party with whom it is not in contractual privity.

In response the plaintiff claims that the Magnuson-Moss Warranty Act guarantees that consumers who receive express warranties enjoy implied warranty protection as well, and that Connecticut law no longer enforces a privity requirement for breach of contractual implied warranty actions.

A. Implied Warranties

Contrary to the plaintiff's position, the Magnuson-Moss Warranty Act does not itself create implied warranties. It merely provides a cause of action for breach of an enforceable implied warranty. 15 U.S.C. §2310(d)(1). State law, rather than Magnuson-Moss, governs the creation and enforcement of implied warranties. . . . In her complaint the plaintiff alleges that "[t]he Vehicle was subject to implied warranties of merchantability, as defined in 15 U.S.C. §2308 and U.C.C. 2-314 and 2-318, running from the Defendants to the Plaintiff." It appears that the plaintiff's claim is that the purported implied warranty she seeks to enforce is derived from the underlying sale of the vehicle from the defendant to the Dealership (the lessor in the lease transaction), and that she is entitled to enforce such a warranty as a third-party beneficiary to that transaction. This inference may be drawn from the fact that Article 2 of the Uniform Commercial Code applies to the sale of goods and §2-318 addresses the rights of third-party beneficiaries to enforce a seller's warranties.

General Statutes §42a-2-314 establishes that a warranty of merchantability from the seller to the buyer is implied in all contracts for the sale of goods. A breach of this warranty occurs, if at all, at "the time of sale . . . or when [the goods] leave the manufacturer's control." [Citations omitted.] Criscuolo v. Mauro Motors, Inc., 58 Conn.App. 537, 546, 754 A.2d 810 (2000). However, the plaintiff was not the buyer in the sale made by the defendant manufacturer, the Dealership was. By its terms, General Statutes §42a-2-314 creates a warranty that is enforceable, if at all, by the Dealership.

The plaintiff also relies on General Statutes §42a-2-318 as a basis for her alleged right to enforce the warranty. Section 42a-2-318, however, only extends the right to enforce the seller's warranty to "any natural person who is in the family or household of his buyer or who is a guest in his home if it is reasonable to expect that such a person may use, consume, or be affected by the goods and who is injured in person by breach of warranty." The plain language explicitly limits the extension of the right of enforcement to individuals who are family members or guests in the Dealership's home and who suffer personal injuries as a result of a breach of the warranty. Therefore, the plaintiff has not pleaded facts which bring her within the application of General Statutes §42a-2-318, nor do the facts alleged give rise to any such inference.

Moreover, plaintiff has not pled any alternative theory pursuant to which she may enforce any implied warranty derived from the sale of the vehicle to the Dealership. . . . Accordingly, the court finds that plaintiff has failed to show that an implied warranty of merchantability was created between the plaintiff and the defendant, or that the plaintiff is entitled to enforce the warranty between the defendant and the Dealership as a beneficiary of that contract.

B. Privity

Even if the court were to find that the plaintiff had the right to enforce an implied warranty of merchantability against the defendant, the court would be constrained to agree with the defendant's second claim that such an action is barred by the lack of privity between the plaintiff and the defendant. The court agrees with the defendant that Connecticut law has maintained a privity requirement that prevents parties who are not in contractual privity with the warrantor from enforcing any implied warranty. See Rosenthal v. Ford Motor Co, Inc., 462 F.Sup.2d 296, 309 (D.Conn. 2006) (noting differences between common-law tortious implied warranty claim and contractual implied warranty claim include the abolition of a privity requirement in the former); Koellmer v. Chrysler Motors Corporation, 6 Conn. Cir. 478, 485, 276 A.2d 807, cert. denied, 160 Conn. 590, 274 A.2d 884 (1971). Similarly, a contractual or buyer-seller relationship between the parties is required to maintain a claim under Article 2 of the UCC which governs the sale of goods. Sylvan R. Shemitz Designs, Inc. v. Newark Corp., Superior Court, judicial district of New Haven, Docket

[continued]

No. 055001029 (May 24, 2006, Blue, J.) (41 Conn. L. Rptr. 440, 2006 Conn. Super. LEXIS 1554).

Connecticut's general rule requiring privity is subject to certain limited exceptions. For example, after reviewing developments in Connecticut law, District Judge Clarie held that the privity requirement is not etched in stone and the doctrine is only applied to situations in which alternative remedies that do not require privity are available. Utica Mutual Ins. Co. v. Denwat Corp., 778 F.Sup. 592, 595-96 (D.Conn. 1991). Courts applying Connecticut law have also recognized that it may be possible to satisfy the privity requirement by pleading facts which establish an agency relationship between a vehicle manufacturer and the Dealership. Koellmer v. Chrysler Motors Corporation., supra, 6 Conn. Cir. 485-86. "The existence of an agency relationship is one of fact." Wesley v. Schaller Subaru, Inc., 277 Conn. 526, 543, 893 A.2d 389 (2006). In Koellmer, however, a directed verdict in favor of the manufacturer was upheld due to the plaintiff's failure to prove an agency relationship where the manufacturer made express written warranties but all direct dealings surrounding the completion of the transaction were between the plaintiff and the dealer.

Other jurisdictions have liberally reduced the role of the privity requirement in breach of implied warranty actions sounding in contract. For example, some courts have found that the extension of the express warranty makes the manufacturer "a party to the retail contract and removes the privity objection as to both express and implied warranties" on the reasoning that the consumer, having received the express warranty, should be entitled to rely on the manufacturer for implied warranties absent a disclaimer. . . . Despite the trend in other jurisdictions to dispense with the privity requirement in contractual breach of implied warranty actions, Connecticut maintains the requirement except under limited circumstances which are not present in this case. There is no allegation in the complaint of an agency relationship between the Dealership and manufacturer nor is it alleged that the plaintiff has no alternative means to obtain a remedy. The no alternative remedies exception also appears particularly inapplicable in light of the plaintiff's claim of breach of express warranty set forth in the second count of her complaint.

C. Conclusion

The court finds that the plaintiff is precluded from maintaining the claim for breach of implied warranty set forth in her third count, on both grounds raised by the defendant. Accordingly, the motion to strike the third count is granted.

Defendant's motion is granted to dismiss the third count.

CRITICAL THINKING

The court emphasizes the privity-of-contract requirement to enforce an implied warranty from the car manufacturer to a subsequent purchaser (through a dealership). However, the court is clear that had certain facts been alleged, the privity requirement may have been relaxed, allowing the plaintiff to maintain her claim. What could those facts be?

ETHICAL DECISION MAKING

Do you find an ethical lapse in the court's arguments in this case regarding privity of contract? Isn't it clearly the intent of the UCC to have the implied warranties extend to foreseeable users? Why is the court so adamant in refusing to recognize this concept?

Warranty Disclaimers and Waivers

LO6

Can warranties be disclaimed?

There really is no question as to whether an implied warranty may be disclaimed. The real question is *how* it is to be disclaimed. Generally speaking, if an implied warranty is to be disclaimed, the seller must do so in clear, unambiguous, conspicuous language. In order to disclaim the implied warranty of fitness for a particular purpose, the seller must disclaim the warranty in writing. The seller may disclaim the warranty of merchantability either orally or in writing; however, some states require that the term *merchantability* must be used in the disclaimer.

The buyer may also waive both implied and express warranties. A buyer may waive these rights by (1) failing to examine goods for which an express warranty was created by a sample or model or (2) failing to comply with the seller's request to inspect the goods. For example, a printer requests that the buyer come into the shop to proof letterhead and envelopes. The buyer refuses, claiming that he is too busy, and tells the printer to go ahead

WARRANTIES IN HONG KONG

An important distinction must be made between *conditions* and *warranties* in Hong Kong business contracts involving the sale of goods. In such contracts, time of payment and delivery are considered warranties unless otherwise specified. If the time of payment or delivery is not fulfilled, the procedures for breach of warranty are followed.

These procedures differ from those that take place if a condition is violated. For example, if advance payment is considered a warranty and the payment is not made, the seller can sue for damages; but if the contract names payment as a condition, the seller can either recall the contract and resell the goods or sue for damages.

and run the stationery. On receipt of the stationery, the buyer discovers that the numbers in the phone number are transposed, making the stationery useless. Unfortunately, the buyer has indeed waived his rights due to his failure to inspect.

A buyer may also waive her warranty rights under the contract by failing to comply with the statute of limitations. Under the UCC, the buyer or seller must bring a lawsuit on a breached contract within four years of when the breach occurred or when the nonbreaching party became aware of it. The buyer and seller are free to negotiate contractually a shorter time period (as long as it is not less than one year), but they are not free to negotiate a longer time period than the four years.

BUT WHAT IF . . .

WHAT IF THE FACTS OF THE CASE OPENER WERE DIFFERENT?

Let's say that, in the Case Opener, the breeder of the puppy said that the puppy was so energetic he would probably live forever but that the potential buyer should take the dog to the vet to get him checked out just in case. The buyer said that she trusted the breeder and was not worried. However, when she got home, it turned out that the dog was a very sickly dog. What is the type of warranty that has been made in this scenario, and what happened to it? Could the buyer still sue the breeder for breach of warranty?

While the UCC remains the primary codification of both state and federal laws regarding sellers' warranties, there has been, in addition to the UCC, specific legislation pertaining to this issue. The 1975 federal law known as the Magnuson-Moss Act requires that if a seller decides to issue a written warranty for a consumer good (the seller is not required to do so), the seller must indicate whether that warranty is a *full* warranty or a *limited* warranty. This applies to any consumer good sold for more than $10. If the written warranty is silent, it is presumed to be a full warranty, which means that if the good fails or is defective, the good or its defective part will be replaced. If replacement cannot be timely effected, the buyer has the right to a refund or a full replacement.

DOES THE IMPLIED WARRANTY OF TITLE EXTEND TO SUBSEQUENT PURCHASERS?

First State Bank & Trust Company of Shawnee, Appellee v. Wholesale Enterprises, Inc., Appellant/Third-Party Plaintiff v. Jim Hazelwood and Lone Star Bank, Third-Party Defendants

1994 OK CIV APP 137, 883 P.2d 207, 1994 Okla. Civ. App. LEXIS 118, 65 O.B.A.J. 3393, 25 U.C.C. Rep. Serv. 2d (Callaghan) 677 (1994)

Someone stole the Corvette in Texas from its original owner, Taylor, and later a title was issued there stating the car was a reconditioned vehicle (i.e., one with parts from other vehicles). In 1988, a Texas bank repossessed the car from a subsequent purchaser and sold it to Hazelwood (a third-party defendant in the trial court). Hazelwood somehow obtained an original vehicle title for the Corvette in Oklahoma and then traded the car to Appellant Wholesale Enterprises, Inc., as partial consideration for his purchase of another car. In October 1990, Wholesale Enterprises sold the Corvette to another individual, Gary Brown. Brown financed his purchase through appellee First State Bank & Trust Company of

Shawnee, granting First State Bank a security interest to secure his loan. Brown subsequently defaulted on the loan, and First State Bank repossessed the car. Meanwhile, Brown filed bankruptcy and was relieved of any further obligation on his car loan. Shortly after repossessing the car, First State Bank tried to resell it through a local auto auction. Employees of the auction house apparently noticed that the car had an original vehicle title yet also had identifiable parts derived from other vehicles. Because of this discrepancy between the title to and the content of the car, the state of Oklahoma filed notice of forfeiture in August 1991, and First State Bank received actual notice of the forfeiture proceedings but failed to answer or defend. At the state's request, the court in the forfeiture proceeding entered a consent judgment in favor of the original owner's insurance company. Then, in September 1991, First State Bank sued Wholesale Enterprises for breach of warranty of title.

The court found for Wholesale Enterprises and ruled that the implied warranty of title did not extend to subsequent purchasers. See the Point/CounterPoint at the end of this chapter for an argument on whether the implied warranty of title should be extended to subsequent purchasers.

If the good is sold for more than $15, the written warranty must disclose a number of items of information—names and addresses of the warrantors, any limitations on the warranty, and the procedures required to activate the warranty remedies—all in readable and easily understood language, in other words, not in *legalese!*

CASE OPENER WRAP-UP

How Much Is That Doggie?

This simple case provides a wonderful template for approaching UCC Article 2 problems. The judge's reasoning lays out an approach for judges and students alike in dealing with these kinds of problems.

1. The court found that a sale of a dog was indeed a sale of a good under UCC Article 2.
2. The seller was a merchant, and as such the implied warranty of merchantability attached to any sale of goods from that merchant.
3. Usually, under a breach-of-contract theory, damages are limited to the contractual loss, in this case the $400 purchase price.
4. But, under the UCC and breach of an implied warranty, forseeable and consequential damages are not only allowed but required in the furtherance of justice.

To that end, the plaintiff was awarded reimbursement for her veterinarian bills.

KEY TERMS

SUMMARY OF KEY TOPICS

A *warranty* is a promise on the part of the seller with respect to certain characteristics of the good.   **Introduction**

Types of Warranties

Express warranties:

1. Description of the good's physical nature or its use.
2. Either general or specific.
3. Material term of the contract.
4. Reliance of buyer on representations.

Implied warranties of title:

1. Passage of good title.
2. Implied promise of no liens or judgments against title.
3. Implied promise that title is not subject to any copyright, patent, or trademark infringement.

Implied warranties of quality:

- *Implied warranty of merchantability:* A warranty based on a reasonable expectation of performance of the purchased good. The good must:
  1. Pass without objection.
  2. Be of fair quality within the description.
  3. Be fit for ordinary uses.
  4. Have even quality.
  5. Be adequately packaged.
  6. Conform to promises made on the label.

- *Implied warranty of fitness:* A warranty that arises when the seller knows the purpose for which the buyer is purchasing goods and the buyer relies on the seller's judgment.

- *Implied warranty of trade usage:* A warranty that arises as a result of generally accepted trade practices.

Third-party beneficiaries of warranties: **Warranty Rights of Third Parties**

1. Seller's warranties may extend to the buyer's household members and guests.
2. Seller's warranties may extend to any reasonable and foreseeable user.
3. Seller's warranties may extend to anyone injured by the good.

Methods of waiving: **Warranty Disclaimers and Waivers**

1. Seller does not make warranties in the first place (express warranty).
2. Seller disclaims in clear, unambiguous, conspicuous language (implied warranty).

3. Buyer fails or refuses to examine goods.

4. Buyer fails to file suit within the time of the statute of limitations.

Magnuson-Moss Act: If a seller decides to issue a written warranty for a consumer good, the seller must indicate whether the warranty is full or limited.

POINT / COUNTERPOINT

Should the Implied Warranty of Title Be Extended to Subsequent Purchasers?	
YES	NO
In the Case Nugget on page 558, Oklahoma courts ruled that the implied warranty of title is not extended to subsequent purchasers. This seems to fly in the face of the logic of the general thrust of the UCC. The UCC operates under the assumption that commercial activity should be enabled and enhanced. Applying the implied warranty of title to subsequent purchasers would facilitate commercial activity by not requiring any purchasers to "look over their shoulders" to ensure that a commercial transaction is not suspect.	Title to goods is so rarely suspect that the necessity of applying the implied warranty of title to subsequent purchasers is really not a practical issue other than in situations involving financing and repossession/foreclosure, as in the Case Nugget. Further, in cases where repossession is involved, the financial institution parties are on notice to verify title. In addition, many of the applications in question deal with stolen goods, but the implied warranty of title never extends to stolen goods and thus they are not subject to its protection.

QUESTIONS & PROBLEMS

1. Poor Sarah Jane not only had a short-lived marriage but found out that her supposedly $45,000 ring was worth only half that amount. It seems that the jeweler had misrepresented the value to her now ex-husband. Sarah Jane brings an action against the jeweler for breach of an express warranty. Does she have the ability to sue even though she was not the purchaser? [*Schauer v. Mandarin Gems of California, Inc.,*] 125 Cal. Rptr. 4th 949 (2005).]

2. Why is it even necessary to have implied warranties when the parties can and should negotiate the terms of the contracts?

3. Review Case 25-2, *Webster v. Blue Ship Tea Room.* Can you think of other situations today for which this case might serve as legal precedent?

4. Carl and Dorothy-Helen Huprich raise Arabian horses for breeding and selling. In 1989, they purchased corn from farmer David Bitto to feed to their horses after having it tested for aflatoxin, a toxin often present in horse feed. The sample tested negative, so the Huprichs purchased a large amount of feed. Soon after they began feeding their horses the corn, two died and a third soon fell ill and died as well. The Huprichs began to suspect that the corn was the culprit after another two horses died and a veterinarian confirmed that the horses had died from leukoencephalomalacia, a fatal brain disease that results from the toxin Fumonisin B-1. This toxin grows on mold known as *Fusarium monoliforme,* a mold often present on feed corn. The Huprichs sued Bitto, alleging breach of implied warranty of merchantability. Should they win on this claim? [*Huprich v. Bitto,* 667 So. 2d 685; 1995 Ala. LEXIS 307; CCH Prod. Liab. Rep. P14, 267; 28 U.C.C. Rep. Serv. 2d (Callaghan) 526.]

5. Duall Building Restoration, Inc., brought an action against the property owner of 1143 East Jersey, alleging that the owner had failed to make the necessary payments specified in the parties' painting

contract. Duall had been contracted to restore the brick walls of the property. The painting job carried a five-year guarantee against peeling or flaking. The property owners counterclaimed, stating that the paint had been defectively applied. Duall had applied Modac paint to the walls, but the paint had peeled from the walls. A brochure for the paint indicated that it was fit for the specific purpose of waterproofing brick walls. The paint manufacturer had assured Duall that the paint would adhere to the brick walls. Who was responsible for the damage? Was this a breach of the implied warranty of merchantability? How do you think the court resolved the conflict? [*Duall Bldg. v. 1143 East Jersey and Monsey Products*, 652 A.2d 1225 (1995).]

6. Kevin Scott purchased a Ford van on credit on May 14, 1987. The total cost of the van was $18,399, and Scott made a down payment of $3,406. After the van was damaged in a traffic accident, Scott failed to make the necessary installment payments required by the contract. The van was repossessed in 1998 and sold at a public auction in 1989. The credit company advised Scott that there was a deficiency of $6,452.56 that he had to pay. Ford Motor Credit Company (FMCC) filed suit for the deficiency on April 16, 1992. Scott argued that the period of limitations for FMCC's claim had passed. Maryland code required that "[a] civil action at law shall be filed within three years from the date it accrues unless another provision of the Code provides a different period of time within which an action shall be commenced." Do you agree with Scott? Why or why not? [*Scott v. Ford Motor Credit Company*, 691 A.2d 1320 (1997).]

7. After living in their home for three years, Roger Nathaniel and Sharon Diamond sold the home to the plaintiffs, Marc Copland and Joan Lund. Nathaniel and Diamond hired a pest control company to inspect the home. The company reported that there was evidence of a previously treated infestation but that no evidence of active infestation was found. This report was provided to Copland and Lund before the sale of the home. The contract specified that the purchaser had inspected the premises and agreed to purchase it "as is." A year later, the plaintiffs discovered that levels of chlordane were present on the property. The plaintiffs discovered that the home had

been treated 10 years earlier for termites. At that time, chlordane was used to remove termites. Despite one toxicologist's report that the level of chlordane did not constitute a health concern, Copland and Lund spent $50,000 removing the contaminated soil from their property. They brought an action against the previous owners, Nathaniel and Diamond. How do you think the court decided? [*Copland v. Nathaniel*, 624. N.Y.S.2d 514 (1995).]

8. Knapp Shoes manufactures and distributes work shoes and sells and distributes shoes made by other shoe companies. One of Knapp's suppliers, Sylvania, produced several models of Knapp shoes. The leather Sylvania used to manufacture the soles tended to fall apart easily. There were additional problems with each line of shoe manufactured by Sylvania. Sylvania claimed that it "stood behind" its product and fully warranted its product against manufacturing defects. Knapp subsequently fell behind on its payments to Sylvania. Sylvania complained to Knapp, but Knapp contended that the defective shoes were jeopardizing important accounts. In 1990 Knapp tried to return two of the models of shoes Sylvania had produced for Knapp in 1988, but Sylvania would not accept the return. Knapp sued Sylvania for breach of express warranty and of implied warranties of merchantability and fitness for a particular purpose. Sylvania countersued for the unpaid bills. How do you think the court decided? [*Knapp Shoes Inc. v. Sylvania Shoe Mfg. Corp.*, 72 F.3d 190 (1995).]

9. Mrs. Cipollone had been a lifetime smoker, starting back in the 1940s. She subsequently died in 1984 from lung cancer. Her husband brought suit against the cigarette companies of the Liggett Group and Philip Morris, citing breach of express warranty and fraud. Mr. Cipollone based these allegations on advertisements that the defendants ran on television, particularly during the *Arthur Godfrey Show*. At trial, the court did not permit the defendants to introduce evidence to show that Mrs. Cipollone did not rely on these advertising representations in deciding whether to continue smoking. Does the plaintiff have the burden to show that the express warranties were in fact relied on? Conversely, may the defense introduce evidence to show just the opposite? [*Cipollone v. Liggett Group Inc.*, 893 F.2d 541 (1992).]

10. Does possible misuse constitute a waiver of the implied warranties? Consider the case of a lessee of a car who, after 18 months, found that the car was running roughly. When the lessee took the car back to the dealership, the lessee was told that several valves in the engine were bent due to misuse by the lessee. The lessee refused to pay the bill of over $500, claiming that the repair should be covered under the warranties. The car dealership's position was that misuse constituted a waiver of the warranties. [*LaBella v. Charlie Thomas Inc. and Mercedes-Benz of North America,* 942 S.W.2d 127.]

Looking for more review materials?

The Online Learning Center at **www.mhhe.com/kubasek3e** contains this chapter's "Assignment on the Internet" and also a list of URLs for more information, entitled "On the Internet." Find both of them in the Student Center portion of the OLC, along with quizzes and other helpful materials.

Negotiable Instruments: Negotiability and Transferability

LEARNING OBJECTIVES

After reading this chapter, you will be able to answer the following questions:

1 Why do we need negotiable instruments?

2 What types of negotiable instruments does the UCC recognize?

3 What are the requirements of negotiability?

4 What are the words of negotiability?

CASE OPENER

Oral Agreements and Negotiable Instruments

As a gambling facility, MGM Desert Inn, Inc., regularly holds and executes negotiable instruments. During a period of two months, patron William E. Shack, Jr., entered MGM and delivered eight checks to the casino in exchange for markers. These checks, which totaled $93,400, were signed by Shack and dated at the time of transfer. When MGM sent Shack's checks to the bank for payment, they were dishonored because the funds in Shack's account were insufficient.

MGM filed an action in district court to obtain the $93,400. Shack contended that a casino host had told him he had sufficient remaining casino credit to receive the markers. The district court judge ruled in favor of MGM, affirming its argument that the checks were negotiable instruments and stating that no evidence of an oral agreement between the casino and Shack was provided. Shack was ordered to pay MGM $5,000 for attorney fees in addition to the $93,400 originally owed on the checks.[1]

1. If you were employed at MGM, what would you do to avoid future disputes with your patrons about the nature of payment agreements?

2. If Shack's claims about an oral agreement with MGM were true, would that affect your decision about whether payment on the checks was currently due?

The Wrap-Up at the end of the chapter will answer these questions.

[1] *MGM Desert Inn, Inc., dba Desert Inn Hotel & Casino v. William E. Shack,* U.S. District Court, District of Nevada, 809 F. Supp. 783 (1993).

Once a sales contract has been created and executed and the parties are aware of their respective obligations under the contract, the next phase is *payment* by the buyer to the seller for the goods purchased. Payment is usually made in one of three ways: in cash, through credit arrangements (discussed in the chapter on secured transactions), or with a *substitute for cash*. This substitute for cash is the focus of this and the next three chapters.

A substitute for cash, or a negotiable instrument, is a written document containing the signature of the creator that makes an unconditional promise or order to pay a certain sum of money, either at a specified time or on demand. Negotiable instruments are executed on a daily basis in the form of checks, certificates of deposit, drafts, and promissory notes in exchange for goods, services, or business financing.

Exhibit 26-1 illustrates where negotiable instruments fit in the process of market exchange for a good or service.

The Need for Negotiable Instruments

L01

Why do we need negotiable instruments?

A currency or cash substitute has existed for centuries in Anglo-American law. England's ancient *lex mercatoria,* or law of merchants, recognized that agreements could be paid for with documents that promised payment, and these documents themselves could be circulated as a substitute for money. However, the English king's court did not at first accept the use of document paper as money. Therefore, merchants had to develop their own system and rules for using documents as payments.

It is easy to see why using documents as payments can greatly facilitate commercial transactions, especially when cash is in short supply or it is dangerous to transfer large amounts of currency or precious metals. These documents of payment were generically called *commercial paper* and under Article 3 of the UCC were specifically labeled *negotiable instruments.*

CONTRACTS AS COMMERCIAL PAPER

We've already discussed one prevalent form of commercial paper: contracts. Whether it is under common law or UCC Article 2, a contract is commercial paper and through assignment may be circulated and transferred throughout the business world. Exhibit 26-2 will help you understand the process of assignment. Follow it step-by-step as you read the following:

Exhibit 26-1

Negotiable Instruments and Market Exchange

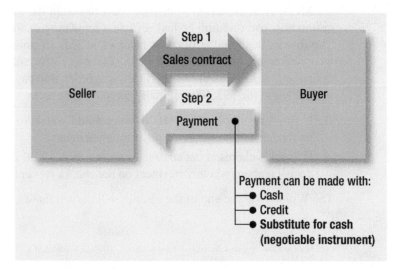

Seller

Step 1
Sales contract

Step 2
Payment

Buyer

Payment can be made with:
• Cash
• Credit
• Substitute for cash
  (negotiable instrument)

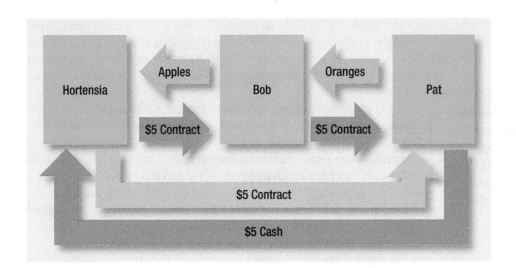

Exhibit 26-2
Negotiable-Instrument
Assignment

Bob sells a bushel of apples to Hortensia; in exchange, Hortensia executes a contract to pay Bob $5 on demand. A few days later, Bob buys some oranges from Pat for $5. Instead of paying Pat $5 cash, Bob *assigns* to Pat Hortensia's obligation to pay him $5. When Pat demands the money from Hortensia, Hortensia will pay Pat and everyone will be square.

Exhibit 26-2 demonstrates that any contractual obligation, except personal and nonassignable ones, may be transferred and thus classified as commercial paper.

PROBLEMS WITH COMMERCIAL PAPER

Our example of Bob, Hortensia, and Pat is a simple one, but it still contains a potential problem. Consider the fact pattern again, but assume that unknown to Hortensia, the apples Bob sold her were rotten.

When Pat demands the $5 from Hortensia, naturally Hortensia will refuse, claiming that Bob breached their original contract by delivering defective apples. She is on legally safe ground, and all Pat can do is go back and sue Bob because the commercial paper he transferred is not acceptable. In other words, these circumstances defeat the purpose of allowing transferability of commercial paper as a substitute for currency.

Types of Negotiable Instruments

Under Article 3, the UCC recognizes four types of negotiable instruments: notes, certificates of deposit (a highly specialized type of note), drafts, and checks (a highly specialized type of draft) (UCC Section 3-104). A note is a promise, by the *maker* of the note, to pay a payee [UCC 3-103(a)(9)]. A draft is an order by a *drawer* to a drawee to pay a payee [UCC 3-103(a)(6)]; in our example, Bob could have drawn a draft ordering Hortensia to pay Pat $5, since Hortensia owed Bob $5. A note is a two-party instrument; by definition a draft is a three-party instrument.

Legal Principle: **Under the UCC, notes, certificates of deposit, checks, and drafts can be negotiable instruments.**

Notes and drafts can be either demand instruments or time instruments. The payee (or subsequent holder) of a demand instrument can demand payment at any time. The

L02

What types of negotiable instruments does the UCC recognize?

UCC defines an instrument "payable on demand" as one that "(i) states that it is payable on demand or at sight, or otherwise indicates that it is payable at the will of the holder, or (ii) does not state any time of payment" [3-108(a)]. Payment on a **time instrument** can be made only at a specific future time, which the UCC says must be easily determined from the document itself [3-108(b)].

To see advantages of certificates of deposit, please see the **Connecting to the Core** activity on the text website at www.mhhe.com/kubasek3e.

Certificates of deposit and checks are specific illustrations of these distinctions. A **certificate of deposit,** or **CD,** is a promise by a bank to pay a payee a certain amount of money at a future time. The UCC defines a certificate of deposit as "an instrument containing an acknowledgment by a bank that a sum of money has been received by the bank and a promise by the bank to repay the sum of money. A certificate of deposit is a note of the bank" [3-104(j)]. Usually, a payee buys a CD from a bank and then collects the principle plus a determined amount of interest in the future.

A **check** is a specific draft, drawn by the owner of a checking account, ordering the bank to pay the payee from that drawer's account [UCC 3-104(f)]. A check is always a demand instrument and can never be a time instrument (postdating does not affect the ability of the holder to cash the check before the postdate). Types of checks include:

- *Cashier's check:* "[A] draft with respect to which the drawer and drawee are the same bank or branches of the same bank" [UCC 3-104(f)].

- *Traveler's check:* "[A]n instrument that (i) is payable on demand, (ii) is drawn on or payable at or through a bank, (iii) is designated by the term 'traveller's check' or by a substantially similar term, and (iv) requires, as a condition to payment, a countersignature by a person whose signature appears on the instrument" [UCC 3-104(i)].

- *Certified check:* "[A] check accepted by the bank on which it is drawn" [UCC 3-409(d)].

Case 26-1 addresses the question of whether a promissory note is a demand instrument.

CASE 26-1 — REGER DEVELOPMENT, LLC v. NATIONAL CITY BANK
U.S. COURT OF APPEALS, SEVENTH CIRCUIT
592 F.3D 759 (2010)

Reger Development borrowed money from National City Bank, using a revolving line of credit supported by a promissory note. At the point that National City discussed the possibility of calling the note, Reger Development sued the bank for breach of contract and fraud.

Reger had met with the bank prior to using the line of credit to discuss the loan. Reger asked about changing the terms of the credit agreement. The bank representative, Duncan, responded that the National City documents were nonnegotiable. Reger then executed the contract. The main question here is whether the promissory instrument entitles National City to demand payment from Reger at will.

CIRCUIT JUDGE FLAUM: The first clause in the Note reads:

PROMISE TO PAY: Reger Development, LLC ("Borrower") promises to pay to National City

Bank ("Lender"), or order, in lawful money of the United States of America, on demand, the principal amount of Seven Hundred Fifty Thousand & 00/100 Dollars ($750,000.00) or so much as may be outstanding, together with interest on the unpaid outstanding principal balance of each advance. Interest shall be calculated from the date of each advance until repayment of each advance.

PAYMENT: Borrower will pay this loan in full immediately upon Lender's demand. Borrower will pay regular monthly payments of all accrued unpaid Interest due as of each payment date, beginning July 25, 2007, with all subsequent Interest payments to be due on the same day of each month after that.

The Note proceeds to reference payment on lender's demand several times in other provisions. It also features a "NO COMMITMENT" clause that states: "NOTWITH-STANDING ANY PROVISION OR INFERENCE TO THE CONTRARY, LENDER SHALL HAVE NO OBLIGATION TO EXTEND ANY CREDIT TO OR FOR THE ACCOUNT OF BORROWER BY REASON OF THIS NOTE." The contract then includes integration language defining it as the final and complete agreement between parties. The Note is governed by federal and Illinois law, to the extent the former does not preempt the latter. Language above the signature line specifies in capital letters that the borrower has read and understood the terms of the document.

On August 19, 2008, National City asked the company to pay down $125,000 towards the principal of the line of credit, which appellant did the next business day. Then, on September 9, 2008, National City asked that Reger Development "term out" $300,000 of the Note by having one of Kevin Reger's other businesses agree to take out a three-year loan in that amount secured by a second mortgage on some real estate.

Kevin Reger "expressed surprise" about these developments and asked if National City would call the line of credit if Reger Development did not agree to the requests. The bank acknowledged that Reger Development was not in default but stated that "there is a possibility that we may demand payment of the line."

Reger Development then filed a complaint in Illinois state court accusing National City of breaching the terms of the Note.

While Illinois law generally holds that "a covenant of fair dealing and good faith is implied into every contract absent express disavowal," the duty to act in good faith does not apply to lenders seeking payment on demand notes. In light of this controlling law, appellant's complaint appears vacuous. Reger Development's allegations are "that National City breached the Contract Documents by arbitrarily and capriciously (1) demanding payment under the Line of Credit even though Reger Development was in good standing and (2) unilaterally changing and attempting to change the fundamental terms of the Contract Documents without Reger Development's consent." Reger Development attempts to substantiate the first part

of the breach claim by pointing to several provisions in the Note that it believes to be fundamentally inconsistent with the nature of a demand instrument. These include the "INTEREST AFTER DEFAULT" provision, which reads, in relevant part, "[u]pon default, including failure to pay upon final maturity, the interest rate on this Note shall be increased by adding a 2.000 percentage point margin"; the prepayment clause, which allows the borrower to pay down "all or a portion of the amount owed earlier than it is due"; and the clause that grants National City the right to access the borrower's financial information. Reger Development describes the latter as a "financial insecurity" provision that conditions the right to demand payment on some economic cause.

We are not persuaded by the suggestion that these references to due dates and default somehow overpower the repeated, explicit contract language setting forth the lender's right to demand payment at any time. A bank that wishes to call the Note can specify some future date on which it needs payment as a "due date." Failure to pay at that point in time, as well as failure to make monthly interest payments required by the Note, would constitute default, but the mere use of the terms "due date" or "default" would not alter the nature of the agreement. Similarly, the "PREPAYMENT" provision cannot bear the interpretive load that appellant wants to place on its shoulders. The clause reads: "Borrower may pay without penalty all or a portion of the amount owed earlier than it is due. Early payments will not, unless agreed to by Lender in writing, relieve Borrower of Borrower's obligation to continue to make payments of accrued unpaid Interest." Both its content and placement (immediately following the "payment" and "variable interest rate" clauses) are innocuous. The language merely reinforces National City's right to collect scheduled monthly interest payments and does not deviate from the structure of a demand note.

For the foregoing reasons, we Affirm the district court's grant of National City's motion to dismiss the Reger Development complaint.

AFFIRMED.

CRITICAL THINKING

What is the ambiguity in the agreement with National City that Reger believes provides him with a proper basis for his cause of action against National City?

ETHICAL DECISION MAKING

What stakeholders are affected by this decision? The law is concerned with much more than the interests of the two parties in the dispute. What other parties are affected by whether Reger won this case?

Exhibit 26-3

Potential Complexity of
Negotiable Instruments

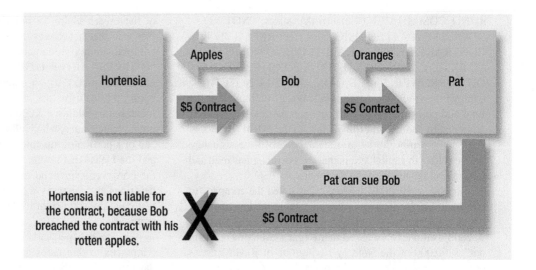

An Overview of the Law of Negotiable Instruments

L03

What are the requirements of negotiability?

A negotiable instrument must meet specific requirements of *negotiability*. However—and this is important—if an instrument fails to qualify as a negotiable instrument, that does *not* mean it fails to be a perfectly good and enforceable contract. All it means is that the special rules regarding negotiable instruments do not apply.

A negotiable instrument confers some special rights on its possessor. Let's go back to Bob, Hortensia, and Pat. Use Exhibit 26-3 to follow the logic of the exchanges.

Hortensia buys apples from Bob and gives him a negotiable note promising to pay $5 on demand. Bob then buys oranges from Pat for $5 and properly transfers (or *negotiates*) the $5 negotiable note to Pat. Pat presents the note to Hortensia for payment, *after* Hortensia has found out that the apples she bought from Bob were bad. Hortensia refuses to pay Pat, and Bob has disappeared. Pat sues Hortensia for the $5. Under the rules of negotiable instruments, Pat could very well prevail, and Hortensia, regardless of Bob's rotten apples, might have to pay.

Here are the issues raised by this chain of events:

1. What constitutes a negotiable instrument?
2. How does someone transfer a negotiable instrument?
3. What is the status of the holder of a negotiable instrument?
4. What happens when the person who created a negotiable instrument has a good defense for not honoring it?

When the contracts for such transactions are not in breach, everything works out fine. Problems do happen, however, and have led to the evolution of the law surrounding negotiable commercial paper. Case 26-2 discusses whether a contract is a negotiable instrument or a common law contract.

CASE 26-2   **SAMUEL JAMES THOMPSON v. FIRST CITIZENS BANK & TRUST CO.**

COURT OF APPEALS OF NORTH CAROLINA

151 N.C. APP., 567 S.E.2D 184 (2002)

On November 5, 1998, Samuel James Thompson borrowed $10,500 from First Citizens Bank & Trust Co. As collateral for the loan First Citizens required Thompson to purchase a $10,000 certificate of deposit. Thompson met with Catherine Huggins, First Citizens' employee, to execute the documents associated with the loan and the purchase of the CD.

Huggins gave him a CD confirmation form with her signature, acknowledging he had opened a CD account with an initial deposit of $10,000. On the same day, Thompson executed an "Assignment of Deposit Account," assigning the CD to the bank as collateral for his loan. In November 1999, Thompson paid off the $10,000 loan from First Citizens and presented the CD confirmation for payment. The bank refused to pay the amount due on the CD and claimed that, notwithstanding the signed confirmation, Thompson had not deposited $10,000 to purchase a CD.

JUDGE BIGGS: . . . Defendant argues that the trial court erred in granting summary judgment for plaintiff, and contends that the evidence raised a genuine issue of material fact regarding whether there was consideration for the CD. The resolution of this issue requires us to examine several features of the commercial transaction at issue. First, plaintiff and defendant disagree about whether the CD is a negotiable instrument as defined by the Uniform Commercial Code (UCC). We conclude that the CD at issue in the present case is not a negotiable instrument, and therefore is not governed by the negotiable instrument provisions of the UCC. The UCC applies only to negotiable instruments.

A "negotiable instrument" is "an unconditional promise or order to pay a fixed amount of money[.]" Negotiable instruments, also called simply "instruments," may include, e.g., a personal check, cashier's check, traveler's check, or CD. N.C.G.S. 25-3-104, however, provides that a financial document such as a CD "is not an instrument if, at the time it is issued or first comes into possession of a holder, it contains a conspicuous statement, however expressed, to the effect that the promise or order is not negotiable or is not an instrument governed by this Article."

In the instant case, the CD confirmation clearly states, in upper case type, "NON-TRANSFERABLE." We conclude that this qualifies as "a conspicuous statement . . . that the promise or order is not negotiable," and, thus, that the CD does not fall within the purview of the negotiable instrument provisions of the UCC.

"Because the certificate of deposit at issue does not fall under the UCC, we must turn to the common law." Holloway at 100, 423 S.E.2d at 755. The CD confirmation is a contract between plaintiff and defendant, and its interpretation is governed by principles of contract law.

. . . Notwithstanding the language of the CD confirmation, defendant contends that language in its "Deposit Account Agreement" booklet establishes that the CD confirmation was issued subject to a condition precedent. This document states that an account "is not opened or valid until we receive . . . the initial deposit in cash or collectible funds." The CD confirmation is, however, the document that verifies or acknowledges that this condition precedent (deposit of money) has already occurred. Therefore, the bank booklet does not raise an issue of fact.

Nor is evidence of a unilateral mistake admissible to contradict the terms of a contract. Goodwin v. Cashwell, 102 N.C. App. 275, 277, 401 S.E.2d 840, 840 (1991) (parol evidence rule excludes consideration of unilateral error made by one party in calculations pertaining to settlement agreement; Court notes that a "unilateral mistake, unaccompanied by fraud, imposition, undue influence, or like oppressive circumstances, is not sufficient to void a contract").

AFFIRMED in favor of defendant.
Judges GREENE and HUDSON concur.

CRITICAL THINKING

Judge Biggs gives only one reason for ruling that the contract was not a negotiable instrument. He says that it is not an instrument if, at the time it is issued or first comes into possession of a holder, it contains a conspicuous statement to the effect that the promise or order is not negotiable. What evidence from this case supports his reasoning that the agreement contains a conspicuous statement to that effect?

ETHICAL DECISION MAKING

Did First Citizens have an ethical obligation to provide further information about the negotiability of the contract? If so, what could the bank do to prevent similar cases in the future?

NEGOTIABLE INSTRUMENT VERSUS SIMPLE CONTRACT

While the Thompson case is a good example of what constitutes a negotiable instrument, it is important to note that a simple contract is very different. First, simple contracts are assigned to an assignee, while negotiable instruments are negotiated to a holder. A holder and an assignee differ because a negotiable instrument gives greater rights to the holder

CAN ALL NEGOTIABLE INSTRUMENTS BE IN ELECTRONIC FORMAT?

Electronic negotiable instruments are often preferable to traditional negotiable instruments because electronic forms foster more efficient business practices by reducing the amount of time a document must wait to be processed. However, the very nature of electronically sent information means that certain types of negotiable instruments should not be in a virtual format. An excellent illustration of this concept is found within the 2008 Kenya Communications Act, which outlines exclusions for electronic negotiable instruments. For example, the act excludes an electronically created or executed will from being upheld as a legal negotiable instrument in court. Exclusions such as this are stipulated because wills and certain other documents are legally significant and binding only if those documents have been signed in their physical form. Considering the ease with which a person could falsify an online signature, it is impractical to allow important documents such as wills to be completed in an electronic format. Specifying what is and is not legally valid in cyberspace is an important step in reducing legal ambiguities and possible conflicts.

Source: http://aitec.usp.net/Banking%20&%20Payment%20Technologies%20EA,17-19Feb2009/MichaelMurungi.pdf.

than the transferor. Second, as you will read below, negotiable instruments lack the requirements of contracts: consideration and both offer and acceptance.

REQUIREMENTS FOR NEGOTIABILITY

To be negotiable (which is *not* the same as *enforceable*) under UCC 3-104(a), the instrument must satisfy seven requirements. It must:

1. Be a written document.
2. Be signed by the creator of the instrument.
3. Have an unconditional promise or order to pay.
4. Specify a fixed sum of money.
5. Specify payment either on demand or at a fixed future time.
6. Contain the words *to the order of* or words indicating it is a bearer instrument.
7. Contain no additional promises.

As you read through the following explanation of the requirements, use Exhibit 26-4 as an example of how they apply to personal checks.

Exhibit 26-4 Requirements of Negotiability in a Check

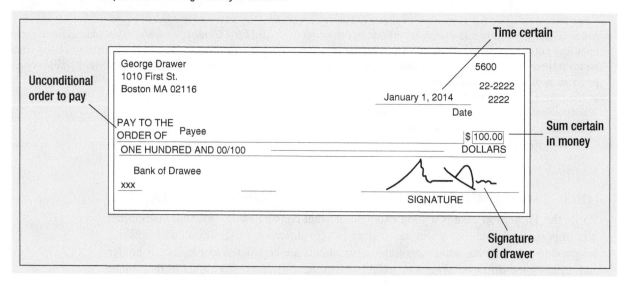

Written Document.   Clearly, the law does not permit an *oral* negotiable instrument. However, under the right circumstances and when the words are provable, such a statement may be a binding, enforceable *contract.*

BUT WHAT IF . . .

WHAT IF THE FACTS OF THE CASE OPENER WERE DIFFERENT?

Recall that, in the Case Opener, Shack contended that an oral agreement had been made between him and the plaintiff about "rolling debt." What if Shack had presented a recording of this particular oral agreement actually being made? Would the judge still rely only on the written negotiable agreement?

Recall that in the Case Opener, the judge ruled in favor of MGM partly because no evidence of an oral agreement was presented. Although Shack claimed that a conversation had occurred, this was not enough evidence for the court. Instead, the judge had to go by the written negotiable agreement. The Case Opener is just one of many examples indicating that the best business practice is to obtain written documentation of all the details pertaining to negotiable instruments.

The written document must have two characteristics: relative permanence and movability. Writing a negotiable instrument in the mud, for example, clearly lacks permanence. Thus, it is not a negotiable instrument. Likewise, mud is not something we can move about in a commercially reasonable or expected manner.

Signature of the Maker or Drawer.   The UCC and precedent cases are fairly liberal in interpreting what constitutes a signature. Anyone's affirmative mark, from a full-blown *John Hancock* to an *X,* will suffice, provided the party intended that the mark be placed on the instrument and uses that mark to identify himself or herself [UCC 1-201(39)]. The UCC specifies that a signature "may be made (i) manually or by means of a device or machine, and (ii) by the use of any name, including a trade or assumed name, or by a word, mark, or symbol executed or adopted by a person with present intention to authenticate a writing" [3-401(b)]. Likewise, a duly authorized agent's signature on behalf of his or her principal binds the principal and satisfies this signature requirement [UCC 3-401(b)].

A handwritten negotiable instrument satisfies the signature requirement even without a formal signature. The handwritten statement "I, Philippe Gauchet, promise to pay Roberta Alexander or the bearer the sum of $20 on Sunday July 4, 2010" would satisfy the signature requirement because the handwriting affirms the maker's intent and, in that handwritten promise, the maker wrote his own name, Philippe Gauchet.

Case 26-3 discusses the extent to which wire transfers and electronic signatures can be governed by the laws set forth by the Uniform Commercial Code.

BUT WHAT IF . . .

WHAT IF THE FACTS OF THE CASE OPENER WERE DIFFERENT?

Let's say, in the Case Opener, that Shack bought a casino marker using a check after he told his assistant to stamp an automated "signature" at the bottom. Would he still be personally liable for the check? Alternatively, what if he signed simply an "H" at the bottom of the check? Would his check be a valid negotiable instrument?

CASE 26-3   STATE v. WARNER
SUPREME COURT OF OHIO
55 OHIO ST. 3D 31, 564 N.E.2D 18 (1990)

On December 13, 1985, defendant-appellant, Marvin L. Warner, controlling shareholder of Home State, and two former Home State Savings Bank presidents, David J. Schiebel and Burton M. Bongard, were indicted and charged with numerous felonies arising from Home State's dealings with ESM Government Securities, Inc. (ESM). The amended indictment charged Warner with forty-two counts of misapplication of funds and forty-one counts of unauthorized acts in violation of Ohio Revised Code 1153.01. Further, Warner was indicted on four counts of securities fraud. . . . The Ohio Revised Code makes it a crime to fraudulently transfer funds by means of a draft or other written instrument. Therefore, one issue before the court in this very complicated securities fraud case is whether an electronic transfer qualifies as a "draft" or "other written instrument." The Ohio Court of Appeals determined it did not and reversed.

JUSTICE HOLMES: Since this issue is one of first impression for this court, we will consider how other jurisdictions have applied laws drafted primarily to address traditional written documents, such as checks, but applied to modern wire transfers. In Richards v. Platte Valley Bank the United States Court of Appeals decided that the word "check" as used in the Uniform Fiduciaries Act could be interpreted to include wire transfers of funds. The Richards court stated:

> We believe wire transfers are analogous to checks for application of the Uniform Fiduciaries Act. The transfer of funds by cable or telegraph is in law a check. Lourie v. Chase Nat'l Bank.
>
> The transfer item must be in some form of writing, such as letter, telegram or magnetic disc. . . . Wire transfers are considered irrevocable after transmission. Delbrueck, 609 F. 2d at 1051.
>
> The wire transfer requirements are similar to the definition of a check under the Uniform Commercial Code. A check is defined as a draft drawn upon a bank and payable on demand, signed by the maker or drawer, containing an unconditional promise to pay a sum certain in money to the order of the payee. A wire transfer is a written order to pay, drawn upon a bank containing an unconditional promise to pay a sum certain in money to the order of the beneficiary. The only element missing is the maker's signature. We do not consider this element significant for

purposes of excluding wire transfers from the operation of the Uniform Fiduciaries Act.

Although the Uniform Commercial Code is not directly applicable to this case due to the nature of the transfer, analogous use of its concepts supports the proposition that wire transfers are written instruments for purposes of R.C. 1153.01. Delbrueck & Co. v. Mfrs. Hanover Trust Co. ("the Uniform Commercial Code ['UCC'] is not applicable to this case because the UCC does not specifically address the problems of electronic funds transfer. However, analogous use of concepts such as the finality of checks once 'accepted' support the irrevocability of these transfers").

In Illinois, ex rel. Lignoul, v. Continental Ill. Natl. Bank & Trust Co. of Chicago, certiorari denied (1976), the United States Court of Appeals, Seventh Circuit, decided that making an electronic transfer of funds through a computer terminal was essentially the same as issuing a check. The Lignoul court observed:

> The check is merely the means used by the bank to attain the desired objective, i.e., the payment of the money to its customer. The card serves the same purpose as the check. It is an order on the bank. Any order to pay which is properly executed by a customer, whether it be check, card or electronic device, must be recognized as a routine banking function when used as here. The relationship between the bank and its customer is the same. . . .

In today's modern banking environment, electronic transfers have become commonplace. On an average day, six hundred billion dollars in funds are transferred by wire or electronic means. . . . As noted in the discussion above, under modern day conditions, transferring assets of a savings and loan association over the Fedwire is the equivalent of sending a check or issuing a draft.

Through R.C. 1553.01, the General Assembly clearly intended to criminalize the unauthorized transfers of an association's assets regardless of form. Thus, the transfer of funds through the Fedwire system qualifies as a "draft" or other "written statement" as those terms are used in R.C. 1153.01. Accordingly, the court of appeals' conclusion that the authorized transfer of Home State's assets over the Fedwire did not constitute a "writing" within the meaning of R.C. 1153.01 was erroneous.

REVERSED in favor of plaintiff.

CRITICAL THINKING

What evidence might the court of appeals have used in its determination that an electronic transfer did not qualify as a draft?

ETHICAL DECISION MAKING

Home State Savings probably suffered negative publicity from this case. One possible safeguard for preventing further unauthorized and fraudulent electronic transfers would be to require that an accountant review all the electronic transactions the controlling shareholder makes on a monthly basis. What types of policies might the company implement to prevent such fraudulent activity in the future? Would those policies assist the relevant stakeholders?

Legal Principle: As a general rule, the promise or order to pay must be specified and not implied.

Unconditional Promise or Order to Pay.   The promise or order to pay must be specific and not implied. The language must be affirmative in nature [UCC 3-103(a)(9)]. For example, simply acknowledging a debt does not create language for payment; therefore, a common IOU is not a promise or an order to pay and cannot be a negotiable instrument. Nevertheless, an IOU is a very strong piece of evidence for demonstrating the existence of a debt and, as such, will prove an enforceable contract. It *can* become a negotiable instrument if the language "payable on demand," or something expressing similar affirmative agreement to pay, is included. In addition, "order" or "bearer" language is required to turn an IOU into a negotiable instrument. For example, a negotiable instrument would include "payable to order or to bearer," as mandated by Section 3-104 of the UCC.

The unconditional nature of the promise or order is often the controversial variable of this requirement of negotiability. Stated as simply as possible, the promise or order to pay cannot be contingent on anything else. An instrument stating, "I promise to pay if the following occurs" is not a negotiable instrument. It may be a perfectly enforceable contract, but it fails to satisfy the terms of negotiability.

BUT WHAT IF . . .
WHAT IF THE FACTS OF THE CASE OPENER WERE DIFFERENT?
Let's say, in the Case Opener, that Shack bought a casino marker, and he, his father, and MGM signed a contract stipulating a certain payment arrangement for that marker. Let's say that the contract says that when the marker comes due, and Shack doesn't pay in cash within 48 hours, his father will pay it. In other words, his father's promise to pay is contingent on whether his son pays within a time frame. Does this document constitute a negotiable instrument? Is the document even an enforceable contract?

Legal Principle: As a general rule, negotiable instruments must promise or order that payment be made in a national currency.

Sum Certain in Money.   Negotiable instruments must promise or order that payment be made in a national currency [UCC 3-104(a)]. For example, U.S. dollars, English pounds, Euros, and Japanese yen all satisfy the currency requirement. While promises to pay in apples or gold or stock may form a perfectly enforceable contract, these are not currencies and the resulting instrument is not a negotiable instrument. An instrument promising payment in "German marks and rare French wine" is not negotiable. Even changing the *and* to an *or* does not salvage negotiability; payment *must* be made in a currency.

> ## ? BUT WHAT IF . . .
>
> ### WHAT IF THE FACTS OF THE CASE OPENER WERE DIFFERENT?
>
> Let's say, in the Case Opener, that Shack bought a casino marker, by giving MGM an IOU with the phrase "payable on demand." Would such a document classify as a negotiable instrument? What if Shack specified an amount of some payment that was payable on demand, stating "1 yacht and 1 million dollars are payable on demand"? Would this document constitute a negotiable instrument?

Payable at a Time Certain or on Demand.   A negotiable instrument must be payable on demand or at a specific time that the parties can compute from the instrument itself. Obviously, if the instrument states a specific date, that is a time certain. If the instrument is dated and states "payment will be made 10 days after above date," the instrument is negotiable because we can calculate the specific date. A dated instrument that states "Payment is to be made at some future time after above date" is clearly nonnegotiable (although, again, it may be enforceable as a contract).

Likewise, an instrument that states "payment will be made 10 days after delivery of the goods" but indicates nowhere in the instrument when that delivery is to be made is not a negotiable instrument. (It might also be nonnegotiable if such a reference is construed to be a condition of payment as well.) Negotiation of an order instrument is by endorsement plus delivery, while negotiation of a bearer instrument is by delivery alone.

There are two noteworthy exceptions to the time-certain requirement. First, an instrument that permits acceleration of payment does not violate this requirement as long as there is a fixed date of payment if the acceleration clause is not satisfied. Second, an instrument that permits an extension of the payment is still negotiable if there is a fixed time for payment. The time of payment may be extended if it is at the election of the holder [UCC 3-108(b)(ii),(iii),(iv)].

Demand instruments, such as checks, are payable as soon as they are issued. If an instrument is silent as to the time of payment, the UCC presumes that it is a demand instrument and thus retains its negotiable status [3-108(a)].

Legal Principle: **For an instrument to be negotiable, the instrument must indicate that it was created for the purpose of being transferred.**

LO4

What are the words of negotiability?

Words of Negotiability.   Finally, for an instrument to be negotiable, the instrument must indicate it was created for the purpose of being transferred. How can the maker or drawer indicate this purpose? By writing the phrase *to the order of* or similar words near the payee's name, such as "Pay to the order of Ichiro Endo" or "Pay to Ichiro Endo on his order." When a specific payee is named, the document is an *order instrument* [UCC 3-109(b)]. Sometimes negotiable instruments have the proper words of negotiability, such as "pay to the order of," and there are still problems with receiving payment.

THE END OF THE FLOAT?

Consumers who rely on "float" (the time it takes for a check to go through the traditional check-clearing process and be paid) have a limited amount of time to enjoy the delay it affords. Businesses in many parts of the country are testing new technology that speeds the check-clearing process. Soon, float might be an outdated tradition.

Nevada State Bank, for instance, allows businesses that purchase a special service to scan checks, send them electronically, and get money for checks drawn on other banks much more quickly than they would otherwise; the delay in check processing is cut by 40 percent. Other banks are testing similar products

and services. In some states, businesses can substitute electronic images of checks for the checks themselves. Here's how the process works: (1) A customer gives a business a check in payment for a product or service, (2) the business scans the check and sends it to the bank providing the new check-clearing products and services, (3) the bank sends the image to the customer's bank, (4) the customer's bank prints a substitute check, and (5) the customer's payment is quickly deposited in the business's account at that business's bank.

It remains to be seen what kinds of litigation will emerge from this expedited process.

BUT WHAT IF . . .

WHAT IF THE FACTS OF THE CASE OPENER WERE DIFFERENT?

Recall in the Case Opener that Shack contended the terms of his old marker payment agreement were not enforceable because he could acquire a new marker to "freshen" the agreement. If Shack had signed a document that simply acknowledged that Shack had acquired a marker, and not that the payment for the marker was due to MGM, would this document qualify as a negotiable instrument?

Negotiable instruments payable to whoever is bearing them are *bearer instruments* [UCC 3-109(a)] and are treated like cash. Anyone who comes into possession of a bearer instrument by any means, including theft, may claim the payment due on it. Endorsing an order instrument, such as a check, converts it into a bearer instrument that may be claimed by anyone in possession of it. Instruments payable to no one, to "X," or to "cash" are also considered bearer instruments.

The phrase *to the order of* is necessary to create a negotiable instrument. Wordings such as "Pay to bearer," "Pay to Ichiro Endo or bearer," "Pay to cash," and "Pay to the order of cash [or bearer]" all make the paper negotiable.

Until the situation moves beyond the two contractual parties, it does not really matter whether an instrument is negotiable. Consider a contractual situation such as that in Exhibit 26-5.

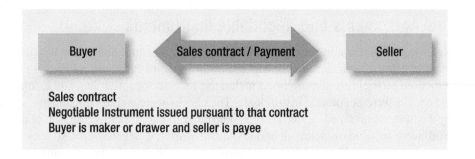

Sales contract
Negotiable Instrument issued pursuant to that contract
Buyer is maker or drawer and seller is payee

Exhibit 26-5

Illustrative Contract Situation with Two Parties

The European Economic Council's (EEC's) Contractual Obligations Convention has addressed how to characterize negotiable instruments, whose definition differs among member countries. Rather than creating one encompassing definition, however, the EEC decided to let each member country decide what types of documents to consider negotiable instruments. While this decision may prevent some problems, it could cause other problems in cross-border transactions. Thus, the convention decided to define a general concept of negotiability. If a transaction is defined as a negotiable instrument within a certain country, it must conform to certain general characteristics outlined by the EEC. These general characteristics are intended to dilute the complexities of cross-border transactions.

The relationship between the buyer and the seller is controlled by the terms of the underlying contract. The status of the negotiable instrument is really irrelevant, as it is a matter between the buyer and the seller. The instrument's being negotiable, however, becomes important when a third party comes into the situation, as in the scenario in Exhibit 26-6.

This situation leads us to the second stage of negotiable instruments: Once the negotiable instrument has been created, how is it transferred? We answer that question in Chapter 27.

Legal Principle: **Definitions of negotiable contracts may vary from country to country, which may make international transactions difficult.**

Exhibit 26-6   Effect of a Third Party

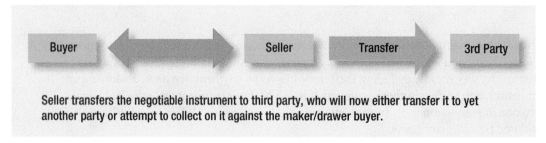

Seller transfers the negotiable instrument to third party, who will now either transfer it to yet another party or attempt to collect on it against the maker/drawer buyer.

CASE OPENER WRAP-UP

Oral Agreements and Negotiable Instruments

Referring to the dispute between MGM Desert Inn, Inc., and Shack, the district court held that the potential oral agreement was irrelevant to the negotiability of the checks. Instead, it focused on the criteria established within the UCC for negotiability, and it concluded that the checks were negotiable instruments. The checks were written documents, were signed by the maker, contained an unconditional promise to pay, specified the sum of money to be paid, were payable on demand, and contained words of negotiability, so they were negotiable instruments. Hence, MGM was considered the holder of the instruments.

KEY TERMS

certificate of deposit (CD)   566

check   566

demand
   instrument   566

draft   565

movability   571

negotiable
   instrument   564

note   565

relative permanence   571

time instrument   566

SUMMARY OF KEY TOPICS

Negotiable Instruments are any contractual obligations, except for personal ones and nonassignable ones. They are a form of commercial paper. A breach of the contract invalidates the commercial paper.

The Need for Negotiable Instruments

There are several types of negotiable instruments.

Types of Negotiable Instruments

1. A *note* is a promise by a maker to pay a payee (e.g., a certificate of deposit).
2. A *draft* is an order by a drawer to a drawee to pay a payee (e.g., a check).

A *demand instrument* is one for which a payee can demand payment at any time.

A *time instrument* is one for which payment will be made only at a designated time.

There are several requirements for negotiability. The following criteria must all be met:

An Overview of the Law of Negotiable Instruments

1. Written document:
   - Relative permanence
   - Movability

2. Signature of the maker or drawer:
   - Affirmative mark
   - Duly authorized agent
   - Handwritten, even without signature
   - Automated signature

3. Unconditional promise or order to pay:
   - Must be specific, not implied

4. Sum certain in money:
   - Currency only; any currency acceptable

5. Payable at a time certain or on demand:
   - Acceleration of payment
   - Extension of payment

6. Words of negotiability:
   - To the order of
   - Order instrument

POINT / COUNTERPOINT

Should Businesses Use Contracts rather than Negotiable Instruments to Set Payment Terms?	
YES	NO
Conditional contractual agreements are preferable.

    Assuming both parties abide by the stipulations in a conditional contract, payment is guaranteed. Payment will not get lost as it travels among many parties—each claiming that a previous party did not fulfill his or her obligations in the contract.

    The conditional aspect of the payment contract makes the sale more appealing to the buyer, who will not have to pay for an item that does not fit the conditions agreed | Unconditional negotiable instruments are a superior form of payment. They allow flexibility in payment and a much higher yield in profits.

    First, negotiable instruments allow only secure monetary payment in a national currency, a restriction ideal for large businesses that cannot calculate the exact worth of gold or diamonds at a future payment date. Businesses operate nationally and internationally with cash, not gems or bottles of fine wine. |

on in the payment contract. Plus, the buyer can feel confident that an unknown individual will not approach him or her to collect money for a debt the original seller transferred. Because the buyer's debt is conditional and payable to the seller *only*, the buyer will always know that his or her debt was paid properly and directly.

The conditional aspect of the contract also keeps all parties honest. The seller cannot secretly transfer the debt to another individual knowing his or her product is poor. The seller is held directly accountable for the product, and the buyer is held directly accountable for payment.

Unconditional negotiable instruments can be paid *only* in a national currency. Under a conditional agreement, which allows for more flexibility, a wine connoisseur can arrange to be paid for a shipment of fine cheese with a bottle of extremely rare 1945 Fonseca—a priceless acquisition.

Second, businesses using negotiable instruments can earn a high yield by investing their excess cash in low-risk certificates of deposit.

Negotiable instruments allow flexibility in payment, either "on demand" or "at time certain." Although these specifications seem rigid, payments can be accelerated or extended, provided a time is always set and not extended indefinitely. This flexibility allows businesses to work well together.

QUESTIONS & PROBLEMS

1. Explain the reason behind the need for negotiable instruments.

2. Are negotiable instruments more similar to money or to contracts? Explain.

3. Identify and define each of the elements of negotiability.

4. Dr. Rodrigue is an obstetrician-gynecologist who in 1989 opened her own practice. The financial support to open her new practice came from North County Women's Health Care Services P.C., which provided her with start-up and relocation assistance and a practice consultant who helped draft and publish an employee manual. In November 1990, Rodrigue missed a sponsored event due to the mishandling of postal mail addressed to the practice. She then required that all mail be given to her, unopened, for her to open personally. In May 1990, she had hired Carol Wiltshire to work as a medical receptionist and secretary. Over the nine years Wiltshire worked for Rodrigue, she held a variety of positions of increasing responsibility and authority within the office. In her position as billing specialist, Wiltshire was responsible for understanding insurance requirements and was the only person in the office trained in the Doctor's Office Management System (DOMS) when Rodrigue converted to the computerized billing

system in 1992. DOMS software is used to manage accounts by tracking charges, payments, and adjustments. From 1992 until her termination in 1999, Wiltshire was solely responsible for entering charges, adjustments, and payments and closing out monthly statements for patient charges via the DOMS software. After learning how to use the software, Wiltshire began stealing checks from the doctor's mail that were sent by various insurance providers and were payable to Rodrigue. During the course of her employment at Rodrigue's office, Wiltshire stole 269 checks, totaling $372,572.18. Around 1994 to 1995, the office began to face financial troubles. Rodrigue finally discovered Wiltshire's embezzlement at the end of November 1999, after her sister-in-law, Denise Rodrigue, told her that she believed Wiltshire had been taking mail into her office, opening it, and stealing insurance checks. Which terms of negotiable instruments does this case fall under or describe? [*Rodrigue v. Olin Employees Credit Union*, 03-2470, 03-2607 (7th Cir. 2005).]

5. In 2001, Cory Babcock and Honest Air Conditioning & Heating, Inc., purchased a new 2001 Chevrolet Corvette from Cox, a car dealer. The retail installment sales contract (RISC) obligated monthly payments on the Corvette to satisfy the total indebtedness of $52,516.20 at a zero percent

interest rate. The RISC was immediately assigned to General Motors Acceptance Corp. (GMAC). On August 22, 2002, Honest Air and Babcock traded the Corvette to Florida Auto Brokers as part of the purchase of another vehicle. In September, Babcock told GMAC that he had traded the vehicle. In December 2002, GMAC was told by Babcock that the local dealership would be mailing GMAC the money due for the Corvette and the vehicle's title as a security interest. Once the check was finally sent to GMAC but not cashed yet, the security interest (the title) was returned to the dealership. However, the check was dishonored for insufficient funds. As a result, GMAC sued Honest Air and Babcock for $35,815.26 as damages resulting from the breach of the terms of the RISC. Cox argued the RISC was a negotiable instrument. What requirements must the RISC meet to be considered a negotiable instrument, and what would this mean for GMAC? [*GMAC v. Honest Air Conditioning & Heating, Inc.,* 2006 933 So. 2d 34, 2006 Fla. App. LEXIS 7255.]

6. Doseung Chung, the plaintiff, a horse player, was at Belmont Park Racetrack, which is owned by the defendant, New York Racing Association. While at the track, Chung was using a voucher to place bets on the races through an automated betting machine. After placing a bet, Chung took his betting ticket but forgot his voucher, which had thousands of dollars left on it. A few minutes later, he returned to the machine, but the voucher was gone. Chung put an electronic stop on the voucher, but the voucher had been cashed out about one minute after it was left in the machine. Chung subsequently sued the racetrack, arguing that the track was negligent in not requiring proof of identity when patrons cash out their vouchers, which constitute negotiable instruments. How did the court rule? Why? [*Doseung Chung v. New York Racing Ass'n,* 714 N.Y.S.2d 429 (2000).]

7. In October 2006, America's Wholesale Lender (AWL) agreed to loan John Horvath $650,000. The loan was stated in an interest-only, fixed-rate note and was secured by a deed of trust on Horvath's home. In exchange for the $650,000, Horvath agreed to repay AWL in monthly installments ranging from about $3,000 to $5,000. The note allowed AWL (and any subsequent holder) to freely transfer the note. In fact, the note provided for "anyone who takes this Note by transfer" to inherit the powers of the "Note Holder," including the right to accelerate payment in the event that Horvath defaulted. Any party who took the note would have the right to enforce it. In 2009, the note was transferred to Bank of New York, and a little over a half year later, Horvath defaulted. His property was foreclosed on, and then he proceeded to sue. Was Horvath right in suing? Why or why not, based on the wording of the note? [*Horvath v. Bank of NY,* 641 F.3d 617, 2011 U.S. App. LEXIS 10152.]

8. Anthony Bango needed several short-term loans to fund a real estate closing. He contacted Dennis Mulholland of Ohio Financial Mortgage Corp. (OFMC), and Mulholland located an interested investor, James Jarvis. Jarvis was faxed a note stating, "Upon the closing of this Real Estate Transaction the lender will be repaid the principal sum of $30,000 along with the closing costs agreed upon by all parties in full by the borrower." Jarvis transferred the money to Mulholland, and Mulholland delivered the money to Bango. Bango, who had a criminal record, requested that the money be delivered in cash. After receiving the money, Bango notified Mulholland that other investors had not come through with their loans and that an additional $20,000 was needed. Again, Jarvis transferred the money to Mulholland to give to Bango. Bango verbally agreed to pay $70,000 in return for the total loan of $50,000. When Bango did not make payment, Mulholland contacted him again. Bango revealed that the real estate transaction did not exist; instead, the money was needed for his personal debts. Jarvis collected only $8,500 of the loan. Jarvis filed a motion for summary judgment against Dennis Mulholland and OFMC. He claimed that the initial fax was a negotiable instrument. The trial court determined that Mulholland's fax did not constitute a promissory note or any other type of negotiable instrument. Do you agree? How does this determination affect the outcome of the case? [*Jarvis v. Silbert,* 1999 Ohio App. LEXIS 4828.]

9. Sirius LC is a Wyoming company co-owned by William Bagley and his wife. Bagley is an attorney whose services Bryce Erickson procured for bankruptcy proceedings. Bagley agreed to represent Erickson for a Chapter 12 bankruptcy proceeding provided that Erickson sign a promissory note payable to Sirius in the amount of $29,173.38 to be secured by a mortgage on property owned by

Erickson in Caribou County, Idaho. Bagley asserts that the amount of the promissory note represented the overdue legal fees Erickson owed him for the Chapter 11 bankruptcy proceeding. Erickson then executed a promissory note payable to Sirius, which provided "[f]or value received, the undersigned Bryce H. Erickson promises to pay to SIRIUS LC . . . the sum of $29,173.38 bearing 10% interest due and payable on June 1, 2001." The case commenced when Sirius filed a complaint to foreclose on Erickson's Caribou County property after he refused to pay the note once it became due. In the proceedings, the district court held that the promissory note "clearly fell within the definition of a negotiable instrument." The case was then appealed. Do you think the decision was affirmed? Does the note have all the proper words of negotiability? [*Sirius LC v. Bryce H. Erickson*, 2007 144 Idaho 38, 156 P.3d 539, LEXIS 74.]

10. A branch of Wachovia bank in Alabama loaned $150,000 to McNamee in early 2003. In order to obtain the $150,000, McNamee was required to sign a promissory note, promising he would repay the loan. At some point, Wachovia lost, misplaced, or destroyed the original note signed by McNamee. The note ($150,000) reached maturity in late 2005, and Wachovia signed the rights of the note over to Atlantic National Trust. The trust sued for recovery of both the principal and the interest owed. However, McNamee claimed that he did not have to repay because the original documentation was lost by Wachovia. What was the result of this case? Why? [*Atlantic National Trust, LLC v. McNamee*, 984 So. 2d 375, 381 (Ala. 2007).]

Looking for more review materials?

The Online Learning Center at **www.mhhe.com/kubasek3e** contains this chapter's "Assignment on the Internet" and also a list of URLs for more information, entitled "On the Internet." Find both of them in the Student Center portion of the OLC, along with quizzes and other helpful materials.

Negotiation, Holder in Due Course, and Defenses

LEARNING OBJECTIVES

After reading this chapter, you will be able to answer the following questions:

1 What is negotiation?

2 What is a holder in due course?

3 What requirements must be met to obtain holder-in-due-course status?

4 What is the shelter principle?

5 In what ways has the holder-in-due-course doctrine been abused?

CASE OPENER

Dishonored Check and Holder-in-Due-Course Status

In July 1993, Cigna Insurance Company issued James Mills a workers' compensation check for $484. Then Mills lied to Cigna and said he had not received the draft due to a change in his address. He requested that payment be stopped and a new draft issued. The insurer complied, stopped payment on the initial draft, and promptly issued a new check for Mills. However, Mills cashed the first check at Sun's Market before the stop-payment notation was placed on the draft. Sun's Market then presented the check for payment through its bank.

As a result of the stop payment on the initial draft, the bank dishonored the check, stamped it "Stop Payment," and returned the check to Sun's bank. After not receiving the cash for the bad check, Sun's Market tacked the check on its bulletin board. An individual, Robert Triffin, purchased the check from Sun's Market and obtained an assignment of Sun's interests in the instrument.

More than two years after the check was returned unpaid, Triffin filed a lawsuit against Cigna for payment on the check. Triffin argued that by purchasing the check from Sun's Market, he gained a special legal status, called *holder-in-due-course* status. This status entitled him to payment on the dishonored check. He argued that he received this special status under the *shelter principle* because the transfer by a holder in due course to a third party, even one with notice of the dishonor, transfers all rights of the holder in due course to the third party.

1. Who do you think should bear the dishonored check? In other words, should Cigna be required to pay Triffin for the dishonored workers' compensation check? Why or why not?

2. Suppose you are a business manager at Sun's Market. You learn that the court holds that Cigna Insurance Company does not have to pay for dishonored checks. Would you make any changes to your business policies? Would you be less likely to accept checks from insurance companies in the future?

The Wrap-Up at the end of the chapter will answer these questions.

As you can see in the Case Opener, financial transactions with negotiable instruments can be risky. A negotiable instrument, as we saw in the preceding chapter, is a written document signed by the maker or drawer with an unconditional promise or order to pay a certain sum of money on demand or at a specified time to the order of bearer (UCC Section 3-104). One important characteristic of negotiable instruments is the ease of transferring them to a third party through negotiation (UCC 3-201). A negotiation occurs when multiple parties enter into an agreement meant to resolve a conflict or another subject of interest. In the opening case, Sun's Market transferred the check through negotiation.

A party who possesses a negotiable instrument payable to the party or bearer of the instrument is a holder of the instrument [UCC 1-201(b)(21)]. A holder's right to an instrument may be limited, and the holder is subject to certain defenses. For example, when a party refuses to make payment on an instrument on the basis of breach of contract, the holder may not be able to collect.

A certain type of holder, however, called a holder in due course (HDC), has more extensive legal rights, including freedom from competing claims and defenses. (Later in the chapter, Exhibit 27-6 provides a list of the specific defenses that can and cannot be used against a holder in due course.) Basically, there are four requirements, described later, for a holder to be of HDC status. Taking a cue from the credit card industry and its platinum cards, you can think of a holder in due course as a "platinum holder."

As a business manager, you will want to know whether your business is a holder or a holder in due course, because your legal rights will vary on the basis of this status. Would Sun's Market or Triffin be considered a holder in due course of the dishonored check and thus be entitled to greater protection? Why?

In this chapter, we begin by examining the characteristics of negotiation. Next, we consider the purpose of the holder-in-due-course doctrine. Then we examine the requirements for HDC status. We also briefly discuss the shelter principle and the HDC, as well as various abuses of the HDC doctrine and their remedies.

Negotiation

LO1

What is negotiation?

The rules of negotiation are slightly different depending on whether the instrument is an order instrument (payable to a specific, named payee) or a bearer instrument (payable to cash or whoever is in possession of the instrument) (UCC Section 3-109). Bearer paper requires only delivery of the instrument to the holder by the payee; order paper requires delivery *and* an endorsement.

THE EVOLUTION OF BILLS OF EXCHANGE IN RUSSIA

The concept of bills of exchange has existed in Russia since the late 17th century. The first statutes regulating them were influenced by German and French models. In the 1930s, however, bills of exchange were outlawed in the USSR, not to reemerge until the 1990s, and then only for use in foreign trade transactions under the Decree of the Presidium, adopted June 24, 1991.

Eventually Russia recognized the benefits of lifting the ban on domestic bills of exchange. Thus, in March 1997, the Russian Federation undertook a rare act in the Russian legal system and reintroduced previously repealed legislation from 1937, declaring that bills of exchange and promissory notes are legitimate documentary transactions in accordance with language of the 1930 Geneva Convention.

DELIVERY

Delivery simply means the physical handing of an instrument from someone entitled to it to the person intended to receive it. A bearer instrument that wafts out a window and lands in someone's hand has not been properly delivered. This lucky person cannot legally demand payment of that instrument because she is not a proper holder. However, she could pass it on to someone who could legally collect on it.

A drawer who is negligent in how he or she makes the delivery may be liable for notes paid with forged or unauthorized endorsements. In *Park State Bank v. Arena Auto Auction,*[1] an Illinois court held that the drawer and not the payor bank was liable for a check cashed by an Illinois business. The drawer had mailed the check to the wrong business, an unrelated firm of the same name as the intended payee but in another state. The payor bank paid the check to the wrong corporation, its client, because the names were the same. When the drawer tried to sue the payor bank, the court ruled that the drawer had acted negligently in delivering the check to the wrong business (which cashed the check in good faith) and therefore the drawer was liable for the amount of the check.

BUT WHAT IF . . .

WHAT IF THE FACTS OF THE CASE OPENER WERE DIFFERENT?

Recall that, in the Case Opener, Triffin purchased the check in question from Sun's Market after seeing it on the bulletin board. What if Sun's Market had thrown the check away and Triffin saw it and picked it up? Would he be able to legally collect on it?

Legal Principle: **A negotiable instrument cannot be delivered if it is accidentally found or is given to the wrong person.**

ENDORSEMENT

Order paper must be *endorsed* as well as *delivered* to be negotiated. The person creating the endorsement is the endorser; the person receiving it is the endorsee. Normally, there is a place on the negotiable instrument for endorsements (such as on the back of a check). If not or if all the room has been taken by other endorsements, an allonge, an additional piece of paper for endorsements, can be attached (firmly, as with staples) [UCC 3-204(a)]. Three kinds of endorsements affect the legal status of a negotiable instrument: unqualified, qualified, and restrictive.

Unqualified Endorsements: Blank and Special Endorsements. There are two kinds of unqualified endorsements: blank and special. A blank endorsement is simply the

[1] 207 N.E.2d 158 (Ill. App. Ct. 1965).

payee's or last endorsee's signature, nothing else [UCC 3-205(b)]. See Exhibit 27-1 for an illustration. An unqualified, blank endorsement turns order paper into bearer paper that can be negotiated by delivery only.

A **special endorsement** is the endorser's signature along with a named endorsee [UCC 3-205(a)]. Exhibit 27-2 illustrates. The words "Pay to Jackie Jones" followed by the endorser's signature create a special endorsement. This type of endorsement keeps order paper as order paper that continues to require endorsement and delivery for further negotiation. The words of negotiability, *to the order of,* are not needed.

Exhibit 27-1   Blank Endorsement

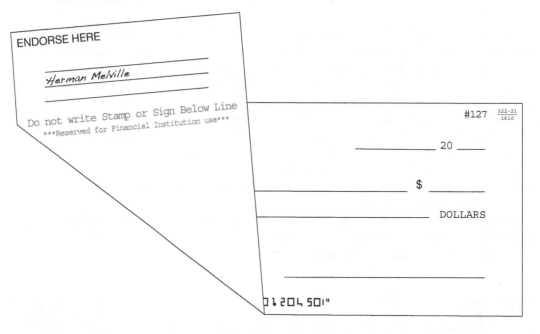

Exhibit 27-2   Special Endorsement

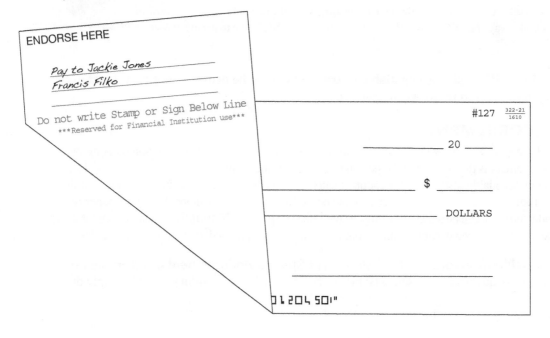

Exhibit 27-3   Blank Qualified Endorsement

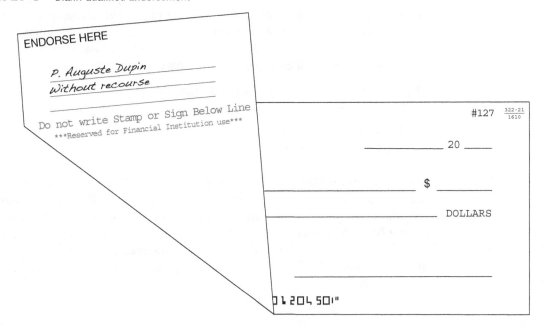

Qualified Endorsements.   Qualified endorsements can also be either blank qualified endorsements or special qualified endorsements. (See Exhibit 27-3 for an illustration.) What makes them qualified is the addition of the words *without recourse*. Ordinarily, when negotiable instruments pass from one party to another, the endorser's signature guarantees payment to a subsequent holder in the event the instrument is not honored by the party who created it [UCC 3-415(a)]. The restrictive endorsement *without recourse* means the endorser does not intend to be bound by this guarantee [UCC 3-415(b)].

For example, people often mistakenly write checks to their insurance agent when the proper recipient is the insurance company. The agent can restrictively endorse the check, following his signature with the statement "without recourse," and hand it over to the agency. The agent has effectively negotiated the check to the company and is not liable for the amount if there is a problem with the check.

While any endorser is free to use them, both blank and special qualified endorsements greatly reduce the marketability and thus the transferability of an instrument. Who would accept an instrument from someone who will endorse it only with qualifications? Such an endorsement is more or less a red flag that there may be a problem with the instrument. Needless to say, it is not widely used, but it is an option for the endorser.

BUT WHAT IF . . .

WHAT IF THE FACTS OF THE CASE OPENER WERE DIFFERENT?

What if Cigna Insurance sent the workers' compensation check to the wrong James Mills? If the incorrect James Mills cashed the check, would Cigna still be liable for the check? Alternatively, let's say the incorrect James Mills signed the check with the words *without recourse* and forwarded the check to the James Mills whom the check was actually intended for. Could the incorrect James Mills be responsible for any part of the payment if there was a problem?

Restrictive Endorsements.

Restrictive endorsements attempt to either limit the transferability of the instrument or control the manner of payment [UCC 3-206(a)]. No type of endorsement can prohibit further transfer; once negotiable, an instrument remains negotiable. But a restrictive endorsement can limit what is done with it.

The UCC gives four examples of restrictive endorsements:

1. The endorsement for deposit or collection only.
2. The endorsement to prohibit further endorsement.
3. The conditional endorsement.
4. The trust endorsement.

Endorsement for Deposit or Collection Only. The most common restrictive endorsement is the endorsement for deposit or collection only. The added words *for deposit only* turn an endorsement into a blank restrictive one [UCC 3-206(c)]. That check cannot be cashed; it can only be deposited into an account—*any* account. To be perfectly safe, the restrictive endorsement should read "for deposit only into National Bank Account #12345" and be signed by the endorser. Case 27-1 discusses endorsement problems.

CASE 27-1   MID-ATLANTIC TENNIS COURTS, INC. v. CITIZENS BANK AND TRUST COMPANY OF MARYLAND

U.S. DISTRICT COURT FOR THE DISTRICT OF MARYLAND
658 F. SUPP. 140 (1987)

In early 1983, Mid-Atlantic Tennis Courts, a small family-held corporation, decided to expand. It hired Loy Smith as a commissioned salesperson authorized to sell tennis court construction jobs and deliver the executed contracts and any customer deposits received directly to the business office of Mid-Atlantic in Clifton, Virginia.

In early 1984, Smith devised a scheme to defraud Mid-Atlantic. Using customer leads from the firm, he entered into eight contracts with potential customers but did not inform Mid-Atlantic of them. In all cases, he accepted deposit checks from the customers made payable either to himself only, to Mid-Atlantic only, or to himself and Mid-Atlantic jointly, and in one case, to himself and an apparently fictitious corporation named SMD. In the summer of 1984, Smith opened two checking accounts with Citizens' Bank in his own name, Loy Thompson Smith, into which he deposited 23 checks, drawn by eight different people on a number of drawees, including Citizens' Bank. For all the checks, the defendant was the depositary bank, as defined in Md. Comm. Law Code Ann. [UCC] § 4-105(a).

DISTRICT JUDGE SMALKIN: In this suit, the plaintiff requests recovery "only for those checks improperly deposited with the endorsement 'for deposit only' or no endorsement" in either one of the two personal checking accounts

Smith opened with the defendant. It is undisputed from the deposition of Citizens' Vice President, Mr. Haste, that these checks (the ones that were not endorsed in any fashion with the name Mid-Atlantic) should not have been accepted by defendant for deposit in *anyone's* account other than Mid-Atlantic's.

The defendant has not answered, in its opposition affidavits, the affidavit assertions of Jim Lieberton, President of Mid-Atlantic, to the effect that Smith deposited the checks in his own account and that Mid-Atlantic has not received the proceeds of the checks, to which it was entitled as payee. Thus, it is clear that the plaintiff was the payee and "owner" of the checks in question, and that they have been converted in the common law sense, *viz.,* that Mid-Atlantic, as the true owner, has been deprived of the checks or the proceeds thereof. The U.C.C., in § 3-419, applies conversion principles to negotiable instruments.

For commercial law analysis purposes, the form of the various instruments must be examined. There are 23 checks listed. Of those, plaintiff seeks recovery for only 13. Of those 13, two were deposited having no endorsement whatever, and the remaining 11 bore "endorsements" that consisted only of the words "for deposit only." The total amount of these 13 items was $72,158.45, which appears to be all the recovery the plaintiff seeks by this lawsuit.

It is utterly clear that the defendant did not act in conformity with the reasonable commercial standards of banking when it took in items with no endorsement at all or with no endorsement, save the restrictive language "for deposit only," that had been deposited in Smith's personal banking account, when the named payee was solely Mid-Atlantic. This was the case with every item for which the plaintiff now seeks compensation. An officer of the defendant has essentially admitted this lapse of conformity to banking standards, there is nothing disputing it in defendant's summary judgment opposition, and the legal conclusion is utterly clear. Thus, defendant, as a depositary bank, has conversion liability to plaintiff whether or not any proceeds of the checks remain in its hands.

It is axiomatic that an item is converted when it is paid on a forged endorsement, because the payment is made to one who has no good title. This is just as true in the case where an endorsement necessary to transfer title is missing, because, without the necessary endorsement, there can be no negotiation of the order paper (such as all this paper was). Although a bank is privileged in some circumstances to supply a missing endorsement, the only endorsement that it can supply is that of *its customer,* and it is clear Mid-Atlantic was not defendant's customer, because it had no account with defendant. Until the bank supplies the missing endorsement of its customer, usually with a rubber stamp, it is not a holder of the item. In this case, the missing endorsement was not that of defendant's customer, Smith, but that of the payee, Mid-Atlantic, who was not defendant's customer. Thus, the depositary bank never became the holder of the checks because of the absence of any endorsement whatever, a deficiency that it could not remedy by a stamp endorsement. Because the depositary bank never became a holder in its own right, and because it took items as to which there was no endorsement whatever, it did not have good title to these items, and, therefore, it converted them when it eventually paid the proceeds over to Smith. Although U.C.C. § 3-419(3) usually protects depositary banks which have no proceeds of the items remaining in their hands that protection is unavailable where, as here, the depositary bank has not adhered to reasonable commercial banking standards.

Thus, the Court concludes there is no genuine dispute of material fact, that plaintiff is entitled to summary judgment against the defendant for all the items deposited bearing no endorsement or the "endorsement" of "for deposit only." The damages are the face amounts of the items.

As an additional ground for recovery, the defendant is liable to the plaintiff for breach of the restrictive endorsement "for deposit only" on the items so marked, for the reason the items were never deposited to the account of Mid-Atlantic, which is the only treatment consistent with a "for deposit only" restrictive endorsement made by, or (even purportedly) on behalf of, a named payee. Thus, the plaintiff has two U.C.C. theories of recovery available with regard to the items that bore nothing more than the language "for deposit only," *i.e.,* conversion and breach of restriction, but either theory entitles it to summary judgment on these items, and the recovery is the same.

Order issued in favor of plaintiff.

CRITICAL THINKING

What reasoning supports the district judge's decision? Are there missing facts in the case that would better enable you to evaluate this reasoning if they were provided?

ETHICAL DECISION MAKING

What values does the court's decision promote? If the bank operated under the ethics-of-care philosophy, would it have forced Mid-Atlantic to court?

Endorsement to Prohibit Further Endorsement. The second kind of restrictive endorsement, the endorsement to prohibit further endorsement, is very rarely used. The operative word in it is *only,* as in *Pay to Oliver Twist only.* While this endorsement does not prohibit further transfer, it does provide Oliver some protection [UCC 3-206(a)]. Even if he endorses this instrument over to someone else, because of the restrictive endorsement he is not liable on the instrument until he is paid.

Conditional Endorsement. The third kind of restrictive endorsement, a conditional endorsement, lets the endorser put a condition on payment (one that would destroy negotiability if it were on the face of the instrument but does not affect it here) [UCC 3-204(a)]. A conditional endorsement, in effect, creates a defense for the endorser in the event that he does not live up to a preconceived promise. However, the conditional endorsement does not affect the instrument's ability to be further negotiated.

BUT WHAT IF . . .

WHAT IF THE FACTS OF THE CASE OPENER WERE DIFFERENT?

Recall that, in the Case Opener, Triffin bought a check issued by Cigna Insurance that totaled $484. Let's say Cigna and Triffin agreed that Cigna would pay Triffin $300 instead of $484 and subsequently Triffin would not sue Cigna for payment on the $484 check. Cigna would send Triffin a new check for $300 and a separate document stipulating certain terms for Triffin's cashing of the $300 check. What kind of restrictive endorsement would this qualify as? Would the check still qualify as a negotiable instrument?

Trust Endorsement. The fourth restrictive endorsement is the trust endorsement, used when the instrument is being transferred to an agent or trustee for the benefit of either the endorser or a third party [UCC 3-206(d)]. It might read "Pay to Jill Rogers in trust for LeBron Watkins" or "Pay to Jill Rogers as agent for LeBron Watkins" and then have either Watkins's or another endorser's signature. This endorsement gives the endorser the rights of a holder.

See Exhibit 27-4 for a summary of types of endorsements.

Exhibit 27-4

Summary of Types of Endorsements

TYPES OF ENDORSEMENTS	DEFINITION
Unqualified Endorsements	
Blank unqualified	An endorsement that is either the payee's or the last endorsee's signature; payable to whoever has possession of the instrument.
Special unqualified	An endorsement that is the endorser's signature followed by a named endorsee, who then becomes the holder of the instrument.
Qualified Endorsements	
Blank qualified	An endorsement that is either the payee's or the last endorsee's signature followed by "without recourse."
Special qualified	An endorsement that is the endorser's signature followed by a named endorsee and "without recourse."
Restrictive Endorsements	
Endorsement for deposit or collection only	An endorsement that restricts the instrument such that it must be collected by a bank for the endorser or for a particular account; the instrument cannot be cashed.
Endorsement that prohibits further endorsement	An endorsement that restricts payment to "only" the endorsee; doesn't prevent further transfer but protects the endorsee from being liable on the instrument until the endorsee receives payment
Conditional endorsement	An endorsement that is followed by a conditional statement that restricts payment; can be used as a defense for the endorser against the endorsee.
Trust endorsement	An endorsement that allows the endorser to have the rights of a holder; used when the instrument is being transferred to a trustee for the benefit of the endorser.

NONCRIMINAL ENDORSEMENT PROBLEMS

It should be no surprise that fraud and forgery create problems with endorsements, and we discuss these criminal issues in the next chapter. Here we consider noncriminal endorsement problems.

Misspelled Name.   If a negotiable instrument contains a misspelled name, the holder may endorse it with the misspelled name, his or her actual name, or (as is typical practice) the misspelled name followed by the actual name.

Payable to a Legal Entity.   Instruments can be made payable to a legal entity. If it is an estate, organization, partnership, or the like, any authorized representative may endorse it. If instruments are made payable to a public office, the person holding the office may endorse it. Upon filing her local taxes, Sarah, not knowing to whom her check should be payable, wrote "Pay to the order of County Tax Collector." Bill Deepockets, the county tax collector, may endorse the check, as he is the person currently holding the office named on it.

Alternative or Joint Payees.   Two possibilities arise when an instrument is payable to more than one person. The first possibility is that there are *alternative payees,* as in "Pay to the order of Jones *or* Smith." Then the endorsement of any one of the listed payees is sufficient.

If, however, there are *joint payees,* the instrument reads, "Pay to the order of Smith *and* Jones." Now the endorsements of *all* listed payees are required before the instrument may be negotiated.

When an instrument is silent as to whether the listed payees are joint or alternative, courts interpret it as containing alternative payees, and the endorsement of only one listed payee is required to negotiate it.

If the instrument is negotiable and the transfer has been a proper negotiation, we can proceed to the third part of the negotiable-instrument process, in which the status and rights of the third-party holder come into play. We cover these in the next chapter. The balance of this chapter discusses the holder-in-due course status and the shelter principle.

BUT WHAT IF . . .

WHAT IF THE FACTS OF THE CASE OPENER WERE DIFFERENT?

What if Cigna Insurance sent Mills a check but misspelled his name as the payee? Would Mills still be able to cash the check, or would it need to be voided and a new check sent?

Holder-in-Due-Course Doctrine

Suppose you contract with a computer seller, Data Corp., to buy 50 computers for your office. As partial payment, you give Data Corp. a note for $30,000. Data Corp. negotiates the note to its landlord, Morgan, for payment of rent.

You discover that the computers are damaged. If Data Corp. still held the $30,000 note, you could refuse to honor it and claim as a defense that Data Corp. breached its contract with you. But Data Corp. negotiated the note to Morgan. If Morgan is simply a holder, you can use the defense of breach of contract against Morgan. However, if Morgan is an HDC, as defined below, you must pay Morgan, because a holder in due course has higher rights to a negotiated instrument than does an ordinary holder.

L02

What is a holder in due course?

Watson Coatings, Inc. v. American Express Travel Services, Inc.
436 F.3d 1036 (2006)

Christine Mayfield used to work for Watson Coatings, Inc., where part of her role was to act as company treasurer. During her employment, Mayfield wrote 45 to 47 checks from Watson's account to American Express to cover her personal debts totaling $745,969.39. American Express credited each check to Mayfield's personal account. After dismissing Mayfield from her job, Watson Coatings discovered the theft and filed suit against American Express for accepting the checks from Mayfield despite their having been clearly labeled as belonging to Watson Coatings, Inc.

The district court granted American Express's motion for summary judgment, but Watson filed an appeal. Judge Smith's opinion explained that because a payee can be considered a holder in due course, American Express qualified as such a holder. However, the court also needed to decide whether this status offered American Express any protection. The appeals court found that it did, even though Watson had brought forth several common law claims, because American Express accepted the checks in good faith. Thus, the appeals court affirmed the district court's grant of summary judgment to American Express.

BUT WHAT IF . . .

WHAT IF THE FACTS OF THE CASE OPENER WERE DIFFERENT?

Recall that, in the Case Opener, Mills was the original holder of the check from Cigna Insurance Company. Cigna sent Mills the check for $484, but Mills said that he never received the check while in reality he cashed the check. So Cigna sent him a new check. Let's say, however, that Cigna realized prior to the cashing of the second check that the first check had been cashed, and due to breach of contract Cigna now attempts to deny payment on the second check. Is Mills a holder of the check or a holder in due course? Depending on his status, will Cigna be able to refuse payment or not?

REASON FOR HOLDER-IN-DUE-COURSE STATUS

Sun's Market, the check-cashing location in the Case Opener, should not be required to shoulder the transaction risks, because it was simply a financial intermediary, and the law wants to encourage companies like Sun's Market to engage in financial interactions. As you read this chapter, keep in mind the purpose of HDC status.

Requirements for Holder-in-Due-Course Status

L03

What requirements must be met to obtain holder-in-due-course status?

To be considered a *holder in due course,* a party must meet four requirements established in UCC Section 3-302:

1. The party must be a holder of a complete and authentic negotiable instrument.
2. The holder must take the instrument for value.
3. The holder must take the instrument in good faith.
4. The holder must take the instrument without notice of defects.

Meeting these requirements is very valuable, as the Case Nugget demonstrates.

Case 27-2 examines the required elements of HDC status. We consider the required elements in closer detail later in this section.

CASE 27-2   MICHAEL J. KANE, JR. v. GRACE KROLL
COURT OF APPEALS OF WISCONSIN
538 N.W.2D 605 (1995)

Michael Kane, Jr., sold Gerald Kroll, Jr., some cows. Gerald could not pay for the cows, so he arranged for his mother, Grace Kroll, to pay Kane. Gerald planned to repay his mother with $6,100, the proceeds from his expected sale of a load of hay. Grace issued a personal check to Kane in the amount of $6,100. However, the next day, Gerald told his mother he would not be able to repay her because the sale of hay fell through. Grace stopped payment on the check to Kane. When Kane presented the check to the bank, the bank refused to pay.

Kane filed suit against Grace to recover the $6,100. Grace argued that she had no legal obligation to repay Gerald's debt and thus no obligation to pay Kane. Kane argued that he was a holder in due course and not subject to Grace's defense of failure of consideration. The trial court held Kane was not a holder in due course because he did not prove he took the check in good faith and without notice of Grace's defenses. Kane appealed.

JUDGE MYSE: Whether Kane is a holder in due course is an issue involving application of § 403.302, STATS., to undisputed facts. A holder must meet three requirements to be a holder in due course under § 403.302, STATS. The holder must take the instrument (1) for value; (2) in good faith; and (3) without notice that it is overdue or has been dishonored or of any defense against or claim to it on the part of any person. We examine each of these elements in turn.

First, a holder must take the instrument for value. Section 403.302(1)(a), STATS. Under § 403.303(2), STATS., a holder takes for value when he takes an instrument in payment for an antecedent claim against *any person*. In this case, Kane took the instrument from Grace in payment of Gerald's debt and thereby satisfied the requirement of § 403.302(1)(a).

Second, a holder must take the instrument in good faith, defined in § 401.201(19), STATS., as "honesty in fact in the conduct or transaction concerned." The holder's initial burden on the issues of notice and good faith is a slight one. As one commentator has noted:

> The burden of proof of the allegations in the Complaint rests upon the plaintiff. It is not necessary, however, that the plaintiff allege in the complaint that good faith was an integral part of the transaction at each stage. That is an affirmative defense which must be raised by the defendant, if at all. [Russell A. Eisenberg, *Good Faith Under The Uniform Commercial Code—A New Look At An Old Problem*, 54 MARQ. L. REV. 1, 14 (1971) (emphasis and footnote omitted)].

In this case, Kane's affidavit supports his contention that he accepted the check in good faith for the payment of Gerald's antecedent debt. Moreover, none of the affidavits supplied by either party suggests evidence of bad faith on Kane's part. In the absence of such evidence, we conclude Kane took the check in good faith as a matter of law.

Finally, the last requirement to become a holder in due course is that the holder take the instrument without notice that it is overdue or has been dishonored or of any defense against it or claim to it on the part of any person. Section 403.302(1)(c), STATS. The knowledge of the defense for purposes of determining holder in due course status must exist at the time of issue. Therefore, we must examine whether Kane had knowledge of any defense at the time he took the check.

Because the requirement that a holder show that it did not have knowledge of a defense or claim to the instrument involves proof of a negative fact, the burden of proof is a slight one. In this case, the facts in Kane's affidavit suggest no knowledge of any claims or defenses, so the burden shifts to Grace to produce evidence that Kane had such knowledge. Grace argues that Kane was on notice that she had no preexisting obligation to pay her son's debt and that this constitutes knowledge of a defense. We disagree. Section 403.303(2), STATS., clearly allows a holder in due course to accept payment from one person for payment of the debt of another. Additionally, the fact that Grace, like any drawer, had the power to stop payment on the check does not constitute a defense that would prevent Kane from being a holder in due course. If it did, no holder would be a holder in due course because any drawer has the power to issue a stop payment order. Since Grace has not alleged that Kane had knowledge of any defense at the time he took the check, we hold that Kane met the requirement of 403.302(1)(c), STATS.

Because Kane took for value, in good faith, without knowledge of claims or defenses to the check, we conclude he was a holder in due course. As a holder in due course, Kane is not subject to Grace's claimed failure of consideration. Therefore, the fact that Gerald broke his promise to repay Grace the day after the check was issued does not affect Kane's status as a holder in due course.

Based upon the foregoing, we conclude that Kane was a holder in due course of the check and therefore not subject to Grace's asserted defenses. Thus, the trial court erred by granting judgment dismissing Kane's complaint. We reverse the judgment and remand to the trial court with directions to enter judgment in Kane's favor.

REVERSED and REMANDED.

CRITICAL THINKING

How do rules of law play into the court's reasoning? Are there ambiguities present in these rules of law?

ETHICAL DECISION MAKING

Think about the WPH process of ethical decision making. What is the ultimate purpose of the judge's decision that Kane was a holder in due course? What value guided this conclusion?

BE A HOLDER OF A COMPLETE AND AUTHENTIC NEGOTIABLE INSTRUMENT

Party Must Be a Holder. As we mentioned earlier, a holder in due course must first be a *holder,* a party in possession of an instrument payable to the party or the bearer [UCC 1-201(20)]. If Adam Brewer possesses a check that states "Payable to Adam Brewer," Adam is a holder. Suppose Adam asked his bank for a cashier's check to buy a boat from his friend, Corey Baum. (See Exhibit 27-5.) Even though Adam possesses the cashier's check and his name appears on it, he is not a holder of it because it is payable to his friend. When Adam gives Corey the cashier's check, Corey becomes its first holder.

If someone steals a check payable to Adam Brewer and forges Adam's signature on the back, the thief is not a holder of the check because it is payable to Adam and not the thief.

Instrument Must Be Negotiable. If an instrument lacks any of the requirements for negotiability we discussed in the previous chapter, the holder cannot be a holder in due course.

Instrument Must Be Complete and Authentic. Third, the negotiable instrument must be complete and authentic [UCC 3-302(a)(1)]. What happens if it is incomplete,

Exhibit 27-5 The Relationship between Being a Payee and Being a Holder

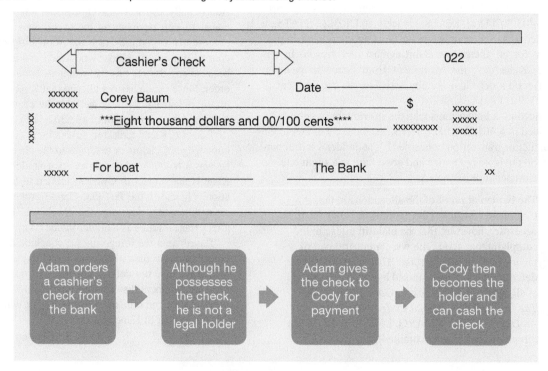

592

DEFINING NEGOTIABLE INSTRUMENTS IN JAPAN

The Japanese Commercial Code does not recognize the term *negotiable instruments.* In fact, the Japanese do not have any term to describe negotiable instruments. Instead, they recognize the legal concept of *yuka shoken,* which means "valuable securities" and encompasses checks, drafts, bonds, and stocks.

Japan does have separate legislation governing the same two general categories of negotiable instruments recognized in the United States, although it does not define them as such or as negotiable instruments. The first is commercial paper, or bills, notes, and checks. The formation, transfer, and defense of these are provided for in the Bills Law and the Checks Law. The second category, covered by several different statutes, is investment securities, including stocks and bonds.

The ambiguity surrounding "valuable securities" has created problems in Japan. Because there is no single definition, judges and scholars interpret *yuka shoken* on the basis of the definition they find most satisfactory at the time. The varying interpretations can lead to arbitrary exercise of judicial power.

---

missing the date for example? The UCC allows the holder to complete the check consistent with the intent of the issuer (3-115). However, if completion is inconsistent with the issuer's intent, the instrument is considered materially altered. If an instrument has been clearly materially altered or is so irregular or incomplete that its authenticity is called into question, the UCC bars a person taking it from becoming a holder in due course [3-302(a)(1)].

After learning about the holder-in-due-course concept, prudent businesses are often motivated to use high-security checks and change their check disbursement procedures to protect themselves. For example, American Express money orders employ intricate watermarks and seals to avoid check fraud. These security measures make it difficult for fraudulent instruments to appear complete and authentic.

TAKE INSTRUMENT FOR VALUE

How an Instrument Is Taken for Value. The holder in due course must take the negotiable instrument "for value." In other areas of the law, taking something for value usually means taking something with consideration, a bargained-for promise. However, the requirement here is more stringent: The party must take the instrument in exchange for a promise that has already been performed; the UCC explicitly excludes promises that have not yet been performed as "value." In other words, the party must suffer an out-of-pocket loss (UCC 3-303). Why? If a party has not yet performed the promise, he or she has not completely committed to the transaction financially and thus should not receive special legal protection. A party who receives a negotiable instrument as a gift or through mistake will be a holder instead of an HDC.

Legal Principle: **One characteristic of an HDC, and not a holder, is that an HDC must take a negotiable instrument for value; in other words, the HDC must take the instrument in exchange for a preexisting promise that has already been performed.**

BUT WHAT IF . . .

WHAT IF THE FACTS OF THE CASE OPENER WERE DIFFERENT?

Recall that, in the Case Opener, Cigna sent Mills a workers' compensation check. What if the check was misprinted, and the monetary amount was never printed on the check? Although Mills knew the check was supposed to be $484, he writes in the monetary amount of $1,000. Would he be able to cash this check considering Cigna made the mistake of not putting in a monetary amount?

Barbour v. Handlos Real Estate[2] offers an example of meeting the requirement of taking for value. Lucile and Alphonse Handlos accepted a note made out to their son as payment for a loan they had previously made to him. Having already given their son the loan, the Handloses had made an investment and thus had taken the note for value previously given. When the note was challenged, the Handloses were afforded holder-in-due-course status.

Legal Principle: **A holder can take an instrument for value if the holder:**

1. **Performs the promise for which the instrument was issued.**
2. **Acquires a security interest or some other lien in the instrument.**
3. **Takes the instrument for payment of a preceding claim.**
4. **Exchanges the instrument for another negotiable instrument.**
5. **Exchanges the instrument for an irrevocable obligation to a third party. [UCC 3-303(a)]**

Banking Transactions and Value.   Other sections of the UCC help determine whether a commercial bank has given value for a check. Section 4-211 says that a bank has given value for the negotiable instrument to the extent it has a security interest in it. Section 4-210 identifies circumstances in which a bank has acquired a security interest in a negotiable instrument. In some of these, although the bank gives value, it does not intend to become an HDC.

Exceptions to the Value Requirement.   UCC Section 3-303(3) states that a holder who takes a negotiable instrument for value does *not* become an HDC if he or she:

1. Purchases the instrument at a judicial sale or under legal process.
2. Acquires it through taking over an estate.
3. Purchases it as part of a bulk transaction not in the regular course of business of the transferor.

TAKE INSTRUMENT IN GOOD FAITH

The HDC must take the negotiable instrument in good faith [UCC 3-302(a)(2)(ii)]. What exactly is *good faith?* Historically, there has been some debate about whether it has an objective or subjective definition. Using the objective sense, some courts would decide whether the holder purchased the instrument with a proper degree of caution through a usual and ordinary manner of conducting business, doing what a reasonable holder *would have done.* However, other courts have looked at good faith in a subjective sense by asking whether the holder acted honestly when taking the instrument—in other words, considering the holder's *actual behavior.*

The UCC defines good faith somewhere between these standards, as "honesty in fact and the observance of reasonable commercial standards of fair dealing" [3-103(a)(4)]. Therefore, to act in good faith, a holder must not deviate from the reasonable commercial standards of fair dealing.

Hartford Ins. Group v. Citizens Fidelity Bank & Trust Co.[3] offers an example of a bank's being considered an HDC because it acted in good faith and within reasonable commercial standards of fair dealing. A customer of Citizens Fidelity Bank deposited a check from his insurance company. There were no

To see how providing HDC status to banks facilitates financial transactions, please see the **Connecting to the Core** activity on the text website at www.mhhe.com/kubasek3e.

[2] 393 N.W.2d 581 (Mich. Ct. App. 1986).
[3] 579 S.W.2d 628 (Ky. Ct. App. 1979).

irregularities on the face of the check, and Citizens' manager, who had known the customer four years, credited his account in accordance with standard bank policy. Thus, the court deemed Citizens a holder in due course and not liable for the check when it was later found that the drawer had told the Citizens' customer not to negotiate it but he did so without telling Citizens about this notification.

When considering whether a holder took the negotiable instrument in good faith, the court looks only at the holder's state of mind. The transferor may have acted in bad faith. Case 27-3 shows how the court determines whether a holder has taken an instrument in good faith.

CASE 27-3   WAWEL SAVINGS BANK v. JERSEY TRACTOR TRAILER TRAINING, INC.
U.S. COURT OF APPEALS FOR THE THIRD CIRCUIT
500 F.3D 147, U.S. APP. LEXIS 19597 (2009)

Wawel Savings Bank entered into a loan agreement with Jersey Tractor Trailer Training (JTTT), Inc., for the amount of $315,000. In the agreement, JTTT pledged all capital equipment and assets of the company as collateral, and Wawel filed Uniform Commercial Code Financing Statements with the New Jersey Department of the Treasury and the Bergen County Clerk's Office. Sometime later, JTTT also entered into a factoring agreement with Yale Factors LLC whereby JTTT agreed to sell the rights to its accounts receivable in return for a 61.5% up-front payment of the amount due on the particular accounts receivable.

On April 4, 2006, JTTT filed a voluntary petition for bankruptcy, and on June 29, 2006, Wawel brought action against JTTT, seeking declaratory relief that its lien on JTTT's accounts receivable had priority over that of Yale's. The Bankruptcy Court found in favor of Wawel, stating that Wawel did not authorize JTTT's factoring agreement with Yale, and that Yale could not be considered a purchaser of instruments or a holder in due course because it did not establish that it acted in "good faith" by observing reasonable commercial standards of fair dealing. Yale appealed the decision.

JUDGE BARRY: Yale asserts that it should be considered a holder in due course, or a purchaser of instruments, and therefore should have priority over Wawel's senior security interest. Yale argues, first, that because the security agreement accompanying Wawel's loan to JTTT did not expressly

prohibit the sale of collateral, Wawel waived its security interest. That argument is without merit, especially given that in its agreement with Wawel, JTTT represented that it "w[ould] not settle any account for less than its full value without your written permission," and that it would "collect all accounts until [told] otherwise." JTTT's sale of its accounts receivable, therefore, ran afoul of the security agreement.

Regardless of whether Wawel waived its security interest, Yale has priority over that interest if it is either a holder in due course or a purchaser of instruments. A holder in due course is one who takes an instrument for value, in good faith, and without notice of dishonor or any defense against or claim to it on the part of any person. "If those requirements are met, a holder in due course take[s] priority over an earlier security interest, even if perfected. . . ." U.C.C. § 9-331(a). The same is true for a purchaser of instruments. To be considered a purchaser of instruments, Yale must have "give[n] value and take[n] possession of the instrument in good faith and without knowledge that the purchase violates the rights of the secured party." "Good faith" is defined in the U.C.C. as "honesty in fact and the observance of reasonable commercial standards of fair dealing." The District Court is to remand this matter to the Bankruptcy Court to determine whether Yale qualifies as a holder in due course or a purchaser of instruments, and to resolve the good faith element of that analysis in accordance with this opinion.

REMANDED.

CRITICAL THINKING

The case entirely rested on the definition of the legal term *good faith.* Suppose that one of your classmates believes the term *good faith* as outlined by the UCC is too ambiguous to make an informed ruling. Would you agree with your classmate about the ambiguity of the term? Why or why not?

ETHICAL DECISION MAKING

Some clues supporting Judge Barry's decision and the UCC's definition of good faith include honesty, transparency, and fairness. Can you think of any value preferences at the forefront of running a business that may conflict with the values outlined by the court and its definition of good faith?

TAKE INSTRUMENT WITHOUT NOTICE

Finally, a holder must take an instrument without notice of various claims to or defects of the negotiable instrument. A holder cannot be an HDC who has notice or is aware of any of the following defects [UCC 3-302(a)]:

1. The instrument is overdue.
2. The instrument has been dishonored.
3. The instrument was issued as part of a series that is in default.
4. The instrument has been altered or contains an unauthorized signature.
5. There is a claim to the instrument. (The claims are described in Section 3-306.)
6. Another party has a defense or claim in recoupment to the instrument.

What Does It Mean to Have Notice?   According to the UCC, a person has notice of a fact who either:

1. Has actual knowledge of the fact.
2. Receives notice or notification of it.
3. Has reason to know the fact exists. [UCC 1-201(25)]

For example, suppose that Sun's Market, the check-cashing business from the Case Opener, received a letter from the insurance company that listed the numbers of checks that had stop-payment orders. As long as Sun's Market received this letter *before* it accidentally accepted the dishonored check, Sun's Market would have notice of a defect and thus could not be a holder in due course. The UCC states that "to be effective, notice must be received at a time and in a manner that gives a reasonable opportunity to act on it" [3-302(f)].

Suppose a person receives an instrument that has clearly been altered but she does not notice the alteration. According to UCC requirements [3-302(a)(1)], the holder's awareness does not matter; the mere existence of such irregularities means that the holder cannot be a holder in due course. Nor can the person who has notice of a defect but still gives value for the instrument.

Overdue Instruments.   Suppose you accept a check from a business associate. Unfortunately, the check falls behind your desk and is lost for the next four months. If you try to negotiate this instrument to another party, he or she will not be permitted to claim HDC status because the check is overdue. How does a holder know an instrument is overdue? The answer depends on the type of instrument. Two types of instruments—demand and time instruments—may be overdue (UCC 3-304).

Demand Instruments.   A demand instrument becomes overdue if it has been outstanding for an unreasonably long period of time after its date [UCC 3-304(a)(3)]. If the demand instrument is a check, it is overdue 90 days after its date [UCC 3-304(a)(2)]. The date on the check gives another party notice of its overdue status; thus the party cannot be an HDC.

Legal Principle: **As a general rule, checks (a type of demand instrument) are overdue 90 days after their due date.**

Time Instruments.   A time instrument becomes overdue at any time after the expressed due date on it. Suppose a customer tries to negotiate a promissory note to you on January 2, 2010. However, the note states that it is payable by January 1, 2010. You have notice that the note is overdue; you must have acquired it before January 1, 2010, for it to be negotiable.

Most of the rules regarding whether a time instrument is overdue depend on its payment structure. If the instrument requires payment in a lump sum rather than in installments, it is overdue if the party does not make the lump-sum payment by the due date [UCC 3-304(b)(2)]. However, overdue status of installments depends on whether payment applies to the principal or the interest. If a party misses payment of an installment of the principal, the instrument is overdue until this installment is paid [UCC 3-304(b)(1)]. If a party misses a payment of interest on this instrument, the instrument is not overdue [UCC 3-304(c)].

Sometimes, parties agree to accelerate the due date of an instrument. Thus, if a party does not make payment on either the principal *or* the interest on the instrument by the accelerated due date, the instrument is overdue [UCC 3-304(b)(3) and 304(c)]. Because it may be difficult for a holder taking an instrument to determine whether there has been an accelerated due date, the UCC permits this holder to become an HDC if he or she had no reason to know about the accelerated due date.

How might a party know that an installment payment on the principal was not made? A bank considering purchasing a consumer note from a retailer, for example, can determine whether all payments have been made on the note by looking at the consumer's credit report. If the credit report indicates an installment had not been paid, the bank would have notice that the instrument was overdue.

Dishonored Instruments. An instrument is dishonored when a party refuses to pay it. Suppose you deposit a check from a customer into your company's account at a Wells Fargo bank. The customer has an account at Chase Bank. Wells Fargo credits your account and later presents the check for payment at Chase.

However, Chase refuses to pay because there are insufficient funds in your customer's account. Chase has dishonored the check and will likely stamp "Insufficient funds" on it. If you then tried to negotiate this check to another party, these words would give notice that the check was dishonored. However, someone who has no reason to know a note has been dishonored (if Chase does not stamp it, for instance) can become an HDC. This hypothetical situation is parallel to the real transactions occurring in the Case Opener. However, by the time Triffin purchased the dishonored check, the words "Stop Payment" were already on it, so Triffin might have had notice that the check was dishonored. To see how this may have affected the court's ruling in this situation, see the Wrap-Up at the end of this chapter.

Legal Principle: **You cannot become a holder in due course if you are aware that the negotiable instrument has been dishonored.**

Claims or Defenses. A party who is aware of any claim or defense to an instrument has notice and cannot become an HDC [UCC 3-302(a)(2)(v),(vi)]. However, a party who had no reason to know various claims or defenses applied to an instrument, even though they exist, is not prevented from becoming an HDC. Exhibit 27-6 presents a summary of defenses related to holder-in-due-course status.

The Shelter Principle and HDC

Generally, if an item is transferred from one person to another, the transferee acquires all the rights the transferor had in the item. This idea is called the shelter principle [UCC Section 3-203(b)]. It means that even a holder who cannot attain holder-in-due-course

L04

What is the shelter principle?

Exhibit 27-6

Defenses and the Holder
in Due Course

The holder in due course may be *free from* the following personal defenses:
1. Lack or failure of consideration
2. Breach of contract
3. Fraud in the inducement in the underlying contract
4. Illegality
5. Duress
6. Unauthorized completion or material alteration of the instrument
7. Unauthorized acquisition of the instrument

The HDC is *subject to* the following real defenses:
1. Fraud in the essence
2. Discharge of the party liable through bankruptcy
3. Forgery
4. Material alteration of a completed instrument
5. Infancy—a party is below the legal age of consent

status can acquire the rights and privileges of an HDC *if* the item is being transferred *from* an HDC. The instrument does not need to be transferred directly from an HDC; under the shelter principle, as long as the holder of an instrument can demonstrate that someone through the line of transfers had obtained the rights of an HDC, then all subsequent holders have these rights.

Therefore, in the Case Opener, plaintiff Triffin received the workers' compensation check from Sun's Market, a holder in due course. If Triffin did not qualify for HDC status on his own, he would have received the rights that Sun's Market, the transferor, had. In other words, Triffin is taking "shelter" in Sun's Market's status as an HDC.

One exception to the shelter principle prevents a person who engages in fraud or other illegal interference with an instrument from becoming an HDC, even if he or she obtains the instrument later from an HDC. For example, Chad and Dave devise a scheme to defraud Jenny. Jenny, unaware of the fraud, writes a check to Dave. Dave negotiates the check to Mariko. Mariko, through the negotiation, becomes an HDC and eventually negotiates the check to Chad. Although Chad should be an HDC under the shelter principle, because he was part of the original fraud against Jenny, he does not obtain the rights of an HDC.

The shelter principle may at first seem contrary to the idea of the HDC principle; however, the purpose of the shelter principle is to encourage the marketability of instruments. The greater protection offered to an HDC is very appealing; thus, allowing parties to achieve it through the shelter principle encourages financial interactions.

Legal Principle: **If an instrument is transferred from a party with holder-in-due-course status, the next party also receives HDC status.**

Abuse of the Holder-in-Due-Course Doctrine

L05

In what ways has the
holder-in-due-course
doctrine been abused?

While HDC status offers great protection to financial intermediaries, the intermediaries might attempt to abuse this protection. Suppose you are starting a small business and a salesperson for Office Supplies Made Easy comes to your new office to sell you high-quality office supplies. You pay for the supplies with a negotiable installment note on which you are supposed to make three installments of $1,000. When you receive your office supplies, you discover they are extremely low-quality and certainly not worth the $3,000 you agreed to pay. You call Office Supplies Made Easy, saying you want to return the supplies. However, an employee tells you that your installment note has been negotiated to a finance company, which became a holder in due course.

The finance company calls your office every day because you have refused to pay for the supplies. You later discover that it negotiates all notes of Office Supplies Made Easy, and the two firms appear to have some kind of arrangement so that the finance company can attain HDC status. Claims or defenses you have against Office Supplies Made Easy do not apply to the finance company.

When cases like this have arisen in court, judges have looked at the connection between the transferor and the transferee. If the companies are closely connected, as in our example, some judges apply the salesperson's knowledge of your claims and defenses to the finance company, preventing the finance company from achieving HDC status.

The FTC created several rules in the 1970s that help protect consumers against the kind of HDC abuse in our example. These rules require every consumer credit contract or any purchase money loan to contain the following statement in 10-point, boldface type:

> Any holder of this consumer credit contract is subject to all claims and defenses which the debtor could assert against the seller of goods or services obtained pursuant hereto or with the proceeds hereof. Recovery hereunder by the debtor shall not exceed amounts paid by the debtor hereunder.[4]

Consequently, no subsequent holder of the contract will have the rights of an HDC.

---

[4] FTC Holder in Due Course Regulations, 16 C.F.R. 433.2 (1978).

CASE OPENER WRAP-UP

Dishonored Check and Holder-in-Due-Course Status

In this case, the court ruled in favor of Triffin and ordered Cigna to pay him $484 plus interest for the check. Even though Triffin knew the check was dishonored when he purchased it, he still was able to receive payment under the shelter principle and holder in due course. That is, the court ruled that the transfer by a holder in due course to a third party, even one with notice of the dishonor, transfers all rights of the holder in due course to the successor in interest.

As discussed earlier in the chapter, the purpose of the holder-in-due-course doctrine is to protect financial intermediaries and encourage them to continue to engage in financial transactions. If you were a manager for Sun's Market and discovered that the insurance company would not be responsible for the dishonored check, you would probably be less likely to accept checks in the future. The holder-in-due-course doctrine and shelter principle encourage market transactions and shield businesses like Sun's Market from unnecessary risks.

KEY TERMS

SUMMARY OF KEY TOPICS

Negotiation	*Delivery:* The physical handing over of a negotiable instrument.
	The two types of endorsements:
	1. Unqualified endorsements
	2. Qualified endorsements
Holder-in-Due-Course Doctrine	The HDC doctrine provides incentive for financial intermediaries to engage in transactions because they receive greater legal protection.
Requirements for Holder-in-Due-Course Status	*The requirements for holder-in-due-course status:*
	1. *Be a holder of a complete and authentic negotiable instrument.*
	2. *Take the instrument for value:* Holder must suffer an out-of-pocket loss.
	3. *Take the instrument in good faith:* Holder must take the instrument with "honesty in fact and the observance of reasonable commercial standards of fair dealing."
	4. *Take the instrument without notice:* Holder must take the instrument without notice of the following defects: It is overdue, dishonored, or part of a series in default; it has been altered or has an unauthorized signature; or it is subject to claims or defenses.
The Shelter Principle and HDC	*Shelter principle:* If a holder cannot attain HDC status, the holder can acquire the rights and privileges of an HDC *if* the item is being transferred *from* an HDC.
Abuse of the Holder-in-Due-Course Doctrine	*FTC rule:* Negotiation of consumer notes may not be subject to HDC status.

POINT / COUNTERPOINT

Should Someone Who Commits an Illegal Activity to Obtain a Negotiable Instrument Still Be Considered a Holder in Due Course?	
YES	**NO**
Someone who commits an illegal activity to obtain a negotiable instrument should still be considered a holder in due course.	A criminal action should prevent HDC status. A person who obtains a negotiable instrument through an illegal activity does not deserve the status of holder in

Suppose a person took a misplaced betting ticket and cashed it (knowing full well the voucher was not his to cash). That person should still be awarded holder-in-due-course status.

The UCC established four requirements a holder must fulfill to be considered a holder in due course. The first requirement is that "the party must be a holder of a complete and authentic negotiable instrument." Assuming the criminal was wise enough to ensure that his recently obtained negotiable instrument is complete and authentic, a criminal can fulfill the first requirement to qualify as a holder in due course.

Another requirement established by the UCC is that "the holder must take the instrument in good faith." Especially because the definition of "good faith" is unclear, a criminal could easily obtain an instrument in good faith. Some criminals may be lucky enough to *find* a misplaced voucher. The criminal has no reason to believe that the voucher belongs to someone else. The "criminal" is fortunate, and he fulfills the good-faith requirement established by the UCC.

Additionally, to be a holder in due course, the holder also "must take the instrument without notice of defects," including notice that it is overdue, dishonored, or altered or has an unauthorized signature. As a person who does not know anything about the instrument's background, the criminal fulfills this requirement.

Meeting the requirements under the UCC should provide any holder the rights of HDC status.

due course. The criminal does not fulfill all the requirements set by the UCC to become a holder in due course.

A criminal does not fulfill two of the four requirements set by the UCC to be deemed a holder in due course. While a criminal may be in possession of a complete and authentic negotiable instrument and the instrument may have been obtained without notice of defects, fulfilling two of the four requirements is not sufficient for the criminal to be considered a holder in due course.

If obtaining the negotiable instrument through thievery, the criminal does not fulfill the second UCC requirement. The second requirement is known as both "taking the instrument for value" and "suffering an out-of-pocket loss." A criminal may "happen upon" a negotiable instrument, but he does not pay anything for the instrument. Therefore, the criminal should not be considered a holder in due course.

A criminal should not be awarded the status of holder in due course for yet another reason. The HDC doctrine was created to provide incentive for financial intermediaries to engage in transactions without fear of liability. The HDC doctrine was *not* designed to encourage or provide incentives for thieves and criminals to dishonestly obtain negotiable instruments.

Providing incentives to financial intermediaries through the holder-in-due-course doctrine is an excellent idea. A party that simply processes a payment should *not* be required to shoulder transaction risks. However, a thief or criminal does not simply process a payment. A criminal does not fulfill the role intended for the holder in due course. Therefore, a criminal should not receive the protection available to a holder in due course.

QUESTIONS & PROBLEMS

1. Evaluate the following statement: "Order paper and bearer paper must be delivered to be negotiated."

2. Explain the rationale for the following statement: "The purpose of holder-in-due-course status is to encourage parties to engage in financial transactions."

3. What are the requirements of holder-in-due-course status?

4. Todd Leparski was an assistant comptroller for Interior Crafts, Inc. Due to extremely lax accounting procedures, Leparski was allowed to both receive and deposit incoming checks from Interior's customers. Consequently, Leparski stole approximately $500,000 from Interior during his four-month employment from October 2000 to February 2001. To steal the money, Leparski took several checks from the incoming mail that were made payable to Interior by customers. He then endorsed the checks "Interior Crafts—For Deposit Only." He took the checks to an ATM machine owned by Pan American Bank and deposited the checks into his own bank account using a deposit envelope. Following the instructions on the deposit envelope, Pan American deposited the funds into Leparski's personal account at Marquette Bank. Eventually,

Marquette Bank alerted Interior to the fact that Leparski was depositing checks into his personal account that were payable to Interior. Interior was able to recover only half the money he had stolen, and it sued Leparski and Pan American Bank to seek recovery for the rest of the stolen money. What type of endorsement was on the negotiable instruments? Did the bank handle this type of endorsement properly? Can a check endorsed "for deposit only" without further limitation be deposited into any account? [*Interior Crafts, Inc. v. Leparski,* 366 Ill. App. 3d 1148, 853 N.E.2d 1244, 2006 Ill. App. LEXIS 589 (2006).]

5. Bond issued a $300,000 note to Goss in 1988. The note was secured by a deed of land. Goss later entered into an agreement to purchase commercial property owned by RAM. In lieu of partial payment, Gaetani, general partner of RAM, accepted the $300,000 note. Supanich, a trustee for Goss, endorsed the note. The note endorsement read: "For value received, the undersigned hereby assigns and transfers all right, title and interest in and to within Note to Toney E. Gaetani, Sr." The endorsement did not contain the words *without recourse.* Bond paid no principal and only partial interest on the note. Gaetani brought an action against Goss, Supanich, and Bond. At issue was whether the endorsement language allowed Gaetani to recover directly against Goss. Despite the lack of the words *without recourse,* the trial court held that Gaetani could not recover from Goss. Do you think the court allowed Gaetani to recover from Goss on appeal? [*Gaetani v. Goss-Golden,* 84 Cal. App. 4th 1118 (2000).]

6. At the end of January 2001, while cleaning out his self-storage locker, Kim Griffith found a certificate of deposit purportedly issued by Mellon Bank, N.A., of Pittsburgh, Pennsylvania, on July 3, 1975, for the amount of $530,000 plus interest to be payable to bearer on August 4, 1975. The CD was in one of several books Griffith had purchased from an unnamed buyer. On its face, the certificate of deposit had not been marked paid. On August 15, 2002, more than a year after finding the certificate of deposit, Griffith presented it for payment in person at a Mellon Bank office in Pennsylvania. Mellon refused to honor the certificate of deposit, arguing that because the bearer certificate of deposit matured 27 years earlier, the certificate was questionable on its face and thus was not genuine. On the basis of Mellon's refusal to honor the certificate of deposit, Griffith filed suit against Mellon. Mellon argues that it has no records of the CD as not being paid and that under Pennsylvania law it falls to Griffith to prove nonpayment. Griffith argues he is a holder in due course and is entitled to payment regardless of any possible defenses Mellon might raise. Is Griffith a holder in due course? Should he be able to collect on the CD? Why or why not? [*Griffith v. Mellon Bank, N.A.,* 328 F. Supp. 2d 536 (2004).]

7. Daniel DeMarais is the former chief financial officer (CFO) of Apex IT. Through a Minnesota Department of Revenue investigation it came to light that DeMarais had embezzled well over $400,000 from the company. DeMarais embezzled funds from Apex in part by using Apex's corporate checks to pay the amounts due on a personal credit card account he maintained with Chase Manhattan Bank USA, N.A. According to Apex, Chase had notice of Apex's claims to these funds because the payments were "unusual, irregular, and large" and were made using business checks from Apex's corporate accounts. Apex demanded that Chase return all funds it received from DeMarais, which Chase refused to do. Apex then sued Chase, seeking equitable relief. Chase contends that Apex's claim must fail because Chase is a holder in due course. Does Chase meet the requirements for a holder in due course? Should Chase have taken more precautions given the unusual nature of the payments? [*Apex IT v. Chase Manhattan Bank USA, N.A.,* 2005 U.S. Dist. LEXIS 3917 (2005).]

8. Delbert Williamson was driving his family home one night when they were struck by a Jeep Wrangler coming in the opposite direction. The accident was caused when the Jeep, which was being hauled by a motor home, came loose and crossed the lane of traffic, hitting the Williamsons' Mazda-MPV minivan head-on. Delbert's wife, Thanh, and their daughter Alexa were also in the car. Thanh later died at the hospital from sustained internal injuries as a result of the accident. Delbert and his daughter were wearing type 2 seatbelts, which have a lap and chest restraint. However, his wife was wearing a type 1 seatbelt, which has only the lap restraint. Williamson sued Mazda, claiming the seatbelt his wife was wearing was defective. Mazda claimed that its permit for seatbelts allows the company to install either type 1 or type 2 in the back-aisle seat of

its vehicles. Do you think that Mazda was liable for the death of Thanh? Why or why not? [*Williamson v. Mazda Motor of America, Inc.*, 562 130 S. Ct. 3348, 176 L. Ed. 2d 1218, 78 U.S.L.W. 3687.]

9. Dr. Rodrigue operated a private practice as a gynecologist-obstetrician. She hired Carol Wiltshire to work as a medical receptionist and secretary, but over her nine years of employment Wiltshire held a variety of positions of increasing responsibility and authority within the office. Wiltshire was responsible for understanding insurance requirements and was the only person in the office trained in the computerized billing system. After learning how to use the billing software, Wiltshire began stealing checks that were sent by various insurance providers and were payable to Rodrigue. In sum, she stole 269 checks, totaling $372,572.18. She forged Rodrigue's endorsement on the insurance checks and deposited them in her own account at the Godfrey, Illinois, branch of Olin Employees Credit Union. Olin required that its tellers obtain a supervisor's approval before accepting third-party checks. The supervisor asked for documentation about the third-party checks, and Wiltshire provided a forged letter of authorization purporting to be from Rodrigue. The bank then began accepting the checks. When Rodrigue found out about the fraudulent checks, she alerted the authorities and brought suit against Olin Employees Credit Union. Olin argues that it did not violate reasonable commercial standards in allowing Wiltshire to cash the insurance reimbursement checks and that it used ordinary care in the negotiable-instrument transactions. Who do you think is liable for the fraudulent checks—Rodrigue or Olin? Why? [*Dr. Linda Rodrigue v. Olin Employees Credit Union*, 406 F.3d 434 (2005).]

10. Stacy and Michael Russell are residents in Harrah, Oklahoma, who live in a trailer. Oklahoma Farm Bureau Mutual Insurance Company was the insurer on the home. Within the Russells' policy a section on loss stated that Farm Bureau "will pay you unless another payee is named on the Declarations page," that "Loss shall be payable to any mortgagee named in the Declarations," and that one of Farm Bureau's responsibilities was to "protect the mortgagee's interests in the insured building." On the Declarations page of the document, Conesco Finance, which held a financial interest in the Russells' home, was named as one of the "payees." A fire completely charred the mobile home in late 2002. A $69,000 settlement amount was agreed on between Russell and Farm Bureau after an insurance claim was made. Conesco was not aware of the fire, nor did it know that a check had been made out to both Conesco and the Russells together to cover damages incurred in the fire. The Russells' deposited the check into their account, with both of their signatures and a stamp from Conesco Finance, which is believed to have been forged, at the Bank of Oklahoma (BOK). The Bank of Nichols Hills (BNH) was the banking provider for the insurance company. About a year later, Conesco learned of the fire and contacted Farm Bureau about being owed more than $50,000, which was paid in full. BNH was notified of the forgery and reimbursed the insurance company for the $50,000. BNH then proceeded to sue BOK, claiming that carelessness was the reason the forgery occurred. Who do you believe is at fault here on the basis of the information presented in the chapter? [*Bank of Nichols Hills v. Bank of Oklahoma*, 196 P.3d 984 (Okla. Civ. App. 2008).]

Looking for more review materials?

The Online Learning Center at **www.mhhe.com/kubasek3e** contains this chapter's "Assignment on the Internet" and also a list of URLs for more information, entitled "On the Internet." Find both of them in the Student Center portion of the OLC, along with quizzes and other helpful materials.

CHAPTER

28 Liability, Defenses, and Discharge

LEARNING OBJECTIVES

After reading this chapter, you will be able to answer the following questions:

1 What information is needed to determine signature liability?

2 What is warranty liability?

3 How does one avoid liability for negotiable instruments?

CASE OPENER

Bank One and the Forged Checks

Dr. Rick LaCombe practiced optometry as a sole proprietorship at LaCombe Eye Center. LaCombe's receptionist, Lana Slyfield, embezzled checks and deposited them in her own account at the bank. She did this by forging LaCombe's signature and writing her account number on the checks. She then put the checks in her account at Bank One. Slyfield successfully cashed the fraudulent checks for four years, amounting to over 500 checks totaling $70,000. When LaCombe discovered the embezzlement and fraud, he sued Bank One for negligence for accepting the forged negotiable instruments.

1. Who do you think should bear the liability for the forged checks—Bank One or LaCombe Eye Center? What values are guiding your decision?

2. As a business manager at LaCombe Eye Center, what kind of practices would you encourage to ensure that employees were not able to easily embezzle money through fraudulent checks?

The Wrap-Up at the end of the chapter will answer these questions.

As you can see from the Bank One opener, it is not always clear who should bear responsibility for the amount of a negotiable instrument. This chapter explains the various ways a party may be liable for a negotiable instrument. First, when a person signs a negotiable instrument, he or she is potentially liable for the instrument. This type of liability is called signature liability. In contrast, a party may be liable if the transfer of the instrument breaches a warranty associated with the instrument. This second type of liability is called warranty liability. After we consider both signature and warranty liability, we examine the defenses to these types of liability. Finally, we investigate how liability for a negotiable instrument may be discharged.

Signature Liability

UCC Section 3-401(a) imposes liability if the party or the party's agent signs the instrument. If a party does not sign, the party cannot be held liable. Thus, because the receptionist at LaCombe Eye Center forged the doctor's name on the checks, should LaCombe be liable?

Because the signature on an instrument leads to liability, it is important to know what counts as a signature. According to the UCC, a signature can be any name, word, mark, or symbol used by a party to authenticate a writing [3-401(b)]. Thus, if you wrote either your full name or an *X* with the intent to authenticate an instrument, either writing would constitute a signature.

When a party signs a negotiable instrument, he or she might be signing as a maker, acceptor, drawer, or endorser of the instrument. The signer's status as a maker, acceptor, drawer, or endorser of the note establishes the extent of the signer's liability. In other words, issuers and acceptors have a certain type of liability, while drawers and endorsers have another type of signature liability. Issuers and acceptors are primarily liable for a negotiable instrument, while drawers and endorsers are secondarily liable. If it is not possible to tell the status of the party, the general rule is that the party is considered an endorser (UCC 3-204, comment 1). Exhibit 28-1 provides a summary of the various endorsing parties and their roles.

L01

What information is needed to determine signature liability?

ENDORSING PARTY	DESCRIPTION	ROLE
Maker	A person promising to pay a set sum to the holder of a promissory note or certificate of deposit	Promises to pay money
Acceptor	A person (drawee) who accepts and signs the draft to agree to pay the draft when it is presented	Pays the money, or is responsible for paying the money, when it is requested
Drawer	A person ordering the drawee to pay	Orders someone (the drawee) to pay
Endorser	A person who signs an instrument to restrict payment of it, negotiate it, or incur liability	Signs an instrument at some point during negotiation

Exhibit 28-1

Parties Signing a Negotiable Instrument

Electronic signatures are an accepted and rather standard method of authorizing payment. However, conducting business through an online payment system puts the company at potential risk. Many banking companies have policies that deem the merchant, rather than the buyer, responsible for the charge if the payment made is fraudulent. For example, Visa advises its business-account customers that make online transactions to know how to protect themselves, as the business owners could be liable if a customer's payment is fraudulent. Businesses have several options for ensuring that their online transaction system can detect fraudulent payment. One of these options is to obtain chargeback insurance to prevent liability for fraud. The second option is to increase safety measures to prevent fraud, such as having online CAPTCHA's or requiring more extensive authentication procedures when a customer makes a payment. Since online business owners are at high risk for this type of fraud, owners should always properly authenticate the customer making a payment.

Source: http://usa.visa.com/download/merchants/visa_risk_management_guide_ecommerce.pdf.

PRIMARY LIABILITY OF MAKERS AND ACCEPTORS

A party who is primarily liable for an instrument must pay the stated amount on the instrument when it is presented for payment. This liability for the stated amount begins as soon as the instrument is issued. Moreover, the primarily liable party must pay without resorting to any other party. For example, suppose you own a business and write a check drawing on your funds in your business account at First National Bank. First National has primary liability for the check; it must pay the stated amount when the check is presented for payment.

The UCC establishes that certain parties—makers and acceptors—are primarily liable. First, a maker is a party who has promised to pay. For example, the maker of a promissory note is primarily liable for the amount of the note because the party has promised to pay the amount of the instrument. Moreover, UCC Section 3-412 states that a party who signs as an issuer of an instrument is liable for the amount of the instrument as soon as it is issued. For example, a bank that issues a cashier's check is primarily liable for the amount of the check as soon as the cashier's check is created (UCC 4-412).

Second, an acceptor, a drawee of a draft who accepts and signs the draft to agree to pay the draft when it is presented, is primarily liable [UCC 3-413(a)]. A party who accepts a draft by signing on the face of the draft is primarily liable (UCC 3-413). For example, when a bank accepts a check, it is primarily liable for the amount of the check (UCC 3-409).

SECONDARY LIABILITY OF DRAWERS AND ENDORSERS

A party who is secondarily liable for an instrument must pay the amount on the instrument if the primarily liable party defaults. Return to the First National Bank example. First National has primary liability for the check; it must pay the stated amount when the check is presented for payment. However, suppose First National dishonors this check because of insufficient funds in your account. Because the primarily liable party, the bank, has defaulted, you, the issuer of the check, are now liable.

Drawers and endorsers are secondarily liable parties. An endorser is a party who signs an instrument to restrict payment of it, negotiate it, or incur liability [UCC 3-204(b)].

A drawer is a person who signs as a party ordering payment [UCC 3-103(a)(5)]. For example, if you write a check from your bank account that is payable to the electric company, you are the drawer of the check, the bank is the drawee, and the electric company is the holder of the check. The holder of the check (the electric company) presents the check to the drawee (the bank) for payment. Presentment is defined in the UCC as making a demand for the drawee to pay [UCC 3-501(a)]. The UCC creates specific rules that govern the time and manner of presentment.

Legal Principle: **Drawers and endorsers are secondarily liable for negotiable instruments.**

Suppose the holder (the electric company) presented your check and the bank dishonored the check because of insufficient funds in your account. The UCC states that drawers of drafts are liable for an instrument only after it has been dishonored (3-414, 3-415). Thus, you (the drawer) are now liable for the check.

By adding a disclaimer to her or his signature on a draft, a drawer might avoid liability if the instrument is dishonored [UCC 3-414(e)]. However, a drawer of a check may not include such a disclaimer of liability.

Three conditions must be met for a drawer or endorser to become liable. First, the holder of the instrument must present the instrument in a proper and timely fashion. Second, the instrument must be dishonored. Third, notice of the dishonor must be given to the drawer.

Presentment.   An instrument must be presented in a proper and timely manner. Exhibit 28-2 provides a summary of the requirements for presentment of a negotiable instrument. First, the instrument must be presented to the proper party. If the instrument is a note, the holder must present the note to the maker of the note. In contrast, if the instrument is a draft, the holder must present the instrument to the drawee. Thus, continuing our electric company example, the electric company must present the check to the bank (the drawee).

Second, the instrument must be presented to the proper party in a proper way. UCC Section 3-501(b) states that an instrument can be presented (1) by any commercially reasonable means, (2) through a clearinghouse procedure, or (3) at the place designated in the instrument.

Third, the instrument must be presented to the proper party in a _timely manner_. Thus, if the instrument is a note, the holder must present the note to the maker on the note's due date. If the instrument is a draft, such as a check, the holder must present the instrument within a _reasonable time._ The failure to present an instrument on time is the most common reason that improper presentment occurs, which ultimately discharges unqualified endorsers from secondary liability.

The UCC states a specific timeline for presentment. If a holder does not present the instrument within a reasonable time, the drawer or endorser may not be held secondarily liable. Therefore, if the electric company waited 60 days to present your check to the bank, it probably cannot hold you secondarily liable because the UCC states that a check must be presented within 30 days of its date to hold the drawer secondarily liable [3-414(f)]. Similarly, to hold an endorser secondarily liable, a holder must present a check within 30 days of the endorsement [UCC 3-415(e)].

1. Presented to the proper party
2. Presented in a proper way
3. Presented in a timely manner

Exhibit 28-2

Proper Presentment of a Negotiable Instrument

Dishonor.   When a holder presents an instrument within a timely and proper manner but acceptance or payment is refused, the instrument has been dishonored. The instrument must be explicitly dishonored; a refusal to pay does not necessarily mean that the instrument has been dishonored. For example, suppose you are a holder of a check that is payable to your business. You present this check for payment, but the bank refuses to pay the check because you cannot present identification [UCC 3-501(b)(2)]. Alternatively, a bank may refuse to pay on an instrument because the endorsement of the instrument is not proper. Again, this refusal to pay does not dishonor the instrument. Situations in which refusals to pay do not constitute dishonorment are found in UCC Section 3-501(b) and are listed in Exhibit 28-3. Remember, a secondarily liable party becomes liable *only* if a primarily liable party dishonors the instrument.

BUT WHAT IF . . .

WHAT IF THE FACTS OF THE CASE OPENER WERE DIFFERENT?

Recall that, in the Case Opener, LaCombe's receptionist Lana Slyfield signed LaCombe's name on the checks and went to the bank to deposit them into her account instead of his company account, where all of LaCombe's checks were legally supposed to be deposited. Slyfield did not provide evidence that this action was authorized by LaCombe. If the bank had refused to pay the checks due to Slyfield's attempting to deposit them into the wrong account, would that mean that the checks had been dishonored?

Exhibit 28-3

Refusals to Pay That Do Not Dishonor an Instrument

REASON FOR REFUSAL	UCC TEXT
Holder's failure to comply with certain requests	Upon demand of the person to whom *presentment* is made, the person making presentment must (i) exhibit the *instrument,* (ii) give reasonable identification and, if presentment is made on behalf of another person, reasonable evidence of authority to do so, and (iii) sign a receipt on the instrument for any payment made or surrender the instrument if full payment is made. [3-501(b)(2)]
Lack of proper endorsement or failure to comply with terms of the instrument	Without dishonoring the *instrument,* the *party* to whom *presentment* is made may (i) return the instrument for lack of a necessary *endorsement,* or (ii) refuse payment or *acceptance* for failure of the presentment to comply with the terms of the instrument, an agreement of the parties, or other applicable law or rule. [3-501(b)(3)]
Presentment after an established cutoff hour	The *party* to whom *presentment* is made may treat presentment as occurring on the next business day after the day of presentment if the party to whom presentment is made has established a cut-off hour not earlier than 2 p.m. for the receipt and processing of *instruments* presented for payment or *acceptance* and presentment is made after the cut-off hour. [3-501(b)(4)]

✳ Notice of Dishonor.   The UCC provides a specific timeline in which notice of dishonor of an instrument must be given to a secondarily liable party (3-503). (The process of determining secondary liability is summarized in Exhibit 28-4.) If the party that dishonors an instrument is a collection bank, it must give notice before midnight of the next day [UCC 3-503(c)]. Other parties must give notice of the dishonor within 30 days of the day on which they receive notice of dishonor. This notice can be given in any commercially reasonable manner: oral, written, or electronic communication [UCC 3-503(b)]. The notice must identify the instrument in question and state that this instrument has been dishonored. If the word *dishonored* appears on the instrument, this writing is enough to constitute notice. As long as the holder gives notice to the secondarily liable parties about the dishonor of the instrument, the holder can sue the other parties.

If all three of these conditions are met, the holder can bring suit against the secondarily liable party. However, in most cases, while a secondarily liable party may have to pay a holder the amount of the instrument, this secondarily liable party can then seek recourse against the primarily liable party. For example, suppose Angie issues a promissory note to Cesar. Cesar endorses the note on the back and transfers this note to Roopa. When the note is due, Roopa presents the note to Angie. However, Angie dishonors the note. Roopa gives notice of dishonor to Cesar and sues Cesar for the value of the instrument. Cesar will be liable; however, he can sue Angie because she was primarily liable for the amount of the promissory note.

In the event that an instrument contains more than one endorsement, each endorser is liable for the full amount to any subsequent endorser or to any holder. For example, Ron issues a note to Jenna. Jenna endorses the note and transfers it to Sally, who endorses and transfers to Bill. Bill presents the note to Ron, who refuses to honor it. Bill can then receive payment from Sally, who transferred the note to him. However, Bill can also seek repayment from Jenna, who endorsed the note before Sally did. If Bill seeks repayment from Sally, Sally can seek repayment from Jenna, who endorsed the note prior to Sally. The secondary liability established through endorsement requires that endorsers pay anyone who endorses the instrument after him or her.

	NOTE	DRAFT
To whom must the holder present the instrument?	Maker	Drawee
When should the instrument be presented?	On due date	Reasonable time; if a check, 30 days within date of check or 30 days within time of endorsement
If the instrument is presented and dishonored, who is usually now liable for the instrument?	Any endorser	Drawer or endorser
What are the requirements for an instrument to be officially dishonored so that a holder may then turn to secondarily liable parties?	1. Present to maker for payment. 2. Maker dishonors. 3. Holder gives notice of dishonor to secondarily liable parties (endorsers).	1. Present to drawee for payment. 2. Drawee dishonors. 3. Holder gives timely notice of dishonor to drawer or endorsers.

Exhibit 28-4
Summary of Process of Determining Secondary Liability

ACCOMMODATION PARTIES

Suppose that, after you graduate from college, you decide to start your own business. You need to borrow a significant amount of money from the bank, and you plan to create a promissory note. However, because you have never owned your own business and have little credit history, the bank is a little wary about whether you will be able to pay the note. Therefore, the bank decides to ask you to have a third party sign the note to ensure that the bank will be paid. Consequently, your business law professor cosigns your note. This third party is called an accommodation party, a party who signs an instrument to provide credit for another party who has also signed the instrument [UCC 3-419(a)].

Accommodation parties may be primarily or secondarily liable for an instrument and can sign as makers, drawers, acceptors, or endorsers. However, accommodation parties more frequently sign as makers or endorsers. As a maker, an accommodation party has primary liability; as an endorser, the party has secondary liability.

Suppose you, in the example above, cannot pay your note, and your business professor, as an accommodation party, pays the note instead. This professor has a right of reimbursement to recover the money from you, the accommodated party [UCC 3-419(e)]. If, however, you, the accommodated party, pay the note when it is due, you cannot force the professor to contribute to the amount due on the loan.

Case 28-1 highlights the importance of the timeliness of <u>notices of dishonor</u> from collection banks.

CASE 28-1   HEARTLAND STATE BANK v. AMERICAN BANK & TRUST
SUPREME COURT OF SOUTH DAKOTA
2010 S.D. LEXIS 122 (2010)

Heartland State Bank routed eight checks to a collections bank, Federal Reserve. Federal Reserve then delivered the checks and additional cash letters to the defendant bank, American Bank & Trust, on April 10, 2002. The defendant bank picked up the checks, and then returned them for insufficient funds before midnight on April 11, 2002. The plaintiff bank, Heartland, sued the defendant payor bank, asserting that the returns were untimely. The trial court granted the defendant's motion for summary judgment, reasoning that under the Uniform Commercial Code midnight-deadline rule for check processing, a payor bank must send notice of dishonor by midnight of the next banking day; therefore, the defendant's return of the checks to Heartland by April 11, 2002, was timely. The plaintiff bank appealed.

JUDGE KONENKAMP: When a bank returned a series of checks for insufficient funds, the returns were challenged as untimely. Under the Uniform Commercial Code midnight-deadline rule for check processing, a payor bank must, after receipt of a check presented for payment, pay the check, return it, or send notice of dishonor by midnight of the next banking day. Otherwise, the payor bank becomes "accountable" for the amount of the check.

When a payor bank receives a check, it is considered "presented," meaning a demand for payment has been made upon the party obligated to pay the check. Once a check has been provisionally settled through a Federal Reserve Bank, a payor bank upon receipt can effect final payment in several ways. But the payor bank may also revoke a provisional settlement and return the check, if the payor bank has not made final payment and returns the check before the midnight deadline. The "midnight deadline" is the "next banking day following the banking day on which [the bank] receives the relevant item or notice or from which the time for taking action commences to run, whichever is later[.]" If the midnight deadline is not met, the payor bank becomes "accountable"—strictly liable—for the amount of the check regardless of whether there were sufficient funds in the customer's account to cover payment.

American requested that the Federal Reserve Bank deliver the checks to its mailing address. The checks were so delivered on April 10, 2002. Because American had until "midnight on its next banking day following the banking day on which it" received the checks, American had until midnight April 11, 2002[,] to return the checks. As the checks were returned by that date, the circuit court properly granted summary judgment to American. We affirm the circuit court's grant of summary judgment.

JUDGMENT AFFIRMED.

[continued]

CRITICAL THINKING

The judge found the defense's evidence persuasive enough to rule that American adhered to the UCC's midnight-deadline rule for presenting notices of dishonor. What evidence seemed to convince the judge? What evidence was the plaintiff relying on to support its conclusion on appeal?

ETHICAL DECISION MAKING

Think about the WPH process of ethical decision making. What is the purpose of creating rules of timeliness for presenting notices of dishonor? Who in the business community is affected when a bank does not adhere to the midnight-deadline rule upheld by the UCC?

AGENTS' SIGNATURES

An agent is a party who has authority to act on behalf of and bind another party, the principal. The agent typically binds the principal through the agent's signature. (Agents' signatures and liability are summarized in Exhibit 28-5.) The agent's binding power through signature similarly applies to negotiable instruments (UCC 3-402). As long as the agent is *authorized* to sign a negotiable instrument on behalf of a principal, the agent's signature can create liability for the principal.

Legal Principle: **The signature of an authorized agent on behalf of the principal party is binding.**

Previously, the UCC required that the agent clearly identify the principal when signing. UCC Section 3-401, which states that a party cannot be liable unless his signature appears on the instrument, was interpreted to mean that if a principal's name was not on the instrument, he could not be held liable. This interpretation has changed. The UCC now states that if an agent signs an instrument truly on behalf of a principal, this principal *can* be held liable even if he or she is not "identified in the instrument" [3-402(a)]. This policy ensures that someone will always be held liable for the instrument. While this new interpretation serves its purpose, what values are in conflict between the old and the new interpretations? Would an ethical dilemma arise when determining whether one was "truly" signing on behalf of a principal?

Can an agent be personally liable for a negotiable instrument? Interpretation of the UCC has changed to make it easier to find that the agent was representing the principal when signing. Now it is a little more difficult to hold an agent personally liable for a negotiable instrument. The authorized agent cannot be liable if she did not sign her own name to the instrument (UCC 3-401). If the authorized agent simply signs her own name to the instrument, she might be liable. If the holder of the instrument is a holder in due course and is not aware and does not have reason to know that the agent has signed on behalf of a principal, the agent may be held personally liable. If the holder of the instrument is not a holder in due course, the agent can usually escape liability by demonstrating that it was not the intent of the principal to hold the agent personally responsible.

AN AGENT MAY BE LIABLE IF:	AN AGENT IS NOT LIABLE IF:
The holder of the instrument has due-course status.	The agent did not sign his or her own name.
The agent is not authorized to sign on behalf of the payee.	The principal is clearly identified.

Exhibit 28-5

Agent Liability

The Negotiable Instruments Law in the People's Republic of China varies from its counterpart in the United States in several ways. First, the law does not address the use of promissory notes by individuals or private parties. Unlike the U.S. law, under which an individual may be an endorsing party, China's Negotiable Instruments Law addresses only banks as endorsers. Article I of the law states that the purpose of this law is to promote the development of the socialist market economy.

Second, the Negotiable Instruments Law also differs from the U.S. law in that the Chinese law mentions the role of a "prior holder," which refers to a debtor who puts his signature or seal to the negotiable instrument before it is acquired by the present signer or holder. Third, the Negotiable Instruments Law in China is very strict in requiring that monetary amounts of instruments must be written out both in Chinese characters and in numbers. The Chinese law states that if there is a conflict or discrepancy between the Chinese characters and the numbers of the instrument, the instrument is void.

There is an exception to agent liability. Even if the holder is a holder in due course and the agent simply signed his name, the agent will not be liable under specific conditions. If the instrument is a check payable from the principal's account and the principal is clearly identified on the check, the agent will not be liable on the check [UCC 3-402(c)].

Finally, the agent can be personally liable if he was not authorized to sign on behalf of the principal. This unauthorized writing falls into a broader category of unauthorized signatures.

Unauthorized Signatures and Endorsements. As a general rule, if a signature to a negotiable instrument is unauthorized, this unauthorized signature will not impose liability to the named party. This rule applies to two cases: forgery and unauthorized agents.

First, return to the accommodation party example above. Suppose you forged your business law professor's name to ensure that you would get your money to start your new business. If you could not pay on the note, your business law professor would not be forced to pay on the basis of the forged signature. Similarly, this rule applies to parties who forge the drawer's signature on a check.

Second, if an agent is not authorized to sign a negotiable instrument on behalf of a principal, the principal will generally not be liable for the instrument. Consequently, the agent would be personally liable for the instrument. However, if the principal decides to ratify, or approve of, the unauthorized agent's signature, the principal will then become liable for the instrument while the agent will escape personal liability [UCC 3-403(a)].

How does a principal ratify an unauthorized signature? A principal could explicitly approve the signature. For example, a Florida court held that a principal could not recover the amount of two checks he gave to his agent because the principal had ratified the signatures.[1] The agent, who was supposed to deposit two checks into the principal's account, forged the principal's signature and deposited the checks into the agent's account. The agent ultimately told the principal about the forged checks and the location of the money. The principal did nothing until the agent later ran away with the money, and the court ruled that the principal's inaction was the same as his approval of his signature.

---

[1] *Fulka v. Florida Commercial Banks, Inc.*, 371 So. 2d 521 (Fla. Dist. Ct. App. 1979).

Alternatively, if the principal accepts the benefits associated with an unauthorized signature, the principal in effect ratifies the signature by his or her conduct. For example, in *Rakestraw v. Rodriguez*,[2] a husband had forged his wife's signature in order to obtain a loan to start a grocery store. A few days later, the wife discovered the forgery, did nothing to correct it, and even participated in the business over the next few years. Part of running the business included sharing in the profits from the grocery store. When the business failed, the wife tried to avoid liability, claiming her husband had forged her signature. The court ruled that her actions in sharing in profits and in helping run the business effectively ratified her signature.

This ratification of an unauthorized signature does not exclusively apply to the agent-principal relationship. Your business law professor could similarly choose to ratify your unauthorized signature of his name so that he would be liable for your promissory note.

However, there are some exceptions to the general rule that an unauthorized signature is not enforceable. (See Exhibit 28-6 for a summary of the enforceability of unauthorized signatures.) Generally, the policy behind these exceptions is that courts want to place the burden on the parties who are in the best position to take a loss or take action to recover a loss. Moreover, particularly in regard to the last two rules that will be discussed here (the imposter rule and the fictitious-payee rule), the court focuses on the intent of the party who is issuing the instrument.

BUT WHAT IF . . .

WHAT IF THE FACTS OF THE CASE OPENER WERE DIFFERENT?

Recall that, in the Case Opener, several years elapsed before LaCombe discovered that his secretary had been putting checks into her account instead of the business account. Let's say that when LaCombe found out about the embezzlement, he didn't try to get the money back because he didn't want her to get in trouble but he talked to her about it. However, much later he decided he wanted the money. Would he be able to get the money back at the much later date?

WHEN IS AN UNAUTHORIZED SIGNATURE ENFORCEABLE?	
If the party fails to exercise ordinary care, observing reasonable commercial standards, then the party substantially contributed to the forged signature and will be held liable.	Negligence rule
If the drawer or maker issues an instrument to an imposter who, posing as the payee, endorses the instrument, the signature is effective as the payee of the instrument and the issuing party is liable.	Imposter rule
If the party issues an instrument to a fictitious payee, an endorsement by any person in the name of the payee is effective and the party is liable and must pay the amount on the instrument when it is presented for payment.	Fictitious-payee rule

Exhibit 28-6
Enforceability of Unauthorized Signatures

[2] 500 P.2d 1401 (Cal. 1972).

Negligence. In some cases, a party's negligence will not permit the party to escape liability for an unauthorized signature. If the party whose signature was forged behaved so negligently as to "substantially contribute to . . . the making of a forged signature," the party may be precluded from escaping liability (UCC 3-406).

For example, in *Thompson Maple Products v. Citizens National Bank,*[3] Thompson was a corporation that manufactured bowling pins from maple logs. Thompson would accept loads of logs from timber owners. When a load arrived at the mill, a Thompson employee filled out a scaling slip that listed the name of the owner, along with the quantity and grade of the logs. Thompson office employees then used these slips to prepare checks for the owner of the logs. A Thompson employee, Emery Albers, took blank scaling slips and filled them out for fictitious loads of logs. The office employees, thinking the slips represented real loads of wood, then prepared checks for payment. Albers then took the checks, forged the name of the owner of the logs, and cashed the checks or deposited them into his bank account at Citizens National Bank. The court ruled that Thompson "substantially contributed" to the forgeries because the blank scaling slips used to record loads of logs were easily accessible. In fact, office employees gave Albers two entire pads of these slips. Moreover, even though it was company policy for the slips to be initialed by authorized employees who were accepting the loads, Thompson office employees created checks for slips that were not authorized. Thus, Thompson's negligence led to the conclusion that Thompson should be liable.

BUT WHAT IF . . .

WHAT IF THE FACTS OF THE CASE OPENER WERE DIFFERENT?

Let's say that LaCombe gave Slyfield a lot of responsibility regarding his business and finances. He even let Slyfield manage his accounting and rarely checked the accounts. Then Slyfield embezzled almost all the checks sent to LaCombe's office for a month. Could LaCombe get that money back when he found out about what Slyfield embezzled?

The Imposter Rule. Suppose that Jamaar, a business manager, has been communicating through e-mail with Carlie, a potential employee. Jamaar has scheduled a meeting with Carlie. However, Samantha, without Carlie's knowledge, decides to impersonate Carlie at the interview. Samantha (as Carlie) tells Jamaar she will strongly consider signing an employment agreement if Jamaar will issue her a $200 check as a presigning bonus. Jamaar agrees and issues the check to Carlie that day. Samantha forges Carlie's name and deposits the check into her own account. Will Jamaar be liable for the amount of the check?

Jamaar's signature has not been forged; he clearly signed the check with intent to transfer money to Carlie. But he did not know Carlie was actually Samantha. Is Samantha's signature considered a forgery? No. Under the UCC's imposter rule, if a maker or drawer issues a negotiable instrument to an imposter, the imposter's endorsement will be effective [3-404(a)]. The court considers the intent of the drawer or maker when issuing the instrument. Because Jamaar intended for Samantha (as Carlie) to have the instrument, her endorsement of the instrument is considered valid. Moreover, it is easier for Jamaar, as maker or drawer, to identify the true identity of Carlie than it would be for a later holder of the check to do so. Perhaps some of you are surprised by the imposter rule. The UCC, as stated, places an immense responsibility on Jamaar to ensure that he is not being duped. What values are in conflict here? Should Jamaar be forced to shoulder this responsibility?

[3] 234 A.2d 32 (Pa. Super. Ct. 1967).

The Fictitious-Payee Rule. Suppose now that Jamaar, who has been authorized to write checks from the company account, draws bonus checks from the company account for five more potential employees. Unfortunately, Jamaar never actually interviewed these employees; thus these people are not entitled to the bonuses. Jamaar takes these checks that are made out to the fictitious potential employees, endorses the checks in their names, and deposits these checks into his personal bank account. These potential employees have no interest (i.e., no right to payment) in the check and are thus called fictitious payees (UCC 3-404, 3-405). As with the endorsement in the imposter case, Jamaar's endorsement of the fictitious payees is not considered forgery [UCC 3-404(b)(2)]. Jamaar's company will be liable for the checks.

Why is the company liable? Courts view the company as being in a better position to bear the loss of the checks. The loss has occurred because Jamaar, a company employee, has acted wrongly. Although the company is liable for the amounts of the checks, the company can recover the money from Jamaar.

Consequently, if we apply this rule to the Bank One opening case, it would seem that LaCombe Eye Center should be held liable because it is in a better position to bear the loss of the checks. Its own employee acted wrongly, and the company is in a better position to monitor the employee's behavior.

> To see how a firm's employee selection process can help avoid situations in which employees mishandle checks, please see the **Connecting to the Core activity** on the text website at www.mhhe.com/kubasek3e.

Warranty Liability

In the previous section, we explained how a party might be liable for an instrument on the basis of his or her signature on the instrument. In this section, we consider another type of liability: warranty liability. A party may be liable for an instrument because of a breach of warranty. There are two relevant types of warranties here: transfer warranties and presentment warranties.

L02

What is warranty liability?

TRANSFER WARRANTY

A negotiable instrument can be transferred from one party to another. A party who transfers a negotiable instrument to another party in good faith for consideration creates transfer warranties regarding the instrument and the transfer itself [UCC 3-416(a)]. Transfer warranties always apply to the party to whom the instrument is transferred (the transferee).

When a party transfers an instrument for consideration, he or she warrants:

1. The transferor is entitled to enforce the negotiable instrument.
2. Signatures on the instrument are authentic and authorized.
3. The instrument has not been altered.
4. The instrument is not subject to a defense or claim in recoupment.
5. The transferor has no knowledge of insolvency proceedings against the maker, acceptor, or drawer of the instrument. [UCC 3-416(a)]

If the transfer is through endorsement, these warranties apply to any future holders. However, if the transfer does not occur through endorsement, the warranties apply only to the transferee. For example, suppose Lisa creates a note payable to Chris. Chris endorses the note and transfers it for consideration to Yolanda. Because Chris has endorsed the instrument and transferred it for consideration, the warranties apply to Yolanda. Moreover, if Yolanda transfers the instrument to another party, the warranties Chris made would apply to this later holder.

These rules on whether the warranties apply to future holders or only to the immediate transferee are important because liability can be imposed for breach of warranty. If the warranties apply and there is a breach of one of the warranties, the parties can bring suit against the transferor, the warrantor, for damages suffered as a result of the breach [UCC

3-416(b)]. Thus, suppose Chris forges Lisa's signature on the note and then transfers the note to Yolanda, who later transfers the note to Gary. This forgery breaches one of the warranties on the instrument. Therefore, because Chris transferred the note through endorsement, Gary, the subsequent holder, can recover damages from Chris.

As soon as a transferee discovers that a breach of warranty has occurred, he or she can bring suit against the transferor. However, the transferee must give notice of the breach-of-warranty claim to the transferor within 30 days of discovering the breach [UCC 3-416(c)]. If the transferee does not give notice within 30 days of discovering the breach, the warranty will be discharged to some extent. If the transferred instrument is a check, the warranties cannot be disclaimed [UCC 3-416(c)].

While warranties on checks cannot be disclaimed, they can be disclaimed on other instruments. When parties agree to a disclaimer, an endorser can disclaim warranties by including in the endorsement the phrase *without warranties*. This endorsement is similar to the restrictive endorsement *without recourse,* which you learned about in the previous chapter. However, *without warranties* disclaims warranty liability, whereas *without recourse* disclaims contract liability.

BUT WHAT IF . . .

WHAT IF THE FACTS OF THE CASE OPENER WERE DIFFERENT?

What if Slyfield had forged LaCombe's signature on a check but, instead of depositing the check into her account, she transferred the check to another person, Bob. Bob then transferred the check to Cindy. Could Cindy recover damages from Slyfield? Also, could Cindy recover any damages if she found out about the breach of warranty a few months later?

PRESENTMENT WARRANTY

In the signature liability section, we discussed the requirements for a negotiable instrument to be properly presented for payment. Certain warranties are associated with the presentment of an instrument. Remember, presentment occurs when a party properly presents an instrument for acceptance and the party to whom it was presented accepts the instrument or pays it in good faith.

Why are presentment warranties needed? Parties who accept or pay instruments may worry that they are not paying the proper party. Thus, while transfer warranties apply to the transferee, presentment warranties cover parties who accept instruments for payment. The party presenting the instrument and any previous transferor of the instrument make these presentment warranties. Therefore, if there is a breach of presentment warranty, the acceptor can recover damages from the presenting party or previous transferors. As with the notice rule for transfer warranties, a party must give notice of a breach-of-presentment warranty within 30 days.

There are two types of presentment warranties. These types depend on what kind of instrument is being presented to a certain kind of party. When a party presents an unaccepted draft to a drawee, the holder guarantees:

1. The warrantor of the instrument is entitled to enforce the instrument.
2. The instrument has not been altered.
3. The warrantor has no knowledge that the drawer's signature or the draft is unauthorized. [UCC 3-417(a)]

These warranties apply only to the drawee who pays or accepts the drafts in good faith.

If the instrument is not an unaccepted draft presented to a drawee, only one presentment warranty applies. The party presenting the instrument guarantees that the warrantor
is or was entitled to payment or authorized to obtain payment [UCC 3-417(d)(1)]. In other
words, only warranty (1) listed above applies to presentments of instruments other than
unaccepted drafts.

Case 28-2 considers whether a bank that cashed forged checks gives presentment and
transfer warranties.

CASE 28-2   HALLIBURTON ENERGY SERVICES, INC. v. FLEET NATIONAL BANK
U.S. DISTRICT COURT FOR THE SOUTHERN DISTRICT OF TEXAS, HOUSTON DIVISION
334 F. SUPP. 2D 930 (2004)

On March 20, 2000, Halliburton issued a check, drawn on a Citibank account, to Arthur Andersen for $215,000.00. The check was deposited in the United States mail. An unknown person stole the check from the mail and then altered the payee to "Paul A. Schumacher."

On March 27, 2000, a person claiming to be "Paul A. Schumacher" opened a Fleet brokerage account from the bank's Internet site. The person posing as "Paul A. Schumacher" endorsed the altered check by signing the name "Paul A. Schumacher" on the back and presented it to Fleet, which honored it. Fleet then presented the check to Citibank, the drawee/payor bank. On March 30, 2000, Citibank charged Halliburton's checking account the sum of $215,000.00 because Citibank had paid the check in full.

On May 15, 2000, Arthur Andersen informed Hallibur-ton it had not received the $215,000.00 check. A Hallibur-ton employee working for Accounts Payable then contacted Citibank and learned that the check had been paid. On May 17, Halliburton requested the original check from Citibank. Upon receiving and examining the check, Halliburton saw that the payee's name had been altered and that the check had been endorsed by the fictitious payee, "Paul A. Schum-acher" "for deposit only."

On June 26, 2000, Citibank notified Fleet that Fleet had honored a fraudulently altered check and asked for prompt reimbursement of what Citibank deemed a wrongful pay-ment. The request was denied. Citibank then assigned any claim it may have against Fleet to Halliburton. Halliburton sued, and filed for summary judgment.

JUDGE LAKE: . . . Section 3.404 covers cases in which an instrument is payable to a fictitious or nonexistent person and in which the payee is a real person but the drawer or maker of the instrument did not intend the payee to have any interest in the instrument. The defense to which section 4.208(c) refers, by incorporating section 3.404(b), is known as the "fictitious payee" or "impostor" rule. An impostor is "one who pretends to be someone else to deceive others,

esp. to receive the benefits of a negotiable instrument," or "a person who practices deception under an assumed character, identity or name."

The impostor rule applies when a bank has honored a check made out to a fictitious payee. If the impostor's endorsement is effective, the collecting bank then becomes a "holder in due course." A "holder in due course is one who takes an instrument (1) for value, (2) in good faith, and (3) without notice of any defense." Even a forger can effectively endorse an instrument. Unless the depository bank knew about the forgery, there is no breach of presentment war-ranty when the depository bank presents it to the drawee. Therefore, in such circumstances, the presenting bank is not liable for the drawer's or drawee's loss.

Under section 3.404(d) the drawee may override the depository/collecting/presenting bank's affirmative defense only if the collecting bank failed "to exercise ordinary care in paying or taking the instrument and that failure contributed to loss resulting from the payment of the instrument." The "ordinary care" standard is just that: It does not mandate that a depository bank engage in peculiar vigilance. In fact, the comments accompanying section 3.404(d) suggest that a col-lecting bank is not liable for breaching its presentment war-ranties unless it knew the instrument had been altered when that bank accepted it.

If the drawee bank can establish that the collecting bank failed to exercise ordinary care, the drawee may recover from the presenting bank "to the extent the failure to exer-cise ordinary care contributed to the loss."

Halliburton has not presented evidence that Fleet was anything other than a holder in due course. In other words, Halliburton has not offered evidence of Fleet's bad faith, e.g., that Fleet's employees connived with the forger. Nor has Halliburton provided any evidence that Fleet had reason to believe the check had been fraudulently altered. Perhaps at trial Halliburton can convince the jury that Fleet, which dealt directly with the impostor, took the forged check with notice of the forgery or accepted the instrument by failing to

[continued]

exercise ordinary care, which would have exposed the forgery. But whether Fleet could have readily ascertained that the check had been fraudulently altered is a fact issue that precludes summary judgment for Halliburton. There are too many questions that need to be answered to support Halliburton's motion for summary judgment.

MOTION DENIED.

CRITICAL THINKING

The motion for summary judgment was denied because there is too much omitted information. As a judge, what information would you deem relevant that is missing from the case? Why is the missing information relevant to this case?

ETHICAL DECISION MAKING

Think about the ethical theories you were presented with earlier. Part of the above case, and the issue of presentment warranties, is who should bear the burden for a fraudulent check. Which party would a deontologist hold responsible for the cashing of a forged check? What about a consequentialist?

Avoiding Liability for Negotiable Instruments

L03

How does one avoid liability for negotiable instruments?

If a party tries to enforce a negotiable instrument, a defendant can try to avoid liability in two ways. First, the defendant can try to claim a defense to liability. Second, the defendant can try to claim that the liability has been discharged.

DEFENSES TO LIABILITY

In the previous chapter, we listed defenses to liability that did or did not apply to a holder in due course. Here, we return to these defenses to liability. There are two categories of defenses: real defenses and personal defenses. Real defenses, also called *universal defenses,* apply to all parties. Personal defenses do not apply to holders in due course.

Real Defenses. A party's right to enforce a negotiable instrument is subject to the following real defenses:

1. Infancy (being below the legal age of consent), to the extent that it makes a contract void.
2. Duress, to the extent that it makes a contract void.
3. Lack of legal capacity, to the extent that it makes a contract void.
4. Illegality of the transaction, to the extent that it makes a contract void.
5. Fraud in the factum.
6. Discharge through insolvency proceedings (bankruptcy).
7. Forgery.
8. Material alteration.

The first six defenses are stated explicitly in UCC Section 3-305. As we discussed earlier in this chapter, the UCC establishes forgery as a defense to liability because a party must have signed the instrument to be held liable. Finally, a material alteration of an instrument discharges a party of a liability [UCC 3-407(a)].

Fraud in the Factum. When a party signs a negotiable instrument without knowing that it is, in fact, a negotiable instrument, the party can claim fraud in the factum (also called *fraud in the execution* and *fraud in the essence*) as a defense. For example, suppose

DEFENSE OF IGNORANCE?

Laborer's Pension Fund v. A & C Envtl., Inc.
301 F.3d 762 (2002)

A & C Environmental, Inc., is a corporation that transports and disposes of nonhazardous waste. In April 1999, A & C was asked to complete a job in Gary, Indiana, which prompted representatives from Laborer's Pension Fund to approach the company. Frattini of the fund asked Clark of A & C to sign a form that would guarantee the five individuals who would work in Gary, Indiana, the coverage of the local union. Clark was hesitant to sign the agreement because he feared that if someone within his company were covered under the union, the entire company would then be covered. It wasn't until after Frattini of the fund guaranteed Clark that the only employees of A & C who would be affected would be those working in Gary, Indiana, that the agreement was signed. When A & C did not pay dues for all of its employees, the fund brought suit for delinquent contributions.

The district court ruled against the fund as a result of the fraud-in-the-execution defense that was brought forth by A & C. The court had decided that any reasonable juror would believe that Clark did not know that he was agreeing to pay the fund dues for each employee of A & C. The fund appealed to the Seventh District of the U.S. Court of Appeals.

In the opinion written by Judge Ripple, the Seventh Circuit found that Clark may not have known what he was agreeing to. Unlike the district court, however, the appeals court found that Clark had a reasonable opportunity to review the document, which was written in English. Although Frattini of the fund had misrepresented the contents of the document to Clark, there was an opportunity to review the document, which established dues for all employees of A & C. Thus, the court of appeals reversed the decision of the district court.

Michael Jordan believes he is signing an autograph for a fan, but he is actually signing a promissory note. Because he did not intend to sign a negotiable instrument, he will not be held liable for the instrument.

Similarly, suppose you, a business manager, are negotiating with another company to purchase materials for your manufacturing business. After your negotiations, the company asks you to sign a document as a preorder for the materials. You hurriedly sign the document and leave. However, instead of signing a preorder, you have actually signed a note. Will you be held liable for this note? In this case, it depends.

For another illustration of these issues, see the Case Nugget.

Although fraud in the factum is a real defense, courts have held that the signer's experience may determine whether the signer should have known what he or she was actually signing. Recall the situation with Jamaar in which he was solely responsible for ensuring the identity of the individual he is signing a check to. However, that level of responsibility is not required of Michael Jordan in this situation. Can you account for the difference in the two situations, pointing out the differing values and ethical norms?

As another example, consider *Schaeffer v. United Bank & Trust Co.*[4] United Bank sued Schaeffer to collect on a promissory note Schaeffer had signed as an accommodation maker. However, the Maryland court ultimately ruled that Schaeffer was not liable due to fraud in the factum. It turns out Schaeffer barely knew how to read, did not understand the document he was signing, and was lied to by the note's maker, who had told Schaeffer that Schaeffer's signature would serve as a character witness. The court ruled that United Bank was not a holder in due course and was subject to Schaeffer's defense even if the bank were a holder in due course as the note was void due to fraud in the factum.

Material Alteration. The UCC defines a *material alteration* as "an unauthorized change in an instrument that purports to modify in any respect the obligation of a party, or an unauthorized addition of words or numbers or other change to an incomplete instrument relating to the obligation of a party" (3-407). Only unauthorized changes that affect the rights of the party are considered material alterations.

[4] 360 A.2d 461 (Md. Ct. Spec. App. 1976).

Suppose Hope creates a promissory note payable to Patrick. Patrick decides Hope should pay him $2 more. If Patrick changes the instrument to reflect the additional $2, he has made an unauthorized change that affects Hope's rights. Changes that typically fall under Section 3-407 include changes to the parties to the instrument, the amount of the instrument, the date the instrument is due, and the applicable interest rate.

If the material alteration is fraudulent, the party whose rights have been affected by the change is completely discharged from the instrument [UCC 3-407(b)]. However, if the material alteration is not fraudulent, the instrument will be enforced only under the original terms. Case 28-3 considers whether changes to a promissory note were material and fraudulent alterations.

Legal Principle: **If a material alteration is not fraudulent, the instrument will be enforced under the original terms.**

CASE 28-3   **GARY DARNALL AND EMILIE DARNALL, APPELLANTS AND CROSS-APPELLEES v. BERNARD PETERSEN, APPELLEE, AND KAY PETERSEN, APPELLEE AND CROSS-APPELLANT**
NEBRASKA COURT OF APPEALS
8 NEB. APP. 185, 592 N.W.2D 505 (1999)

Gary Darnall gave a business loan to Bernard and Kay Petersen to be used for the purchase of a flower shop. The parties executed a promissory note for $55,000 plus interest. The note was due on demand and provided for 13 percent interest and 18 percent default interest. Gary Darnall received only two payments in the amount of $45,000 and $2,500 for the note. The Darnalls made demand for the remainder of the money owed and wrote the Petersens a letter demanding that payment be made and threatening legal action if the note was not paid. As a result, the Darnalls brought suit to recover the remainder of the promissory note and interest.

The Petersens alleged that when they signed the note, the blanks for the interest rate and the default interest rate were not filled in. Mrs. Petersen said when the note was presented to her, no interest rate was shown on the note and that it was her understanding that no interest would be charged on the note. As a result, she argued the note had been materially altered without any authority and that no interest or due date was specified on the note she originally signed.

However, Gary Darnall, the person who loaned the Petersens the money, argued he and Bernard discussed the interest rate prior to execution of the promissory note and that at the time the Petersens signed the note, the blanks for the interest rate, the default interest rate, and the due date contained the terms agreed to by the parties.

JUDGE MUES:

1. Were Terms on Note When Petersens Signed It?
We begin by addressing the issue of whether the promissory note was altered after the Petersens signed it.

Section 3-115 addresses situations where an instrument has been altered after a party has signed it. It provides:

(1) When a paper whose contents at the time of signing show that it is intended to become an instrument is signed while still incomplete in any necessary respect it cannot be enforced until completed, but when it is completed in accordance with authority given it is effective as completed.

(2) If the completion is unauthorized the rules as to material alteration apply (Section 3-407), even though the paper was not delivered by the maker or drawer; but the burden of establishing that any completion is unauthorized is on the party so asserting.

In a bench trial of a law action, the court, as the trier of fact, is the sole judge of the credibility of the witnesses and the weight to be given their testimony. The trial court found Kay's testimony on the alteration issues to be more credible than that of the Darnalls. While we may have reached a different conclusion if we were reviewing the evidence de novo, we cannot say that the trial court's factual findings on these issues are clearly erroneous.

2. Material Alteration.
Section 3-407 provides:

(1) Any alteration of an instrument is material which changes the contract of any party thereto in any respect, including any such change in . . .

(b) an incomplete instrument, by completing it otherwise than as authorized. . . .

(2) As against any person other than a subsequent holder in due course

(a) alteration by the holder which is both fraudulent and material discharges any party whose contract is thereby changed unless that party assents or is precluded from asserting the defense;

(b) no other alteration discharges any party and the instrument may be enforced according to its original tenor, or as to incomplete instruments according to the authority given.

The trial court found that the alterations were unauthorized but determined that the changes were not done fraudulently. Kay's cross-appeal asserts that the changes were both material and fraudulent and contends that the trial court erred in not discharging her from any obligation under the note. Kay is obviously contending that the trial court's finding in this regard was clearly erroneous. We do not agree.

The changes were clearly material. As we have already determined, the changes were made after the execution of the note and without the Petersens' authority. See § 3-407(1)(b). However, a material alteration does not discharge a party from his or her obligation unless it is made for a fraudulent purpose. See § 3-407(2)(a) and (b).

> An alteration is fraudulent when the holder intends to achieve an advantage for himself to which he has reason to know he is not entitled. Thus, where the holder believes that the party has authorized or consented to the alteration or completion, the fact that no such consent or authorization actually exists does not make the alteration fraudulent. Likewise, where the holder believes that he has the right to alter the instrument to reflect the true agreement of the parties, it is not fraudulent. (William D. Hawkland & Lary Lawrence, Uniform Commercial Code Series § 3-407:07 at 741 (1994)).

Although Kay proved that the note was altered, she presented no evidence that the alteration was made for a fraudulent purpose. In fact, in her pleadings Kay did not allege that the alteration was fraudulently made and did not pray that she be discharged from her obligation. Rather, she alleged merely that the note had been materially altered and prayed that the court find that the Darnalls were entitled to collect the principal only.

Cases are heard in the state appellate courts on the theory upon which they are tried. An issue not presented to the trial court may not be raised on appeal, inasmuch as a lower court cannot commit error in resolving an issue it was never given an opportunity to resolve. Moreover, the trial court's factual finding that the alterations were not fraudulent is not clearly erroneous. Accordingly, the trial court did not err in failing to discharge Kay from her obligations under the note, and Kay's cross-appeal is without merit.

3. Effect of Nonfraudulent Material Alteration.

The Darnalls argue that the trial court's factual conclusions regarding the alteration of the interest rates rendered its usury analysis unnecessary and, as a matter of law, incorrect. We agree.

To review, the court concluded as a matter of fact that the interest "blanks" had been filled in without the authority of Kay. Under § 3-407(1)(b), this was a material alteration. The court also concluded the alteration was not a fraudulent one. Therefore, the provisions of § 3-407(2)(a) do not come into play to discharge the parties. It was at this juncture that the trial court, determining that the 18-percent default rate was usurious, found that the Darnalls could recover no interest under the note. However, as the Darnalls correctly point out, when a note is materially altered but not fraudulently so, the instrument may be enforced according to its original tenor, or as to incomplete instruments according to the authority given. § 3-407(2)(b). The trial court found that the interest figures were inserted without Kay's authorization and knowledge. However, the Darnalls were still entitled, under these findings, to enforce the note according to its "original tenor."

4. Conclusion

The trial court's finding that the promissory note was altered without any authority after Kay signed it was not clearly erroneous. However, the trial court's finding that the Darnalls did not fraudulently alter the instrument was also not clearly wrong, and therefore the Darnalls were entitled to enforce it according to its original terms.

Affirmed in part, and in part reversed and remanded with directions.

CRITICAL THINKING

Regarding whether the blanks were filled in on the note, the judge states, "The trial court found Kay's testimony on the alteration issues to be more credible than that of the Darnalls. While we may have reached a different conclusion if we were reviewing the evidence de novo [in a new trial],

ETHICAL DECISION MAKING

In a discussion about values in this case, your classmate says that "justice" was not served in this case because even though the promissory note was materially altered, it still had to be enforced by its original terms because it was not a fraudulent alteration. What might this classmate's definition

[continued]

we cannot say that the trial court's factual findings on these issues are clearly erroneous." How strong do you think this reasoning is?

If the court could hear a new case regarding the promissory note, what type of additional information might lead the judge to determine the note was entirely filled in when it was signed?

of justice be? Can you provide an alternative meaning of justice that would lead you to conclude justice was served in this case?

Personal Defenses.   Personal defenses apply to holders, not holders in due course. Personal defenses can be divided into two categories. First, there are general defenses that can be asserted against the defendant on general contract theory.

Second, the UCC lists specific personal defenses created by provisions of Article 3.

DISCHARGE OF LIABILITY ON INSTRUMENTS

When a party's liability for a negotiable instrument is terminated, this party's liability has been discharged. In other words, the party is released from liability. Discharge can occur through a variety of ways (see Exhibit 28-7). For example, as stated earlier, discharge of endorsers can occur if a party who has a right to enforce the instrument has materially altered an instrument. Keep in mind that discharge is not effective against a holder in due course (UCC 3-601).

Discharge through Payment and Tender of Payment.   Earlier in this chapter, we discussed how a party becomes liable for an instrument by signing the instrument. If a party (or another party on the first party's behalf) who has signed an instrument as

Exhibit 28-7

Ways to Be Discharged from Liability for a Negotiable Instrument

Discharge by payment or tender of payment	Once payment of the stated amount on the instrument is made to the payee, all parties who are liable will be discharged.
Discharge by cancellation or renunciation	If the holder or enforcer cancels the instrument either by mutilating the document or surrendering it to the party who was to pay, that party is no longer liable to pay the stated amount.
Discharge by reacquisition	If the instrument becomes reacquired by a former holder of the instrument, all endorsements made after the reacquirer initially became the holder are canceled and thus those endorsers are discharged from liability.
Discharge by impairment of recourse	If the endorser's ability to seek recourse has been impaired by a previous holder, the endorser is discharged from liability.
Discharge by impairment of collateral	If the holder of collateral impairs the value of the collateral, the party who posted the collateral is discharged from liability to the extent of the damage to the collateral.

an obligation to pay then pays the full amount due, all parties who are liable will be discharged (UCC 3-602).

For example, Stuart creates a note in which he promises to pay Vanessa $1,000. If Stuart pays the $1,000 on the due date, he will be discharged from liability on the note. However, if Stuart makes the payment on the note to John, knowing that John stole the note from Vanessa and is wrongfully possessing it, Stuart's obligation will not be discharged. Paying John does not discharge Stuart's liability because John, who stole the note, is not a holder and is not entitled to the amount on the note [UCC 3-602(b)(2)].

Moreover, some parties' obligations on an instrument will be discharged if the obliged party tenders full payment on the due date but the holder of the instrument refuses to accept the money [UCC 3-603(b)]. If Stuart makes a proper tender of the full amount ($1,000) to Vanessa on the note's due date but she improperly refuses to accept the money, Stuart will still be liable for the $1,000 but will not have to pay interest on the amount. However, if any endorsers or accommodation parties are liable for Stuart's note, these parties' obligation will be discharged.

Discharge by Cancellation or Renunciation.   A party who is entitled to enforce an instrument may decide to cancel the instrument with or without consideration. Canceling the instrument discharges the obligation of a party who must pay the instrument (UCC 3-604). The party who decides to cancel the instrument may engage in an intentional voluntary act to cancel the instrument. For example, the party might write "Paid" on the instrument, intentionally destroy or mutilate the instrument, or give the instrument to the obliged party.

Alternatively, a party may renounce an instrument by promising not to sue to enforce the instrument. Renunciation occurs when a party agrees, in writing, not to sue the obliged party.

BUT WHAT IF . . .
WHAT IF THE FACTS OF THE CASE OPENER WERE DIFFERENT?
Let's say that a patient of LaCombe's called about a check she had given him and said she could not afford to pay the check because she had just lost her job. LaCombe decided to send her a letter saying he would not sue her to get the money from the check. If LaCombe later tells the patient he wants to deposit the check, is the patient already discharged from the obligation of paying the instrument or does she legally have to allow LaCombe to deposit the check?

Discharge by Reacquisition.   Reacquisition occurs when a former holder of an instrument has the instrument transferred back to him or her by negotiation or other means. When reacquisition occurs, anyone who endorsed the instrument in between the initial acquisition and the reacquisition by the holder has his or her endorsement canceled. When an endorsement is canceled, discharge occurs. The holder who reacquired the instrument can further negotiate the instrument, but the intermediate endorsers will not be held liable (UCC 3-207).

For example, suppose Gina acquires a note through negotiation. Gina endorses and transfers the note to Jeremy. Jeremy endorses and transfers to Amanda, who endorses and transfers to Ben. Ben then endorses the note and transfers it back to Gina. When Gina endorses the note, she cancels Jeremy's, Amanda's, and Ben's endorsements. Were the note to be dishonored, Jeremy, Amanda, and Ben would all not be liable on the amount of the instrument.

Discharge by Impairment of Recourse.   A right to recourse is the ability of a party to seek reimbursement. Typically, when a holder presents an instrument to an endorser, the endorser presented with the instrument can seek recourse from prior endorsers, the maker, the drawer, or accommodating parties. However, if the holder has in some way impaired the endorser's ability to seek recourse from any of these parties, the endorser is not liable on the instrument [UCC 3-605(i)].

For example, Mary is the holder of a promissory note. She presents the note to Peter, a previous endorser. Normally Peter would have to pay the note and would be entitled to collect from a number of other parties. However, Mary carelessly defaced the note in such a way as to make the note worthless. Since Peter cannot invoke his right to recourse because of Mary's actions, he is not liable on the note and does not have to pay Mary.

Discharge by Impairment of Collateral.   If a party posts collateral to ensure his performance of the negotiable instrument and the holder of the collateral impairs the value of the collateral, the party to the instrument is discharged from the instrument to the extent of the damage to the collateral [UCC 3-605(d)].

CASE OPENER WRAP-UP

Bank One and the Forged Checks

The district court held for LaCombe. The bank appealed. The appellate court considered whether the bank and/or LaCombe failed to exercise ordinary care, whether either party was negligent, and whether this negligence substantially contributed to the making of the forged signatures on the checks.

The appellate court found that LaCombe was given no reason to suspect that any wrongdoing was taking place. Neither his business reports nor statements raised any "red flags." Slyfield covered her illegal activity well, choosing checks that would not be easily missed. LaCombe's accounting system was reasonable under the circumstances. Accordingly, the court found that LaCombe exercised "ordinary care" in the conduct of his practice and did not substantially contribute to the making of his forged signature on the checks.

However, Bank One failed to act in accordance with its own policies. It was the bank's policy that a check made out to a business, including a check made out to a sole proprietorship, had to be deposited into an account bearing the business's name. However, LaCombe's checks were not deposited into the business account. Therefore, Bank One failed to exercise ordinary care in taking the forged instruments. As a result, the appellate court affirmed the trial court's determination that the bank was 100 percent liable for the forged checks. This led to the conclusion that LaCombe should be reimbursed for the embezzled checks.

Several lessons can be drawn from this case. First, it emphasizes that as a business manager, you will need to carefully select your employees because hiring decisions can have an enormous impact on the financial success of your company. Second, it emphasizes the importance of paying close attention to your financial accounts. Perhaps if LaCombe had paid better attention in the first place, he would not have to deal with the stress of a lawsuit against Bank One. This case also demonstrates the importance of following proper procedures and exercising care in all business practices. The cost to LaCombe to avoid such embezzlement would have been far higher than that to the bank, which has specific procedures for check cashing of sole proprietorships.

KEY TERMS

SUMMARY OF KEY TOPICS

A party can be held liable for an instrument only if the party has signed the instrument.   **Signature Liability**

Primary liability of makers and acceptors: They must pay the stated amount on the instrument when it is presented for payment.

Secondary liability of drawers and endorsers: They must pay the amount on the instrument if the primarily liable party dishonors the instrument and the following three conditions are met:

1. Presentment
2. Dishonor
3. Notice of dishonor

Accommodation party: An accommodation party is one who signs an instrument to provide credit for another party who has also signed the instrument.

Agent's signature: As long as the agent is *authorized* to sign a negotiable instrument on behalf of a principal, the agent's signature can create liability for the principal.

Unauthorized signature: If a signature to a negotiable instrument is unauthorized, this unauthorized signature will not impose liability to the named party.

1. Negligence
2. Imposter rule
3. Fictitious-payee rule

Transfer warranty: When a party transfers an instrument to another party for consideration, the   **Warranty Liability**
transferring party makes certain promises or warranties regarding the instrument and the transfer itself.

Presentment warranty: When a party properly presents an instrument for acceptance, the party makes certain promises regarding the instrument and the party who is entitled to payment.

1. *Defenses to liability:* The arguments as to why a party should not be held liable for an instrument   **Avoiding Liability for**
    include: **Negotiable Instruments**
    a. Real defenses
    b. Personal defenses

2. *Discharge of liability:* Release from liability can occur through:
    a. Discharge by payment or tender of payment.
    b. Discharge by cancellation or renunciation.
    c. Discharge by reacquisition.
    d. Discharge by impairment of recourse.
    e. Discharge by impairment of collateral.

POINT / COUNTERPOINT

Should a Company Be Held Liable When an Employee's Work-Related Illegal Actions Include the Endorsement of Fraudulent Checks?	
YES	**NO**
A company should always be held liable for an employee's work-related illegal actions. The company hired the employee and put him in a position where he could commit an illegal action, so the company should be held responsible.	Companies should not be held liable for an employee's fraudulent checks. The employees, not the companies, should be held liable.
A company benefits from the work of each of its employees. If employees are profitable, company profits increase, shareholder stock increases, and salaries increase; everyone benefits. Thus, because the company *benefits* when the employee is *profitable,* the company should also experience *losses* when the employee is *unprofitable* or *harmful.*	Every employee is an individual who controls his or her own actions. Although a company can try to monitor employee activities, if an employee wants to commit an illegal act, she will. Most companies hire smart, well-qualified people. Smart people can always find a way around even the best company security systems.
One of the factors in assigning liability for fraudulent checks is the ability of a party to bear the loss of the checks. A company is better equipped to bear a loss of funds than an individual. The losses occurred because of the actions of a specific *company* employee. Therefore, a company should shoulder the blame and pay for the losses from the fraudulent checks. After the company bears the losses of the checks, the company can then assess how to penalize the employee who endorsed the fraudulent checks.	Employees also need to feel the consequences of their own actions. If a corporation always takes the hit for an employee's poor decision, the employee cannot learn to change his behavior.
	Companies should not be blamed for an employee's fraudulent checks because, sometimes, the bank responsible for paying out the fraudulent checks should be held responsible. Banks are companies as well, and as such, they should be aware of suspicious activities. When cashing large checks, the bank could easily require a verification code that would be known only by someone authorized to give checks.
A company should be held liable for an employee's actions because the company has the ability to monitor employee activities and the company chose to use the employee to represent the company.	Employees make their own decisions and are not forced to act against the law. Therefore, the employees should be held personally accountable.

QUESTIONS & PROBLEMS

1. What is the distinction between primary and secondary liability for a signed negotiable instrument?

2. Evaluate the following statement: "A party can never be held liable for a negotiable instrument if he or she did not sign the check."

3. What are the similarities and differences between transfer and presentment warranties?

4. Joshua Herrera found a purse in a dumpster. He contacted the owner of the purse, and it was returned to its owner. After returning the purse, Herrera returned to the dumpster. He found a check written out to "cash." Herrera testified that he thought that meant that he "could get money for the check." He presented the check at a bank, and the bank teller instructed him to put his name on the payee line next to cash. Herrera added the words "to Joshua Herrera" to the payee line and endorsed the check. The trial court found Herrera guilty of forgery. On appeal, Herrera argued that he did not alter the check because he did not change the legal efficacy of the check. Herrera claimed that the check was a bearer instrument and payable to anyone possessing the instrument. How do you think the court decided? [*State of New Mexico v. Joshua Herrera,* 2000 N.M. App. LEXIS 100 (2001).]

5. In 1992, Eric M. Schmitz executed two "Limited Power of Attorney" forms with Georgetown

Financial, a Wisconsin company that provided investment, insurance, and financial services. James O'Hearn was the sole owner and chief executive officer of Georgetown Financial. Georgetown Financial purchased mutual funds through Putnam Investments for Schmitz. Putnam issued two checks and mailed them to Schmitz, in care of Georgetown Financial, as designated in the account application. O'Hearn presented both checks to Firstar Bank for deposit into a Georgetown Financial account. The larger check did not include an endorsement by or on behalf of Schmitz. The smaller check included an endorsement bearing Schmitz's name that Schmitz claims is a forged signature. Both checks were stamped with a Georgetown Financial deposit stamp and marked "for deposit only." Firstar Bank deposited the face value of both checks into a Georgetown Financial account. Schmitz never received the funds deposited into the account. Schmitz argued that because Georgetown Financial did not have authority to endorse the larger check, Firstar Bank was liable as a matter of law for making payment on this check, which was presented by Georgetown Financial without his actual or purported signature. Should Firstar Bank be held liable for cashing both checks? How did the court decide? [*Schmitz v. Firstar Bank Milwaukee,* 2003 WI 21 (2003).]

6. Olga Ensenat, an 88-year-old woman, had substantial investment accounts. Eventually her niece, Diana Flores, moved in to take care of Ensenat. While living with her, Flores withdrew on Ensenat's accounts, forged Ensenat's signature, and deposited the money into Flores's accounts. In the end Flores embezzled $157,386.30, all of which was deposited at Hancock Bank, where Flores had an account. Ensenat alleged that she did not herself withdraw or authorize any other person to withdraw retirement funds from her accounts. Ensenat sued Hancock Bank, claiming that it was responsible because it allowed the checks to be paid or deposited without her endorsement, signature, or authorization. Did the court agree with Ensenat and find Hancock Bank liable for the deposited checks? Why or why not? [*Hancock Bank v. Ensenat,* 819 So. 2d 3 (2001).]

7. Robert Carter, an employee of National Accident Insurance, intercepted insurance premium checks totaling more than $10 million that customers made payable to the insurance agency. Carter then altered those checks by adding a slash (/) and additional payees, such as "Sherman" or "Sherman Imports, Inc." These changes to the checks were made either in a different typewritten font or different handwriting than the other payee listed. After altering the checks, he endorsed and deposited the checks in his "Sherman account" at Citibank. After Citibank was taken to court for cashing the fraudulent checks, Citibank relied on the fictitious-payee rule, arguing that this is a situation in which the bank honors a check bearing the forged endorsement of a fictional payee. Thus, Citibank believes that the rule should relieve its liability and place the loss on the drawer of the checks. Do you think the fictitious-payee rule applies in this case? Would any additional information help you make your decision? [*National Accident Insurance Underwriters v. Citibank,* 243 F. Supp. 2d 763 (2002).]

8. The late Dr. Fred Clark had a bank account at Toronto Dominion Bank. Unauthorized withdrawals were made from his account to allegedly pay for outstanding balances owed by numerous unidentified customers of the various retail defendants. Somehow one or more of the defendants improperly obtained access to Clark's account and began withdrawing money through a series of electronic fund transfers. The bank is not liable for withdrawals that were not made known to the bank within one year of the withdrawals. What additional considerations would determine whether Clark or the defendant is liable for the withdrawals from Clark's account? In other words, use the "but what if" logic to show you understand this area of business law. [*Estate of Clark v. Toronto Dominion Bank,* 2013 WL 1159014 (E.D. Pa. 2013).]

9. In this strange case, Albertson has already been convicted of passing checks that were ultimately dishonored because of insufficient funds in Albertson's checking account. Both Albertson and a witness claim that the person to whom the checks were issued had an agreement with Albertson that the drawee would hold on to the checks until Albertson had sufficient funds to cover the checks. The drawee was a used-car dealer who admitted in court that he had hold-check agreements with others but could not recall whether he had one with Albertson. Naturally, Albertson does not want to be liable for the checks that were later dishonored. Given the principles of law you learned in this chapter, what

facts would need to be true for Albertson to have a reasonable argument on his behalf? [*Albertson v. State*, 2013 WL 3233378 (Md. App. 2013).]

10. A Chapter 7 bankruptcy trustee is filing an action to recover funds from the wife of a debtor. The wife signed a debtor's instrument in which her husband borrowed funds to construct utility barns and fencing necessary for his horse-raising business. The debtor and his wife used the property on which the horse-raising facilities were built as their residence. The purchase of the materials to construct the barns and fence was not made with any intention of increasing the value of their residential property. What additional information would you need to determine whether the wife was an "accommodation party" for purposes of determining liability regarding the debt instrument that she signed? [*In re Simpson*, 474 B.R. 656 (Bkrtcy. S.D. Ind. 2012).]

Looking for more review materials?

The Online Learning Center at **www.mhhe.com/kubasek3e** contains this chapter's "Assignment on the Internet" and also a list of URLs for more information, entitled "On the Internet." Find both of them in the Student Center portion of the OLC, along with quizzes and other helpful materials.

Checks and Electronic Fund Transfers

LEARNING OBJECTIVES

After reading this chapter, you will be able to answer the following questions:

1   What are the components of a check?

2   What are the differences among the various types of checks?

3   How and where are deposits accepted?

4   When may a bank charge a customer's account?

5   What are the different types of electronic fund transfers?

CASE OPENER

Fraudulent Electronic Fund Transfers

Patco Construction Company was a customer that had an account at Ocean Bank. Patco argued that its account was subject to the authorization of six fraudulent withdrawals from the account after a perpetrator supplied the correct security answers for access to Patco's account. The perpetrator successfully wired Patco's money to multiple individual accounts to which Patco had never before sent funds. Although Ocean Bank's security system flagged these transactions as "unusually high risk," given that the electronic fund transfers were inconsistent with Patco's usual payment orders, the bank still did not notify Patco and allowed the payments, totaling $588,851.26. Ocean Bank eventually recovered $243,406.83, leaving a loss of $345,444.43 with Patco.

Patco argued that the bank should bear this loss because its security system was not "commercially reasonable" under Article 4(A) of the Uniform Commercial Code. This article of the UCC is meant to govern the rights, duties, and liabilities of banks and their customers in regard to electronic fund transfers. More specifically, Patco argued that the bank's security system was not commercially reasonable because it failed to incorporate additional security measures such as monitoring high-risk transactions or immediately notifying customers of high-risk transactions.

On the other hand, the bank asserted that the security system was in fact commercially reasonable, and because Patco agreed to the security system in use, the bank was entitled to summary judgment on all six counts of the complaint by Patco.

1. Suppose that you are a business manager at a new bank. You are determining bank policy regarding your bank's security system. What additional components should you include in your policy to ensure that your bank meets the standards of the UCC in respect to electronic fund transfers?

2. Now suppose that you have created that policy. How would you decide to communicate this policy to your customers?

The Wrap-Up at the end of the chapter will answer these questions.

The relationship between a bank and its customers is quite complicated. When a customer opens an account at a bank, he or she creates a contractual relationship with the bank. Within this relationship, both the customer and the bank have certain rights and duties. This relationship is governed by Article 4 of the UCC. For example, the customer has the right to order a stop payment on a check for any or no reason. The corresponding duty of the bank is to follow this order.

As we explained in previous chapters, checks are considered negotiable instruments under Article 3 of the UCC. However, Article 4 of the UCC is also relevant; this section of the UCC governs the transfer of checks between banks. Thus, both Article 3 and Article 4 are relevant to this chapter.

Article 3 of the UCC outlines the requirements that negotiable instruments, including checks, must meet. Article 3 also establishes the rights and responsibilities pertaining to parties to negotiable instruments. Article 4 creates a framework controlling deposit and checking agreements between banks and customers. In addition, Article 4 directs the relationships between banks as checks are processed among different banks. Moreover, according to UCC Section 4-102(a), when conflicts arise between rules in Articles 3 and 4, Article 4 is to take precedence.

In 2009, Americans wrote approximately 70 billion checks. Clearly, checks are an enormous part of the bank-customer relationship. In fact, of all the negotiable instruments regulated by the UCC, checks are the most common type used. Thus, we begin this chapter by taking a closer look at different types of checks. Then we examine the process of check collection: If the bank accepts a check, how is the money from one account actually transferred to another account? Next, we consider when a bank may charge a customer's account in the context of potential problems with checks, such as stale, postdated, and forged checks. Finally, we turn to an increasingly important element of the banking process: the electronic transfer of funds.

Checks

L01

What are the components of a check?

Although you have likely written a check, do you know what the actual characteristics of checks are? (The key terms and an illustration are provided in Exhibits 29-1 and 29-2.) According to the UCC, a check is a special kind of draft. A draft is an instrument that is an order. Three parties are related to an order. First, a drawer is the party that gives the order. Second, a drawee is the party that must obey the order. Finally, the payee is the party that receives the benefit of the order. Thus, when you write a check at the grocery store, you are the drawer ordering the drawee (your bank) to make a payment to the payee (the grocery store).

A check is a special draft that orders the drawee, a bank, to pay a fixed amount of money on demand [UCC Section 3-104(f)]. The UCC defines a bank as "any business

Exhibit 29-1
Key Terms for Checks

Draft	An instrument whereby one party orders a second party to pay an amount of money to the party listed on the instrument
Drawer	The party giving the order to pay on a draft
Drawee	The party ordered to pay on a draft
Payee	The party receiving the money from the draft

Exhibit 29-2   A Check

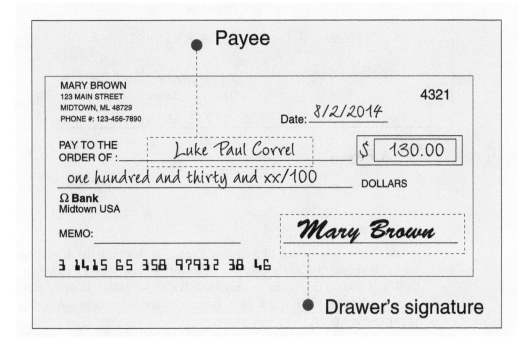

engaged in the business of banking" [4-105(1)]. Consequently, savings banks, savings and loans, credit unions, and trust companies are all considered banks. The drawer of a check writes the check and thus orders the bank to pay. The payee is the party to whom the check is written.

CASHIER'S CHECKS

A **cashier's check** is a check for which both the drawer and the drawee are the same bank [UCC 3-104(g)]. (See Exhibit 29-3 for an example.) The payee of the check is a specific person. In other words, the bank is drawing on itself and thus assumes the responsibility for paying the check to that specific person.

Customers often purchase cashier's checks to give to creditors who want to be sure the funds represented by the check are available. Cashier's checks are useful because they are considered by many in the business community to be the near equivalent of cash. For example, suppose Dave is buying a used car for $9,000 and wants to pay with a personal check. The seller of the car, Hudson, is not sure Dave actually has $9,000 in his checking account. Thus, Hudson asks Dave to pay for the car with a cashier's check. Dave goes to his bank and transfers the $9,000 to the bank. The bank then creates a check for $9,000 payable to Hudson.

L02

What are the differences among the various types of checks?

Exhibit 29-3   A Cashier's Check

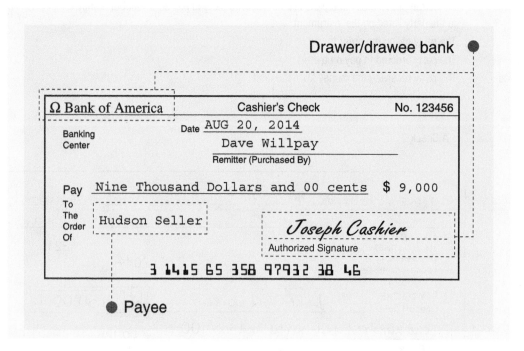

TELLER'S CHECKS

A teller's check is similar to a cashier's check in that both the drawer and the drawee are banks. However, a teller's check is different because it is a check that is drawn by one bank and usually drawn on another bank [UCC 3-104(h)]. In other words, bank A is the drawer, while bank B is the drawee. In some cases, the drawee is a nonbank, but the check is payable at a bank.

TRAVELER'S CHECKS

A traveler's check is an instrument that must have the following characteristics (see Exhibit 29-4):

1. Is payable on demand.
2. Is drawn on or through a bank.
3. Is designated by the phrase *traveler's check*.
4. Requires a countersignature by a person whose signature appears on the instrument. [UCC 3-104(i)]

The drawer of a traveler's check is usually a large financial organization, such as American Express. The person who signs the traveler's check must sign it when she buys the checks. When the person is ready to use the traveler's check to make some kind of payment, the same person must sign the traveler's check in the presence of the acceptor.

MONEY ORDERS

Money orders (see Exhibit 29-5), particularly personal money orders, are usually in the same form as personal checks and are considered checks under UCC Section 3-104. Both banks and nonbanks sell money orders. The money order states that a certain amount of

Exhibit 29-4   A Traveler's Check

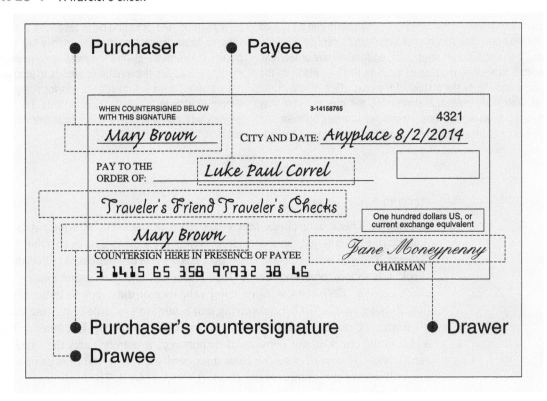

Exhibit 29-5   A Money Order

money is to be paid to a particular person. The amount of money to be paid is usually already imprinted on the money order. The person purchasing the money order signs the money order as the drawer and fills in the name of the person who is to receive the money.

Legal Principle: **A bank is primarily liable for a certified check.**

Unlike in the United States, in India, money orders can be issued only by the post office. The money order can be verified by a signature, a thumb mark or fingerprint, or both. Money orders can be written in various languages, such as English, Hindi, or the language specific to the district of the post office. While in the United States the individual purchasing the money order may be referred to as a *purchaser, sender,* or *remitter,* in India, the law refers to the individual who is writing the money order only as a *remitter.* The person who is receiving the money order is referred to as the *payee.* After the money has been paid to the payee, the remitter always receives acknowledgment of payment to the payee. If the remitter wishes to stop payment on the money order, there are no stipulations for doing so; the remitter simply returns to the post office, notifies the personnel of the payee's address, and offers the receipt from the issued money order.

CERTIFIED CHECKS

A certified check is a check that is accepted at the bank at which it is drawn [UCC 3-409(d)]. For example, suppose Hope writes a check to Jeremiah from her account at Citizens National Bank (CNB). Hope asks CNB to certify her check. CNB then accepts the check, withdraws the money from Hope's account, and places that money in its certified check account. CNB then signs or stamps the face of the check to indicate that it is certified. In other words, CNB is promising that funds are available to pay the check.

Banks are not required to certify checks [UCC 3-409(d)]. If a bank refuses to certify a check, the check is not considered dishonored; it merely lacks the extra protection of certification. However, once the bank does certify a check, the drawer of the check is no longer liable for the amount of the check [UCC 3-414(c)]. The bank has become primarily liable for the check.

WHY USE CASHIER'S, TELLER'S, OR CERTIFIED CHECKS?

There are a number of reasons to use a cashier's, teller's, or certified check as opposed to a regular check when conducting business exchanges. While all of these types of drafts are different, one thing they have in common is an increased guarantee of being paid. That is, a cashier's, teller's, or certified check is less likely to be denied by a bank.

Cashier's checks are a valuable business tool because the bank, and not the individual, is the drawer as well as the drawee. When a cashier's check is presented for payment, the bank, and not the individual, must pay for the cashier's check. The added guarantee of knowing that the bank is paying for the cashier's check makes the cashier's check a veritable guarantee to pay. One downside of the cashier's check is that it must be paid for in advance, including a small fee. However, because the cashier's check is paid for first, it can be purchased at any bank, regardless of whether one has an account at the bank.

Teller's checks function like cashier's checks. Teller's checks tend to carry with them a similar guarantee to be paid. However, because the teller's check is drawn on a bank other than the one issuing the teller's check, the process is a step removed from the one regarding cashier's checks. That is, the bank ordering payment is not the bank making the payment, so the guarantee of sufficient funds is not as strong as it is with cashier's checks. Given the weaker guarantee, a teller's check is used primarily when a customer wants to buy a cashier's check from a bank that does not currently have the funds to cover the cashier's check and thus issues a teller's check. Consequently, although a cashier's check is preferred to a teller's check, the teller's check is almost as good as the cashier's check.

Certified checks are useful in business because when a bank certifies a check, it essentially says that it cannot refuse liability on the check. A certified check is one that the bank sets aside money for and agrees to pay when the certified check is presented. Despite the

Exhibit 29-6   Relationship among Cashier's, Teller's, and Certified Checks

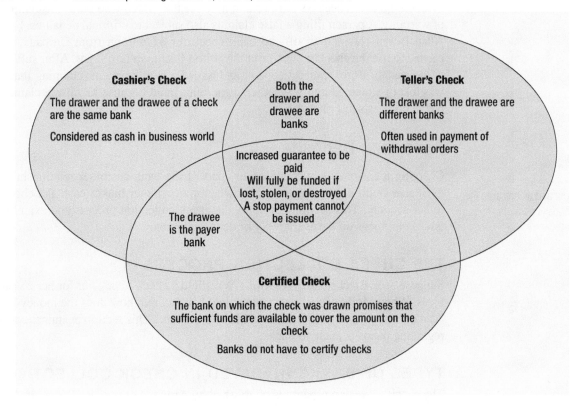

added guarantee, there are two main drawbacks to a certified check. The first is that a person must have an account at a specific bank to obtain a certified check. That is, unlike cashier's or teller's checks, if a person does not have an account at the bank, he or she cannot obtain a certified check from that bank. The second drawback is that banks do not have to certify checks. Banks may refuse to certify any check for any reason. Refusing to certify is not the same as dishonoring a check, but it does not provide the same guarantee that a certified check has. While banks do not have to certify a check, they are not allowed to refuse to sell a cashier's or teller's check as long as the payment is valid.

Exhibit 29-6 summarizes the relationship among cashier's, teller's, and certified checks.

LOST, STOLEN, OR DESTROYED CASHIER'S, TELLER'S, OR CERTIFIED CHECKS

In the event a cashier's, teller's, or certified check is lost, stolen, or destroyed, the UCC allows for recovery. According to UCC Section 3-312, the remitter (the party who purchased the check) or the payee may request a refund because the check was lost, stolen, or destroyed. With proper identification, the party should be able to obtain a full refund for the amount on the check.

The claim is enforceable when the claim is made; if it is a cashier's or teller's check, 90 days after the check was made; or if it is a certified check, 90 days after acceptance, whichever occurs last [UCC 3-312(b)(1)]. After the claim becomes enforceable, if no one presented the check for payment, a refund is issued and the bank is discharged of liability [UCC 3-312(b)(4)]. When a claim is made, the person making the claim warrants to the bank and any party who has an interest in the check that the check was really lost, stolen, or destroyed.

If the check was not lost, stolen, or destroyed, the holder barred from receiving payment on the check because of the claim may sue the person who made the claim for breach of warranty. A person filing a false claim is also subject to criminal penalties. For example, Allan Boren obtained an official bank check for $1 million from Citibank. Boren proceeded to use the check to gamble at the Hilton Casino in Las Vegas. After suffering losses at the casino, Boren called Citibank and issued a stop payment, claiming that the check was lost or stolen. Boren was indicted for bank fraud because he falsely claimed that his bank check was lost or stolen.

Accepting Deposits

L03

How and where are deposits accepted?

Charging a customer's account is only part of the bank-customer relationship; the bank must also credit a customer's account when the customer makes cash and check deposits to her account. This section considers the check collection process and examines several issues that focus on the availability of deposited money.

THE CHECK COLLECTION PROCESS

Suppose Jack Blackstone gives Molly Whetfield a check to pay her for her consulting services. When Molly deposits that check into her account, how does the money from Jack's account actually get transferred into Molly's account? This section examines several issues regarding deposits made to banks.

TYPES OF BANKS INVOLVED IN CHECK COLLECTION

The check collection process is established by Article 4 of the UCC. Section 4-105 of the UCC defines the four types of banks that may be involved in the check collection process. Return to the Jack and Molly example. First, suppose Molly presents Jack's check to her bank for deposit in her account. Molly's bank is called the depositary bank, the first bank that receives a check for payment. Second, Jack's bank is called the payor bank, the bank on which a check is drawn. Third, any kind of bank (besides the payor bank) that handles Jack's check during the collection process is called a collecting bank. Finally, any bank (besides the payor bank and depositary bank) to which the check is transferred is called an intermediary bank.

A bank involved in the check collection process may be classified as several of these types of banks at the same time. For example, when Molly deposits Jack's check at her bank, her bank is both the depositary bank and the collecting bank.

CHECK COLLECTION WITHIN THE SAME BANK

Sometimes the depositary bank is the same bank as the payor bank. When the depositary bank is the same bank as the payor bank, the check is referred to as an "on-us item." For example, suppose Molly's and Jack's accounts are at the same bank. When Molly deposits Jack's check into her account, the check does not have to be sent to another bank because she and Jack share the same bank. Instead, the bank gives a "provisional" credit to Molly's account. If this bank does not dishonor the check on the second day, the check is paid [UCC 4-215(e)(2)]. Finally, on the third day, the provisional credit becomes an actual payment.

CHECK COLLECTION BETWEEN DIFFERENT BANKS

Suppose that Jack and Molly have accounts at different banks. Molly's account is in Los Angeles, while Jack's account is in Miami. When Molly deposits Jack's check at her bank in Los Angeles, her bank is the depositary bank. When a depositary bank receives a check, it must present the check at the payor bank or send it through intermediary banks to reach the payor bank. Once a bank receives a check, it must pass the check on before midnight of the next day [UCC 4-202(b)]. When the check finally reaches the payor bank, the payor bank must respond to the check by dishonoring it or becoming liable for the face amount of the check (UCC 4-302).

The UCC allows banks to establish cutoff hours for making entries on their books. For example, a bank may determine that 2 p.m. or later is the cutoff hour for handling checks (UCC 4-108). If the bank receives a check after this deadline, the bank will defer posting this check to its customer's account until the next day.

FEDERAL RESERVE SYSTEM FOR CLEARING CHECKS

The Federal Reserve System, consisting of 12 central banks, acts as a clearinghouse for the check collection process. (A *clearinghouse* is an institution created to facilitate banks in their exchange of checks and drafts drawn on one another, as well as to enable banks to settle their daily balances.) These 12 banks are located in the following cities: Atlanta, Boston, Chicago, Cleveland, Dallas, Kansas City, Minneapolis, New York, Philadelphia, Richmond, Saint Louis, and San Francisco. Most banks have accounts with the Federal Reserve. Thus, when Molly deposits Jack's check at her bank in Los Angeles, this bank will deposit the check in the San Francisco Federal Reserve Bank. The San Francisco Federal Reserve Bank will transfer the check to the Atlanta Federal Reserve Bank, which serves Miami. Finally, the Atlanta Federal Reserve Bank will transfer the check to Jack's bank in Miami.

ELECTRONIC CHECK PRESENTMENT

In the past, checks were physically presented to each bank in the chain of collection. Now, checks are transmitted electronically from bank to bank (UCC 4-110). Through electronic check presentment, a check can be processed on the day on which it is deposited. An item is encoded with information that is transferred from one bank's computer to another bank's computer. The person who enters the information into the computer (i.e., encodes the information) warrants that the information is correct (UCC 4-209). Alternatively, the image of a check may be transmitted for payment to other banks.

Substitute Checks. To further facilitate electronic presentment, in 2004 Congress passed the *Check Clearing for the 21st Century Act* (also known as *Check 21* or the *Check Truncation Act*). Check 21 allows banks to forgo sending original checks as part of the collection or return process and instead send a truncated version. In place of the original paper check, a bank may send (1) a substitute check or (2), by agreement, an electronic image of the check along with data from the magnetic ink character recognition (MICR) line on the original check.

A substitute check is similar to the electronic image that may be sent in lieu of the original paper check. Check 21 defines a substitute check as a paper reproduction of the original check that conforms to the following requirements:

1. Contains a clear replication of the front and back of the original paper check.
2. Bears an MICR line with all the information on the original check's MICR line.
3. Conforms with generally applicable industry standards for paper stock, dimensions, and other general qualities.
4. Is suitable for automated processing in the same manner as the original paper check.

Check 21 provides the guidelines for the issuance and use of substitute checks. The act also allows for the use of digital or paper substitutions for the original paper check.

AVAILABILITY SCHEDULE FOR DEPOSITED CHECKS

Once a check is considered deposited in a customer's account, when are the funds available to the customer? In the past, banks placed extended holds (e.g., 10 days) on deposited funds to allow for ensuring that the payor bank would not dishonor the check. If the check was from out of state, the bank might place a two-week hold on the check.

Because customers were frustrated with such extended holds on checks, Congress enacted the Expedited Funds Availability Act of 1987. This act created explicit timelines that mandate when banks must make deposited funds available to customers. If the risk of dishonor is low, the funds must be made available very quickly. For example, the first $100 of any amount deposited must be available to the depositor on the business day following the day of deposit [12 C.F.R. Section 229.10(a)–(c)]. The availability of the rest of the funds depends on whether the check is local, what the amount of the check is, and how the depositor wishes to withdraw the funds.

Legal Principle: **If the deposited check is drawn on a bank within the same Federal Reserve Bank area, the depositary bank must make the deposited funds available to the customer on the second business day following the deposit day [12 C.F.R. 229.10(b)].**

Legal Principle: **If the deposited check is outside the same Federal Reserve Bank area, the depositary bank must make the funds available on the fifth business day following the day of deposit [12 C.F.R. 229.12(c)].**

There are some exceptions to these rules. For example, if a customer makes a deposit at an ATM not owned by the bank that is receiving the deposit, the bank places a five-day hold on the deposit, including cash deposits. Moreover, if a customer makes a deposit over $5,000, the depositary bank may place an eight-day hold on the funds.

When a Bank May Charge a Customer's Account

L04

When may a bank charge a customer's account?

The following sections consider certain problems related to a bank's accepting and paying a customer's check. See Exhibit 29-7 for a summary of who bears responsibility when these problems arise.

WRONGFUL DISHONOR

When a customer opens a checking account, both the customer and the bank accept certain duties and rights. Generally, the customer assumes a duty to keep sufficient funds in her account to cover the checks written on her account. If the customer does not have enough funds to cover a check, the bank will dishonor the check and the customer becomes liable for the amount of the check.

Similarly, under the *properly payable rule,* the bank has a duty to pay checks from the customer's account as long as the check is "properly payable" [UCC Section 4-401(a)]. In other words, the check must be authorized by the drawer and must not violate the agreement between the bank and the customer. Generally, for a check to be considered properly payable, it must:

1. Have the drawer's authorized signature on the check.
2. Be paid to a person entitled to enforce the check.

Exhibit 29-7   Who Is Responsible for the Check?

The customer presents a properly payable check, and the banks fails to pay it, thus wrongfully dishonoring the check.	**The bank is responsible.**
The customer does not have enough funds in her account to cover the check, so the bank dishonors the check.	**The customer is liable.**
The customer issues a stop-payment order orally and does not submit a written stop-payment order, and the bank cashes the check 20 days later.	**The customer is responsible.**
The customer writes a postdated check and notifies the bank, but the bank processes the check early and the customer does not have sufficient funds to pay the amount.	**The bank is responsible.**
The customer presents a check for payment eight months after the draft was written.	**No one; the check is stale and nonpayable.**
The customer has been adjudicated incompetent, but the bank does not have knowledge of this.	**The bank is responsible.**
The customer dies, and a check from the deceased customer is presented for payment 11 days after his death.	**No one; the check is nonpayable.**
The bank cashes a check with an unauthorized signature of the drawer ordering payment.	**The bank is responsible.**
The bank cashes a check with an unauthorized signature of the drawer ordering payment, but the customer's negligence contributed to the forgery.	**The customer is responsible.**
The bank cashes a check with an unauthorized drawer signature, but the customer notifies the bank of this two months after the statement was made available.	**The customer is responsible.**
The bank pays a check that has been fraudulently endorsed, but the customer reports the forgery four years later.	**The customer is responsible**
The bank cashes a check that has been altered.	**The bank is responsible.**
The customer loses her ATM card and notifies the bank right away.	**The customer is liable only for the first $50.**
The customer's ATM card is stolen, and the customer does not notify the bank.	**The customer is liable for the first $500.**
The customer notifies the bank of an erroneous electronic transfer three months after the statement is made available.	**The customer is responsible.**

3. Not have been altered.
4. Not have been completed by addition of unauthorized terms if the check was incomplete.
5. Be paid on or after the date of the check.
6. Not be subject to a stop payment from the drawer.

BUT WHAT IF . . .

WHAT IF THE FACTS OF THE CASE OPENER WERE DIFFERENT?

What if Patco Construction Company had written a check to Stoneworld Masonry for $500, but the check was altered to read $5,000 and was subsequently cashed, resulting in $5,000 being taken out of Patco's account? When Patco discovered this wrongful payment, would the bank be required to redeposit the $5,000 in the Patco account?

If the bank wrongfully fails to pay a check—wrongfully dishonoring the check—the bank may be liable to the customer for damages. The UCC clearly states that banks can be held liable, but it does not cite a specific theory for recovery. Therefore, someone whose check was dishonored need prove only that the dishonoring was wrongful, and he or she will be entitled to recovery. Case 29-1 provides an example of the damages a customer may potentially recover from a bank for wrongful dishonor. The case also illustrates another important aspect of recovering damages from a wrongful dishonor. UCC 4-402 authorizes a cause of action against a bank for wrongfully dishonoring a check of a "customer." Case 29-1 illustrates the difficulty of determining who a "customer" is when corporations are involved.

CASE 29-1

PAMELA JANA v. WACHOVIA
COMMON PLEAS COURT OF PHILADELPHIA
2006 PHILA. CT. COM. PL. LEXIS 479, 61 U.C.C. REP. SERV. 2D (CALLAGHAN) 583 (2006)

Since 1991, Pamela and Jerry Jana were involved in investment opportunities which consisted of acquiring certificates of deposit ("CDs") in their own names and the name of their minor son, Jerry A. Jana. The CDs were in savings and loan and/or mutual savings banks and the Janas held the CDs until such time that the banks converted to publicly owned banks, whereupon certificate holders were entitled to purchase shares of the converting bank's stock at a favorable price. To conduct their business, the Janas formed corporations in several states to acquire the CDs because the banks preferred to deal with customers within their community.

An investment opportunity arose in September of 2003, and the Janas sought to purchase shares in a bank by three separate checks. The checks the defendant provided to the Janas did not have the account number micro-encoded on the checks but rather was written by hand. The checks at issue were made payable to the savings bank the Janas were buying stock in and were in the names of "Pamela Jana," "Jerry A. Jana" (Pamela's minor son), and "Altoona Inc." (one of the Jana's companies). The defendant subsequently dishonored the checks due to alleged micro-encoding errors. Later the defendant agreed to honor these checks, but since the deadline had passed, the Janas' investment opportunity refused to fill the stock purchase requests. As a result, the Janas claimed $306,872 in damages due to lost profits from the wrongful dishonor of the checks. The defendants motioned for summary judgment claiming that the company, not the individual members of the Jana family, were customers to the bank. Under the UCC, a person must be a "customer" to recover damages from a wrongful dishonor of checks.

JUDGE SHEPPARD: 13 Pa.C.S. § 4402(b) sets forth the liability of a bank in the event of a wrongful dishonor:

A payor bank is liable to its customer for damages proximately caused by the wrongful dishonor of

an item. Liability is limited to actual damages proved and may include damages for an arrest or prosecution of the customer or other consequential damages. Whether any consequential damages are proximately caused by the wrongful dishonor is a question of fact to be determined in each case.

"Customer" is defined as "a person having an account with a bank or for whom a bank has agreed to collect items, including a bank that maintains an account at another bank." 13 Pa.C.S. § 4104.

The issue presented is whether Pamela Jana and her minor son may properly be considered "customers" for purposes of 13 Pa.C.S. § 4402(b). The account at issue was in the name of "Heronwood." Pamela and Jerry Jana were the authorized signatories on the account. Their minor son was not a signatory or otherwise named on the account.

This court is unaware of any Federal, Pennsylvania or other state decisions similar to the facts before this court. However, courts in various other jurisdictions have considered factual scenarios which are instructive. For example, in *Murdaugh Volkswagen, Inc. v. First Nat. Bank*, 801 F.2d 719 (4th Cir. 1986), an individual who was the president and sole stockholder of a corporation sought to bring an action for wrongful dishonor of a corporate check under UCC § 4-402. The bank argued that the plaintiff had no standing to assert such a claim because she did not have an account with the bank (the account was in the corporation's name). The Fourth Circuit found the bank's construction of § 4-402 to be unjustifiably narrow based on the facts presented because the evidence demonstrated a close link between the president and her corporation—the bank treated the president and the corporate depositor as one entity. The bank consistently and repeatedly looked to the president to assume the corporation's obligations by requiring her to mortgage her own home and personally borrow funds for the company's benefit. The court said that, under these facts, the president was a customer of the bank for purposes of § 4-402.

In *Parrett v. Platte Valley State Bank & Trust Co.,* 236 Neb. 139, 459 N.W.2d 371 (Neb. 1990), the Nebraska Supreme Court held that liability under UCC § 4-402 for wrongful dishonor could extend to a corporate officer who signed the check on behalf of the corporation, even though the check was written on the corporate account. The officer was the principal shareholder, president, and chief operating officer of the corporation, as well as a signatory to the corporate account. The evidence demonstrated that the officer personally participated in the business relationship between the corporation and the bank, including giving his personal guarantee to the bank for all obligations owed by the corporation to the bank. The court found that the officer was a "customer" of the bank within the meaning of § 4-402, observing that the parties' business relationship was such that it was foreseeable that dishonoring the corporation's check would reflect directly on the officer, against whom criminal charges had been brought in connection with the dishonored check.

Other courts, however, have adopted a more narrow approach. In *Loucks v. Albuquerque National Bank,* 76 N.M. 735, 418 P.2d 191 (N.M. 1966), Loucks and Martinez, as partners, had a partnership checking account at Albuquerque National. The bank dishonored the partnership's check after it had improperly charged the partnership account with a payment on a debt owed by Martinez. Loucks and Martinez individually sued the bank for wrongful dishonor of the partnership check. In determining that Loucks and Martinez, as individuals, had no cause of action against the bank for the alleged wrongful dishonor, the court stated:

> The relationship, in connection with which the wrongful conduct of the bank arose, was the relationship between the bank and the partnership. The partnership was the customer, and any damages arising from the dishonor belonged to the partnership and not to the partners individually.

However, many of the courts which adopted this strict approach seemed to leave the door open for situations where the evidence demonstrates that the corporation and the individual were one and the same or that the bank regarded the officer as its customer. See e.g., *Thrash v. Georgia State Bank,* 189 Ga. App. 21, 375 S.E.2d 112 (Ga. App. 1988) (found that the president of a corporation was not a "customer" for purposes of UCC § 4-402 where president was only a minority shareholder of the corporation who had merely joined with the other shareholders in guaranteeing the corporation's debt to the bank, and where the evidence failed to demonstrate that the president and the corporation were one and the same); *Koger v. East First Nat. Bank,* 443 So.2d 141 (Fla. App. 1983) (found that the trial court acted properly in dismissing an individual corporate stockholder's action under UCC § 4-402, since the individual was not the named customer on the account, noting that there was no allegation that the corporation was "undercapitalized" or a mere "transparent shell"); *Kesner v. Liberty Bank & Trust Co.,* 7 Mass. App. Ct. 934, 390 N.E.2d 259 (Mass. App. 1979) (held that the treasurer of a corporation could not bring an action under UCC § 4-402 since there was no ambiguity as to who had the account with the bank and where there was no suggestion that the corporation was a mere transparent shell rather than a separate and distinct legal entity with independent liability); *Farmers Bank v. Sinwellan Corp.,* 367 A.2d 180 (Del. Sup. 1976) (corporation's president was not a "customer" of the bank under plain language of statute where there was no evidence in the record supporting a finding that the bank regarded the president as its customer).

This case law suggests that where a dishonored check was drawn on the account of a small business entity, such as a closely held corporation, the wrongful dishonor can result in some actionable damage to the persons who control the corporation. In such instances, evidence may be presented to show that the person injured bore such a close relationship to the corporation that he or she should be permitted to bring an action for wrongful dishonor under the Commercial Code. Such evidence can include the failure to issue stock, undercapitalization of the business or corporation, the person's guarantee of the business' obligations, or the fact that the bank, in some way, treated the person and the business as a single entity. Such a finding would be precluded where there is evidence that the account on which the item was written carried only the corporate name and not the person's name, that the bank did not regard the person and the business as a single entity, or that the business entity was not undercapitalized.

Here, Jerry A. Jana, the minor plaintiff, has failed to satisfy this criteria. He was not a signatory or otherwise formally connected to the Account. It is admitted that he was never an officer or employee of Heronwood and never held any role in the company or had any direct dealings with the bank. As such, Jerry A. Jana, the minor plaintiff, cannot be considered a "customer" for purposes of § 4402, as a matter of law. Accordingly, summary judgment is granted in favor of defendants on this issue. Jerry A. Jana's claim is dismissed.

However, the court finds that a factual issue exists as to whether Pamela Jana can be considered a "customer." In order to survive summary judgment on this issue, Ms. Jana must produce evidence to show that she bore such a close relationship to the corporation that she should be permitted to bring an action for wrongful dishonor under § 4402 (b). This court finds that Ms. Jana has presented sufficient evidence to submit the issue to a jury, in that there is documentation to support her claim that the bank viewed she and her husband as their customers, rather than Heronwood. Based on the foregoing, summary judgment is granted in favor of defendants as to the claims of minor plaintiff Jerry A. Jana and of Heronwood, Inc. Defendants' Motion for Summary Judgment is denied with respect to the claims of Pamela Jana, individually.

Motion granted in part, denied in part.

CRITICAL THINKING

Judge Sheppard uses several cases to make analogies with the Jana case. Do you think these analogies are effective? Are there any differences between those cases and the facts in this case that suggest that Judge Sheppard should not have relied so heavily on them?

How should the judge decide on the case when there is no clear precedent about what to do in this situation?

ETHICAL DECISION MAKING

Return to the WPH framework and ask yourself, "Who are the relevant stakeholders?" A classmate agrees with the judge and believes that the minor in the case is not a relevant stakeholder. Make an argument suggesting that the minor is a relevant stakeholder, even though he is not a legal adult.

OVERDRAFTS

Suppose you write 10 checks on your company's account to pay your employees' salaries. Unfortunately, you do not have sufficient funds to cover the full amount of the last check; you are short $50. The bank has two options: (1) Dishonor the last check, or (2) create an overdraft by paying the check and charging the account the amount short [UCC 4-401(a)]. Thus, when you make your next deposit, $50 will be deducted from that deposit.

How frequently do banks have to dishonor checks because of insufficient funds? In Europe, less than 1 percent of personal checks are returned because of insufficient funds. Approximately 1 percent of checks are returned because of insufficient funds in the United States. In contrast, 9.5 percent of personal checks bounce in Qatar, while 3.4 percent are returned in Saudi Arabia.

Many banks offer overdraft protection to their customers. In other words, some banks will promise to credit their customers' accounts if there are insufficient funds. However, these banks may charge the customers for this service. Alternatively, banks may give several options to customers to prevent overdrafts. For example, the bank may link the checking account to the customer's savings account or credit card; thus, if a customer has insufficient funds in her checking account, the bank may draw on the savings account or credit card.

If the bank chooses to dishonor the check, the holder can attempt to resubmit the check at a later date. However, as we explained in Chapter 26, once the check has been dishonored, the holder must notify the endorsers of the check of the dishonor. If the holder does not give proper notice, the endorsers will not be responsible for the amount of the check.

Legal Principle: **If a bank does not honor a customer's stop-payment order, the bank is liable for any damages the customer suffers.**

STOP-PAYMENT ORDER

A customer can issue a stop-payment order, an order by a drawer to the drawee bank not to pay a check that has been drawn on the customer's account (UCC 4-403). A customer issues a stop-payment order when she has issued a check that has not yet been accepted and she wishes the check not to be accepted. For example, Angelina orders a pair of boots from her favorite store and writes a check to cover the cost in advance. Angelina is informed the next day that the boots have been discontinued and she will not be receiving the boots. Given that Angelina has already issued the check, she can issue a stop-payment order for her check because the check is no longer covering the purchase of her boots. If the bank pays a check in violation of a stop-payment order, the bank will incur liability for the damages suffered by the customer due to the stop payment [UCC 4-403(b)].

To be effective, the stop order must meet two requirements: (1) The customer must give the order in a reasonable time, and (2) the customer must describe the item with "reasonable certainty" [UCC 4-403(a)]. For example, the stop-payment order must be given so that the bank has enough time to instruct its tellers and other employees that they should not pay the check. Moreover, the UCC states that the stop-payment order must reach the bank by a certain cutoff time. Generally, the stop-payment order should list:

1. The date of the check
2. The name of the payee
3. The amount of the check
4. The number of the check
5. The checking account number

There are several issues regarding stop-payment orders. First, how is the stop-payment order given? A stop-payment order may be given orally or in writing. If it is an oral order, it is valid for just 14 days unless the order is later confirmed in writing. If the order is given through writing, the order is valid for six months and can be extended for another six months [UCC 4-403(b)]. Note that not all states allow stop-payment orders to be delivered orally. In the event that oral stop-payment orders are not allowed, they must be given in writing.

Second, if the customer issues a stop payment and does not have a valid legal ground for this order, the holder of the instrument will likely sue the customer. Not only will the customer be liable for the value of the check, but he will also probably be liable for any damages incurred by the payee of the check because of the stop-payment order. Even with a valid legal reason, if the holder of the check is a holder in due course, the drawer's defenses will not apply and he will still be liable for the check.

Third, payment cannot be stopped on certified checks, cashier's checks, or teller's checks [UCC 3-411(b)].

BUT WHAT IF . . .

WHAT IF THE FACTS OF THE CASE OPENER WERE DIFFERENT?

Assume that Patco Construction Company had written a check to a supplier and then found out that the supplier had supplied inferior-quality materials, so Patco decided to return the materials and cancel the check. Patco immediately issued a stop-payment order over the phone, and the bank teller said the oral order was sufficient, but 21 days later the supplier cashed the check and Patco's account was debited in the amount of the check. Does Patco have any recourse against the bank?

POSTDATED CHECKS

Under previous versions of Articles 3 and 4 of the UCC, a check could not be charged to a customer's account until the date of the check. Thus, some customers attempted to hold off payment on a check by postdating the check and giving it to the payee. However, because banks generally use an automated system to process checks, checks are now frequently paid without regard to the date. If a bank pays a check before its date and thus depletes a customer's account, the bank could be liable to the customer for damages. Thus, some banks include certain clauses in their customer agreements that state they may pay checks regardless of the date.

The UCC presents a middle ground that protects a bank from liability while permitting customers to postdate checks. Section 4-401(c) states that customers can postdate checks but they must give the bank notice of the postdated check. Therefore, the bank can assume that it can pay all checks on presentment unless the bank has received notice. Most banks charge a processing fee for notice of a postdated check.

STALE CHECKS

If a check is not presented to a bank within six months of its date, the check is considered a stale check. If a payee presents an uncertified stale check to a bank, the bank is not required to pay the amount of the check (UCC 4-404). However, if the bank pays the check in good faith, it may charge the drawer's account. Case 29-2 explores how long a bank must honor an oral stop-payment order.

CASE 29-2   SCOTT D. LEIBLING, P.C. v. MELLON PSFS (NJ) NATIONAL ASSOCIATION
SUPERIOR COURT OF NEW JERSEY, LAW DIVISION, SPECIAL CIVIL PART, CAMDEN COUNTY
710 A.2D 1067 (1998)

Scott D. Liebling, P.C., an attorney, had an attorney trust account ("Account") at Mellon Bank (NJ) National Association. Mellon uses a computerized system to process checks for payment. Liebling represented Fredy Ramos in a personal injury case that led to a settlement.

In May 1995, Liebling issued check number 1031 for over $8,000 to Ramos as a result of the settlement. However, a few days later, Liebling mistakenly issued check number 1043 in the same amount to Ramos. Mellon honored this first check on May 26, 1995. Around May 30, 1995, Liebling called Ramos and explained that check 1043 was issued in error and should be destroyed. Moreover, Liebling called the bank and ordered an oral stop payment on the second check. On December 21, 1996, Ramos cashed check number 1043.

Liebling filed a complaint against Mellon, arguing Mellon breached their duty of good faith, payment of a stale check, and breach of contract as a result of Mellon honoring the second check, check 1043.

JUDGE RAND:
Issue

Whether the defendant bank acted in good faith when it honored a check that was presented for payment nineteen months after it was issued and subsequent to the expiration of an oral stop payment order?

Discussion

It is important to consider the relevant New Jersey statute sections before discussing what actions constitute "good faith." Under N.J.S.A. 12A:4-403(b):

A stop payment order is effective for six months, but it lapses after 14 calendar days if the original

order was oral and was not confirmed in writing within that period. A stop payment order may be renewed for additional six-month periods by a writing given to the bank within a period during which the stop-payment order is effective.

In addition, N.J.S.A. 12A:4-404 states:

A bank is under no obligation to a customer having a checking account to pay a check . . . which is presented more than six months after its date, but it *may charge its customer's account for a payment made thereafter in good faith.*

Thus, the issue in the present case turns on whether Mellon acted in good faith when it honored Plaintiff's check. Good faith under N.J. Uniform Commercial Code has been defined in N.J.S.A. 12A:3-103(a)(4) as "honesty in fact and the observance of reasonable commercial standards of fair dealing." Since there is no New Jersey case law directly on point, it is necessary to consider alternate sources.

. . . Plaintiff's argument centers on the proposition that the bank's duty of good faith required it to inquire or consult with Plaintiff before honoring a stale check that had a previous oral stop payment order on it. This argument was upheld in the Pre-Code case of Goldberg v. Manufacturers Hanover Trust Co., 199 Misc. 167, 102 N.Y.S.2d 144 (NY Mun. Ct. 1951). In that case, the bank was held liable to the drawer for payment of a 27 month old check even though a stop payment order had expired. The Court predicated liability on the bank's payment of the check without inquiring into its own records which would have revealed the lapsed stop payment order and put the bank on notice. The [1962] N.J.

Study Comment to N.J.S.A. 12A:4-404 cites Redfield, The Law of Commercial Paper § 584, noting that the "practical way out of this dilemma is the simple expedient of making inquiry."

However, in the Uniform Commercial Code Treatise, "Hawkland § 4-404:01," Mr. Hawkland stated that the above case [is] not consistent with the Uniform Commercial Code. Specifically, "the duty [of inquiry] is inconsistent with the provisions of subsection 4-403(2) on the expiration of the 'effectiveness' of stop orders. Such a duty is hardly practical today."

Plaintiff counters that . . . this Court should give total credence to the explanatory comments drafted many years before the most recent code § 4-404 revisions. Pursuant to § 4-404, the bank may charge the customer's account for a check presented more than six months after it is dated as long as the bank acts in good faith. N.J.S.A. § 12A:3-103(a)(4) defines good faith. The definition "honesty in fact and the observance of reasonable commercial standards of fair dealings" is a revision from the 1961 version of the Code. It interjects a subjective analysis into the concept of fair dealings.

In 1990, Articles III and IV of the Code were substantially revised relating to, among other things, bank deposits and collections to become effective on June 1, 1995. The Court is satisfied as pointed out by the Defendant that those Amendments were enacted in order to address the effect of automated systems utilized by banks with the substantial increase in check usage after the original enactment of the Code. The Official Code Comment to the 1995 Amendments for § 12A:4-101, states as follows:

2. . . . An important goal of the 1990 revision of Article 4 is to promote the efficiency of the check collection process by making the provisions of Article 4 more compatible with the needs of an automated system and, by doing so, increase the speed and lower the cost of check collection for those who write and receive checks. [Code Comment to N.J.S.A. § 12A:4-101 (1995) (Supp. p. 157).]

The 1995 Amendments to § 12A:4-404 New Jersey Study Comment include different language than that on which the Plaintiff totally relied. Plaintiff's reliance upon the 1962 Study Comment is misplaced and outdated. The more modern and up to date approach requires a rejection of the 1962 Study Comment upon which Plaintiff's argument solely rests.

Thus, in determining whether defendant bank in the present action acted in good faith, the above cited material must be analyzed and applied. First, it appears clear that the Uniform Commercial Code acknowledges that computerized check processing systems are common and accepted banking procedures in the United States. Therefore, it can not be said that defendant bank acted in bad faith by using a computerized system when it honored Plaintiff's "stale" check. Furthermore, it appears that the test for good faith is a subjective test. Thus, based on all of the foregoing material, as long as defendant bank used an adequate computer system for processing checks (here there is no proof to the contrary), it appears to have acted in good faith even though it did not consult the Plaintiff before it honored the "stale" check that had an expired oral stop-payment order on it. [T]he obligation of a bank to stop payment on a check does not continue in perpetuity once the stop payment order expires.

The bank's conduct was fair and in accordance with reasonable commercial standards.

Judgment for defendant Mellon.

CRITICAL THINKING

What evidence does the judge rely on to come to the conclusion that the bank was not liable? Do you think the judge ignores any important evidence? Is there any missing information that would help you come to a conclusion regarding the bank's liability?

ETHICAL REASONING

What are the values associated with not holding the bank responsible to honor an expired stop-payment order? What values are in conflict? Do you think the values promoted by the decision are appropriate for the situation? Why or why not?

FORGERIES AND ALTERATIONS

In 1999, attempted check fraud in the United States rose to approximately $2.2 billion, while merchants and banks suffered actual losses approximating $679 million through check fraud. Thus, banks are clearly concerned about the acceptance of altered or forged checks.

  Legal Principle: **If a bank cashes a check with a forged or fraudulent signature, the bank is liable.**

Checks Bearing Forged Signatures.

Under the properly payable rule, the bank may pay a check only if it is authorized by the customer. Who is liable if a bank cashes a check signed by an unauthorized person? In other words, what happens when someone forges a drawer's signature on a check?

The UCC establishes that a forged signature has no legal effect as a signature of the drawer [3-403(a)]. Consequently, in most cases, if a bank pays a check when the drawer's signature has been forged, the bank will be liable for the amount of the check.

However, there are some exceptions to this rule. First, if the customer's negligence substantially contributed to a forged signature and the bank pays the check in good faith, the bank is not required to repay the customer [UCC 3-406(a)]. For example, if the customer is an employer who keeps a rubber stamp of his signature in an unlocked drawer, and an employee uses the signature stamp to create a check payable to the employee, the customer has substantially contributed to the forged signature and will likely not be able to recover the amount of the check.

Yet, if the bank that pays the check is also negligent, the customer may be able to recover part of the money. For example, suppose the employer-customer notified the bank of the employee's unauthorized use of the signature stamp but the bank paid the check anyway. The customer's liability for the amount of the check may be reduced by the bank's negligence in paying the check when it had been notified that the check was unauthorized.

Another exception to the forgery liability rule is related to the customer's duty to examine the bank statement. Banks make a customer's statement available to the customer approximately once a month. This statement lists or includes all the checks that have been charged against the customer's account over that past month. A customer must examine her bank statement reasonably promptly for any forgeries or unauthorized payments. If the customer discovers a forgery or unauthorized payment, she must notify the bank promptly [UCC 4-406(c)]. Under the UCC, if the customer does not notify the bank of an unauthorized signature within 30 days after the statement has been made available, she cannot hold the bank liable for the payment [4-406(d)].

The duty to examine the bank statement is particularly important in cases where there have been multiple forgeries by the same forger, or "same wrongdoer." If a customer examines a statement and does not notify the bank of the first forgery within 30 days, the customer will be liable for future forgeries on the customer's account by the same wrongdoer. For example, in one case, a customer was not aware of 17 forged checks totaling $13,000 paid on his account over a period of four months. In the fifth month, he discovered five checks forged on his account and reported these to the bank. The customer discovered his grandson had been the forger on these checks. The customer asked the bank to credit his account for the five unauthorized payments in the fifth month. When the bank refused, the customer sued. The court held that because the customer did not review his statement in the first month and all unauthorized signatures were from the same forger, the customer could not recover any of the subsequent forgeries.

Case 29-3 provides an example of alleged unauthorized electronic transfers in which the bank asserted that the consumer schemed against the bank to falsely allege unauthorized transfers.

CASE 29-3   MERISIER v. BANK OF AMERICA
U.S. COURT OF APPEALS FOR THE 11TH DISTRICT
2012 U.S. APP. LEXIS 15784 (2012)

Caroline Merisier was a customer of Bank of America. Merisier and a group of friends all opened their checking accounts with Bank of America within six months of one another. On March 5, 2010, Merisier was in Florida when her check card was rejected because of a fraud block. Merisier then completed a fraud affidavit, in which she flagged several transactions totaling $15,775.76 as unauthorized withdrawals from her account. Bank of America investigated Merisier's claim, and denied it after the investigation had verified the earliest of the withdrawals as legitimate. The bank reasoned that there were several security verifications following fraud blocks, existing security of Merisier's debit card and PIN, exclusively PIN-based transactions, and several structured deposits into the account before the alleged fraudulent withdrawals. Based on its investigation, the bank ultimately determined that Merisier was colluding with the various friends whom she had all sign up for checking accounts at the same time with the bank, and that together, they had drawn down her account and were scheming to defraud Bank of America.

On September 8, 2010, Merisier filed an instant action suit against Bank of America, asserting that the bank failed to conduct a reasonable investigation of her claim, and failed to follow the Electronic Fund Transfer Act's claim resolution procedures, consequently holding her unlawfully liable for unauthorized transactions. Merisier claimed that she was entitled to recover the damages of the unauthorized electronic funds withdrawn from her account. The District Court found that Bank of America was not liable for the amount withdrawn from Merisier's account. On appeal, Merisier contended that the District Court erred in finding that Bank of America did not violate any provision of EFTA.

JUDGE TJOFLAT: This is a case under the Electronic Fund Transfer Act ("EFTA"). A bank customer sued her bank to recover for unauthorized withdrawals from her checking account, made using her check card and personal identification number ("PIN"). EFTA requires a bank to investigate such disputed transactions, to notify the customer if it has verified the transactions as authorized, and to re-credit the account if the withdrawals were unauthorized; failure to do so renders the bank liable to the customer for up to treble damages. The bank investigated the withdrawals at issue in this case, found that they were the product of a scheme to defraud the bank, and denied liability for the withdrawals.

After a two-day bench trial, the District Court rejected the customer's EFTA claims and entered judgment for the bank. Specifically, the District Court found that the transactions were authorized because they were part of a scheme to defraud the bank. The customer appealed. Although the briefs are inartfully drawn, she appears to challenge the District Court's finding as clearly erroneous. . . . On appeal, Merisier contends that the District Court erred in finding that Bank of America did not violate any provision of EFTA. In this respect, Merisier argues that the District Court applied the wrong burden of proof to her at trial, contending that, under EFTA, Bank of America bore the burden to demonstrate the transfers were authorized. Essentially, she maintains that the District Court's finding that the subject transactions were authorized was clearly erroneous. She contends the District Court mistakenly considered the following factors because they were mischaracterized by the trial judge or irrelevant: (a) evidence of a scheme to defraud; (b) ostensible evasion of cash-deposit reporting requirements; and (c) the source of the deposits to Merisier's account.

EFTA requires banks to follow one of two paths in response to such an alleged error on an account: (1) to investigate and correct the error if an unauthorized transfer has occurred, or (2) to investigate and inform the customer that no error occurred if the transfer was authorized by the customer. The bank followed the steps of path (2) after it determined that Merisier had in fact authorized the transactions at issue. Merisier thinks the bank ought to have followed path (1) because she insists to this day that the disputed transactions were unauthorized. She thinks the District Court improperly forced her to prove the bank ought to have followed path (1) and found for the bank when she did not. . . .

On appeal, Merisier has advanced no reason to disturb the District Court's findings. That the transactions were authorized is a factual determination that we will reverse only for clear error. "A finding is clearly erroneous 'when although there is evidence to support it, the reviewing court on the entire evidence is left with the definite and firm conviction that a mistake has been committed.'" Merisier has failed to make such a showing; her arguments focus on her perception that the District Court erroneously required her to prove that the withdrawals were unauthorized. It is thus undisputed that substantial evidence supports the District Court's finding that the transactions were authorized. See id. We are thus left with no "definite and firm conviction that a mistake has been committed." The District Court therefore did not err in finding that the transactions were authorized and, consequently, that Bank of America had not violated EFTA. . . . After thorough review, we find no error and therefore affirm.

Judgment of the District Court is AFFIRMED.

[continued]

CRITICAL THINKING

The court ruled that on the basis of the evidence provided by Bank of America, the plaintiff's transactions were in fact authorized. Can you think of anything problematic about the evidence provided by Bank of America to conclude that Merisier's transactions were authorized? What evidence could Merisier have provided the court that may have changed the court's ruling in the bank's favor?

ETHICAL DECISION MAKING

Take a look at the WPH framework and attempt to think of an ethical justification for this ruling. What value do you think is at play in regard to the purpose of the Electronic Fund Transfer Act?

Again, if the bank was negligent in paying the forged checks, the customer's liability for the checks may be diminished through comparative negligence [UCC 4-406(e)]. Regardless of the 30-day requirement for multiple forgeries or the care used in cashing a check, a customer must report a forgery within one year from the date the statement is available to the customer or he will lose the right to recover this money [UCC 4-406(f)].

Finally, because a drawer is generally not liable for a forged check, the bank must credit a drawer's account for a paid forged check. The bank would likely then try to recover the money from the forger; a forged signature is effective as the signature of the forger [UCC 3-403(a)]. In other words, if Christina Simpson forges Ricky McIntyre's signature on his check, forging "Ricky McIntyre" functions to make Christina liable for the amount of the check.

Checks Bearing Forged Endorsements.   If a bank pays a check that has been fraudulently endorsed, who is responsible? In the same way that a drawer is not responsible for a check that bears the drawer's forged signature, the drawer is similarly not responsible for a check that has been fraudulently endorsed. Generally, when an endorsement has been forged, the first party to accept the forged instrument is ultimately liable for the loss because a forged endorsement does not legally transfer title [UCC 4-207(a)(2)]. However, the drawer again has a duty to examine her statement for fraudulent endorsements and then notify the bank. As such, the drawer must report all forged endorsements within a three-year period after the customer was returned the forged items or given his or her statement containing the forged items. If the customer does not report the forgery within three years, the bank is no longer liable for the customer's loss (UCC 4-111).

Altered Checks.   Remember, under the properly payable rule, a bank is to pay only those checks that are authorized. When a party makes an unauthorized change or alteration to a check, the check becomes unauthorized. The UCC defines alteration as a change (without consent) that modifies the obligation of a party to the instrument. Generally, if a bank pays a check that has been altered, the bank will be liable for the alteration.

For example, suppose a drawer writes a check for $5. The payee changes the amount paid to $55 and presents the check for payment. The bank pays $55 to the payee. The drawer discovers the alteration on his statement and reports it to the bank. The bank will then credit the drawer's account with $50; the drawer remains liable for the original amount of the check. The bank is liable for the $50 (UCC 4-111).

Again, a customer's substantial contribution to the alteration will limit the customer's ability to require that the bank credit his or her account. In other words, if the customer leaves large blank spaces open on the check so that another party may easily alter the check, the customer will likely be liable for the altered amount of the check. Similarly, suppose you, as a business manager, send an employee to purchase some supplies for a company picnic. You give the employee a check payable to the store, but you do not fill in

VSoft Corporation provides technological solutions to financial institutions. VSoft has released software that captures images at ATM locations. These images are used for processing and image exchange. The significance of this software is that it makes ATM envelopes unnecessary. Financial institutions with the VSoft technology capture a check image and related data at the ATM, and then integrate that information with validation from back-office operations. Banks can now engage in virtual sorting and deposit review. The software provides customers with a receipt that includes an image of the deposited check. This software promises service and convenience to customers. It also reduces the financial institution's operating costs and reduces opportunities for fraud.

Source: "VSoft Announces the New 5.20 Release of Its Centrum Gateway TM-ATM Software," *Business Wire,* September 17, 2008.

---

the dollar amount of the check. The employee then writes in an amount that is $20 more than the total cost of the goods and asks for $20 in cash back. You do not become aware of the employee's action until you receive your bank statement. Under the UCC, any drawer who leaves the dollar amount blank may not later protest paying whatever amount has been written on the check [4-401(d)(2)].

As in the case of forged signatures, the customer's duty to examine his bank statement also applies to looking for altered checks. Thus, if the customer does not discover the altered check or does not report the altered check within a reasonable time, the bank's liability for the altered check is reduced. Similarly, if both the customer and the bank are negligent in contributing to and paying an altered check, both parties will be responsible for a portion of the check.

Moreover, if a bank proves that losses from later altered checks occurred due to the customer's failure to identify and report the illegally altered checks, the bank will have a reduced liability due to the customer's contributory negligence (UCC 4-406). The bank may assert the defense of contributory negligence only if the bank exercised ordinary care (adherence to standard practices in the industry) when it cashed the altered check.

Electronic Fund Transfers

The application of technology to the banking system has made the banking process more efficient and less reliant on paperwork. When money is transferred by an electronic terminal, telephone, or computer, this transfer is called an **electronic fund transfer (EFT).** Consumer fund transfers are governed by the Electronic Fund Transfer Act of 1978, while commercial electronic fund transfers are governed by Article 4(A) of the UCC. By 1996, all 50 states had adopted Article 4(A).

L05

What are the different types of electronic fund transfers?

TYPES OF EFT SYSTEMS

The most common types of electronic fund systems are automated teller machines, point-of-sale systems, direct deposits and withdrawals, pay-by-telephone systems, and online systems. (See Exhibit 29-8.)

Automated Teller Machines.   **Automated teller machines (ATMs),** machines connected to a bank's computer, are located in convenient places so that customers may conduct banking transactions without actually going into a bank. Customers may withdraw and deposit money, as well as check the balance of their savings and checking accounts. Customers use an ATM bank card and a personal identification number to access their accounts through the ATM.

Point-of-Sale Systems.   A **point-of-sale system** allows a consumer to directly transfer funds from a banking account to a merchant. For example, Jay buys a CD from Best Buy

Exhibit 29-8

Types of Electronic Fund
Transfer Systems

Automated teller machines (ATMs)	Convenient electronic teller machines allow customers to conduct banking transactions without going to a bank.
Point of sale	Using a debit card, customers can transfer funds directly out of their accounts to the merchant's account.
Pay by telephone	Customers can make payments or transfer funds between accounts over the phone.
Online banking	Customers can make payments or transfer funds between accounts online.
Direct deposits and withdrawals	Customers can preauthorize deposits and withdrawals performed on their accounts electronically.

and pays for the CD with his debit card. The Best Buy employee swipes Jay's debit card to determine whether there are enough funds in Jay's account to pay for the CD. Jay signs a receipt like a credit card receipt, and the amount of the sale is charged to Jay's bank account.

Direct Deposits and Withdrawals.   A direct deposit or withdrawal is a preauthorized action performed on a customer's account through an electronic terminal. For example, an employee may now choose to have her paycheck directly deposited into her checking account instead of receiving a check from the employer. A customer can similarly authorize a direct withdrawal. For instance, a customer might have his phone bill directly withdrawn from his bank account each month.

To see the issues involved with direct-deposit employee payment, please see the **Connecting to the Core** activity on the text website at www.mhhe.com/kubasek3e.

Pay-by-Telephone Systems.   Some merchants allow customers to use the telephone to make payments or transfer funds. For example, a customer may transfer money from a savings account to a checking account over the phone. Moreover, the IRS permits taxpayers to file and pay over the telephone.

Online Payments and Banking.   Various banks and credit card companies allow customers to engage in banking transactions online. Customers may access their account statements and transfer funds online. Similarly, credit card companies allow customers to make monthly payments. Companies are moving toward offering more and more online services.

CONSUMER FUND TRANSFERS

Consumer fund transactions are governed by the *Electronic Fund Transfer Act of 1978 (EFTA)*. This act sets out the rights and liabilities of the parties involved in electronic fund transfers. Regulation E of the act allows the Federal Reserve Board to issue rules and regulations to enforce EFTA. The following transactions are considered consumer fund transactions: transactions in which a retail customer pays for an item with a debit card that allows the customer's bank account to be instantly charged, ATM transactions, and direct deposits of paychecks.

Customer and Bank Rights and Responsibilities.   EFTA requires that merchants inform customers of their rights regarding EFTs. First, if a customer's ATM card is lost or stolen, the customer must notify the bank within two days. The customer is then liable for only the first $50 stolen. If the customer does not notify the bank, the customer will then be held liable for up to $500 that is stolen. Second, the bank has a duty to provide a monthly statement that includes electronic fund transfers, and the customer has a duty to examine this bank statement for any unauthorized electronic fund transfers or errors.

Third, the customer has a duty to notify the bank of any errors in the electronic transactions within 60 days of receiving the statement. Fourth, a bank is required to provide customers with receipts for electronic transactions. Fifth, the bank must notify the customer that preauthorized payments may be stopped; however, the customer must stop the payment by notifying the bank at any time up to three days before the preauthorized payment is scheduled. While a customer may stop a preauthorized payment, a customer cannot order a stop payment on an EFT because such transfers occur instantaneously.

Unauthorized Transfers. Under EFTA, an unauthorized electronic transfer is a federal felony punishable through criminal sanctions, such as a $10,000 fine or 10-year prison sentence. An electronic transfer is unauthorized if (1) it is initiated by a person who has no authority to transfer, (2) the customer receives no benefit from the transfer, and (3) the customer did not give his personal identification number to the unauthorized party.

When banks violate EFTA, consumers may recover actual and punitive damages, where the punitive damages total between $100 and $1,000. If the consumers are part of a class action suit, the punitive damages are capped at $500,000 or 1 percent of the institution's net worth.

As suggested in the Case Opener, the relationship between a bank and its customers is quite complicated. When a customer opens an account at a bank, he or she creates a contractual relationship with the bank. Within this relationship, both the customer and the bank have certain rights and duties. This relationship is governed by Article 4 of the UCC. For example, the customer has the right to order a stop payment on a check for any or no reason. The corresponding duty of the bank is to follow this order.

COMMERCIAL FUND TRANSFERS

Because EFTA did not cover all situations in which funds may be electronically transferred, Article 4(A) of the UCC was issued to address commercial fund transfers. An important type of commercial fund transfer is a wire transfer. Funds are "wired" between two commercial parties. There are two major payment systems that coordinate wire payments: the Federal Reserve wire transfer network (Fedwire) and the New York Clearing House Interbank Payments Systems (CHIPS). These two systems account for the transfer of more than $1 trillion daily. This sum is substantially more than is transferred by any other means.

E-Money and Online Banking

With the rapid advancements in technology, the banking system is also finding itself changing rapidly. Electronic payments, or e-payments, are becoming increasingly prevalent in daily life. Increasingly, bank transactions are being conducted electronically, marking a shift away from physical currency. In fact, it is possible for electronic forms of money to completely replace physical currency such as paper and coin money. Digital cash, money stored electronically on microchips, magnetic strips, or other computer media, would allow for the elimination of physical currency.

Helping to lead the digital banking revolution are the various forms of e-money (electronic money). The most common example of e-money is stored-value cards. Stored-value cards are typically plastic cards that contain a magnetic strip. The magnetic strip, similar to the ones on credit cards and ATM cards, contains data regarding the value of the card. For example, suppose a new laundry facility opened up near your apartment. However, instead of your using quarters, the facility requires that you get a card and use a machine to put a balance on the card. Then, when you are ready to do your laundry, you insert the card into the washer and the cost of a load of laundry is deducted automatically from the card. Because the information regarding the amount on the card is stored in the magnetic strip on the card, the card is referred to as a *stored-value card.*

Another, newer, type of e-money is the smart card. Smart cards are the same size as regular check and ATM cards and look the same from the front. However, instead of having a magnetic strip, smart cards contain microchips for storing data. The advantage of the microchip over the magnetic strip is that the microchip can hold a far greater amount of data than a magnetic strip. However, because this is still a new technology, not all businesses are equipped to read smart cards yet. As the technology expands, expect to see a large influx in the use of smart cards.

Related to the expansion of technology in banking is the increase in use of online banking. With online banking, banks allow customers electronic access to their accounts so that they can check their accounts, transfer money, order payments, pay bills, check their investments, and, through some banks, even trade stock. While services vary from bank to bank, more banks are offering at least some form of online banking to their customers.

ONLINE BANKING SERVICES

There are three services most banks with online banking offer. These three services are (1) bill consolidation and payment, (2) transfer of funds from one account to another, and (3) loan applications (an appearance at the bank to sign the loan is typically required to finalize the loan process). By offering these three services, banks help cut down on their own costs as well as allow customers greater control over their funds.

Despite the number of banking services offered online, not all banking services can be conducted over the Internet. For example, depositing and withdrawing funds are two services that cannot be conducted from a computer with an Internet connection. However, the smart-card technology might allow for withdrawals and deposits from home computers hooked up to the Internet. The microchips in the smart cards could be read by devices attached to a home computer, allowing for withdrawals or deposits; but this technology has not yet been developed and marketed to consumers.

REGULATORY COMPLIANCE

In the main, banks are in favor of the increased use of online banking. Part of the reason banks like online banking is that it helps reduce the bank's operating cost and thus increase its profits. One way online banking reduces cost is through paperless billing. By not having to send paper statements to their customers, banks save on paper, ink, and envelopes, as well as postage. The bank posts all the information to the user's account online, which does not cost the bank much at all.

Another reason banks are in favor of online banking is that it decreases what is known as "float" time. *Float time* is the period between the time a check is written and the time it is presented for final payment, during which a customer can still use his or her funds. As the check does not have to transfer between banks, accounts can be credited or debited more quickly.

However, as with other areas of the Internet, it is not clear which laws apply to online banking. Part of the problem is related to the legal definition of *bank*. Banks are required by law to have a geographically defined market area, as well as to report to the proper authorities regarding their deposits and loans. These requirements are designed to ensure that all Americans have access to banks and that banks are not discriminating by choosing only certain locations for operation. The requirements are established primarily in two pieces of legislation: the Home Mortgage Disclosure Act, 12 U.S.C. Sections 2801–2810, and the Community Reinvestment Act (CRA) of 1977, 12 U.S.C. Sections 2901–2908. The CRA requires that a bank's market area surround the bank and be divided on the basis of normal divisions, such as standard metropolitan areas or county lines.

The requirement of a defined market area poses a problem for cyberbanks. How exactly would a cyberbank establish a geographic market region? Consequently, banks with online services are in a bit of a gray area when it comes to legal compliance. Not only is it hard for such banks to comply with the Home Mortgage Disclosure Act and the CRA, but it is not yet clear if these banks need to comply with these two laws.

PRIVACY PROTECTION

Are e-money institutions the same as traditional financial institutions? Do the same laws apply? These two questions hold the key to the question: How secure are e-payments and e-money? The answer is, "We do not know."

E-Money Payment Information.   Which laws apply to e-money is still mostly untested legal ground. That is, there is little clarity regarding which laws do apply to e-money. The Federal Reserve has explicitly stated that Regulation E, which regulates traditional electronic fund transfers, does not apply to e-money transactions. Nonetheless, laws regarding computer files, not directly related to banking, might apply to e-money, such as laws against unauthorized access of electronic files or communication. There are several such laws regarding electronic files and communication, and it is not clear if they apply to e-money.

E-Money Issuer's Financial Records.   In 1978 Congress passed the *Right to Financial Privacy Act* [12 U.S.C. Section 3401 et seq.]. Under this act, financial institutions, such as banks, may not give a federal agency information regarding a person's finances without either that person's explicit consent or a warrant. The Right to Financial Privacy Act may apply to digital cash providers if the provider is considered a legal bank or credit provider that supplies customers with a card considered to be similar to a credit or debit card. However, given the lack of a physical location for the digital cash provider, it is also possible that the Right to Financial Privacy Act does not apply, in which case digital cash providers may release your financial information freely to any federal agency.

Consumer Financial Data.   In an effort to further protect people's financial privacy, Congress passed the *Financial Services Modernization Act,* also known as the *Gramm-Leach-Bliley Act* (12 U.S.C. Sections 24a, 248b, 1820a, 1828b). The act's purpose is to control how financial institutions handle customer information, ultimately providing greater privacy protections to financial institution customers. Financial institutions are prohibited from disclosing personal information about their clients to third parties unless certain requirements set forth in the act are met. In addition, financial institutions are legally required to present customers with the institution's privacy policies and practices.

CASE OPENER WRAP-UP

Fraudulent Electronic Fund Transfers

On August 4, 2011, the district court granted Ocean Bank's motion for summary judgment on all six counts of Patco's complaint and denied Patco's motion for summary judgment on Count I of liability under the UCC. On September 6, 2011, Patco appealed.

On appeal, the court found that the bank failed to introduce additional security measures, despite the fact that these additional security measures are common in the industry and are easy to implement. Further, the court ruled that this failure to implement additional security measures was especially unreasonable given that the bank was knowledgeable about ongoing fraud with electronic fund transfers. The court advised that "when Ocean Bank had warning that such fraud was likely occurring with a transaction, the bank should have monitored that transaction, and provided notice to its customers." In conclusion, the appellate court rendered Ocean Bank's security procedures commercially unreasonable under the standards of Article 4(A) of the UCC, and it reversed the district court's grant of summary judgment in favor of the bank.

However, the appellate court reversed only part of the district court's decision. In addition to the reversal of the summary judgment in favor of the bank, the appellate court also affirmed the district court's denial of Patco's motion for summary judgment. The court argued that there remained several disputed issues of fact that may be material to determining whether Patco satisfied its own obligations under the UCC. Thus, the court left these questions open for remand, especially for the purposes of mitigation of damages.

KEY TERMS

alteration 648	digital cash 651	intermediary bank 636	stale check 644
automated teller machines (ATMs) 649	direct deposit 650	money orders 632	stop-payment order 642
	draft 630	overdraft 642	stored-value cards 651
cashier's check 631	drawee 630	payee 630	teller's check 632
certified check 634	drawer 630	payor bank 636	traveler's check 632
check 630	electronic fund transfer (EFT) 649	point-of-sale system 649	
collecting bank 636		smart card 652	
depository bank 636	e-money 651		

SUMMARY OF KEY TOPICS

Checks

Draft: An instrument that is an order.

Drawer: The party that gives the order.

Drawee: The party that must obey the order.

Payee: The party that receives the benefit of the order.

Check: A special draft that orders the drawee, a bank, to pay a fixed amount of money on demand.

Cashier's check: A check for which both the drawer and the drawee of a check are the same bank.

Teller's check: A check that is drawn by one bank and usually drawn on another bank.

Traveler's check: An instrument that is payable on demand, is drawn on or through a bank, is designated by the phrase *traveler's check,* and requires a countersignature by a person whose signature appears on the instrument.

Money order: An instrument stating that a certain amount of money is to be paid to a particular person.

Certified check: A check that is accepted at the bank at which it is drawn.

Depositary bank: The first bank that receives a check for payment.

Payor bank: The bank on which a check is drawn.

Collecting bank: Any kind of bank (besides the payor bank) that handles a check during the collection process.

Intermediary bank: Any bank (besides the payor bank and depositary bank) to which the check is transferred.

Accepting Deposits

Properly payable rule: A bank may pay an instrument only when it is authorized by the drawer and does not violate the agreement between the bank and the customer.

Wrongful dishonor: A bank refuses to pay a properly payable check; the bank incurs liability.

Overdraft: If there are insufficient funds in the customer's account, the bank may (1) dishonor the check or (2) create an overdraft by paying the check and charging the account the amount short.

Stop-payment order: A drawer orders the drawee bank to not pay a check that has been drawn on the customer's account.

Postdated check: A customer can postdate a check but must give the bank notice of the postdated check.

Stale check: A check is not presented to a bank within six months of its date.

Forgeries and alterations:

1. *Check bearing a forged signature:* Generally, the drawer is not liable for a forged check unless the drawer substantially contributed to the forgery.

2. *Check bearing a forged endorsement:* Neither the drawer nor the drawer's bank is liable for a forged endorsement.

3. *Altered check:* If an unauthorized change modifies the obligation of a party to the instrument, the drawer is generally not liable for the altered amount unless he or she negligently contributed to the alteration.

When a Bank May Charge a Customer's Account

Money is transferred by an electronic terminal, telephone, or computer.

Types of EFT systems:

ATMs (automated teller machines): Machines connected to a bank's computer, located in convenient places, that allow customers to conduct banking transactions without actually going into a bank.

Point-of-sale system: System that allows a consumer to directly transfer funds from a bank account to a merchant.

Direct deposits and withdrawals: Preauthorized actions performed on a customer's account through an electronic terminal.

Pay-by-telephone system: System whereby merchants allow customers to use the telephone to make payments or transfer funds.

Online banking: System in which banks grant customers electronic access to account data to perform banking tasks, such as transferring funds between accounts, online.

Electronic Fund Transfers

E-Money and Online Banking

Digital cash: Money stored electronically on microchips, magnetic strips, or other computer media.

Stored-value cards: Plastic cards that have magnetic strips, similar to those on credit cards or ATM cards, containing data regarding the value of the card.

Smart cards: Cards that are the same size as regular check and ATM cards but that contain microchips, instead of a magnetic strip, for storing larger amounts of data.

POINT / COUNTERPOINT

Should a Company Be Allowed to Require that Employees Receive Payment through Direct Deposit?

YES	NO
A company should be allowed to require that employees receive payment through direct deposit because direct-deposit payment is the most efficient form of payment for both employers and employees.	A company should not be allowed to require that its employees receive payment through direct deposit. While direct deposit is a good option for employers to provide to employees, the choice of payment form should be left to the employees.

A company should be allowed to require that employees receive payment through direct deposit because direct-deposit payment is the most efficient form of payment for both employers and employees.

Direct deposit allows employers and employees security they would not have with mailed paychecks. Companies can keep track of employee payments more accurately when employees are paid through one payment method.

Through direct deposit, employers are assured that *all employees* are paid at the same time, on the same day. Neither employees nor employers need to be concerned with lost, stolen, delayed, or damaged paychecks.

Many people have already chosen the convenience of online banking for their other banking needs; adding direct deposit only simplifies their lives. In fact, studies show that the average worker spends between 8.5 and 24 hours each year cashing and depositing payroll checks.*

Direct deposit allows for a separate payroll account and more exact bookkeeping. The losses normally associated with stolen and doubled paychecks can be reinvested in the company, eventually allowing for potential salary/ wage increases for all. Furthermore, a company saves a lot of money on paper costs alone by switching to direct deposit.

Many people willingly choose to directly deposit their paychecks. A company establishing a requirement of direct-deposit payment would only streamline and simplify the process for everyone involved.

A company should not be allowed to require that its employees receive payment through direct deposit. While direct deposit is a good option for employers to provide to employees, the choice of payment form should be left to the employees.

First, very few guidelines have been established regarding direct-deposit procedures. Employees would not necessarily be provided an in-depth statement discussing the details of each pay period. With direct deposit, employees have more difficulty ensuring that pay statements are accurate.

Wage-based employees, for example, need to know exactly what they are paid per hour, for how many hours, so that the employees know whether they need to be paid overtime wages. Some direct-deposit statements list only the amount of money transferred to the employee's account.

Some employees simply prefer to literally hold and personally deposit a physical check. They also have a physical copy of their pay stub for paper records. The absence of a physical receipt creates "holes" in an individual's paper records. These holes can create problems when an individual gathers documents in preparation for tax season.

Direct deposit can also cause problems with an individual's banking practices. When money is automatically (though sometimes not regularly) deposited, the individual can have difficulty keeping track of deductions and bank account balances.

While companies can and should present to employees a list of the advantages of direct deposit, the ultimate decision should be left to the employees, because the employees are most heavily affected if their paychecks are not deposited properly.

*www.msmoney.com.

QUESTIONS & PROBLEMS

1. Who are the three parties involved in the transfer of money through a check?

2. What types of banks are involved in the check collection process? How are these banks different?

3. Explain the reason for the following policy: "A customer has a duty to examine his or her bank statement."

4. Evaluate the following statement: "If a signature on a check is forged, the customer will never be responsible for the amount on the check."

5. Dustin Barwick is a resident of Arkansas who in 2009 married Lucy Sheets. Sheets then proceeded to purchase insurance from GEICO Co. GEICO is an insurance agency that issues automobile insurance to individuals along with the option of medical coverage. In applying for this insurance, Sheets waived the section including medical coverage in case of an accident. In early 2010, Barwick was hit by another car and then proceeded to submit a claim to GEICO for reimbursement in the amount of $6,284. Barwick was denied reimbursement with the reasoning that his spouse, electronically, denied medical coverage. Her signature, according to GEICO, was binding and therefore Barwick could not receive the benefit. Is an electronic signature enough to validate a document? If so, under what act or acts does this fall? [*Barwick v. GEICO*, 10-1076 (Ark. S. Ct. 2011).]

6. Mary Christelle, the mother of the president of Essential Technologies of Illinois (ETI), purchased a $50,000 cashier's check from Charter One Bank payable to ETI. Subsequently, ETI deposited the check in its MidAmerica Bank account. Four days later, Mary Christelle asked Charter One to stop payment on the check. Charter One issued a stop-payment order on the cashier's check, and it then refused to honor the check when MidAmerica presented it for payment. Charter One returned it to MidAmerica stamped with "stop payment." MidAmerica then removed $50,000 from ETI's account to recover the money from the stop-payment check. After removing the $50,000, ETI's account was closed due to a negative balance after additional deposited checks were returned for insufficient funds. In 2006, MidAmerica filed suit against Charter One to recover the value of the check. MidAmerica alleged that Charter One wrongfully stopped payment on the cashier's check. A worker for Charter One testified that Charter One permits stop-payment orders on a cashier's check only if the check is lost, destroyed, or stolen and that bank policy permits it to seek indemnification from the person who placed the stop-payment order. The bank also requires an affidavit to support the stop-payment order, but Charter One did not have an affidavit in this case. Do you think the court ruled in favor of Charter One or MidAmerica in regard to the stop payment and dishonoring of the cashier's check? Would any additional information help you reach your conclusion? [*MidAmerica Bank v. Charter One Bank*, 232 Ill. 2d 560, 905 N.E.2d 839 (2009).]

7. Casey Anthony, a Florida resident, has recently gained "fame" in the murder trial of her daughter, Kaylee. Among the charges brought against Anthony in court were check fraud and murder. The check fraud charge came about after an investigation revealed that Anthony had stolen the checkbook of her friend, Amy Huizenga, and written checks amounting to $650. She wrote the checks to pay her bills, without Huizenga's knowledge. Anthony received no additional jail time and was ordered to serve one year probation. What topics of this chapter can we apply to this case? [*Anthony v. State of Florida*, 11-2357 (Fla. Dist. Ct. App. 2012).].

8. Nicholas Fredich placed an advertisement in a newspaper seeking applications for the job of bookkeeper. He then stole the résumé and identity of one of the respondents and used the person's information to apply for a bookkeeping position at Clean World Engineering, Ltd. After two weeks of working at Clean World, he claimed he had an emergency and he took several days off. Then it was discovered that many checks were missing and Fredich had forged the checks. Fredich had complete access to the checks during his employment at Clean World. Some of these forged checks were deposited into a bank and paid by MidAmerica Bank. MidAmerica did not contest the fact that it paid the checks bearing the forged signatures, but it

argued that Clean World did not exercise ordinary care. Given these facts, who should bear the loss, MidAmerica or Clean World? [*Clean World Engineering, Ltd. v. MidAmerica Federal Savings Bank,* 341 Ill. App. 3d 992, 793 N.E.2d 110 (2003).]

9. In January 2008, $243,000 was transferred from William Ryder's account at Universal City Studios Credit Union to a bank in Hong Kong. The credit union said that someone who identified himself as Ryder called to change a telephone number supposedly associated with the account. The caller identified Ryder's date of birth, Social Security number, and mother's maiden name, as well as certain account activity. Five days later a wire transfer of funds from Ryder's line of credit to the Hong Kong account was received. After verification of the signature on the Fax, the credit union called the new telephone number to verify the request from a person who said he was Ryder. The transfer was made. The credit union submitted a claim to its insurance company for the amount of the transfer. The insurance company refused to pay because the security agreement with the credit union required that wire transfers be made through a secure telephone number that had been in place for at least 30 days prior to the transfer request. Would a court decision allowing the credit union to collect advance any values important to market exchange? [*Universal City Studios Credit Union v. CUMIS Insurance Society, Inc.,* B226868 (Cal. App. 2d 2012).]

10. On November 30, 2000, Walmart issued a check made payable to Alcon Laboratories, Inc., in the amount of $563,288.95, written on a Wachovia Bank checking account. Walmart mailed the check, but Alcon never received it. On December 7, 2000, an individual named Pit Foo Wong deposited the check in his account at Asia Bank. The payee on the check had been altered from "Alcon Laboratories, Inc." to "Pit Foo Wong." In accordance with Federal Reserve procedures, Asia Bank presented the check to the Federal Reserve Bank (FRB) of New York, which then presented the check to the FRB in Richmond. On December 8, 2000, the FRB presented the check to Wachovia, and Wachovia issued payment. Wachovia, in accordance with its internal policy, did not manually review the copy of the check presented by the FRB. However, it did review the check information through an electronic tracking system. No fraud was detected at this time. Although the employees at Asia Bank allowed Wong to deposit the check, their suspicions were aroused by his deposit of over $500,000 and a hold was placed on the funds. Asia Bank twice contacted Walmart, which informed Asia Bank that the check was "good." After Alcon determined that it had not received the check, Alcon called Walmart. Walmart indicated that the check had been paid and that its policy was to wait 30 days before tracing missing checks. When Walmart discovered that the Alcon check had been altered, it notified Wachovia, which sought reimbursement from Asia Bank. By this time the hold had expired and Wong wired the money out of his account. Asia Bank refused to reimburse Wachovia, and Wachovia brought suit against the FRB for breach of presentment and transfer warranties under the UCC and federal regulations. The FRB filed a third-party complaint against Walmart, alleging that Walmart's failure to exercise ordinary care substantially contributed to the alteration of the check. The district court granted summary judgment in favor of both Wachovia and Walmart. The parties appealed. How do you think the court ruled on appeal? Should Walmart have detected the alteration earlier? [*Wachovia Bank, N.A. v. FRB,* 338 F.3d 318 (2003).]

Looking for more review materials?

The Online Learning Center at **www.mhhe.com/kubasek3e** contains this chapter's "Assignment on the Internet" and also a list of URLs for more information, entitled "On the Internet." Find both of them in the Student Center portion of the OLC, along with quizzes and other helpful materials.

APPENDIX B

UNIFORM COMMERCIAL CODE

Article 2—Sales

PART 1: SHORT TITLE, GENERAL CONSTRUCTION AND SUBJECT MATTER

§ 2–101. Short Title. This Article shall be known and may be cited as Uniform Commercial Code—Sales.

§ 2–102. Scope; Certain Security and Other Transactions Excluded from This Article. Unless the context otherwise requires, this Article applies to transactions in goods; it does not apply to any transaction which although in the form of an unconditional contract to sell or present sale is intended to operate only as a security transaction nor does this Article impair or repeal any statute regulating sales to consumers, farmers or other specified classes of buyers.

§ 2–103. Definitions and Index of Definitions.

(1) In this Article unless the context otherwise requires
    (a) "Buyer" means a person who buys or contracts to buy goods.
    (b) "Good faith" in the case of a merchant means honesty in fact and the observance of reasonable commercial standards of fair dealing in the trade.
    (c) "Receipt" of goods means taking physical possession of them.
    (d) "Seller" means a person who sells or contracts to sell goods.
(2) Other definitions applying to this Article or to specified Parts thereof, and the sections in which they appear are:

"Acceptance"	Section 2–606.
"Banker's credit"	Section 2–325.
"Between merchants"	Section 2–104.
"Cancellation"	Section 2–106(4).
"Commercial unit"	Section 2–105.
"Confirmed credit"	Section 2–325.
"Conforming to contract"	Section 2–106.
"Contract for sale"	Section 2–106.
"Cover"	Section 2–712.
"Entrusting"	Section 2–403.
"Financing agency"	Section 2–104.
"Future goods"	Section 2–105.
"Goods"	Section 2–105.
"Identification"	Section 2–501.
"Installment contract"	Section 2–612.
"Letter of credit"	Section 2–325.
"Lot"	Section 2–105.

"Merchant"	Section 2–104.
"Overseas"	Section 2–323.
"Person in position of seller"	Section 2–707.
"Present sale"	Section 2–106.
"Sale"	Section 2–106.
"Sale on approval"	Section 2–326.
"Sale or return"	Section 2–326.
"Termination"	Section 2–106.

(3) The following definitions in other Articles apply to this Article:

"Check"	Section 3–104.
"Consignee"	Section 7–102.
"Consignor"	Section 7–102.
"Consumer goods"	Section 9–109.
"Dishonor"	Section 3–502.
"Draft"	Section 3–104.

(4) In addition Article 1 contains general definitions and principles of construction and interpretation applicable throughout this Article.

As amended in 1994.
See Appendix XI for material relating to changes made in text in 1994.

§ 2–104. Definitions: "Merchant"; "Between Merchants"; "Financing Agency".

(1) "Merchant" means a person who deals in goods of the kind or otherwise by his occupation holds himself out as having knowledge or skill peculiar to the practices or goods involved in the transaction or to whom such knowledge or skill may be attributed by his employment of an agent or broker or other intermediary who by his occupation holds himself out as having such knowledge or skill.

(2) "Financing agency" means a bank, finance company or other person who in the ordinary course of business makes advances against goods or documents of title or who by arrangement with either the seller or the buyer intervenes in ordinary course to make or collect payment due or claimed under the contract for sale, as by purchasing or paying the seller's draft or making advances against it or by merely taking it for collection whether or not documents of title accompany the draft. "Financing agency" includes also a bank or other person who similarly intervenes between persons who are in the position of seller and buyer in respect to the goods (Section 2–707).

(3) "Between merchants" means in any transaction with respect to which both parties are chargeable with the knowledge or skill of merchants.

§ 2–105. Definitions: "Transferability"; "Goods"; "Future" Goods; "Lot"; "Commercial Unit".

(1) "Goods" means all things (including specially manufactured goods) which are movable at the time of identification to the contract for sale other than the money in which the price is to be paid, investment securities (Article 8) and things in action. "Goods" also includes the unborn young of animals and growing crops and other identified things attached to realty as described in the section on goods to be severed from realty (Section 2–107).

(2) Goods must be both existing and identified before any interest in them can pass. Goods which are not both existing and identified are "future" goods. A purported present sale of future goods or of any interest therein operates as a contract to sell.

(3) There may be a sale of a part interest in existing identified goods.

(4) An undivided share in an identified bulk of fungible goods is sufficiently identified to be sold although the quantity of the bulk is not determined. Any agreed proportion of such a bulk or any quantity thereof agreed upon by number, weight or other measure may to the extent of the seller's interest in the bulk be sold to the buyer who then becomes an owner in common.

(5) "Lot" means a parcel or a single article which is the subject matter of a separate sale or delivery, whether or not it is sufficient to perform the contract.

(6) "Commercial unit" means such a unit of goods as by commercial usage is a single whole for purposes of sale and division of which materially impairs its character or value on the market or in use. A commercial unit may be a single article (as a machine) or a set of articles (as a suite of furniture or an assortment of sizes) or a quantity (as a bale, gross, or carload) or any other unit treated in use or in the relevant market as a single whole.

§ 2–106. Definitions: "Contract"; "Agreement"; "Contract for Sales"; "Sale"; "Present Sale"; "Conforming" to Contract; "Termination"; "Cancellation".

(1) In this Article unless the context otherwise requires "contract" and "agreement" are limited to those relating to the present or future sale of goods. "Contract for sale" includes both a present sale of goods and a contract to sell goods at a future time. A "sale" consists in the passing of title from the seller to the buyer for a price (Section 2–401). A "present sale" means a sale which is accomplished by the making of the contract.

(2) Goods or conduct including any part of a performance are "conforming" or conform to the contract when they are in accordance with the obligations under the contract.

(3) "Termination" occurs when either party pursuant to a power created by agreement or law puts an end to the contract otherwise than for its breach. On "termination" all obligations which are still executory on both sides are discharged but any right based on prior breach or performance survives.

(4) "Cancellation" occurs when either party puts an end to the contract for breach by the other and its effect is the same as that of "termination" except that the cancelling party also retains any remedy for breach of the whole contract or any unperformed balance.

§ 2–107. Goods to Be Severed from Realty: Recording.

(1) A contract for the sale of minerals or the like (including oil and gas) or a structure or its materials to be removed from realty is a contract for the sale of goods within this Article if they are to be severed by the seller but until severance a purported present sale thereof which is not effective as a transfer of an interest in land is effective only as a contract to sell.

(2) A contract for the sale apart from the land of growing crops or other things attached to realty and capable of severance without material harm thereto but not described in subsection (1) or of timber to be cut is a contract for the sale of goods within this Article whether the subject matter is to be severed by the buyer or by the seller even though it forms part of the realty at the time of contracting, and the parties can by identification effect a present sale before severance.

(3) The provisions of this section are subject to any third party rights provided by the law relating to realty records, and the contract for sale may be executed and recorded as a document transferring an interest in land and shall then constitute notice to third parties of the buyer's rights under the contract for sale. As amended in 1972.

PART 2: FORM, FORMATION AND READJUSTMENT OF CONTRACT

§ 2–201. Formal Requirements; Statute of Frauds.

(1) Except as otherwise provided in this section a contract for the sale of goods for the price of $500 or more is not enforceable by way of action or defense unless there is some writing sufficient to indicate that a contract for sale has been made between the parties and signed

by the party against whom enforcement is sought or by his authorized agent or broker. A writing is not insufficient because it omits or incorrectly states a term agreed upon but the contract is not enforceable under this paragraph beyond the quantity of goods shown in such writing.

(2) Between merchants if within a reasonable time a writing in confirmation of the contract and sufficient against the sender is received and the party receiving it has reason to know its contents, it satisfies the requirements of subsection (1) against such party unless written notice of objection to its contents is given within 10 days after it is received.

(3) A contract which does not satisfy the requirements of subsection (1) but which is valid in other respects is enforceable
   (a) if the goods are to be specially manufactured for the buyer and are not suitable for sale to others in the ordinary course of the seller's business and the seller, before notice of repudiation is received and under circumstances which reasonably indicate that the goods are for the buyer, has made either a substantial beginning of their manufacture or commitments for their procurement; or
   (b) if the party against whom enforcement is sought admits in his pleading, testimony or otherwise in court that a contract for sale was made, but the contract is not enforceable under this provision beyond the quantity of goods admitted; or
   (c) with respect to goods for which payment has been made and accepted or which have been received and accepted (Section 2–606).

§ 2–202. Final Written Expression: Parol or Extrinsic Evidence.
Terms with respect to which the confirmatory memoranda of the parties agree or which are otherwise set forth in a writing intended by the parties as a final expression of their agreement with respect to such terms as are included therein may not be contradicted by evidence of any prior agreement or of a contemporaneous oral agreement but may be explained or supplemented

   (a) by course of dealing or usage of trade (Section 1–205) or by course of performance (Section 2–208); and
   (b) by evidence of consistent additional terms unless the court finds the writing to have been intended also as a complete and exclusive statement of the terms of the agreement.

§ 2–203. Seals Inoperative.
The affixing of a seal to a writing evidencing a contract for sale or an offer to buy or sell goods does not constitute the writing a sealed instrument and the law with respect to sealed instruments does not apply to such a contract or offer.

§ 2–204. Formation in General.

(1) A contract for sale of goods may be made in any manner sufficient to show agreement, including conduct by both parties which recognizes the existence of such a contract.
(2) An agreement sufficient to constitute a contract for sale may be found even though the moment of its making is undetermined.
(3) Even though one or more terms are left open a contract for sale does not fail for indefiniteness if the parties have intended to make a contract and there is a reasonably certain basis for giving an appropriate remedy.

§ 2–205. Firm Offers.
An offer by a merchant to buy or sell goods in a signed writing which by its terms gives assurance that it will be held open is not revocable, for lack of consideration, during the time stated or if no time is stated for a reasonable time, but in no event may such period of irrevocability exceed three months; but any such term of assurance on a form supplied by the offeree must be separately signed by the offeror.

§ 2–206. Offer and Acceptance in Formation of Contract.

(1) Unless otherwise unambiguously indicated by the language or circumstances
    (a) an offer to make a contract shall be construed as inviting acceptance in any manner and by any medium reasonable in the circumstances;
    (b) an order or other offer to buy goods for prompt or current shipment shall be construed as inviting acceptance either by a prompt promise to ship or by the prompt or current shipment of conforming or non-conforming goods, but such a shipment of non-conforming goods does not constitute an acceptance if the seller seasonably notifies the buyer that the shipment is offered only as an accommodation to the buyer.
(2) Where the beginning of a requested performance is a reasonable mode of acceptance an offeror who is not notified of acceptance within a reasonable time may treat the offer as having lapsed before acceptance.

§ 2–207. Additional Terms in Acceptance or Confirmation.

(1) A definite and seasonable expression of acceptance or a written confirmation which is sent within a reasonable time operates as an acceptance even though it states terms additional to or different from those offered or agreed upon, unless acceptance is expressly made conditional on assent to the additional or different terms.
(2) The additional terms are to be construed as proposals for addition to the contract. Between merchants such terms become part of the contract unless:
    (a) the offer expressly limits acceptance to the terms of the offer;
    (b) they materially alter it; or
    (c) notification of objection to them has already been given or is given within a reasonable time after notice of them is received.
(3) Conduct by both parties which recognizes the existence of a contract is sufficient to establish a contract for sale although the writings of the parties do not otherwise establish a contract. In such case the terms of the particular contract consist of those terms on which the writings of the parties agree, together with any supplementary terms incorporated under any other provisions of this Act.

§ 2–208. Course of Performance or Practical Construction.

(1) Where the contract for sale involves repeated occasions for performance by either party with knowledge of the nature of the performance and opportunity for objection to it by the other, any course of performance accepted or acquiesced in without objection shall be relevant to determine the meaning of the agreement.
(2) The express terms of the agreement and any such course of performance, as well as any course of dealing and usage of trade, shall be construed whenever reasonable as consistent with each other; but when such construction is unreasonable, express terms shall control course of performance and course of performance shall control both course of dealing and usage of trade (Section 1–205).
(3) Subject to the provisions of the next section on modification and waiver, such course of performance shall be relevant to show a waiver or modification of any term inconsistent with such course of performance.

§ 2–209. Modification, Rescission and Waiver.

(1) An agreement modifying a contract within this Article needs no consideration to be binding.
(2) A signed agreement which excludes modification or rescission except by a signed writing cannot be otherwise modified or rescinded, but except as between merchants such a requirement on a form supplied by the merchant must be separately signed by the other party.

(3) The requirements of the statute of frauds section of this Article (Section 2–201) must be satisfied if the contract as modified is within its provisions.

(4) Although an attempt at modification or rescission does not satisfy the requirements of subsection (2) or (3) it can operate as a waiver.

(5) A party who has made a waiver affecting an executory portion of the contract may retract the waiver by reasonable notification received by the other party that strict performance will be required of any term waived, unless the retraction would be unjust in view of a material change of position in reliance on the waiver.

§ 2–210. Delegation of Performance; Assignment of Rights.

(1) A party may perform his duty through a delegate unless otherwise agreed or unless the other party has a substantial interest in having his original promisor perform or control the acts required by the contract. No delegation of performance relieves the party delegating of any duty to perform or any liability for breach.

(2) Unless otherwise agreed all rights of either seller or buyer can be assigned except where the assignment would materially change the duty of the other party, or increase materially the burden or risk imposed on him by his contract, or impair materially his chance of obtaining return performance. A right to damages for breach of the whole contract or a right arising out of the assignor's due performance of his entire obligation can be assigned despite agreement otherwise.

(3) Unless the circumstances indicate the contrary a prohibition of assignment of "the contract" is to be construed as barring only the delegation to the assignee of the assignor's performance.

(4) An assignment of "the contract" or of "all my rights under the contract" or an assignment in similar general terms is an assignment of rights and unless the language or the circumstances (as in an assignment for security) indicate the contrary, it is a delegation of performance of the duties of the assignor and its acceptance by the assignee constitutes a promise by him to perform those duties. This promise is enforceable by either the assignor or the other party to the original contract.

(5) The other party may treat any assignment which delegates performance as creating reasonable grounds for insecurity and may without prejudice to his rights against the assignor demand assurances from the assignee (Section 2–609).

PART 3: GENERAL OBLIGATION AND CONSTRUCTION OF CONTRACT

§ 2–301. General Obligations of Parties. The obligation of the seller is to transfer and deliver and that of the buyer is to accept and pay in accordance with the contract.

§ 2–302. Unconscionable Contract or Clause.

(1) If the court as a matter of law finds the contract or any clause of the contract to have been unconscionable at the time it was made the court may refuse to enforce the contract, or it may enforce the remainder of the contract without the unconscionable clause, or it may so limit the application of any unconscionable clause as to avoid any unconscionable result.

(2) When it is claimed or appears to the court that the contract or any clause thereof may be unconscionable the parties shall be afforded a reasonable opportunity to present evidence as to its commercial setting, purpose and effect to aid the court in making the determination.

§ 2–303. Allocation or Division of Risks. Where this Article allocates a risk or a burden as between the parties "unless otherwise agreed", the agreement may not only shift the allocation but may also divide the risk or burden.

§ 2–304. Price Payable in Money, Goods, Realty, or Otherwise.

(1) The price can be made payable in money or otherwise. If it is payable in whole or in part in goods each party is a seller of the goods which he is to transfer.

(2) Even though all or part of the price is payable in an interest in realty the transfer of the goods and the seller's obligations with reference to them are subject to this Article, but not the transfer of the interest in realty or the transferor's obligations in connection therewith.

§ 2–305. Open Price Term.

(1) The parties if they so intend can conclude a contract for sale even though the price is not settled. In such a case the price is a reasonable price at the time for delivery if
   (a)   nothing is said as to price; or
   (b)   the price is left to be agreed by the parties and they fail to agree; or
   (c)   the price is to be fixed in terms of some agreed market or other standard as set or recorded by a third person or agency and it is not so set or recorded.

(2) A price to be fixed by the seller or by the buyer means a price for him to fix in good faith.

(3) When a price left to be fixed otherwise than by agreement of the parties fails to be fixed through fault of one party the other may at his option treat the contract as cancelled or himself fix a reasonable price.

(4) Where, however, the parties intend not to be bound unless the price be fixed or agreed and it is not fixed or agreed there is no contract. In such a case the buyer must return any goods already received or if unable so to do must pay their reasonable value at the time of delivery and the seller must return any portion of the price paid on account.

§ 2–306. Output, Requirements and Exclusive Dealings.

(1) A term which measures the quantity by the output of the seller or the requirements of the buyer means such actual output or requirements as may occur in good faith, except that no quantity unreasonably disproportionate to any stated estimate or in the absence of a stated estimate to any normal or otherwise comparable prior output or requirements may be tendered or demanded.

(2) A lawful agreement by either the seller or the buyer for exclusive dealing in the kind of goods concerned imposes unless otherwise agreed an obligation by the seller to use best efforts to supply the goods and by the buyer to use best efforts to promote their sale.

§ 2–307. Delivery in Single Lot or Several Lots. Unless otherwise agreed all goods called for by a contract for sale must be tendered in a single delivery and payment is due only on such tender but where the circumstances give either party the right to make or demand delivery in lots the price if it can be apportioned may be demanded for each lot.

§ 2–308. Absence of Specified Place for Delivery. Unless otherwise agreed

   (a)   the place for delivery of goods is the seller's place of business or if he has none his residence; but
   (b)   in a contract for sale of identified goods which to the knowledge of the parties at the time of contracting are in some other place, that place is the place for their delivery; and
   (c)   documents of title may be delivered through customary banking channels.

§ 2–309. Absence of Specific Time Provisions; Notice of Termination.

(1) The time for shipment or delivery or any other action under a contract if not provided in this Article or agreed upon shall be a reasonable time.

(2) Where the contract provides for successive performances but is indefinite in duration it is valid for a reasonable time but unless otherwise agreed may be terminated at any time by either party.

(3) Termination of a contract by one party except on the happening of an agreed event requires that reasonable notification be received by the other party and an agreement dispensing with notification is invalid if its operation would be unconscionable.

§ 2–310. Open Time for Payment or Running of Credit; Authority to Ship Under Reservation. Unless otherwise agreed

(a) payment is due at the time and place at which the buyer is to receive the goods even though the place of shipment is the place of delivery; and

(b) if the seller is authorized to send the goods he may ship them under reservation, and may tender the documents of title, but the buyer may inspect the goods after their arrival before payment is due unless such inspection is inconsistent with the terms of the contract (Section 2–513); and

(c) if delivery is authorized and made by way of documents of title otherwise than by subsection (b) then payment is due at the time and place at which the buyer is to receive the documents regardless of where the goods are to be received; and

(d) where the seller is required or authorized to ship the goods on credit the credit period runs from the time of shipment but postdating the invoice or delaying its dispatch will correspondingly delay the starting of the credit period.

§ 2–311. Options and Cooperation Respecting Performance.

(1) An agreement for sale which is otherwise sufficiently definite (subsection (3) of Section 2–204) to be a contract is not made invalid by the fact that it leaves particulars of performance to be specified by one of the parties. Any such specification must be made in good faith and within limits set by commercial reasonableness.

(2) Unless otherwise agreed specifications relating to assortment of the goods are at the buyer's option and except as otherwise provided in subsections (1)(c) and (3) of Section 2–319 specifications or arrangements relating to shipment are at the seller's option.

(3) Where such specification would materially affect the other party's performance but is not seasonably made or where one party's cooperation is necessary to the agreed performance of the other but is not seasonably forthcoming, the other party in addition to all other remedies

(a) is excused for any resulting delay in his own performance; and

(b) may also either proceed to perform in any reasonable manner or after the time for a material part of his own performance treat the failure to specify or to cooperate as a breach by failure to deliver or accept the goods.

§ 2–312. Warranty of Title and Against Infringement; Buyer's Obligation Against Infringement.

(1) Subject to subsection (2) there is in a contract for sale a warranty by the seller that

(a) the title conveyed shall be good, and its transfer rightful; and

(b) the goods shall be delivered free from any security interest or other lien or encumbrance of which the buyer at the time of contracting has no knowledge.

(2) A warranty under subsection (1) will be excluded or modified only by specific language or by circumstances which give the buyer reason to know that the person selling does not claim title in himself or that he is purporting to sell only such right or title as he or a third person may have.

(3) Unless otherwise agreed a seller who is a merchant regularly dealing in goods of the kind warrants that the goods shall be delivered free of the rightful claim of any third person by way of infringement or the like but a buyer who furnishes specifications to the seller must hold the seller harmless against any such claim which arises out of compliance with the specifications.

§ 2–313. Express Warranties by Affirmation, Promise, Description, Sample.

(1) Express warranties by the seller are created as follows:

    (a) Any affirmation of fact or promise made by the seller to the buyer which relates to the goods and becomes part of the basis of the bargain creates an express warranty that the goods shall conform to the affirmation or promise.

    (b) Any description of the goods which is made part of the basis of the bargain creates an express warranty that the goods shall conform to the description.

    (c) Any sample or model which is made part of the basis of the bargain creates an express warranty that the whole of the goods shall conform to the sample or model.

(2) It is not necessary to the creation of an express warranty that the seller use formal words such as "warrant" or "guarantee" or that he have a specific intention to make a warranty, but an affirmation merely of the value of the goods or a statement purporting to be merely the seller's opinion or commendation of the goods does not create a warranty.

§ 2–314. Implied Warranty: Merchantability; Usage of Trade.

(1) Unless excluded or modified (Section 2–316), a warranty that the goods shall be merchantable is implied in a contract for their sale if the seller is a merchant with respect to goods of that kind. Under this section the serving for value of food or drink to be consumed either on the premises or elsewhere is a sale.

(2) Goods to be merchantable must be at least such as

    (a) pass without objection in the trade under the contract description; and

    (b) in the case of fungible goods, are of fair average quality within the description; and

    (c) are fit for the ordinary purposes for which such goods are used; and

    (d) run, within the variations permitted by the agreement, of even kind, quality and quantity within each unit and among all units involved; and

    (e) are adequately contained, packaged, and labeled as the agreement may require; and

    (f) conform to the promise or affirmations of fact made on the container or label if any.

(3) Unless excluded or modified (Section 2–316) other implied warranties may arise from course of dealing or usage of trade.

§ 2–315. Implied Warranty: Fitness for Particular Purpose.
Where the seller at the time of contracting has reason to know any particular purpose for which the goods are required and that the buyer is relying on the seller's skill or judgment to select or furnish suitable goods, there is unless excluded or modified under the next section an implied warranty that the goods shall be fit for such purpose.

§ 2–316. Exclusion or Modification of Warranties.

(1) Words or conduct relevant to the creation of an express warranty and words or conduct tending to negate or limit warranty shall be construed wherever reasonable as consistent with each other; but subject to the provisions of this Article on parol or extrinsic evidence (Section 2–202) negation or limitation is inoperative to the extent that such construction is unreasonable.

(2) Subject to subsection (3), to exclude or modify the implied warranty of merchantability or any part of it the language must mention merchantability and in case of a writing must be conspicuous, and to exclude or modify any implied warranty of fitness the exclusion must be by a writing and conspicuous. Language to exclude all implied warranties of fitness is sufficient if it states, for example, that "There are no warranties which extend beyond the description on the face hereof."

(3) Notwithstanding subsection (2)

    (a) unless the circumstances indicate otherwise, all implied warranties are excluded by expressions like "as is", "with all faults" or other language which in common understanding calls the buyer's attention to the exclusion of warranties and makes plain that there is no implied warranty; and

(b) when the buyer before entering into the contract has examined the goods or the sample or model as fully as he desired or has refused to examine the goods there is no implied warranty with regard to defects which an examination ought in the circumstances to have revealed to him; and

(c) an implied warranty can also be excluded or modified by course of dealing or course of performance or usage of trade.

(4) Remedies for breach of warranty can be limited in accordance with the provisions of this Article on liquidation or limitation of damages and on contractual modification of remedy (Sections 2–718 and 2–719).

§ 2–317. Cumulation and Conflict of Warranties Express or Implied.

Warranties whether express or implied shall be construed as consistent with each other and as cumulative, but if such construction is unreasonable the intention of the parties shall determine which warranty is dominant. In ascertaining that intention the following rules apply:

(a) Exact or technical specifications displace an inconsistent sample or model or general language of description.

(b) A sample from an existing bulk displaces inconsistent general language of description.

(c) Express warranties displace inconsistent implied warranties other than an implied warranty of fitness for a particular purpose.

§ 2–318. Third Party Beneficiaries of Warranties Express or Implied.

Note: *If this Act is introduced in the Congress of the United States this section should be omitted. (States to select one alternative.)*

Alternative A

A seller's warranty whether express or implied extends to any natural person who is in the family or household of his buyer or who is a guest in his home if it is reasonable to expect that such person may use, consume or be affected by the goods and who is injured in person by breach of the warranty. A seller may not exclude or limit the operation of this section.

Alternative B

A seller's warranty whether express or implied extends to any natural person who may reasonably be expected to use, consume or be affected by the goods and who is injured in person by breach of the warranty. A seller may not exclude or limit the operation of this section.

Alternative C

A seller's warranty whether express or implied extends to any person who may reasonably be expected to use, consume or be affected by the goods and who is injured by breach of the warranty. A seller may not exclude or limit the operation of this section with respect to injury to the person of an individual to whom the warranty extends.

As amended in 1966.

§ 2–319. F.O.B. and F.A.S. Terms.

(1) Unless otherwise agreed the term F.O.B. (which means "free on board") at a named place, even though used only in connection with the stated price, is a delivery term under which

(a) when the term is F.O.B. the place of shipment, the seller must at that place ship the goods in the manner provided in this Article (Section 2–504) and bear the expense and risk of putting them into the possession of the carrier; or

(b) when the term is F.O.B. the place of destination, the seller must at his own expense and risk transport the goods to that place and there tender delivery of them in the manner provided in this Article (Section 2–503);

(c) when under either (a) or (b) the term is also F.O.B. vessel, car or other vehicle, the seller must in addition at his own expense and risk load the goods on board. If the term is F.O.B. vessel the buyer must name the vessel and in an appropriate case the seller must comply with the provisions of this Article on the form of bill of lading (Section 2–323).

(2) Unless otherwise agreed the term F.A.S. vessel (which means "free alongside") at a named port, even though used only in connection with the stated price, is a delivery term under which the seller must

    (a) at his own expense and risk deliver the goods alongside the vessel in the manner usual in that port or on a dock designated and provided by the buyer; and

    (b) obtain and tender a receipt for the goods in exchange for which the carrier is under a duty to issue a bill of lading.

(3) Unless otherwise agreed in any case falling within subsection (1)(a) or (c) or subsection (2) the buyer must seasonably give any needed instructions for making delivery, including when the term is F.A.S. or F.O.B. the loading berth of the vessel and in an appropriate case its name and sailing date. The seller may treat the failure of needed instructions as a failure of cooperation under this Article (Section 2–311). He may also at his option move the goods in any reasonable manner preparatory to delivery or shipment.

(4) Under the term F.O.B. vessel or F.A.S. unless otherwise agreed the buyer must make payment against tender of the required documents and the seller may not tender nor the buyer demand delivery of the goods in substitution for the documents.

§ 2–320. C.I.F. and C. & F. Terms.

(1) The term C.I.F. means that the price includes in a lump sum the cost of the goods and the insurance and freight to the named destination. The term C. & F. or C.F. means that the price so includes cost and freight to the named destination.

(2) Unless otherwise agreed and even though used only in connection with the stated price and destination, the term C.I.F. destination or its equivalent requires the seller at his own expense and risk to

    (a) put the goods into the possession of a carrier at the port for shipment and obtain a negotiable bill or bills of lading covering the entire transportation to the named destination; and

    (b) load the goods and obtain a receipt from the carrier (which may be contained in the bill of lading) showing that the freight has been paid or provided for; and

    (c) obtain a policy or certificate of insurance, including any war risk insurance, of a kind and on terms then current at the port of shipment in the usual amount, in the currency of the contract, shown to cover the same goods covered by the bill of lading and providing for payment of loss to the order of the buyer or for the account of whom it may concern; but the seller may add to the price the amount of the premium for any such war risk insurance; and

    (d) prepare an invoice of the goods and procure any other documents required to effect shipment or to comply with the contract; and

    (e) forward and tender with commercial promptness all the documents in due form and with any indorsement necessary to perfect the buyer's rights.

(3) Unless otherwise agreed the term C. & F. or its equivalent has the same effect and imposes upon the seller the same obligations and risks as a C.I.F. term except the obligation as to insurance.

(4) Under the term C.I.F. or C. & F. unless otherwise agreed the buyer must make payment against tender of the required documents and the seller may not tender nor the buyer demand delivery of the goods in substitution for the documents.

§ 2–321. C.I.F. or C. & F.: "Net Landed Weights"; "Payment on Arrival"; Warranty of Condition on Arrival. Under a contract containing a term C.I.F. or C. & F.

(1) Where the price is based on or is to be adjusted according to "net landed weights", "delivered weights", "out turn" quantity or quality or the like, unless otherwise agreed the seller must reasonably estimate the price. The payment due on tender of the documents called for

by the contract is the amount so estimated, but after final adjustment of the price a settlement must be made with commercial promptness.

(2) An agreement described in subsection (1) or any warranty of quality or condition of the goods on arrival places upon the seller the risk of ordinary deterioration, shrinkage and the like in transportation but has no effect on the place or time of identification to the contract for sale or delivery or on the passing of the risk of loss.

(3) Unless otherwise agreed where the contract provides for payment on or after arrival of the goods the seller must before payment allow such preliminary inspection as is feasible; but if the goods are lost delivery of the documents and payment are due when the goods should have arrived.

§ 2–322. Delivery "Ex-Ship".

(1) Unless otherwise agreed a term for delivery of goods "ex-ship" (which means from the carrying vessel) or in equivalent language is not restricted to a particular ship and requires delivery from a ship which has reached a place at the named port of destination where goods of the kind are usually discharged.

(2) Under such a term unless otherwise agreed
   (a) the seller must discharge all liens arising out of the carriage and furnish the buyer with a direction which puts the carrier under a duty to deliver the goods; and
   (b) the risk of loss does not pass to the buyer until the goods leave the ship's tackle or are otherwise properly unloaded.

§ 2–323. Form of Bill of Lading Required in Overseas Shipment; "Overseas".

(1) Where the contract contemplates overseas shipment and contains a term C.I.F. or C. & F. or F.O.B. vessel, the seller unless otherwise agreed must obtain a negotiable bill of lading stating that the goods have been loaded in board or, in the case of a term C.I.F. or C. & F., received for shipment.

(2) Where in a case within subsection (1) a bill of lading has been issued in a set of parts, unless otherwise agreed if the documents are not to be sent from abroad the buyer may demand tender of the full set; otherwise only one part of the bill of lading need be tendered. Even if the agreement expressly requires a full set
   (a) due tender of a single part is acceptable within the provisions of this Article on cure of improper delivery (subsection (1) of Section 2–508); and
   (b) even though the full set is demanded, if the documents are sent from abroad the person tendering an incomplete set may nevertheless require payment upon furnishing an indemnity which the buyer in good faith deems adequate.

(3) A shipment by water or by air or a contract contemplating such shipment is "overseas" insofar as by usage of trade or agreement it is subject to the commercial, financing or shipping practices characteristic of international deep water commerce.

§ 2–324. "No Arrival, No Sale" Term. Under a term "no arrival, no sale" or terms of like meaning, unless otherwise agreed,

   (a) the seller must properly ship conforming goods and if they arrive by any means he must tender them on arrival but he assumes no obligation that the goods will arrive unless he has caused the non-arrival; and
   (b) where without fault of the seller the goods are in part lost or have so deteriorated as no longer to conform to the contract or arrive after the contract time, the buyer may proceed as if there had been casualty to identified goods (Section 2–613).

§ 2–325. "Letter of Credit" Term; "Confirmed Credit".

(1) Failure of the buyer seasonably to furnish an agreed letter of credit is a breach of the contract for sale.

(2) The delivery to seller of a proper letter of credit suspends the buyer's obligation to pay. If the letter of credit is dishonored, the seller may on seasonable notification to the buyer require payment directly from him.

(3) Unless otherwise agreed the term "letter of credit" or "banker's credit" in a contract for sale means an irrevocable credit issued by a financing agency of good repute and, where the shipment is overseas, of good international repute. The term "confirmed credit" means that the credit must also carry the direct obligation of such an agency which does business in the seller's financial market.

§ 2–326. Sale on Approval and Sale or Return; Consignment Sales and Rights of Creditors.

(1) Unless otherwise agreed, if delivered goods may be returned by the buyer even though they conform to the contract, the transaction is
  (a)   a "sale on approval" if the goods are delivered primarily for use, and
  (b)   a "sale or return" if the goods are delivered primarily for resale.

(2) Except as provided in subsection (3), goods held on approval are not subject to the claims of the buyer's creditors until acceptance; goods held on sale or return are subject to such claims while in the buyer's possession.

(3) Where goods are delivered to a person for sale and such person maintains a place of business at which he deals in goods of the kind involved, under a name other than the name of the person making delivery, then with respect to claims of creditors of the person conducting the business the goods are deemed to be on sale or return. The provisions of this subsection are applicable even though an agreement purports to reserve title to the person making delivery until payment or resale or uses such words as "on consignment" or "on memorandum". However, this subsection is not applicable if the person making delivery
  (a)   complies with an applicable law providing for a consignor's interest or the like to be evidenced by a sign, or
  (b)   establishes that the person conducting the business is generally known by his creditors to be substantially engaged in selling the goods of others, or
  (c)   complies with the filing provisions of the Article on Secured Transactions (Article 9).

(4) Any "or return" term of a contract for sale is to be treated as a separate contract for sale within the statute of frauds section of this Article (Section 2–201) and as contradicting the sale aspect of the contract within the provisions of this Article on parol or extrinsic evidence (Section 2–202).

§ 2–327. Special Incidents of Sale on Approval and Sale or Return.

(1) Under a sale on approval unless otherwise agreed
  (a)   although the goods are identified to the contract the risk of loss and the title do not pass to the buyer until acceptance; and
  (b)   use of the goods consistent with the purpose of trial is not acceptance but failure seasonably to notify the seller of election to return the goods is acceptance, and if the goods conform to the contract acceptance of any part is acceptance of the whole; and
  (c)   after due notification of election to return, the return is at the seller's risk and expense but a merchant buyer must follow any reasonable instructions.

(2) Under a sale or return unless otherwise agreed
  (a)   the option to return extends to the whole or any commercial unit of the goods while in substantially their original condition, but must be exercised seasonably; and
  (b)   the return is at the buyer's risk and expense.

§ 2–328. Sale by Auction.

(1) In a sale by auction if goods are put up in lots each lot is the subject of a separate sale.

(2) A sale by auction is complete when the auctioneer so announces by the fall of the hammer or in other customary manner. Where a bid is made while the hammer is falling in

acceptance of a prior bid the auctioneer may in his discretion reopen the bidding or declare the goods sold under the bid on which the hammer was falling.

(3) Such a sale is with reserve unless the goods are in explicit terms put up without reserve. In an auction with reserve the auctioneer may withdraw the goods at any time until he announces completion of the sale. In an auction without reserve, after the auctioneer calls for bids on an article or lot, that article or lot cannot be withdrawn unless no bid is made within a reasonable time. In either case a bidder may retract his bid until the auctioneer's announcement of completion of the sale, but a bidder's retraction does not revive any previous bid.

(4) If the auctioneer knowingly receives a bid on the seller's behalf or the seller makes or procures such a bid, and notice has not been given that liberty for such bidding is reserved, the buyer may at his option avoid the sale or take the goods at the price of the last good faith bid prior to the completion of the sale. This subsection shall not apply to any bid at a forced sale.

PART 4: TITLE, CREDITORS AND GOOD FAITH PURCHASERS

§ 2–401. Passing of Title; Reservation for Security; Limited Application of This Section.
Each provision of this Article with regard to the rights, obligations and remedies of the seller, the buyer, purchasers or other third parties applies irrespective of title to the goods except where the provision refers to such title. Insofar as situations are not covered by the other provisions of this Article and matters concerning title become material the following rules apply:

(1) Title to goods cannot pass under a contract for sale prior to their identification to the contract (Section 2–501), and unless otherwise explicitly agreed the buyer acquires by their identification a special property as limited by this Act. Any retention or reservation by the seller of the title (property) in goods shipped or delivered to the buyer is limited in effect to a reservation of a security interest. Subject to these provisions and to the provisions of the Article on Secured Transactions (Article 9), title to goods passes from the seller to the buyer in any manner and on any conditions explicitly agreed on by the parties.

(2) Unless otherwise explicitly agreed title passes to the buyer at the time and place at which the seller completes his performance with reference to the physical delivery of the goods, despite any reservation of a security interest and even though a document of title is to be delivered at a different time or place; and in particular and despite any reservation of a security interest by the bill of lading
   (a) if the contract requires or authorizes the seller to send the goods to the buyer but does not require him to deliver them at destination, title passes to the buyer at the time and place of shipment; but
   (b) if the contract requires delivery at destination, title passes on tender there.

(3) Unless otherwise explicitly agreed where delivery is to be made without moving the goods,
   (a) if the seller is to deliver a document of title, title passes at the time when and the place where he delivers such documents; or
   (b) if the goods are at the time of contracting already identified and no documents are to be delivered, title passes at the time and place of contracting.

(4) A rejection or other refusal by the buyer to receive or retain the goods, whether or not justified, or a justified revocation of acceptance revests title to the goods in the seller. Such revesting occurs by operation of law and is not a "sale".

§ 2–402. Rights of Seller's Creditors Against Sold Goods.

(1) Except as provided in subsections (2) and (3), rights of unsecured creditors of the seller with respect to goods which have been identified to a contract for sale are subject to the buyer's rights to recover the goods under this Article (Sections 2–502 and 2–716).

(2) A creditor of the seller may treat a sale or an identification of goods to a contract for sale as void if as against him a retention of possession by the seller is fraudulent under any rule of law of the state where the goods are situated, except that retention of possession in good faith and current course of trade by a merchant-seller for a commercially reasonable time after a sale or identification is not fraudulent.

(3) Nothing in this Article shall be deemed to impair the rights of creditors of the seller

    (a) under the provisions of the Article on Secured Transactions (Article 9); or

    (b) where identification to the contract or delivery is made not in current course of trade but in satisfaction of or as security for a pre-existing claim for money, security or the like and is made under circumstances which under any rule of law of the state where the goods are situated would apart from this Article constitute the transaction a fraudulent transfer or voidable preference.

§ 2–403. Power to Transfer; Good Faith Purchase of Goods; "Entrusting".

(1) A purchaser of goods acquires all title which his transferor had or had power to transfer except that a purchaser of a limited interest acquires rights only to the extent of the interest purchased. A person with voidable title has power to transfer a good title to a good faith purchaser for value. When goods have been delivered under a transaction of purchase the purchaser has such power even though

    (a) the transferor was deceived as to the identity of the purchaser, or

    (b) the delivery was in exchange for a check which is later dishonored, or

    (c) it was agreed that the transaction was to be a "cash sale", or

    (d) the delivery was procured through fraud punishable as larcenous under the criminal law.

(2) Any entrusting of possession of goods to a merchant who deals in goods of that kind gives him power to transfer all rights of the entruster to a buyer in ordinary course of business.

(3) "Entrusting" includes any delivery and any acquiescence in retention of possession regardless of any condition expressed between the parties to the delivery or acquiescence and regardless of whether the procurement of the entrusting or the possessor's disposition of the goods have been such as to be larcenous under the criminal law.

[*Publisher's Editorial Note: If a state adopts the repealer of Article 6—Bulk Transfers (Alternative A), subsec. (4) should read as follows:*]

(4) The rights of other purchasers of goods and of lien creditors are governed by the Articles on Secured Transactions (Article 9) and Documents of Title (Article 7).

[*Publisher's Editorial Note: If a state adopts Revised Article 6—Bulk Sales (Alternative B), subsec. (4) should read as follows:*]

(4) The rights of other purchasers of goods and of lien creditors are governed by the Articles on Secured Transactions (Article 9), Bulk Sales (Article 6) and Documents of Title (Article 7).

As amended in 1988.

For material relating to the changes made in text in 1988, see section 3 of Alternative A (Repealer of Article 6—Bulk Transfers) and Conforming Amendment to Section 2–403 following end of Alternative B (Revised Article 6—Bulk Sales).

PART 5: PERFORMANCE

§ 2–501. Insurable Interest in Goods; Manner of Identification of Goods.

(1) The buyer obtains a special property and an insurable interest in goods by identification of existing goods as goods to which the contract refers even though the goods so identified are non-conforming and he has an option to return or reject them. Such identification can be made at any time and in any manner explicitly agreed to by the parties. In the absence of explicit agreement identification occurs

(a) when the contract is made if it is for the sale of goods already existing and identified;

(b) if the contract is for the sale of future goods other than those described in paragraph (c), when goods are shipped, marked or otherwise designated by the seller as goods to which the contract refers;

(c) when the crops are planted or otherwise become growing crops or the young are conceived if the contract is for the sale of unborn young to be born within twelve months after contracting or for the sale of crops to be harvested within twelve months or the next normal harvest season after contracting whichever is longer.

(2) The seller retains an insurable interest in goods so long as title to or any security interest in the goods remains in him and where the identification is by the seller alone he may until default or insolvency or notification to the buyer that the identification is final substitute other goods for those identified.

(3) Nothing in this section impairs any insurable interest recognized under any other statute or rule of law.

§ 2–502. Buyer's Right to Goods on Seller's Insolvency.

(1) Subject to subsection (2) and even though the goods have not been shipped a buyer who has paid a part or all of the price of goods in which he has a special property under the provisions of the immediately preceding section may on making and keeping good a tender of any unpaid portion of their price recover them from the seller if the seller becomes insolvent within ten days after receipt of the first installment on their price.

(2) If the identification creating his special property has been made by the buyer he acquires the right to recover the goods only if they conform to the contract for sale.

§ 2–503. Manner of Seller's Tender of Delivery.

(1) Tender of delivery requires that the seller put and hold conforming goods at the buyer's disposition and give the buyer any notification reasonably necessary to enable him to take delivery. The manner, time and place for tender are determined by the agreement and this Article, and in particular

(a) tender must be at a reasonable hour, and if it is of goods they must be kept available for the period reasonably necessary to enable the buyer to take possession; but

(b) unless otherwise agreed the buyer must furnish facilities reasonably suited to the receipt of the goods.

(2) Where the case is within the next section respecting shipment tender requires that the seller comply with its provisions.

(3) Where the seller is required to deliver at a particular destination tender requires that he comply with subsection (1) and also in any appropriate case tender documents as described in subsections (4) and (5) of this section.

(4) Where goods are in the possession of a bailee and are to be delivered without being moved

(a) tender requires that the seller either tender a negotiable document of title covering such goods or procure acknowledgment by the bailee of the buyer's right to possession of the goods; but

(b) tender to the buyer of a non-negotiable document of title or of a written direction to the bailee to deliver is sufficient tender unless the buyer seasonably objects, and receipt by the bailee of notification of the buyer's rights fixes those rights as against the bailee and all third persons; but risk of loss of the goods and of any failure by the bailee to honor the non-negotiable document of title or to obey the direction remains on the seller until the buyer has had a reasonable time to present the document or direction, and a refusal by the bailee to honor the document or to obey the direction defeats the tender.

(5) Where the contract requires the seller to deliver documents

(a) he must tender all such documents in correct form, except as provided in this Article with respect to bills of lading in a set (subsection (2) of Section 2–323); and

(b) tender through customary banking channels is sufficient and dishonor of a draft accompanying the documents constitutes non-acceptance or rejection.

§ 2–504. Shipment by Seller. Where the seller is required or authorized to send the goods to the buyer and the contract does not require him to deliver them at a particular destination, then unless otherwise agreed he must

(a) put the goods in the possession of such a carrier and make such a contract for their transportation as may be reasonable having regard to the nature of the goods and other circumstances of the case; and

(b) obtain and promptly deliver or tender in due form any document necessary to enable the buyer to obtain possession of the goods or otherwise required by the agreement or by usage of trade; and

(c) promptly notify the buyer of the shipment.

Failure to notify the buyer under paragraph (c) or to make a proper contract under paragraph (a) is a ground for rejection only if material delay or loss ensues.

§ 2–505. Seller's Shipment Under Reservation.

(1) Where the seller has identified goods to the contract by or before shipment:

(a) his procurement of a negotiable bill of lading to his own order or otherwise reserves in him a security interest in the goods. His procurement of the bill to the order of a financing agency or of the buyer indicates in addition only the seller's expectation of transferring that interest to the person named.

(b) a non-negotiable bill of lading to himself or his nominee reserves possession of the goods as security but except in a case of conditional delivery (subsection (2) of Section 2–507) a non-negotiable bill of lading naming the buyer as consignee reserves no security interest even though the seller retains possession of the bill of lading.

(2) When shipment by the seller with reservation of a security interest is in violation of the contract for sale it constitutes an improper contract for transportation within the preceding section but impairs neither the rights given to the buyer by shipment and identification of the goods to the contract nor the seller's powers as a holder of a negotiable document.

§ 2–506. Rights of Financing Agency.

(1) A financing agency by paying or purchasing for value a draft which relates to a shipment of goods acquires to the extent of the payment or purchase and in addition to its own rights under the draft and any document of title securing it any rights of the shipper in the goods including the right to stop delivery and the shipper's right to have the draft honored by the buyer.

(2) The right to reimbursement of a financing agency which has in good faith honored or purchased the draft under commitment to or authority from the buyer is not impaired by subsequent discovery of defects with reference to any relevant document which was apparently regular on its face.

§ 2–507. Effect of Seller's Tender; Delivery on Condition.

(1) Tender of delivery is a condition to the buyer's duty to accept the goods and, unless otherwise agreed, to his duty to pay for them. Tender entitles the seller to acceptance of the goods and to payment according to the contract.

(2) Where payment is due and demanded on the delivery to the buyer of goods or documents of title, his right as against the seller to retain or dispose of them is conditional upon his making the payment due.

§ 2–508. Cure by Seller of Improper Tender or Delivery; Replacement.

(1) Where any tender or delivery by the seller is rejected because non-conforming and the time for performance has not yet expired, the seller may seasonably notify the buyer of his intention to cure and may then within the contract time make a conforming delivery.

(2) Where the buyer rejects a non-conforming tender which the seller had reasonable grounds to believe would be acceptable with or without money allowance the seller may if he seasonally notifies the buyer have a further reasonable time to substitute a conforming tender.

§ 2–509. Risk of Loss in the Absence of Breach.

(1) Where the contract requires or authorizes the seller to ship the goods by carrier
    (a) if it does not require him to deliver them at a particular destination, the risk of loss passes to the buyer when the goods are duly delivered to the carrier even though the shipment is under reservation (Section 2–505); but
    (b) if it does require him to deliver them at a particular destination and the goods are there duly tendered while in the possession of the carrier, the risk of loss passes to the buyer when the goods are there duly so tendered as to enable the buyer to take delivery.

(2) Where the goods are held by a bailee to be delivered without being moved, the risk of loss passes to the buyer
    (a) on his receipt of a negotiable document of title covering the goods; or
    (b) on acknowledgment by the bailee of the buyer's right to possession of the goods; or
    (c) after his receipt of a non-negotiable document of title or other written direction to deliver, as provided in subsection (4)(b) of Section 2–503.

(3) In any case not within subsection (1) or (2), the risk of loss passes to the buyer on his receipt of the goods if the seller is a merchant; otherwise the risk passes to the buyer on tender of delivery.

(4) The provisions of this section are subject to contrary agreement of the parties and to the provisions of this Article on sale on approval (Section 2–327) and on effect of breach on risk of loss (Section 2–510).

§ 2–510. Effect of Breach on Risk of Loss.

(1) Where a tender or delivery of goods so fails to conform to the contract as to give a right of rejection the risk of their loss remains on the seller until cure or acceptance.

(2) Where the buyer rightfully revokes acceptance he may to the extent of any deficiency in his effective insurance coverage treat the risk of loss as having rested on the seller from the beginning.

(3) Where the buyer as to conforming goods already identified to the contract for sale repudiates or is otherwise in breach before risk of their loss has passed to him, the seller may to the extent of any deficiency in his effective insurance coverage treat the risk of loss as resting on the buyer for a commercially reasonable time.

§ 2–511. Tender of Payment by Buyer; Payment by Check.

(1) Unless otherwise agreed tender of payment is a condition to the seller's duty to tender and complete any delivery.

(2) Tender of payment is sufficient when made by any means or in any manner current in the ordinary course of business unless the seller demands payment in legal tender and gives any extension of time reasonably necessary to procure it.

(3) Subject to the provisions of this Act on the effect of an instrument on an obligation (Section 3–310), payment by check is conditional and is defeated as between the parties by dishonor of the check on due presentment.

As amended in 1994.

See Appendix XI for material relating to changes made in text in 1994.

§ 2–512. Payment by Buyer Before Inspection.

(1) Where the contract requires payment before inspection non-conformity of the goods does not excuse the buyer from so making payment unless

(a)   the non-conformity appears without inspection; or

(b)   despite tender of the required documents the circumstances would justify injunction against honor under this Act (Section 5–109(b)).

(2)   Payment pursuant to subsection (1) does not constitute an acceptance of goods or impair the buyer's right to inspect or any of his remedies.

As amended in 1995.

See Appendix XIV for material relating to changes made in text in 1995.

§ 2–513. Buyer's Right to Inspection of Goods.

(1)   Unless otherwise agreed and subject to subsection (3), where goods are tendered or delivered or identified to the contract for sale, the buyer has a right before payment or acceptance to inspect them at any reasonable place and time and in any reasonable manner. When the seller is required or authorized to send the goods to the buyer, the inspection may be after their arrival.

(2)   Expenses of inspection must be borne by the buyer but may be recovered from the seller if the goods do not conform and are rejected.

(3)   Unless otherwise agreed and subject to the provisions of this Article on C.I.F. contracts (subsection (3) of Section 2–321), the buyer is not entitled to inspect the goods before payment of the price when the contract provides

(a)   for delivery "C.O.D." or on other like terms; or

(b)   for payment against documents of title, except where such payment is due only after the goods are to become available for inspection.

(4)   A place or method of inspection fixed by the parties is presumed to be exclusive but unless otherwise expressly agreed it does not postpone identification or shift the place for delivery or for passing the risk of loss. If compliance becomes impossible, inspection shall be as provided in this section unless the place or method fixed was clearly intended as an indispensable condition failure of which avoids the contract.

§ 2–514. When Documents Deliverable on Acceptance; When on Payment.

Unless otherwise agreed documents against which a draft is drawn are to be delivered to the drawee on acceptance of the draft if it is payable more than three days after presentment; otherwise, only on payment.

§ 2–515. Preserving Evidence of Goods in Dispute. In furtherance of the adjustment of any claim or dispute

(a)   either party on reasonable notification to the other and for the purpose of ascertaining the facts and preserving evidence has the right to inspect, test and sample the goods including such of them as may be in the possession or control of the other; and

(b)   the parties may agree to a third party inspection or survey to determine the conformity or condition of the goods and may agree that the findings shall be binding upon them in any subsequent litigation or adjustment.

PART 6: BREACH, REPUDIATION AND EXCUSE

§ 2–601. Buyer's Rights on Improper Delivery. Subject to the provisions of this Article on breach in installment contracts (Section 2–612) and unless otherwise agreed under the sections on contractual limitations of remedy (Sections 2–718 and 2–719), if the goods or the tender of delivery fail in any respect to conform to the contract, the buyer may

(a)   reject the whole; or

(b)   accept the whole; or

(c)   accept any commercial unit or units and reject the rest.

§ 2–602. Manner and Effect of Rightful Rejection.

(1) Rejection of goods must be within a reasonable time after their delivery or tender. It is ineffective unless the buyer seasonably notifies the seller.

(2) Subject to the provisions of the two following sections on rejected goods (Sections 2–603 and 2–604),

    (a) after rejection any exercise of ownership by the buyer with respect to any commercial unit is wrongful as against the seller; and

    (b) if the buyer has before rejection taken physical possession of goods in which he does not have a security interest under the provisions of this Article (subsection (3) of Section 2–711), he is under a duty after rejection to hold them with reasonable care at the seller's disposition for a time sufficient to permit the seller to remove them; but

    (c) the buyer has no further obligations with regard to goods rightfully rejected.

(3) The seller's rights with respect to goods wrongfully rejected are governed by the provisions of this Article on Seller's remedies in general (Section 2–703).

§ 2–603. Merchant Buyer's Duties as to Rightfully Rejected Goods.

(1) Subject to any security interest in the buyer (subsection (3) of Section 2–711), when the seller has no agent or place of business at the market of rejection a merchant buyer is under a duty after rejection of goods in his possession or control to follow any reasonable instructions received from the seller with respect to the goods and in the absence of such instructions to make reasonable efforts to sell them for the seller's account if they are perishable or threaten to decline in value speedily. Instructions are not reasonable if on demand indemnity for expenses is not forthcoming.

(2) When the buyer sells goods under subsection (1), he is entitled to reimbursement from the seller or out of the proceeds for reasonable expenses of caring for and selling them, and if the expenses include no selling commission then to such commission as is usual in the trade or if there is none to a reasonable sum not exceeding ten percent on the gross proceeds.

(3) In complying with this section the buyer is held only to good faith and good faith conduct hereunder is neither acceptance nor conversion nor the basis of an action for damages.

§ 2–604. Buyer's Options as to Salvage of Rightfully Rejected Goods.

Subject to the provisions of the immediately preceding section on perishables if the seller gives no instructions within a reasonable time after notification of rejection the buyer may store the rejected goods for the seller's account or reship them to him or resell them for the seller's account with reimbursement as provided in the preceding section. Such action is not acceptance or conversion.

§ 2–605. Waiver of Buyer's Objections by Failure to Particularize.

(1) The buyer's failure to state in connection with rejection a particular defect which is ascertainable by reasonable inspection precludes him from relying on the unstated defect to justify rejection or to establish breach

    (a) where the seller could have cured it if stated seasonably; or

    (b) between merchants when the seller has after rejection made a request in writing for a full and final written statement of all defects on which the buyer proposes to rely.

(2) Payment against documents made without reservation of rights precludes recovery of the payment for defects apparent on the face of the documents.

§ 2–606. What Constitutes Acceptance of Goods.

(1) Acceptance of goods occurs when the buyer

    (a) after a reasonable opportunity to inspect the goods signifies to the seller that the goods are conforming or that he will take or retain them in spite of their non-conformity; or

(b) fails to make an effective rejection (subsection (1) of Section 2–602), but such acceptance does not occur until the buyer has had a reasonable opportunity to inspect them; or

(c) does any act inconsistent with the seller's ownership; but if such act is wrongful as against the seller it is an acceptance only if ratified by him.

(2) Acceptance of a part of any commercial unit is acceptance of that entire unit.

§ 2–607. Effect of Acceptance; Notice of Breach; Burden of Establishing Breach After Acceptance; Notice of Claim or Litigation to Person Answerable Over.

(1) The buyer must pay at the contract rate for any goods accepted.

(2) Acceptance of goods by the buyer precludes rejection of the goods accepted and if made with knowledge of a non-conformity cannot be revoked because of it unless the acceptance was on the reasonable assumption that the non-conformity would be seasonably cured but acceptance does not of itself impair any other remedy provided by this Article for non-conformity.

(3) Where a tender has been accepted

(a) the buyer must within a reasonable time after he discovers or should have discovered any breach notify the seller of breach or be barred from any remedy; and

(b) if the claim is one for infringement or the like (subsection (3) of Section 2–312) and the buyer is sued as a result of such a breach he must so notify the seller within a reasonable time after he receives notice of the litigation or be barred from any remedy over for liability established by the litigation.

(4) The burden is on the buyer to establish any breach with respect to the goods accepted.

(5) Where the buyer is sued for breach of a warranty or other obligation for which his seller is answerable over

(a) he may give his seller written notice of the litigation. If the notice states that the seller may come in and defend and that if the seller does not do so he will be bound in any action against him by his buyer by any determination of fact common to the two litigations, then unless the seller after seasonable receipt of the notice does come in and defend he is so bound.

(b) if the claim is one for infringement or the like (subsection (3) of Section 2–312) the original seller may demand in writing that his buyer turn over to him control of the litigation including settlement or else be barred from any remedy over and if he also agrees to bear all expense and to satisfy any adverse judgment, then unless the buyer after seasonable receipt of the demand does turn over control the buyer is so barred.

(6) The provisions of subsections (3), (4) and (5) apply to any obligation of a buyer to hold the seller harmless against infringement or the like (subsection (3) of Section 2–312).

§ 2–608. Revocation of Acceptance in Whole or in Part.

(1) The buyer may revoke his acceptance of a lot or commercial unit whose non-conformity substantially impairs its value to him if he has accepted it

(a) on the reasonable assumption that its non-conformity would be cured and it has not been seasonably cured; or

(b) without discovery of such non-conformity if his acceptance was reasonably induced either by the difficulty of discovery before acceptance or by the seller's assurances.

(2) Revocation of acceptance must occur within a reasonable time after the buyer discovers or should have discovered the ground for it and before any substantial change in condition of the goods which is not caused by their own defects. It is not effective until the buyer notifies the seller of it.

(3) A buyer who so revokes has the same rights and duties with regard to the goods involved as if he had rejected them.

§ 2–609. Right to Adequate Assurance of Performance.

(1) A contract for sale imposes an obligation on each party that the other's expectation of receiving due performance will not be impaired. When reasonable grounds for insecurity arise with respect to the performance of either party the other may in writing demand adequate assurance of due performance and until he receives such assurance may if commercially reasonable suspend any performance for which he has not already received the agreed return.

(2) Between merchants the reasonableness of grounds for insecurity and the adequacy of any assurance offered shall be determined according to commercial standards.

(3) Acceptance of any improper delivery or payment does not prejudice the aggrieved party's right to demand adequate assurance of future performance.

(4) After receipt of a justified demand failure to provide within a reasonable time not exceeding thirty days such assurance of due performance as is adequate under the circumstances of the particular case is a repudiation of the contract.

§ 2–610. Anticipatory Repudiation.

When either party repudiates the contract with respect to a performance not yet due the loss of which will substantially impair the value of the contract to the other, the aggrieved party may

(a) for a commercially reasonable time await performance by the repudiating party; or

(b) resort to any remedy for breach (Section 2–703 or Section 2–711), even though he has notified the repudiating party that he would await the latter's performance and has urged retraction; and

(c) in either case suspend his own performance or proceed in accordance with the provisions of this Article on the seller's right to identify goods to the contract notwithstanding breach or to salvage unfinished goods (Section 2–704).

§ 2–611. Retraction of Anticipatory Repudiation.

(1) Until the repudiating party's next performance is due he can retract his repudiation unless the aggrieved party has since the repudiation cancelled or materially changed his position or otherwise indicated that he considers the repudiation final.

(2) Retraction may be by any method which clearly indicates to the aggrieved party that the repudiating party intends to perform, but must include any assurance justifiably demanded under the provisions of this Article (Section 2–609).

(3) Retraction reinstates the repudiating party's rights under the contract with due excuse and allowance to the aggrieved party for any delay occasioned by the repudiation.

§ 2–612. "Installment Contract"; Breach.

(1) An "installment contract" is one which requires or authorizes the delivery of goods in separate lots to be separately accepted, even though the contract contains a clause "each delivery is a separate contract" or its equivalent.

(2) The buyer may reject any installment which is non-conforming if the non-conformity substantially impairs the value of that installment and cannot be cured or if the non-conformity is a defect in the required documents; but if the non-conformity does not fall within subsection (3) and the seller gives adequate assurance of its cure the buyer must accept that installment.

(3) Whenever non-conformity or default with respect to one or more installments substantially impairs the value of the whole contract there is a breach of the whole. But the aggrieved party reinstates the contract if he accepts a non-conforming installment without seasonably notifying of cancellation or if he brings an action with respect only to past installments or demands performance as to future installments.

§ 2–613. Casualty to Identified Goods. Where the contract requires for its performance goods identified when the contract is made, and the goods suffer casualty without fault of either party before the risk of loss passes to the buyer, or in a proper case under a "no arrival, no sale" term (Section 2–324) then

    (a) if the loss is total the contract is avoided; and

    (b) if the loss is partial or the goods have so deteriorated as no longer to conform to the contract the buyer may nevertheless demand inspection and at his option either treat the contract as avoided or accept the goods with due allowance from the contract price for the deterioration or the deficiency in quantity but without further right against the seller.

§ 2–614. Substituted Performance.

(1) Where without fault of either party the agreed berthing, loading, or unloading facilities fail or an agreed type of carrier becomes unavailable or the agreed manner of delivery otherwise becomes commercially impracticable but a commercially reasonable substitute is available, such substitute performance must be tendered and accepted.

(2) If the agreed means or manner of payment fails because of domestic or foreign governmental regulation, the seller may withhold or stop delivery unless the buyer provides a means or manner of payment which is commercially a substantial equivalent. If delivery has already been taken, payment by the means or in the manner provided by the regulation discharges the buyer's obligation unless the regulation is discriminatory, oppressive or predatory.

§ 2–615. Excuse by Failure of Presupposed Conditions. Except so far as a seller may have assumed a greater obligation and subject to the preceding section on substituted performance:

    (a) Delay in delivery or non-delivery in whole or in part by a seller who complies with paragraphs (b) and (c) is not a breach of his duty under a contract for sale if performance as agreed has been made impracticable by the occurrence of a contingency the non-occurrence of which was a basic assumption on which the contract was made or by compliance in good faith with any applicable foreign or domestic governmental regulation or order whether or not it later proves to be invalid.

    (b) Where the causes mentioned in paragraph (a) affect only a part of the seller's capacity to perform, he must allocate production and deliveries among his customers but may at his option include regular customers not then under contract as well as his own requirements for further manufacture. He may so allocate in any manner which is fair and reasonable.

    (c) The seller must notify the buyer seasonably that there will be delay or non-delivery and, when allocation is required under paragraph (b), of the estimated quota thus made available for the buyer.

§ 2–616. Procedure on Notice Claiming Excuse.

(1) Where the buyer receives notification of a material or indefinite delay or an allocation justified under the preceding section he may by written notification to the seller as to any delivery concerned, and where the prospective deficiency substantially impairs the value of the whole contract under the provisions of this Article relating to breach of installment contracts (Section 2–612), then also as to the whole,

    (a) terminate and thereby discharge any unexecuted portion of the contract; or

    (b) modify the contract by agreeing to take his available quota in substitution.

(2) If after receipt of such notification from the seller the buyer fails so to modify the contract within a reasonable time not exceeding thirty days the contract lapses with respect to any deliveries affected.

(3) The provisions of this section may not be negated by agreement except in so far as the seller has assumed a greater obligation under the preceding section.

PART 7: REMEDIES

§ 2–701. Remedies for Breach of Collateral Contracts Not Impaired. Remedies for breach of any obligation or promise collateral or ancillary to a contract for sale are not impaired by the provisions of this Article.

§ 2–702. Seller's Remedies on Discovery of Buyer's Insolvency.

(1) Where the seller discovers the buyer to be insolvent he may refuse delivery except for cash including payment for all goods theretofore delivered under the contract, and stop delivery under this Article (Section 2–705).

(2) Where the seller discovers that the buyer has received goods on credit while insolvent he may reclaim the goods upon demand made within ten days after the receipt, but if misrepresentation of solvency has been made to the particular seller in writing within three months before delivery the ten day limitation does not apply. Except as provided in this subsection the seller may not base a right to reclaim goods on the buyer's fraudulent or innocent misrepresentation of solvency or of intent to pay.

(3) The seller's right to reclaim under subsection (2) is subject to the rights of a buyer in ordinary course or other good faith purchaser under this Article (Section 2–403). Successful reclamation of goods excludes all other remedies with respect to them.

As amended in 1966.

§ 2–703. Seller's Remedies in General. Where the buyer wrongfully rejects or revokes acceptance of goods or fails to make a payment due on or before delivery or repudiates with respect to a part or the whole, then with respect to any goods directly affected and, if the breach is of the whole contract (Section 2–612), then also with respect to the whole undelivered balance, the aggrieved seller may

    (a) withhold delivery of such goods;

    (b) stop delivery by any bailee as hereafter provided (Section 2–705);

    (c) proceed under the next section respecting goods still unidentified to the contract;

    (d) resell and recover damages as hereafter provided (Section 2–706);

    (e) recover damages for non-acceptance (Section 2–708) or in a proper case the price (Section 2–709);

    (f) cancel.

§ 2–704. Seller's Right to Identify Goods to the Contract Notwithstanding Breach or to Salvage Unfinished Goods.

(1) An aggrieved seller under the preceding section may

    (a) identify to the contract conforming goods not already identified if at the time he learned of the breach they are in his possession or control;

    (b) treat as the subject of resale goods which have demonstrably been intended for the particular contract even though those goods are unfinished.

(2) Where the goods are unfinished an aggrieved seller may in the exercise of reasonable commercial judgment for the purposes of avoiding loss and of effective realization either complete the manufacture and wholly identify the goods to the contract or cease manufacture and resell for scrap or salvage value or proceed in any other reasonable manner.

§ 2–705. Seller's Stoppage of Delivery in Transit or Otherwise.

(1) The seller may stop delivery of goods in the possession of a carrier or other bailee when he discovers the buyer to be insolvent (Section 2–702) and may stop delivery of carload, truckload, planeload or larger shipments of express or freight when the buyer repudiates or fails to make a payment due before delivery or if for any other reason the seller has a right to withhold or reclaim the goods.

(2) As against such buyer the seller may stop delivery until
 (a) receipt of the goods by the buyer; or
 (b) acknowledgment to the buyer by any bailee of the goods except a carrier that the bailee holds the goods for the buyer; or
 (c) such acknowledgment to the buyer by a carrier by reshipment or as warehouseman; or
 (d) negotiation to the buyer of any negotiable document of title covering the goods.
(3) (a) To stop delivery the seller must so notify as to enable the bailee by reasonable diligence to prevent delivery of the goods.
 (b) After such notification the bailee must hold and deliver the goods according to the directions of the seller but the seller is liable to the bailee for any ensuing charges or damages.
 (c) If a negotiable document of title has been issued for goods the bailee is not obliged to obey a notification to stop until surrender of the document.
 (d) A carrier who has issued a non-negotiable bill of lading is not obliged to obey a notification to stop received from a person other than the consignor.

§ 2–706. Seller's Resale Including Contract for Resale.

(1) Under the conditions stated in Section 2–703 on seller's remedies, the seller may resell the goods concerned or the undelivered balance thereof. Where the resale is made in good faith and in a commercially reasonable manner the seller may recover the difference between the resale price and the contract price together with any incidental damages allowed under the provisions of this Article (Section 2–710), but less expenses saved in consequence of the buyer's breach.
(2) Except as otherwise provided in subsection (3) or unless otherwise agreed resale may be at public or private sale including sale by way of one or more contracts to sell or of identification to an existing contract of the seller. Sale may be as a unit or in parcels and at any time and place and on any terms but every aspect of the sale including the method, manner, time, place and terms must be commercially reasonable. The resale must be reasonably identified as referring to the broken contract, but it is not necessary that the goods be in existence or that any or all of them have been identified to the contract before the breach.
(3) Where the resale is at private sale the seller must give the buyer reasonable notification of his intention to resell.
(4) Where the resale is at public sale
 (a) only identified goods can be sold except where there is a recognized market for a public sale of futures in goods of the kind; and
 (b) it must be made at a usual place or market for public sale if one is reasonably available and except in the case of goods which are perishable or threaten to decline in value speedily the seller must give the buyer reasonable notice of the time and place of the resale; and
 (c) if the goods are not to be within the view of those attending the sale the notification of sale must state the place where the goods are located and provide for their reasonable inspection by prospective bidders; and
 (d) the seller may buy.
(5) A purchaser who buys in good faith at a resale takes the goods free of any rights of the original buyer even though the seller fails to comply with one or more of the requirements of this section.
(6) The seller is not accountable to the buyer for any profit made on any resale. A person in the position of a seller (Section 2–707) or a buyer who has rightfully rejected or justifiably revoked acceptance must account for any excess over the amount of his security interest, as hereinafter defined (subsection (3) of Section 2–711).

§ 2–707. "Person in the Position of a Seller".

(1) A "person in the position of a seller" includes as against a principal an agent who has paid or become responsible for the price of goods on behalf of his principal or anyone who otherwise holds a security interest or other right in goods similar to that of a seller.

(2) A person in the position of a seller may as provided in this Article withhold or stop delivery (Section 2–705) and resell (Section 2–706) and recover incidental damages (Section 2–710).

§ 2–708. Seller's Damages for Non-acceptance or Repudiation.

(1) Subject to subsection (2) and to the provisions of this Article with respect to proof of market price (Section 2–723), the measure of damages for non-acceptance or repudiation by the buyer is the difference between the market price at the time and place for tender and the unpaid contract price together with any incidental damages provided in this Article (Section 2–710), but less expenses saved in consequence of the buyer's breach.

(2) If the measure of damages provided in subsection (1) is inadequate to put the seller in as good a position as performance would have done then the measure of damages is the profit (including reasonable overhead) which the seller would have made from full performance by the buyer, together with any incidental damages provided in this Article (Section 2–710), due allowance for costs reasonably incurred and due credit for payments or proceeds of resale.

§ 2–709. Action for the Price.

(1) When the buyer fails to pay the price as it becomes due the seller may recover, together with any incidental damages under the next section, the price
   (a) of goods accepted or of conforming goods lost or damaged within a commercially reasonable time after risk of their loss has passed to the buyer; and
   (b) of goods identified to the contract if the seller is unable after reasonable effort to resell them at a reasonable price or the circumstances reasonably indicate that such effort will be unavailing.

(2) Where the seller sues for the price he must hold for the buyer any goods which have been identified to the contract and are still in his control except that if resale becomes possible he may resell them at any time prior to the collection of the judgment. The net proceeds of any such resale must be credited to the buyer and payment of the judgment entitles him to any goods not resold.

(3) After the buyer has wrongfully rejected or revoked acceptance of the goods or has failed to make a payment due or has repudiated (Section 2–610), a seller who is held not entitled to the price under this section shall nevertheless be awarded damages for non-acceptance under the preceding section.

§ 2–710. Seller's Incidental Damages.
Incidental damages to an aggrieved seller include any commercially reasonable charges, expenses or commissions incurred in stopping delivery, in the transportation, care and custody of goods after the buyer's breach, in connection with return or resale of the goods or otherwise resulting from the breach.

§ 2–711. Buyer's Remedies in General; Buyer's Security Interest in Rejected Goods.

(1) Where the seller fails to make delivery or repudiates or the buyer rightfully rejects or justifiably revokes acceptance then with respect to any goods involved, and with respect to the whole if the breach goes to the whole contract (Section 2–612), the buyer may cancel and whether or not he has done so may in addition to recovering so much of the price as has been paid
   (a) "cover" and have damages under the next section as to all the goods affected whether or not they have been identified to the contract; or
   (b) recover damages for non-delivery as provided in this Article (Section 2–713).

(2) Where the seller fails to deliver or repudiates the buyer may also
   (a) if the goods have been identified recover them as provided in this Article (Section 2–502); or
   (b) in a proper case obtain specific performance or replevy the goods as provided in this Article (Section 2–716).

(3) On rightful rejection or justifiable revocation of acceptance a buyer has a security interest in goods in his possession or control for any payments made on their price and any expenses reasonably incurred in their inspection, receipt, transportation, care and custody and may hold such goods and resell them in like manner as an aggrieved seller (Section 2–706).

§ 2–712. "Cover"; Buyer's Procurement of Substitute Goods.

(1) After a breach within the preceding section the buyer may "cover" by making in good faith and without unreasonable delay any reasonable purchase of or contract to purchase goods in substitution for those due from the seller.

(2) The buyer may recover from the seller as damages the difference between the cost of cover and the contract price together with any incidental or consequential damages as hereinafter defined (Section 2–715), but less expenses saved in consequence of the seller's breach.

(3) Failure of the buyer to effect cover within this section does not bar him from any other remedy.

§ 2–713. Buyer's Damages for Non-delivery or Repudiation.

(1) Subject to the provisions of this Article with respect to proof of market price (Section 2–723), the measure of damages for non-delivery or repudiation by the seller is the difference between the market price at the time when the buyer learned of the breach and the contract price together with any incidental and consequential damages provided in this Article (Section 2–715), but less expenses saved in consequence of the seller's breach.

(2) Market price is to be determined as of the place for tender or, in cases of rejection after arrival or revocation of acceptance, as of the place of arrival.

§ 2–714. Buyer's Damages for Breach in Regard to Accepted Goods.

(1) Where the buyer has accepted goods and given notification (subsection (3) of Section 2–607) he may recover as damages for any non-conformity of tender the loss resulting in the ordinary course of events from the seller's breach as determined in any manner which is reasonable.

(2) The measure of damages for breach of warranty is the difference at the time and place of acceptance between the value of the goods accepted and the value they would have had if they had been as warranted, unless special circumstances show proximate damages of a different amount.

(3) In a proper case any incidental and consequential damages under the next section may also be recovered.

§ 2–715. Buyer's Incidental and Consequential Damages.

(1) Incidental damages resulting from the seller's breach include expenses reasonably incurred in inspection, receipt, transportation and care and custody of goods rightfully rejected, any commercially reasonable charges, expenses or commissions in connection with effecting cover and any other reasonable expense incident to the delay or other breach.

(2) Consequential damages resulting from the seller's breach include

    (a) any loss resulting from general or particular requirements and needs of which the seller at the time of contracting had reason to know and which could not reasonably be prevented by cover or otherwise; and

    (b) injury to person or property proximately resulting from any breach of warranty.

§ 2–716. Buyer's Right to Specific Performance or Replevin.

(1) Specific performance may be decreed where the goods are unique or in other proper circumstances.

(2) The decree for specific performance may include such terms and conditions as to payment of the price, damages, or other relief as the court may deem just.

(3) The buyer has a right of replevin for goods identified to the contract if after reasonable effort he is unable to effect cover for such goods or the circumstances reasonably indicate that such effort will be unavailing or if the goods have been shipped under reservation and satisfaction of the security interest in them has been made or tendered.

§ 2–717. Deduction of Damages from the Price. The buyer on notifying the seller of his intention to do so may deduct all or any part of the damages resulting from any breach of the contract from any part of the price still due under the same contract.

§ 2–718. Liquidation or Limitation of Damages; Deposits.

(1) Damages for breach by either party may be liquidated in the agreement but only at an amount which is reasonable in the light of the anticipated or actual harm caused by the breach, the difficulties of proof of loss, and the inconvenience or nonfeasibility of otherwise obtaining an adequate remedy. A term fixing unreasonably large liquidated damages is void as a penalty.

(2) Where the seller justifiably withholds delivery of goods because of the buyer's breach, the buyer is entitled to restitution of any amount by which the sum of his payments exceeds
  (a) the amount to which the seller is entitled by virtue of terms liquidating the seller's damages in accordance with subsection (1), or
  (b) in the absence of such terms, twenty percent of the value of the total performance for which the buyer is obligated under the contract or $500, whichever is smaller.

(3) The buyer's right to restitution under subsection (2) is subject to offset to the extent that the seller establishes
  (a) a right to recover damages under the provisions of this Article other than subsection (1), and
  (b) the amount or value of any benefits received by the buyer directly or indirectly by reason of the contract.

(4) Where a seller has received payment in goods their reasonable value or the proceeds of their resale shall be treated as payments for the purposes of subsection (2); but if the seller has notice of the buyer's breach before reselling goods received in part performance, his resale is subject to the conditions laid down in this Article on resale by an aggrieved seller (Section 2–706).

§ 2–719. Contractual Modification or Limitation of Remedy.

(1) Subject to the provisions of subsections (2) and (3) of this section and of the preceding section on liquidation and limitation of damages,
  (a) the agreement may provide for remedies in addition to or in substitution for those provided in this Article and may limit or alter the measure of damages recoverable under this Article, as by limiting the buyer's remedies to return of the goods and repayment of the price or to repair and replacement of non-conforming goods or parts; and
  (b) resort to a remedy as provided is optional unless the remedy is expressly agreed to be exclusive, in which case it is the sole remedy.

(2) Where circumstances cause an exclusive or limited remedy to fail of its essential purpose, remedy may be had as provided in this Act.

(3) Consequential damages may be limited or excluded unless the limitation or exclusion is unconscionable. Limitation of consequential damages for injury to the person in the case of consumer goods is prima facie unconscionable but limitation of damages where the loss is commercial is not.

§ 2–720. Effect of "Cancellation" or "Rescission" on Claims for Antecedent Breach. Unless the contrary intention clearly appears, expressions of "cancellation" or "rescission" of the contract or the like shall not be construed as a renunciation or discharge of any claim in damages for an antecedent breach.

§ 2–721. Remedies for Fraud. Remedies for material misrepresentation or fraud include all remedies available under this Article for non-fraudulent breach. Neither rescission or a claim for rescission of the contract for sale nor rejection or return of the goods shall bar or be deemed inconsistent with a claim for damages or other remedy.

§ 2–722. Who Can Sue Third Parties for Injury to Goods. Where a third party so deals with goods which have been identified to a contract for sale as to cause actionable injury to a party to that contract

 (a) a right of action against the third party is in either party to the contract for sale who has title to or a security interest or a special property or an insurable interest in the goods; and if the goods have been destroyed or converted a right of action is also in the party who either bore the risk of loss under the contract for sale or has since the injury assumed that risk as against the other;

 (b) if at the time of the injury the party plaintiff did not bear the risk of loss as against the other party to the contract for sale and there is no arrangement between them for disposition of the recovery, his suit or settlement is, subject to his own interest, as a fiduciary for the other party to the contract;

 (c) either party may with the consent of the other sue for the benefit of whom it may concern.

§ 2–723. Proof of Market Price: Time and Place.

(1) If an action based on anticipatory repudiation comes to trial before the time for performance with respect to some or all of the goods, any damages based on market price (Section 2–708 or Section 2–713) shall be determined according to the price of such goods prevailing at the time when the aggrieved party learned of the repudiation.

(2) If evidence of a price prevailing at the times or places described in this Article is not readily available the price prevailing within any reasonable time before or after the time described or at any other place which in commercial judgment or under usage of trade would serve as a reasonable substitute for the one described may be used, making any proper allowance for the cost of transporting the goods to or from such other place.

(3) Evidence of a relevant price prevailing at a time or place other than the one described in this Article offered by one party is not admissible unless and until he has given the other party such notice as the court finds sufficient to prevent unfair surprise.

§ 2–724. Admissibility of Market Quotations. Whenever the prevailing price or value of any goods regularly bought and sold in any established commodity market is in issue, reports in official publications or trade journals or in newspapers or periodicals of general circulation published as the reports of such market shall be admissible in evidence. The circumstances of the preparation of such a report may be shown to affect its weight but not its admissibility.

§ 2–725. Statute of Limitations in Contracts for Sale.

(1) An action for breach of any contract for sale must be commenced within four years after the cause of action has accrued. By the original agreement the parties may reduce the period of limitation to not less than one year but may not extend it.

(2) A cause of action accrues when the breach occurs, regardless of the aggrieved party's lack of knowledge of the breach. A breach of warranty occurs when tender of delivery is made, except that where a warranty explicitly extends to future performance of the goods and discovery of the breach must await the time of such performance the cause of action accrues when the breach is or should have been discovered.

(3) Where an action commenced within the time limited by subsection (1) is so terminated as to leave available a remedy by another action for the same breach such other action may be commenced after the expiration of the time limited and within six months after the termination of the first action unless the termination resulted from voluntary discontinuance or from dismissal for failure or neglect to prosecute.

(4) This section does not alter the law on tolling of the statute of limitations nor does it apply to causes of action which have accrued before this Act becomes effective.

Article 2A—Leases

PART 1: GENERAL PROVISIONS

§ 2A–101. Short Title. This Article shall be known and may be cited as the Uniform Commercial Code—Leases.

See Appendix VI [following Amendment 24 therein] for material relating to changes in the Official Comment to conform to the 1990 amendments to various sections of Article 2A.

§ 2A–102. Scope. This Article applies to any transaction, regardless of form, that creates a lease.

§ 2A–103. Definitions and Index of Definitions.

(1) In this Article unless the context otherwise requires:
  (a) "Buyer in ordinary course of business" means a person who in good faith and without knowledge that the sale to him [or her] is in violation of the ownership rights or security interest or leasehold interest of a third party in the goods buys in ordinary course from a person in the business of selling goods of that kind but does not include a pawnbroker. "Buying" may be for cash or by exchange of other property or on secured or unsecured credit and includes receiving goods or documents of title under a preexisting contract for sale but does not include a transfer in bulk or as security for or in total or partial satisfaction of a money debt.
  (b) "Cancellation" occurs when either party puts an end to the lease contract for default by the other party.
  (c) "Commercial unit" means such a unit of goods as by commercial usage is a single whole for purposes of lease and division of which materially impairs its character or value on the market or in use. A commercial unit may be a single article, as a machine, or a set of articles, as a suite of furniture or a line of machinery, or a quantity, as a gross or carload, or any other unit treated in use or in the relevant market as a single whole.
  (d) "Conforming" goods or performance under a lease contract means goods or performance that are in accordance with the obligations under the lease contract.
  (e) "Consumer lease" means a lease that a lessor regularly engaged in the business of leasing or selling makes to a lessee who is an individual and who takes under the lease primarily for a personal, family, or household purpose [, if the total payments to be made under the lease contract, excluding payments for options to renew or buy, do not exceed $_____].
  (f) "Fault" means wrongful act, omission, breach, or default.
  (g) "Finance lease" means a lease with respect to which:
    (i) the lessor does not select, manufacture, or supply the goods;
    (ii) the lessor acquires the goods or the right to possession and use of the goods in connection with the lease; and

(iii) one of the following occurs:

    (A) the lessee receives a copy of the contract by which the lessor acquired the goods or the right to possession and use of the goods before signing the lease contract;

    (B) the lessee's approval of the contract by which the lessor acquired the goods or the right to possession and use of the goods is a condition to effectiveness of the lease contract;

    (C) the lessee, before signing the lease contract, receives an accurate and complete statement designating the promises and warranties, and any disclaimers of warranties, limitations or modifications of remedies, or liquidated damages, including those of a third party, such as the manufacturer of the goods, provided to the lessor by the person supplying the goods in connection with or as part of the contract by which the lessor acquired the goods or the right to possession and use of the goods; or

    (D) if the lease is not a consumer lease, the lessor, before the lessee signs the lease contract, informs the lessee in writing (a) of the identity of the person supplying the goods to the lessor, unless the lessee has selected that person and directed the lessor to acquire the goods or the right to possession and use of the goods from that person, (b) that the lessee is entitled under this Article to the promises and warranties, including those of any third party, provided to the lessor by the person supplying the goods in connection with or as part of the contract by which the lessor acquired the goods or the right to possession and use of the goods, and (c) that the lessee may communicate with the person supplying the goods to the lessor and receive an accurate and complete statement of those promises and warranties, including any disclaimers and limitations of them or of remedies.

(h) "Goods" means all things that are movable at the time of identification to the lease contract, or are fixtures (Section 2A–309), but the term does not include money, documents, instruments, accounts, chattel paper, general intangibles, or minerals or the like, including oil and gas, before extraction. The term also includes the unborn young of animals.

(i) "Installment lease contract" means a lease contract that authorizes or requires the delivery of goods in separate lots to be separately accepted, even though the lease contract contains a clause "each delivery is a separate lease" or its equivalent.

(j) "Lease" means a transfer of the right to possession and use of goods for a term in return for consideration, but a sale, including a sale on approval or a sale or return, or retention or creation of a security interest is not a lease. Unless the context clearly indicates otherwise, the term includes a sublease.

(k) "Lease agreement" means the bargain, with respect to the lease, of the lessor and the lessee in fact as found in their language or by implication from other circumstances including course of dealing or usage of trade or course of performance as provided in this Article. Unless the context clearly indicates otherwise, the term includes a sublease agreement.

(l) "Lease contract" means the total legal obligation that results from the lease agreement as affected by this Article and any other applicable rules of law. Unless the context clearly indicates otherwise, the term includes a sublease contract.

(m) "Leasehold interest" means the interest of the lessor or the lessee under a lease contract.

(n) "Lessee" means a person who acquires the right to possession and use of goods under a lease. Unless the context clearly indicates otherwise, the term includes a sublessee.

(o) "Lessee in ordinary course of business" means a person who in good faith and without knowledge that the lease to him [or her] is in violation of the ownership rights or security interest or leasehold interest of a third party in the goods, leases in ordinary course from a person in the business of selling or leasing goods of that kind but does not include a pawnbroker. "Leasing" may be for cash or by exchange of other property or on secured or unsecured credit and includes receiving goods or documents of title under a preexisting lease contract but does not include a transfer in bulk or as security for or in total or partial satisfaction of a money debt.

(p) "Lessor" means a person who transfers the right to possession and use of goods under a lease. Unless the context clearly indicates otherwise, the term includes a sublessor.

(q) "Lessor's residual interest" means the lessor's interest in the goods after expiration, termination, or cancellation of the lease contract.

(r) "Lien" means a charge against or interest in goods to secure payment of a debt or performance of an obligation, but the term does not include a security interest.

(s) "Lot" means a parcel or a single article that is the subject matter of a separate lease or delivery, whether or not it is sufficient to perform the lease contract.

(t) "Merchant lessee" means a lessee that is a merchant with respect to goods of the kind subject to the lease.

(u) "Present value" means the amount as of a date certain of one or more sums payable in the future, discounted to the date certain. The discount is determined by the interest rate specified by the parties if the rate was not manifestly unreasonable at the time the transaction was entered into; otherwise, the discount is determined by a commercially reasonable rate that takes into account the facts and circumstances of each case at the time the transaction was entered into.

(v) "Purchase" includes taking by sale, lease, mortgage, security interest, pledge, gift, or any other voluntary transaction creating an interest in goods.

(w) "Sublease" means a lease of goods the right to possession and use of which was acquired by the lessor as a lessee under an existing lease.

(x) "Supplier" means a person from whom a lessor buys or leases goods to be leased under a finance lease.

(y) "Supply contract" means a contract under which a lessor buys or leases goods to be leased.

(z) "Termination" occurs when either party pursuant to a power created by agreement or law puts an end to the lease contract otherwise than for default.

(2) Other definitions applying to this Article and the sections in which they appear are:

"Accessions"	Section 2A–310(1).
"Construction mortgage"	Section 2A–309(1) (d).
"Encumbrance"	Section 2A–309(1) (e).
"Fixtures"	Section 2A–309(1) (a).
"Fixture filing"	Section 2A–309(1) (b).
"Purchase money lease"	Section 2A–309(1) (c).

(3) The following definitions in other Articles apply to this Article:

"Account"	Section 9–106.
"Between merchants"	Section 2–104(3).
"Buyer"	Section 2–103(1) (a).
"Chattel paper"	Section 9–105(1) (b).
"Consumer goods"	Section 9–109(1).
"Document"	Section 9–105(1) (f).
"Entrusting"	Section 2–403(3).
"General intangibles"	Section 9–106.
"Good faith"	Section 2–103(1) (b).
"Instrument"	Section 9–105(1) (i).
"Merchant"	Section 2–104(1).
"Mortgage"	Section 9–105(1) (j).

"Pursuant to commitment"	Section 9–105(1) (k).
"Receipt"	Section 2–103(1) (c).
"Sale"	Section 2–106(1).
"Sale on approval"	Section 2–326.
"Sale or return"	Section 2–326.
"Seller"	Section 2–103(1) (d).

(4) In addition Article 1 contains general definitions and principles of construction and interpretation applicable throughout this Article.

As amended in 1990.

§ 2A–104. Leases Subject to Other Law.

(1) A lease, although subject to this Article, is also subject to any applicable:
   (a) certificate of title statute of this State: (list any certificate of title statutes covering automobiles, trailers, mobile homes, boats, farm tractors, and the like);
   (b) certificate of title statute of another jurisdiction (Section 2A–105); or
   (c) consumer protection statute of this State, or final consumer protection decision of a court of this State existing on the effective date of this Article.
(2) In case of conflict between this Article, other than Sections 2A–105, 2A–304(3), and 2A–305(3), and a statute or decision referred to in subsection (1), the statute or decision controls.
(3) Failure to comply with an applicable law has only the effect specified therein.

As amended in 1990.

§ 2A–105. Territorial Application of Article to Goods Covered by Certificate of Title.
Subject to the provisions of Sections 2A–304(3) and 2A–305(3), with respect to goods covered by a certificate of title issued under a statute of this State or of another jurisdiction, compliance and the effect of compliance or noncompliance with a certificate of title statute are governed by the law (including the conflict of laws rules) of the jurisdiction issuing the certificate until the earlier of (a) surrender of the certificate, or (b) four months after the goods are removed from that jurisdiction and thereafter until a new certificate of title is issued by another jurisdiction.

§ 2A–106. Limitation on Power of Parties to Consumer Lease to Choose Applicable Law and Judicial Forum.

(1) If the law chosen by the parties to a consumer lease is that of a jurisdiction other than a jurisdiction in which the lessee resides at the time the lease agreement becomes enforceable or within 30 days thereafter or in which the goods are to be used, the choice is not enforceable.
(2) If the judicial forum chosen by the parties to a consumer lease is a forum that would not otherwise have jurisdiction over the lessee, the choice is not enforceable.

§ 2A–107. Waiver or Renunciation of Claim or Right After Default.
Any claim or right arising out of an alleged default or breach of warranty may be discharged in whole or in part without consideration by a written waiver or renunciation signed and delivered by the aggrieved party.

§ 2A–108. Unconscionability.

(1) If the court as a matter of law finds a lease contract or any clause of a lease contract to have been unconscionable at the time it was made the court may refuse to enforce the lease contract, or it may enforce the remainder of the lease contract without the unconscionable

clause, or it may so limit the application of any unconscionable clause as to avoid any unconscionable result.

(2) With respect to a consumer lease, if the court as a matter of law finds that a lease contract or any clause of a lease contract has been induced by unconscionable conduct or that unconscionable conduct has occurred in the collection of a claim arising from a lease contract, the court may grant appropriate relief.

(3) Before making a finding of unconscionability under subsection (1) or (2), the court, on its own motion or that of a party, shall afford the parties a reasonable opportunity to present evidence as to the setting, purpose, and effect of the lease contract or clause thereof, or of the conduct.

(4) In an action in which the lessee claims unconscionability with respect to a consumer lease:

    (a) If the court finds unconscionability under subsection (1) or (2), the court shall award reasonable attorney's fees to the lessee.

    (b) If the court does not find unconscionability and the lessee claiming unconscionability has brought or maintained an action he [or she] knew to be groundless, the court shall award reasonable attorney's fees to the party against whom the claim is made.

    (c) In determining attorney's fees, the amount of the recovery on behalf of the claimant under subsections (1) and (2) is not controlling.

§ 2A–109. Option to Accelerate at Will.

(1) A term providing that one party or his [or her] successor in interest may accelerate payment or performance or require collateral or additional collateral "at will" or "when he [or she] deems himself [or herself] insecure" or in words of similar import must be construed to mean that he [or she] has power to do so only if he [or she] in good faith believes that the prospect of payment or performance is impaired.

(2) With respect to a consumer lease, the burden of establishing good faith under subsection (1) is on the party who exercised the power; otherwise the burden of establishing lack of good faith is on the party against whom the power has been exercised.

PART 2: FORMATION AND CONSTRUCTION OF LEASE CONTRACT

§ 2A–201. Statute of Frauds.

(1) A lease contract is not enforceable by way of action or defense unless:

    (a) the total payments to be made under the lease contract, excluding payments for options to renew or buy, are less than $1,000; or

    (b) there is a writing, signed by the party against whom enforcement is sought or by that party's authorized agent, sufficient to indicate that a lease contract has been made between the parties and to describe the goods leased and the lease term.

(2) Any description of leased goods or of the lease term is sufficient and satisfies subsection (1) (b), whether or not it is specific, if it reasonably identifies what is described.

(3) A writing is not insufficient because it omits or incorrectly states a term agreed upon, but the lease contract is not enforceable under subsection (1) (b) beyond the lease term and the quantity of goods shown in the writing.

(4) A lease contract that does not satisfy the requirements of subsection (1), but which is valid in other respects, is enforceable:

    (a) if the goods are to be specially manufactured or obtained for the lessee and are not suitable for lease or sale to others in the ordinary course of the lessor's business, and the lessor, before notice of repudiation is received and under circumstances that reasonably indicate that the goods are for the lessee, has made either a substantial beginning of their manufacture or commitments for their procurement;

    (b) if the party against whom enforcement is sought admits in that party's pleading, testimony or otherwise in court that a lease contract was made, but the lease contract is not enforceable under this provision beyond the quantity of goods admitted; or

    (c) with respect to goods that have been received and accepted by the lessee.

(5) The lease term under a lease contract referred to in subsection (4) is:
- (a) if there is a writing signed by the party against whom enforcement is sought or by that party's authorized agent specifying the lease term, the term so specified;
- (b) if the party against whom enforcement is sought admits in that party's pleading, testimony, or otherwise in court a lease term, the term so admitted; or
- (c) a reasonable lease term.

§ 2A–202. Final Written Expression: Parol or Extrinsic Evidence.

Terms with respect to which the confirmatory memoranda of the parties agree or which are otherwise set forth in a writing intended by the parties as a final expression of their agreement with respect to such terms as are included therein may not be contradicted by evidence of any prior agreement or of a contemporaneous oral agreement but may be explained or supplemented:

- (a) by course of dealing or usage of trade or by course of performance; and
- (b) by evidence of consistent additional terms unless the court finds the writing to have been intended also as a complete and exclusive statement of the terms of the agreement.

§ 2A–203. Seals Inoperative.

The affixing of a seal to a writing evidencing a lease contract or an offer to enter into a lease contract does not render the writing a sealed instrument and the law with respect to sealed instruments does not apply to the lease contract or offer.

§ 2A–204. Formation in General.

(1) A lease contract may be made in any manner sufficient to show agreement, including conduct by both parties which recognizes the existence of a lease contract.

(2) An agreement sufficient to constitute a lease contract may be found although the moment of its making is undetermined.

(3) Although one or more terms are left open, a lease contract does not fail for indefiniteness if the parties have intended to make a lease contract and there is a reasonably certain basis for giving an appropriate remedy.

§ 2A–205. Firm Offers.

An offer by a merchant to lease goods to or from another person in a signed writing that by its terms gives assurance it will be held open is not revocable, for lack of consideration, during the time stated or, if no time is stated, for a reasonable time, but in no event may the period of irrevocability exceed 3 months. Any such term of assurance on a form supplied by the offeree must be separately signed by the offeror.

§ 2A–206. Offer and Acceptance in Formation of Lease Contract.

(1) Unless otherwise unambiguously indicated by the language or circumstances, an offer to make a lease contract must be construed as inviting acceptance in any manner and by any medium reasonable in the circumstances.

(2) If the beginning of a requested performance is a reasonable mode of acceptance, an offeror who is not notified of acceptance within a reasonable time may treat the offer as having lapsed before acceptance.

§ 2A–207. Course of Performance or Practical Construction.

(1) If a lease contract involves repeated occasions for performance by either party with knowledge of the nature of the performance and opportunity for objection to it by the other, any course of performance accepted or acquiesced in without objection is relevant to determine the meaning of the lease agreement.

(2) The express terms of a lease agreement and any course of performance, as well as any course of dealing and usage of trade, must be construed whenever reasonable as consistent with each other; but if that construction is unreasonable, express terms control course of performance, course of performance controls both course of dealing and usage of trade, and course of dealing controls usage of trade.

(3) Subject to the provisions of Section 2A–208 on modification and waiver, course of performance is relevant to show a waiver or modification of any term inconsistent with the course of performance.

§ 2A–208. Modification, Rescission and Waiver.

(1) An agreement modifying a lease contract needs no consideration to be binding.

(2) A signed lease agreement that excludes modification or rescission except by a signed writing may not be otherwise modified or rescinded, but, except as between merchants, such a requirement on a form supplied by a merchant must be separately signed by the other party.

(3) Although an attempt at modification or rescission does not satisfy the requirements of subsection (2), it may operate as a waiver.

(4) A party who has made a waiver affecting an executory portion of a lease contract may retract the waiver by reasonable notification received by the other party that strict performance will be required of any term waived, unless the retraction would be unjust in view of a material change of position in reliance on the waiver.

§ 2A–209. Lessee Under Finance Lease as Beneficiary of Supply Contract.

(1) The benefit of a supplier's promises to the lessor under the supply contract and of all warranties, whether express or implied, including those of any third party provided in connection with or as part of the supply contract, extends to the lessee to the extent of the lessee's leasehold interest under a finance lease related to the supply contract, but is subject to the terms of the warranty and of the supply contract and all defenses or claims arising therefrom.

(2) The extension of the benefit of a supplier's promises and of warranties to the lessee (Section 2A–209(1)) does not: (i) modify the rights and obligations of the parties to the supply contract, whether arising therefrom or otherwise, or (ii) impose any duty or liability under the supply contract on the lessee.

(3) Any modification or rescission of the supply contract by the supplier and the lessor is effective between the supplier and the lessee unless, before the modification or rescission, the supplier has received notice that the lessee has entered into a finance lease related to the supply contract. If the modification or rescission is effective between the supplier and the lessee, the lessor is deemed to have assumed, in addition to the obligations of the lessor to the lessee under the lease contract, promises of the supplier to the lessor and warranties that were so modified or rescinded as they existed and were available to the lessee before modification or rescission.

(4) In addition to the extension of the benefit of the supplier's promises and of warranties to the lessee under subsection (1), the lessee retains all rights that the lessee may have against the supplier which arise from an agreement between the lessee and the supplier or under other law.

As amended in 1990.

§ 2A–210. Express Warranties.

(1) Express warranties by the lessor are created as follows:
   (a) Any affirmation of fact or promise made by the lessor to the lessee which relates to the goods and becomes part of the basis of the bargain creates an express warranty that the goods will conform to the affirmation or promise.
   (b) Any description of the goods which is made part of the basis of the bargain creates an express warranty that the goods will conform to the description.
   (c) Any sample or model that is made part of the basis of the bargain creates an express warranty that the whole of the goods will conform to the sample or model.

(2) It is not necessary to the creation of an express warranty that the lessor use formal words, such as "warrant" or "guarantee," or that the lessor have a specific intention to make a warranty, but an affirmation merely of the value of the goods or a statement purporting to be merely the lessor's opinion or commendation of the goods does not create a warranty.

§ 2A–211. Warranties Against Interference and Against Infringement; Lessee's Obligation Against Infringement.

(1) There is in a lease contract a warranty that for the lease term no person holds a claim to or interest in the goods that arose from an act or omission of the lessor, other than a claim by way of infringement or the like, which will interfere with the lessee's enjoyment of its leasehold interest.

(2) Except in a finance lease there is in a lease contract by a lessor who is a merchant regularly dealing in goods of the kind a warranty that the goods are delivered free of the rightful claim of any person by way of infringement or the like.

(3) A lessee who furnishes specifications to a lessor or a supplier shall hold the lessor and the supplier harmless against any claim by way of infringement or the like that arises out of compliance with the specifications.

§ 2A–212. Implied Warranty of Merchantability.

(1) Except in a finance lease, a warranty that the goods will be merchantable is implied in a lease contract if the lessor is a merchant with respect to goods of that kind.

(2) Goods to be merchantable must be at least such as
   (a) pass without objection in the trade under the description in the lease agreement;
   (b) in the case of fungible goods, are of fair average quality within the description;
   (c) are fit for the ordinary purposes for which goods of that type are used;
   (d) run, within the variation permitted by the lease agreement, of even kind, quality, and quantity within each unit and among all units involved;
   (e) are adequately contained, packaged, and labeled as the lease agreement may require; and
   (f) conform to any promises or affirmations of fact made on the container or label.

(3) Other implied warranties may arise from course of dealing or usage of trade.

§ 2A–213. Implied Warranty of Fitness for Particular Purpose.
Except in a finance lease, if the lessor at the time the lease contract is made has reason to know of any particular purpose for which the goods are required and that the lessee is relying on the lessor's skill or judgment to select or furnish suitable goods, there is in the lease contract an implied warranty that the goods will be fit for that purpose.

§ 2A–214. Exclusion or Modification of Warranties.

(1) Words or conduct relevant to the creation of an express warranty and words or conduct tending to negate or limit a warranty must be construed wherever reasonable as consistent with each other; but, subject to the provisions of Section 2A–202 on parol or extrinsic evidence, negation or limitation is inoperative to the extent that the construction is unreasonable.

(2) Subject to subsection (3), to exclude or modify the implied warranty of merchantability or any part of it the language must mention "merchantability", be by a writing, and be conspicuous. Subject to sub-section (3), to exclude or modify any implied warranty of fitness the exclusion must be by a writing and be conspicuous. Language to exclude all implied warranties of fitness is sufficient if it is in writing, is conspicuous and states, for example, "There is no warranty that the goods will be fit for a particular purpose".

(3) Notwithstanding subsection (2), but subject to subsection (4),
   (a) unless the circumstances indicate otherwise, all implied warranties are excluded by expressions like "as is," or "with all faults," or by other language that in common

understanding calls the lessee's attention to the exclusion of warranties and makes plain that there is no implied warranty, if in writing and conspicuous;

(b) if the lessee before entering into the lease contract has examined the goods or the sample or model as fully as desired or has refused to examine the goods, there is no implied warranty with regard to defects that an examination ought in the circumstances to have revealed; and

(c) an implied warranty may also be excluded or modified by course of dealing, course of performance, or usage of trade.

(4) To exclude or modify a warranty against interference or against infringement (Section 2A–211) or any part of it, the language must be specific, be by a writing, and be conspicuous, unless the circumstances, including course of performance, course of dealing, or usage of trade, give the lessee reason to know that the goods are being leased subject to a claim or interest of any person.

§ 2A–215. Cumulation and Conflict of Warranties Express or Implied.

Warranties, whether express or implied, must be construed as consistent with each other and as cumulative, but if that construction is unreasonable, the intention of the parties determines which warranty is dominant. In ascertaining that intention the following rules apply:

(a) Exact or technical specifications displace an inconsistent sample or model or general language of description.

(b) A sample from an existing bulk displaces inconsistent general language of description.

(c) Express warranties displace inconsistent implied warranties other than an implied warranty of fitness for a particular purpose.

§ 2A–216. Third Party Beneficiaries of Express and Implied Warranties.

Alternative A

A warranty to or for the benefit of a lessee under this Article, whether express or implied, extends to any natural person who is in the family or household of the lessee or who is a guest in the lessee's home if it is reasonable to expect that such person may use, consume, or be affected by the goods and who is injured in person by breach of the warranty. This section does not displace principles of law and equity that extend a warranty to or for the benefit of a lessee to other persons. The operation of this section may not be excluded, modified, or limited, but an exclusion, modification, or limitation of the warranty, including any with respect to rights and remedies, effective against the lessee is also effective against any beneficiary designated under this section.

Alternative B

A warranty to or for the benefit of a lessee under this Article, whether express or implied, extends to any natural person who may reasonably be expected to use, consume, or be affected by the goods and who is injured in person by breach of the warranty. This section does not displace principles of law and equity that extend a warranty to or for the benefit of a lessee to other persons. The operation of this section may not be excluded, modified, or limited, but an exclusion, modification, or limitation of the warranty, including any with respect to rights and remedies, effective against the lessee is also effective against the beneficiary designated under this section.

Alternative C

A warranty to or for the benefit of a lessee under this Article, whether express or implied, extends to any person who may reasonably be expected to use, consume, or be affected by the goods and who is injured by breach of the warranty. The operation of this section may not be excluded, modified, or limited with respect to injury to the person of an individual to whom the warranty extends, but an exclusion, modification, or limitation of the warranty, including any with respect to rights and remedies, effective against the lessee is also effective against the beneficiary designated under this section.

§ 2A–217. Identification. Identification of goods as goods to which a lease contract refers may be made at any time and in any manner explicitly agreed to by the parties. In the absence of explicit agreement, identification occurs:

(a) when the lease contract is made if the lease contract is for a lease of goods that are existing and identified;

(b) when the goods are shipped, marked, or otherwise designated by the lessor as goods to which the lease contract refers, if the lease contract is for a lease of goods that are not existing and identified; or

(c) when the young are conceived, if the lease contract is for a lease of unborn young of animals.

§ 2A–218. Insurance and Proceeds.

(1) A lessee obtains an insurable interest when existing goods are identified to the lease contract even though the goods identified are nonconforming and the lessee has an option to reject them.

(2) If a lessee has an insurable interest only by reason of the lessor's identification of the goods, the lessor, until default or insolvency or notification to the lessee that identification is final, may substitute other goods for those identified.

(3) Notwithstanding a lessee's insurable interest under subsections (1) and (2), the lessor retains an insurable interest until an option to buy has been exercised by the lessee and risk of loss has passed to the lessee.

(4) Nothing in this section impairs any insurable interest recognized under any other statute or rule of law.

(5) The parties by agreement may determine that one or more parties have an obligation to obtain and pay for insurance covering the goods and by agreement may determine the beneficiary of the proceeds of the insurance.

§ 2A–219. Risk of Loss.

(1) Except in the case of a finance lease, risk of loss is retained by the lessor and does not pass to the lessee. In the case of a finance lease, risk of loss passes to the lessee.

(2) Subject to the provisions of this Article on the effect of default on risk of loss (Section 2A–220), if risk of loss is to pass to the lessee and the time of passage is not stated, the following rules apply:

    (a) If the lease contract requires or authorizes the goods to be shipped by carrier

        (i) and it does not require delivery at a particular destination, the risk of loss passes to the lessee when the goods are duly delivered to the carrier; but

        (ii) if it does require delivery at a particular destination and the goods are there duly tendered while in the possession of the carrier, the risk of loss passes to the lessee when the goods are there duly so tendered as to enable the lessee to take delivery.

    (b) If the goods are held by a bailee to be delivered without being moved, the risk of loss passes to the lessee on acknowledgment by the bailee of the lessee's right to possession of the goods.

    (c) In any case not within subsection (a) or (b), the risk of loss passes to the lessee on the lessee's receipt of the goods if the lessor, or, in the case of a finance lease, the supplier, is a merchant; otherwise the risk passes to the lessee on tender of delivery.

§ 2A–220. Effect of Default on Risk of Loss.

(1) Where risk of loss is to pass to the lessee and the time of passage is not stated:

    (a) If a tender or delivery of goods so fails to conform to the lease contract as to give a right of rejection, the risk of their loss remains with the lessor, or, in the case of a finance lease, the supplier, until cure or acceptance.

(b) If the lessee rightfully revokes acceptance, he [or she], to the extent of any deficiency in his [or her] effective insurance coverage, may treat the risk of loss as having remained with the lessor from the beginning.

(2) Whether or not risk of loss is to pass to the lessee, if the lessee as to conforming goods already identified to a lease contract repudiates or is otherwise in default under the lease contract, the lessor, or, in the case of a finance lease, the supplier, to the extent of any deficiency in his [or her] effective insurance coverage may treat the risk of loss as resting on the lessee for a commercially reasonable time.

§ 2A–221. Casualty to Identified Goods.

If a lease contract requires goods identified when the lease contract is made, and the goods suffer casualty without fault of the lessee, the lessor or the supplier before delivery, or the goods suffer casualty before risk of loss passes to the lessee pursuant to the lease agreement or Section 2A–219, then:

(a) if the loss is total, the lease contract is avoided; and

(b) if the loss is partial or the goods have so deteriorated as to no longer conform to the lease contract, the lessee may nevertheless demand inspection and at his [or her] option either treat the lease contract as avoided or, except in a finance lease that is not a consumer lease, accept the goods with due allowance from the rent payable for the balance of the lease term for the deterioration or the deficiency in quantity but without further right against the lessor.

PART 3: EFFECT OF LEASE CONTRACT

§ 2A–301. Enforceability of Lease Contract.

Except as otherwise provided in this Article, a lease contract is effective and enforceable according to its terms between the parties, against purchasers of the goods and against creditors of the parties.

§ 2A–302. Title to and Possession of Goods.

Except as otherwise provided in this Article, each provision of this Article applies whether the lessor or a third party has title to the goods, and whether the lessor, the lessee, or a third party has possession of the goods, notwithstanding any statute or rule of law that possession or the absence of possession is fraudulent.

§ 2A–303. Alienability of Party's Interest Under Lease Contract or of Lessor's Residual Interest in Goods; Delegation of Performance; Transfer of Rights.

(1) As used in this section, "creation of a security interest" includes the sale of a lease contract that is subject to Article 9, Secured Transactions, by reason of Section 9–102(1) (b).

(2) Except as provided in subsections (3) and (4), a provision in a lease agreement which (i) prohibits the voluntary or involuntary transfer, including a transfer by sale, sublease, creation or enforcement of a security interest, or attachment, levy, or other judicial process, of an interest of a party under the lease contract or of the lessor's residual interest in the goods, or (ii) makes such a transfer an event of default, gives rise to the rights and remedies provided in subsection (5), but a transfer that is prohibited or is an event of default under the lease agreement is otherwise effective.

(3) A provision in a lease agreement which (i) prohibits the creation or enforcement of a security interest in an interest of a party under the lease contract or in the lessor's residual interest in the goods, or (ii) makes such a transfer an event of default, is not enforceable unless, and then only to the extent that, there is an actual transfer by the lessee of the lessee's right of possession or use of the goods in violation of the provision or an actual delegation of a material performance of either party to the lease contract in violation of the provision. Neither the granting nor the enforcement of a security interest in (i) the lessor's interest under the lease contract or (ii) the lessor's residual interest in the goods is a transfer that materially impairs the prospect of obtaining return performance by, materially changes the

duty of, or materially increases the burden or risk imposed on, the lessee within the purview of subsection (5) unless, and then only to the extent that, there is an actual delegation of a material performance of the lessor.

(4) A provision in a lease agreement which (i) prohibits a transfer of a right to damages for default with respect to the whole lease contract or of a right to payment arising out of the transferor's due performance of the transferor's entire obligation, or (ii) makes such a transfer an event of default, is not enforceable, and such a transfer is not a transfer that materially impairs the prospect of obtaining return performance by, materially changes the duty of, or materially increases the burden or risk imposed on, the other party to the lease contract within the purview of subsection (5).

(5) Subject to subsections (3) and (4):

   (a) if a transfer is made which is made an event of default under a lease agreement, the party to the lease contract not making the transfer, unless that party waives the default or otherwise agrees, has the rights and remedies described in Section 2A–501(2);

   (b) if paragraph (a) is not applicable and if a transfer is made that (i) is prohibited under a lease agreement or (ii) materially impairs the prospect of obtaining return performance by, materially changes the duty of, or materially increases the burden or risk imposed on, the other party to the lease contract, unless the party not making the transfer agrees at any time to the transfer in the lease contract or otherwise, then, except as limited by contract, (i) the transferor is liable to the party not making the transfer for damages caused by the transfer to the extent that the damages could not reasonably be prevented by the party not making the transfer and (ii) a court having jurisdiction may grant other appropriate relief, including cancellation of the lease contract or an injunction against the transfer.

(6) A transfer of "the lease" or of "all my rights under the lease", or a transfer in similar general terms, is a transfer of rights and, unless the language or the circumstances, as in a transfer for security, indicate the contrary, the transfer is a delegation of duties by the transferor to the transferee. Acceptance by the transferee constitutes a promise by the transferee to perform those duties. The promise is enforceable by either the transferor or the other party to the lease contract.

(7) Unless otherwise agreed by the lessor and the lessee, a delegation of performance does not relieve the transferor as against the other party of any duty to perform or of any liability for default.

(8) In a consumer lease, to prohibit the transfer of an interest of a party under the lease contract or to make a transfer an event of default, the language must be specific, by a writing, and conspicuous.

As amended in 1990.

§ 2A–304. Subsequent Lease of Goods by Lessor.

(1) Subject to Section 2A–303, a subsequent lessee from a lessor of goods under an existing lease contract obtains, to the extent of the leasehold interest transferred, the leasehold interest in the goods that the lessor had or had power to transfer, and except as provided in subsection (2) and Section 2A–527(4), takes subject to the existing lease contract. A lessor with voidable title has power to transfer a good leasehold interest to a good faith subsequent lessee for value, but only to the extent set forth in the preceding sentence. If goods have been delivered under a transaction of purchase, the lessor has that power even though:

   (a) the lessor's transferor was deceived as to the identity of the lessor;

   (b) the delivery was in exchange for a check which is later dishonored;

   (c) it was agreed that the transaction was to be a "cash sale"; or

   (d) the delivery was procured through fraud punishable as larcenous under the criminal law.

(2) A subsequent lessee in the ordinary course of business from a lessor who is a merchant dealing in goods of that kind to whom the goods were entrusted by the existing lessee of that lessor before the interest of the subsequent lessee became enforceable against that

lessor obtains, to the extent of the leasehold interest transferred, all of that lessor's and the existing lessee's rights to the goods, and takes free of the existing lease contract.

(3) A subsequent lessee from the lessor of goods that are subject to an existing lease contract and are covered by a certificate of title issued under a statute of this State or of another jurisdiction takes no greater rights than those provided both by this section and by the certificate of title statute.

As amended in 1990.

§ 2A–305. Sale or Sublease of Goods by Lessee.

(1) Subject to the provisions of Section 2A–303, a buyer or sublessee from the lessee of goods under an existing lease contract obtains, to the extent of the interest transferred, the leasehold interest in the goods that the lessee had or had power to transfer, and except as provided in subsection (2) and Section 2A–511(4), takes subject to the existing lease contract. A lessee with a voidable leasehold interest has power to transfer a good leasehold interest to a good faith buyer for value or a good faith sublessee for value, but only to the extent set forth in the preceding sentence. When goods have been delivered under a transaction of lease the lessee has that power even though:
   (a) the lessor was deceived as to the identity of the lessee;
   (b) the delivery was in exchange for a check which is later dishonored; or
   (c) the delivery was procured through fraud punishable as larcenous under the criminal law.
(2) A buyer in the ordinary course of business or a sublessee in the ordinary course of business from a lessee who is a merchant dealing in goods of that kind to whom the goods were entrusted by the lessor obtains, to the extent of the interest transferred, all of the lessor's and lessee's rights to the goods, and takes free of the existing lease contract.
(3) A buyer or sublessee from the lessee of goods that are subject to an existing lease contract and are covered by a certificate of title issued under a statute of this State or of another jurisdiction takes no greater rights than those provided both by this section and by the certificate of title statute.

§ 2A–306. Priority of Certain Liens Arising by Operation of Law. If a person in the ordinary course of his [or her] business furnishes services or materials with respect to goods subject to a lease contract, a lien upon those goods in the possession of that person given by statute or rule of law for those materials or services takes priority over any interest of the lessor or lessee under the lease contract or this Article unless the lien is created by statute and the statute provides otherwise or unless the lien is created by rule of law and the rule of law provides otherwise.

§ 2A–307. Priority of Liens Arising by Attachment or Levy on, Security Interests in, and Other Claims to Goods.

(1) Except as otherwise provided in Section 2A–306, a creditor of a lessee takes subject to the lease contract.
(2) Except as otherwise provided in subsections (3) and (4) and in Sections 2A–306 and 2A–308, a creditor of a lessor takes subject to the lease contract unless:
   (a) the creditor holds a lien that attached to the goods before the lease contract became enforceable;
   (b) the creditor holds a security interest in the goods and the lessee did not give value and receive delivery of the goods without knowledge of the security interest; or
   (c) the creditor holds a security interest in the goods which was perfected (Section 9–303) before the lease contract became enforceable.
(3) A lessee in the ordinary course of business takes the leasehold interest free of a security interest in the goods created by the lessor even though the security interest is perfected (Section 9–303) and the lessee knows of its existence.

(4) A lessee other than a lessee in the ordinary course of business takes the leasehold interest free of a security interest to the extent that it secures future advances made after the secured party acquires knowledge of the lease or more than 45 days after the lease contract becomes enforceable, whichever first occurs, unless the future advances are made pursuant to a commitment entered into without knowledge of the lease and before the expiration of the 45-day period.

As amended in 1990.

§ 2A–308. Special Rights of Creditors.

(1) A creditor of a lessor in possession of goods subject to a lease contract may treat the lease contract as void if as against the creditor retention of possession by the lessor is fraudulent under any statute or rule of law, but retention of possession in good faith and current course of trade by the lessor for a commercially reasonable time after the lease contract becomes enforceable is not fraudulent.

(2) Nothing in this Article impairs the rights of creditors of a lessor if the lease contract (a) becomes enforceable, not in current course of trade but in satisfaction of or as security for a preexisting claim for money, security, or the like, and (b) is made under circumstances which under any statute or rule of law apart from this Article would constitute the transaction a fraudulent transfer or voidable preference.

(3) A creditor of a seller may treat a sale or an identification of goods to a contract for sale as void if as against the creditor retention of possession by the seller is fraudulent under any statute or rule of law, but retention of possession of the goods pursuant to a lease contract entered into by the seller as lessee and the buyer as lessor in connection with the sale or identification of the goods is not fraudulent if the buyer bought for value and in good faith.

§ 2A–309. Lessor's and Lessee's Rights When Goods Become Fixtures.

(1) In this section:
   (a) goods are "fixtures" when they become so related to particular real estate that an interest in them arises under real estate law;
   (b) a "fixture filing" is the filing, in the office where a mortgage on the real estate would be filed or recorded, of a financing statement covering goods that are or are to become fixtures and conforming to the requirements of Section 9–402(5);
   (c) a lease is a "purchase money lease" unless the lessee has possession or use of the goods or the right to possession or use of the goods before the lease agreement is enforceable;
   (d) a mortgage is a "construction mortgage" to the extent it secures an obligation incurred for the construction of an improvement on land including the acquisition cost of the land, if the recorded writing so indicates; and
   (e) "encumbrance" includes real estate mortgages and other liens on real estate and all other rights in real estate that are not ownership interests.

(2) Under this Article a lease may be of goods that are fixtures or may continue in goods that become fixtures, but no lease exists under this Article of ordinary building materials incorporated into an improvement on land.

(3) This Article does not prevent creation of a lease of fixtures pursuant to real estate law.

(4) The perfected interest of a lessor of fixtures has priority over a conflicting interest of an encumbrancer or owner of the real estate if:
   (a) the lease is a purchase money lease, the conflicting interest of the encumbrancer or owner arises before the goods become fixtures, the interest of the lessor is perfected by a fixture filing before the goods become fixtures or within ten days thereafter, and the lessee has an interest of record in the real estate or is in possession of the real estate; or
   (b) the interest of the lessor is perfected by a fixture filing before the interest of the encumbrancer or owner is of record, the lessor's interest has priority over any conflicting interest of a predecessor in title of the encumbrancer or owner, and the lessee has an interest of record in the real estate or is in possession of the real estate.

(5) The interest of a lessor of fixtures, whether or not perfected, has priority over the conflicting interest of an encumbrancer or owner of the real estate if:
   (a) the fixtures are readily removable factory or office machines, readily removable equipment that is not primarily used or leased for use in the operation of the real estate, or readily removable replacements of domestic appliances that are goods subject to a consumer lease, and before the goods become fixtures the lease contract is enforceable; or
   (b) the conflicting interest is a lien on the real estate obtained by legal or equitable proceedings after the lease contract is enforceable; or
   (c) the encumbrancer or owner has consented in writing to the lease or has disclaimed an interest in the goods as fixtures; or
   (d) the lessee has a right to remove the goods as against the encumbrancer or owner. If the lessee's right to remove terminates, the priority of the interest of the lessor continues for a reasonable time.
(6) Notwithstanding subsection (4) (a) but otherwise subject to subsections (4) and (5), the interest of a lessor of fixtures, including the lessor's residual interest, is subordinate to the conflicting interest of an encumbrancer of the real estate under a construction mortgage recorded before the goods become fixtures if the goods become fixtures before the completion of the construction. To the extent given to refinance a construction mortgage, the conflicting interest of an encumbrancer of the real estate under a mortgage has this priority to the same extent as the encumbrancer of the real estate under the construction mortgage.
(7) In cases not within the preceding subsections, priority between the interest of a lessor of fixtures, including the lessor's residual interest, and the conflicting interest of an encumbrancer or owner of the real estate who is not the lessee is determined by the priority rules governing conflicting interests in real estate.
(8) If the interest of a lessor of fixtures, including the lessor's residual interest, has priority over all conflicting interests of all owners and encumbrancers of the real estate, the lessor or the lessee may (i) on default, expiration, termination, or cancellation of the lease agreement but subject to the agreement and this Article, or (ii) if necessary to enforce other rights and remedies of the lessor or lessee under this Article, remove the goods from the real estate, free and clear of all conflicting interests of all owners and encumbrancers of the real estate, but the lessor or lessee must reimburse any encumbrancer or owner of the real estate who is not the lessee and who has not otherwise agreed for the cost of repair of any physical injury, but not for any diminution in value of the real estate caused by the absence of the goods removed or by any necessity of replacing them. A person entitled to reimbursement may refuse permission to remove until the party seeking removal gives adequate security for the performance of this obligation.
(9) Even though the lease agreement does not create a security interest, the interest of a lessor of fixtures, including the lessor's residual interest, is perfected by filing a financing statement as a fixture filing for leased goods that are or are to become fixtures in accordance with the relevant provisions of the Article on Secured Transactions (Article 9).

As amended in 1990.

§ 2A–310. Lessor's and Lessee's Rights When Goods Become Accessions.

(1) Goods are "accessions" when they are installed in or affixed to other goods.
(2) The interest of a lessor or a lessee under a lease contract entered into before the goods became accessions is superior to all interests in the whole except as stated in subsection (4).
(3) The interest of a lessor or a lessee under a lease contract entered into at the time or after the goods became accessions is superior to all subsequently acquired interests in the whole except as stated in subsection (4) but is subordinate to interests in the whole existing at the time the lease contract was made unless the holders of such interests in the whole have in writing consented to the lease or disclaimed an interest in the goods as part of the whole.

(4) The interest of a lessor or a lessee under a lease contract described in subsection (2) or (3) is subordinate to the interest of

   (a) a buyer in the ordinary course of business or a lessee in the ordinary course of business of any interest in the whole acquired after the goods became accessions; or

   (b) a creditor with a security interest in the whole perfected before the lease contract was made to the extent that the creditor makes subsequent advances without knowledge of the lease contract.

(5) When under subsections (2) or (3) and (4) a lessor or a lessee of accessions holds an interest that is superior to all interests in the whole, the lessor or the lessee may (a) on default, expiration, termination, or cancellation of the lease contract by the other party but subject to the provisions of the lease contract and this Article, or (b) if necessary to enforce his [or her] other rights and remedies under this Article, remove the goods from the whole, free and clear of all interests in the whole, but he [or she] must reimburse any holder of an interest in the whole who is not the lessee and who has not otherwise agreed for the cost of repair of any physical injury but not for any diminution in value of the whole caused by the absence of the goods removed or by any necessity for replacing them. A person entitled to reimbursement may refuse permission to remove until the party seeking removal gives adequate security for the performance of this obligation.

§ 2A–311. Priority Subject to Subordination.   Nothing in this Article prevents subordination by agreement by any person entitled to priority.

As added in 1990.

PART 4: PERFORMANCE OF LEASE CONTRACT: REPUDIATED, SUBSTITUTED AND EXCUSED

§ 2A–401. Insecurity: Adequate Assurance of Performance.

(1) A lease contract imposes an obligation on each party that the other's expectation of receiving due performance will not be impaired.

(2) If reasonable grounds for insecurity arise with respect to the performance of either party, the insecure party may demand in writing adequate assurance of due performance. Until the insecure party receives that assurance, if commercially reasonable the insecure party may suspend any performance for which he [or she] has not already received the agreed return.

(3) A repudiation of the lease contract occurs if assurance of due performance adequate under the circumstances of the particular case is not provided to the insecure party within a reasonable time, not to exceed 30 days after receipt of a demand by the other party.

(4) Between merchants, the reasonableness of grounds for insecurity and the adequacy of any assurance offered must be determined according to commercial standards.

(5) Acceptance of any nonconforming delivery or payment does not prejudice the aggrieved party's right to demand adequate assurance of future performance.

§ 2A–402. Anticipatory Repudiation.   If either party repudiates a lease contract with respect to a performance not yet due under the lease contract, the loss of which performance will substantially impair the value of the lease contract to the other, the aggrieved party may:

   (a) for a commercially reasonable time, await retraction of repudiation and performance by the repudiating party;

   (b) make demand pursuant to Section 2A–401 and await assurance of future performance adequate under the circumstances of the particular case; or

   (c) resort to any right or remedy upon default under the lease contract or this Article, even though the aggrieved party has notified the repudiating party that the aggrieved party would await the repudiating party's performance and assurance and has urged retraction. In addition, whether or not the aggrieved party is pursuing one of the foregoing remedies, the aggrieved party may suspend performance or, if the aggrieved party is the lessor, proceed in accordance with the provisions of this Article on the lessor's right to identify goods to the lease contract notwithstanding default or to salvage unfinished goods (Section 2A–524).

§ 2A–403. Retraction of Anticipatory Repudiation.

(1) Until the repudiating party's next performance is due, the repudiating party can retract the repudiation unless, since the repudiation, the aggrieved party has cancelled the lease contract or materially changed the aggrieved party's position or otherwise indicated that the aggrieved party considers the repudiation final.

(2) Retraction may be by any method that clearly indicates to the aggrieved party that the repudiating party intends to perform under the lease contract and includes any assurance demanded under Section 2A–401.

(3) Retraction reinstates a repudiating party's rights under a lease contract with due excuse and allowance to the aggrieved party for any delay occasioned by the repudiation.

§ 2A–404. Substituted Performance.

(1) If without fault of the lessee, the lessor and the supplier, the agreed berthing, loading, or unloading facilities fail or the agreed type of carrier becomes unavailable or the agreed manner of delivery otherwise becomes commercially impracticable, but a commercially reasonable substitute is available, the substitute performance must be tendered and accepted.

(2) If the agreed means or manner of payment fails because of domestic or foreign governmental regulation:

(a) the lessor may withhold or stop delivery or cause the supplier to withhold or stop delivery unless the lessee provides a means or manner of payment that is commercially a substantial equivalent; and

(b) if delivery has already been taken, payment by the means or in the manner provided by the regulation discharges the lessee's obligation unless the regulation is discriminatory, oppressive, or predatory.

§ 2A–405. Excused Performance. Subject to Section 2A–404 on substituted performance, the following rules apply:

(a) Delay in delivery or nondelivery in whole or in part by a lessor or a supplier who complies with paragraphs (b) and (c) is not a default under the lease contract if performance as agreed has been made impracticable by the occurrence of a contingency the nonoccurrence of which was a basic assumption on which the lease contract was made or by compliance in good faith with any applicable foreign or domestic governmental regulation or order, whether or not the regulation or order later proves to be invalid.

(b) If the causes mentioned in paragraph (a) affect only part of the lessor's or the supplier's capacity to perform, he [or she] shall allocate production and deliveries among his [or her] customers but at his [or her] option may include regular customers not then under contract for sale or lease as well as his [or her] own requirements for further manufacture. He [or she] may so allocate in any manner that is fair and reasonable.

(c) The lessor seasonably shall notify the lessee and in the case of a finance lease the supplier seasonably shall notify the lessor and the lessee, if known, that there will be delay or nondelivery and, if allocation is required under paragraph (b), of the estimated quota thus made available for the lessee.

§ 2A–406. Procedure on Excused Performance.

(1) If the lessee receives notification of a material or indefinite delay or an allocation justified under Section 2A–405, the lessee may by written notification to the lessor as to any goods involved, and with respect to all of the goods if under an installment lease contract the value of the whole lease contract is substantially impaired (Section 2A–510):

    (a)   terminate the lease contract (Section 2A–505(2)); or

    (b)   except in a finance lease that is not a consumer lease, modify the lease contract by accepting the available quota in substitution, with due allowance from the rent payable for the balance of the lease term for the deficiency but without further right against the lessor.

(2) If, after receipt of a notification from the lessor under Section 2A–405, the lessee fails so to modify the lease agreement within a reasonable time not exceeding 30 days, the lease contract lapses with respect to any deliveries affected.

§ 2A–407. Irrevocable Promises: Finance Leases.

(1) In the case of a finance lease that is not a consumer lease the lessee's promises under the lease contract become irrevocable and independent upon the lessee's acceptance of the goods.

(2) A promise that has become irrevocable and independent under subsection (1):

    (a)   is effective and enforceable between the parties, and by or against third parties including assignees of the parties; and

    (b)   is not subject to cancellation, termination, modification, repudiation, excuse, or substitution without the consent of the party to whom the promise runs.

(3) This section does not affect the validity under any other law of a covenant in any lease contract making the lessee's promises irrevocable and independent upon the lessee's acceptance of the goods.

As amended in 1990.

PART 5: DEFAULT

§ 2A–501. Default: Procedure.

(1) Whether the lessor or the lessee is in default under a lease contract is determined by the lease agreement and this Article.

(2) If the lessor or the lessee is in default under the lease contract, the party seeking enforcement has rights and remedies as provided in this Article and, except as limited by this Article, as provided in the lease agreement.

(3) If the lessor or the lessee is in default under the lease contract, the party seeking enforcement may reduce the party's claim to judgment, or otherwise enforce the lease contract by self-help or any available judicial procedure or nonjudicial procedure, including administrative proceeding, arbitration, or the like, in accordance with this Article.

(4) Except as otherwise provided in Section 1–106(1) or this Article or the lease agreement, the rights and remedies referred to in subsections (2) and (3) are cumulative.

(5) If the lease agreement covers both real property and goods, the party seeking enforcement may proceed under this Part as to the goods, or under other applicable law as to both the real property and the goods in accordance with that party's rights and remedies in respect of the real property, in which case this Part does not apply.

As amended in 1990.

§ 2A–502. Notice After Default. Except as otherwise provided in this Article or the lease agreement, the lessor or lessee in default under the lease contract is not entitled to notice of default or notice of enforcement from the other party to the lease agreement.

§ 2A–503. Modification or Impairment of Rights and Remedies.

(1) Except as otherwise provided in this Article, the lease agreement may include rights and remedies for default in addition to or in substitution for those provided in this Article and may limit or alter the measure of damages recoverable under this Article.

(2) Resort to a remedy provided under this Article or in the lease agreement is optional unless the remedy is expressly agreed to be exclusive. If circumstances cause an exclusive or limited remedy to fail of its essential purpose, or provision for an exclusive remedy is unconscionable, remedy may be had as provided in this Article.

(3) Consequential damages may be liquidated under Section 2A–504, or may otherwise be limited, altered, or excluded unless the limitation, alteration, or exclusion is unconscionable. Limitation, alteration, or exclusion of consequential damages for injury to the person in the case of consumer goods is prima facie unconscionable but limitation, alteration, or exclusion of damages where the loss is commercial is not prima facie unconscionable.

(4) Rights and remedies on default by the lessor or the lessee with respect to any obligation or promise collateral or ancillary to the lease contract are not impaired by this Article.

As amended in 1990.

§ 2A–504. Liquidation of Damages.

(1) Damages payable by either party for default, or any other act or omission, including indemnity for loss or diminution of anticipated tax benefits or loss or damage to lessor's residual interest, may be liquidated in the lease agreement but only at an amount or by a formula that is reasonable in light of the then anticipated harm caused by the default or other act or omission.

(2) If the lease agreement provides for liquidation of damages, and such provision does not comply with subsection (1), or such provision is an exclusive or limited remedy that circumstances cause to fail of its essential purpose, remedy may be had as provided in this Article.

(3) If the lessor justifiably withholds or stops delivery of goods because of the lessee's default or insolvency (Section 2A–525 or 2A–526), the lessee is entitled to restitution of any amount by which the sum of his [or her] payments exceeds:
   (a) the amount to which the lessor is entitled by virtue of terms liquidating the lessor's damages in accordance with subsection (1); or
   (b) in the absence of those terms, 20 percent of the then present value of the total rent the lessee was obligated to pay for the balance of the lease term, or, in the case of a consumer lease, the lesser of such amount or $500.

(4) A lessee's right to restitution under subsection (3) is subject to offset to the extent the lessor establishes:
   (a) a right to recover damages under the provisions of this Article other than subsection (1); and
   (b) the amount or value of any benefits received by the lessee directly or indirectly by reason of the lease contract.

§ 2A–505. Cancellation and Termination and Effect of Cancellation, Termination, Rescission, or Fraud on Rights and Remedies.

(1) On cancellation of the lease contract, all obligations that are still executory on both sides are discharged, but any right based on prior default or performance survives, and the cancelling party also retains any remedy for default of the whole lease contract or any unperformed balance.

(2) On termination of the lease contract, all obligations that are still executory on both sides are discharged but any right based on prior default or performance survives.

(3) Unless the contrary intention clearly appears, expressions of "cancellation," "rescission," or the like of the lease contract may not be construed as a renunciation or discharge of any claim in damages for an antecedent default.

(4) Rights and remedies for material misrepresentation or fraud include all rights and remedies available under this Article for default.

(5) Neither rescission nor a claim for rescission of the lease contract nor rejection or return of the goods may bar or be deemed inconsistent with a claim for damages or other right or remedy.

§ 2A–506. Statute of Limitations.

(1) An action for default under a lease contract, including breach of warranty or indemnity, must be commenced within 4 years after the cause of action accrued. By the original lease contract the parties may reduce the period of limitation to not less than one year.

(2) A cause of action for default accrues when the act or omission on which the default or breach of warranty is based is or should have been discovered by the aggrieved party, or when the default occurs, whichever is later. A cause of action for indemnity accrues when the act or omission on which the claim for indemnity is based is or should have been discovered by the indemnified party, whichever is later.

(3) If an action commenced within the time limited by subsection (1) is so terminated as to leave available a remedy by another action for the same default or breach of warranty or indemnity, the other action may be commenced after the expiration of the time limited and within 6 months after the termination of the first action unless the termination resulted from voluntary discontinuance or from dismissal for failure or neglect to prosecute.

(4) This section does not alter the law on tolling of the statute of limitations nor does it apply to causes of action that have accrued before this Article becomes effective.

§ 2A–507. Proof of Market Rent: Time and Place.

(1) Damages based on market rent (Section 2A–519 or 2A–528) are determined according to the rent for the use of the goods concerned for a lease term identical to the remaining lease term of the original lease agreement and prevailing at the times specified in Sections 2A–519 and 2A–528.

(2) If evidence of rent for the use of the goods concerned for a lease term identical to the remaining lease term of the original lease agreement and prevailing at the times or places described in this Article is not readily available, the rent prevailing within any reasonable time before or after the time described or at any other place or for a different lease term which in commercial judgment or under usage of trade would serve as a reasonable substitute for the one described may be used, making any proper allowance for the difference, including the cost of transporting the goods to or from the other place.

(3) Evidence of a relevant rent prevailing at a time or place or for a lease term other than the one described in this Article offered by one party is not admissible unless and until he [or she] has given the other party notice the court finds sufficient to prevent unfair surprise.

(4) If the prevailing rent or value of any goods regularly leased in any established market is in issue, reports in official publications or trade journals or in newspapers or periodicals of general circulation published as the reports of that market are admissible in evidence. The circumstances of the preparation of the report may be shown to affect its weight but not its admissibility.

As amended in 1990.

§ 2A–508. Lessee's Remedies.

(1) If a lessor fails to deliver the goods in conformity to the lease contract (Section 2A–509) or repudiates the lease contract (Section 2A–402), or a lessee rightfully rejects the goods (Section 2A–509) or justifiably revokes acceptance of the goods (Section 2A–517), then

with respect to any goods involved, and with respect to all of the goods if under an installment lease contract the value of the whole lease contract is substantially impaired (Section 2A–510), the lessor is in default under the lease contract and the lessee may:

(a) cancel the lease contract (Section 2A–505(1));

(b) recover so much of the rent and security as has been paid and is just under the circumstances;

(c) cover and recover damages as to all goods affected whether or not they have been identified to the lease contract (Sections 2A–518 and 2A–520), or recover damages for nondelivery (Sections 2A–519 and 2A–520);

(d) exercise any other rights or pursue any other remedies provided in the lease contract.

(2) If a lessor fails to deliver the goods in conformity to the lease contract or repudiates the lease contract, the lessee may also:

(a) if the goods have been identified, recover them (Section 2A–522); or

(b) in a proper case, obtain specific performance or replevy the goods (Section 2A–521).

(3) If a lessor is otherwise in default under a lease contract, the lessee may exercise the rights and pursue the remedies provided in the lease contract, which may include a right to cancel the lease, and in Section 2A–519(3).

(4) If a lessor has breached a warranty, whether express or implied, the lessee may recover damages (Section 2A–519(4)).

(5) On rightful rejection or justifiable revocation of acceptance, a lessee has a security interest in goods in the lessee's possession or control for any rent and security that has been paid and any expenses reasonably incurred in their inspection, receipt, transportation, and care and custody and may hold those goods and dispose of them in good faith and in a commercially reasonable manner, subject to Section 2A–527(5).

(6) Subject to the provisions of Section 2A–407, a lessee, on notifying the lessor of the lessee's intention to do so, may deduct all or any part of the damages resulting from any default under the lease contract from any part of the rent still due under the same lease contract.

As amended in 1990.

§ 2A–509. Lessee's Rights on Improper Delivery; Rightful Rejection.

(1) Subject to the provisions of Section 2A–510 on default in installment lease contracts, if the goods or the tender or delivery fail in any respect to conform to the lease contract, the lessee may reject or accept the goods or accept any commercial unit or units and reject the rest of the goods.

(2) Rejection of goods is ineffective unless it is within a reasonable time after tender or delivery of the goods and the lessee seasonably notifies the lessor.

§ 2A–510. Installment Lease Contracts: Rejection and Default.

(1) Under an installment lease contract a lessee may reject any delivery that is nonconforming if the nonconformity substantially impairs the value of that delivery and cannot be cured or the nonconformity is a defect in the required documents; but if the nonconformity does not fall within subsection (2) and the lessor or the supplier gives adequate assurance of its cure, the lessee must accept that delivery.

(2) Whenever nonconformity or default with respect to one or more deliveries substantially impairs the value of the installment lease contract as a whole there is a default with respect to the whole. But, the aggrieved party reinstates the installment lease contract as a whole if the aggrieved party accepts a nonconforming delivery without seasonably notifying of cancellation or brings an action with respect only to past deliveries or demands performance as to future deliveries.

§ 2A–511. Merchant Lessee's Duties as to Rightfully Rejected Goods.

(1) Subject to any security interest of a lessee (Section 2A–508(5)), if a lessor or a supplier has no agent or place of business at the market of rejection, a merchant lessee, after rejection of goods in his [or her] possession or control, shall follow any reasonable instructions received from the lessor or the supplier with respect to the goods. In the absence of those instructions, a merchant lessee shall make reasonable efforts to sell, lease, or otherwise dispose of the goods for the lessor's account if they threaten to decline in value speedily. Instructions are not reasonable if on demand indemnity for expenses is not forthcoming.

(2) If a merchant lessee (subsection (1)) or any other lessee (Section 2A–512) disposes of goods, he [or she] is entitled to reimbursement either from the lessor or the supplier or out of the proceeds for reasonable expenses of caring for and disposing of the goods and, if the expenses include no disposition commission, to such commission as is usual in the trade, or if there is none, to a reasonable sum not exceeding 10 percent of the gross proceeds.

(3) In complying with this section or Section 2A–512, the lessee is held only to good faith. Good faith conduct hereunder is neither acceptance or conversion nor the basis of an action for damages.

(4) A purchaser who purchases in good faith from a lessee pursuant to this section or Section 2A–512 takes the goods free of any rights of the lessor and the supplier even though the lessee fails to comply with one or more of the requirements of this Article.

§ 2A–512. Lessee's Duties as to Rightfully Rejected Goods.

(1) Except as otherwise provided with respect to goods that threaten to decline in value speedily (Section 2A–511) and subject to any security interest of a lessee (Section 2A–508(5)):
  (a) the lessee, after rejection of goods in the lessee's possession, shall hold them with reasonable care at the lessor's or the supplier's disposition for a reasonable time after the lessee's seasonable notification of rejection;
  (b) if the lessor or the supplier gives no instructions within a reasonable time after notification of rejection, the lessee may store the rejected goods for the lessor's or the supplier's account or ship them to the lessor or the supplier or dispose of them for the lessor's or the supplier's account with reimbursement in the manner provided in Section 2A–511; but
  (c) the lessee has no further obligations with regard to goods rightfully rejected.

(2) Action by the lessee pursuant to subsection (1) is not acceptance or conversion.

§ 2A–513. Cure by Lessor of Improper Tender or Delivery; Replacement.

(1) If any tender or delivery by the lessor or the supplier is rejected because nonconforming and the time for performance has not yet expired, the lessor or the supplier may seasonably notify the lessee of the lessor's or the supplier's intention to cure and may then make a conforming delivery within the time provided in the lease contract.

(2) If the lessee rejects a nonconforming tender that the lessor or the supplier had reasonable grounds to believe would be acceptable with or without money allowance, the lessor or the supplier may have a further reasonable time to substitute a conforming tender if he [or she] seasonably notifies the lessee.

§ 2A–514. Waiver of Lessee's Objections.

(1) In rejecting goods, a lessee's failure to state a particular defect that is ascertainable by reasonable inspection precludes the lessee from relying on the defect to justify rejection or to establish default:
  (a) if, stated seasonably, the lessor or the supplier could have cured it (Section 2A–513); or

(b) between merchants if the lessor or the supplier after rejection has made a request in writing for a full and final written statement of all defects on which the lessee proposes to rely.

(2) A lessee's failure to reserve rights when paying rent or other consideration against documents precludes recovery of the payment for defects apparent on the face of the documents.

§ 2A–515. Acceptance of Goods.

(1) Acceptance of goods occurs after the lessee has had a reasonable opportunity to inspect the goods and
   (a) the lessee signifies or acts with respect to the goods in a manner that signifies to the lessor or the supplier that the goods are conforming or that the lessee will take or retain them in spite of their nonconformity; or
   (b) the lessee fails to make an effective rejection of the goods (Section 2A–509(2)).
(2) Acceptance of a part of any commercial unit is acceptance of that entire unit.

§ 2A–516. Effect of Acceptance of Goods; Notice of Default; Burden of Establishing Default After Acceptance; Notice of Claim or Litigation to Person Answerable Over.

(1) A lessee must pay rent for any goods accepted in accordance with the lease contract, with due allowance for goods rightfully rejected or not delivered.
(2) A lessee's acceptance of goods precludes rejection of the goods accepted. In the case of a finance lease, if made with knowledge of a nonconformity, acceptance cannot be revoked because of it. In any other case, if made with knowledge of a nonconformity, acceptance cannot be revoked because of it unless the acceptance was on the reasonable assumption that the nonconformity would be seasonably cured. Acceptance does not of itself impair any other remedy provided by this Article or the lease agreement for nonconformity.
(3) If a tender has been accepted:
   (a) within a reasonable time after the lessee discovers or should have discovered any default, the lessee shall notify the lessor and the supplier, if any, or be barred from any remedy against the party not notified;
   (b) except in the case of a consumer lease, within a reasonable time after the lessee receives notice of litigation for infringement or the like (Section 2A–211) the lessee shall notify the lessor or be barred from any remedy over for liability established by the litigation; and
   (c) the burden is on the lessee to establish any default.
(4) If a lessee is sued for breach of a warranty or other obligation for which a lessor or a supplier is answerable over the following apply:
   (a) The lessee may give the lessor or the supplier, or both, written notice of the litigation. If the notice states that the person notified may come in and defend and that if the person notified does not do so that person will be bound in any action against that person by the lessee by any determination of fact common to the two litigations, then unless the person notified after seasonable receipt of the notice does come in and defend that person is so bound.
   (b) The lessor or the supplier may demand in writing that the lessee turn over control of the litigation including settlement if the claim is one for infringement or the like (Section 2A–211) or else be barred from any remedy over. If the demand states that the lessor or the supplier agrees to bear all expense and to satisfy any adverse judgment, then unless the lessee after seasonable receipt of the demand does turn over control the lessee is so barred.
(5) Subsections (3) and (4) apply to any obligation of a lessee to hold the lessor or the supplier harmless against infringement or the like (Section 2A–211).

As amended in 1990.

§ 2A–517. Revocation of Acceptance of Goods.

(1) A lessee may revoke acceptance of a lot or commercial unit whose nonconformity substantially impairs its value to the lessee if the lessee has accepted it:
    (a) except in the case of a finance lease, on the reasonable assumption that its nonconformity would be cured and it has not been seasonably cured; or
    (b) without discovery of the nonconformity if the lessee's acceptance was reasonably induced either by the lessor's assurances or, except in the case of a finance lease, by the difficulty of discovery before acceptance.

(2) Except in the case of a finance lease that is not a consumer lease, a lessee may revoke acceptance of a lot or commercial unit if the lessor defaults under the lease contract and the default substantially impairs the value of that lot or commercial unit to the lessee.

(3) If the lease agreement so provides, the lessee may revoke acceptance of a lot or commercial unit because of other defaults by the lessor.

(4) Revocation of acceptance must occur within a reasonable time after the lessee discovers or should have discovered the ground for it and before any substantial change in condition of the goods which is not caused by the nonconformity. Revocation is not effective until the lessee notifies the lessor.

(5) A lessee who so revokes has the same rights and duties with regard to the goods involved as if the lessee had rejected them.

As amended in 1990.

§ 2A–518. Cover; Substitute Goods.

(1) After a default by a lessor under the lease contract of the type described in Section 2A–508(1), or, if agreed, after other default by the lessor, the lessee may cover by making any purchase or lease of or contract to purchase or lease goods in substitution for those due from the lessor.

(2) Except as otherwise provided with respect to damages liquidated in the lease agreement (Section 2A–504) or otherwise determined pursuant to agreement of the parties (Sections 1–102(3) and 2A–503), if a lessee's cover is by a lease agreement substantially similar to the original lease agreement and the new lease agreement is made in good faith and in a commercially reasonable manner, the lessee may recover from the lessor as damages (i) the present value, as of the date of the commencement of the term of the new lease agreement, of the rent under the new lease agreement applicable to that period of the new lease term which is comparable to the then remaining term of the original lease agreement minus the present value as of the same date of the total rent for the then remaining lease term of the original lease agreement, and (ii) any incidental or consequential damages, less expenses saved in consequence of the lessor's default.

(3) If a lessee's cover is by lease agreement that for any reason does not qualify for treatment under subsection (2), or is by purchase or otherwise, the lessee may recover from the lessor as if the lessee had elected not to cover and Section 2A–519 governs.

As amended in 1990.

§ 2A–519. Lessee's Damages for Nondelivery, Repudiation, Default, and Breach of Warranty in Regard to Accepted Goods.

(1) Except as otherwise provided with respect to damages liquidated in the lease agreement (Section 2A–504) or otherwise determined pursuant to agreement of the parties (Sections 1–102(3) and 2A–503), if a lessee elects not to cover or a lessee elects to cover and the cover is by lease agreement that for any reason does not qualify for treatment under Section 2A–518(2), or is by purchase or otherwise, the measure of damages for nondelivery or repudiation by the lessor or for rejection or revocation of acceptance by the lessee is the present value, as of the date of the default, of the then market rent minus the present value as

of the same date of the original rent, computed for the remaining lease term of the original lease agreement, together with incidental and consequential damages, less expenses saved in consequence of the lessor's default.

(2) Market rent is to be determined as of the place for tender or, in cases of rejection after arrival or revocation of acceptance, as of the place of arrival.

(3) Except as otherwise agreed, if the lessee has accepted goods and given notification (Section 2A–516(3)), the measure of damages for nonconforming tender or delivery or other default by a lessor is the loss resulting in the ordinary course of events from the lessor's default as determined in any manner that is reasonable together with incidental and consequential damages, less expenses saved in consequence of the lessor's default.

(4) Except as otherwise agreed, the measure of damages for breach of warranty is the present value at the time and place of acceptance of the difference between the value of the use of the goods accepted and the value if they had been as warranted for the lease term, unless special circumstances show proximate damages of a different amount, together with incidental and consequential damages, less expenses saved in consequence of the lessor's default or breach of warranty.

As amended in 1990.

§ 2A–520. Lessee's Incidental and Consequential Damages.

(1) Incidental damages resulting from a lessor's default include expenses reasonably incurred in inspection, receipt, transportation, and care and custody of goods rightfully rejected or goods the acceptance of which is justifiably revoked, any commercially reasonable charges, expenses or commissions in connection with effecting cover, and any other reasonable expense incident to the default.

(2) Consequential damages resulting from a lessor's default include:
  (a) any loss resulting from general or particular requirements and needs of which the lessor at the time of contracting had reason to know and which could not reasonably be prevented by cover or otherwise; and
  (b) injury to person or property proximately resulting from any breach of warranty.

§ 2A–521. Lessee's Right to Specific Performance or Replevin.

(1) Specific performance may be decreed if the goods are unique or in other proper circumstances.

(2) A decree for specific performance may include any terms and conditions as to payment of the rent, damages, or other relief that the court deems just.

(3) A lessee has a right of replevin, detinue, sequestration, claim and delivery, or the like for goods identified to the lease contract if after reasonable effort the lessee is unable to effect cover for those goods or the circumstances reasonably indicate that the effort will be unavailing.

§ 2A–522. Lessee's Right to Goods on Lessor's Insolvency.

(1) Subject to subsection (2) and even though the goods have not been shipped, a lessee who has paid a part or all of the rent and security for goods identified to a lease contract (Section 2A–217) on making and keeping good a tender of any unpaid portion of the rent and security due under the lease contract may recover the goods identified from the lessor if the lessor becomes insolvent within 10 days after receipt of the first installment of rent and security.

(2) A lessee acquires the right to recover goods identified to a lease contract only if they conform to the lease contract.

§ 2A–523. Lessor's Remedies.

(1) If a lessee wrongfully rejects or revokes acceptance of goods or fails to make a payment when due or repudiates with respect to a part or the whole, then, with respect to any goods involved, and with respect to all of the goods if under an installment lease contract the

value of the whole lease contract is substantially impaired (Section 2A–510), the lessee is in default under the lease contract and the lessor may:

(a)   cancel the lease contract (Section 2A–505(1));

(b)   proceed respecting goods not identified to the lease contract (Section 2A–524);

(c)   withhold delivery of the goods and take possession of goods previously delivered (Section 2A–525);

(d)   stop delivery of the goods by any bailee (Section 2A–526);

(e)   dispose of the goods and recover damages (Section 2A–527), or retain the goods and recover damages (Section 2A–528), or in a proper case recover rent (Section 2A–529);

(f)   exercise any other rights or pursue any other remedies provided in the lease contract.

(2)   If a lessor does not fully exercise a right or obtain a remedy to which the lessor is entitled under subsection (1), the lessor may recover the loss resulting in the ordinary course of events from the lessee's default as determined in any reasonable manner, together with incidental damages, less expenses saved in consequence of the lessee's default.

(3)   If a lessee is otherwise in default under a lease contract, the lessor may exercise the rights and pursue the remedies provided in the lease contract, which may include a right to cancel the lease. In addition, unless otherwise provided in the lease contract:

(a)   if the default substantially impairs the value of the lease contract to the lessor, the lessor may exercise the rights and pursue the remedies provided in subsections (1) or (2); or

(b)   if the default does not substantially impair the value of the lease contract to the lessor, the lessor may recover as provided in subsection (2).

As amended in 1990.

§ 2A–524. Lessor's Right to Identify Goods to Lease Contract.

(1)   After default by the lessee under the lease contract of the type described in Section 2A–523(1) or 2A–523(3) (a) or, if agreed, after other default by the lessee, the lessor may:

(a)   identify to the lease contract conforming goods not already identified if at the time the lessor learned of the default they were in the lessor's or the supplier's possession or control; and

(b)   dispose of goods (Section 2A–527(1)) that demonstrably have been intended for the particular lease contract even though those goods are unfinished.

(2)   If the goods are unfinished, in the exercise of reasonable commercial judgment for the purposes of avoiding loss and of effective realization, an aggrieved lessor or the supplier may either complete manufacture and wholly identify the goods to the lease contract or cease manufacture and lease, sell, or otherwise dispose of the goods for scrap or salvage value or proceed in any other reasonable manner.

As amended in 1990.

§ 2A–525. Lessor's Right to Possession of Goods.

(1)   If a lessor discovers the lessee to be insolvent, the lessor may refuse to deliver the goods.

(2)   After a default by the lessee under the lease contract of the type described in Section 2A–523(1) or 2A–523(3) (a) or, if agreed, after other default by the lessee, the lessor has the right to take possession of the goods. If the lease contract so provides, the lessor may require the lessee to assemble the goods and make them available to the lessor at a place to be designated by the lessor which is reasonably convenient to both parties. Without removal, the lessor may render unusable any goods employed in trade or business, and may dispose of goods on the lessee's premises (Section 2A–527).

(3)   The lessor may proceed under subsection (2) without judicial process if it can be done without breach of the peace or the lessor may proceed by action.

As amended in 1990.

§ 2A–526. Lessor's Stoppage of Delivery in Transit or Otherwise.

(1) A lessor may stop delivery of goods in the possession of a carrier or other bailee if the lessor discovers the lessee to be insolvent and may stop delivery of carload, truckload, planeload, or larger shipments of express or freight if the lessee repudiates or fails to make a payment due before delivery, whether for rent, security or otherwise under the lease contract, or for any other reason the lessor has a right to withhold or take possession of the goods.

(2) In pursuing its remedies under subsection (1), the lessor may stop delivery until
    (a) receipt of the goods by the lessee;
    (b) acknowledgment to the lessee by any bailee of the goods, except a carrier, that the bailee holds the goods for the lessee; or
    (c) such an acknowledgment to the lessee by a carrier via reshipment or as warehouseman.

(3) (a) To stop delivery, a lessor shall so notify as to enable the bailee by reasonable diligence to prevent delivery of the goods.
    (b) After notification, the bailee shall hold and deliver the goods according to the directions of the lessor, but the lessor is liable to the bailee for any ensuing charges or damages.
    (c) A carrier who has issued a nonnegotiable bill of lading is not obliged to obey a notification to stop received from a person other than the consignor.

§ 2A–527. Lessor's Rights to Dispose of Goods.

(1) After a default by a lessee under the lease contract of the type described in Section 2A–523(1) or 2A–523(3) (a) or after the lessor refuses to deliver or takes possession of goods (Section 2A–525 or 2A–526), or, if agreed, after other default by a lessee, the lessor may dispose of the goods concerned or the undelivered balance thereof by lease, sale, or otherwise.

(2) Except as otherwise provided with respect to damages liquidated in the lease agreement (Section 2A–504) or otherwise determined pursuant to agreement of the parties (Sections 1–102(3) and 2A–503), if the disposition is by lease agreement substantially similar to the original lease agreement and the new lease agreement is made in good faith and in a commercially reasonable manner, the lessor may recover from the lessee as damages (i) accrued and unpaid rent as of the date of the commencement of the term of the new lease agreement, (ii) the present value, as of the same date, of the total rent for the then remaining lease term of the original lease agreement minus the present value, as of the same date, of the rent under the new lease agreement applicable to that period of the new lease term which is comparable to the then remaining term of the original lease agreement, and (iii) any incidental damages allowed under Section 2A–530, less expenses saved in consequence of the lessee's default.

(3) If the lessor's disposition is by lease agreement that for any reason does not qualify for treatment under subsection (2), or is by sale or otherwise, the lessor may recover from the lessee as if the lessor had elected not to dispose of the goods and Section 2A–528 governs.

(4) A subsequent buyer or lessee who buys or leases from the lessor in good faith for value as a result of a disposition under this section takes the goods free of the original lease contract and any rights of the original lessee even though the lessor fails to comply with one or more of the requirements of this Article.

(5) The lessor is not accountable to the lessee for any profit made on any disposition. A lessee who has rightfully rejected or justifiably revoked acceptance shall account to the lessor for any excess over the amount of the lessee's security interest (Section 2A–508(5)).

As amended in 1990.

§ 2A–528. Lessor's Damages for Nonacceptance, Failure to Pay, Repudiation, or Other Default.

(1) Except as otherwise provided with respect to damages liquidated in the lease agreement (Section 2A–504) or otherwise determined pursuant to agreement of the parties (Sections 1–102(3) and 2A–503), if a lessor elects to retain the goods or a lessor elects to dispose of the goods and the disposition is by lease agreement that for any reason does not qualify for treatment under Section 2A–527(2), or is by sale or otherwise, the lessor may recover from the lessee as damages for a default of the type described in Section 2A–523(1) or 2A–523(3) (a), or, if agreed, for other default of the lessee, (i) accrued and unpaid rent as of the date of default if the lessee has never taken possession of the goods, or, if the lessee has taken possession of the goods, as of the date the lessor repossesses the goods or an earlier date on which the lessee makes a tender of the goods to the lessor, (ii) the present value as of the date determined under clause (i) of the total rent for the then remaining lease term of the original lease agreement minus the present value as of the same date of the market rent at the place where the goods are located computed for the same lease term, and (iii) any incidental damages allowed under Section 2A–530, less expenses saved in consequence of the lessee's default.

(2) If the measure of damages provided in subsection (1) is inadequate to put a lessor in as good a position as performance would have, the measure of damages is the present value of the profit, including reasonable overhead, the lessor would have made from full performance by the lessee, together with any incidental damages allowed under Section 2A–530, due allowance for costs reasonably incurred and due credit for payments or proceeds of disposition.

As amended in 1990.

§ 2A–529. Lessor's Action for the Rent.

(1) After default by the lessee under the lease contract of the type described in Section 2A–523(1) or 2A–523(3) (a) or, if agreed, after other default by the lessee, if the lessor complies with subsection (2), the lessor may recover from the lessee as damages:

    (a) for goods accepted by the lessee and not repossessed by or tendered to the lessor, and for conforming goods lost or damaged within a commercially reasonable time after risk of loss passes to the lessee (Section 2A–219), (i) accrued and unpaid rent as of the date of entry of judgment in favor of the lessor, (ii) the present value as of the same date of the rent for the then remaining lease term of the lease agreement, and (iii) any incidental damages allowed under Section 2A–530, less expenses saved in consequence of the lessee's default; and

    (b) for goods identified to the lease contract if the lessor is unable after reasonable effort to dispose of them at a reasonable price or the circumstances reasonably indicate that effort will be unavailing, (i) accrued and unpaid rent as of the date of entry of judgment in favor of the lessor, (ii) the present value as of the same date of the rent for the then remaining lease term of the lease agreement, and (iii) any incidental damages allowed under Section 2A–530, less expenses saved in consequence of the lessee's default.

(2) Except as provided in subsection (3), the lessor shall hold for the lessee for the remaining lease term of the lease agreement any goods that have been identified to the lease contract and are in the lessor's control.

(3) The lessor may dispose of the goods at any time before collection of the judgment for damages obtained pursuant to subsection (1). If the disposition is before the end of the remaining lease term of the lease agreement, the lessor's recovery against the lessee for damages is governed by Section 2A–527 or Section 2A–528, and the lessor will cause an appropriate credit to be provided against a judgment for damages to the extent that the amount of the judgment exceeds the recovery available pursuant to Section 2A–527 or 2A–528.

(4) Payment of the judgment for damages obtained pursuant to subsection (1) entitles the lessee to the use and possession of the goods not then disposed of for the remaining lease term of and in accordance with the lease agreement.

(5) After default by the lessee under the lease contract of the type described in Section 2A–523(1) or Section 2A–523(3) (a) or, if agreed, after other default by the lessee, a lessor who is held not entitled to rent under this section must nevertheless be awarded damages for nonacceptance under Section 2A–527 or Section 2A–528.

As amended in 1990.

§ 2A–530. Lessor's Incidental Damages. Incidental damages to an aggrieved lessor include any commercially reasonable charges, expenses, or commissions incurred in stopping delivery, in the transportation, care and custody of goods after the lessee's default, in connection with return or disposition of the goods, or otherwise resulting from the default.

§ 2A–531. Standing to Sue Third Parties for Injury to Goods.

(1) If a third party so deals with goods that have been identified to a lease contract as to cause actionable injury to a party to the lease contract (a) the lessor has a right of action against the third party, and (b) the lessee also has a right of action against the third party if the lessee:
   (i)   has a security interest in the goods;
   (ii)   has an insurable interest in the goods; or
   (iii)   bears the risk of loss under the lease contract or has since the injury assumed that risk as against the lessor and the goods have been converted or destroyed.

(2) If at the time of the injury the party plaintiff did not bear the risk of loss as against the other party to the lease contract and there is no arrangement between them for disposition of the recovery, his [or her] suit or settlement, subject to his [or her] own interest, is as a fiduciary for the other party to the lease contract.

(3) Either party with the consent of the other may sue for the benefit of whom it may concern.

§ 2A–532. Lessor's Rights to Residual Interest. In addition to any other recovery permitted by this Article or other law, the lessor may recover from the lessee an amount that will fully compensate the lessor for any loss of or damage to the lessor's residual interest in the goods caused by the default of the lessee.

As added in 1990.

Article 3—Negotiable Instruments

PART 1: GENERAL PROVISIONS AND DEFINITIONS

§ 3–101. Short Title. This Article may be cited as Uniform Commercial Code—Negotiable Instruments.

§ 3–102. Subject Matter.

   (a)   This Article applies to negotiable instruments. It does not apply to money, to payment orders governed by Article 4A, or to securities governed by Article 8.

   (b)   If there is conflict between this Article and Article 4 or 9, Articles 4 and 9 govern.

   (c)   Regulations of the Board of Governors of the Federal Reserve System and operating circulars of the Federal Reserve Banks supersede any inconsistent provision of this Article to the extent of the inconsistency.

§ 3–103. Definitions.

(a) In this Article:

    (1) "Acceptor" means a drawee who has accepted a draft.

    (2) "Consumer account" means an account established by an individual primarily for personal, family, or household purposes.

    (3) "Consumer transaction" means a transaction in which an individual incurs an obligation primarily for personal, family, or household purposes.

    (4) "Drawee" means a person ordered in a draft to make payment.

    (5) "Drawer" means a person who signs or is identified in a draft as a person ordering payment.

    (6) ["Good faith" means honesty in fact and the observance of reasonable commercial standards of fair dealing.]

    (7) "Maker" means a person who signs or is identified in a note as a person undertaking to pay.

    (8) "Order" means a written instruction to pay money signed by the person giving the instruction. The instruction may be addressed to any person, including the person giving the instruction, or to one or more persons jointly or in the alternative but not in succession. An authorization to pay is not an order unless the person authorized to pay is also instructed to pay.

    (9) "Ordinary care" in the case of a person engaged in business means observance of reasonable commercial standards, prevailing in the area in which the person is located, with respect to the business in which the person is engaged. In the case of a bank that takes an instrument for processing for collection or payment by automated means, reasonable commercial standards do not require the bank to examine the instrument if the failure to examine does not violate the bank's prescribed procedures and the bank's procedures do not vary unreasonably from general banking usage not disapproved by this Article or Article 4.

    (10) "Party" means a party to an instrument.

    (11) "Principal obligor," with respect to an instrument, means the accommodated party or any other party to the instrument against whom a secondary obligor has recourse under this article.

    (12) "Promise" means a written undertaking to pay money signed by the person undertaking to pay. An acknowledgment of an obligation by the obligor is not a promise unless the obligor also undertakes to pay the obligation.

    (13) "Prove" with respect to a fact means to meet the burden of establishing the fact (Section 1–201(8)).

    (14) ["Record" means information that is inscribed on a tangible medium or that is stored in electronic or other medium and is retrievable in perceivable form.]

    (15) "Remitter" means a person who purchases an instrument from its issuer if the instrument is payable to an identified person other than the purchaser.

    (16) "Remotely-created consumer item" means an item drawn on a consumer account, which is not created by the payor bank and does not bear a handwritten signature purporting to be the signature of the drawer.

    (17) "Secondary obligor," with respect to an instrument, means (a) an indorser or an accommodation party, (b) a drawer having the obligation described in Section 3–414(d), or (c) any other party to the instrument that has recourse against another party to the instrument pursuant to Section 3–116(b).

(b) Other definitions applying to this Article and the sections in which they appear are:

"Acceptance"	Section 3–409.
"Accommodated party"	Section 3–419.
"Accommodation party"	Section 3–419.

"Account"	Section 4–104.
"Alteration"	Section 3–407.
"Anomalous indorsement"	Section 3–205.
"Blank indorsement"	Section 3–205.
"Cashier's check"	Section 3–104.
"Certificate of deposit"	Section 3–104.
"Certified check"	Section 3–409.
"Check"	Section 3–104.
"Consideration"	Section 3–303.
"Draft"	Section 3–104.
"Holder in due course"	Section 3–302.
"Incomplete instrument"	Section 3–115.
"Indorsement"	Section 3–204.
"Indorser"	Section 3–204.
"Instrument"	Section 3–104.
"Issue"	Section 3–105.
"Issuer"	Section 3–105.
"Negotiable instrument"	Section 3–104.
"Negotiation"	Section 3–201.
"Note"	Section 3–104.
"Payable at a definite time"	Section 3–108.
"Payable on demand"	Section 3–108.
"Payable to bearer"	Section 3–109.
"Payable to order"	Section 3–109.
"Payment"	Section 3–602.
"Person entitled to enforce"	Section 3–301.
"Presentment"	Section 3–501.
"Reacquisition"	Section 3–207.
"Special indorsement"	Section 3–205.
"Teller's check"	Section 3–104.
"Transfer of instrument"	Section 3–203.
"Traveler's check"	Section 3–104.
"Value"	Section 3–303.

(c) The following definitions in other Articles apply to this Article:

"Banking day"	Section 4–104.
"Clearing house"	Section 4–104.
"Collecting bank"	Section 4–105.
"Depositary bank"	Section 4–105.
"Documentary draft"	Section 4–104.
"Intermediary bank"	Section 4–105.
"Item"	Section 4–104.
"Payor bank"	Section 4–105.
"Suspends payments"	Section 4–104.

(d) In addition, Article 1 contains general definitions and principles of construction and inter-
     pretation applicable throughout this Article.

*Legislative Note. A jurisdiction that enacts this statute that has not yet enacted the revised ver-
sion of UCC Article 1 should add to Section 3–103 the definition of "good faith" that appears
in the official version of Section 1–201(b)(20) and the definition of "record" that appears in
the official version of Section 1–201(b)(31). Sections 3–103(a)(6) and (14) are reserved for that
purpose. A jurisdiction that already has adopted or simultaneously adopts the revised Article
1 should not add those definitions, but should leave those numbers "reserved." If jurisdictions follow the numbering suggested here, the subsections will have the same numbering in all
jurisdictions that have adopted these amendments (whether they have or have not adopted the
revised version of UCC Article 1).*

§ 3–104. Negotiable Instrument.

(a) Except as provided in subsections (c) and (d), "negotiable instrument" means an uncondi-
     tional promise or order to pay a fixed amount of money, with or without interest or other
     charges described in the promise or order, if it:
     (1) is payable to bearer or to order at the time it is issued or first comes into possession of
          a holder;
     (2) is payable on demand or at a definite time; and
     (3) does not state any other undertaking or instruction by the person promising or order-
          ing payment to do any act in addition to the payment of money, but the promise or
          order may contain (i) an undertaking or power to give, maintain, or protect collateral
          to secure payment, (ii) an authorization or power to the holder to confess judgment or
          realize on or dispose of collateral, or (iii) a waiver of the benefit of any law intended
          for the advantage or protection of an obligor.
(b) "Instrument" means a negotiable instrument.
(c) An order that meets all of the requirements of subsection (a), except paragraph (1), and
     otherwise falls within the definition of "check" in subsection (f) is a negotiable instrument
     and a check.
(d) A promise or order other than a check is not an instrument if, at the time it is issued or first
     comes into possession of a holder, it contains a conspicuous statement, however expressed,
     to the effect that the promise or order is not negotiable or is not an instrument governed by
     this Article.
(e) An instrument is a "note" if it is a promise and is a "draft" if it is an order. If an instrument
     falls within the definition of both "note" and "draft," a person entitled to enforce the instru-
     ment may treat it as either.
(f) "Check" means (i) a draft, other than a documentary draft, payable on demand and drawn
     on a bank or (ii) a cashier's check or teller's check. An instrument may be a check even
     though it is described on its face by another term, such as "money order."
(g) "Cashier's check" means a draft with respect to which the drawer and drawee are the same
     bank or branches of the same bank.
(h) "Teller's check" means a draft drawn by a bank (i) on another bank, or (ii) payable at or
     through a bank.
(i) "Traveler's check" means an instrument that (i) is payable on demand, (ii) is drawn on or
     payable at or through a bank, (iii) is designated by the term "traveler's check" or by a sub-
     stantially similar term, and (iv) requires, as a condition to payment, a countersignature by a
     person whose specimen signature appears on the instrument.
(j) "Certificate of deposit" means an instrument containing an acknowledgment by a bank that
     a sum of money has been received by the bank and a promise by the bank to repay the sum
     of money. A certificate of deposit is a note of the bank.

§ 3–105. Issue of Instrument.

(a) "Issue" means the first delivery of an instrument by the maker or drawer, whether to a
     holder or nonholder, for the purpose of giving rights on the instrument to any person.

(b) An unissued instrument, or an unissued incomplete instrument that is completed, is binding on the maker or drawer, but nonissuance is a defense. An instrument that is conditionally issued or is issued for a special purpose is binding on the maker or drawer, but failure of the condition or special purpose to be fulfilled is a defense.

(c) "Issuer" applies to issued and unissued instruments and means a maker or drawer of an instrument.

§ 3–106. Unconditional Promise or Order.

(a) Except as provided in this section, for the purposes of Section 3–104(a), a promise or order is unconditional unless it states (i) an express condition to payment, (ii) that the promise or order is subject to or governed by another record, or (iii) that rights or obligations with respect to the promise or order are stated in another record. A reference to another record does not of itself make the promise or order conditional.

(b) A promise or order is not made conditional (i) by a reference to another record for a statement of rights with respect to collateral, prepayment, or acceleration, or (ii) because payment is limited to resort to a particular fund or source.

(c) If a promise or order requires, as a condition to payment, a countersignature by a person whose specimen signature appears on the promise or order, the condition does not make the promise or order conditional for the purposes of Section 3–104(a). If the person whose specimen signature appears on an instrument fails to countersign the instrument, the failure to countersign is a defense to the obligation of the issuer, but the failure does not prevent a transferee of the instrument from becoming a holder of the instrument.

(d) If a promise or order at the time it is issued or first comes into possession of a holder contains a statement, required by applicable statutory or administrative law, to the effect that the rights of a holder or transferee are subject to claims or defenses that the issuer could assert against the original payee, the promise or order is not thereby made conditional for the purposes of Section 3–104(a); but if the promise or order is an instrument, there cannot be a holder in due course of the instrument.

§ 3–107. Instrument Payable in Foreign Money.

Unless the instrument otherwise provides, an instrument that states the amount payable in foreign money may be paid in the foreign money or in an equivalent amount in dollars calculated by using the current bank offered spot rate at the place of payment for the purchase of dollars on the day on which the instrument is paid.

§ 3–108. Payable on Demand or at Definite Time.

(a) A promise or order is "payable on demand" if it (i) states that it is payable on demand or at sight, or otherwise indicates that it is payable at the will of the holder, or (ii) does not state any time of payment.

(b) A promise or order is "payable at a definite time" if it is payable on elapse of a definite period of time after sight or acceptance or at a fixed date or dates or at a time or times readily ascertainable at the time the promise or order is issued, subject to rights of (i) prepayment, (ii) acceleration, (iii) extension at the option of the holder, or (iv) extension to a further definite time at the option of the maker or acceptor or automatically upon or after a specified act or event.

(c) If an instrument, payable at a fixed date, is also payable upon demand made before the fixed date, the instrument is payable on demand until the fixed date and, if demand for payment is not made before that date, becomes payable at a definite time on the fixed date.

§ 3–109. Payable to Bearer or to Order.

(a) A promise or order is payable to bearer if it:
  (1) states that it is payable to bearer or to the order of bearer or otherwise indicates that the person in possession of the promise or order is entitled to payment;
  (2) does not state a payee; or
  (3) states that it is payable to or to the order of cash or otherwise indicates that it is not payable to an identified person.
(b) A promise or order that is not payable to bearer is payable to order if it is payable (i) to the order of an identified person or (ii) to an identified person or order. A promise or order that is payable to order is payable to the identified person.
(c) An instrument payable to bearer may become payable to an identified person if it is specially indorsed pursuant to Section 3–205(a). An instrument payable to an identified person may become payable to bearer if it is indorsed in blank pursuant to Section 3–205(b).

§ 3–110. Identification of Person to Whom Instrument Is Payable.

(a) The person to whom an instrument is initially payable is determined by the intent of the person, whether or not authorized, signing as, or in the name or behalf of, the issuer of the instrument. The instrument is payable to the person intended by the signer even if that person is identified in the instrument by a name or other identification that is not that of the intended person. If more than one person signs in the name or behalf of the issuer of an instrument and all the signers do not intend the same person as payee, the instrument is payable to any person intended by one or more of the signers.
(b) If the signature of the issuer of an instrument is made by automated means, such as a check writing machine, the payee of the instrument is determined by the intent of the person who supplied the name or identification of the payee, whether or not authorized to do so.
(c) A person to whom an instrument is payable may be identified in any way, including by name, identifying number, office, or account number. For the purpose of determining the holder of an instrument, the following rules apply:
  (1) If an instrument is payable to an account and the account is identified only by number, the instrument is payable to the person to whom the account is payable. If an instrument is payable to an account identified by number and by the name of a person, the instrument is payable to the named person, whether or not that person is the owner of the account identified by number.
  (2) If an instrument is payable to:
    (i) a trust, an estate, or a person described as trustee or representative of a trust or estate, the instrument is payable to the trustee, the representative, or a successor of either, whether or not the beneficiary or estate is also named;
    (ii) a person described as agent or similar representative of a named or identified person, the instrument is payable to the represented person, the representative, or a successor of the representative;
    (iii) a fund or organization that is not a legal entity, the instrument is payable to a representative of the members of the fund or organization; or
    (iv) an office or to a person described as holding an office, the instrument is payable to the named person, the incumbent of the office, or a successor to the incumbent.
(d) If an instrument is payable to two or more persons alternatively, it is payable to any of them and may be negotiated, discharged, or enforced by any or all of them in possession of the instrument. If an instrument is payable to two or more persons not alternatively, it is payable to all of them and may be negotiated, discharged, or enforced only by all of them. If an instrument payable to two or more persons is ambiguous as to whether it is payable to the persons alternatively, the instrument is payable to the persons alternatively.

§ 3–111. Place of Payment. Except as otherwise provided for items in Article 4, an instrument is payable at the place of payment stated in the instrument. If no place of payment is stated, an instrument is payable at the address of the drawee or maker stated in the instrument. If no address is stated, the place of payment is the place of business of the drawee or maker. If a drawee or maker has more than one place of business, the place of payment is any place of business of the drawee or maker chosen by the person entitled to enforce the instrument. If the drawee or maker has no place of business, the place of payment is the residence of the drawee or maker.

§ 3–112. Interest.

(a) Unless otherwise provided in the instrument, (i) an instrument is not payable with interest, and (ii) interest on an interest bearing instrument is payable from the date of the instrument.

(b) Interest may be stated in an instrument as a fixed or variable amount of money or it may be expressed as a fixed or variable rate or rates. The amount or rate of interest may be stated or described in the instrument in any manner and may require reference to information not contained in the instrument. If an instrument provides for interest, but the amount of interest payable cannot be ascertained from the description, interest is payable at the judgment rate in effect at the place of payment of the instrument and at the time interest first accrues.

§ 3–113. Date of Instrument.

(a) An instrument may be antedated or postdated. The date stated determines the time of payment if the instrument is payable at a fixed period after date. Except as provided in Section 4–401(c), an instrument payable on demand is not payable before the date of the instrument.

(b) If an instrument is undated, its date is the date of its issue or, in the case of an unissued instrument, the date it first comes into possession of a holder.

§ 3–114. Contradictory Terms of Instrument. If an instrument contains contradictory terms, typewritten terms prevail over printed terms, handwritten terms prevail over both, and words prevail over numbers.

§ 3–115. Incomplete Instrument.

(a) "Incomplete instrument" means a signed writing, whether or not issued by the signer, the contents of which show at the time of signing that it is incomplete but that the signer intended it to be completed by the addition of words or numbers.

(b) Subject to subsection (c), if an incomplete instrument is an instrument under Section 3–104, it may be enforced according to its terms if it is not completed, or according to its terms as augmented by completion. If an incomplete instrument is not an instrument under Section 3–104, but, after completion, the requirements of Section 3–104 are met, the instrument may be enforced according to its terms as augmented by completion.

(c) If words or numbers are added to an incomplete instrument without authority of the signer, there is an alteration of the incomplete instrument under Section 3–407.

(d) The burden of establishing that words or numbers were added to an incomplete instrument without authority of the signer is on the person asserting the lack of authority.

§ 3–116. Joint and Several Liability; Contribution.

(a) Except as otherwise provided in the instrument, two or more persons who have the same liability on an instrument as makers, drawers, acceptors, indorsers who indorse as joint payees, or anomalous indorsers are jointly and severally liable in the capacity in which they sign.

(b) Except as provided in Section 3–419(f) or by agreement of the affected parties, a party having joint and several liability who pays the instrument is entitled to receive from any party having the same joint and several liability contribution in accordance with applicable law.

§ 3–117. Other Agreements Affecting Instrument. Subject to applicable law regarding exclusion of proof of contemporaneous or previous agreements, the obligation of a party to an instrument to pay the instrument may be modified, supplemented, or nullified by a separate agreement of the obligor and a person entitled to enforce the instrument, if the instrument is issued or the obligation is incurred in reliance on the agreement or as part of the same transaction giving rise to the agreement. To the extent an obligation is modified, supplemented, or nullified by an agreement under this section, the agreement is a defense to the obligation.

§ 3–118. Statute of Limitations.

(a) Except as provided in subsection (e), an action to enforce the obligation of a party to pay a note payable at a definite time must be commenced within six years after the due date or dates stated in the note or, if a due date is accelerated, within six years after the accelerated due date.

(b) Except as provided in subsection (d) or (e), if demand for payment is made to the maker of a note payable on demand, an action to enforce the obligation of a party to pay the note must be commenced within six years after the demand. If no demand for payment is made to the maker, an action to enforce the note is barred if neither principal nor interest on the note has been paid for a continuous period of 10 years.

(c) Except as provided in subsection (d), an action to enforce the obligation of a party to an unaccepted draft to pay the draft must be commenced within three years after dishonor of the draft or 10 years after the date of the draft, whichever period expires first.

(d) An action to enforce the obligation of the acceptor of a certified check or the issuer of a teller's check, cashier's check, or traveler's check must be commenced within three years after demand for payment is made to the acceptor or issuer, as the case may be.

(e) An action to enforce the obligation of a party to a certificate of deposit to pay the instrument must be commenced within six years after demand for payment is made to the maker, but if the instrument states a due date and the maker is not required to pay before that date, the six-year period begins when a demand for payment is in effect and the due date has passed.

(f) An action to enforce the obligation of a party to pay an accepted draft, other than a certified check, must be commenced (i) within six years after the due date or dates stated in the draft or acceptance if the obligation of the acceptor is payable at a definite time, or (ii) within six years after the date of the acceptance if the obligation of the acceptor is payable on demand.

(g) Unless governed by other law regarding claims for indemnity or contribution, an action (i) for conversion of an instrument, for money had and received, or like action based on conversion, (ii) for breach of warranty, or (iii) to enforce an obligation, duty, or right arising under this Article and not governed by this section must be commenced within three years after the [cause of action] accrues.

§ 3–119. Notice of Right to Defend Action. In an action for breach of an obligation for which a third person is answerable over pursuant to this Article or Article 4, the defendant may give the third person notice of the litigation in a record, and the person notified may then give similar notice to any other person who is answerable over. If the notice states (i) that the person notified may come in and defend and (ii) that failure to do so will bind the person notified in an action later brought by the person giving the notice as to any determination of fact common to the two litigations, the person notified is so bound unless after seasonable receipt of the notice the person notified does come in and defend.

PART 2: NEGOTIATION, TRANSFER, AND INDORSEMENT

§ 3–201. Negotiation.

(a) "Negotiation" means a transfer of possession, whether voluntary or involuntary, of an instrument by a person other than the issuer to a person who thereby becomes its holder.

(b) Except for negotiation by a remitter, if an instrument is payable to an identified person, negotiation requires transfer of possession of the instrument and its indorsement by the holder. If an instrument is payable to bearer, it may be negotiated by transfer of possession alone.

§ 3–202. Negotiation Subject to Rescission.

(a) Negotiation is effective even if obtained (i) from an infant, a corporation exceeding its powers, or a person without capacity, (ii) by fraud, duress, or mistake, or (iii) in breach of duty or as part of an illegal transaction.

(b) To the extent permitted by other law, negotiation may be rescinded or may be subject to other remedies, but those remedies may not be asserted against a subsequent holder in due course or a person paying the instrument in good faith and without knowledge of facts that are a basis for rescission or other remedy.

§ 3–203. Transfer of Instrument; Rights Acquired by Transfer.

(a) An instrument is transferred when it is delivered by a person other than its issuer for the purpose of giving to the person receiving delivery the right to enforce the instrument.

(b) Transfer of an instrument, whether or not the transfer is a negotiation, vests in the transferee any right of the transferor to enforce the instrument, including any right as a holder in due course, but the transferee cannot acquire rights of a holder in due course by a transfer, directly or indirectly, from a holder in due course if the transferee engaged in fraud or illegality affecting the instrument.

(c) Unless otherwise agreed, if an instrument is transferred for value and the transferee does not become a holder because of lack of indorsement by the transferor, the transferee has a specifically enforceable right to the unqualified indorsement of the transferor, but negotiation of the instrument does not occur until the indorsement is made.

(d) If a transferor purports to transfer less than the entire instrument, negotiation of the instrument does not occur. The transferee obtains no rights under this Article and has only the rights of a partial assignee.

§ 3–204. Indorsement.

(a) "Indorsement" means a signature, other than that of a signer as maker, drawer, or acceptor, that alone or accompanied by other words is made on an instrument for the purpose of (i) negotiating the instrument, (ii) restricting payment of the instrument, or (iii) incurring indorser's liability on the instrument, but regardless of the intent of the signer, a signature and its accompanying words is an indorsement unless the accompanying words, terms of the instrument, place of the signature, or other circumstances unambiguously indicate that the signature was made for a purpose other than indorsement. For the purpose of determining whether a signature is made on an instrument, a paper affixed to the instrument is a part of the instrument.

(b) "Indorser" means a person who makes an indorsement.

(c) For the purpose of determining whether the transferee of an instrument is a holder, an indorsement that transfers a security interest in the instrument is effective as an unqualified indorsement of the instrument.

(d) If an instrument is payable to a holder under a name that is not the name of the holder, indorsement may be made by the holder in the name stated in the instrument or in the holder's name or both, but signature in both names may be required by a person paying or taking the instrument for value or collection.

§ 3–205. Special Indorsement; Blank Indorsement; Anomalous Indorsement.

(a) If an indorsement is made by the holder of an instrument, whether payable to an identified person or payable to bearer, and the indorsement identifies a person to whom it makes the instrument payable, it is a "special indorsement." When specially indorsed, an instrument becomes payable to the identified person and may be negotiated only by the indorsement of that person. The principles stated in Section 3–110 apply to special indorsements.

(b) If an indorsement is made by the holder of an instrument and it is not a special indorsement, it is a "blank indorsement." When indorsed in blank, an instrument becomes payable to bearer and may be negotiated by transfer of possession alone until specially indorsed.

(c) The holder may convert a blank indorsement that consists only of a signature into a special indorsement by writing, above the signature of the indorser, words identifying the person to whom the instrument is made payable.

(d) "Anomalous indorsement" means an indorsement made by a person who is not the holder of the instrument. An anomalous indorsement does not affect the manner in which the instrument may be negotiated.

§ 3–206. Restrictive Indorsement.

(a) An indorsement limiting payment to a particular person or otherwise prohibiting further transfer or negotiation of the instrument is not effective to prevent further transfer or negotiation of the instrument.

(b) An indorsement stating a condition to the right of the indorsee to receive payment does not affect the right of the indorsee to enforce the instrument. A person paying the instrument or taking it for value or collection may disregard the condition, and the rights and liabilities of that person are not affected by whether the condition has been fulfilled.

(c) If an instrument bears an indorsement (i) described in Section 4–201(b), or (ii) in blank or to a particular bank using the words "for deposit," "for collection," or other words indicating a purpose of having the instrument collected by a bank for the indorser or for a particular account, the following rules apply:

   (1) A person, other than a bank, who purchases the instrument when so indorsed converts the instrument unless the amount paid for the instrument is received by the indorser or applied consistently with the indorsement.

   (2) A depositary bank that purchases the instrument or takes it for collection when so indorsed converts the instrument unless the amount paid by the bank with respect to the instrument is received by the indorser or applied consistently with the indorsement.

   (3) A payor bank that is also the depositary bank or that takes the instrument for immediate payment over the counter from a person other than a collecting bank converts the instrument unless the proceeds of the instrument are received by the indorser or applied consistently with the indorsement.

   (4) Except as otherwise provided in paragraph (3), a payor bank or intermediary bank may disregard the indorsement and is not liable if the proceeds of the instrument are not received by the indorser or applied consistently with the indorsement.

(d) Except for an indorsement covered by subsection (c), if an instrument bears an indorsement using words to the effect that payment is to be made to the indorsee as agent, trustee, or other fiduciary for the benefit of the indorser or another person, the following rules apply:

   (1) Unless there is notice of breach of fiduciary duty as provided in Section 3–307, a person who purchases the instrument from the indorsee or takes the instrument from the indorsee for collection or payment may pay the proceeds of payment or the value given for the instrument to the indorsee without regard to whether the indorsee violates a fiduciary duty to the indorser.

(2) A subsequent transferee of the instrument or person who pays the instrument is neither given notice nor otherwise affected by the restriction in the indorsement unless the transferee or payor knows that the fiduciary dealt with the instrument or its proceeds in breach of fiduciary duty.

(e) The presence on an instrument of an indorsement to which this section applies does not prevent a purchaser of the instrument from becoming a holder in due course of the instrument unless the purchaser is a converter under subsection (c) or has notice or knowledge of breach of fiduciary duty as stated in subsection (d).

(f) In an action to enforce the obligation of a party to pay the instrument, the obligor has a defense if payment would violate an indorsement to which this section applies and the payment is not permitted by this section.

§ 3–207. Reacquisition. Reacquisition of an instrument occurs if it is transferred to a former holder, by negotiation or otherwise. A former holder who reacquires the instrument may cancel indorsements made after the reacquirer first became a holder of the instrument. If the cancellation causes the instrument to be payable to the reacquirer or to bearer, the reacquirer may negotiate the instrument. An indorser whose indorsement is canceled is discharged, and the discharge is effective against any subsequent holder.

PART 3: ENFORCEMENT OF INSTRUMENTS

§ 3–301. Person Entitled to Enforce Instrument. "Person entitled to enforce" an instrument means (i) the holder of the instrument, (ii) a nonholder in possession of the instrument who has the rights of a holder, or (iii) a person not in possession of the instrument who is entitled to enforce the instrument pursuant to Section 3–309 or 3–418(d). A person may be a person entitled to enforce the instrument even though the person is not the owner of the instrument or is in wrongful possession of the instrument.

§ 3–302. Holder in Due Course.

(a) Subject to subsection (c) and Section 3–106(d), "holder in due course" means the holder of an instrument if:
  (1) the instrument when issued or negotiated to the holder does not bear such apparent evidence of forgery or alteration or is not otherwise so irregular or incomplete as to call into question its authenticity; and
  (2) the holder took the instrument (i) for value, (ii) in good faith, (iii) without notice that the instrument is overdue or has been dishonored or that there is an uncured default with respect to payment of another instrument issued as part of the same series, (iv) without notice that the instrument contains an unauthorized signature or has been altered, (v) without notice of any claim to the instrument described in Section 3–306, and (vi) without notice that any party has a defense or claim in recoupment described in Section 3–305(a).

(b) Notice of discharge of a party, other than discharge in an insolvency proceeding, is not notice of a defense under subsection (a), but discharge is effective against a person who became a holder in due course with notice of the discharge. Public filing or recording of a document does not of itself constitute notice of a defense, claim in recoupment, or claim to the instrument.

(c) Except to the extent a transferor or predecessor in interest has rights as a holder in due course, a person does not acquire rights of a holder in due course of an instrument taken (i) by legal process or by purchase in an execution, bankruptcy, or creditor's sale or similar proceeding, (ii) by purchase as part of a bulk transaction not in ordinary course of business of the transferor, or (iii) as the successor in interest to an estate or other organization.

(d) If, under Section 3–303(a)(1), the promise of performance that is the consideration for an instrument has been partially performed, the holder may assert rights as a holder in due course of the instrument only to the fraction of the amount payable under the instrument equal to the value of the partial performance divided by the value of the promised performance.

(e) If (i) the person entitled to enforce an instrument has only a security interest in the instrument and (ii) the person obliged to pay the instrument has a defense, claim in recoupment, or claim to the instrument that may be asserted against the person who granted the security interest, the person entitled to enforce the instrument may assert rights as a holder in due course only to an amount payable under the instrument which, at the time of enforcement of the instrument, does not exceed the amount of the unpaid obligation secured.

(f) To be effective, notice must be received at a time and in a manner that gives a reasonable opportunity to act on it.

(g) This section is subject to any law limiting status as a holder in due course in particular classes of transactions.

§ 3–303. Value and Consideration.

(a) An instrument is issued or transferred for value if:
  (1) the instrument is issued or transferred for a promise of performance, to the extent the promise has been performed;
  (2) the transferee acquires a security interest or other lien in the instrument other than a lien obtained by judicial proceeding;
  (3) the instrument is issued or transferred as payment of, or as security for, an antecedent claim against any person, whether or not the claim is due;
  (4) the instrument is issued or transferred in exchange for a negotiable instrument; or
  (5) the instrument is issued or transferred in exchange for the incurring of an irrevocable obligation to a third party by the person taking the instrument.

(b) "Consideration" means any consideration sufficient to support a simple contract. The drawer or maker of an instrument has a defense if the instrument is issued without consideration. If an instrument is issued for a promise of performance, the issuer has a defense to the extent performance of the promise is due and the promise has not been performed. If an instrument is issued for value as stated in subsection (a), the instrument is also issued for consideration.

§ 3–304. Overdue Instrument.

(a) An instrument payable on demand becomes overdue at the earliest of the following times:
  (1) on the day after the day demand for payment is duly made;
  (2) if the instrument is a check, 90 days after its date; or
  (3) if the instrument is not a check, when the instrument has been outstanding for a period of time after its date which is unreasonably long under the circumstances of the particular case in light of the nature of the instrument and usage of the trade.

(b) With respect to an instrument payable at a definite time the following rules apply:
  (1) If the principal is payable in installments and a due date has not been accelerated, the instrument becomes overdue upon default under the instrument for nonpayment of an installment, and the instrument remains overdue until the default is cured.
  (2) If the principal is not payable in installments and the due date has not been accelerated, the instrument becomes overdue on the day after the due date.
  (3) If a due date with respect to principal has been accelerated, the instrument becomes overdue on the day after the accelerated due date.

(c) Unless the due date of principal has been accelerated, an instrument does not become overdue if there is default in payment of interest but no default in payment of principal.

§ 3–305. Defenses and Claims in Recoupment; Claims in Consumer Transactions.

(a) Except as otherwise provided in this section, the right to enforce the obligation of a party to pay an instrument is subject to the following:

    (1) a defense of the obligor based on (i) infancy of the obligor to the extent it is a defense to a simple contract, (ii) duress, lack of legal capacity, or illegality of the transaction which, under other law, nullifies the obligation of the obligor, (iii) fraud that induced the obligor to sign the instrument with neither knowledge nor reasonable opportunity to learn of its character or its essential terms, or (iv) discharge of the obligor in insolvency proceedings;

    (2) a defense of the obligor stated in another section of this Article or a defense of the obligor that would be available if the person entitled to enforce the instrument were enforcing a right to payment under a simple contract; and

    (3) a claim in recoupment of the obligor against the original payee of the instrument if the claim arose from the transaction that gave rise to the instrument; but the claim of the obligor may be asserted against a transferee of the instrument only to reduce the amount owing on the instrument at the time the action is brought.

(b) The right of a holder in due course to enforce the obligation of a party to pay the instrument is subject to defenses of the obligor stated in subsection (a)(1), but is not subject to defenses of the obligor stated in subsection (a)(2) or claims in recoupment stated in subsection (a)(3) against a person other than the holder.

(c) Except as stated in subsection (d), in an action to enforce the obligation of a party to pay the instrument, the obligor may not assert against the person entitled to enforce the instrument a defense, claim in recoupment, or claim to the instrument (Section 3–306) of another person, but the other person's claim to the instrument may be asserted by the obligor if the other person is joined in the action and personally asserts the claim against the person entitled to enforce the instrument. An obligor is not obliged to pay the instrument if the person seeking enforcement of the instrument does not have rights of a holder in due course and the obligor proves that the instrument is a lost or stolen instrument.

(d) In an action to enforce the obligation of an accommodation party to pay an instrument, the accommodation party may assert against the person entitled to enforce the instrument any defense or claim in recoupment under subsection (a) that the accommodated party could assert against the person entitled to enforce the instrument, except the defenses of discharge in insolvency proceedings, infancy, and lack of legal capacity.

(e) In a consumer transaction, if law other than this article requires that an instrument include a statement to the effect that the rights of a holder or transferee are subject to a claim or defense that the issuer could assert against the original payee, and the instrument does not include such a statement:

    (1) the instrument has the same effect as if the instrument included such a statement;

    (2) the issuer may assert against the holder or transferee all claims and defenses that would have been available if the instrument included such a statement; and

    (3) the extent to which claims may be asserted against the holder or transferee is determined as if the instrument included such a statement.

(f) This section is subject to law other than this article that establishes a different rule for consumer transactions.

Legislative Note: If a consumer protection law in this state addresses the same issue as subsection (g), it should be examined for consistency with subsection (g) and, if inconsistent, should be amended.

§ 3–306. Claims to an Instrument.
A person taking an instrument, other than a person having rights of a holder in due course, is subject to a claim of a property or possessory right in the instrument or its proceeds, including a claim to rescind a negotiation and to recover the instrument or its proceeds. A person having rights of a holder in due course takes free of the claim to the instrument.

§ 3–307. Notice of Breach of Fiduciary Duty.

(a) In this section:
   (1) "Fiduciary" means an agent, trustee, partner, corporate officer or director, or other representative owing a fiduciary duty with respect to an instrument.
   (2) "Represented person" means the principal, beneficiary, partnership, corporation, or other person to whom the duty stated in paragraph (1) is owed.

(b) If (i) an instrument is taken from a fiduciary for payment or collection or for value, (ii) the taker has knowledge of the fiduciary status of the fiduciary, and (iii) the represented person makes a claim to the instrument or its proceeds on the basis that the transaction of the fiduciary is a breach of fiduciary duty, the following rules apply:
   (1) Notice of breach of fiduciary duty by the fiduciary is notice of the claim of the represented person.
   (2) In the case of an instrument payable to the represented person or the fiduciary as such, the taker has notice of the breach of fiduciary duty if the instrument is (i) taken in payment of or as security for a debt known by the taker to be the personal debt of the fiduciary, (ii) taken in a transaction known by the taker to be for the personal benefit of the fiduciary, or (iii) deposited to an account other than an account of the fiduciary, as such, or an account of the represented person.
   (3) If an instrument is issued by the represented person or the fiduciary as such, and made payable to the fiduciary personally, the taker does not have notice of the breach of fiduciary duty unless the taker knows of the breach of fiduciary duty.
   (4) If an instrument is issued by the represented person or the fiduciary as such, to the taker as payee, the taker has notice of the breach of fiduciary duty if the instrument is (i) taken in payment of or as security for a debt known by the taker to be the personal debt of the fiduciary, (ii) taken in a transaction known by the taker to be for the personal benefit of the fiduciary, or (iii) deposited to an account other than an account of the fiduciary, as such, or an account of the represented person.

§ 3–308. Proof of Signatures and Status as Holder in Due Course.

(a) In an action with respect to an instrument, the authenticity of, and authority to make, each signature on the instrument is admitted unless specifically denied in the pleadings. If the validity of a signature is denied in the pleadings, the burden of establishing validity is on the person claiming validity, but the signature is presumed to be authentic and authorized unless the action is to enforce the liability of the purported signer and the signer is dead or incompetent at the time of trial of the issue of validity of the signature. If an action to enforce the instrument is brought against a person as the undisclosed principal of a person who signed the instrument as a party to the instrument, the plaintiff has the burden of establishing that the defendant is liable on the instrument as a represented person under Section 3–402(a).

(b) If the validity of signatures is admitted or proved and there is compliance with subsection (a), a plaintiff producing the instrument is entitled to payment if the plaintiff proves entitlement to enforce the instrument under Section 3–301, unless the defendant proves a defense or claim in recoupment. If a defense or claim in recoupment is proved, the right to payment of the plaintiff is subject to the defense or claim, except to the extent the plaintiff proves that the plaintiff has rights of a holder in due course which are not subject to the defense or claim.

§ 3–309. Enforcement of Lost, Destroyed, or Stolen Instrument.

(a) A person not in possession of an instrument is entitled to enforce the instrument if:
   (1) the person seeking to enforce the instrument:
      (i) was entitled to enforce the instrument when loss of possession occurred; or
      (ii) has directly or indirectly acquired ownership of the instrument from a person who was entitled to enforce the instrument when loss of possession occurred.

    (2) the loss of possession was not the result of a transfer by the person or a lawful seizure; and

    (3) the person cannot reasonably obtain possession of the instrument because the instrument was destroyed, its whereabouts cannot be determined, or it is in the wrongful possession of an unknown person or a person that cannot be found or is not amenable to service of process.

(b) A person seeking enforcement of an instrument under subsection (a) must prove the terms of the instrument and the person's right to enforce the instrument. If that proof is made, Section 3–308 applies to the case as if the person seeking enforcement had produced the instrument. The court may not enter judgment in favor of the person seeking enforcement unless it finds that the person required to pay the instrument is adequately protected against loss that might occur by reason of a claim by another person to enforce the instrument. Adequate protection may be provided by any reasonable means.

§ 3–310. Effect of Instrument on Obligation for Which Taken.

(a) Unless otherwise agreed, if a certified check, cashier's check, or teller's check is taken for an obligation, the obligation is discharged to the same extent discharge would result if an amount of money equal to the amount of the instrument were taken in payment of the obligation. Discharge of the obligation does not affect any liability that the obligor may have as an indorser of the instrument.

(b) Unless otherwise agreed and except as provided in subsection (a), if a note or an uncertified check is taken for an obligation, the obligation is suspended to the same extent the obligation would be discharged if an amount of money equal to the amount of the instrument were taken, and the following rules apply:

    (1) In the case of an uncertified check, suspension of the obligation continues until dishonor of the check or until it is paid or certified. Payment or certification of the check results in discharge of the obligation to the extent of the amount of the check.

    (2) In the case of a note, suspension of the obligation continues until dishonor of the note or until it is paid. Payment of the note results in discharge of the obligation to the extent of the payment.

    (3) Except as provided in paragraph (4), if the check or note is dishonored and the obligee of the obligation for which the instrument was taken is the person entitled to enforce the instrument, the obligee may enforce either the instrument or the obligation. In the case of an instrument of a third person which is negotiated to the obligee by the obligor, discharge of the obligor on the instrument also discharges the obligation.

    (4) If the person entitled to enforce the instrument taken for an obligation is a person other than the obligee, the obligee may not enforce the obligation to the extent the obligation is suspended. If the obligee is the person entitled to enforce the instrument but no longer has possession of it because it was lost, stolen, or destroyed, the obligation may not be enforced to the extent of the amount payable on the instrument, and to that extent the obligee's rights against the obligor are limited to enforcement of the instrument.

(c) If an instrument other than one described in subsection (a) or (b) is taken for an obligation, the effect is (i) that stated in subsection (a) if the instrument is one on which a bank is liable as maker or acceptor, or (ii) that stated in subsection (b) in any other case.

§ 3–311. Accord and Satisfaction by Use of Instrument.

(a) If a person against whom a claim is asserted proves that (i) that person in good faith tendered an instrument to the claimant as full satisfaction of the claim, (ii) the amount of the claim was unliquidated or subject to a bona fide dispute, and (iii) the claimant obtained payment of the instrument, the following subsections apply.

(b) Unless subsection (c) applies, the claim is discharged if the person against whom the claim is asserted proves that the instrument or an accompanying written communication contained a conspicuous statement to the effect that the instrument was tendered as full satisfaction of the claim.

(c) Subject to subsection (d), a claim is not discharged under subsection (b) if either of the following applies:

(1) The claimant, if an organization, proves that (i) within a reasonable time before the tender, the claimant sent a conspicuous statement to the person against whom the claim is asserted that communications concerning disputed debts, including an instrument tendered as full satisfaction of a debt, are to be sent to a designated person, office, or place, and (ii) the instrument or accompanying communication was not received by that designated person, office, or place.

(2) The claimant, whether or not an organization, proves that within 90 days after payment of the instrument, the claimant tendered repayment of the amount of the instrument to the person against whom the claim is asserted. This paragraph does not apply if the claimant is an organization that sent a statement complying with paragraph (1)(i).

(d) A claim is discharged if the person against whom the claim is asserted proves that within a reasonable time before collection of the instrument was initiated, the claimant, or an agent of the claimant having direct responsibility with respect to the disputed obligation, knew that the instrument was tendered in full satisfaction of the claim.

§ 3–312. Lost, Destroyed, or Stolen Cashier's Check, Teller's Check, or Certified Check.

(a) In this section:

(1) "Check" means a cashier's check, teller's check, or certified check.

(2) "Claimant" means a person who claims the right to receive the amount of a cashier's check, teller's check, or certified check that was lost, destroyed, or stolen.

(3) "Declaration of loss" means a statement, made in a record under penalty of perjury, to the effect that (i) the declarer lost possession of a check, (ii) the declarer is the drawer or payee of the check, in the case of a certified check, or the remitter or payee of the check, in the case of a cashier's check or teller's check, (iii) the loss of possession was not the result of a transfer by the declarer or a lawful seizure, and (iv) the declarer cannot reasonably obtain possession of the check because the check was destroyed, its whereabouts cannot be determined, or it is in the wrongful possession of an unknown person or a person that cannot be found or is not amenable to service of process.

(4) "Obligated bank" means the issuer of a cashier's check or teller's check or the acceptor of a certified check.

(b) A claimant may assert a claim to the amount of a check by a communication to the obligated bank describing the check with reasonable certainty and requesting payment of the amount of the check, if (i) the claimant is the drawer or payee of a certified check or the remitter or payee of a cashier's check or teller's check, (ii) the communication contains or is accompanied by a declaration of loss of the claimant with respect to the check, (iii) the communication is received at a time and in a manner affording the bank a reasonable time to act on it before the check is paid, and (iv) the claimant provides reasonable identification if requested by the obligated bank. Delivery of a declaration of loss is a warranty of the truth of the statements made in the declaration. If a claim is asserted in compliance with this subsection, the following rules apply:

(1) The claim becomes enforceable at the later of (i) the time the claim is asserted, or (ii) the 90th day following the date of the check, in the case of a cashier's check or teller's check, or the 90th day following the date of the acceptance, in the case of a certified check.

(2) Until the claim becomes enforceable, it has no legal effect and the obligated bank may pay the check or, in the case of a teller's check, may permit the drawee to pay the check. Payment to a person entitled to enforce the check discharges all liability of the obligated bank with respect to the check.

(3) If the claim becomes enforceable before the check is presented for payment, the obligated bank is not obliged to pay the check.

(4) When the claim becomes enforceable, the obligated bank becomes obliged to pay the amount of the check to the claimant if payment of the check has not been made to a person entitled to enforce the check. Subject to Section 4–302(a)(1), payment to the claimant discharges all liability of the obligated bank with respect to the check.

(c) If the obligated bank pays the amount of a check to a claimant under subsection (b)(4) and the check is presented for payment by a person having rights of a holder in due course, the claimant is obliged to (i) refund the payment to the obligated bank if the check is paid, or (ii) pay the amount of the check to the person having rights of a holder in due course if the check is dishonored.

(d) If a claimant has the right to assert a claim under subsection (b) and is also a person entitled to enforce a cashier's check, teller's check, or certified check which is lost, destroyed, or stolen, the claimant may assert rights with respect to the check either under this section or Section 3–309.

PART 4: LIABILITY OF PARTIES

§ 3–401. Signature.

(a) A person is not liable on an instrument unless (i) the person signed the instrument, or (ii) the person is represented by an agent or representative who signed the instrument and the signature is binding on the represented person under Section 3–402.

(b) A signature may be made (i) manually or by means of a device or machine, and (ii) by the use of any name, including a trade or assumed name, or by a word, mark, or symbol executed or adopted by a person with present intention to authenticate a writing.

§ 3–402. Signature by Representative.

(a) If a person acting, or purporting to act, as a representative signs an instrument by signing either the name of the represented person or the name of the signer, the represented person is bound by the signature to the same extent the represented person would be bound if the signature were on a simple contract. If the represented person is bound, the signature of the representative is the "authorized signature of the represented person" and the represented person is liable on the instrument, whether or not identified in the instrument.

(b) If a representative signs the name of the representative to an instrument and the signature is an authorized signature of the represented person, the following rules apply:

(1) If the form of the signature shows unambiguously that the signature is made on behalf of the represented person who is identified in the instrument, the representative is not liable on the instrument.

(2) Subject to subsection (c), if (i) the form of the signature does not show unambiguously that the signature is made in a representative capacity or (ii) the represented person is not identified in the instrument, the representative is liable on the instrument to a holder in due course that took the instrument without notice that the representative was not intended to be liable on the instrument. With respect to any other person, the representative is liable on the instrument unless the representative proves that the original parties did not intend the representative to be liable on the instrument.

(c) If a representative signs the name of the representative as drawer of a check without indication of the representative status and the check is payable from an account of the represented person who is identified on the check, the signer is not liable on the check if the signature is an authorized signature of the represented person.

§ 3–403. Unauthorized Signature.

(a) Unless otherwise provided in this Article or Article 4, an unauthorized signature is ineffective except as the signature of the unauthorized signer in favor of a person who in good faith pays the instrument or takes it for value. An unauthorized signature may be ratified for all purposes of this Article.

(b) If the signature of more than one person is required to constitute the authorized signature of an organization, the signature of the organization is unauthorized if one of the required signatures is lacking.

(c) The civil or criminal liability of a person who makes an unauthorized signature is not affected by any provision of this Article which makes the unauthorized signature effective for the purposes of this Article.

§ 3–404. Impostors; Fictitious Payees.

(a) If an impostor, by use of the mails or otherwise, induces the issuer of an instrument to issue the instrument to the impostor, or to a person acting in concert with the impostor, by impersonating the payee of the instrument or a person authorized to act for the payee, an indorsement of the instrument by any person in the name of the payee is effective as the indorsement of the payee in favor of a person who, in good faith, pays the instrument or takes it for value or for collection.

(b) If (i) a person whose intent determines to whom an instrument is payable (Section 3–110(a) or (b)) does not intend the person identified as payee to have any interest in the instrument, or (ii) the person identified as payee of an instrument is a fictitious person, the following rules apply until the instrument is negotiated by special indorsement:

    (1) Any person in possession of the instrument is its holder.

    (2) An indorsement by any person in the name of the payee stated in the instrument is effective as the indorsement of the payee in favor of a person who, in good faith, pays the instrument or takes it for value or for collection.

(c) Under subsection (a) or (b), an indorsement is made in the name of a payee if (i) it is made in a name substantially similar to that of the payee or (ii) the instrument, whether or not indorsed, is deposited in a depositary bank to an account in a name substantially similar to that of the payee.

(d) With respect to an instrument to which subsection (a) or (b) applies, if a person paying the instrument or taking it for value or for collection fails to exercise ordinary care in paying or taking the instrument and that failure substantially contributes to loss resulting from payment of the instrument, the person bearing the loss may recover from the person failing to exercise ordinary care to the extent the failure to exercise ordinary care contributed to the loss.

§ 3–405. Employer's Responsibility for Fraudulent Indorsement by Employee.

(a) In this section:

    (1) "Employee" includes an independent contractor and employee of an independent contractor retained by the employer.

    (2) "Fraudulent indorsement" means (i) in the case of an instrument payable to the employer, a forged indorsement purporting to be that of the employer, or (ii) in the case of an instrument with respect to which the employer is the issuer, a forged indorsement purporting to be that of the person identified as payee.

    (3) "Responsibility" with respect to instruments means authority (i) to sign or indorse instruments on behalf of the employer, (ii) to process instruments received by the employer for bookkeeping purposes, for deposit to an account, or for other disposition, (iii) to prepare or process instruments for issue in the name of the employer,

(iv) to supply information determining the names or addresses of payees of instruments to be issued in the name of the employer, (v) to control the disposition of instruments to be issued in the name of the employer, or (vi) to act otherwise with respect to instruments in a responsible capacity. "Responsibility" does not include authority that merely allows an employee to have access to instruments or blank or incomplete instrument forms that are being stored or transported or are part of incoming or outgoing mail, or similar access.

(b) For the purpose of determining the rights and liabilities of a person who, in good faith, pays an instrument or takes it for value or for collection, if an employer entrusted an employee with responsibility with respect to the instrument and the employee or a person acting in concert with the employee makes a fraudulent indorsement of the instrument, the indorsement is effective as the indorsement of the person to whom the instrument is payable if it is made in the name of that person. If the person paying the instrument or taking it for value or for collection fails to exercise ordinary care in paying or taking the instrument and that failure substantially contributes to loss resulting from the fraud, the person bearing the loss may recover from the person failing to exercise ordinary care to the extent the failure to exercise ordinary care contributed to the loss.

(c) Under subsection (b), an indorsement is made in the name of the person to whom an instrument is payable if (i) it is made in a name substantially similar to the name of that person or (ii) the instrument, whether or not indorsed, is deposited in a depositary bank to an account in a name substantially similar to the name of that person.

§ 3–406. Negligence Contributing to Forged Signature or Alteration of Instrument.

(a) A person whose failure to exercise ordinary care substantially contributes to an alteration of an instrument or to the making of a forged signature on an instrument is precluded from asserting the alteration or the forgery against a person who, in good faith, pays the instrument or takes it for value or for collection.

(b) Under subsection (a), if the person asserting the preclusion fails to exercise ordinary care in paying or taking the instrument and that failure substantially contributes to loss, the loss is allocated between the person precluded and the person asserting the preclusion according to the extent to which the failure of each to exercise ordinary care contributed to the loss.

(c) Under subsection (a), the burden of proving failure to exercise ordinary care is on the person asserting the preclusion. Under subsection (b), the burden of proving failure to exercise ordinary care is on the person precluded.

§ 3–407. Alteration.

(a) "Alteration" means (i) an unauthorized change in an instrument that purports to modify in any respect the obligation of a party, or (ii) an unauthorized addition of words or numbers or other change to an incomplete instrument relating to the obligation of a party.

(b) Except as provided in subsection (c), an alteration fraudulently made discharges a party whose obligation is affected by the alteration unless that party assents or is precluded from asserting the alteration. No other alteration discharges a party, and the instrument may be enforced according to its original terms.

(c) A payor bank or drawee paying a fraudulently altered instrument or a person taking it for value, in good faith and without notice of the alteration, may enforce rights with respect to the instrument (i) according to its original terms, or (ii) in the case of an incomplete instrument altered by unauthorized completion, according to its terms as completed.

§ 3–408. Drawee Not Liable on Unaccepted Draft. A check or other draft does not of itself operate as an assignment of funds in the hands of the drawee available for its payment, and the drawee is not liable on the instrument until the drawee accepts it.

§ 3–409. Acceptance of Draft; Certified Check.

(a) "Acceptance" means the drawee's signed agreement to pay a draft as presented. It must be written on the draft and may consist of the drawee's signature alone. Acceptance may be made at any time and becomes effective when notification pursuant to instructions is given or the accepted draft is delivered for the purpose of giving rights on the acceptance to any person.

(b) A draft may be accepted although it has not been signed by the drawer, is otherwise incomplete, is overdue, or has been dishonored.

(c) If a draft is payable at a fixed period after sight and the acceptor fails to date the acceptance, the holder may complete the acceptance by supplying a date in good faith.

(d) "Certified check" means a check accepted by the bank on which it is drawn. Acceptance may be made as stated in subsection (a) or by a writing on the check which indicates that the check is certified. The drawee of a check has no obligation to certify the check, and refusal to certify is not dishonor of the check.

§ 3–410. Acceptance Varying Draft.

(a) If the terms of a drawee's acceptance vary from the terms of the draft as presented, the holder may refuse the acceptance and treat the draft as dishonored. In that case, the drawee may cancel the acceptance.

(b) The terms of a draft are not varied by an acceptance to pay at a particular bank or place in the United States, unless the acceptance states that the draft is to be paid only at that bank or place.

(c) If the holder assents to an acceptance varying the terms of a draft, the obligation of each drawer and indorser that does not expressly assent to the acceptance is discharged.

§ 3–411. Refusal to Pay Cashier's Checks, Teller's Checks, and Certified Checks.

(a) In this section, "obligated bank" means the acceptor of a certified check or the issuer of a cashier's check or teller's check bought from the issuer.

(b) If the obligated bank wrongfully (i) refuses to pay a cashier's check or certified check, (ii) stops payment of a teller's check, or (iii) refuses to pay a dishonored teller's check, the person asserting the right to enforce the check is entitled to compensation for expenses and loss of interest resulting from the nonpayment and may recover consequential damages if the obligated bank refuses to pay after receiving notice of particular circumstances giving rise to the damages.

(c) Expenses or consequential damages under subsection (b) are not recoverable if the refusal of the obligated bank to pay occurs because (i) the bank suspends payments, (ii) the obligated bank asserts a claim or defense of the bank that it has reasonable grounds to believe is available against the person entitled to enforce the instrument, (iii) the obligated bank has a reasonable doubt whether the person demanding payment is the person entitled to enforce the instrument, or (iv) payment is prohibited by law.

§ 3–412. Obligation of Issuer of Note or Cashier's Check. The issuer of a note or cashier's check or other draft drawn on the drawer is obliged to pay the instrument (i) according to its terms at the time it was issued or, if not issued, at the time it first came into possession of a holder, or (ii) if the issuer signed an incomplete instrument, according to its terms when completed, to the extent stated in Sections 3–115 and 3–407. The obligation is owed to a person entitled to enforce the instrument or to an indorser who paid the instrument under Section 3–415.

§ 3–413. Obligation of Acceptor.

(a) The acceptor of a draft is obliged to pay the draft (i) according to its terms at the time it was accepted, even though the acceptance states that the draft is payable "as originally drawn" or equivalent terms, (ii) if the acceptance varies the terms of the draft, according to the terms of the draft as varied, or (iii) if the acceptance is of a draft that is an incomplete instrument, according to its terms when completed, to the extent stated in Sections 3–115 and 3–407. The obligation is owed to a person entitled to enforce the draft or to the drawer or an indorser who paid the draft under Section 3–414 or 3–415.

(b) If the certification of a check or other acceptance of a draft states the amount certified or accepted, the obligation of the acceptor is that amount. If (i) the certification or acceptance does not state an amount, (ii) the amount of the instrument is subsequently raised, and (iii) the instrument is then negotiated to a holder in due course, the obligation of the acceptor is the amount of the instrument at the time it was taken by the holder in due course.

§ 3–414. Obligation of Drawer.

(a) This section does not apply to cashier's checks or other drafts drawn on the drawer.

(b) If an unaccepted draft is dishonored, the drawer is obliged to pay the draft (i) according to its terms at the time it was issued or, if not issued, at the time it first came into possession of a holder, or (ii) if the drawer signed an incomplete instrument, according to its terms when completed, to the extent stated in Sections 3–115 and 3–407. The obligation is owed to a person entitled to enforce the draft or to an indorser who paid the draft under Section 3–415.

(c) If a draft is accepted by a bank, the drawer is discharged, regardless of when or by whom acceptance was obtained.

(d) If a draft is accepted and the acceptor is not a bank, the obligation of the drawer to pay the draft if the draft is dishonored by the acceptor is the same as the obligation of an indorser under Section 3–415(a) and (c).

(e) If a draft states that it is drawn "without recourse" or otherwise disclaims liability of the drawer to pay the draft, the drawer is not liable under subsection (b) to pay the draft if the draft is not a check. A disclaimer of the liability stated in subsection (b) is not effective if the draft is a check.

(f) If (i) a check is not presented for payment or given to a depositary bank for collection within 30 days after its date, (ii) the drawee suspends payments after expiration of the 30–day period without paying the check, and (iii) because of the suspension of payments, the drawer is deprived of funds maintained with the drawee to cover payment of the check, the drawer to the extent deprived of funds may discharge its obligation to pay the check by assigning to the person entitled to enforce the check the rights of the drawer against the drawee with respect to the funds.

§ 3–415. Obligation of Indorser.

(a) Subject to subsections (b), (c), (d), (e) and to Section 3–419(d), if an instrument is dishonored, an indorser is obliged to pay the amount due on the instrument (i) according to the terms of the instrument at the time it was indorsed, or (ii) if the indorser indorsed an incomplete instrument, according to its terms when completed, to the extent stated in Sections 3–115 and 3–407. The obligation of the indorser is owed to a person entitled to enforce the instrument or to a subsequent indorser who paid the instrument under this section.

(b) If an indorsement states that it is made "without recourse" or otherwise disclaims liability of the indorser, the indorser is not liable under subsection (a) to pay the instrument.

(c) If notice of dishonor of an instrument is required by Section 3–503 and notice of dishonor complying with that section is not given to an indorser, the liability of the indorser under subsection (a) is discharged.

(d) If a draft is accepted by a bank after an indorsement is made, the liability of the indorser under subsection (a) is discharged.

(e) If an indorser of a check is liable under subsection (a) and the check is not presented for payment, or given to a depositary bank for collection, within 30 days after the day the indorsement was made, the liability of the indorser under subsection (a) is discharged.

§ 3–416. Transfer Warranties.

(a) A person who transfers an instrument for consideration warrants to the transferee and, if the transfer is by indorsement, to any subsequent transferee that:
   (1) the warrantor is a person entitled to enforce the instrument;
   (2) all signatures on the instrument are authentic and authorized;
   (3) the instrument has not been altered;
   (4) the instrument is not subject to a defense or claim in recoupment of any party which can be asserted against the warrantor;
   (5) the warrantor has no knowledge of any insolvency proceeding commenced with respect to the maker or acceptor or, in the case of an unaccepted draft, the drawer; and
   (6) with respect to a remotely-created consumer item, that the person on whose account the item is drawn authorized the issuance of the item in the amount for which the item is drawn.

(b) A person to whom the warranties under subsection (a) are made and who took the instrument in good faith may recover from the warrantor as damages for breach of warranty an amount equal to the loss suffered as a result of the breach, but not more than the amount of the instrument plus expenses and loss of interest incurred as a result of the breach.

(c) The warranties stated in subsection (a) cannot be disclaimed with respect to checks. Unless notice of a claim for breach of warranty is given to the warrantor within 30 days after the claimant has reason to know of the breach and the identity of the warrantor, the liability of the warrantor under subsection (b) is discharged to the extent of any loss caused by the delay in giving notice of the claim.

(d) A [cause of action] for breach of warranty under this section accrues when the claimant has reason to know of the breach.

§ 3–417. Presentment Warranties.

(a) If an unaccepted draft is presented to the drawee for payment or acceptance and the drawee pays or accepts the draft, (i) the person obtaining payment or acceptance, at the time of presentment, and (ii) a previous transferor of the draft, at the time of transfer, warrant to the drawee making payment or accepting the draft in good faith that:
   (1) the warrantor is, or was, at the time the warrantor transferred the draft, a person entitled to enforce the draft or authorized to obtain payment or acceptance of the draft on behalf of a person entitled to enforce the draft;
   (2) the draft has not been altered;
   (3) the warrantor has no knowledge that the signature of the drawer of the draft is unauthorized; and
   (4) with respect to any remotely-created consumer item, that the person on whose account the item is drawn authorized the issuance of the item in the amount for which the item is drawn.

(b) A drawee making payment may recover from any warrantor damages for breach of warranty equal to the amount paid by the drawee less the amount the drawee received or is entitled to receive from the drawer because of the payment. In addition, the drawee is entitled to compensation for expenses and loss of interest resulting from the breach. The right of the drawee to recover damages under this subsection is not affected by any failure of the drawee to exercise ordinary care in making payment. If the drawee accepts the draft, breach of warranty is a defense to the obligation of the acceptor. If the acceptor makes payment with respect to the draft, the acceptor is entitled to recover from any warrantor for breach of warranty the amounts stated in this subsection.

(c) If a drawee asserts a claim for breach of warranty under subsection (a) based on an unauthorized indorsement of the draft or an alteration of the draft, the warrantor may defend by proving that the indorsement is effective under Section 3–404 or 3–405 or the drawer is precluded under Section 3–406 or 4–406 from asserting against the drawee the unauthorized indorsement or alteration.

(d) If (i) a dishonored draft is presented for payment to the drawer or an indorser or (ii) any other instrument is presented for payment to a party obliged to pay the instrument, and (iii) payment is received, the following rules apply:

   (1) The person obtaining payment and a prior transferor of the instrument warrant to the person making payment in good faith that the warrantor is, or was, at the time the warrantor transferred the instrument, a person entitled to enforce the instrument or authorized to obtain payment on behalf of a person entitled to enforce the instrument.

   (2) The person making payment may recover from any warrantor for breach of warranty an amount equal to the amount paid plus expenses and loss of interest resulting from the breach.

(e) The warranties stated in subsections (a) and (d) cannot be disclaimed with respect to checks. Unless notice of a claim for breach of warranty is given to the warrantor within 30 days after the claimant has reason to know of the breach and the identity of the warrantor, the liability of the warrantor under subsection (b) or (d) is discharged to the extent of any loss caused by the delay in giving notice of the claim.

(f) A [cause of action] for breach of warranty under this section accrues when the claimant has reason to know of the breach.

§ 3–418. Payment or Acceptance by Mistake.

(a) Except as provided in subsection (c), if the drawee of a draft pays or accepts the draft and the drawee acted on the mistaken belief that (i) payment of the draft had not been stopped pursuant to Section 4–403 or (ii) the signature of the drawer of the draft was authorized, the drawee may recover the amount of the draft from the person to whom or for whose benefit payment was made or, in the case of acceptance, may revoke the acceptance. Rights of the drawee under this subsection are not affected by failure of the drawee to exercise ordinary care in paying or accepting the draft.

(b) Except as provided in subsection (c), if an instrument has been paid or accepted by mistake and the case is not covered by subsection (a), the person paying or accepting may, to the extent permitted by the law governing mistake and restitution, (i) recover the payment from the person to whom or for whose benefit payment was made or (ii) in the case of acceptance, may revoke the acceptance.

(c) The remedies provided by subsection (a) or (b) may not be asserted against a person who took the instrument in good faith and for value or who in good faith changed position in reliance on the payment or acceptance. This subsection does not limit remedies provided by Section 3–417 or 4–407.

(d) Notwithstanding Section 4–215, if an instrument is paid or accepted by mistake and the payor or acceptor recovers payment or revokes acceptance under subsection (a) or (b), the instrument is deemed not to have been paid or accepted and is treated as dishonored, and the person from whom payment is recovered has rights as a person entitled to enforce the dishonored instrument.

§ 3–419. Instruments Signed for Accommodation.

(a) If an instrument is issued for value given for the benefit of a party to the instrument ("accommodated party") and another party to the instrument ("accommodation party") signs the instrument for the purpose of incurring liability on the instrument without being a direct beneficiary of the value given for the instrument, the instrument is signed by the accommodation party "for accommodation."

(b) An accommodation party may sign the instrument as maker, drawer, acceptor, or indorser and, subject to subsection (d), is obliged to pay the instrument in the capacity in which the accommodation party signs. The obligation of an accommodation party may be enforced notwithstanding any statute of frauds and whether or not the accommodation party receives consideration for the accommodation.

(c) A person signing an instrument is presumed to be an accommodation party and there is notice that the instrument is signed for accommodation if the signature is an anomalous indorsement or is accompanied by words indicating that the signer is acting as surety or guarantor with respect to the obligation of another party to the instrument. Except as provided in Section 3–605, the obligation of an accommodation party to pay the instrument is not affected by the fact that the person enforcing the obligation had notice when the instrument was taken by that person that the accommodation party signed the instrument for accommodation.

(d) If the signature of a party to an instrument is accompanied by words indicating unambiguously that the party is guaranteeing collection rather than payment of the obligation of another party to the instrument, the signer is obliged to pay the amount due on the instrument to a person entitled to enforce the instrument only if (i) execution of judgment against the other party has been returned unsatisfied, (ii) the other party is insolvent or in an insolvency proceeding, (iii) the other party cannot be served with process, or (iv) it is otherwise apparent that payment cannot be obtained from the other party.

(e) If the signature of a party to an instrument is accompanied by words indicating that the party guarantees payment or the signer signs the instrument as an accommodation party in some other manner that does not unambiguously indicate an intention to guarantee collection rather than payment, the signer is obliged to pay the amount due on the instrument to a person entitled to enforce the instrument in the same circumstances as the accommodated party would be obliged, without prior resort to the accommodated party by the person entitled to enforce the instrument.

(f) An accommodation party who pays the instrument is entitled to reimbursement from the accommodated party and is entitled to enforce the instrument against the accommodated party. In proper circumstances, an accommodation party may obtain relief that requires the accommodated party to perform its obligations on the instrument. An accommodated party that pays the instrument has no right of recourse against, and is not entitled to contribution from, an accommodation party.

§ 3–420. Conversion of Instrument.

(a) The law applicable to conversion of personal property applies to instruments. An instrument is also converted if it is taken by transfer, other than a negotiation, from a person not entitled to enforce the instrument or a bank makes or obtains payment with respect to the instrument for a person not entitled to enforce the instrument or receive payment. An action for conversion of an instrument may not be brought by (i) the issuer or acceptor of the instrument or (ii) a payee or indorsee who did not receive delivery of the instrument either directly or through delivery to an agent or a co-payee.

(b) In an action under subsection (a), the measure of liability is presumed to be the amount payable on the instrument, but recovery may not exceed the amount of the plaintiff's interest in the instrument.

(c) A representative, other than a depositary bank, who has in good faith dealt with an instrument or its proceeds on behalf of one who was not the person entitled to enforce the instrument is not liable in conversion to that person beyond the amount of any proceeds that it has not paid out.

PART 5: DISHONOR

§ 3–501. Presentment.

(a) "Presentment" means a demand made by or on behalf of a person entitled to enforce an instrument (i) to pay the instrument made to the drawee or a party obliged to pay the instrument or, in the case of a note or accepted draft payable at a bank, to the bank, or (ii) to accept a draft made to the drawee.

(b) The following rules are subject to Article 4, agreement of the parties, and clearing-house rules and the like:

    (1) Presentment may be made at the place of payment of the instrument and must be made at the place of payment if the instrument is payable at a bank in the United States; may be made by any commercially reasonable means, including an oral, written, or electronic communication; is effective when the demand for payment or acceptance is received by the person to whom presentment is made; and is effective if made to any one of two or more makers, acceptors, drawees, or other payors.

    (2) Upon demand of the person to whom presentment is made, the person making presentment must (i) exhibit the instrument, (ii) give reasonable identification and, if presentment is made on behalf of another person, reasonable evidence of authority to do so, and (iii) sign a receipt on the instrument for any payment made or surrender the instrument if full payment is made.

    (3) Without dishonoring the instrument, the party to whom presentment is made may (i) return the instrument for lack of a necessary indorsement, or (ii) refuse payment or acceptance for failure of the presentment to comply with the terms of the instrument, an agreement of the parties, or other applicable law or rule.

    (4) The party to whom presentment is made may treat presentment as occurring on the next business day after the day of presentment if the party to whom presentment is made has established a cut-off hour not earlier than 2 p.m. for the receipt and processing of instruments presented for payment or acceptance and presentment is made after the cut-off hour.

§ 3–502. Dishonor.

(a) Dishonor of a note is governed by the following rules:

    (1) If the note is payable on demand, the note is dishonored if presentment is duly made to the maker and the note is not paid on the day of presentment.

    (2) If the note is not payable on demand and is payable at or through a bank or the terms of the note require presentment, the note is dishonored if presentment is duly made and the note is not paid on the day it becomes payable or the day of presentment, whichever is later.

    (3) If the note is not payable on demand and paragraph (2) does not apply, the note is dishonored if it is not paid on the day it becomes payable.

(b) Dishonor of an unaccepted draft other than a documentary draft is governed by the following rules:

    (1) If a check is duly presented for payment to the payor bank otherwise than for immediate payment over the counter, the check is dishonored if the payor bank makes timely return of the check or sends timely notice of dishonor or nonpayment under Section 4–301 or 4–302, or becomes accountable for the amount of the check under Section 4–302.

    (2) If a draft is payable on demand and paragraph (1) does not apply, the draft is dishonored if presentment for payment is duly made to the drawee and the draft is not paid on the day of presentment.

    (3) If a draft is payable on a date stated in the draft, the draft is dishonored if (i) presentment for payment is duly made to the drawee and payment is not made on the day the draft becomes payable or the day of presentment, whichever is later, or (ii) presentment for acceptance is duly made before the day the draft becomes payable and the draft is not accepted on the day of presentment.

(4) If a draft is payable on elapse of a period of time after sight or acceptance, the draft is dishonored if presentment for acceptance is duly made and the draft is not accepted on the day of presentment.

(c) Dishonor of an unaccepted documentary draft occurs according to the rules stated in subsection (b)(2), (3), and (4), except that payment or acceptance may be delayed without dishonor until no later than the close of the third business day of the drawee following the day on which payment or acceptance is required by those paragraphs.

(d) Dishonor of an accepted draft is governed by the following rules:

(1) If the draft is payable on demand, the draft is dishonored if presentment for payment is duly made to the acceptor and the draft is not paid on the day of presentment.

(2) If the draft is not payable on demand, the draft is dishonored if presentment for payment is duly made to the acceptor and payment is not made on the day it becomes payable or the day of presentment, whichever is later.

(e) In any case in which presentment is otherwise required for dishonor under this section and presentment is excused under Section 3–504, dishonor occurs without presentment if the instrument is not duly accepted or paid.

(f) If a draft is dishonored because timely acceptance of the draft was not made and the person entitled to demand acceptance consents to a late acceptance, from the time of acceptance the draft is treated as never having been dishonored.

§ 3–503. Notice of Dishonor.

(a) The obligation of an indorser stated in Section 3–415(a) and the obligation of a drawer stated in Section 3–414(d) may not be enforced unless (i) the indorser or drawer is given notice of dishonor of the instrument complying with this section or (ii) notice of dishonor is excused under Section 3–504(b).

(b) Notice of dishonor may be given by any person; may be given by any commercially reasonable means, including an oral, written, or electronic communication; and is sufficient if it reasonably identifies the instrument and indicates that the instrument has been dishonored or has not been paid or accepted. Return of an instrument given to a bank for collection is sufficient notice of dishonor.

(c) Subject to Section 3–504(c), with respect to an instrument taken for collection by a collecting bank, notice of dishonor must be given (i) by the bank before midnight of the next banking day following the banking day on which the bank receives notice of dishonor of the instrument, or (ii) by any other person within 30 days following the day on which the person receives notice of dishonor. With respect to any other instrument, notice of dishonor must be given within 30 days following the day on which dishonor occurs.

§ 3–504. Excused Presentment and Notice of Dishonor.

(a) Presentment for payment or acceptance of an instrument is excused if (i) the person entitled to present the instrument cannot with reasonable diligence make presentment, (ii) the maker or acceptor has repudiated an obligation to pay the instrument or is dead or in insolvency proceedings, (iii) by the terms of the instrument presentment is not necessary to enforce the obligation of indorsers or the drawer, (iv) the drawer or indorser whose obligation is being enforced has waived presentment or otherwise has no reason to expect or right to require that the instrument be paid or accepted, or (v) the drawer instructed the drawee not to pay or accept the draft or the drawee was not obligated to the drawer to pay the draft.

(b) Notice of dishonor is excused if (i) by the terms of the instrument notice of dishonor is not necessary to enforce the obligation of a party to pay the instrument, or (ii) the party whose obligation is being enforced waived notice of dishonor. A waiver of presentment is also a waiver of notice of dishonor.

(c) Delay in giving notice of dishonor is excused if the delay was caused by circumstances beyond the control of the person giving the notice and the person giving the notice exercised reasonable diligence after the cause of the delay ceased to operate.

§ 3–505. Evidence of Dishonor.

(a) The following are admissible as evidence and create a presumption of dishonor and of any notice of dishonor stated:
   (1) a document regular in form as provided in subsection (b) which purports to be a protest;
   (2) a purported stamp or writing of the drawee, payor bank, or presenting bank on or accompanying the instrument stating that acceptance or payment has been refused unless reasons for the refusal are stated and the reasons are not consistent with dishonor;
   (3) a book or record of the drawee, payor bank, or collecting bank, kept in the usual course of business which shows dishonor, even if there is no evidence of who made the entry.

(b) A protest is a certificate of dishonor made by a United States consul or vice consul, or a notary public or other person authorized to administer oaths by the law of the place where dishonor occurs. It may be made upon information satisfactory to that person. The protest must identify the instrument and certify either that presentment has been made or, if not made, the reason why it was not made, and that the instrument has been dishonored by non-acceptance or nonpayment. The protest may also certify that notice of dishonor has been given to some or all parties.

PART 6: DISCHARGE AND PAYMENT

§ 3–601. Discharge and Effect of Discharge.

(a) The obligation of a party to pay the instrument is discharged as stated in this Article or by an act or agreement with the party which would discharge an obligation to pay money under a simple contract.

(b) Discharge of the obligation of a party is not effective against a person acquiring rights of a holder in due course of the instrument without notice of the discharge.

§ 3–602. Payment.

(a) Subject to subsection (e), an instrument is paid to the extent payment is made by or on behalf of a party obliged to pay the instrument, and to a person entitled to enforce the instrument.

(b) Subject to subsection (e), a note is paid to the extent payment is made by or on behalf of a party obliged to pay the note to a person that formerly was entitled to enforce the note only if at the time of the payment the party obliged to pay has not received adequate notification that the note has been transferred and that payment is to be made to the transferee. A notification is adequate only if it is signed by the transferor or the transferee; reasonably identifies the transferred note; and provides an address at which payments subsequently are to be made. Upon request, a transferee shall seasonably furnish reasonable proof that the note has been transferred. Unless the transferee complies with the request, a payment to the person that formerly was entitled to enforce the note is effective for purposes of subsection (c) even if the party obliged to pay the note has received a notification under this paragraph.

(c) Subject to subsection (e), to the extent of a payment under subsections (a) and (b), the obligation of the party obliged to pay the instrument is discharged even though payment is made with knowledge of a claim to the instrument under Section 3–306 by another person.

(d) Subject to subsection (e), a transferee, or any party that has acquired rights in the instrument directly or indirectly from a transferee, including any such party that has rights as a holder in due course, is deemed to have notice of any payment that is made under subsection (b) after the date that the note is transferred to the transferee but before the party obliged to pay the note receives adequate notification of the transfer.

(e) The obligation of a party to pay the instrument is not discharged under subsections (a) through (d) if:

   (1) a claim to the instrument under Section 3–306 is enforceable against the party receiving payment and (i) payment is made with knowledge by the payor that payment is prohibited by injunction or similar process of a court of competent jurisdiction, or (ii) in the case of an instrument other than a cashier's check, teller's check, or certified check, the party making payment accepted, from the person having a claim to the instrument, indemnity against loss resulting from refusal to pay the person entitled to enforce the instrument; or

   (2) the person making payment knows that the instrument is a stolen instrument and pays a person it knows is in wrongful possession of the instrument.

(f) As used in this section, "signed," with respect to a record that is not a writing, includes the attachment to or logical association with the record of an electronic symbol, sound, or process with the present intent to adopt or accept the record.

§ 3–603. Tender of Payment.

(a) If tender of payment of an obligation to pay an instrument is made to a person entitled to enforce the instrument, the effect of tender is governed by principles of law applicable to tender of payment under a simple contract.

(b) If tender of payment of an obligation to pay an instrument is made to a person entitled to enforce the instrument and the tender is refused, there is discharge, to the extent of the amount of the tender, of the obligation of an indorser or accommodation party having a right of recourse with respect to the obligation to which the tender relates.

(c) If tender of payment of an amount due on an instrument is made to a person entitled to enforce the instrument, the obligation of the obligor to pay interest after the due date on the amount tendered is discharged. If presentment is required with respect to an instrument and the obligor is able and ready to pay on the due date at every place of payment stated in the instrument, the obligor is deemed to have made tender of payment on the due date to the person entitled to enforce the instrument.

§ 3–604. Discharge by Cancellation or Renunciation.

(a) A person entitled to enforce an instrument, with or without consideration, may discharge the obligation of a party to pay the instrument (i) by an intentional voluntary act, such as surrender of the instrument to the party, destruction, mutilation, or cancellation of the instrument, cancellation or striking out of the party's signature, or the addition of words to the instrument indicating discharge, or (ii) by agreeing not to sue or otherwise renouncing rights against the party by a signed record.

(b) Cancellation or striking out of an indorsement pursuant to subsection (a) does not affect the status and rights of a party derived from the indorsement.

(c) In this section, "signed," with respect to a record that is not a writing, includes the attachment to or logical association with the record of an electronic symbol, sound, or process with the present intent to adopt or accept the record.

§ 3–605. Discharge of Secondary Obligors.

(a) If a person entitled to enforce an instrument releases the obligation of a principal obligor in whole or in part, and another party to the instrument is a secondary obligor with respect to the obligation of that principal obligor, the following rules apply:

   (1) Any obligations of the principal obligor to the secondary obligor with respect to any previous payment by the secondary obligor are not affected. Unless the terms of the release preserve the secondary obligor's recourse, the principal obligor is discharged, to the extent of the release, from any other duties to the secondary obligor under this article.

(2) Unless the terms of the release provide that the person entitled to enforce the instrument retains the right to enforce the instrument against the secondary obligor, the secondary obligor is discharged to the same extent as the principal obligor from any unperformed portion of its obligation on the instrument. If the instrument is a check and the obligation of the secondary obligor is based on an indorsement of the check, the secondary obligor is discharged without regard to the language or circumstances of the discharge or other release.

(3) If the secondary obligor is not discharged under paragraph (2), the secondary obligor is discharged to the extent of the value of the consideration for the release, and to the extent that the release would otherwise cause the secondary obligor a loss.

(b) If a person entitled to enforce an instrument grants a principal obligor an extension of the time at which one or more payments are due on the instrument and another party to the instrument is a secondary obligor with respect to the obligation of that principal obligor, the following rules apply:

(1) Any obligations of the principal obligor to the secondary obligor with respect to any previous payment by the secondary obligor are not affected. Unless the terms of the extension preserve the secondary obligor's recourse, the extension correspondingly extends the time for performance of any other duties owed to the secondary obligor by the principal obligor under this article.

(2) The secondary obligor is discharged to the extent that the extension would otherwise cause the secondary obligor a loss.

(3) To the extent that the secondary obligor is not discharged under paragraph (2), the secondary obligor may perform its obligations to a person entitled to enforce the instrument as if the time for payment had not been extended or, unless the terms of the extension provide that the person entitled to enforce the instrument retains the right to enforce the instrument against the secondary obligor as if the time for payment had not been extended, treat the time for performance of its obligations as having been extended correspondingly.

(c) If a person entitled to enforce an instrument agrees, with or without consideration, to a modification of the obligation of a principal obligor other than a complete or partial release or an extension of the due date and another party to the instrument is a secondary obligor with respect to the obligation of that principal obligor, the following rules apply:

(1) Any obligations of the principal obligor to the secondary obligor with respect to any previous payment by the secondary obligor are not affected. The modification correspondingly modifies any other duties owed to the secondary obligor by the principal obligor under this article.

(2) The secondary obligor is discharged from any unperformed portion of its obligation to the extent that the modification would otherwise cause the secondary obligor a loss.

(3) To the extent that the secondary obligor is not discharged under paragraph (2), the secondary obligor may satisfy its obligation on the instrument as if the modification had not occurred, or treat its obligation on the instrument as having been modified correspondingly.

(d) If the obligation of a principal obligor is secured by an interest in collateral, another party to the instrument is a secondary obligor with respect to that obligation, and a person entitled to enforce the instrument impairs the value of the interest in collateral, the obligation of the secondary obligor is discharged to the extent of the impairment. The value of an interest in collateral is impaired to the extent the value of the interest is reduced to an amount less than the amount of the recourse of the secondary obligor, or the reduction in value of the interest causes an increase in the amount by which the amount of the recourse exceeds the value of the interest. For purposes of this subsection, impairing the value of an interest in collateral includes failure to obtain or maintain perfection or recordation of the interest in collateral, release of collateral without substitution of collateral of equal value or equivalent reduction of the underlying obligation, failure to perform a duty to preserve the value of collateral owed, under Article 9 or other law, to a debtor or other person secondarily liable, and failure to comply with applicable law in disposing of or otherwise enforcing the interest in collateral.

(e) A secondary obligor is not discharged under subsections (a)(3), (b), (c), or (d) unless the person entitled to enforce the instrument knows that the person is a secondary obligor or has notice under Section 3–419(c) that the instrument was signed for accommodation.

(f) A secondary obligor is not discharged under this section if the secondary obligor consents to the event or conduct that is the basis of the discharge, or the instrument or a separate agreement of the party provides for waiver of discharge under this section specifically or by general language indicating that parties waive defenses based on suretyship or impairment of collateral. Unless the circumstances indicate otherwise, consent by the principal obligor to an act that would lead to a discharge under this section constitutes consent to that act by the secondary obligor if the secondary obligor controls the principal obligor or deals with the person entitled to enforce the instrument on behalf of the principal obligor.

(g) A release or extension preserves a secondary obligorís recourse if the terms of the release or extension provide that:

(1) the person entitled to enforce the instrument retains the right to enforce the instrument against the secondary obligor; and

(2) the recourse of the secondary obligor continues as if the release or extension had not been granted.

(h) Except as otherwise provided in subsection (i), a secondary obligor asserting discharge under this section has the burden of persuasion both with respect to the occurrence of the acts alleged to harm the secondary obligor and loss or prejudice caused by those acts.

(i) If the secondary obligor demonstrates prejudice caused by an impairment of its recourse, and the circumstances of the case indicate that the amount of loss is not reasonably susceptible of calculation or requires proof of facts that are not ascertainable, it is presumed that the act impairing recourse caused a loss or impairment equal to the liability of the secondary obligor on the instrument. In that event, the burden of persuasion as to any lesser amount of the loss is on the person entitled to enforce the instrument.

Online Supplements

ConnectPlus Online Access for Dynamic Business Law, Third Edition

McGraw-Hill ConnectPlus® provides an online eBook and immediate feedback on online assignments, quizzes, and practice tests, providing a learning experience that is personalized for YOU. Study more efficiently and engage with your learning process – Connect with future success!

HOW TO REGISTER

Using a <u>Print Book</u>?
To register and activate your ConnectPlus account, simply follow these easy steps:
1. **Go to the ConnectPlus course web address provided by your instructor or visit the Connect link set up on your instructor's course within your campus learning management system.**
2. **Click on the link to register.**
3. **When prompted, enter the ConnectPlus code found on the inside back cover of your book and click Submit. Complete the brief registration form that follows to begin using Connect.**

Using an <u>eBook</u>?
To register and activate your ConnectPlus account, simply follow these easy steps:
1. **Upon purchase of your eBook, you will be granted automatic access to ConnectPlus.**
2. **Go to the ConnectPlus course web address provided by your instructor or visit the Connect link set up on your instructor's course within your campus learning management system.**
3. **Sign in using the same email address and password you used to register on the eBookstore. Complete your registration and begin using Connect.**

Note: Access Code is for one use only. If you did not purchase this book new, the access code included in this book is no longer valid.

Need help? Visit mhhe.com/support